Apache, MySQL, and PHP
Web Development

ALL-IN-ONE DESK REFERENCE

FOR

DUMMIES®

Apache, MySQL, and PHP Web Development

ALL-IN-ONE DESK REFERENCE

FOR

DUMMIES®

by Jeffrey Cogswell

WILEY

Wiley Publishing, Inc.

Apache®, MySQL®, and PHP Web Development All-in-One Desk Reference For Dummies®

Published by
Wiley Publishing, Inc.
111 River Street
Hoboken, NJ 07030-5774

Copyright © 2004 by Wiley Publishing, Inc., Indianapolis, Indiana

Published by Wiley Publishing, Inc., Indianapolis, Indiana

Published simultaneously in Canada

For general information on our other products and services or to obtain technical support, please contact our Customer Care Department within the U.S. at 800-762-2974, outside the U.S. at 317-572-3993, or fax 317-572-4002.

Wiley also publishes its books in a variety of electronic formats. Some content that appears in print may not be available in electronic books.

Library of Congress Control Number available from publisher

ISBN: 0-7645-4969-3

Manufactured in the United States of America

10 9 8 7 6 5 4 3 2 1

1O/RZ/RR/QT/IN

0 1021 0188388 6

WILEY   is a trademark of Wiley Publishing, Inc.

About the Author

Jeff Cogswell is an accomplished software engineer, teacher, and writer. Having written ten books about programming, he is known to be one of the best teachers around. He has tutored and taught more students than he can count and has worked on many professional software projects. He has lived all over the United States but still hasn't been to Europe.

Dedication

This book is dedicated to all my friends for supporting me through the changes in my life over the past couple of years.

Author's Acknowledgments

You've heard it before: A book isn't just created by the author. While as I stare at the computer in my home office I sometimes feel alone, the fact is many people are helping out behind the scenes. Additionally, I've had a lot of people provide me valuable feedback — not just on this book, but on life in general.

Thanks to:

- The editors: Melody Layne, Chris Morris, Jerry Reed, and Kim Darosett
- My agent and good friend, Margot Maley Hutchison of Waterside Productions. Also thanks to the whole team at Waterside, including Kimberly Valentini, Bill Gladstone, and Maureen Maloney.
- All my writing friends, and especially Dave Taylor for moral support.
- My friends: In alphabetical order by first name, Amy Sue Page (she's also my sister), Andrea Vaduva, Carousel Castillo, Charla Silver, Greg and Jennifer Wood, Jen Lesh and Michael Bownds, Jennifer and Karl Mueller, and Michele Fender. Thanks and love to you all.

Publisher's Acknowledgments

We're proud of this book; please send us your comments through our online registration form located at `www.dummies.com/register/`.

Some of the people who helped bring this book to market include the following:

Acquisitions, Editorial, and Media Development

Project Editor: Christopher Morris

Acquisitions Editor: Melody Layne

Senior Copy Editor: Kim Darosett

Technical Editor: Jerry Reed

Editorial Manager: Kevin Kirschner

Permissions Editor: Laura Moss

Media Development Supervisor: Richard Graves

Editorial Assistant: Amanda Foxworth

Cartoons: Rich Tennant (`www.the5thwave.com`)

Production

Project Coordinator: Courtney MacIntyre

Layout and Graphics: Seth Conley, Joyce Haughey, Stephanie D. Jumper, Kristin McMullan, Jacque Schneider, Julie Trippetti

Proofreaders: Andy Hollandbeck, Betty Kish, Carl William Pierce, Dwight Ramsey, Brian H. Walls

Indexer: Tom Dinse

Publishing and Editorial for Technology Dummies

    Richard Swadley, Vice President and Executive Group Publisher

    Andy Cummings, Vice President and Publisher

    Mary C. Corder, Editorial Director

Publishing for Consumer Dummies

    Diane Graves Steele, Vice President and Publisher

    Joyce Pepple, Acquisitions Director

Composition Services

    Gerry Fahey, Vice President of Production Services

    Debbie Stailey, Director of Composition Services

Contents at a Glance

Table of Contents

Introduction

*W*elcome to LAMP! What is LAMP, you ask? LAMP stands for Linux, Apache, MySQL, and Perl. The P sometimes stands for PHP, or it stands for both Perl and PHP. In this book, I cover all these topics, but I don't limit the book to Linux. I talk about Windows, too, because Apache runs just fine on a Windows computer. That's a good thing if you're working with a remote hosting service for your Web server, and the service runs Apache but you run Windows at home. You can successfully set up your Windows computer with Apache, MySQL, Perl, and PHP and test out your Web server locally before uploading it to the remote Apache system. Life is good.

About This Book

Here are the parts that make up LAMP:

✦ **Linux:** This is the operating system you use for your Web servers.

✦ **Apache:** This is the Web server software — well, sort of anyway. Apache actually refers to a whole set of open-source software projects dealing with Web servers. When many of us say *Apache,* we're referring to the *HTTP Server* portion of Apache, which is the Web server. In this book if I say Apache, I'm referring to the Web server called HTTP Server.

✦ **MySQL:** This is a free database product that is widely used on the Web. Like Apache, MySQL is the name for a group of database-related products, and the one I'm really talking about is the MySQL Database Server. Throughout this book, when I say MySQL, I'm talking about the Database Server portion of the product.

✦ **Perl:** This is a popular programming language that sports some seriously powerful text-processing features.

✦ **PHP:** This is an amazing programming language that you embed right in Web pages. The Web server runs PHP, which processes the code that builds a dynamic Web page on the fly.

All of these products are open source, which means you can obtain the source code for them and make changes to them (if you want). In this book, I don't talk about the source code to these products. I think the products work great, and I see no reason to change them.

In this book, I also talk about the following topics that are important to LAMP Web development:

✦ **Tcl/Tk:** Although Tcl and Tk are two separate things, they are often used together. Tcl is a simple yet powerful programming language based on a command concept. Tk is an entire system for building graphical user interfaces (you know, windows, buttons, menus, list boxes — all that good stuff). This book focuses on accessing Tk through Tcl programs, although you can also access Tk through several other languages as well.

✦ **Regular expressions:** Regular expressions are a mystery to many people. Regular expressions are ways of specifying patterns that you can use for matching text. For example, if you search for the pattern `/.ook/` in the string "Look at the book," you find the characters `Look` and `book`. Regular expressions are for processing documents and building Web pages.

Foolish Assumptions

As much as I tried to start each minibook out from square one, I do make some basic assumptions about what you already know. I don't define what a mouse or a Web page is, for example. But here are some things that I assume you know before embarking on this book:

✦ You know what HTML is and you have a basic understanding of HTML tags, such as `<body>` and `<img src="mypic.jpg">`.

✦ You know how to work a text editor, and how to open and save files.

✦ You know how to open up a command prompt on your computer (whether it's Windows or Linux or Unix), and you know how to type commands; further, you're familiar with many of the basic commands, such as `cd`, `cp`, and `ls` on Unix/Linux, or `cd`, `copy`, and `dir` on Windows.

✦ You can perform square roots in your head to 12-digit precision in less than five seconds. Just kidding.

✦ You know how to upload files to your Web site.

✦ You know what using a third-party hosting service means, and you know whether or you're using one.

I can think of many things I *don't* assume you know because you don't need to know it for this book, like who the second emperor of Rome was or what Planks constant is.

If you have some programming knowledge already, you'll have a definite advantage in understanding this book. However, I do *not* assume you already know how to program. In Book III, I cover many introductory programming topics (ranging from variables to object-oriented programming) to help you get started.

Conventions Used in This Book

When you see something in `monofont` in this book, it's a computer word that you type into the computer or read on the computer screen. Monofont is also used for URLs, e-mail addresses, and filenames.

When computer code appears on a single line, it looks like this:

```
var email = document.form1.email.value;
```

When computer code appears on multiple lines, it looks like this:

```
if (document.form1.email.value !=
document.form1.remail.value) {
```

How This Book Is Organized

If you're reading this part, congratulations; I know that most people like to skip the Introduction and maybe even tear out the pages and throw them in the dumpster. But if you take a moment and scan through the following list, you'll get an idea of what you can expect to find in each minibook.

Book I: Configuring Linux and Windows for Apache

In this book, I help you get your Linux or Windows system ready for Apache. I start off by discussing how to configure Linux, how to install a firewall, and how to facilitate logging. Then I show you how to configure Windows and how to make Windows secure. Soon you'll be ready to install Apache — which is the subject of Book II.

Book II: Building an Apache Web Site

This book takes you through the process of getting Apache set up and running. Apache is generally easy to set up, but if you run into problems, this book gets you through those problems without a hitch.

In this book I first discuss how Apache works, its advantages, architecture, and how it communicates with browsers. Next I show you how to install, compile, and run Apache. In subsequent chapters I discuss how to configure Apache, how to install and use Apache modules, and what you can do to keep your server secure.

Book III: Perl Web Site Automation

This book features the Perl programming language. The discussion starts with the basics of Perl and the basics of programming. I explain how to create variables using Perl's limited number of data types. From there I show how you can compare variables and expressions, and create sophisticated if statements and how to use various *control structures* to make sure that certain portions of your code repeat several times. Next I include an entire chapter on processing text files, since that's one of the more common uses of Perl. I also include a chapter on advanced Perl programming, as I explore some of the object-oriented features of Perl. Finally, I show you how to use Perl in your CGI scripts, allowing you to create dynamic web sites.

Book IV: Tcl/Tk Front End Development

This book talks about the Tcl language and helps you create GUIs (sometimes called *front ends*) for your programs using the Tk toolkit. This book really consists of two parts; the first focuses on the Tcl language, where I show you how to use the unusual syntax of Tcl, create variables in Tcl, and use various control structures. In the second part, I focus on Tk, and I discuss how to create windows and add controls to them.

Book V: PHP Web Pages for Dynamic Content

Using this book, you can quickly get up to speed writing dynamic Web pages. PHP is one of my favorite programming languages, and in this book I introduce it. PHP is a full-featured language, and in this book I show you how to create variables in PHP, use the different control structures, and create arrays and functions. Then I move on to interacting with HTML forms, and advanced programming techniques in PHP, such as using references, converting between variables, and creating classes and objects. After that I cover graphics; using PHP, you can dynamically create graphic images and send these images down to the web browser. Finally, I take a look at many of the functions in PHP's rich, built-in function library.

Book VI: MySQL Databases on the Web

This book shows you how to build databases. I explain what a database is; I take you through the process of designing the parts of databases called tables; and I give you the scoop on Structured Query Language (SQL), all under the auspices of the MySQL Database Server. I then show you how to create your tables in such a way that the data between the tables is related, resulting in a *relational database*. Next I have a chapter on using MySQL from within a PHP program. The next chapter gets into more detail on retrieving data from a MySQL database (a process called *querying*). After that I cover accessing MySQL from a Perl program. And finally, I have a chapter devoted to an entire sample user login program for a website.

Book VII: Processing Web Files with Regular Expressions

Not enough people understand and use regular expressions. That's why I decided to include an entire book on them. A regular expression is, in short, a pattern that you can use for searching text. This book shows you what you need to know to start using regular expressions. I take you through the simple but unusual and powerful syntax of regular expressions, while using examples from the languages covered in this book—Perl, PHP, and Tcl. I then move on to cover such topics as splitting and joining strings and processing HTML files, which are both some common uses of regular expressions.

Book VIII: Appendixes

Most open-source development teams use a system called CVS (Concurrent Version System) for sharing files. CVS is available for most operating systems, making it ideal for sharing code. Appendix A gets you up to speed with CVS.

Appendix B explains open-source licenses. The open-source revolution includes some different kinds of licensing issues. Although I'm not a lawyer and don't claim to be, I give you some thoughts on understanding the open-source licenses and what they mean for you.

Icons Used in This Book

What would a Dummies book be without the great cartoons and cute icons? A very boring book indeed. To help you find your way while reading, I sprinkle some great visual clues along the way. Here's what they mean:

During my many years of programming, I've picked up a thing or two that are worth passing on. I highlight these useful nuggets with this Tip icon.

When I'm writing about something I think you should commit to memory, I drop this Remember icon in place.

This icon notifies you of times when you need to need to pay special attention to avoid potential pitfalls.

These sections are optional. They're intended for those of you who want to go the extra mile and find out a few extra pieces of information.

When I want to highlight a particular Web reference, I include this icon.

Getting Started

If you've made it this far, you're probably ready and raring to go. The beauty of this book is that it's a reference guide, so you can either read it straight through or, more likely, pick and choose the topics you're interested in. Good luck and may your Web site be powerful and receive lots of hits.

If you're interested in checking out the official Web sites for the technologies covered in this book, here are the addresses:

✦ **Apache:** www.apache.org
✦ **MySQL:** www.mysql.com
✦ **Perl:** www.perl.org
✦ **PHP:** www.php.net
✦ **Tcl/Tk:** www.tcl.tk

Book I

Configuring Linux and Windows for Apache

The 5th Wave   By Rich Tennant

"Can't I just give you riches or something?"

Contents at a Glance

Chapter 1: Configuring Linux

In This Chapter

✔ **Removing unused services**

✔ **Installing a firewall and IP security**

✔ **Using logging**

*T*o make your Linux system secure enough to resist being compromised, you should focus on two general areas:

✦ The Linux system itself, which is the focus of this chapter

✦ The security of the network to which the Linux system is connected

You need to secure the Linux system before attaching it to the network. It is difficult to ensure the security of a system if it has been connected to a public network before you begin configuring it for secure operation. Because this chapter focuses on prevention, you need to begin with a clean slate — in other words, a system that you are certain has not been turned into a hacker's willing pawn.

If your Linux system will be exposed to the Internet, you want to protect it from as much foul play as possible. You also want to protect your private network resources from the Internet and the Linux system allowing public access. To do this, you need to design a detailed security plan and develop what is commonly called an isolation LAN or demilitarized zone (DMZ) on your network. The simplest form of a secure LAN consists of two routers, as shown in Figure 1-1.

The *outside* router controls access to systems within the secure LAN and restricts (generally blocks entirely) connections that originate from hosts on the internet that are targeting either the private network or the inside router. The *inside* router is designed to allow private LAN traffic to pass outside the network and act as a second barrier between the private network and the internet. It blocks all inbound connections and specifically blocks connections initiated by hosts on the secure LAN and the outside router itself. This ensures that if a secure LAN host or the outside router is compromised, intruders will not have gained access to the private network. Even with a secure LAN configuration, your Linux host needs to be securely configured. Although the secure LAN goes a long way towards protecting your private network resources, your hosts on the secure LAN are exposed to the Internet.

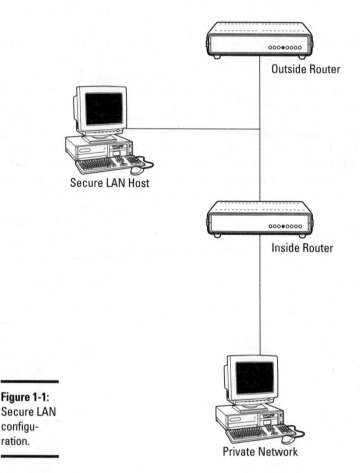

Figure 1-1:
Secure LAN
configu-
ration.

Outside Router

Secure LAN Host

Inside Router

Private Network

Getting a Handle on TCP and UDP Services

When you finish your Linux installation and before installing any other software, you need to remove the default network services that won't be used. By default, the services running on your new Linux installation are providing what the install package's creator deems commonly used services. Because your system will provide Web services (exclusively if possible) and because it may be directly connected to the Internet, you will want to remove many of the default services. Any service can provide an unscrupulous remote user with a potential avenue into your system. If the service is available to network users and is running, you should consider it a potential weakness. Even though many hours are spent testing and identifying flaws in the Linux system, testing can't catch everything. However, you can minimize potential threats by removing unneeded services.

Inetd

Identifying and controlling services, network services in particular, is fairly straightforward on most current versions of Linux, including Red Hat, Mandrake, and SuSE. Within the `/etc` directory, you will find a file called `inetd.conf`. This file is used at system startup to load most of the system's networking services. Rather than have a large number of active processes listening for network connections, the inetd "super server" plays traffic cop between service requests and available services, which results in a more efficient use of system resources. Basically, inetd is a server service that listens for requests that relate to TCP and UDP connections. Any requests for services are then passed to the appropriate service if one is available. If no service is available, the request is dropped. For example, if a Linux server is allowing Web and FTP connections for hundreds of users, inetd allows the creation of sessions for each individual connection rather than have numerous instances of the ftpd or httpd processes idling all the time waiting for users to connect. This frees up memory and CPU time for other uses.

The inetd process relies on a corresponding conf file to determine which processes are available for use. Figure 1-2 shows an example of an `inetd.conf` file.

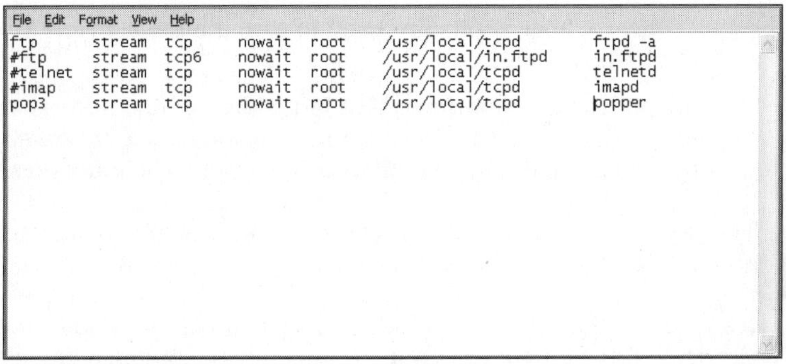

Figure 1-2:
Sample
`inetd.`
`conf.`

```
File  Edit  Format  View  Help
ftp        stream  tcp    nowait  root   /usr/local/tcpd      ftpd -a
#ftp       stream  tcp6   nowait  root   /usr/local/in.ftpd   in.ftpd
#telnet    stream  tcp    nowait  root   /usr/local/tcpd      telnetd
#imap      stream  tcp    nowait  root   /usr/local/tcpd      imapd
pop3       stream  tcp    nowait  root   /usr/local/tcpd      popper
```

What you find in the `inetd` file varies depending on the distribution you use, but how you can control it is the same across most distributions. You can open the file with the text editor of your choice and add or remove entries as needed. For example, the inetd server ignores any line with the # symbol. Using the # symbol is also known as "commenting out" the code that follows.

"Commenting out" allows you to disable startup services without removing the configuration. This is useful if you have a service you will use only occasionally and you want to start it manually instead of at startup. You can also temporarily disable one of the services by inserting the # symbol and restarting the inetd. As the phrase "comment out" suggests, you can also use this symbol to insert comments into the file. For example you might want to note why you added or removed a particular entry. The process for restarting inetd varies in some distributions, but in general, you can go to the directory where the inetd is stored (/etc/rc.d/inet.d on Red Hat) and type the `inetd restart` command. You need to run this command as root or with root privileges. If this command doesn't work on your distribution, search that product's support information for the relevant process to restart the inetd process.

The `inetd.conf` file contains six attributes for each item. Here are the attributes from left to right as shown in Figure 1-2:

✦ **The service name:** In the example, the first line has a service named ftp, indicating it is an ftp service. The name of the service is taken from the corresponding entry in the /etc/services file.

✦ **The socket type:** The socket type can be either stream or datagram. In most cases, it's stream.

✦ **The protocol type:** This can be specified as either TCP or UDP.

✦ **The wait/nowait option:** This option determines if a new process is spawned for each request (nowait) or if each request is processed sequentially one at a time (wait).

✦ **The user whose rights are used to execute the service:** The user is root in the example.

✦ **The path to the command that launches the daemon:** The path is /usr/local/tcpd in the example. A *daemon* is a program that waits in the background until called upon by a user to actually do something.

The seventh field is optional. If you don't need to specify any execution arguments, feel free to omit this field.

Many Linux distributions include graphical tools for configuring the startup services. Typically these configuration applets contain a list of startup services and corresponding check boxes. To disable a service, you simply clear the corresponding check box. In most cases, you need to manually shut down the service by using a command in a terminal window or by restarting the system. For more information about the specific tools available, consult the developers of your desktop environment (KDE or Gnome).

Xinetd

On many current distributions, the xinetd daemon is used instead of inetd. Conceptually, xinetd does the same thing inetd does. However, for the most part, this similarity is only skin deep. The processes for configuring files and for the construction of the configuration files are quite different. There are some other critical operational differences. For example, any user can use xinetd to start servers that do not need privileged ports. This is possible because, unlike inetd, xinetd does not require that the services in its configuration file (`xinet.d`) also appear in `/etc/services`.

In the list below, the key enhancements (what xinetd does that inetd does not) are outlined.

✦ Access control works on multi-threaded and single-threaded services.

✦ Xinetd kills those services that no longer meet the existing access control criteria and those that have been removed from the `xinet.d` configuration file.

✦ It can place limits on the number of processes a single host can spawn, the number of servers a particular service can start, and the size of log files. These configurable limitations go a long way towards preventing denial-of-service attacks, which attempt to disrupt the system by overutilizing available resources.

As noted earlier, the configuration file (`/etc/xinetd.conf`) for the xinetd service is also notably different than the file used by inetd. The example below (Figure 1-3) shows telnet, IMAP, and the default entries. By itself, this configuration is not entirely useful; I've included it because it illustrates the differences between the layout of inetd and xinetd.

```
Untitled - Notepad
File  Edit  Format  View  Help

defaults
{
        instances       = 25
        log_type        = FILE /var/log/servicelog
        log_on_success  = HOST PID
        log_on_failure  = HOST RECORD
#       only_from       = 192.168.0.22
#       only_from       = localhost
        disabled        = tftp
}

service imap
{
        socket_type     = stream
        protocol        = tcp
        wait            = no
        user            = root
        only_from       = 192.168.0.20 localhost
        banner          = /usr/local/etc/deny_banner
        server          = /usr/local/sbin/imapd
}

service telnet
{
        flags           = REUSE
        socket_type     = stream
        wait            = no
        user            = root
        redirect        = 192.168.0.1 23
        bind            = 127.0.0.1
        log_on_failure += USERID
}

service telnet
{
        flags           = REUSE
        socket_type     = stream
        wait            = no
        user            = root
        server          = /usr/sbin/in.telnetd
        bind            = 192.168.0.1
        log_on_failure += USERID
}
```

Figure 1-3:
Example
xinetd
configu-
ration file.

If you would like to convert an `inet.d` configuration file to be compatible with xinetd, you can make use of one of a couple of conversion tools. Both itox and `xconv.pl` come with full distributions of xinetd and are relatively painless to use. For guidance, check out the information located here (under the configuration section): `www.linuxfocus.org/English/November2000/ article175.shtml`.

No Sharing: NFS/RPC

Unless you're dying for someone to turn your Linux server into the technological equivalent of Typhoid Mary, avoid the Remote Procedure Call (RPC) and Network File Service (NFS). Keep in mind I'm talking about a Linux server exposed to the Internet. RPC and NFS can be very useful on a private network but have no business on at-risk systems. Both services are designed to allow remote users to access resources:

✦ RPC allows the sharing of processing resources among computers. With RPC, a single program can use the resources of several computers collectively in a clustery arrangement.

✦ NFS is used to facilitate disk access. Remote users who have the appropriate access rights can mount and access data on an NFS-enabled hard disk.

It is painfully easy to misconfigure these services, NFS in particular, in a manner that creates huge holes. For example, a misconfigured NFS implementation allows anyone to mount and access data on the NFS-capable drive.

The portmapper controls the use of NFS and RPC. The portmapper is another daemon and is typically housed at `/etc/rc.d/rc.inet2`, though the location can vary depending on the distribution. If you do not know the location, you can try running the `find` command on the `/etc` directory. For example, the following line finds instances of words containing *map:*

```
find /etc -name "*map*" -print | more
```

You can replace the *map* argument with *nfs*, *port*, or *rpc* to thoroughly scan the `/etc/rc.d` directories for the startup locations of the NFS and RPC services. Like other configuration files, find the relevant entries and place a # in front of the execution lines or simply delete the entries. After the services have been disabled, you need to restart the system to unload them.

If you want to access your server remotely, Telnet is not a good option because it has no system for protecting information passed between the connecting client and the server. Instead, you should use the Secure Shell (SSH) client-server utility. SSH encrypts all the data that passes between the client and the server. Not only is the logon information protected, but the data transferred is protected as well. Virtually all modern Linux distributions include an SSH implementation, but if it is not present, you can download it. To install SSH, you can download the source, run the ./configure script, and then run the make and make install commands. For more information on the installation process for SSH, see www.openssh.com.

Misleading Binaries (SUID/GUID Binaries)

In addition to network services, some of the programs on your Linux system can be real liabilities because they need root privileges to do much. Some programs use a specialized bit (set on the binary itself) — called either Set User ID (SUID) or Group User ID (GUID) — to gain more privileges than the user who might run the program or use its services. For example, if users want to send e-mail, they need to use the services of an SMTP server such as Sendmail. However, they probably won't have all the rights needed to perform all the tasks that the mail server needs to do. To perform the needed tasks, Sendmail often runs with the Set User ID bit set to use root account privileges.

Any program that uses SUID/GUID to run with elevated privileges is a liability. If a malicious user gains control of the application, that user may be able to interact with the system using the elevated system rights provided by the SUID/GUID setting. Fortunately, you can easily identify the binaries that have been configured to use the SUID/GUID funtionality. If you check the file attributes of a binary and see an s where you would normally see an r or x (r-sr-xr-x, for example), you have a binary using SUID/GUID. So how do you find and, if not needed, disable these binaries? The easiest method is to use the find command to search the entire system and build a list of the SUID/GUID-enabled applications. Here's an elegant solution that uses the find command with the option to dump the output to a text file:

```
find / \( -perm -4000 -o -perm -2000 \) -exec ls -ldb {} \;
>> /tmp/suids
```

This command creates the text file suids in the /tmp directory with information about all the binaries using the SUID/GUID capability. You can find and delete any binaries that you know you don't need. If you determine that some of the binaries may prove useful, you can refine their access rules (by using the CHMOD command) so that not just anyone can run them. This is especially useful if one of the remaining binaries needs to be granted root access.

Here are a couple handy ways to help you determine if you need a particular service or program:

✦ Visit the home page of your Linux distribution and search for the program.

✦ Search for "man *program/service*" using a search engine like Yahoo! or Google. The manual (man) pages typically reveal a wealth of information about the program/service and its usage.

Protection with Firewalls

Although many third-party security products, including firewalls, are available for Linux, several handy features are included with the operating system out of the box. Having a firewall on your Linux system is exceptionally important if the system is outside any other firewalls. For example, if the resources for setting up a secure LAN are not available, the Linux server you build needs a local firewall installed if it is connected to the Internet. Even if you're using a secure LAN configuration, an additional, local firewall adds an extra line of defense to stave off intruders if they compromise one of your existing routers.

Ipchains

Ipchains is a long-standing firewalling mechanism that is available on most Linux distributions that use kernel version 2.2.x. To get started, you need to enable ipchains. If your system is using the IP address 10.50.4.55 with the mask 255.255.255.0 (internally), you need to run the following commands with root privileges:

```
echo 1 > /proc/sys/net/ipv4/ip_forwardipchains -A forward -j
MASQ -s 10.50.4.0/24 -d 0.0.0.0/0
```

The first command enables `ip_forwarding`, and the second entry configures the server with which network to grant Internet access. If you want to load the ipchains service at startup, you need to place the two preceding commands into the `etc/rc.d/rc.local` file. After you have the firewall running, you can use the `ipchains -L` command to see the configured IP filtering rules. Of course to start with, there is not much to see. The output of this command looks something like Figure 1-4.

In the figure, three chains are in place by default. The chains are for inbound, outbound, and forwarded packets. But because you have not configured the behavior of these chains, nothing useful is happening at this point. To set a rule, you need to invoke the `ipchains` command and tell it what to do. Take a look at the following example:

```
ipchains -A input -p icmp -i eth0 -j REJECT
```

Here's a closer look at the components of this example:

✦ The `ipchains -A input` portion indicates that you're appending (A) a
new rule to the ipchains `input` chain. In place of `-A`, you can use `-L` to
see the current ipchains rules and `-D` to delete a rule from a chain.

✦ The option `-p` specifies that you're going to set a rule for a protocol.

✦ Net is the type (used with the `-p` option), and in this case, that is all
ICMP traffic.

✦ `Eth0` is the network interface to apply the rule to.

✦ The `-j REJECT` option specifies that the ICMP traffic should be rejected
at the interface. The result is that any inbound ICMP traffic on the `Eth0`
interface is summarily rejected.

See Book I, Chapter 3, for information about products that make ipchains
and other firewall configuration easier. This chapter only touches on the
capabilities of the ipchains tool. If you're interested in finding out more
about ipchains, visit `www.rt.com/man/ipchains.8.html` or type "man
ipchains" on your Linux server to see the almost overwhelming number of
ipchains run-time options.

```
File  Edit  Format  View  Help
# ipchains -L


Chain input (policy ACCEPT):
Chain forward (policy ACCEPT):
Chain output (policy ACCEPT):
```

Figure 1-4:
Example
ipchains
rules
configu-
ration.

Iptables

Another option for implementing a firewall on your Linux system is through
the use of iptables. They are similar in function (they both control network
access); however, iptables has several advantages over ipchains. The advantages are noteworthy enough that if you are using a 2.4.x or newer kernel
version (any build of Red Hat newer than 7.1, for example) you should use
iptables. Below are some of the ways in which iptables differs from ipchains.

✦ Iptables, unlike ipchains, uses a single chain to process filtered packets.
Because of this, iptables allows you to exert finer control over the kinds
of filtering options you choose. For example, a packet forwarded by an
ipchains host must traverse the input, forward, and output chains to
make it to its destination. An iptables host must only check the packet

against the output filter. If the host is using iptables, a conflicting rule on the input chain won't stop the forwarding of the packet.

✦ The iptables host processes inbound packets using only the inbound rules, and outbound packets using only the outbound rules. If you want to specify the network interface to be used with a particular rule, you must use the appropriate option in your configuration. The -i option must be used with the inbound or forward chains and the -o option must be used with the outbound chains. Remember that the inbound interface will not use outbound rules and the outbound interface will not use inbound rules. If you mix your options, the rule will not have the intended effect.

✦ Unlike ipchains, you must specify the source or destination port after the protocol declaration (ICMP, TCP, or UDP). In ipchains the order was not all that important, however with iptables the rules will fail to operate as expected if the proper order is not used.

As you might expect, the configuration file (typically located in /etc/sysconfig/iptables) has changed considerably as well. The overall arrangement is a bit cleaner and if you use comments, it is fairly straightforward to understand what is going on in the configuration. In Figure 1-5, the configuration first sets a rule that allows the local host (running iptables) to pass any traffic to or from *localhost*. The next entry allows the passage of ICMP type 3 traffic. Type 3 "Destination Unreachable" messages are used when systems that forward data to another host cannot find the targeted host. Next, there are mountd and NFS connections allowed. These would probably be essential if you needed to connect to your system over a network to send data (to upload Web page content for example), but if you are working locally on the machine, these could be eliminated. The mountd entry in this example only works if you go to the NFS configuration file /etc/rc.d/init.d/nfs and assign the mountd service to a single port (33333 in this case). By default, the port is picked during system startup and varies between 32000 and 42000. Finally, the configuration file allows the passing of http traffic on port 80. If you need to use https as well, you could duplicate this last entry and change the destination port (dport) and source port (sport) values to 443.

In Figure 1-4, note that three chains are in place by default.

I strongly recommended that you become familiar with the syntax and use of ipchains and iptables before you use either in a production environment. It's easy to overlook something and leave your system exposed. Make a plan for the kinds of traffic you need to allow in and out of your server and for the services and ports that need to be blocked. With a clear plan, your results will be much better. To find additional information about ipchains configurations, check out www.linux.org/docs/ldp/howto/IPCHAINS-HOWTO.html. If you will be working with iptables, there is a great source of general information and configuration examples located at www.jollycom.ca/iptables-tutorial/iptables-tutorial.html.

Figure 1-5:
Example
iptables
configu-
ration.

Playing Games: IP Masquerade

Network Address Translation (NAT) is used to hide a group host address behind a single public address. Typically NAT is used to allow multiple private hosts to use a single public IP address to access the Internet. Everyone on the private network sharing the single public IP is effectively "masked" — hence the moniker *Masquerade* — from the Internet. The individual host can use a private IP address (192.168.1.22, for example) and use NAT to access public networks with a different IP address that is routable on the Internet. The advantage to this configuration is that an organization with many internal hosts needs only a single publicly known IP address for all of its resources.

To use IP Masquerade, you need a build that already supports it, or you may need to recompile your kernel to use IP Masquerade. Most current Linux releases support IP Masquerade. To check your system, you can run this command:

```
uname -a
```

The results reveal the kernel version your system is using. To use IP Masquerade, you need kernel version 2.0.x or greater. On the Red Hat distribution, within the /etc/rc.d/rc.local script is an entry that loads the

/etc/rc.d/rc.firewall script during system startup. The purpose of the rc.firewall script is to load all the needed modules to run IP Masquerade and process its relevant configuration files. This file is where you enter the traffic restrictions (rule sets) like the ipchains and iptables examples earlier in this chapter. Many sample IP Masquerade configurations are available, including www.tldp.org/HOWTO/IP-Masquerade-HOWTO/, which helps you get your masquerade configuration up and running.

Keeping on Top with Logging

Although it's important to have a handle on the services running on your system and use firewalling if possible, comprehensive logging is one of the most useful methods for ensuring that your system remains secure. The syslog daemon is used on Linux and Unix systems to facilitate logging. On most Linux installations, a global configuration file controls the behavior of the syslog component. The /etc/syslog.conf file passes the logging instructions to the syslog daemon. Most default Linux installations are designed to balance security and functionality, and as a result, the default logging behavior needs improvement.

Within the syslog.conf file, you will find entries that look like this:

```
*.=info;*.=notice        /usr/log/notice.log
```

Each entry has three elements:

✦ The first item is the source of the log information, called a *facility* — in other words, which processes should be monitored for logging output. * is used to specify "all available" log sources.

✦ The information following the * specifies the kinds of events that will be captured, known as *priority*. For example, in *.=notice, all log sources are monitored, and only the notice priority events are captured.

✦ The last element specifies what will be done with the logging information, and in most cases where the log information will be stored. In the example, the logging output is stored in the file /usr/log/notice.log.

It is fairly useful to log different facilities to different log files. Although this can increase the amount of disk space used by log files, it can make locating information about particular events easier.

Several facilities that you should track may not be logged by default. To begin logging these items, you need to create a new entry in the syslog. conf log file. Table 1-1 shows some of the common facilities that you should use.

Table 1-1	Common Logging Facility Options
Facility	*Use*
Auth/Security	Log information relating to user authentication.
Authpriv	A more detailed version of auth.
Cron	Logs activity of the cron daemon, which is used to schedule events.
Daemon	Collects information about *all* system daemons.
Mail	Tracks mail server activity. This is a must have if you're running a mail server.
Syslog	Information about the syslog server itself.

Along with this selection of facilities, you need to understand the priorities that are available. How much detail you need is up to you. Keep in mind that if a problem occurs and you don't have enough information to identify the source, the logs are essentially useless. However, if you collect every transaction and message in the log, it may be nearly impossible to locate meaningful information. Table 1-2 describes the available priorities.

Table 1-2	Logging Priorities
Priority	*Use*
Info	Logs general informational messages
Notice	Logs occurrences that require special interaction (that is, user prompts)
Warning	System warning, "might be a problem"
Err	System error, "a problem occurred"
Crit	Critical condition, "a big problem has occurred"
Alert	Intervention required, "problem happening, need help"
Emerg	Serious system failure, "something is hosed"
Panic	System panic, "HUGE problem"
Debug	Logs nearly everything

Chapter 2: Configuring Windows

*I*f you decide to use the Windows operating system as the host for your Web server, you need to spend some time making sure it's secure. Although a lot of media attention has focused on the security risks of Windows operating systems, you need to focus on a couple of general truths:

✦ Most of the severe security-related events directed at Windows (CodeRed, Sobig, MSBlast, and so forth) occurred *after* Microsoft had released a patch that removed the exploited vulnerability. If a system had the patch installed, it would not have been directly affected by the event. Thus, you need to keep on top of the available security patches by checking for them on a weekly basis at minimum. If you find a new, critical patch make sure you install it ASAP.

✦ Many of the common attacks against Windows systems don't require special vulnerabilities. Typically, the default settings for Windows operating systems are very insecure. With casual network access and a brute-force password cracker, any illicit user has better than a 50 percent chance of cracking any newly installed Windows PC.

Fortunately, you can perform a few basic tasks to remedy most of these issues and greatly reduce your risk of being violated. In this chapter, I use Windows 2000 Server for all the examples. The policies and procedures translate to any other version of Windows, but some details may differ slightly.

Securing Windows during Setup

To make your system resilient enough for duty as a publicly exposed Web server, you need to start securing it from the very beginning of the installation process. During the operating system installation, set a strong administrator password and disable networking services that you don't plan to use.

Setting an administrator password

According to the SANS institute (www.sans.org), a good password (not just *administrator*) should meet the following minimum criteria:

✦ Is at least eight alphanumeric characters long

✦ Contains both upper and lowercase characters (that is, a–z, A–Z)

✦ Has digits and punctuation characters as well as letters — that is, 0–9, !@#$%^&*()_+|~-=\`{}[]:";'<>?,./

✦ Does not use entire words in any language, slang, dialect, jargon, and so on

✦ Does not use personal information, family member names, and so on

One way to come up with good passwords is to build passwords based on phrases. For example, take the phrase "I like to eat pizza at the park" and apply the preceding rules. Using the first letter of each word, you might come up with the password ill2eP@tP. By using a phrase and then some kind of patterned substitution, you can create a password that is both memorable and effective.

If you follow the suggestions in the previous list, your password is virtually immune to attacks that rely on victims using dictionary words. Most password-cracking tools come with a dictionary attack component. This tool takes the entire contents of a collection of dictionaries and uses all the words as passwords for a particular user name. The attack is effective against passwords that are dictionary words like "procrastination" or "beautiful" even if you reverse the words or just add a number to the end or beginning. For example, "beautiful1" is not really much better than just plain "beautiful." To get an idea about how commonly certain passwords are used, take a look at www.openwall.com/passwords/ordlists/common.txt. Do you see any of your old passwords on this list?

Disabling network services

After you have set a strong password for the administrator account, make sure that there are no networking services running that you won't use.

Disabling services during setup

During the later stages of the setup process, you are prompted to configure the networking configuration. If you select the option to customize these settings, you can deselect any of the services that you don't plan on using. For example, if your server will exclusively be a platform for Apache, PHP, and MySQL, you can pretty much scrap everything other than TCP/IP itself. However, this won't nab all the services you'll want disabled. After the installation completes, you need to do a little extra work.

Administrative shares exist by default on all Windows NT–based systems (Windows NT, Windows 2000, Windows XP, and Windows Server 2003). These shares are designed to allow remote access to authorized users but have no place on a single-purpose Web server. To remove these shares, you can use the `net use` *driveletter* `/delete` command. For example, you can use this command:

```
net use c$ /delete
```

Each hard drive has an administrative share (C:\ = c$), and there are two special shares, `ipc$` and `admin$`. Because these shares are restored on startup in certain configurations, you may need to create a batch file with the needed `net use` command entries and load the batch file into the system startup group. For a system with a single hard drive C:, you need to enter the following lines:

```
net share c$ /delete
net share admin$ /delete
net share ipc$ /delete
```

Disabling services after setup

After you have completed the system install and you have logged onto the system as a user with administrative privileges (and before the system is connected to a public network), you need to disable a large number of services. To access and disable the services, follow these steps:

1. **Right-click the My Computer icon on the desktop.**

2. **Select Manage from the context menu that appears.**

The Microsoft Management Console (MMC) window appears.

3. **Locate the Services and Applications entry. Click the + symbol next to it to expand the menu, as shown in Figure 2-1.**

4. **Find and click the Services entry.**

The right side of the MMC window lists the services currently running on your system.

5. **Right-click the listed service and select the Properties option from the context menu that appears.**

The General tab of the Properties window appears, as shown in Figure 2-2.

6. **Select Disabled from the Startup Type drop-down list.**

The service is now disabled.

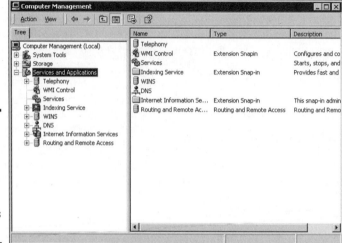

Figure 2-1:
Computer
Manage-
ment
Services
and
Applications
console.

Figure 2-2:
Services
Properties
Sheet:
General tab.

On the General tab of the Properties window for a service, you can also stop, start, pause, or resume a service. The functions on the General tab enable you to do most of what you need to at this point. The other two tabs you need to know about are Log On (see Figure 2-3) and Dependencies (see Figure 2-4):

✦ **Log On:** Somewhat like the SUID/GUID options for configuring how binaries run under Linux, the Log On properties allow you to control the authority that a service has. For example, if a service runs with the

SYSTEM account, it can pretty much get to anything. If hackers compromised the service, it is likely that they could then execute arbitrary code allowing them to do all kinds of horrible things.

Though many of these services won't work (well or at all) without high-level access, you can use the Log On tab to modify their rights in an attempt to rein them in. This process is trial and error. The best method is to assign the relevant user credentials and then attempt to restart the service. If it works, you could be in business, but you need to initiate a process that uses the service to be sure. If errors result, change the Log On settings back to their defaults and try another tactic.

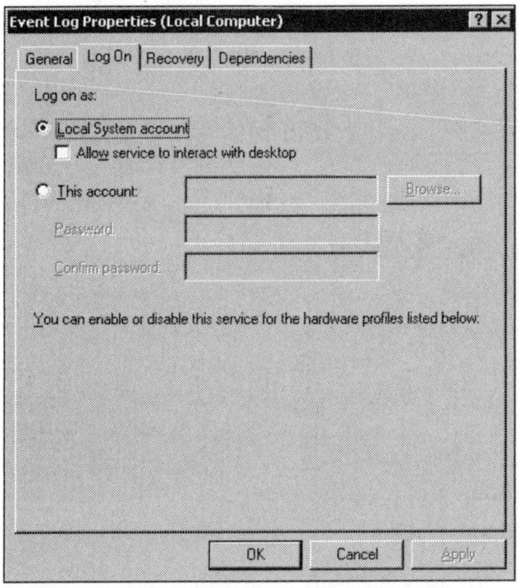

Figure 2-3:
Services
Properties
Sheet:
Logon tab.

✦ **Dependencies:** On this tab, you find the services that depend on the service in question, and those services on which it depends. For example, if you want to disable the Event Log (see Figure 2-4), you notice that the Event log depends on no other services. This means you can disable any service without affecting the Event Log. However, several services require the Event Log in order to work. For example, if you disable the Event Log, the File Replication Service will no longer work.

For every service you want to disable, make sure that you're not going to inadvertently break a service you need. You should also note that you can set a service to manual startup rather than automatic or disabled. This is a useful setting if you're unsure if an application will require it. If an application does need the service, it will be able to start it.

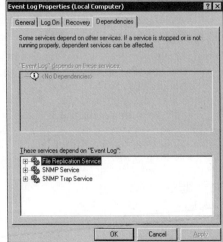

Figure 2-4: Services Properties Sheet: Dependencies tab.

Deciding what services to disable

So which services can you live without? On your Web server, the following services can safely be stopped and disabled. Microsoft includes restrictions on the number of external user connections allowed on non-server operating systems, which is typically ten users. Because you're likely to want more than ten users on your server at a time, the following list focuses on services running on Windows 2000 Server with Service Pack 4. You should disable the following services:

- ✦ Alerter
- ✦ Application Layer Gateway Service
- ✦ Automatic Updates
- ✦ ClipBook
- ✦ COM+ Event System
- ✦ COM+ System Application
- ✦ Computer Browser
- ✦ DHCP Client
- ✦ Distributed Link Tracking Client
- ✦ Distributed Transaction Coordinator

- ✦ Fax Service
- ✦ FTP Publishing Service
- ✦ IIS Admin
- ✦ Indexing Service
- ✦ IPSEC Services
- ✦ Logical Disk Manager
- ✦ Logical Disk Manager Administrative Service
- ✦ Messenger
- ✦ Net Login
- ✦ NetMeeting Remote Desktop Sharing
- ✦ Network DDE
- ✦ Network DDE DSDM

- ✦ Network Location Awareness (NLA)
- ✦ NT LM Security Support Provider
- ✦ Performance Logs and Alerts
- ✦ QoS RSVP
- ✦ Remote Procedure Call (RPC) Locator
- ✦ Remote Registry Service
- ✦ Routing and Remote Access

- ✦ Smart Card
- ✦ Smart Card Helper
- ✦ TCP/IP NetBIOS Helper Service
- ✦ Telephony
- ✦ Telnet
- ✦ Uninterruptible Power Supply
- ✦ Wireless Configuration
- ✦ World Wide Web Publishing Service

Keeping Up with Patches and Updates

Because new issues arise with Windows (and just about every other operating system) on a regular basis, you need to have a plan for updating your system. The place to start is the Microsoft Windows Update Web site at `windowsupdate.microsoft.com`. Once on the Web site, you may need to interact with a couple of security pop-ups. If you click the OK option in the pop-ups, eventually you see an option (green link) that says Scan for Updates, as shown in Figure 2-5. Click this option to start the scanning process.

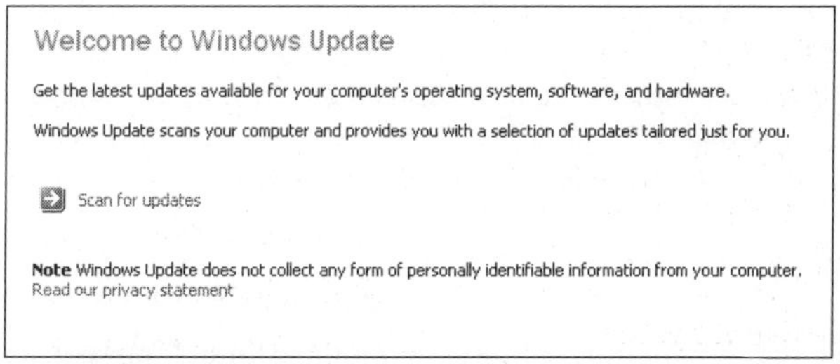

Figure 2-5:
The Scan
for Updates
screen.

Welcome to Windows Update

Get the latest updates available for your computer's operating system, software, and hardware.

Windows Update scans your computer and provides you with a selection of updates tailored just for you.

Scan for updates

Note Windows Update does not collect any form of personally identifiable information from your computer. Read our privacy statement

After your system has been scanned, three classes of updates may be identified:

- ✦ **Critical updates and service packs:** You should install all critical updates and service packs regardless of how the computer is being used. For example, several high-profile worms used vulnerabilities that had been identified and resolved (via available patches) months or years before the actual worm was created and released. All of the files needed to prevent infection are available on the Windows Update Web site. In general you need to download and install all updates listed as "critical." Other updates should be considered entirely optional. The other two groups of updates are discussed briefly below.

✦ **Generic updates:** These updates add some kind of functionality but do not correct critical system issues.

✦ **Driver updates:** Generally speaking, if you're not having any problems related to drivers, you should avoid these driver updates. If you have a newer driver on your system that is not certified by Microsoft, the drivers options suggest replacing your driver anyway; the result is that the Windows Update site could end up downgrading your driver.

If you want to make an update package that does not require the system being updated to be online, you can collect the updates individually and place them on a CD-R or whatever medium you prefer for later use. To collect the individual updates, go to www.microsoft.com/downloads and click the Windows (Security & Updates) link in the table of contents on the left. A variety of files appear, including critical updates and service packs. Select the items you desire, download them, and you're ready to go. This method can be particularly useful if a critical patch needs to be installed while the system is offline.

Analyzing with MBSA

As a final step to make sure your system is as secure as can be, you can use the Microsoft Baseline Security Analyzer (MBSA). This tool provides users with a method of identifying common configuration problems. The current version of the MBSA tool is 1.1.1. This version includes options for using the standard graphical interface as well as a command-line version. One of the benefits of this arrangement is that the tool is easy to use locally, and it has the potential to be automated via batch scripting.

This tool is compatible with Windows 2000, Windows XP, and Windows Server 2003 systems as hosts. MBSA will scan the following system types for need-to-be-patched items and configuration weaknesses: Windows NT 4.0, Windows 2000, Windows XP, and Windows Server 2003. MBSA will also scan a number of service and supplemental applications, including Internet Information Server (IIS) 4.0 and 5.0, SQL Server 7.0 and 2000, Internet Explorer, and Office 2000 and 2002 for unpatched components. The HFNetChk tool (previously a separate tool) is used to scan for missing updates in the supplementary applications and services. In addition to identifying the needed system updates, the MBSA tool creates a report for every system scanned when groups of systems are scanned at one time.

Getting Windows behind a Firewall

Okay, you have Windows all patched with nonessential services disabled. Now are you safe? Unfortunately the answer is somewhere between "probably not" and "if so, probably not for long." No operating system that provides a wide range of end user services should be directly connected to the Internet. This includes Windows, Linux, Unix and NetWare just to name a few. Along with patching, securing, and limiting operating services, you also should use a hardware firewall. A *firewall* is hardware or software that acts as a security agent for your network or server. A firewall sits physically between your protected system (such as your Web server) and any unsecured networks (such as the Internet). All data coming to your Web server first must come through your firewall. Though the features vary by manufacturer and model, firewalls can be configured to refuse certain kinds of connections, block traffic from a denial-of-service attack, and log suspicious activity.

Firewalls vary widely in cost and ease of use. If you are protecting a small network or a single host you don't necessarily need to spend a fortune on a firewall. However, a few features should be considered essential. The list below outlines the minimum features your firewall needs to have. Other features such as DHCP and Virtual Private Network (VPN) hosting services could be useful depending on your network layout, but they are not essential.

✦ Stateful packet inspection

✦ Denial-of-service (DoS) prevention

✦ Configurable Port Forwarding

✦ Easy to configure management interface

Stateful packet inspection involves the examination of data traffic coming into the firewall from the Internet. It is designed to prevent a kind of attack known as *spoofing,* where an external user tries to fool the firewall into believing a local host is actually located on the Internet. A successful spoof allows the external user to bypass the security that the router provides. With a firewall, the inbound traffic is checked to see if it is in response to a request that an internal host made. If it is, then the traffic is forwarded along. If the traffic is not legitimate, it is discarded.

The denial-of-service protection provided by a firewall can come in several forms. A denial-of-service attack typically involves either sending large volumes of traffic or malformed data to a host. The idea is to cause the host (router or firewall) to become so overloaded it stops forwarding traffic. The attack thus denies the users (who depend on the router/firewall for network access) any use of their service. Hence the name Denial of Service.

The firewall's method of preventing the attack often involves blocking or ignoring traffic from a host or set of hosts. This is extremely effective. After the firewall ceases processing traffic from the attacking host there is very little chance that a prolonged service outage will occur.

Port forwarding is only essential if you intend to allow inbound (from the Internet) connections. An *inbound connection* occurs when an Internet-based user gains access to some resource on your network. A relevant example is your Web server. To allow users access to your internal Web server, the firewall must be configured to forward Web traffic (on TCP port 80) to the internal IP address of your Web server.

Make sure that when you purchase a firewall you research the device thoroughly. You will probably want functionality beyond just the basic items outlined above. Develop a list of features you deem essential. Read the product literature and select a device that best matches your needs. There are many great firewall producers out there. The list below outlines some of the most popular.

+ Cisco Systems: www.cisco.com
+ Netgear: www.netgear.com
+ Sonic Wall: www.sonicwall.com
+ Nokia: www.nokia.com
+ 3Com: www.3com.com

Chapter 3: Ten Third-Party Packages That Enhance Security

In This Chapter

✔ **Bastille Hardening System**

✔ **LIDS**

✔ **Guarddog**

✔ **Firestarter**

✔ **WinRoute**

✔ **ZoneAlarm**

✔ **SNORT**

✔ **ACID**

✔ **Pandora**

✔ **Nessus**

*I*n your quest to secure your server, you don't need to depend solely on the tools that came with your operating system. Many third-party vendors make security-enhancing products. In the Linux community, these tools not only are powerful but often have little or no retail costs associated with them. This chapter examines ten excellent products designed to help you keep your system secure.

Locking Down with Bastille

The program known as the Bastille Hardening System is used to perform a systemic hardening of supported operating systems. This tool currently supports a variety of Linux distributions including Red Hat, Debian, Mandrake, SuSE, and Turbo Linux, as well as other operating systems such as HP-UX and Mac OS X. Essentially, Bastille is a collection of scripts that when executed removes a large number of known configuration weaknesses. These scripts are built by a collection of developers who are experts in their respective fields. The scripts are designed to reconfigure the system on which they're executed. Along with individual expert input, accepted industry guidelines, such as the SANS institute's recommendations for securing Linux, are used.

Go to `www.bastille-linux.org` to download the installer for your operating system, such as the RPM package for Red Hat and the perl-TK or perl-Curses package. To run the script, simply type `bastille` in a terminal window. The hardening script then executes and walks you through the process of hardening the system.

Linux Intrusion Detection with LIDS

The Linux Intrusion Detection System (LIDS) is a collection of components that updates the Linux kernel's security options. Access rules are put in place that control the default abilities of the kernel. These access options expand the ability to control access to the level where even root can be restricted from accessing various system resources. In addition, LIDS extends the system capabilities allowing it to control the whole system as well as some network and file-system security features. The LIDS developers promote it as "A Protection, Detection, and Response in the Linux system." You use rules along with LIDS to define which events are tracked, how LIDS should respond to network-intrusion attempts, and so forth. The following list outlines some of the key features of LIDS:

✦ It allows the configuration of file access in such a manner that not even root can make changes to the file.

✦ It can protect processes from being killed.

✦ It enables you to restrict RAW IO operations, protect your hard drive, and protect the Master Boot Record.

✦ When your LIDS-enabled system is the target of a port scan, LIDS can detect it and send an alert to the user in charge of maintaining the system. Any violation of the defined rules can also be logged and generate alerts.

✦ When someone violates the rules, LIDS can log the detail message about the violated action to the system log file or to your syslog server, either of which may be protected by LIDS.

✦ Also in response to rule violations, LIDS can notify an administrator or even kill the offending session/connection.

For more information about LIDS, including usage and configuration, check out `www.lids.org/`.

Starting Easy with Guarddog

Guarddog is a KDE-based graphical firewall-configuration utility that helps simplify the process of configuring your Linux firewall. This product was designed to help beginners, as well as save more advanced users the trouble of dealing with complex scripts and ipchains configurations. Along with easy setup, Guarddog enables you to continually tweak and adjust your firewall. Like the initial setup, easy-to-navigate graphical tools are used. Here are some of the key features of Guarddog:

✦ Enables you to divide hosts/networks into zones. Different zones can have different security policies if needed. For example, one zone may contain computers used for public access with nonsensitive information (minimal security needs) and another zone could contain mission-critical servers (maximum security needs).

✦ Supports a huge number of networking protocols, including FTP, SSH, Telnet, SMTP, DNS, HTTP, HTTPS, and POP.

✦ Enables you to add at a later date any protocols not supported by the default configuration.

✦ Works with local router configurations (if your system is performing routing).

✦ Runs on KDE 2 or 3, and Linux 2.2 and 2.4 series kernels.

✦ Works with iptables features including connection tracking and rate-limited logging.

✦ Enables you to import/export firewall scripts.

✦ Uses a fail-safe default configuration that denies all activities that are not implicitly allowed.

For more information on Guarddog, check out `www.simonzone.com/software/guarddog/`.

Taking Control with Firestarter

Another graphical tool for configuring Linux firewalls is Firestarter. This tool uses GTK+/GNOME. The product developers tout Firestarter as a user-friendly means of configuring Linux firewalls using GNOME. When compared to Guarddog, Firestarter seems to be slightly more feature-rich. For many users, particularly beginners who are comfortable with a particular desktop environment, the best option is to select the GUI configuration tool that works with their configuration. The following list highlights some of the most interesting and useful features of Firestarter:

✦ Provides a configuration wizard that enables the program to work in a useful way for both beginners and experts.

✦ Provides multilanguage support.

✦ Comes with predefined rule sets, as well as tools for adding your own access and monitoring rules.

✦ Comes with a list of known network exploits and various malware signatures. *Malware* is short for "Malicious Software." Malware generally includes worms, Trojans, virii, backdoor utilities, and any other tool used for malicious activities.

✦ Enables *granular service control,* which means, plainly, that you have the ability to control even the most detailed setting.

✦ Comes with ICMP tools usable in preventing some denial-of-service (DoS) attacks.

✦ Provides Type of Service (ToS) support.

✦ Provides full-featured Network Address Translation (NAT) and IP port forwarding functions.

✦ Provides user-configurable Advanced Kernel Tuning Features.

✦ Works with glibc's sysctl tuning to enhance system reliability and protect the firewall from flooding, broadcasting, and IP spoofing.

✦ Supports Linux kernels 2.2, 2.4 and 2.5.

For downloads, installation HOWTO's, and a wealth of other information, check out `firestarter.sourceforge.net`.

WinRoute Firewall

If you use the Microsoft Windows family of operating systems to host your networked application, you need a third-party firewall. In particular, firewalling your server is especially important if the system will be accessed by users coming from the Internet. Kerio's WinRoute Firewall product (`www.kerio.com/kwf_home.html`) is one of the more cost effective (yet entirely functional) firewall products available. This application is easy to install, configure, and maintain.

Here are some of the key features of the WinRoute Firewall package:

✦ It provides full routing capabilities.

✦ Stateful packet inspection can be applied to both inbound and outbound traffic.

✦ It has a network rules wizard that makes configuring the firewall painless.

✦ Antivirus capabilities are available. WinRoute Firewall can scan inbound and outbound HTTP and FTP traffic for viruses.

✦ It supports VPN through its NAT firewall. This is particularly useful if you need to remotely manage your server because it provides encrypted access.

ZoneAlarm

ZoneAlarm is a powerful software firewall for Windows. It is free to private and nonprofit users, and available for a modest fee to businesses. ZoneAlarm performs the same functions as most firewalls (stateful packet inspection, filtering, and so on) but has a security wizard that is a little different than most. When you choose a high security level during installation, you are prompted to allow or deny all of the outbound traffic the host sees. For example, if a process tries to access DNS services on a remote host, a window pops up asking if you want to allow this traffic to pass. You can elect to let it pass in that particular instance, or you can tell ZoneAlarm to always let it pass.

Any inbound connections are blocked. You have to use the configuration wizard to allow any inbounds you need (such as http or port 80). You get to interactively "train" the firewall to handle your traffic. If you choose another security level (lower), the firewall allows more traffic to pass (by default). For more information about ZoneAlarm, check out the Zone Labs Web site at www.zonelabs.com.

Snort

In the world of software Intrusion Detection Systems (IDSs), Snort is one of the most useful products. In addition to being a top-performing software package, Snort is an open-source IDS that is available for free. With relatively minimal hardware requirements, Snort can monitor access and perform traffic analysis in real time. Snort is effective at identifying or stopping a wide range of network intrusions and attacks including the following:

+ Buffer overflows

+ Stealth port scans

+ CGI attacks

+ SMB probes

+ OS fingerprinting attempts

+ Brute-force crackers

The underlying detection engine and rules language are what make Snort so effective. Using the included language, you can specify what kinds of traffic should be allowed to pass on or around your network and what Snort should do if it encounters forbidden activity. You can drop most of Snort's output to a syslog server where it can then be manually inspected. Or using something like ACID (described in the next section) on the syslog server, Snort can provide dynamic alerting and reporting. Although getting Snort up and running can be a complex task, a wealth of useful implementation guides are available on the Snort Web site at www.snort.org.

ACID

ACID (Analysis Console for Intrusion Databases) is a collection of PHP code that powers an engine used for searching security logs and security databases. For example, you can use ACID to provide reporting on databases used by programs such as syslog, but you can also access a wide range of security records. Rather than plug in a number of text-driven queries or manually scan files, ACID enables you to quickly make inquiries and see the results displayed graphically. You can also configure ACID to generate alerts based on its data analysis. For example, if it finds records of certain types of activities (such as Nessus running on your network; see "Getting In with Nessus," later in this chapter), it can highlight the results in your query or generate administrative alerts via e-mail.

If you care at all about meaningful reporting, ACID is a can't-do-without kind of tool. You can find ACID in a number of locations, including `sourceforge.net/projects/acidlab`. Although the quality of documentation relating to the use of ACID is sometimes a bit scattered, the Web site `www.andrew.cmu.edu/~rdanyliw/snort/acid_config.html` provides a good general reference for using Snort.

Opening the Box: Pandora

Pandora is a powerful network-security auditing tool. Some folks might call it a hacking tool, but that depends on your perspective. Regardless, it is marketed as an auditing tool.

Pandora builds on a long list of multi-OS vulnerabilities and intrusion techniques to test your network for weaknesses. Primarily a NetWare auditing tool (as far as password cracking and direct server scanning), support for Linux is expected soon. In the interim, the network-attack tools are useful for testing regardless of the server platform in use. Some of the noteworthy abilities of Pandora include the following:

✦ Provides password-cracking feature.

✦ Can be used as a browser for accessing all NDS (NetWare) objects. Enables you to enumerate shares, users, groups and so forth.

✦ Can attach to servers using only the password hash (if you do not wish to crack them).

✦ Can collect information about servers. Identifies vulnerabilities to IP spoofing.

✦ Can initiate denial-of-service attacks.

For installation binaries, source code, documentation and more, visit the development site at `www.nmrc.org/pandora/`.

Getting In with Nessus

First off, do not download and use this tool on your network unless everyone (that is, the boss) knows what you're up to. You can possibly crash a server with this tool if you use all its features. It is almost a given as well that any IDS system worth its salt will go bonkers the minute you begin running this tool because Nessus is used for evil as well as good.

Nessus is probably the best security-auditing tool available. To use a cliché, "It's all that, and a bucket of chicken." Nessus does something that many security scanners don't do: It attempts to steer away from assumptions about your network configuration. For example, if a service such as FTP is running on a port other than 21 (3728, for example), Nessus will find it and test it. Nothing is perfect, and something somewhere will probably be missed. However, Nessus is one of the best at finding holes in the largest number of networks. Here are some the key features of Nessus:

✦ Nessus supports expansion with the use of plug-ins. Each plug-in contains information about a known weakness, new attack type, and so forth so that the repertoire of vectors for testing your network remains current and potent (if you install new plug-ins as they're developed).

✦ It supports multithreading to allow the analysis of large numbers of hosts and devices at a single time. Your only limitation is CPU horsepower.

✦ Relational multihost testing is used to probe not only a single system, but also all of its related network hosts. For example, all the hosts in the domain, IP subnet, or systems currently connected via RPC are probed as well. This testing identifies indirect means of compromising a specific host.

✦ The reporting system is relatively easy to use. Nessus uses a graphical interface to display the holes in the scanned network that have been found.

For more information, downloads, and product tours, check out the Nessus home page, www.nessus.org/.

Book II

Building an Apache Web Site

The 5th Wave   By Rich Tennant

©RICHTENNANT

"Just how accurately should my Web site reflect my place of business?"

Contents at a Glance

Chapter 1: Introducing the Apache Web Server

In This Chapter

✔ **Understanding how Apache works**

✔ **Introducing the HTTP protocol**

✔ **Examining the parts of a URL**

✔ **Exploring the Apache architecture**

Apache is an open-source Web server. A Web server delivers the files on the Web site to the visitor who wants to see the Web pages. In this chapter, I show you the basics of Apache, including why it's popular and how it works.

The Advantages to Using the Apache Web Server

Apache is the most popular Web server on the World Wide Web. Approximately 60 percent of the Web sites on the Internet use Apache, according to surveys at www.netcraft.com/survey and www.security space.com/s_survey/data/. The following list highlights some advantages to using Apache:

✦ **It's free.** Like the other open-source software in this book, Apache is free.

✦ **It runs on a wide variety of operating systems.** Apache runs on Windows, Linux, Mac OS, FreeBSD, and most varieties of Unix.

✦ **It's popular.** Over half of all Web sites use Apache. This wouldn't be true if it didn't work well. Also, this means that a lot of information about Apache is available on the Web and that many Apache users can provide help.

✦ **It's reliable.** After Apache is up and running, it should run as long as your computer runs. Emergency problems with Apache are rare.

✦ **It's customizable.** The open-source license allows programmers to modify the Apache software, adding or modifying modules as needed to fit their own environments.

✦ **It's secure.** Free software is available that runs with Apache to make it into a secure SSL server. Security is an essential issue if you're using the site for e-commerce.

Understanding How Apache Works

The Apache Web server is the engine that powers your Web site. It handles requests for information and sends the information to the requestor. The process that Apache uses to deliver your Web pages to the world works as follows:

1. A user types a URL for a Web page on your site into his or her browser.

2. The browser sends a request via the Internet, asking for the file specified in the URL.

3. Apache on your Web site receives the request from the browser.

4. Apache looks on your Web site for the file specified in the URL.

5. If Apache finds the requested file, it sends the file to the browser that requested it. If Apache doesn't find the file or can't send it for some reason, it sends a numeric error code to the browser.

6. The browser interprets the information it receives from Apache as HTML and displays the resulting Web page in the browser window. If the information received is an error code, the browser displays the message associated with the error code.

Communication between Apache and the browser

Apache and the Web browser communicate using the Hypertext Transfer Protocol, generally referred to as HTTP. HTTP is a language that both Apache and the browser understand, and it's used to transfer information between them. An HTTP message is sent in an HTTP *header,* the first message sent in a communication.

Communication between Apache and the browser proceeds in a request/response format: The browser sends a request message in an HTTP header, and Apache responds. For instance, when the browser sends a request via the Internet for a file, an HTTP header containing an HTTP message similar to the following is sent:

```
GET /productInfo.html HTTP/1.1
Host: www.myfinecompany.com
```

In this example, the GET request header asks for the productInfo.html file. The GET header also includes the version of HTTP that is being used — in this case version 1.1. The second line tells Apache that the file is located on the computer with the domain name www.myfinecompany.com.

Your Apache server stores all the requests it receives in its log file. You can look at the log to see what requests are being sent to your server. The Apache log files are discussed in more detail in Book II, Chapter 3.

When Apache receives the request header, it looks for the specified file. It then sends an HTTP response based on whether it was successful in finding and sending the file to the requestor.

If the request is unsuccessful, the HTTP message is similar to the following:

```
HTTP/1.1 404 Not found
```

This message shows the HTTP version and the status, which consists of a numeric error code and a short phrase describing why the request failed. Another common message for an unsuccessful request is as follows:

```
HTTP/1.1 403 Forbidden
```

This message means the file was located, but the requestor isn't authorized to access it.

If the request is successful, the first line is a status message, as follows:

```
HTTP/1.1 200 OK
```

In addition to status information, the HTTP message also contains the following data:

✦ **Information about the file being sent.** This information may include the date, the type of file, the server name, and information that is specific to the individual Apache setup.

✦ **The contents of the file that was requested.** This is the last element of the HTTP message.

Receiving requests

Apache is responsible for responding to requests for Web page files. It is always running on your Web site, sitting quietly in the background, listening for requests. Apache's job is to send files from your Web site to users who request them.

Apache recognizes requests and accepts them based on the URL (Uniform Resource Locator) specified in the request. A URL is an address on the World Wide Web, and every Web page has a unique URL. Apache recognizes the URL for the Web site and accepts the requests that are addressed to the Web site where it's installed.

The format of a URL is as follows:

`http://servername:portnumber/path`

Here's a breakdown of the parts that make up the URL:

✦ `http://`: This specifies the HTTP protocol, which is the main protocol discussed in this book. Other protocols include FTP and HTTPS. FTP tells the server to download the file using FTP rather than HTTP. HTTPS tells Apache to access the file using SSL, the secure server protocol; SSL is discussed in Book II, Chapter 4. If this part of the URL is left out, Apache assumes that the protocol is HTTP.

✦ `servername`: This tells Apache the name of the computer where the Web site is located. This part of the URL is required. You can reach many Web sites by using only the servername. For instance, you can reach the Amazon and Google Web sites by using only `amazon.com` and `google.com`, respectively, as the URLs.

✦ `:portnumber`: Apache exchanges information with the Internet at a particular port on the computer. Most of the time, Apache is set up to communicate via port 80. If the port number is not specified, port 80 is assumed.

In some unusual circumstances, a Web server may use a different port number, in which case the port number must be specified. The most common reason for using a different port number is to set up a test Web site on another port, such as 8080, that is available only to developers and testers, not customers. When the site is ready for customers, it is made available on port 80.

✦ `path`: This is the path to the file, which follows the rules of any path on the computer where the Web site is located. The root of the path is the main Web site directory. For instance, `productInfo.html` is the path part of the URL `www.myfinecompany.com/productInfo.html`.

Locating the requested file

After Apache accepts a request, it attempts to locate the requested Web page file and send it to the user. Apache is configured to look for Web page files in a particular directory, sometimes called its *Web space*. The directory is specified in the Apache configuration file as DOCUMENTROOT. The Apache configuration file is discussed in Book II, Chapter 3.

The default location for Web page files is in the `htdocs` subdirectory, which is located in the directory where Apache was installed. Web page files can be accessed from `htdocs` or any subdirectory of `htdocs`. You can change the location where Apache looks for Web page files by changing the value for DOCUMENTROOT in the Apache configuration file. Some Linux distributions set the document root to a different location. For example, Red Hat sets the document root to `/var/www/html`.

If the URL specifies a directory rather than a file, Apache looks for a default file in the specified directory. The default filename is set in the Apache configuration file. Usually, the default file is called `index.html`, but you can set any name you want by editing the value for `DirectoryIndex` in the Apache configuration file.

**Book II
Chapter 1**

**Introducing the
Apache Web Server**

If Apache can't find a file with the default name in the directory specified in the URL, it may display a list of the files in the directory. This is a serious security hazard; you don't want visitors to your Web site to see all the files and be able to access them. You can control whether Apache displays a list of files in the directory by changing a setting in the configuration file (discussed in Book II, Chapter 3). Look for the following setting:

```
Options Indexes
```

This setting tells Apache to display a list of the files in the directory. Change the setting to the following:

```
Options -Indexes
```

With this setting, if Apache can't find a default file in a directory, it displays the following message:

```
Forbidden
You don't have permission to access /dirname on this server.
```

Processing files as scripts

In many cases, Apache returns the requested file to the browser, as is, as described at the beginning of this chapter. However, Apache has the ability to treat the file as a script. Apache can run the script by using outside software (such as the bash shell, PHP, or Perl), receive the output produced by running the script, and then send that output to the browser. In that case, the steps described at the beginning of the chapter expand, as follows:

1. A user types a URL for a Web page on your Web site into his or her browser.

2. The browser sends a request to the host computer for your site via the Internet, asking for the file specified in the URL.

3. Apache receives the request for the file.

4. Apache looks on your Web site for the file specified in the URL.

5. If Apache finds the requested file, it does the following:

    i. It checks whether the file needs to be treated as a script. If so, it runs the script, using the designated software to execute the script file.

    ii. It receives the output from the other software and sends that output to the browser that requested the file.

    If Apache doesn't find the file or can't send it for some reason, it sends a numeric error code to the browser.

6. The browser interprets the information it receives from Apache as HTML and displays the resulting Web page in the browser window. If the information received is an error code, the browser displays the message associated with the error code.

Outside software is often used to make a Web site interactive. For instance, if you display an HTML form, you need to use other software to process the information the user types into the form. As another example, you may need outside software for your Web site to interact with a database.

Apache knows to treat the file as a script and execute it using outside software based on directives in its configuration file, as discussed in Book II, Chapter 3. You can tell Apache to run the file using outside software if the file is in a certain directory, if the file has a certain extension, or if the file is a certain type. For instance, if the requested file is in the CGI directory (the configuration file specifies which directory is the CGI directory; the default is cgi-bin), Apache assumes the file is a script and runs it. The script needs to have a pound-bang line — a line in the top of the script that tells the shell which software (often Perl) to use to run the script. Another example is when directives in the configuration file tell Apache to send any file with the extension .php to PHP to be processed before returning the output to the browser.

Using cookies

Cookies are text strings generated by Apache and stored in files on users' hard disks. The filenames include your Web site's name. Cookies serve as long-term memory, storing information the server wants to remember about the Web site visitor. When the browser sends any future requests for a Web page from the same Web site, the cookie is sent along with the request, providing the stored information to the server.

Taking a Look at the Apache Architecture

The Apache Web server software consists of core software plus many modules that can be added to Apache:

✦ **Base modules** are included with Apache by default.

✦ **Extensions** are modules downloaded with Apache, but not enabled by default; you have to enable them when you install Apache in order to use them.

✦ **External modules** — third-party modules — are available to add to Apache, but they are not included by default.

In addition, you can write your own Apache module with features that you need and add it to Apache.

The behavior of Apache is set in a configuration file using statements called *directives*. Many directives are made available as part of the Apache core features. Other directives are made available and handled by modules. You can't use a specific directive unless the module that handles the directive is added to Apache.

When you install Apache and start it, Apache reads the configuration file and behaves according to the directives in this file. You can change some of Apache's behavior by editing the configuration file and restarting Apache so that it reads the new directives. The configuration file and its directives are discussed in Book II, Chapter 3.

Apache logs its activities in log files. Directives control what events are logged and where the log files are stored. By default, an error log named `error_log` is set up, and in it, Apache writes messages whenever errors occur. The error log is stored in the subdirectory logs in the directory in which Apache is installed. Also by default, Apache logs all requests and responses in a file called `access_log` in the same directory.

Chapter 2: Installing Apache

In This Chapter

✔ **Selecting an Apache version**

✔ **Compiling Apache**

✔ **Starting Apache**

✔ **Running more than one Apache server**

*A*pache is an open-source Web server, which means that you can install it for free on the host computer for your Web site. In this chapter, I show you how to obtain and install Apache on your computer.

Getting Apache from the Web

In most cases, you want to get Apache from the Web and install it yourself. Although Apache may already be installed on your computer (because most Linux distributions include Apache), it's unlikely to be the latest version. Or Apache may not have been installed with the options you need. Because of this, in most cases you're better off installing Apache yourself.

Selecting a version of Apache

Apache is currently available in two versions: Apache 1.3 and Apache 2. Apache 2 is the newer version, released in April 2002. Apache 2 is a major rewrite of Apache, changing some fundamental internal functioning to make Apache run more efficiently on different operating systems and to make it easier to port Apache from one operating system to another. Apache 2 handles processes and threads very differently than Apache 1.3.

Currently, many developers are using Apache 2 and are quite happy with it. Many Linux machines come with Apache 2 installed. However, sometimes Apache 2 is not the right choice. Apache modules that run with Apache 1.3 won't run with Apache 2. Therefore, if you need to use a module, it must be rewritten before you can use it with Apache 2. Many modules have been rewritten, but some have not. For example, PHP — the most popular Apache module — currently cautions against using PHP in a production environment on its Web site at `www.php.net/manual/en/install.apache2.php#install.apache2.unix`.

When deciding which version to install, check the Web sites for the modules you plan to use to determine their compatibility with Apache 2. For example, if you use the SSL module, check the www.modssl.org Web site. You can usually find the Web site name for a module by entering the module name at www.google.com. If the modules are compatible, install Apache 2.

The information in this book is based on Apache 2. Most of it applies just as well to Apache 1.3. In some places, I mention that the information applies only to Apache 2.

Apache 2

At this time, the current version of Apache 2 is version 2.0.47. This version contains bug fixes for previous versions and also fixes a security problem. Try to install the most current Apache version. Apache 2 is released frequently, so check the Apache Web site (httpd.apache.org) for the most current information on versions.

Apache 1.3

The current version of Apache 1.3 is version 1.3.28. This release fixes some security issues. For security reasons, you should install this version or a later version. New features are no longer being added to Apache 1.3, but bugs are still being fixed, and security issues are being addressed. New versions of Apache 1.3 continue to be released, but on a less frequent basis than for Apache 2.

Upgrading from Apache 1.3 to Apache 2

As mentioned earlier, modules that run with Apache 1.3 do not run with Apache 2. Therefore, if you're running modules with Apache 1.3, you need to upgrade the modules when you upgrade Apache. Check the Web sites for the modules and download a version that has been rewritten to run with Apache 2.

Selecting the type of file to install

You can download and install two types of Apache software:

+ A binary — a precompiled machine language file made specifically for your operating system

+ A source file that you compile yourself and then install

Binary files

Binary files are available for installation on most operating systems. Binary files are easier to install than source files because they're already compiled. However, the binary file for a version is generally released a little later than the source file. Therefore, the binary file is probably not the very latest version.

Binary files are available from the Apache Web site. You select the appropriate binary for your operating system. The Web site has a README file for each binary with information about the binary, including which modules are compiled into the binary. The binary files, all necessary supporting files (including a README.bindist), and installation instructions (in the file INSTALL.bindist) are compressed and packed into one file — called a *tarball* — that you download. You unpack the file to access the files you need and then install the files in the appropriate location.

If you're familiar with Linux RPM files, you may want to install Linux as an RPM. Download the RPM file from the Web site for your Linux distribution. That is, if you're running Red Hat Linux, download the RPM from the Red Hat Web site.

Source files

Installing Apache from source files is more difficult than installing it from binary files, but doing so enables you to install the latest version with exactly the options you need.

Before installing Apache

Before installing Apache, check your host computer for the following requirements:

✦ **Disk space:** You may need as much as 50MB of disk space while installing. Apache will probably use 10MB after installation, although the amount varies depending on the options used and modules installed.

✦ **C compiler:** Your computer has an ANSI-compliant C compiler installed. GNU C (gcc) is a good choice.

Installing Apache from Source Files

To install Apache from source files, follow these steps:

1. **Point your Web browser to** `httpd.apache.org`, **the Apache home page.**

2. **Click the From a Mirror link under Download on the left side of the page.**

3. **Scroll down to the section labeled Mirror.**

   A specific mirror is selected for you. If you do not want to use this mirror, select another. Or if you have problems downloading from this mirror, return to this page and select another.

4. **Scroll farther down the same page to the section for Apache 2 or for Apache 1.3, whichever you want to install. Locate and highlight the file you want to download.**

   For instance, at this time, the most recent version for Linux is `httpd-2.0.47.tar.gz`.

5. **Click the latest version to download it.**

6. **Select the option to save the file.**

7. **Navigate to where you want to save the source code (for example, `/usr/src`). Then click Save.**

8. **After the download, change to the download directory (for example, `cd-/usr/src`).**

   You see a file named `httpd-`, followed by the version name and `tar.gz`. This file is called a tarball because it contains many files compressed into the tarball file by a program called tar.

   Be sure you're using an account that has permission to write into `/usr/src`, such as root.

9. **Verify the downloaded file to be sure it hasn't been tampered with. To verify the file, follow these steps:**

   i. Download two files from `www.apache.org/dist/httpd/`: KEYS and a file with the same version number as the source with a filename that ends in `.asc`.

   ii. Type one of the following lines, depending on which version of PGP is installed on your computer:

   ```
   pgp <KEYS
   gpg --import KEYS
   ```

   Several lines of output are displayed.

   iii. Type one of the following lines, with the correct version number.

   ```
   pgp httpd-2.0.47.tar.gz.asc
   gpg --verify httpd-2.0.47.tar.gz.asc
   ```

You should see something similar to the following:

```
Good signature from user "Sander Striker"
```

This is what you're looking for. Several messages may be displayed, but the preceding message is the important one. You may also see a message stating that the relationship between the key and the signer of the key cannot be verified. This is okay.

If you don't get a message that the signature is good, the file may have been tampered with and may be dangerous. In this case, repeat the process starting with Step 1 and select a different mirror to download from.

10. **Unpack the tarball.**

The command to unpack the tarball for version 2.0.47 is the following:

```
gunzip -c httpd-2.0.47.tar.gz | tar -xf -
```

A new directory called `httpd-2.0.47` is created with several subdirectories containing all the files that you just unpacked from the tarball.

11. **Change to the new directory that was created when you unpacked the tarball.**

For example, you can use a command like the following:

```
cd httpd-2.0.47
```

12. **Type the `configure` command.**

The `configure` command consists of `./configure` followed by all the necessary options. If you can use all the default options, you can use `configure` as follows:

```
./configure
```

One of the more important installation options you may want to use is `prefix`, which sets a different location where you want Apache to be installed. By default, Apache is installed at `/usr/local/apache` or `usr/local/apache2`. You can change the installation location with the following line:

```
./configure --prefix=/software/apache2
```

Additional installation options are discussed later in this chapter in the section "Installation Options." You can see a list of all the available options by typing the following line:

```
./configure --help
```

This script may take a while to finish running. As it runs, it displays output. When the script is done, the system prompt is displayed. If `configure` encounters a problem, it displays a descriptive error message.

13. **Type the following command:**

    ```
    make
    ```

    This command builds the Apache server. It may take several minutes to finish running. As it runs, it displays messages telling you what it's doing. There may be occasional longer pauses as it completes some action. When it's finished, it returns to the system prompt. If it has a problem, it displays a descriptive error message.

14. **Type the following command:**

    ```
    make install
    ```

    This command installs the Apache software in the proper locations, based on the `configure` command you used in Step 11.

15. **Start the Apache Web server.**

    See the section "Starting Apache," later in this chapter, for details.

16. **Type the URL for your Web site (for example, `www.mysite.com` or `localhost`) into a browser to test Apache.**

    If all goes well, you see the Apache message telling you that Apache is working. If you don't see this message, something is amiss, and you should read the section "Troubleshooting Apache," later in this chapter.

Installing Apache from Binaries

Installing Apache from binaries is similar to installing Apache from source. Use the following steps to install Apache from binaries:

1. **Point your Web browser to** `www.apache.org/dist/httpd/binaries/linux/`.

2. **Click the latest version to download it.**

    The most recent binary is currently `httpd-2.0.45-x86_64-unknown-linux-gnu.tar.gz`. The binary version is usually slightly older than the source version.

3. **Select the option to save the file.**

4. **Navigate to where you want to save the source code (for example, `/usr/local/bindir`). Then click Save.**

5. **After the download is complete, change to the download directory (for example, `cd-/usr/local/bindir`).**

You see a file named `httpd-`, followed by the version name and `tar.gz`. This file is called a *tarball*.

Be sure you're using an account that has permission to write into `/usr/src`, such as root.

6. **Verify the downloaded file to be sure it hasn't been tampered with. To verify the file, follow these steps:**

   i. Download two files from `www.apache.org/dist/httpd/`: KEYS and a file with the same version number as the source with a filename that ends in `.asc`.

   ii. Type one of the following lines, depending on which version of PGP is installed on your computer:

       ```
       pgp <KEYS
       gpg --import KEYS
       ```

   Several lines of output are displayed.

   iii. Type one of the following lines, with the correct version number:

       ```
       pgp httpd-2.0.47.tar.gz.asc
       gpg --verify httpd-2.0.47.tar.gz.asc
       ```

   You should see something similar to the following:

       ```
       Good signature from user "Sander Striker"
       ```

   This is what you're looking for. Several messages may be displayed, but the preceding message is the important one. You may also see a message stating that the relationship between the key and the signer of the key can't be verified. This is okay.

   If you don't get a message that the signature is good, the file may have been tampered with and may be dangerous. In this case, repeat the process starting with Step 1 and select a different mirror to download from.

7. **Unpack the tarball.**

   The command to unpack the tarball for version 2.0.45 is the following:

   ```
   gunzip -c httpd-2.0.45.tar.gz | tar -xf -
   ```

   A new directory called `httpd-2.0.45` is created with several subdirectories containing all the files that you just unpacked from the tarball.

8. **Change to the new directory that was created when you unpacked the tarball.**

   For example, you can use a command like the following:

   ```
   cd httpd-2.0.45
   ```

9. **Type this:**

   ```
   ./install-bindist.sh
   ```

   If you want to install Apache in a location other than the default, which is /usr/local/apache2, you can specify a different installation location as follows:

   ```
   ./install-bindist.sh /usr/mine/apache2
   ```

10. **Start the Apache Web server.**

    See the section "Starting Apache," later in this chapter, for details.

11. **Type the URL for your Web site (for example, www.mysite.com or localhost) into a browser to test Apache.**

    If all goes well, you see the Apache message telling you that Apache is working. If you don't see this message, something is amiss, and you should read the section "Troubleshooting Apache," later in this chapter.

Installation Options

In Step 11 when installing Apache from source files (see "Installing Apache from Source Files"), you can use installation options with the configure command to change the way that Apache is installed. This section describes different installation options that you can use.

Setting paths

Apache is installed in a default location if you don't use an option with the configure command to change the location. The default path to the main Apache directory is /usr/local/apache for Apache 1.3 and /usr/local/apache2 for Apache 2. To change the location where the Apache files are installed, use one of the following three installation options:

✦ prefix=PREFIX: Sets the main Apache directory to PREFIX. The default location is /usr/local/apache for Apache 1.3 and /usr/local/apache2 for Apache 2.

✦ exec-prefix=EPREFIX: Sets the directory where architecture-dependent files are installed to EPREFIX. Architecture-dependent files are files that are specific to the operating system (such as the Apache server binary file), as opposed to files that are the same on every operating system (such as the configuration file httpd.conf, which is the same text file on every operating system). By default, EPREFIX is PREFIX.

✦ `enable-layout=LAYOUT`: Uses the layout named LAYOUT in the file named `config.layout` to specify where files are installed.

To use an option, include it in the `configure` command, preceded by two hyphens (`--`), as follows:

`./configure --prefix=/usr/apache --exec-prefix=/usr/apexec`

You can use the layout file to specify where all the files should be installed. The layout file, named `config.layout`, contains several sample layouts that you can use. You can also edit one of the existing layouts or add your own layout. The standard Apache layout, used when you don't change anything, is included in the file and looks like the following:

**Book II
Chapter 2**

Installing Apache

```
<Layout Apache>
    prefix:           /usr/local/apache2
    exec_prefix:      ${prefix}
    bindir:           ${exec_prefix}/bin
    sbindir:          ${exec_prefix}/bin
    libdir:           ${exec_prefix}/lib
    libexecdir:       ${exec_prefix}/modules
    mandir:           ${prefix}/man
    sysconfdir:       ${prefix}/conf
    datadir:          ${prefix}
    installbuilddir:  ${datadir}/build
    errordir:         ${datadir}/error
    iconsdir:         ${datadir}/icons
    htdocsdir:        ${datadir}/htdocs
    manualdir:        ${datadir}/manual
    cgidir:           ${datadir}/cgi-bin
    includedir:       ${prefix}/include
    localstatedir:    ${prefix}
    runtimedir:       ${localstatedir}/logs
    logfiledir:       ${localstatedir}/logs
    proxycachedir:    ${localstatedir}/proxy
</Layout>
```

The layout is enclosed by starting and ending layout lines, as follows:

```
<Layout Apache>
</Layout>
```

In this example, `Apache` is the name of the layout. If you want to use this layout, use the following option with the `configure` command:

`./configure -enable-layout=Apache`

The layout then specifies the paths to directories for various types of files, as follows:

```
prefix: main Apache directory
exec_prefix: architecture dependent files
bindir: user executable binary files
sbindir: system executable binary files
libdir: libraries
libexecdir: architecture dependent libraries
mandir: man pages
sysconfdir: configuration files
    datadir: read-only data files
    installbuilddir: datafiles used in the build
    errordir: error files
    iconsdir: image files containing icons
    htdocsdir: Web page files
    manualdir: HTML manual files
    cgidir: CGI programs
    includedir: include files
    localstatedir: writeable data files
    runtimedir: runtime data files
    logfiledir: log files
    proxycachedir: proxy cache files
```

You can edit this layout by changing the directory names. For example, the layout specifies the following path for the CGI directory:

```
cgidir:          ${datadir}/cgi-bin
```

You can change this path by editing the line as follows:

```
cgidir:          ${datadir}/mycgi-bin
```

The file contains several other layouts you can use. At the present time, the layouts are GNU, Mac OS X Server, Darwin, Red Hat, opt, beos, SuSE, BSDI, Solaris, OpenBSD, and Debian. You can also edit any of these layouts if you want, or you can add a new layout of your own.

Setting environmental variables

One type of installation option sets environmental variables that are used during the build process (Steps 9 and 12 in "Installing Apache from Source Files"). You can set the environmental variables separately before issuing the `configure` command. Or you can set the variables on the same line as the `configure` command, as follows:

```
CC="gcc" ./configure
```

The `configure` command prepares the way for the `make` command, preparing a file called `makefile`. Then the `make` command starts the build process, which looks for certain environmental variables, based on the instructions contained in the makefile. You may be familiar with `make` and makefiles if you have experience using C. If not, you probably have no need to set these environmental variables. You can read more about `make` on the GNU Web site at `www.gnu.org`. Table 2-1 shows environmental variables that you may want to set.

Table 2-1	Setting Environmental Variables
Option	*Tells Apache To . . .*
`CC="COMP"`	Use `COMP` as the name of the C compiler when performing the build (the `make` command).
`CPPPFLAGS="FLAGS"`	Use `FLAGS` as miscellaneous options for the C compiler.
`CFLAGS="FLAGS"`	Use `FLAGS` as debugging and optimization options for the C compiler.
`LDFLAGS="FLAGS"`	Pass `FLAGS` to the linker during the build.
`LIBS="LOCATIONS"`	Pass library `LOCATIONS` to the linker during the build.
`INCLUDES="DIRS"`	Use `DIRS` as directories to search for header files during the build.
`TARGET="NAME"`	Give the compiled file the name `NAME`. The default is `httpd`.

Enabling modules

Modules must be enabled before you can use them. Many modules are enabled by default when Apache is installed. Others must be enabled using an installation option during installation. For information about using modules, see Book II, Chapter 4.

Starting and Stopping Apache

A script named `apachectl` is available to control the server. By default, the script is stored in a subdirectory called `bin` in the directory where Apache is installed. Some Linux distributions may put it in another directory.

The script requires a keyword. The most common keywords are `start`, `stop`, and `restart`. The general syntax is as follows:

```
path/apachectl keyword
```

For example, if Apache was installed in the default directory, type the following line to start Apache:

```
/usr/local/apache2/bin/apachectl start
```

Starting Apache

The `apachectl` script starts the Apache server. The server then runs in the background, listening for HTTP requests. By default, the compiled Apache server is named `httpd` and is stored in the same directory as the `apachectl` script, although you can change the name and location when you install Apache. The `apachectl` script serves as an interface to the compiled server, called `httpd`.

You can run the `httpd` server directly, but it's better to use `apachectl` as an interface. The `apachectl` script manages and checks data that `httpd` commands require. Use the `apachectl` script to start Apache with the following command:

```
/usr/local/apache2/bin/apachectl start
```

The `apachectl` script contains a line that runs `httpd`. By default, `apachectl` looks for `httpd` in the default location — `/usr/local/apache/bin` or `/usr/local/apache2/bin`. If you installed Apache in a nonstandard location, you may need to edit `apachectl` to use the correct path. Open `apachectl` and then search for the following line:

```
HTTPD='/usr/local/apache2/bin/httpd'
```

Change the path to the location where you installed `httpd`. For example, the new line might be this:

```
HTTPD='/usr/mystuff/bin/httpd'
```

After you start Apache, you can check whether Apache is running by looking at the processes on your computer. Type the following command to see what processes are running:

```
ps -A
```

If Apache is running, the list of processes displayed includes some `httpd` processes.

Using Apache start options

You can use several options to start the Apache server. For example, you may want to use a configuration file with a different name. You may want to call the configuration file `myhttpd.conf` rather than `httpd.conf`. You can tell Apache to look for a different file when you start it, as follows:

```
/usr/local/apache2/bin/httpd -f conf/myhttpd.conf
```

If you want to use any of the `httpd` options when starting Apache, add the options to the `apachectl` file, as follows:

```
HTTPD='/usr/local/apache2/bin/httpd -f conf/myhttpd.conf'
```

Table 2-2 shows some options that are available for `httpd`.

Table 2-2	httpd Options
Option	*Tells Apache To . . .*
`-d serverroot`	Use `serverroot` as the main directory to search for Apache files. The default is `/usr/local/apache` or `/usr/local/apache2`.
`-f path/filename`	Use `path/filename` as the configuration file. The path is relative to `serverroot`. The default is `conf/httpd.conf`.
`-k action`	Signals Apache to start, stop, or restart. The command used in `apachectl` to start `httpd` is `httpd -k start`.
`-C directive`	Process `directive` before reading the configuration file. Can use any directive. Directives are discussed in Book II, Chapter 3.
`-c directive`	Process `directive` after reading the configuration file. Can use any directive. Directives are discussed in Book II, Chapter 3.
`-D`	Set a configuration parameter. See Book II, Chapter 3, for details.
`-e`	Set the level for error reporting. See Book II, Chapter 3, for a description of the possible levels.
`-E file`	Send error messages to `file`.
`-h`	Display a list of possible options and then exit.
`-l`	Display a list of modules that are compiled into the server and then exit.
`-L`	Display a list of available directives and then exit.
`-S`	Show settings from the configuration file and then exit.
`-t`	Run syntax tests only. Returns "Syntax OK" if no errors are found in the configuration file.
`-v`	Show version of Apache and then exit.
`-V`	Show version and build parameters of Apache and then exit.
`-X`	Run Apache in debug mode.

Several of the options in Table 2-1 display information only and don't start the `httpd` server. These options are not suitable to add to the `apachectl` script. You should run these commands directly. For example, you can see what version of Apache you have installed by using the following command:

```
/usr/local/apache2/bin/httpd -v
```

Or you can see what modules are compiled into Apache with the following command:

```
/usr/local/apache2/bin/httpd -l
```

Restarting Apache

Whenever you change the configuration file, the new directives take effect the next time Apache starts. If Apache is shut down when you make the changes, you can start Apache as described earlier in "Starting Apache." However, if Apache is running, you can't use `start` to restart it. Using `start` results in an error message saying that Apache is already running. You can use the following command to restart Apache when it's currently running:

```
/usr/local/apache2/bin/apachectl restart
```

Although the `restart` command usually works, sometimes it doesn't. If you restart Apache and the new settings don't seem to be in effect, try stopping Apache and starting it again. Sometimes this solves the problem.

Stopping Apache

To stop Apache, use the following command:

```
/usr/local/apache2/bin/apachectl stop
```

You can check to see that Apache is stopped by checking the processes that are running on your computer with the following command:

```
ps -A
```

The output from `ps` should not include any `httpd` processes.

Troubleshooting Apache

Occasionally, you encounter problems when installing Apache. This section describes problems you might encounter and how to handle the problems.

If you have tried everything and still can't get Apache working, you can ask for help on the Apache user support list. The many Apache users on the list will help you solve your problem. To subscribe to the list, send an empty e-mail message to `users-subscribe@httpd.apache.org`. In addition, archives of the list are available (`marc.theaimsgroup.com/?l=apache-httpd-users`), so you can also search past messages for the answer you need. Another method for finding information about a problem is to search `www.google.com` for the text of the error message or some descriptive words. If it's a common problem, you may find some information on it.

Problems compiling Apache

If you encounter problems while the `configure`, `make`, or `make install` commands are running, an error message is displayed that tells you what the problem is. In most cases, the problem is that the installation script can't find the software that it needs. Either the software is not installed on your computer, or the software is not installed in the location where the script expects to find it. Sometimes, the software installed on your computer is an older version and needs to be upgraded. Read the error message carefully and install/upgrade the software as needed.

If the message is not clear, you can try asking on the Apache discussion list or searching for the message at Google.

Book II
Chapter 2

Installing Apache

Problems starting Apache

When Apache starts, it reads a configuration file to obtain information that it needs. When Apache is installed, it creates this file. Usually, you can start Apache with the information put into the file at installation. However, if Apache doesn't start correctly, a problem in the configuration file may be to blame. The configuration file is discussed in detail in Book II, Chapter 3.

Unless you specified otherwise during installation, the configuration file is located at `/usr/local/apache2/conf/httpd.conf`. You can check where Apache is looking for the configuration file by typing the following line in the directory where Apache is installed:

```
bin/httpd -V
```

The output is a list of settings. The setting `SERVER_CONFIG_FILE` shows where Apache is looking for its configuration file. Make sure that the file exists.

If you get a permission-denied error when you attempt to start Apache, you may have a permissions problem. The account you're using to start Apache may not have the permissions it needs. For example, the account may not have permission to run `httpd` or to open the configuration file. You may need to use an account with more permissions to start Apache. It is common to use the root account to start Apache.

Apache listens for requests on a port specified in the configuration file. If a server is already using that port, you see an error message. You can change the port that the server is listening on by editing the configuration file. Find the following line:

```
Listen 80
```

Then change 80 to another port number, such as 8080.

Running Multiple Apache Servers

You may want to run more than one Apache server. For example, you may want to have one Apache server for your production Web site and another for a test environment. Or you may want to have more than one version of Apache running to test the differences. Running multiple Apache servers is not a problem.

Install each Apache server in a different directory. That is, specify different main Apache directories by using the `--prefix` option with the `configure` command. This builds two different Apache servers in two different directories.

You can start and stop each server, running only one at a time for testing purposes. Or you can run both servers at the same time. You can have one server listening on a single port, such as port 80, and another server listening on a different port. You tell Apache which port to listen on by editing the configuration file (for example, `conf/httpd.conf`) and changing the number of the port in the following line:

```
Listen 80
```

Each Apache server also needs to read its own configuration file. By default, the configuration file is installed as `conf/httpd.conf`. If you install two servers in different directories, each server is reading its own configuration file, such as `/usr/local/apacheA/conf/httpd.conf` and `/usr/local/apacheB/conf/httpd.conf`. Make sure that you don't change the location of the configuration file so that both servers are reading the same configuration file.

Chapter 3: Configuring Apache

In This Chapter

✓ Finding Apache configuration files

✓ Adding and changing directives in the configuration files

✓ Using virtual hosting

Much of Apache's behavior is controlled by settings in plain-text configuration files. Settings control which outside hosts can access which parts of the Web site, what character sets are used, what errors are reported, what resources are available, and many other Apache features. The statements in the configuration file are called *directives*. Directives can apply to the entire Web site or only to certain directories, URLs, or files on the Web site.

In addition, one Apache server can serve Web pages for many Web sites on the same computer, called *virtual hosting*. You can set directives to apply to one or more Web sites in a virtual hosting environment, rather than to all the Web sites served by the Apache server.

Apache has many directives. This chapter describes the directives that are used most frequently — a small percentage of the available directives. All the directives are documented in the documentation on the Apache Web site (`httpd.apache.org`). Check out the directives to see what additional functionality is available for Apache.

Understanding Configuration Files

When Apache starts, it reads information from a configuration file. If Apache can't read the configuration file, it can't start. Unless you tell Apache to use a different configuration file, it looks for the file `conf/httpd.conf` in the directory where Apache is installed. You can direct Apache to look for a file with a different name or in a different location by using startup options, as described in Book II, Chapter 2.

The configuration file is a text file that you can edit to change configuration settings. The file has numerous comments in it, describing the various directives. Any line that begins with a `#` is a comment line.

The configuration file is divided into three sections:

- ✦ **Global Environment:** Directives that control the operation of Apache as a whole.

- ✦ **Main Server Configuration:** Directives that apply to the main server, not to virtual hosts. These directives are also the defaults for virtual hosts, if the settings are not defined for the virtual host.

- ✦ **Virtual Hosts:** Directives that apply only to virtual hosts.

Additional configuration files are allowed but not required. You can put a configuration file into any directory in your Web space. The file is usually called .htaccess, but you can change the name using the AccessFileName directive in the main configuration file. The .htaccess file enables you to set configuration values for a specific directory only.

You can put one or more directives in the .htaccess file, and the directives will apply to the directory and all subdirectories where the .htaccess file is placed. Not all directives are valid in an .htaccess file, though. The documentation on the Apache Web site (httpd.apache.org) provides information on each directive's context — that is, whether it is valid in an .htaccess file.

What types of directives can be used in the .htaccess file is controlled by the AllowOverride directive in the main configuration file. The AllowOverride directive is used only with directories; it does not apply to Apache as a whole. To prevent the use of directives in an .htaccess file, use the following directive:

AllowOverride none

To allow the use of all directives in an .htaccess file, use the following directive:

AllowOverride all

You can also use a directive that specifies a type of directive, such as the following:

AllowOverride AuthConfig

You can specify the following types of directives:

- ✦ **AuthConfig:** Authorization directives
- ✦ **FileInfo:** Directives controlling document types

+ **Indexes:** Directives controlling directory indexing

+ **Limit:** Directives limiting host access

+ **Option:** Directives controlling directory features

For more information on specific directives, see the next section, "Using Directives."

The .htaccess file can be a security risk. It's better to set directory-specific settings in the main configuration file. Use .htaccess files only if you're unable to set directory options in the main configuration file — such as when you don't have access to the main configuration file.

Using Directives

Many Apache directives are made available as part of the Apache core features. Other directives are made available and handled by modules. Some modules are compiled into Apache by default, but some must be specifically enabled when Apache is installed. You can't use a directive unless the module that handles the directive is added to Apache. The documentation on the Apache Web site (httpd.apache.org) provides information on its availability for each module, as follows:

+ **Core:** A Core directive is provided by the Apache core and is always available.

+ **MPM:** An MPM directive is provided by a Multi-Processing Module. MPM is a type of module in Apache 2. A specific MPM is installed based on your operating system. Which directives are available depends on which MPM is installed. The documentation tells you which MPM is installed.

+ **Base:** A Base directive is provided by modules that are included in Apache by default. The directives are always available unless you specifically disabled a module during installation.

+ **Extension:** An Extension directive is provided by modules that are downloaded with Apache but not compiled into Apache by default. You must enable the module during installation before the directive is available.

+ **Experimental:** An Experimental directive is provided with Apache but is not yet considered stable. Use it at your own peril.

Directives have the following format:

```
Directive setting
```

You place each directive on a separate line; you can't put two directives on the same line.

For example, the `Listen` directive that was discussed earlier has the following format:

```
Listen 80
```

In general, the setting does not require quotes around it. However, when a directory path includes special characters, such as a colon (`:`), enclose the path in double quotes. For example, `d:/apache/` needs to be enclosed in quotes like this: `"d:/apache/"`. The underscore (`_`) and the hyphen (`-`) don't require quotes.

You do not use any punctuation at the end of the line with a directive, contrary to how many languages indicate the end of a statement. The directive ends at the end of the line.

Configuring the server

This section describes some directives that you can use to control the general behavior of Apache. Most of these directives are set with a default value during installation, but at some point, you may want to change them.

The following information includes a general description of the directive, the format of the directive, what the possible settings are, and the context in which the directive is valid (whether it can be applied to the whole server, to directories, or to files, or used in the `.htaccess` file). If the directive was recently introduced, the information includes what versions of Apache recognize the directive.

AccessFileName

Description: This directive sets the filename that Apache uses for directory-specific directives.

Format: `AccessFileName filename`

You can use any filename you want. The default filename is `.htaccess`.

Context in Which It Is Valid: Server, virtual host

DirectoryIndex

Description: This directive tells Apache which files to display when it receives a request that asks for a directory.

Format: `DirectoryIndex listoffiles`

If more than one file is listed, Apache returns the first one it finds. If it can't find any of the files, Apache's behavior depends on the setting for Indexes. If Indexes is turned on, Apache displays an index of the directory. If Indexes is turned off, an error code is sent.

Example:

```
DirectoryIndex index.html index.htm
```

The file can also be a script, as in the following directive:

```
DirectoryIndex index.html /cgi-bin/list.pl
```

With this directive, if Apache doesn't find `index.html` in the requested directory, it runs the script `list.pl` in the `cgi-bin` directory.

Context in Which It Is Valid: Server, virtual host, directory, `.htaccess`

**Book II
Chapter 3**

Configuring Apache

DocumentRoot

Description: This directive sets the path to the top directory of your Web space — the directory where Apache looks for Web page files in response to HTTP requests. When Web users type your domain name (for example, `www.myfinecompany.com`) into their browsers, `DocumentRoot` is the directory they're connected to.

Format: `DocumentRoot` *pathtodir*

Don't include a forward slash (/) on the end of the directory path. The default path is `/usr/local/apache2/htdocs`.

Example: `DocumentRoot /usr/myserver/Apache2/webpages`

Context in Which It Is Valid: Server, virtual host

Listen

Description: This directive tells Apache which IP address and which port to listen to. If no IP address is specified, Apache listens to all IP interfaces configured on the computer. You can use more than one `Listen` directive, telling Apache to listen on more than one IP address and on more than one port. `Listen` understands IPv6 addresses, but they must be enclosed in brackets.

`Listen` has been a required directive since Apache 2. If `Listen` is not included in the main configuration file, Apache 2 won't start. Previous versions of Apache did not require `Listen`.

Format: `Listen` *`ipaddress`*`:`*`portnumber`*

The following are all valid `Listen` directives:

```
Listen 80
Listen 8080
Listen 192.173.1.4:8000
Listen [fe80::b07:30ef:fea0:ccea]:80
```

Context in Which It Is Valid: Server

PidFile
Description: When Apache starts, it stores its process ID (PID) in a file. The `PidFile` directive specifies the name of the file where the PID is stored. The default filename is `logs/httpd.pid`.

Format: `PidFile` *`path/filename`*

Example: `PidFile logs/pid`

Context in Which It Is Valid: Server

ServerAdmin
Description: This directive provides an e-mail address that is used in error messages that Apache sends to the browser.

Format: `ServerAdmin` *`email-address`*

Example: `ServerAdmin webAdmin@mycompanyemailaddress.com`

Context in Which It Is Valid: Server, virtual host

ServerName
Description: This directive defines a server name and port number that Apache uses to identify itself.

Prior to Apache 2, you specified the port number using a `Port` directive. As of Apache 2, the port number is specified as part of `ServerName`, and the `Port` directive is no longer used.

Format: `ServerName` *`servername`*`:`*`portnumber`*

You must use a fully qualified domain name for the *`servername`*, or you can use the IP address for the *`servername`*.

Example: `ServerName mybestcompany.com:80`

Context in Which It Is Valid: Server, virtual host

Serverroot

Description: This directive sets the directory path for the main Apache directory, the directory where Apache is installed. The default path is `/usr/local/apache` or `/usr/local/apache2`. If you used the prefix option to change this path when installing Apache, the changed directory path is set in the configuration file.

Format: `Serverroot path`

Example: `Serverroot /myplace/apache2`

Context in Which It Is Valid: Server

User

Description: Sets the user ID under which Apache will respond to requests. In most cases, it's best to set up a user specifically for running Apache. Frequently, the user *nobody* is used for this purpose.

Format: `user username`

The server must be started by root to have the permissions necessary to change to the user with lesser privileges. The account should not be able to access files that are not intended to be available to the world on your Web site.

Context in Which It Is Valid: Server

Configuring log files

Apache can log many of its actions. Log files are a valuable resource for managing your Web site. Log files contain error messages for problems that occur and all requests and responses processed by Apache. Apache writes two separate log files: one for errors and one for requests. By default, error messages are stored in `logs/error_log`.

You can change the filename and location of the error log with the `ErrorLog` directive, as follows:

```
ErrorLog filename
```

For example, you can use the following directive:

```
ErrorLog /etc/apache_error_log
```

You can send the error log entries to a script, rather than a file, by using the following format:

```
ErrorLog |/bin/process_aerrors
```

In this directive, `process_aerrors` is a script that processes the error entries. You can use the `ErrorLog` directive in the server or the virtual host context.

You can also change the error-reporting level, specifying that Apache log lower or higher levels of errors. You can use the `LogLevel` directive to specify the error-reporting level, as follows:

```
LogLevel level
```

You can specify the following error levels:

- `emerg`: System is not usable
- `alert`: Requires immediate action
- `crit`: Critical condition
- `error`: Error condition
- `warn`: Warning condition
- `notice`: Probably normal, but unusual
- `info`: Informational only
- `debug`: Debug level message

When you specify an error level (such as `error`), all levels above the specified level (`crit`, `alert`, and `emerg`) are also logged. The default error level is `warn`. You can use `LogLevel` in the server or the virtual host context. For security, don't let anyone except the user running Apache write in the directories where logs are stored.

Apache also logs all requests it receives. By default, the log file is `logs/access_log`. You can change the name and location of the log file and what is stored in each log entry.

The information and format of the log entry is determined by the `LogFormat` directive. The location is determined by the `CustomLog` directive.

Some formats for log entries are defined in the main configuration file by default. Check your file to see what formats are defined. One format is usually defined and called common. This format is used for the default format for your log file. The following two sections show how to use the LogFormat directive and the CustomLog directive to change your log files if needed.

CustomLog

Description: Logs requests to the server. You specify the format for the log entries.

Format: CustomLog *file|pipe format|nickname*

Book II
Chapter 3

Configuring Apache

CustomLog takes two arguments. Each argument can take one of two formats. The arguments are as follows:

✦ **First argument:** Specifies where log entries are sent. The argument can be either a filename or a command that sends (pipes) the log entries to a script.

  • **Filename:** Filename where log entries will be stored.

  • **Pipe:** A pipe character (|) followed by the name of a script/program that you want to process the log entries. For example, the argument might be | /usr/bin/apachelog.pl, where apachelog.pl is a script that processes and stores the log entries.

✦ **Second argument:** Specifies the format for the log entry. The argument can be either a string log format or a nickname for a log format.

  • **Log format:** A text string that defines a format for the log entry. The symbols that are available for use in the text string are shown in Table 3-1 in the description for LogFormat.

  • **Nickname:** The nickname under which a log format was stored using the LogFormat directive.

Example:

```
CustomLog logs/mylog_file "%h %u %t %r: %s"
```

This directive sends the log entry to a file called logs/mylog_file. Each entry contains the remote host name (h), the remote username (u), the time of the request (t), the first line of the request (r), and the response to the request (s). The % tells Apache that a format character comes next.

Context in Which It Is Valid: Server, virtual host

LogFormat

Description: Defines a log format and saves the log format under a nickname.

Format: `LogFormat "format" nickname`

The format is a string that defines the information that is stored in the log entry. The string is saved under the nickname, and the nickname can be used in the `CustomLog` directive. Table 3-1 shows some of the formatting characters you can use in the format. See the documentation on the Apache Web site for the complete list of format characters.

Table 3-1	Format Characters
Character	*Meaning*
a	Remote IP address
A	Local IP address
B	Bytes sent
D	Time, in microseconds, to serve the request
h	Remote host
q	Query string
r	First line of request
s	Status of request
t	Time that event is logged
T	Time, in seconds, to serve the request
u	Remote user

Example:

```
LogFormat "%T %r" shortentry
```

This directive saves the specified log format with the nickname `shortentry`. The `CustomLog` directive can now use the nickname `shortentry` to start a new log file, as follows:

```
CustomLog logs/short_log shortentry
```

Context in Which It Is Valid: Server, virtual host

Running Scripts

One useful Apache feature enables Apache to run scripts, receive the output from the scripts, and send the output to the browser. Directives in the main configuration file tell Apache that certain files should be run as scripts when they are requested and that certain software should be used to run them.

One type of script is the CGI (Common Gateway Interface) script. A CGI script is used to process information and return the output to Apache. Apache then sends the output to the browser, as if it were any other HTML code.

Apache has a specific directory that is the CGI script directory. Apache assumes that any file requested from this directory is a script. The script is run by the shell running on Linux in the same manner as any other script. Shells read the first line of the script, looking for a line that identifies the program that should be used to execute the script. For example, a script may contain the following line as its first line:

```
#!/bin/bash
```

This line (called a pound-bang line) tells the shell to execute this file using the program at `/bin/bash`. In this example, the program is a bash shell script. You can use other common software, such as the following:

```
#!/usr/local/bin/perl  (Perl)
```

You define the CGI directory with the `ScriptAlias` directive. The directive tells Apache that any program found in this directory should be treated as a script and executed. The format is as follows:

```
ScriptAlias alias dirpath
```

The `alias` is a short name that you can use to refer to the directory from now on. The `dirpath` is the actual path to the directory where you want to store your CGI scripts. For example, you can use the following directive to set up your CGI directory:

```
ScriptAlias /cgi-bin/ /usr/local/apache2/cgi-bin/
```

Notice that the path to the `cgi-bin` directory ends with a slash. This is required when the alias ends with a slash. Thus, if you say `/cgi-bin/`, you must include the slash at the end of the second parameter.

MIME types

MIME (Multipurpose Internet Mail Extensions) types are unique identifiers used for different file types. MIME is an official standard originally developed for use with Internet mail, but it has evolved for use with the Web. Different types of files — such as text files, graphics files, audio files, and so on — must be handled differently, so the software receiving the file needs to know what type of file it is receiving. MIME types tell the software what type of file has arrived.

MIME types have the following format:

```
type/subtype
```

The following are some common MIME types used on the Web:

```
text/plain
text/html
text/xml
image/jpeg
image/gif
video/mpeg
application/pdf
application/zip
```

When Apache sends a file to a browser, it sends a message with the file that tells the browser what type of file it's sending. The format of the message is as follows:

```
content-type: mimetype
```

Unless you're using the module `mime_magic`, which looks inside the file to determine the MIME type, Apache determines the MIME type of a file based on the filename extension. Apache looks in the file `mime.types` to see which MIME type is associated with which extension. (This file is located in the conf subdirectory of the directory where Apache is installed.) The file lists many standard MIME types. Some have extensions listed after the MIME type, as follows:

```
text/html               html htm
```

The following line tells Apache that a file with an `.html` extension or an `.htm` extension should be sent with the message:

```
content--type: text/html
```

If Apache can't determine the content type, it sends a default type set with the directive `DefaultType`. The default type, unless you change it, is `test/plain`.

You can edit the `mime.types` file to add MIME types or associate different file extensions with MIME types. You can also add MIME types with the `AddType` directive as described in the numbered list on the next page.

By convention, the CGI directory is usually called `cgi-bin`. Any time Apache receives a request for a file in this directory, it runs the file as a script. You can request the file from one of your Web pages. A common way to use CGI files is to process HTML forms. The form tag might be this:

```
<form action="/cgi-bin/processform.cgi" method="POST">
```

When the form is submitted, a request for the file `/cgi-bin/processform.cgi` is sent to Apache. Apache looks for the file in `/usr/local/apache2/cgi-bin` and runs it as a script.

When you have many files that you want Apache to process as CGI by using a specific program, you can tell Apache that any files of a certain type should be run as a script. This may require two steps:

1. **Add the MIME type.**

If the MIME type you want to use is already defined in the MIME type definition file (default: `/conf/mime.types`), you can skip this step. If the MIME type you need is not in the MIME type definitions file, use the `AddType` directive to add the type, as follows:

```
AddType mime-type extension
```

For example, to add a MIME type for PHP, use the following line:

```
AddType application/x-httpd-php .php
```

The directive adds a line to the MIME type file telling Apache that files with the `.php` extension have the MIME type `application/x-httpd-php`.

2. **Tell Apache to run a particular script when it receives a request for a file of a specified MIME type.**

The `Action` directive serves this purpose. Its format is as follows:

```
Action mime-type script
```

For example, you can create an action that handles all png images with a specified CGI script, as follows:

```
Action image/png /cgi-bin/processPNG.cgi
```

Or you can create an action for PHP using the MIME type created in Step 1, as follows:

```
Action application/x-httpd-php /php/php.exe
```

In this case, you need to have set up `/php/` to be a script directory, using the `ScriptAlias` directive described earlier in this section.

Configuring Directories and Files

All Apache directives have a context. The directive can be applied to the Apache server as a whole, to directories, to files, or to virtual hosts. In the previous sections of this chapter, I discuss directives as applied to the server as a whole. In the next few sections, I discuss using directives with directories and files.

Setting up a default directory

For security purposes, it's important that Apache doesn't have any more access to directories than is necessary. The most common way to do this is to set up a restricted default directory and provide additional access to directories only when necessary. A default directory is automatically set up in your main configuration file during installation. The directives for the default directory are similar to the following:

```
<Directory />
    Options FollowSymLinks
    AllowOverride None
</Directory>
```

The options in this directory apply to all the directories that Apache has access to. AllowOverride is set to none for all directories, meaning that an .htaccess file can't be used in any directory. Directives that are frequently used in directory and file context are discussed in the later section "Using directives with directories." In the configuration file, after the default directory is defined, set options, access, and other features for the directories that users need to access, such as your DocumentRoot directory. Use a Directory block for each directory that users need to access, using only those directives needed to give the directories the features that are needed — but no more features than are necessary.

Identifying directories

The directives that apply to a directory are enclosed in the directory tags, as follows:

```
<Directory dirpath>
    directives
</Directory>
```

The directives apply to the directory and all its subdirectories. The *dirpath* is the path to the directory. The path is the full path to the directory, as follows:

```
<Directory /usr/local/apache2/htdocs>
```

You can use wildcards in the directory, following the rules for Linux filenames — ? is a wildcard for a single character, and * is a wildcard meaning a string of characters. Therefore, you can use the following statement:

```
<Directory /usr/local/apache2/htdocs/dir*>
```

This statement identifies all directories in `htdocs` that begin with *dir* and end with any string of characters, such as `dir1`, `dir2`, `directly`, `dir27`, and so on. If you need to identify a set of directories with more complicated names, you can use `DirectoryMatch` with regular expressions, as follows:

```
<DirectoryMatch "regular expression">
```

Directories are processed in order from the shortest path to the longest path. That is, the directives for the directory `/usr/local/apache2/htdocs` are processed before directives for `/usr/local/apache2/htdocs/dir1`. The directives that you apply to `htdocs` are processed first and apply to `htdocs/dir1`, because directives apply to all the subdirectories. However, the directives for `htdocs/dir1` are processed later and change the settings for `htdocs/dir1`, without affecting the settings for all other subdirectories of `htdocs`.

Book II
Chapter 3

Configuring Apache

Using directives with directories

Not all directives can be applied to directories. Most of the directives discussed so far in this chapter can be used only in the context of the server or a virtual host. In this section, I discuss some directives that are often used for directories, directives that restrict/allow access to the directory or allow certain features to be used in the directory.

Configuring access

Access is a fundamental issue for directories. You can make access to a directory as open or restricted as you want. Three directives work together to provide access to directories: `Allow`, `Deny`, and `Order`.

The `Allow` directive and the `Deny` directive specify who is allowed access to the directory. The format is as follows:

```
Allow from identifier
Deny from identifier
```

The `identifier` can be one of the following:

✦ **All:** The word *all* specifies all hosts.

✦ **Domain name:** A host name or domain name, such as `allmyaffiliates.com` or `pooh.myfinecompany.com`. Any host name that matches or ends with this identifier is allowed or denied.

✦ **IP address:** An IP address, such as 192.72.3.1. An IPv6 address can be used.

✦ **Partial IP address:** A partial IP address — such as 197.72 — that would represent a subnet.

The `Order` directive tells Apache whether to process `Deny` first and `Allow` second or vice versa. Whichever directive is processed last overrides the access specified in the first. For example, suppose you have the following directives:

```
<Directory /usr/local/apache/htdocs/secret>
  Order Deny,Allow
  Allow from myfinecompany.com
  Deny from all
</Directory>
```

Following the `Order` directive, the `Deny` directive is processed first, even though it is listed second. The `Deny` directive denies access to all hosts. Therefore, no one can access the directory. Next, the `Allow` directive is processed, which allows any host from the `myfinecompany.com` domain to access the directory. The result is that only hosts from the `myfinecompany.com` domain can access the directory; no other host can access the directory.

Now suppose the following directives are used instead:

```
Order Allow,Deny
Allow from myfinecompany.com
Deny from all
```

In this case, the `Allow` directive is processed first, allowing access to hosts from the `myfinecompany.com` domain. However, the `Deny` directive is processed next, denying access to all hosts. The final result is that no host can access the directory.

Enabling features

In addition to controlling access to directories, you often want to restrict what features are available in the directory. For example, you may want users to be able to see the directory index, but not execute CGI scripts in the directory. For security, you don't want any features available that users don't need.

The `Options` directive controls what features are available in a directory. The format for this directive is as follows:

```
Options features
```

One or more features are listed for *features*. Here are some possible features:

- ✦ `All`: Turns on all features.
- ✦ `ExecCGI`: CGI scripts can be executed.
- ✦ `FollowSymLinks`: Apache follows symbolic links.

✦ `Includes`: Server-side includes (SSI) are allowed. SSIs are statements that can be added to an HTML file and interpreted by Apache to allow some dynamic content in your page. See the Apache documentation on the Apache Web site for more information.

✦ `Indexes`: Displays an index of files for the directory.

✦ `None`: No features are available.

✦ `SymLinksIfOwnerMatch`: Follows symbolic links only if the target is owned by the same user ID as the link.

You can apply the features directly, or you can add or remove a feature from an existing setting by using plus (+) or minus (-) signs. Consider the following examples:

Book II
Chapter 3

Configuring Apache

```
<Directory /usr/local/apache2/htdocs>
    options Indexes Includes
</Directory>

<Directory /usr/local/apache2/htdocs/dir3>
    options -Indexes +ExecCGI
</Directory>
```

The directive for the first directory turns on `Indexes` and `Includes`, for `htdocs` and all its subdirectories, including `dir3`. The directive for the second directory removes the feature `Indexes` and adds the `ExecCGI` feature for `htdocs/dir3`, but not for any other directory. The final result gives `htdocs/dir3` the features `Includes` and `ExecCGI`. Now, suppose the directive for the second directory did not include the plus and minus signs, as follows:

```
options Indexes ExecCGI
```

In this case, the result is different. The options replace the previous features, rather than change them, so the result is that `htdocs/dir3` has the features `Indexes` and `ExecCGI`.

Using directives with files

You can restrict access to files in the same way you restrict access to directories, using the `Files` directive. The format of the `Files` directive is similar to the `Directory` directive, as follows:

```
<Files filename>
    directives
</Files>
```

As for `Directory`, you can use wildcards in the filename, as follows:

```
<Files *.gif>
```

This directive identifies all files with a `.gif` extension, in any directory to which Apache has access.

You can also use regular expressions by using the `FilesMatch` directive. You can put a `File` directive or a `FilesMatch` directive inside a Directory section or in an `.htaccess` file.

To restrict access to files, you use the `Allow`, `Deny`, and `Order` directives in the same way you use them for directories, as described in the earlier section "Configuring access."

Configuring Virtual Hosts

One Apache Web server can serve more than one Web site. Setting up several Web sites on the same computer is called *virtual hosting.* You can implement virtual hosting in one of the following ways:

+ **Name-based virtual hosts:** All virtual hosts have the same IP address but different names. This method is simpler and uses fewer IP addresses. Therefore, this method is usually preferred.

+ **IP-based virtual hosts:** Each virtual host has a different IP address. This method is required for SSL secure servers because of the nature of the SSL protocol. Also, some operating systems use software that can't recognize different hosts unless they're on different IP addresses.

You must tell Apache which IP address to listen on to receive requests for name-based virtual hosts. Use the `NameVirtualHost` directive, with the following format:

```
NameVirtualHost IPaddress:portnumber
```

You can use * for the *IPaddress*, which tells Apache to listen on all interfaces. If you want to name two or more IP addresses specifically, use one directive for each IP address. The port number is not required. If you specify an IPv6 address, enclose it in square brackets.

The `NameVirtualHost` directive does not take the place of the `Listen` directive. A `Listen` directive is still required.

Next, you need to create a block of directives for each virtual host you want to serve, using the `VirtualHost` directive. The same identifier must be used in the `VirtualHost` directive that was used in the `NameVirtualHost` directive. The block must contain, at the least, a `ServerName` directive and a `DocumentRoot` directive. The following directives set up two virtual hosts:

```
NameVirtualHost *

<VirtualHost *>
    ServerName www.mysite.com
    DocumentRoot /usr/local/apache/htdocs/mysite
</VirtualHost>

<VirtualHost *>
    ServerName www.mysite2.com
    DocumentRoot /usr/local/apache/htdocs/mysite2
</VirtualHost>
```

When Apache receives a request on any IP address, it treats the request as a request for a virtual host because the `NameVirtualHost` directive specified *, meaning all IP addresses. Apache looks through all the virtual host blocks identified with * to find a match for the server name received in the request. When it finds a match, it uses the directives included for that virtual host. If it can't find a match for the server name in any of the virtual host `ServerName` directives, it uses the first virtual host block in the configuration file, treating the first virtual host definition as the default.

Here are a few additional points to remember about virtual host blocks:

✦ Directives used outside the virtual host block are in effect unless they're overridden by a directive inside the virtual host block.

✦ You can use almost any directive in a virtual host block.

✦ You can set up a different e-mail address for the server administrator and configure different log files.

✦ You can set up different CGI directories.

✦ You can use `Directory` and `File` directives inside a virtual host.

✦ You can use different access directive settings. Your virtual hosts are almost completely independent, and you can set up each one differently from the others.

Chapter 4: Apache Modules

In This Chapter

✓ **Understanding Apache modules**

✓ **Installing Apache modules**

✓ **Finding out about useful Apache modules**

Modules provide many of Apache's features. The following types of modules are available:

✦ **Base modules:** These modules are included with the Apache distribution and are enabled by default, meaning they're always available unless you disable them when installing Apache.

✦ **Extension modules:** These modules are also included in the Apache distribution, but they're not compiled by default. You must specifically enable these modules when installing Apache.

✦ **External modules:** These are third-party modules created for Apache.

Installing Modules

You can compile modules in one of two ways:

✦ **Statically:** The module is compiled with Apache as part of the Apache binary. To add or remove the module, you must recompile Apache.

✦ **Dynamically:** You compile the module separately from Apache, as a Dynamically Shared Object (DSO). You use the `LoadModule` directive to include the module features as part of Apache at start up.

Compiling modules

You can compile modules when Apache is installed. You enable modules during the configuration step in the installation procedure (see Book II, Chapter 2). To include a module, use the installation option, as follows:

```
./configure --enable-modulename
```

For example, to compile and include `mod_info` when installing Apache, use the following installation option:

```
./configure --enable-info
```

This option compiles `mod_info` statically and includes it as part of the Apache binary.

To compile a module dynamically, use the following format:

```
./configure --enable-modulename=shared
```

A dynamically compiled module usually has the extension `.so`. For Apache to use the module, you must include a `LoadModule` directive in the main configuration file that loads the module, as follows:

```
LoadModule moduleIdentifier pathtoDSOfile
```

The `moduleIdentifier` is listed in the documentation for the module. For example, the following directive loads `mod_status`:

```
LoadModule status_module modules/mod_status.so
```

Using base and extension modules

Many modules are included in the Apache distribution. When you unpack the tarball, the module source files are unpacked into the modules subdirectory in the source directory. Some of these modules are base modules; some are extension modules. The base modules are compiled and included by default when you install Apache. The extension modules are not included by default.

The base modules are compiled statically and are included in Apache during installation by default. You can use the following command to see which modules are compiled into Apache:

```
httpd -l
```

If you don't want one of the base modules installed, you need to disable it during installation by using an option similar to the following:

```
./configure --disable-info
```

The extension modules are not included in Apache by default. If you want to add one of the extension modules, use one of the following options:

```
./configure --enable-headers
./configure --enable-headers=shared
```

If you enable the module as a DSO, using `shared`, the compiled module is stored in the modules subdirectory in the Apache main directory. A `LoadModule` directive is needed in the main configuration file to tell Apache to load the module and provide the location of the module. During the build process, the `LoadModule` directive is automatically added to the configuration file for you, along with the correct location for the module.

If you install the module as a DSO, you have more flexibility. You can remove or add the module whenever you need to with the `LoadModule` directive, without needing to recompile Apache.

Using external modules

Many third-party modules are available for use with Apache. If you want to use an external module, check the third party's Web site for information about the module. Use the installation instructions provided with the module. Some modules need to be installed statically; some work better as a DSO.

Some Useful Modules

The following sections describe some modules with useful features.

PHP

PHP is a scripting language used to make Web sites dynamic. PHP is the most popular Apache module, according to a survey of Apache module use conducted by SecuritySpace (`www.securityspace.com/s_survey`). Over 13 million domains use PHP, according to Netcraft (`www.php.net/usage.php`).

PHP is open-source software that runs on most operating systems and works with most Web servers, not just on Linux with Apache. The PHP project is supported by the Apache Software Foundation, the same group that supports the development of Apache. Consequently, PHP runs particularly well with Apache. PHP can be statically compiled and run as part of Apache or can run as a DSO module.

PHP was designed specifically for use on Web sites and is particularly well suited for that purpose. Book V discusses PHP in detail.

Secure Sockets Layer (SSL) module

If you plan to send any important information between Apache and Web site visitors' browsers, you need to use the Secure Sockets Layer (SSL) protocol. With SSL, information sent between Apache and the browser is encrypted, preventing anyone who intercepts the information from being able to understand it. In addition, the SSL server holds a digital certificate, issued by certificate authorities that verify the server's identity.

When a server is communicating using SSL, the protocol is HTTPS, not HTTP. The server listens for HTTPS requests on port 443 rather than port 80. Apache can support both HTTP and HTTPS at the same time. Any files on the Web site can be sent using HTTP or HTTPS, whichever is specified in the URL.

The Apache distribution includes mod_ssl as an extension, which means you must enable mod_ssl at installation with the option:

```
./configure --enable-ssl
```

However, mod_ssl uses a library called OpenSSL, so you also need to download and install OpenSSL. The following steps provide a quick overview of installing OpenSSL; the OpenSSL download includes more complete installation instructions:

1. **Download the latest version of OpenSSL from** www.openssl.org/source/ **and save it in an appropriate directory, such as** /usr/local/src.

2. **Unpack the tarball.**

   You must be using an account that has permission to write in the directory where the tarball is being unpacked, such as root.

3. **CD (change directory) to the OpenSSL directory created when the tarball was unpacked.**

4. **Type** ./configure.

5. **Type** make.

6. **Type** make test.

   This step tests the libraries built in Step 5. If the test fails, informative error messages are displayed. Solve the problems and repeat the steps starting from Step 5. If the test is successful, continue to Step 7.

7. **Type:** make install.

Installing OpenSSL creates a directory containing the OpenSSL libraries, libcrypto and libssl. The default location for the directory is /usr/local/ssl. After the OpenSSL libraries are installed, you can use the OpenSSL command-line tool to install your certificate, either a fake certificate for testing purposes or a real certificate obtained from an organization that issues certificates, such as VeriSign. In addition, the directives provided by mod_ssl to configure SSL for your server are available for use. See the Apache documentation for descriptions of the directives available.

The installation process creates a configuration file called `conf/ssl.conf` that contains the configuration directives for your SSL server. For example, the file contains a `Listen` directive for port 443. You may need to edit this configuration file. When you install SSL with Apache, you need to start Apache with the following command:

```
/usr/local/apache2/bin/apachectl startssl
```

Perl

You can use the module `mod_perl` to execute Perl CGI scripts. Scripts executed with `mod_perl` run much faster than Perl scripts executed as CGI scripts.

The `mod_perl` project is supported by the Apache Software Foundation. A Web page for `mod_perl` provides the software and documentation at `perl.apache.org`. Two versions of `mod_perl` are provided: `mod_perl` 1 for Apache 1.3 and `mod_perl` 2 for Apache 2. The `mod_perl` module is installed statically, as part of Apache. The documentation on the Web site provides detailed installation instructions.

Python

You can use the `mod_python` module to execute Python programs with Apache. These programs execute much faster than traditional CGI scripts. You can also use the more advanced features provided by Python. Python is an open-source, object-oriented computer language, comparable to Perl or Java.

The `mod_python` project is supported by the Apache Software Foundation. You can download the source at `httpd.apache.org/modules/python-download.cgi`. Version 3.0 is available for Apache 2, and version 2.7 is available for Apache 1.3. Documentation and other information are available at `www.modpython.org`. You can subscribe to a Python mailing list by sending an e-mail with the word *subscribe* in the subject line to `mod_python-request@modpython.org`.

The `mod_python` module is installed dynamically as a DSO. The Python source must also be available, as well as Python libraries. If you installed Python from source on your system, you have everything you need. If you installed Python from an RPM, installing just binaries, you need to download the source.

Chapter 5: Ten Security Tips

In This Chapter

✔ Limiting access to your Web server

✔ Monitoring Web server activity

*W*eb sites are particularly vulnerable to outside attacks because they accept information from visitors. Although the vast majority of visitors are good guys, trying to use the Web site for its intended purpose, a few people have intentions that are not so pure, such as stealing information or destroying your Web site for fun or profit. This chapter provides security tips to help make your Apache Web server more secure.

Update Regularly

Some new versions of Apache fix security problems in older versions. Make sure that you're using software that has been fixed. For example, version 2.0.47 addresses four security issues, so you should be using at least that version or later. Apache 1.3.28 also fixes security issues. Check the Apache Web site frequently for security information and subscribe to the announce list (httpd.apache.org/lists.html#http-announce) to receive notices of new releases.

Restrict Access to the Apache Directory

Apache is installed in a main directory, such as /usr/local/apache2. Unauthorized persons should not be able to write into this directory. Create this directory using a root account with root permissions so that only a root account can write to the directory.

Don't Run Your Server as Root

Although you must start your server using the root account to access port 80, change to another user with restricted permissions to run the server and respond to requests. Use the User directive and the Group directive to change from the root account to another account, preferably an account created specifically to run your Web server.

Monitor Server Requests

All requests to Apache are logged in your log files. Review these requests frequently to look for suspicious requests, such as requests for the `passwd` file or multiple denied requests from the same user.

Use a Restricted Default Directory

Set up your default directory (`<directory />`) to have restricted access, such as `Deny from all`. Then use the `Allow` directive to provide access to only those directories that users need to access, such as your `DocumentRoot` (for example, `htdocs` or `/var/www`).

Don't Let Users See Your Files

Don't allow indexes in any directories, unless you specifically want the directory to serve as an index of files. In most cases, you don't want Web site visitors to see a list of all your files so they can try each file. Don't set the `Option` directive to `Indexes` in your default directory, only in any directory that you want to serve as a file index. You can also restrict the files displayed in the index to certain filenames.

Limit CGI Scripts

Limit the execution of CGI scripts to specific directories, such as `cgi-bin`. Don't allow CGI execution in any other directories unless you really trust the users that have access to the directory. CGI scripts can be a source of security issues because they allow users to execute code outside of Apache, in your shell.

Any directories that allow the execution of CGI scripts should not be writable by the account under which Apache is running. Also, no uploads or FTP should be allowed into any directory that can execute CGI scripts.

Don't Allow .htaccess Files

Allowing `.htaccess` files to override configuration settings is a security risk. Use `AllowOverride none` unless you have a very good reason to allow `.htaccess` files.

Use suEXEC Carefully

When CGI scripts are run, they run under the same user ID that the Web server runs under, with the same privileges. You can use suEXEC to run the CGI script under a different user ID, with fewer privileges. However, use it carefully and be sure you understand how it functions, or you may accidentally create a larger security problem.

Use SSL for Important Communications

If you're exchanging important information with your users, such as credit card numbers, you need to use SSL. SSL is discussed in Book II, Chapter 4.

Book II
Chapter 5

Ten Security Tips

Book III

Perl Web Site Automation

Contents at a Glance

Chapter 1: Introducing Perl

In This Chapter

✔ Becoming familiar with the Perl mindset

✔ Trying out a simple Perl program

✔ Adding comments to your Perl code

✔ Using the -W option to keep Perl on its toes

✔ Ending a Perl program

✔ Exploring different uses for Perl

✔ Navigating the Perl online help

Depending on which programming languages you've worked with, Perl may strike you as one of the strangest. (I wouldn't say it's the strangest of all, though. LISP is pretty bizarre.) Perl requires a slightly different mindset from other languages. However, after you use Perl and start to understand its way of doing things, you can easily begin to appreciate its power.

Before I get into the mechanics of Perl, I want to share with you one quick pointer that will make your Perl programming life much easier: Perl has a *default variable*. When you have a for loop, for example, you can skip the loop variable name and use the default variable. When you want to compare a string with a regular expression, you can plug the string into the default variable and then not specify which string you want to compare the regular expression to; the Perl interpreter will use the default variable.

In this first chapter, I give you a few examples of what Perl is usually used for, and I give you a sprinkling of Perl code to help you become familiar with using it.

Trying Out a Simple Perl Program

To get you started in the wonderful world of Perl, here's a simple Perl program that writes two lines of text to the console. First, here's the code:

```
print "This is a simple program!\n";
print "And this is a second line!\n";
```

This Perl program consists of only two lines of code. Each line starts with the word `print`, is followed by some text inside double quotes, and ends with a semicolon. To create this program, type it into your favorite text editor and save it with the filename `simple.pl`. Start up the command-line prompt, and make sure you're in the directory containing `simple.pl`. Then type the following line:

```
perl simple.pl
```

The output is as follows:

```
This is a simple program!
And this is a second line!
```

The first line of code prints out the line of text inside the double quotes. The double quotes don't appear in the output; they simply tell Perl where the text begins and ends. At the end of each line (still inside the quotes) is the strange combination of characters \n (a backslash followed by an n). This tells Perl to print a newline.

Each line of code in Perl ends with a semicolon. When I say "line of code," I mean an entire sentence in a Perl program, not a single line of text in a code file. Just as an English sentence makes a complete statement, starts with a capital letter, ends with a period, and can span multiple lines on a page in a book, a Perl sentence has its own special but similar format. A Perl sentence always ends with a semicolon and can span multiple lines in a single code file. For example, you could write the preceding Perl code like this:

```
print
    "This is a simple program!\n";
print
    "And this is a second line!\n";
```

This short program functions just as if the quoted string were on the same line as the `print` statement. You can put carriage returns wherever you want, provided you don't break up a single word. (For example, you can't write `pr` on one line and `int` on the next and expect Perl to interpret that as `print`.) But anywhere you have a space, you can use tabs, multiple spaces, and carriage returns.

Use whitespace (spaces, tabs, carriage returns) liberally in your code. The more whitespace you include, the easier your programs will be to read. To format your code, follow the examples throughout this book, noting how I format my code. My way isn't the only way (even though I like to believe it is), and you will likely come up with your own conventions for formatting code. But please include blank lines to separate logical portions of your code, and indent your code when using loops and other constructs.

Commenting your code

In most programming languages, you're encouraged (by me and all the other computer people out there) to include *comments* in your code. Comments are notes and thoughts about the program that you type into the code in a human language (such as English, French, German, or whatever). Perl doesn't use these comments; they're simply there for you and other humans to read when looking at the code.

The idea is that code can sometimes get a little complex, and if you write code that somebody else may be reading, you'll want to include comments explaining some of the things you do. Here's an example; the comments start with a # character:

```
# Write out an introductory message
print "Greetings!\n";

# Change to a different directory
chdir "/";
```

This code is functionally identical to the following code.

```
print "Greetings!\n";
chdir "/";
```

The lines that start with a # character are simply comments, and the Perl interpreter ignores them. You can also place a comment at the end of a line:

```
print "Hi\n"; # Write a friendly greeting
```

Perl treats everything from the # sign to the end of the line as a comment. Therefore, you can't include code after a comment on a single line. If you want to include code after a comment, you must put the code on the next line.

In certain situations, Perl does not regard the # character as a comment. In particular, when you put the character inside a string, as in the following example, Perl doesn't consider it the start of a comment.

```
print "This # is not a comment!\n";
```

The # character has different names, and although a lot of noncomputer people prefer to call it a *number sign,* we computer people call it a *pound sign.* (Some even call it a *hash.*) The term *pound sign* refers to the fact that # is often used as an abbreviation for the unit of weight measure called pounds — which has nothing whatsoever to do with computers. Nevertheless, we still call it a pound sign.

Keeping Perl on its toes with the -W option

When you run Perl programs, you may occasionally type in some code that seems to work but doesn't do exactly what you expected it to do. The program runs, but you may find it behaving in a strange way.

Perl has a handy feature that I recommend you always use: It's called the "minus W option," and it keeps Perl on its toes. Whenever you run a Perl program, I recommend that you type -W after the word Perl, like so:

```
perl -W simple.pl
```

The -W instructs Perl to be more sensitive to possible mistakes and to print out a warning message if it finds a mistake. I recommend always running your programs with the -W option. Otherwise, Perl won't print out a warning if it finds a mistake and will just go on its merry way.

Ending a Perl program

This is a strange feature of Perl, and, frankly, I have mixed feelings about it. If something goes wrong in a Perl program, you can use the word die to stop the Perl program in its tracks and print out a message that you have specified. Most programmers use this feature, and it's a handy way to handle error situations. I have problems with it because it's not a user friendly way to deal with errors. (Users don't want to see your error messages; they want a program that works smoothly.) Nevertheless, the feature is available, and almost everybody uses it.

The simple program I show you at the beginning of the chapter prints some information to the console. In the following example, I change the current working directory. But if the directory doesn't exist, the program will *die*. First, here's a Windows version:

```
chdir "c:/temp100" or die "Can't change to c:/temp100";
```

And here's a Unix version:

```
chdir "/home/jeff" or die "Can't change to /home/jeff";
```

Each of these two lines of code attempts to change to a given directory. But if that directory doesn't exist, the program stops and prints out one of these two messages, respectively:

```
Can't change to c:/temp100 at die.pl line 3.
Can't change to /home/jeff at die.pl line 6.
```

People use the `die` statement all the time in Perl, and again, that's why I'm showing it to you. However, I prefer to make my software a bit more robust and handle the situation more appropriately. If the program can't switch to the directory, then perhaps the program can create the directory, or can figure out why the directory doesn't exist and print out a better message, explaining that the user needs to create the directory. But please, don't just complain to users that your program can't switch to the directory, leaving the users to their own devices — because you never know what those devices may be.

Processing Text Files

One of Perl's great strengths is in the processing of text files. If you have a file filled with text (whether it's a source code file, or an HTML file, or whatever), you can write some powerful Perl programs that will process the text in the file. What will this processing yield? Here are some examples:

✦ You can count the number of lines in the file.

✦ You can replace the variable `Spinach` with the variable `Broccoli`.

✦ You can extract all the `img` tags from the `.html` file.

✦ You can find the lines containing a particular string.

✦ You can find all the words in the file that match a particular regular expression.

In Book III, Chapter 5, I give you the lowdown on processing text files. As a preview of what's to come, here's a quick sample file that opens a text file, reads each line in the text file, and writes out the lines to the console:

```
while (<>) {
    print $_;
}
```

Believe it or not, that's the whole kit and caboodle. Save this code to a file called `file.pl`. Then create a sample text file to use with it. Here's a sample file I made called `test.txt`:

```
This is a sample text file.
It contains several lines.
Yeah, uh huh.
```

Now you can run the program like so:

```
perl file.pl test.txt
```

**Book III
Chapter 1**

Introducing Perl

You see the contents of `test.txt` appear on the screen. The first line in the code uses a `while` loop to grind through each line in the file. The strange `<>` inside parentheses instructs the Perl interpreter to read the name of the file from the command-line arguments (in this case, `test.txt`).

Inside the braces (you use braces to delimit blocks of text in Perl), the line `print $_;` prints out the value of the *default variable.* The default variable is called `$_` in Perl, and inside this `while` loop, the default variable contains the single line of text.

In Book III, Chapter 4, I tell you more about the `while` loop, as well as the other kinds of control structures you can use in Perl.

Running as a CGI script

Because this book is about creating Web sites, you'll be happy to know that you can use Perl scripts in your `cgi-bin` directory, where you have your CGI scripts. A CGI script is a program that runs in response to an HTTP request. For example, if you open your browser and visit `www.jeffcogswell.com/cgi-bin/dummies.cgi`, you see a Perl script run, which prints out the following text:

```
<h1>Hello readers!</h1>
```

This, of course, is HTML-speak for the string `Hello readers` in Header 1 text.

Here's the Perl script, which I saved as filename `dummies.cgi`:

```
#!/usr/bin/perl
print "Content-type: text/html\n\n";
print "<h1>Hello readers!</h1>\n";
```

The first line is a special line that instructs the Web server where to find the Perl interpreter. I talk more about that line — called a pound-bang line — in Book III, Chapter 7.

The next two lines are `print` statements. When the program operates as a CGI program, these two lines don't print to the console. Instead, they print out to the Web server and ultimately become the `.html` file.

The first of the `print` statements is required when you're writing an `.html` file. The next line is the source of the `.html` file, which is a level-1 header. Nice and sweet.

I talk all about CGI scripts in Book III, Chapter 7.

Interacting with Web Servers

Perl lets you use a URL to connect to a Web server and download an `.html` file in the same way that a Web browser does. Then you can process the file as if it's a text file, using all the cool features of Perl.

But you can do more than just download files from the Internet and process them. With Perl, you can write scripts that connect to Web sites, set cookies, retrieve headers, and do sophisticated processing. You can also write scripts that send data to Web servers in the same way that an HTML form sends data to a Web server.

Your scripts can run on a client computer, in which case you may write them to interact with a remote Web server (or even a local Web server). For example, you may write a script that sends data to a Web site expecting data from a form, thereby automating a form entry.

Or you may create scripts that sit on a server and interact with a client browser; such scripts may be the receiving end of a form entry. And you may need for these scripts to, in turn, contact another Web server. For example, I wrote a script for a client that receives data from an online bill-paying system and then sends the data to another server, where the user information is stored in a database. The script that receives the billing info and sends it to the database is a Perl script.

To accomplish all this network communication, Perl has several extra libraries, which are add-ons that Perl enthusiasts have written. Many of these libraries have become so popular that the designers of Perl now ship them as part of Perl itself.

Navigating the Perl Online Help

The Perl designers have created an enormous volume of online help for Perl, which you can find at `www.perl.org/docs.html`. Unfortunately, the organization of the online help is a bit of a disaster.

I recommend installing the ActiveState version of the Perl documentation, which ships with the ActiveState version of Perl. This is the same documentation you can find at the `perl.org` Web site; however, ActiveState has created a frame set that lists all the names of the Perl documents in a left-hand frame for easy navigation.

Each Perl document has a unique, rather cryptic name that starts with the word *perl* in all lowercase letters. Some examples are perlsyn, perldata, perlfunc, and perlre.

To help you find your way around the piles of documentation, the following list describes the documents that I find the most useful:

✦ perlfunc: Probably the single most important document in the Perl documentation library. This document contains information about all the built-in subroutines (also called functions) inside Perl. This document provides a wealth of information, and I strongly recommend reading it.

✦ perltoc: The main table of contents to all the other Perl documents.

✦ perlintro: A pretty good introduction to Perl.

✦ perldsc: A Perl data structures cookbook. Perl has lots of documents called "cookbooks" that are filled with handy tricks and tips. This one deals with data structures.

✦ perlstyle: A handy reference for general notes about programming in Perl; helps you understand the Perl frame of mind.

✦ perlfaq1, perlfaq2, perlfaq3, perlfaq4, perlfaq5, perlfaq6, perlfaq7, perlfaq8, and perlfaq9: Several Frequently Asked Questions documents about Perl.

✦ perlsyn: Information about `while` loops, `for` loops, and other control structures in Perl.

✦ perldata: Information about the different data types in Perl.

✦ perlop: Information about all the different operators in Perl.

✦ perlsub: Information about how to write subroutines in Perl.

✦ perlrun: The different ways to run the Perl program itself.

Chapter 2: Simple Data Types

In This Chapter

✔ **Storing data in a variable**

✔ **Working with scalars**

✔ **Putting special characters and variables inside a string**

✔ **Storing lists of data**

✔ **Storing associated data with hashes**

*P*erl has an incredibly simple data type system. Although other languages have a dozen data types for numbers alone, Perl has only three main data types:

✦ Scalars

✦ Lists

✦ Hashes

In addition, Perl has two other specialized data types:

✦ File handles for reading files

✦ Directory handles for reading directories

If you're already familiar with a programming language, you'll be interested to know that even though you can have strings and numbers in Perl, they're all treated as a single data type. I explain how this is possible in the section "Storing Single Items as Scalars."

In this chapter, I introduce the three main data types: scalars, lists, and hashes. You can find information about file handles and directory handles in Book III, Chapter 5.

To really understand the Perl mindset, I encourage you to read the final section of this chapter, "Talking about Scalar Context and List Context." The information in this section helps you fully understand how Perl handles functions and other features. (The information will help you remain sane and keep all your hair later on.)

Storing Data in Variables

If you're already familiar with variables, you can safely skip this section. However, be sure to read the final "Remember" point in this section. There I explain how Perl uses three characters — $, @, and % — to specify the three types of data.

Computers are good at remembering things, which is probably no surprise to you. (I know I wish one certain computer at one certain police station would forget that I owe a parking ticket. But that's another story.) You can store data on your hard drive, or you can store data in memory while your program is running. One way to store data in memory while your program is running is to create a storage bin for your data. You give this storage bin a name, and then you can put something in it. Such a storage bin is called a *variable*.

What can you put inside a variable? Lots of things, including the following:

✦ Numbers, such as 500 or 325 or 3.1415926

✦ Strings, such as abcdef or Sam or http://www.dummies.com.

✦ Lists of data, like 1, 2, 3, 4, 5.

A variable can hold only one thing at a time. For example, if you put the number 500 in a variable and then later put 325 in the same variable, the 500 is replaced by 325. The only exception to this rule is the list, which can hold multiple things. But still, each item in the list is a single item.

In Perl, you distinguish between the single-item variables and the lists of variables. The single-item variables are called *scalars* (another math term). A list is called, well, a *list*. But Perl has another kind of data item that's similar to a list called a *hash*. A hash is a list where each item in the list gets its own name. For example, a hash may have a first item called Name that contains the string "Fido" and a second item called Age that contains the number 5. A list, in contrast, doesn't provide names for the individual items in the list. A list would just have "Fido" and 5 in it.

A variable name in Perl is made up of any combination of letters, underscores, and numbers, with the only special rule being that the first character can't be a number. Here are some examples of valid variable names:

✦ MyName

✦ _height

✦ counter1000

✦ person_name

✦ I_am_really_good

Here are some examples of invalid variable names:

✦ 3MyName is invalid because it starts with a number.

✦ All&My&Luck is invalid because it contains characters other than letters, underscores, and numbers.

When you create a variable in Perl, you must specify whether it holds a scalar, a list, or a hash. You do this by putting one of the following characters before the variable:

✦ $ specifies a scalar. Thus, the variable $MyName will hold a single value.

✦ @ specifies a list. Thus, @names will hold a list.

✦ % specifies a hash. Thus, %people will hold a hash.

Now for a bizarre rule about names. Perl keeps a separate list of names for scalars, a separate list for lists, and a separate list for hashes. That means you can have two separate variables of the same name but different types. You can have a scalar variable called $goodfood and a list stored in @goodfood. The variables $goodfood and @goodfood are separate variables. But here's my suggestion: Don't do that. I'm only telling you about this rule for completeness in case you come across it someday and need to decipher the horrible, nasty code. But please don't write original code that uses the same name for different types. It makes the code hard to read and work with.

Storing Single Items as Scalars

If you want to store a single item such as a number or a string in Perl, you use a scalar variable. A scalar variable gets a $ symbol before its name.

Although a scalar is a single type, you can put some subtypes inside it. By subtypes (which is not the actual term, but one I'm using here because there really isn't a word for it), I mean specific types such as numbers and strings.

Perl can handle strings, integers (that is, whole numbers), and floating point numbers (that is, numbers that have a decimal part).

If you want to store the number 42 inside the variable $life, write a line of code like this:

```
$life = 42;
```

You start with the variable name (notice it begins with a $, meaning scalar), then an equal sign, and then the value 42. End the statement with a semicolon. (Always end statements with semicolons in Perl.)

If you want to put the value 3.1415 inside the variable $pi, write this line of code:

```
$pi = 3.1415;
```

Perl provides many ways for storing strings inside variables. One way is to specify the string using single quotes, like so:

```
$MyName = 'Jeff';
```

You can also use double quotes:

```
$MyName = "Jeff";
```

In the section "Putting special characters in strings," later in this chapter, I talk about the difference between single quotes and double quotes, and how you can put another variable's data inside a string. It's fun stuff, so be sure to read it.

Although most languages consider a character a single type, Perl doesn't distinguish between strings and characters. Characters are simply strings that take up only one, well, character.

Writing out variables

Writing out the contents of a variable to the console is easy; you simply use the print statement, like so:

```
print $MyName;
```

Listing 2-1 is a complete Perl program that fills some variables with data and writes the data to the console.

Listing 2-1:   A Program That Fills Variables with Data and Prints the Data

```
$MyName = 'Hal';
$MyAge = 98;
$MyTemperature = 98.6;

print $MyName;
print "\n";
print $MyAge;
print "\n";
print $MyTemperature;
print "\n";
```

Save this program as `Listing2_1.pl`. (I know, what an exciting filename.) To run this program, type the following:

```
perl Listing2_1.pl
```

Then you see this output:

```
Hal
98
98.6
```

The first three lines store data in three different variables: `MyName`, `MyAge`, and `MyTemperature` respectively. The next line prints out the value stored in `MyName`. The line after that is a special line for printing out a newline. The backslash followed by an n doesn't actually print out a backslash followed by an n. Instead, the Perl interpreter sees the two characters together and interprets it as a newline. And thus, Perl prints out a newline. I talk more about this special character in the next section.

Putting special characters in strings

Sometimes you want to print things that don't have an equivalent character that you can simply type. For example, you may want to print some text, then a tab, then some more text, and then start a new line where you print even more text.

To print a newline, you put a `\n` inside the double quotes in your `print` statement, like so:

```
print "\n";
```

For this to work, you must use double quotes. If you use single quotes, you won't get a newline. You'll just get a backslash followed by the letter *n*.

You can also put other characters inside your string. Look at this line of code:

```
print "Hi\nthere";
```

This prints the following:

```
Hi
there
```

The code printed the characters `Hi`; then it "printed" a newline, which means the output moved to the next line; and finally, it printed the characters `there`.

How do you put a tab in your output? You use a \t, like so:

```
print "Hi\tthere";
```

This prints the following:

```
Hi      there
```

You can use the special characters \n and \t to line up text so it looks nice and neat. Look at this example:

```
print "Name\tage\n";
print "Hank\t28\n";
print "Sue\t29\n";
print "Mary\t30\n";
```

Look closely at the \t and \n characters embedded in the strings. The first line has the characters Name followed by a tab, followed by the characters age, followed by a newline. Here's the output that you see:

```
Name    age
Hank    28
Sue     29
Mary    30
```

But what if you want to actually print the characters \n or \t or just a back-slash? The key is to use *two* backslashes. The reason is that Perl treats the backslash as a special character; every time it encounters the backslash, Perl does something special, depending on the character that follows the backslash. These combinations are called *escape sequences*. Backslash-n produces a newline. Backslash-t produces a tab. And backslash-backslash produces a backslash. Got all that?

Here's an example:

```
print "\\";
```

This code prints a single backslash:

```
\
```

If you want to print \n and \t, you would use this:

```
print "\\n\\t";
```

Here's the output:

```
\n\t
```

If you don't plan to do any conversions in your string (which includes embedded variables, a topic I talk about in the section "Writing strings and variables together," later in this chapter), you can use single quotes instead of double quotes. Here's an example:

```
print '\n\t';
```

This example prints \n\t, not a newline followed by a tab.

How do you print a double quote inside a double-quoted string, or a single-quote inside a single-quoted string? You use a backslash followed by the quote. Here's an example:

```
print '\'';
```

(That's a single quote, then a backslash, then a single quote, and then another single quote.) This line of code prints a single quote.

Here's another example:

```
print "\"";
```

This line of code prints a double quote.

If you have a sharp eye, you may notice a slight contradiction with something I said. I said that with single quotes, no conversions take place. However, the backslash before a single quote is an exception to that rule, because it lets you include a single quote inside a single-quoted string.

Table 2-1 lists many special characters available to you.

Table 2-1	Special Characters You Can Use in Perl
Special Character	*Translates To*
\t	Tab character.
\n	Newline.
\r	Carriage return.
\f	Form feed, which is primarily useful when sending output to a printer.
\b	Backspace, which simply backspaces over the previous character.
\a	Annoying beeping sound (the "a" stands for "alarm").
\e	Escape character.
\033	Octal char whose ASCII code is given by the three digits. If you're really into octal for some reason, this does the trick.

(continued)

Table 2-1 *(continued)*

Special Character	Translates To
\x1b	Hexadecimal character. The \x is required; next comes two digits representing the character's ASCII code.
\x{263a}	Wide-hexadecimal character.
\c[	The control character.
\l	Lowercase the next character. Thus, \lA prints a.
\u	Uppercase the next character; see the example that follows this table.
\L	Lowercase until \E.
\U	Uppercase until \E; see the example that follows this table.
\E	End case modification.
\Q	Quote non-word characters until \E.

Here's an example of some of the case-modification sequences in Table 2-1:

```
$name = "jeff";
print "\u$name\n";
print "\U$name\E";
```

This prints Jeff (with a capital *j*), a newline, and then JEFF in all caps.

Writing strings and variables together

Since the beginning of time (or, at least, since the beginning of modern computer languages), language designers have come up with new ways to write out a string of characters mixed with the values stored in various variables.

In Perl, you can *embed* your variables in the string. For example, suppose the variable $MyName contains the string Jeff, and you want to print out the following message:

```
Hello Jeff, I am your computer and I quit.
```

You can embed the variable $MyName inside a string, like so:

```
$MyName = "Jeff";
print "Hello $MyName, I am your computer and I quit.";
```

Notice that I simply put the variable name inside the double-quoted string.

Embedding variables doesn't work in single-quoted strings, as is also the case with escape sequences such as \n. If you used single quotes rather than double quotes in the preceding example, your output would be this:

```
Hello $MyName, I am your computer and I quit.
```

You can also embed characters inside a string and put the string inside a scalar variable. Here's an example:

```
$MyName = "Jeff";
$ComputerTalk =
    "Hello $MyName, I am your computer and I quit.";
print $ComputerTalk;
```

Storing Lists of Items

Perl lets you store lists of scalars in a single variable. The variable itself is called an *array*, and the array variable holds a *list*. Each element of the array is itself a *scalar*. (If you're familiar with multidimensional arrays, I take those up in Book III, Chapter 6.)

Suppose you want to put a list of names into an array variable. Here's a line of code that will work:

```
@names = ("Amy", "Bob", "Carl", "Danielle",
    "Egbert", "Frank");
```

(This code stretches two lines in this book, but it's really just one line of code.) This code puts the six names listed into the array called `names`. Notice that `names` starts with an @ character, which means that `names` is an array.

How do you get to the individual scalars within the list? Like this:

```
print $names[0];
print "\n";
print $names[1];
print "\n";
```

This prints out the first item in the list, then a newline, then the second item from the list, and then a newline. Look closely at how I got to the first item in the list:

```
$names[0]
```

I started with a $ character, not an @ character. The reason for this is a bit strange (and not very consistent with the rest of the language). Because I'm accessing a scalar of `@names`, I put a $ in front of it. I know, I know, that's not a very good rule. And, in fact, you can do this to get to the first element:

```
@names[0]
```

However, @names[0] is itself a list, not a scalar, because it starts with an @ character. It's a list containing one item, which isn't anything different in Perl from just a scalar, and that's why either works. Still, the Perl creators have made the rules that you must follow: Use $names[0] instead of @names[0].

TIP

Just use $names[0] when trying to access the first element of the array. That is, use a $ character, not an @ character, even though Perl allows you to use the @ character. (I know that early in this chapter I stated that $good-food and @goodfood were two separate variables. This time, however, the $ and @ amount to the same variable. This is just another rule to follow.)

You access the first element in the list by using [0], as in $names[0]. You access the second element in the list by using [1]. The number inside brackets is called the *index*. Thus, the first index is 0. The second index is 1.

You can also access the items starting at the end of the list. $names[-1] gives you the final item in the list:

```
print $names[-1];
```

This prints out Frank. Then $names[-2] will give you the second from the last item in the list, which is Egbert.

You can also access the elements using a scalar variable, like this:

```
$index = 3;
print $names[$index];
print "\n";
```

In this example, I save the number 3 in the scalar variable $index, and I access the "$index'th" element of the @names array, printing out the contents. This example prints the name Danielle, which is index 3 (but the *fourth* item).

If you're familiar with foreach loops (which I discuss in Book III, Chapter 4), you can loop through the elements of the array using a foreach loop, like so:

```
foreach (@names) {
    print $_;
    print "\n";
}
```

This prints out each name in the list. Inside the loop, each name gets put into the *default variable,* which is called $_. All I do is print out the contents of the default variable and then a newline. Easy!

Changing an item in a list

Changing an item is easy. All you do is access the item within the list, put it on the left side of an equal sign, and put something new on the right side. Suppose your list looks like this:

```
@names = ("Amy", "Bob", "Carl", "Danielle",
    "Egbert", "Frank");
```

Then you use this line of code:

```
$names[2] = 'Carrie';
```

Your list now has Amy, Bob, Carrie, Danielle, Egbert, and Frank in it. (Remember, the first item has index 0, so $names[2] refers to the third item in the list, which is Carl.)

Now, suppose you use this line:

```
print $names[2];
```

The name Carrie prints out. The original data, Carl, is gone for good . . . at least until you do this:

```
$names[2] = 'Carl';
```

Carl is now back in the list, and Carrie is gone.

Each item in the list is a scalar. Thus, when you have this line:

```
$names[2] = 'Carrie';
```

the previous value in the element, Carl, gets replaced by the value Carrie. You *don't* end up with both Carl and Carrie in the array at once. You can't because the element is a scalar, not a list.

Embedding list elements in a string

If you want to put a list element inside a string, type it into the string as you would any other variable. Here's an example:

```
print "Hello $names[0], how are you?\n";
```

If your array @names contains a list of strings and the first one is Amy, you see the following output:

```
Hello Amy, how are you?
```

You can also add a bit of complexity by using index variables:

```
$current = 3;
print "Hello $names[$current], good to see you!\n";
```

When you embed a particular element in the array as I did in the preceding code, make sure that you include the $ character before the index variable name. For example, if you mistakenly use $names[current] instead of $names[current], you'll get strange behavior when you run your program. Try it yourself; you'll always get the first element of the array because the Perl compiler thinks current without the $ character is a string, and it tries to convert current to a number and just gets 0, because current is not a number.

Obtaining slices of a list

Perl makes it easy to get a *slice* of a list, which means a new list consisting of just a portion of the original list. Suppose this is your list:

```
@names = ("Amy", "Bob", "Carl", "Danielle",
    "Egbert", "Frank");
```

You want to get the second element, third element, and fourth element and save them in a new list. Here's an amazingly short line of code that does all this:

```
@somenames = @names[1..3];
```

The two dots mean you're obtaining a range of elements, from index 1 (which is the *second* element) up to and including index 3. This means @somenames now has the elements Bob, Carl, and Danielle.

The original array is left unchanged. That means after you run the preceding code, your original array — @names — still has Amy, Bob, Carl, Danielle, Egbert, and Frank in it. The array @somenames has Bob, Carl, and Danielle in it, which are copies. Now suppose that after copying the slice, you change the original array like this:

```
$names[1] = 'Bridgette';
```

Now @names contains Amy, Bridgette, Carl, Danielle, Egbert, and Frank, and @somenames still has Bob, Carl, and Danielle in it.

This new variable is an array holding a list, so you can access it with its own indexes, which have nothing in common with the indexes of the original array:

```
print $somenames[0];
print "\n";
print $somenames[1];
print "\n";
print $somenames[2];
print "\n";
```

This prints out the following:

```
Bob
Carl
Danielle
```

Different languages have different rules about slices and ranges. In Perl, the higher number (that would be 3 in [1..3]) gets included in the range. Some other languages (Python comes to mind, even though I don't discuss it in this book) return a slice up to but not including the final number. Not Perl: You get what you ask for.

You can also extract particular elements in the list and save them into a new array, by separating the indexes with commas. Here's an example:

```
@morenames = @names[1,2,4];
```

This extracts the names Bob, Carl, and Egbert, which are the names with indexes 1, 2, and 4, respectively. Pretty good, eh?

Putting slices into individual variables

If you have several elements in a list that you want to store in individual variables, Perl has a handy syntax that helps you do so. Suppose this is your list:

```
@food = ("Asparagus", "Broccoli", "Cabbage",
    "Donut", "Eggplant");
```

Now you want to copy three of these food items to three separate variables. You can do so like this:

```
($goodfood, $badfood, $funfood) = @food[0,3,4];
```

Then if you print each of these, you can see that the process works:

```
print "$goodfood\n";
print "$badfood\n";
print "$funfood\n";
```

Make sure that you understand why it works. The code @food[0,3,4] returns a list of three elements. The left half of the equal sign is also a list of three elements, and Perl copies the elements one by one from the right side to the left side.

Now look at this code:

```
@pres = ("Washington", "Adams", "Jefferson");
($first, $second, $third) = @pres;
```

The first line creates a list and puts it in the @pres array; no big deal. The second line copies the individual elements from the list stored in @pres to the list on the left. Thus, the first element, Washington, ends up in the $first variable; the second, Adams, ends up in the $second variable; and the third, Jefferson, ends up in the $third variable.

If the list on the right has more elements than the list on the left, only as many elements as necessary are copied. Take a look at this slightly modified code:

```
@pres = ("Washington", "Adams", "Jefferson");
($tallguy, $funguy) = @pres;
```

The list on the right side of the equal sign has more elements than the list on the left, but that's okay. After the second line of code is run, $tallguy contains the string Washington, and $funguy contains the string Adams. The third string, Jefferson, isn't used.

When working with arrays and copying the elements elsewhere, remember that you're just copying the elements. For example, when you do something like this, the original array, @pres, remains unchanged:

```
($tallguy, $funguy) = @pres;
```

Thus, if @pres contains Washington, Adams, and Jefferson, respectively, then after this code runs, $tallguy will contain Washington, and $pres[0] will still contain Washington as well.

If you explore functions later on (or if you already have), you'll be interested in knowing that when you call a function that returns a list, the list hangs around in limbo until you store it in a variable. However, you can also yank out only certain elements of the list and store them in individual variables using the technique I'm describing in the present section. The following code shows how to do this:

```
$longname = "Abraham Honest Abe Lincoln";
($fname, $mname1, $mname2, $lname) = split(' ',$longname);
print "$fname\n";
print "$mname1\n";
print "$mname2\n";
print "$lname\n";
```

The `split` function returns a list. Instead of storing the list in an array, how-ever, I store the individual elements in four separate scalar variables. If you want to extract only certain portions, put parentheses around the function and then put brackets after the function, specifying the elements. In the following example, I extract the first and last elements:

```
($firstname, $lastname) = (split(' ',$longname))[0,-1];
```

If `$longname` still contains `Abraham Honest Abe Lincoln`, the `split` array returns a list of four strings. Then the `[0,-1]` indexes return a list consisting of the first element (the 0 index) and the last element (the -1 index). Thus, `$firstname` contains `Abraham`, and `$lastname` contains `Lincoln`.

Associating Data with Hashes

If you want to store data in a list but want to be able to access the data via a name instead of an index, you can use a *hash*. A hash is the Perl name for what is commonly known as an *associative array*. An associative array is an array in which you store indexed information so that the index can be any data, not just a whole number or 0. (The reason for the strange name *hash* is that Perl uses a special way of organizing the data; this special way is called a *hash* by computer scientists. Why the computer scientists call it a hash, I have no idea.)

Here's an example to help you understand what a hash is. Suppose you have a list of names, and you want to be able to look up the first name, based on the last name. You can store this data like so:

```
%names = (
    "Lincoln" => "Abraham",
    "Washington" => "George",
    "Jefferson" => "Thomas"
);
```

This code creates a hash in which the element indexed by `Lincoln` contains the value `Abraham`; the element indexed by `Washington` contains the value `George`; and the value indexed by `Jefferson` contains the value `Thomas`. Here's a line of code that outputs the value indexed by `Jefferson`:

```
print $names{'Jefferson'};
```

This line prints out the following:

```
Thomas
```

Notice the similarity between a hash and an array. An array has a fixed set of indexes, starting with 0, then 1, and then 2. A hash can have any scalar for the index. In this preceding example, the indexes are `Lincoln`, `Washington`, and `Jefferson`.

Understanding Scalar Context and List Context

Perl is unlike any other language. (To some people, that's a good thing; to others, it's a bad thing.) One odd thing about the language is that it maintains a *context*. In Perl, you work with data in either a *scalar context* or a *list context*. Depending on your choice, various statements (such as calling functions or subroutines, something I discuss in Book III, Chapter 3) will behave differently.

The context dictates how a certain statement in Perl will behave. Take a look at this example:

```
@words = ("hi", "there", "everybody");
$more = @words;
print "$more\n";
```

The first line creates a list of three words and stores the list in the array called `@words`. The second line is where the fun is: When I assign the list to the `$more` variable, Perl puts the list into scalar context because `$more` is a scalar. In scalar *context*, a list consists of a number representing how many elements are in the list. The list, when taken in scalar context, is the number of elements in the list. Thus, `$more` is 3, and the final line, the `print` statement, prints out the number 3.

Let me say that another way to help clarify the point. You can look at almost everything in Perl two ways: a scalar way and a list way. With a list, you can look at it the list way, in which case you see the actual list. Or you can look at it the scalar way, in which case you see a number representing the number of items in the list.

If you need a visual representation, you can look at it the way mathematicians look at things like this: Imagine that you have a candy bar (yes, mathematicians are known for their chocolate weakness), and printed on the front of the candy bar is not the name of your favorite chocolate manufacturer, but rather the items in the `@words` list, as shown in Figure 2-1. Printed on the end of the candy bar is the number 3, which represents how many items are in the list.

Figure 2-1:
The candy
bar is an
ideal way of
imagining
how to look
at an item
as either a
list or a
scalar.

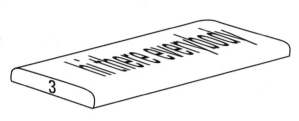

As you get ready to eat the candy bar, you can look at it from the top, straight down, in which case you see the list; that's the list context. Or you can look at the end straight on, in which case you see the number 3; that's the scalar context. It's the same candy bar, but you can look at it two different ways.

The same idea works in Perl, except you can't eat the language, and even if you could, it probably wouldn't taste very good. But either way, almost everything in Perl has both a scalar context and a list context.

If you've read about functions and subroutines, here's an example that demonstrates context. If your function returns a list, you don't need to store the list in an array. Instead, you can take the list in scalar context and store the result in a scalar.

For example, the `split` function splits the words in a string, returning a list of the words. If you store that list in a scalar variable rather than an array value, you do the split in scalar context and get back the size of the list. In other words, you find out how many words are in the string.

Here's an example:

```
$longname = "Abraham Honest Abe Lincoln";
$count = split(' ',$longname);
print "$count\n";
```

The `split` function returns a list containing the strings `Abraham`, `Honest`, `Abe`, and `Lincoln`. But because this code takes the list in scalar context, you end up with the number `4` in the variable `$count`, which is the number of elements in the list. Thus, this code prints out `4`.

Chapter 3: Comparing and Testing Variables

In This Chapter

✔ Testing conditions

✔ Performing actions based on conditions

✔ Making consecutive comparisons

✔ Comparing in different ways

✔ Performing comparisons together

*O*ne of the most important features in a computer language is the capability to make comparisons. For example, you may want to write out code that checks the time and writes "Good morning!" if the time is before noon, and "Good afternoon!" if the time is after noon. You can do this by making a comparison (of time and noon) and printing out the appropriate message. In this chapter, you find out how to perform comparisons and test conditions.

Testing Conditions

Perl includes several constructs for testing conditions and executing blocks of code if those conditions are satisfied. Suppose you want to write a program that tests whether a username and password are correct. Take a look at this sample Perl code:

```perl
$username = "jeff";

if ($username eq "jeff") {
    print "Hello jeff, welcome back\n";
}
else {
    print "Who are you?? Go away! Go away!\n";
}
print "All done!\n";
```

The first line stores the string `jeff` in the scalar variable called `$username`. Next, the program performs a comparison using an `if` statement. The line starts with the word `if` and is followed by a condition inside parentheses. The condition is as follows:

```
$username eq "jeff"
```

This condition tests if `$username` contains the string `jeff`. The word `eq` stands for *equals*. Next, you'll notice the code has an open brace and, later on, a closed brace. The code between these braces executes only if the expression `$username eq "jeff"` is true — that is, if `$username` contains the string `jeff`. The statements between these braces are known as the *if block*.

If `$username` does contain `jeff`, the program prints the following message:

```
Hello jeff, welcome back
```

Next comes the word `else`, followed by an open brace, some code, and a closed brace. The code inside these braces runs if the expression `$username eq "jeff"` is *not* true — that is, if `$username` does not contain the string `jeff`. The statements between these braces are known as the *else block*.

After either the `if` block or the `else` block runs, the code continues with the remaining statement. In this case, the remaining statement is the final `print` statement, which prints `All done!\n`.

The results of this conditional test may be a little obvious. Because you put the string `jeff` inside the variable `$username` just before the program tests if `$username` contains `jeff`, the `if` block runs, not the `else` block. However, if you were to use code like this in a real system, such as a login system, you probably wouldn't be defining the `$username` string yourself — you'd get it from somewhere such as a Web form, where a user would type in his or her name.

The `else` block is optional. If you have no need for an `else` block, you can omit it, like so:

```
if ($username eq "jeff") {
    print "Hello jeff, welcome back\n";
}
```

This tests whether `$username` contains the string `jeff` and, if so, prints the message. Otherwise, the code does nothing. Regardless of the results of the condition, the program continues running any lines that follow the `if` statement.

Although you use the word `eq` to compare strings, you don't use it to compare numbers. For comparing numbers, you use two equal signs, `==`. Here's an example:

```
$num = 10;
$another = 10;
if ($num == $another) {
    print "We're equal in all regards.\n";
}
```

This compares the number stored in `$num` to the number stored in `$another`. If you want Perl to remind you if you accidentally use the `==` operator to compare two strings, run Perl with the `-W` option. (See Book III, Chapter 1, for more information on `-W`.)

Here's some sample code that will cause a problem:

```
$username = "jeff";
if ($username == "jeff") {
    print "Hello jeff, welcome back\n";
}
```

I used `==` when I should have used `eq`. Here's the warning that you'll see:

```
Argument "jeff" isn't numeric in
numeric eq (==) at warning.pl line 2.
```

Use two equal signs in a row when you want to test for equality between numbers. If you forget and accidentally use one equal sign, your program will behave strangely. For example, look at this line:

```
$favorite = 10;
if ($favorite = 20) { # wrong
    print $favorite;
}
```

The first line stores the number 10 in the variable `$favorite`. Then the program attempts to compare the `$favorite` variable to the number 20. However, this code has a mistake in it; it has only one equal sign. So when Perl encounters the statement `$favorite = 20` while inside the `if` block, it sees the statement as a variable assignment and stores the number 20 in the variable `$favorite`. And because a storage statement such as this always returns true, the `if` statement succeeds, and the line inside the `if` block runs, printing out the following:

```
20
```

Shorter ways to `if`

The `if` statement is handy if you have several lines of code. But if you need to make a short comparison, you can tighten up your code by using a shortened version of the `if` statement. Here's an example:

```
print "Hi Jeff" if ($username eq "jeff");
```

Although this code may look a little bizarre if you've programmed in other languages, this is a simple `if` statement. It prints the line `Hi Jeff` only if the `$username` variable contains the string `jeff`. This code is equivalent to the following longer code, which uses a regular `if` statement:

```
if ($username eq "jeff") {
    print "Hi Jeff";
}
```

Because Perl requires you to use braces in a regular `if` statement, the shortened version lets you squeeze the whole thing onto a single line of code.

Here's another short way to write an `if` statement:

```
$a = ($username eq "jeff") ? "Hi" :
        "Bye";
print $a;
```

This method is for assigning variables. If `$username` contains the string `jeff`, `$a` gets the string `Hi`. Otherwise, `$a` gets the string `Bye`. The right side of the equal sign — `($username eq "jeff") ? "Hi" : "Bye"` — returns a value, either `Hi` or `Bye`, depending on the condition.

Oops — that's not what was supposed to happen. If you make the mistake of using a single equal sign in a comparison, you will not get an error. Instead, the value you're trying to compare to your variable will get placed inside the variable, and the code inside the `if` block will run every time.

Although I just said Perl won't issue an error, that's not entirely true. If you run Perl with the `-W` option (which most Perl programmers do), you will see a warning. Here's the warning you'll see if you use a single equal sign inside a comparison:

```
Found = in conditional, should be == at mistake.pl line 2.
```

(The term *conditional* refers to the expression inside parentheses in the `if` statement.) That warning is helpful and lets you know that you need to add an equal sign.

If you come from a C or C++ background, please note that you are not allowed to leave off the braces following an if or else statement. In C and C++, if you have just one line of code, you are free to leave off the braces. But in Perl, you must include the braces, even if you have only a single line of code.

Also, if you come from a C or C++ background, you may be troubled by the fact that you use a different comparison operator for strings or numbers. But remember, C or C++ does the same thing: The == operator doesn't work on pointers to characters, which is the traditional way of storing strings.

Performing Actions Based on Conditions

Another way to perform an if statement is to tell the computer that you want to execute some code *unless* something is true. This is another bizarre Perl-ism that is not present in other languages, and people who use Perl regularly enjoy using constructs such as this.

Here's an example:

```
unless ($username eq "jeff") {
    print "Hey, you're not Jeff! Why are you here?\n";
}
else {
    print "Oh good, it's you Jeff.\n";
}
```

Book III
Chapter 3

I know, this is kind of strange. I personally never use this because I think it looks weird. But you're welcome to use it. And remember, the preceding code works the same way as the following, more traditional version:

```
if ($username ne "jeff") {
    print "Hey, you're not Jeff! Why are you here?\n";
}
else {
    print "Oh good, it's you Jeff.\n";
}
```

In the first example, I'm saying, "unless such and such is true, do this." In the second example, I'm saying, "if such and such is not true, do this." These examples are really saying the same thing.

Comparing and
Testing Variables

In the `if` statement in the second example, I use the expression `$username ne "jeff"`. The word `ne` stands for *not equal* and applies only to strings. If you want to do the same not-equal comparison for numbers, you use code like this:

```
$num = 10;
if ($num != 20) {
    print "$num is not equal to 20!\n";
}
```

The exclamation point (which computer people call a *bang* — I'm not kidding) followed by an equal sign means *not equal*. Thus, == means *equal,* and != means *not equal*. Thus, `$username != "jeff"` means "$username doesn't contain the string `jeff`." In the section, "Comparing in Different Ways," later in this chapter, I give a rundown of the different comparisons you can make.

Making Consecutive Comparisons

When you start writing code that runs in response to comparisons, you'll quickly find that you often have multiple situations. For example, you may want one set of code instructions to run if the `$username` variable contains the string `maude`, another set to run if the `$username` variable contains `henry`, and a third set to run if the variable contains anything else.

You can make consecutive comparisons by adding another piece to the `if`-block puzzle: the keyword `elsif` (yes, the `e` is missing; take the word `else`, drop the `e`, and add `if`).

elsif

Here's an example of `elsif` in action:

```
$username = "henry";
if ($username eq "henry") {
    print "Greetings, Henry!\n";
}
elsif ($username eq "maude") {
    print "Good to see you, Maude!\n";
}
else {
    print "I don't know you, but nice to meet you!\n";
}

$day = (localtime())[6];
print $day;
```

This code saves the string henry in the variable $username and then compares $username to the string henry. If the condition is true, the program writes out a friendly message. If the condition isn't true (that is, if the name doesn't equal henry), the program compares $username to maude. If this comparison matches, the program prints out a message. If it fails, the program prints out a generic message.

Another way to do consecutive if statements is to use a switch statement, which I describe next.

switch

The switch statement is available starting with Perl version 5.8. You can find out your version of Perl by typing the following statement at the command prompt:

```
perl -v
```

If your version number is lower than 5.8, you have to use an if statement followed by several elsif statements, as described in the preceding section.

The example in the preceding section isn't particularly useful because I saved the string henry in the variable and immediately started comparing it. As a better example, first let me show you how to obtain the current day of the week. Look at this line of code:

```
$day = (localtime())[6];
```

This code saves the day of the week as a number in the $day variable. (For details on the localtime() function, see the "Getting the time" sidebar, elsewhere in this chapter.) If the current day is Sunday, $day is 0. If it's Monday, $day is 1, and so on.

Here's an example of the switch statement:

```
use Switch;
$day = (localtime())[6];
switch ($day) {
    case 0 {
        print "Sunday, I love eating sundaes";
    }
    case 1 {
        print "Monday is a slow day";
    }
    case 2 {
        print "Two for Tuesday";
```

```
    }
    case 3 {
        print "It's midweek!!!!";
    }
    case 4 {
        print "Thirsty on Thursday";
    }
    case 5 {
        print "French fries for Friday";
    }
    else {
        print "Fly to Saturn on Saturday";
    }
}
```

The first line, use Switch;, is a special line that tells the Perl system to make use of an extra language add-in called Switch. You need this line because the switch statement isn't a built-in part of the language. By including the use Switch; line, you are adding the switch capabilities to the language. (This type of add-in is called a *module*.)

The next line grabs the day of the week, as I described earlier. Then comes the switch statement. Think of the switch statement as a shorthand version of an if block. The switch statement in this case checks the value of the $day variable. At the top of the switch statement, you place the variable you want to check inside parentheses. (Or you can place a function there, and the switch statement will use the result of the function.) Next comes an open brace, and at the end of the switch block is a closed brace.

Inside the switch block, you list several case statements. Each case statement begins with the word case followed by the value you want to compare the variable against. In this example, I compare the $day variable against 0 (on the line starting with case 0), then against 1 (on the line starting with case 1), and so on.

If $day is 0, I print the string Sunday, I love eating sundaes. Otherwise, if $day is 1, I print the string Monday is a slow day. This continues on through the value of 5, which represents Friday. If none of the cases satisfies the condition, I follow these case statements with an else block. For this example, because the only remaining possibility is 6, which represents Saturday, I print out a message for Saturday.

The switch statement is useful if you have a single item and you want to compare it to several things and execute code for each particular situation. The item inside parentheses can be a variable; an expression, such as ($day + 1); or the result of a function. Further, you don't have to compare the item against just numbers. You can compare it against strings or even regular expressions. (I discuss regular expressions in Book VII.)

Getting the time

Perl measures the current time in seconds. The current time is given as the number of seconds since sometime around 1970. (I say "sometime" because different operating systems use a different start date, which is near January 1, 1970.) You can use the `localtime` function to figure out information about a specific time, such as the day, month, and year. For example, the time 1000000000 corresponds to sometime on September 8, 2001.

The `localtime` function creates a list of nine items. Here's what these nine items represent, in order:

- The seconds portion of the time. This first item is index 0.

- The minutes portion of the time. This second item is index 1.

- The hours.

- The date in the month.

- A number representing the month.

- The year. (The year is strange; 99 means the year 1999, 100 means the year 2000, 101 means 2001, and so on.)

- A number for the day of the week. (0 means Sunday, 1 means Monday, and so on.)

- The number of the day within the year. (1 is January 1, 200 is June 20 on non-leap years, and 365 is December 31 on non-leap years.)

- 1 if the time is during daylight-savings time; 0 otherwise.

To use the `localtime` function, you either pass a number representing a time in seconds, or don't pass anything to get information about the current time.

The number representing the current time isn't consistent across different computers and especially operating systems. Therefore, after you get the current time, I recommend running it through `localtime` to get a list that will be the same across systems.

Comparing in Different Ways

You can use several different comparison operators. To test if two numbers are equal, you use two equal signs together, as in ==. To test if the numbers are not equal, you use a bang followed by an equal sign, as in !=. You can test numbers or strings. Here are a couple of examples:

```perl
$num = 10;
$another = 20;

if ($num != $another) {
    print "$num does not equal $another.\n";
}
```

This sample code stores numbers in the two variables. Then the code tests if the numbers are not equal. If they are not equal, it prints out a message stating that fact. When you run this code, you see the following output:

```
10 does not equal 20.
```

Table 3-1 lists the available comparisons.

Table 3-1	The Functions of Many Operators in Perl
Operator	*Function*
==	Tests if two numbers are equal.
!=	Tests if two numbers are not equal.
eq	Tests if two strings are equal.
ne	Tests if two strings are not equal.
<	Tests if the first item is less than the second item. This works for numbers and for strings containing only numbers.
>	Tests if the first item is greater than the second item. As with less than, this works for numbers and for strings containing only numbers.
>=	Tests if the first item is greater than or equal to.
<=	Tests if the first item is less than or equal to.
!	Reverses the results of a test. See the text that follows for more on this operator.

Most of these comparison operators are pretty straightforward, but a few require some additional explanation.

The >, <, >=, and <= operators, as described in Table 3-1, work with both numbers and with strings containing only numbers. Here's an example of such a comparison:

```
$a = "10";
$b = "20";
if ($a < $b) {
    print "$a is less than $b\n";
}
```

The final operator in Table 3-1 may be confusing if you're new to programming. Take a look at this example:

```
$num = 10;
if (!($num > 100)) {
    print "$num is NOT greater than 100!\n";
}
```

In this example, the ! character takes the comparison $num > 100 and reverses it. Thus, the code inside braces runs if $num is *not* greater than 100.

One more interesting comparison operator is <=>, which is a less-than sign followed by an equal sign, followed by a greater-than sign. I didn't include this operator in Table 3-1 because you use it in a slightly different way than the other operators. You use the <=> operator to compare two numbers. (It doesn't apply to strings.) But instead of putting it in an if statement, you save its results in a variable, and then test if the variable is negative, 0, or positive, like so:

```
$num = 10;
$another = 20;
$compare = $num <=> $another;
if ($compare < 0 ) {
    print "$num is less than $another\n";
}
elsif ($compare == 0) {
    print "$num equals $another\n";
}
else {
    print "$num is greater than $another\n";
}
```

Here's how the <=> operator works. As you can see in this example, first I stored numbers in two variables, called $num and $another. Then I did the comparison, storing the results in the variable called $compare. At this point, $compare will contain -1 if the first variable is less than the second (that is, if 10 is less than 20, which it is), $compare will contain 0 if the two numbers are equal, or $compare will contain 1 if the first variable is greater than the second.

Then I begin the if statement. The first if statement checks if $compare is less than 0, which is true if the first variable is less than the second. The second comparison checks if $compare is 0, which means the two numbers are equal, and the third checks if $compare is greater than 0, meaning the first number is greater.

Mathematically speaking, you can accomplish the same thing as the <=> operator by doing a simple subtraction and then testing whether the result is negative, zero, or positive. However, the <=> operator is simpler because instead of returning just any negative number, it will return -1, or instead of returning just any positive number, it will return 1.

Performing Comparisons Together

Often in programming, you want to test two or more separate conditions and then run some code if all the conditions are true. Or you may want to run some code if at least one of the conditions is true. To perform these comparisons, you can use an and comparison or an or comparison.

Suppose you want to run some code if the variable $username contains the string maude *and* the variable $password contains the string pizza. This is an ideal situation for an and comparison, and here's how you could code it:

```
$username = "maude";
$password = "pizza";
if ($username eq "maude" && $password eq "pizza") {
    print "Welcome maude to the house of pizza!\n";
}
```

The comparison in the if statement contains two comparisons. The first is $username eq "maude". The second is $password eq "pizza". Between the two comparisons, I include the operator &&, which means *and*. Thus, the code inside the braces runs only if the first comparison is true *and* the second comparison is true: The && means *and* and is considered a *logical operator*.

Another logical operator is the or operator. The or operator consists of two vertical-bar characters, | |. As an example, you may want to allow two different passwords into a system, either maude or claude. Thus, you write this code:

```
$username = "claude";
if ($username eq "maude" || $username eq "claude") {
    print "Hello maude or claude.\n";
}
```

In this example, $username can be maude, *or* $username can be claude. If either is true, the code inside braces runs.

If you have two conditions separated by an or operator, and if *both* conditions are true, the code will still run. You don't need to have only one condition that's true. Thus, an or condition is true if either or both conditions are true.

Chapter 4: Controlling the Structure of Your Program

In This Chapter

✔ Looping

✔ Breaking out of a loop or continuing with the next iteration

✔ Writing a subroutine

✔ Passing data to and from subroutines

✔ Keeping data local to subroutines

Sophisticated programs are more than just a sequence of actions that must be completed one after another, from the beginning of the code file to the end. Instead, sophisticated code usually takes more complicated twists and turns. Take a look at this sample code:

```
$us = "aliens";
print "Hello\n";
print "$us\n";
print "and\n";
print "earthlings\n";
```

When you run this, the program runs the first line of code, which stores the string aliens inside the $us variable. Then the program runs the next line, which prints out the string Hello followed by a newline. Then the third line runs, then the fourth, and finally the fifth.

Everything in this program happens in order, line by line. But this is a simple example. What if you have a more complex task? (Personally, when I'm faced with a complex task, my instinct is to run.) Not everything on this planet happens in a linear sequence of steps. For example, when you log on to check your bank statement, the bank's computer first pulls up your list of accounts. If you have multiple accounts, you will see a balance for each account. Here a sequence of steps must be repeated, over and over, for each account you have.

In this chapter, I take you through the different ways you can control the structure of your program. The *structure* refers to the way the program is organized, which affects the flow of the program. The *flow* of the program is the step-by-step sequence the program takes through your code, however simple or complex it may be.

Looping

Often when you're developing programs, you need to repeat a group of instructions over and over. Sometimes you need to repeat these instructions a specific number of times; sometimes they must be repeated as long as a certain condition is true. (Such conditions are within the computer, however. I don't mean conditions like "while my boss is still paying me" or "while I still have caffeine inside of me.") For example, you may be reading in lines from a text file, and you want to process (print out, remove the HTML, or whatever) each line. You want to do this for each line in the file. Or, another example: You may be reading information coming down over the Internet, and you will keep reading as long as more information arrives, only stopping your reading when the data ends.

Both of these examples share a common element: They both perform a certain task over and over. In the sections that follow, I show you how you can make things happen over and over using — you guessed it — Perl.

Looping for each item in a list: foreach loops

The easiest way to repeat a sequence of instructions over and over is by using a foreach loop. The foreach loop operates in the way that its name implies. This example shows you what I mean by that:

```
foreach (0,1,1,2,3,5,8,13,21) {
    print "$_\n";
}
```

This foreach loop runs the code inside the braces once for each number inside the list. Each time the loop runs, the default variable ($_) takes on the value of the current item from the list. During the first iteration through the loop, $_ is 0. Then the loop goes through another iteration, but this time, $_ is 1. Then it's 1 again, then 2, then 3, then 5, and so on. Here's the output:

```
0
1
```

```
1
2
3
5
8
13
21
```

Often, you won't need to specify the items of the list as I do in this example. Instead, list items can be provided for you. For example, you may use the results of a function that returns a list. Or you can build up a list, store it in a variable, and then step through the elements. Consider this example:

```
$sentence = "The goose climbed out of the river.";
$num = 0;
foreach (split(' ', $sentence)) {
    print "Word $num is $_\n";
    $num++;
}
```

The first line stores a set of words in the $sentence variable. The next line stores the number 0 in the variable $num. Now for the exciting part. The foreach loop calls split, which splits up the string stored in the $sentence variable into a list of words. The foreach loop then iterates for each word in the array, printing out each word as it cycles through. Thus, here is the output:

```
Word 0 is The
Word 1 is goose
Word 2 is climbed
Word 3 is out
Word 4 is of
Word 5 is the
Word 6 is river.
```

If you don't like the default variable (many people familiar with other programming languages don't feel comfortable with it), you can also specify your own variable and use that instead of the default variable. Here's an example:

```
$sentence = "I think the spaghetti sauce is rotten";
foreach $word (split(' ', $sentence)) {
    print "$word\n";
}
```

In this example, each iteration of the loop inserts the current word inside the $word variable, and *not* in the default variable, $_.

Suppose you have a list stored in a variable and you want to use the list in a foreach loop. If you use the default variable to access the individual items of the list inside the loop, and then you modify the variable, you modify the items in the list, too. Here's an example:

```
@list = ('a', 'b', 'c', 'd');
foreach (@list) {
    $_ = "letter $_";
}
foreach (@list) {
    print "$_\n";
}
```

The first foreach loop runs through the list, modifying each item in the list. The characters a, b, c, and d are converted to the strings letter a, letter b, letter c, and letter d. And then just to show that the modifications really did stick, the next foreach loop runs through the list again, printing out each item. Here's the output:

```
letter a
letter b
letter c
letter d
```

The first item in the list is now letter a, not just a. That means the first foreach loop did indeed modify the items in the list. And further, if you specify your own variable and use that instead of the default variable, changing that variable will modify the entries in the list as well. Be careful!

If you want to modify the default variable in a foreach list without changing the data in the list, simply copy the variable to another variable, like this:

```
@list = ('a', 'b', 'c', 'd');
foreach (@list) {
    $letter = $_;
    # . . . more code would follow using $letter . . .
```

In this example, I assign the default variable to the $letter variable. I am now free to modify the $letter variable all I want, without having to worry about any unintentional modifications to the entries in the list.

Looping for a reason: for loops

The `for` statement is another way to create a loop. With the `for` statement, you specify three things upfront:

✦ The initial setup

✦ The conditions under which the loop will continue to run

✦ What to do at the end of each iteration

Before I explain each of these bullet items, take a look at the following example:

```
for ($i=0; $i<10; $i++) {
    print "$i\n";
}
```

This `for` loop counts from 0 to 9, inclusively, and prints each number. Here's the output:

```
0
1
2
3
4
5
6
7
8
9
```

The key to the `for` loop is the junk — er, I mean *expressions* — inside parentheses in the first line. The three items inside those parentheses are each separated by commas; these correspond to the bullet items I mentioned earlier. The first item in this parentheses is this:

```
$i=0
```

This creates a counter variable called `$i` that you can use inside the loop — much like the default variable in a `foreach` loop — and initializes it to 0. The next item is this:

```
$i<10
```

This means the loop will run as long as the counter variable, $i, is less than 10. If this condition becomes false (that is, if $i is 10 or greater), the loop will finish and continue running any code that follows the loop. Here's the third item:

```
$i++
```

This means that at the end of each iteration, the program will add 1 to the value stored in $i, thus increasing the counter. All three items add up to the single fact that this loop will run 10 times, starting at $i = 0, going through $i = 9.

If you have a for loop where the condition starts out false, nothing in the for loop will run. Here's an example of this:

```
$a = 50;
for ($x = $a; $x < 40; $x++) {
    print "$x\n";
}
```

While my loop gently runs: while loops

If you have some lines of code that you want to repeat over and over as long as a condition is true, your code is a perfect candidate for a while loop.

The while loop is a block of code that repeats as long as a condition is true, and at the point the condition is not true, the program continues with the code following the while loop. Here's an example:

Technically speaking, they're interchangeable

In the earlier section "Looping for each item in a list: foreach loops," I explain how the foreach statement loops through the items in a list. In the section "Looping for a reason: for loops," also in this chapter, I show how you can use the for statement to loop for a set number of iterations.

Now for the strange part: The two keywords for and foreach are interchangeable. But please don't interchange them. Don't use foreach if you mean for, and don't use for if you mean foreach. That will just confuse the poor souls that work in the cubes around you.

So why am I sharing this secret piece of information? So that you won't be the poor soul who gets confused if you encounter code where (ahem) *somebody else* used for in place of foreach or vice versa. (What nerve.)

```
$num = 1;
while ($num < 10000) {
    print "$num\n";
    $num = $num * 2;
}
print "All done!\n";
```

And here's the output from this code:

```
1
2
4
8
16
32
64
128
256
512
1024
2048
4096
8192
All done!
```

This code starts out by storing the number 1 inside the $num variable. If $num is less than 10000, the program prints out $num and then doubles $num. It keeps doing so as long as $num is less than 10000. When $num is no longer less than 10000, the program continues with the line following the while loop.

If the condition at the beginning of the while loop is false right off the bat, the code inside the while loop doesn't run at all, and the program jumps to the code following the while loop. Here's a silly example that demonstrates this:

```
$a = 10;
while ($a == 11) {
    print "This line will never run!\n";
}
```

Because $a is 10 and the while loop checks if $a is 11, the code inside the while loop never runs. This is silly, however, because I wouldn't write code like this — it has no practical application. A more common example of a while loop is when you open a file, start reading text, and immediately discover the file is empty. Your while loop might be coded to run "while more data is in the file." But because no data is present in the file, the program skips right over the code in the file.

Until the end of time (or a condition happens): until loops

One way to perform a loop is to repeat some lines of code *until* a certain condition happens. This is somewhat conversely similar to a `while` loop. Here's a quick example to demonstrate how the `until` loop works:

```
$a = 10;
until ($a > 15) {
    print "$a\n";
    $a++;
}
```

This code starts out with a 10 stored in the `$a` variable. Next, the code inside braces runs until `$a > 15`. Initially, `$a` is `10;`, so the loop runs and then increments `$a`. Then `$a` is 11. Because `$a` still isn't greater than 15, the loop runs again. This continues until `$a` reaches 16, at which point the code inside the loop doesn't run, and the program runs any code following the `while` loop. Here's the output:

```
10
11
12
13
14
15
```

But what if the condition is not true to begin with? Then the code inside the loop doesn't run; the program just skips over it. Here's a really awesome example that I just came up with: Suppose you're writing a program in a chemistry lab that measures the size of a single-celled organism that has outgrown its petri dish and is beginning to expand to monstrous proportions. (I'll call it a *blob* for this discussion.) You want to keep recording the size of the blob until it reaches two tons, at which point you're going to high-tail it out of there.

Suppose you hook up the instruments to the blob and discover it's already at three tons before you even start measuring. What should you do? Well, I'd suggest that you just skip the code, so to speak, and get on out of there. (But that's just a suggestion.) In other words, the condition is already true, so don't bother executing the loop. The same is true for the `until` loop in Perl. Here's the example in code:

```
$weight = 3000;
until ($weight > 2000) {
    print "Still safe!\n";
}
print "Yikes! Get out!\n";
```

In this example, the `Still safe!\n` message never prints because the condition is already true (`$weight` is indeed greater than 2000). So the program skips the code inside braces and jumps right to the code following the `until` loop.

Doing something at least once: do-until loops

If you have a `while` loop or an `until` loop and the initial condition is not met, the code inside the loop won't execute. But sometimes you want to execute the code at least once, and only check for a condition afterwards. In such a case, you can use a `do-until` loop. Here's a short example that doesn't involve any chemistry or alien blobs:

```
$i = 10;
do {
    print "$i\n";
    $i++;
} until $i > 15;
```

This code starts out with the counter variable, `$i`, being assigned the value 10. Then the program performs the code inside the loop. At that point, if `$i` is greater than 15 (which it isn't), the loop ends. Otherwise, the loop repeats again, until `$i` is greater than 15. Here's the output:

```
10
11
12
13
14
15
```

Messing up the final conditions

Be careful when you're working with `while`, `until`, and `do-until` loops, especially when dealing with numbers. Look closely at this code:

```
$i = 10;
do {
    $i++;
} until $i > 15;
print $i;
```

The code prints `$i` only after the loop is finished. After the loop runs, do you think the code will print 15 or 16? The answer is 16. The reason is that each time the loop executes, `$i` increases by 1. This keeps happening until `$i` is greater than 15, when `$i` is equal to 16. Understanding this will help prevent a common error of running a loop either one too few times or one too many times.

Breaking out of or continuing with a loop

If you ever want to break out of a loop or get on with the next iteration (an *iteration* is one trip through a loop) without finishing the remaining code in the loop, you can use the last or next statements, respectively.

The next statement forces the loop to end the current iteration and immediately begin the next iteration. As an example of this, imagine you're reading in a file line by line. You have a while loop that reads a single line with each iteration. If you encounter some data you're not interested in, instead of processing the data, you can skip over it by calling next. When you do, the program jumps back to the beginning of the while loop and then continues with the next iteration.

Here's an example that shows the file mechanism I'm describing. It reads in a text file line by line, and if it encounters a line that contains the word *pizza*, it skips over it (because I'm on a diet).

First, here's the text file you can type in. Call it pizza.txt and type a carriage return at the end of each line. (Otherwise, your Perl program will read it all in as a single line.)

```
This is a story about a (let's get pizza) little computer.
The computer is a sad computer. (He never gets any pizza.)
One day the computer found exactly what he was looking
for. What was he looking for? Why pizza, of course.
The end. (Pizza.)
```

Now here's the code. Save this code in a file called next.pl:

```
while (<>) {
    next if /pizza/i;
    print "$_";
}
```

Here's what you type to run the program:

```
perl next.pl pizza.txt
```

When you run this code, here's what you see:

```
One day the computer found exactly what he was looking
```

This is the only line that doesn't contain the word *pizza* (without regard for uppercase or lowercase letters). This `while` loop is a bit strange at first sight. The `<>` inside the parentheses causes the program to open whatever file is listed on the command prompt (in the example, that file is `pizza.txt`) and read each line into an array. The `while` loop runs for each line in the array — that is, each line in the file. Each line is then placed in the default variable, `$_`.

The next line is the `next` construct. To use this, you type `next`, followed by `if`, followed by a condition. If the condition is true, the program skips to the next iteration of the `while` loop, without running any remaining instructions inside the loop. In this example, the condition is whether the line in the default variable matches the regular expression `/pizza/i`. This is true if the line contains the word `pizza`, or any uppercase or lowercase variation thereof, such as `Pizza`. (The lowercase `i` at the end of the regular expression means it's case insensitive. Without it, the program would match `pizza` and not `Pizza`.)

If the line doesn't contain the word `pizza`, the program continues with the code inside the braces. The next line to run is the `print` statement, which prints out the current line. Thus, the program prints out only those lines not containing any `pizza` (like my stomach right now, unfortunately).

If you're familiar with C or C++, the `next` statement in Perl is analogous to the `continue` statement in C or C++. Similarly, the `last` statement in Perl is equivalent to the `break` statement in C or C++.

Here's an example of the `last` statement. Because I'm not supposed to eat any pizza, I'd better get up and run if I encounter any pizza. In computer terms, that means I'll get right out of the loop — completely out, not just out of this particular iteration — and continue with any lines after the loop. Here's how to do that:

```
while (<>) {
    last if /pizza/i;
    print "$_";
}
print "All done!\n";
```

This code is just like the previous code, except I added a line after the `while` loop, and the `while` loop has the word `last` in place of the word `next`. When the program encounters the first instance of the word pizza, it will jump right out of the `while` loop without continuing any more iterations.

**Book III
Chapter 4**

**Controlling the
Structure of
Your Program**

Using the `pizza.txt` file I described earlier, you can run the code like this:

```
perl last.pl pizza.txt
```

Because the first line in the `pizza.txt` file contains some *pizza,* the program doesn't even make it to the first `print` statement. All you see in the output is the output from the code that follows the `while` loop:

```
All done!
```

Subroutines

One of the best ways to write software is to divide your code into different parts called *subroutines.* And the best way to understand what I mean by this is through an example. Take a look at this code:

```
sub dosomething {
    print "Inside the subroutine!\n";
}

print "Starting!\n";
dosomething();
print "Finishing!\n";
```

The first three lines are a *subroutine* and don't run at first. Instead, the flow skips to the first line after the subroutine, which is `print "Starting!\n";`. Then the next line, `dosomething();`, *calls* the subroutine, which diverts the flow of the program to start running the lines inside the subroutine.

In this case, the subroutine has only one line inside it:

```
print "Inside the subroutine!\n";
```

After running this line of code, the program returns to where it left off before entering the subroutine and runs the final line, `print "Finishing!\n";`. When you run the program, you see this output:

```
Starting!
Inside the subroutine!
Finishing!
```

Think of subroutines like this: Suppose you're going to run some errands. You may first go to the bank, then head for the grocery store, and then drop off the recycling. In this scenario, you have divided your process (running errands) into three separate smaller processes (bank, grocery store, recycling). Each smaller process has its own steps. You can write a program for this like so:

```
sub Bank {
    print "Driving to the bank...\n";
    print "Depositing a million dollars!\n";
    print "Leaving the bank.\n";
}

sub GroceryStore {
    print "Driving to the grocery store...\n";
    print "Buying apples!\n";
    print "Buying more apples since I have millions!\n";
    print "Paying for the apples!\n";
    print "Leaving the grocery store.\n";
}

sub Recycling {
    print "Driving to the recycle plant.\n";
    print "Avoiding hitting the broken bottles.\n";
    print "Smashing bottles into bins.\n";
    print "Driving away.\n";
}

Bank();
GroceryStore();
Recycling();
print "Found more money!\n";
Bank();
GroceryStore();
```

This program defines three subroutines, Bank, GroceryStore, and Recycling. The main part of the program then calls the subroutines one by one. Then the main part prints out a message, calls the Bank subroutine a second time, and then calls the GroceryStore subroutine a second time.

You can call the subroutines whenever you need to and as often as you need to. That's the idea behind subroutines: If you have common code you need to repeat periodically, you can put it in a subroutine rather than retype it over and over.

You don't need to call the subroutines in the order in which you declare them. If you want to rearrange your errands and drop off the recycling first, then you don't need to rearrange the order of the subroutines — only the code that *calls* the subroutines.

By itself, a subroutine does nothing. The subroutine runs only when you have code in your program that *calls* the subroutine. To call the subroutine, you type the name of the subroutine (such as Bank) followed by a set of parentheses. (In the next section, "Passing data to a subroutine," I show you how you can put variables inside those parentheses.)

Many other languages (including C++ and PHP) use the term *function* instead of *subroutine*. In fact, Perl is a little inconsistent in its terminology because some of the official documentation uses the term *function*. Therefore, I use the terms function and subroutine interchangeably. (Note, however, that some languages, most notably Pascal, distinguish between subroutines and functions. A function is a special kind of subroutine that *returns* data to the caller. I talk about returning data in the section, "Returning data to the caller," later in this chapter.)

Passing data to a subroutine

A subroutine is useful, but a subroutine that has data is even more useful. Here's an example: Suppose you have a subroutine called Bank, and each time you call it, you want to deposit a different amount of money. For example, one day you want to deposit $13,527,985, and the next day you can only deposit a measly $995,219. Instead of writing two separate subroutines, you can write one that can handle different amounts.

Here's the code to do this:

```
sub Bank {
    $amount = $_[0];
    print "Wow! Depositing $amount! I'm rich!\n";
}
Bank(13527985);
Bank(995219);
```

First, look at the two lines in the main part of the program that call the subroutine. Each line consists of the word Bank followed by a number inside parentheses, which is the amount of the deposit. The first line *passes* 13527985 to the Bank subroutine. The second line passes 995219 to the Bank subroutine.

Now look at the code for the subroutine. Miraculously, this code figures out what number was passed to it. That's what the first line inside the subroutine does: $amount = $_[0];.

This line obtains the passed parameter and stores it in the variable called $amount. Yes, this code is strange. The @_ thing is really an array. (Remember, array variables start with an @ symbol.) Next comes the index of the array, [0], which is the first item in the array. In other words, you are grabbing the first item in the default array and storing it in the variable called $amount. This first item in the default array is the passed parameter.

When you run the preceding code, you see the following output:

```
Wow! Depositing 13527985! I'm rich!
Wow! Depositing 995219! I'm rich!
```

 If you're experienced in another language, this method of extracting parameters through an array may seem bizarre — and it is. I can't speak for the Perl designers, so I can't say what possessed them to choose this method. But remember, as weird as it is, the general idea is simple: The passed parameters all come in to a subroutine through the default array, @_.

Passing multiple parameters to a subroutine

Although passing a single parameter to a subroutine is fun and exciting, passing multiple parameters is even more fun and exciting. Suppose you have a subroutine called Bank, and when you call the subroutine, you want to pass both an amount and an account number. Inside your Bank routine, you can extract the values from the @_ array as you would with a single parameter, except this time you'll have two items inside the array. The first parameter is stored as @_[0], and the second parameter is stored as @_[1]. (The second parameter is the second item in the array.)

Here's a sample program that does the trick:

```
sub Bank {
    $amount = $_[0];
    $account = $_[1];
    print "Depositing $amount into account $account!\n";
}

Bank(13527985, 1);
Bank(995219, 2);
```

And here's the output from this program:

```
Depositing 13527985 into account 1!
Depositing 995219 into account 2!
```

Keeping variables local to the subroutine

If you're inside a subroutine and you create a variable, that variable will be accessible to parts of the program outside the subroutine. For example, if you have a subroutine called Bank that creates a variable called $amount, that variable will still exist after you call the subroutine, like so:

```
sub Bank {
    $amount = $_[0];
    print "Wow! Depositing $amount! I'm rich!\n";
}

Bank(13527985);
print "The amount is still $amount.\n";
```

When you run this code, you see the following output:

```
Wow! Depositing 13527985! I'm rich!
The amount is still 13527985.
```

Even though the Bank subroutine created a variable called $amount, that variable is now available to the rest of the program. Generally computer scientists (and normal people as well) consider this a bad thing: When a subroutine (or function, as other languages call it) creates a variable, that variable should be available only to the subroutine itself. When the subroutine ends, the variable should go away. This is called information hiding, which is a good thing: Only make information available where it is needed, so the rest of the program doesn't have to worry about it.

When a subroutine creates a variable and the variable exists only while the subroutine is running, we say that the variable's *scope* is the subroutine. The word *scope* refers to the part of the program where the variable exists.

If you want to limit a variable's scope to the subroutine itself (which is called keeping a variable *local* to the subroutine), you can use the word my. The following code is the same as the preceding example code, except the scope is now limited:

```
sub Bank {
    my $amount = $_[0];
    print "Wow! Depositing $amount! I'm rich!\n";
}

Bank(13527985);
print "The amount is still $amount.\n";
```

Inside the function, when I created the variable $amount, I put the word my in front of it. In doing so, I'm telling the Perl system that the variable's scope is limited to the function — that is, the variable is local to the function.

Here's the output from the program :

```
Wow! Depositing 13527985! I'm rich!
The amount is still .
```

(***Note:*** I'm running this without the -W option because otherwise you'll get some errors; Perl knows that I'm trying to fake it out here.) The final line of the program doesn't know about the $amount variable in the subroutine and prints nothing. The subroutine's $amount variable is gone when the subroutine finishes.

When I try to access the $amount variable outside the subroutine, I'm actually using a separate variable *also* called $amount. That's the interesting thing about the my word: You can use it to create a separate variable in each subroutine and use whatever names you want without having to worry about the variable name being in use elsewhere in the program. Take a look at the following code, which has two subroutines, each with a separate variable called $amount, as well as a main section that also has its own $amount variable:

```
sub Bank {
    my $amount = $_[0];
    print "Wow! Depositing $amount! I'm rich!\n";
}

sub Grocery {
    my $amount = $_[0];
    print "I am about to spend $amount in groceries!\n";
}

$amount = 10000;
print "I have $amount dollars in my pocket.\n";
Bank(50);
Grocery(25);
print "The amount in my pocket is still $amount!\n";
```

The $amount variable inside the Bank subroutine is a separate $amount variable from the one in the Grocery subroutine, and these are both separate from the main $amount variable. Here's the output:

```
I have 10000 dollars in my pocket.
Wow! Depositing 50! I'm rich!
I am about to spend 25 in groceries!
The amount in my pocket is still 10000!
```

If you're familiar with other languages, the idea that variables are global by default will seem strange. In Perl, if you declare a variable inside a subroutine, by default that variable becomes part of the global scope. To prevent this from happening, declare the variable using the my keyword.

Returning data to the caller

Although passing a single or multiple items to a subroutine is exciting, the most amazing thing you can possibly imagine is for a subroutine to return data *back to the caller.* If you haven't experienced this, then your life has been far from complete.

Just as you can pass a set of parameters to a subroutine as a list, you can pass a set of data back out of the subroutine as a list. Or, you can pass a single item of data, which is a scalar.

Take a look at this example.

```
sub Multiply {
    $first = @_[0];
    $second = @_[1];
    return $first * $second;
}

$total = Multiply(10,20);
print "The total is $total\n";
```

The Multiply subroutine accepts two parameters. It then multiplies these two parameters and returns the single number as a scalar. In the main code, the call to the subroutine is on the right side of an equal sign. That means that when the subroutine returns, you get back a single number, and you store that number in the variable called $total. Then in the next line, you print out that number.

Here's the output from this program:

```
The total is 200
```

The subroutine returned a value, 200, and you were able to store that value inside a variable.

You don't have to return just a scalar. You can also return an entire list, as in this example:

```
sub Sequence {
    $start = $_[0];
    return ($start, $start+1, $start+2, $start+3);
}

@mylist = Sequence(10);
foreach (@mylist) {
    print "$_\n";
}
```

Here's the output from this program:

```
10
11
12
13
```

Chapter 5: Processing Text Files and Directories

*O*ne of the most important uses of Perl is the processing of text files. Although Perl allows you to do much more than this, processing text files is one of its strong points and is among its most common uses.

In this chapter, I show you the different ways to open files, read and process the contents of those files, write new text files, and manipulate directories of files. Note, however, that in order to get the most out of Perl, you must use various *modules* in Perl. Modules are additions to Perl that make life easier. Over time, Perl users found the need for additional functionality that the language did not offer, so they wrote these additional parts themselves.

The samples in this chapter that use an extra module have the word use at the start of the code, followed by the name of the module. To use the module, all you have to do is type in the code I provide.

In this chapter, I show you the basics of reading and writing text files, in addition to processing directories. Generally, when reading files, you will want to process the data using *regular expressions*. See Book VII for further discussion of the topic of processing text files with regular expressions.

Processing Directories

Perl has built-in features for processing directories. With these features, you can get the current working directory, set the current working directory, or get a list of files and subdirectories within a directory. In the following sections, I show you how to do all this with remarkable ease.

Getting and setting the working directory

The easiest way to get the current working directory is by using a module called Cwd and then calling `getcwd`. Here's some code that does this:

```
use Cwd;
print getcwd;
```

The first line tells Perl that you want to use the Cwd module. The next line calls `getcwd` and prints out the results, which is the current working directory.

Setting the current working directory is even easier; you don't need to use the Cwd module. You can do it in a single line of code:

```
chdir "/tmp";
```

The `chdir` command is actually a subroutine, and Perl lets you call subroutines without parentheses. This line sets the current working directory to `/tmp` for the current program. (When Perl ends, the shell will still be in the directory it was in before the program ran.)

If you're working in Windows, you can use forward slashes, `/`, between directory names, instead of the standard backslash. Doing so has the advantage that you don't need to double up the backslashes as in `\\`, because a single backslash is an escape character used in such escape sequences as `\n`.

Obtaining a directory listing

Perl has directory listing features built right into the language. To get a directory listing, you have to open the directory. Yes, this may seem a bit odd; how do you open a directory? Don't you just open files? Well, yes, that's correct, but Perl uses an *open* metaphor for the directories. To open a directory, you call the `opendir` subroutine, passing a variable that will hold a *directory handle* (which is a variable you can use in later directory operations) along with the directory you want to read. From there, you call `readdir` over and over until you get back a false value (that is, an empty string, which Perl treats as a false value). Each time you call readdir and get back a true value, you will have another file in the listing. Here's some sample code that does this:

```
opendir(DIR, "/tmp");
while ($file = readdir(DIR)) {
    print "/tmp/$file\n";
}
closedir(DIR);
```

The readdir function returns a string containing the name of the item in the directory. (I say *item* because it can be either a file or a subdirectory.) Or, if the listing has been exhausted, you will get back a false value, and the loop will end. Then remember to call closedir at the end of the directory operation. (Because Perl lets you open a directory, you must also close it.)

But what if you want to list only the files and not the subdirectories? Then you use a special built-in function called -d (which stands for *directory*). Yes, -d is a function, even though it doesn't look like one. To use -d, you follow it with a string, and if the string represents the full path and name of a directory, you get back a value of true. You can augment the preceding code by including a test to determine if the filename is a directory. If it is, just continue with the next iteration of the loop using the next keyword, like so:

```
opendir(DIR, "/tmp");
while ($file = readdir(DIR)) {
    $fullpath = "/tmp/$file";
    if (-d $fullpath) { next };
    print "$fullpath\n";
}
closedir(DIR);
```

What if you only want subdirectories? No problem. Put a logical NOT operation (using an exclamation point) before the call to -d, like so:

```
opendir(DIR, "/tmp");
while ($file = readdir(DIR)) {
    $fullpath = "/tmp/$file";
    if (! -d $fullpath) { next };
    print "$fullpath\n";
}
closedir(DIR);
```

**Book III
Chapter 5**

**Processing Text
Files and
Directories**

This says, "If the filename is *not* a directory, continue with the next iteration." And remember, as usual, you need to call `closedir` after all this directory searching is finished.

Recursively listing a directory

If you want to find out not only the filenames and subdirectories in a directory, but also the filenames and subdirectories in the *subdirectories* (that is, you want to get a recursive listing, which means you want to get every subdirectory of every subdirectory of every subdirectory . . .), I suggest not using the `opendir` and `readdir` procedure. Instead, use the File module's `Find` function. Doing so is easy, as you can see in the following code:

```
use File::Find;

sub PrintFile {
    $name = $File::Find::name;
    print "$name\n";
}

find (\&PrintFile, "/tmp");
```

The first line of this code says you want to use the `Find` function inside the `File` module. The next line begins the definition of a subroutine that will serve as a *callback function*. When you perform your search using the `Find` function, the `Find` function calls your callback function for each file that it finds. Inside this subroutine, I extract the name of that file using this expression:

```
$File::Find::name
```

I save this value in the `$name` string, and then I print out the string. But remember, this is all inside a subroutine that will get called for each file. The next line is the call to `Find` that recursively finds all the files. The first parameter in the call to `Find` is odd looking; it's a reference to the subroutine. (The `\&` means you're obtaining a reference to the subroutine.) The next parameter is the string representing the directory where you want to start your search.

Here's some sample output where I have a `/tmp` directory containing four files (`a.txt`, `b.txt`, `c.txt`, and `d.txt`), and two subdirectories (`subdir1` and `subdir2`). Additionally, `subdir1` has a single file in it called `a1.txt`.

```
/tmp
/tmp/b.txt
```

```
/tmp/c.txt
/tmp/d.txt
/tmp/e.txt
/tmp/subdir2
/tmp/subdir1
/tmp/subdir1/a1.txt
```

If you're on a multiuser system, you might see some permission denied errors for some of the files in /tmp. You can ignore those.

Processing Files

Perl has numerous features for processing files. In the following sections, I give you the lowdown on opening files and processing them line by line.

Opening a file specified as a command-line argument

Often you will be using Perl to write command-line utilities that will process a file. You may run Perl from the command-line prompt, or you may spawn a process. Either way, you may have a command such as this:

```
perl cmdline.pl a.txt
```

The first parameter, cmdline.pl, is the name of the Perl program. The second parameter, a.txt, is the name of the file you want to process in your cmdline.pl program. In other words, a.txt is the name of a file passed into your cmdline.pl program as a command-line parameter. Here's a simple Perl program that opens a.txt and outputs each line in it:

```
foreach (<>) {
    print "$_";
}
```

Save this code as cmdline.pl and create a sample a.txt file such as this:

```
hello
there
fellow
dummies
readers
```

Then run `perl cmdline.pl a.txt`, and `a.txt` is printed out to the command line. The key to this Perl program is this part of the code:

```
foreach (<>)
```

The magical thing inside parentheses, `<>`, opens the file named on the command line and puts each line of the file into a list. Thus, the `foreach` statement walks through the list — that is, each line in the file. Inside the loop, I print out each item in the list using the default variable; each item in the list is a line in the file. Therefore, I'm printing out each line in the file. It's like magic!

Chomping your lines

Take a close look at this code, which is from the preceding section:

```
foreach (<>) {
    print "$_";
}
```

Then look at the output. You may notice something strange: The `print` statement prints the default variable, `$_`, and nothing more. But each line prints to the screen on a separate line, as if I had included a `\n` inside quotes after the `$_`. But I didn't. What's going on?

When you read in each line from the file, you get not only the text from the line, but also the newline at the end of the line. That newline ends up as a part of the line. Thus, the first line is not just the string `hello`, but rather `hello\n`.

The inclusion of this newline may or may not be what you want. Often people don't want the newline, especially when reading in data. For example, you wouldn't want to read in the newline when your text file is a list of e-mail addresses you want to process. (You want e-mail addresses to read something like `president@whitehouse.gov`, not `president@whitehouse.gov\n`, with a newline at the end.) In cases such as this, you want to *chomp* the newline. (Yes, *chomp* is the official Perl word for removing the newline. I'm not making this up.)

If you've ever written code in another language that reads in lines of text, and you've wanted to remove the extra newline, you probably found that the process isn't clear cut. You don't just remove the final character because you may accidentally remove some important data. Sure, this code isn't very long; only a few lines, but why rewrite it over and over each time you write a program that processes a text file? The Perl designers recognized this and therefore came up with the `chomp` function.

Here's an example of the chomp function in action; save this file as chomp1.pl:

```
foreach (<>) {
    chomp;
    print "$_";
}
```

The chomp function, when issued without parameters, chomps the default variable. Thus, suppose that you type this:

```
perl chomp.pl a.txt
```

And suppose that a.txt contains this:

```
hello
there
fellow
dummies
readers
```

Here's the output you see:

```
hellotherefellowdummiesreaders
```

The code read in the first line, hello\n, chomps off the \n, and prints out hello. But without the presence of a newline, the next output appears on the same line. Thus, the next line is there\n, which gets chomped to there, and the program writes there on the same line as before. All lines thereafter end up on that single line.

As you can see from this example, after calling chomp, the newline is gone. Perl makes sure, however, that it doesn't remove anything if no newline is present. And Perl is smart enough to know that different operating systems use different newline characters, and the program will remove whatever newline character is present, be it \n, \r\n, or \r.

What if you prefer to chomp one of your own variables rather than the default variable? Not a problem; just follow chomp with the name of your variable. Here's a modified form of the previous example:

```
foreach $line (<>) {
    chomp $line;
    print "$line";
}
```

This reads each line into the $line variable (instead of the default variable). Then to call chomp, you pass the name of the variable you want to chomp: chomp $line;. And it works perfectly.

Unlike many functions, which return a new string but don't actually modify the original string, chomp modifies the string you pass to it. So be careful.

Creating and writing to a file

Perl provides you with an easy way to create and write to files using the open function. To use the open function, pass as a parameter the name of a variable you want to represent the file after it's open. However, this variable is not a scalar, an array, or a hash. It's called a *file handle,* and its name isn't preceded by a special character like $, @ or %. Because of this, people usually specify file handles in all capital letters so they stand out. Here's an example:

```
open (MYFILE, ">/tmp/a.txt");
print MYFILE "hello\n";
print MYFILE "there\n";
print MYFILE "fellow\n";
print MYFILE "Dummies\n";
print MYFILE "readers!\n";
close (MYFILE);
```

This program opens the file called /tmp/a.txt. In doing so, the code opens the file for write access. I specified write access by placing a greater-than symbol inside the string just before the filename, like so:

```
">/tmp/a.txt"
```

Without the presence of the greater-than symbol, Perl tries to open the file for read access *only.* Perl doesn't open the file for write access, and your attempt to write to the file fails.

The next lines write to the file using an alternate form of the print statement. These print statements look like any other print statement, except that after the word print they have the file handle variable, MYFILE. The first of these print lines writes the string hello\n to the file. The final line closes the file.

Always remember to close your files!

To try out this program, make sure that you have a directory called /tmp (or \tmp on Windows, but you don't need to change the code to use back-slashes). Then save the code as print.pl and run it like so:

```
perl print.pl
```

Now you have a file called a.txt in the /tmp directory with five lines of text in it.

Opening and reading from a file

If a file already exists, you can easily open the file and read from it. The earlier section "Opening a file specified as a command-line argument" explains how to do this for a filename specified on the command line. But if you don't want to use a filename from the command line, you have to use the open function.

To use the open function to read a file, first pass the name of a file handle variable (put it in all caps and don't precede it with a $, @, or %). Then place the name of the file you want to read. Next, use a while loop, as in the following example:

```
open (READFILE, "/tmp/a.txt");
while (<READFILE>) {
    print $_;
}
close READFILE;
```

Book III
Chapter 5

Notice that the while loop has the file-handle variable inside angled brackets, < and >. This causes the whole file to be read in as a list; each line is a separate entry in the list. The while loop then steps through the items in the list, meaning that the loop runs through each line in the file. This sample program then prints out each line. Finally, the program closes the file.

Just as when you read a file specified as a command-line argument, the lines in your file will have a newline character. If you want, you can chomp each line, thereby removing the newline character. Here's an example:

```
open (READFILE2, "/tmp/a.txt");
while (<READFILE2>) {
    chomp;
    print $_;
}
close READFILE2;
```

Processing Text
Files and
Directories

Appending to an existing file

Sometimes you want to write to a file that already exists by appending to it. For example, say you're keeping a log file on your Web site, and each time somebody visits your site, you want to make an entry into the log file. But you don't want to wipe out the existing entries by starting over each time; you want to keep adding entries to the existing information.

To do so, you can open a file in an *append* state. You do this by placing two greater-than symbols before the filename in the call to open. Then Perl will open the file, if the file exists, in an append state. If the file doesn't exist, then Perl will create the file.

Here is a short example:

```
open (APPENDFILE, ">/tmp/a.txt");
print APPENDFILE "Me again!\n";
close APPENDFILE;
```

Each time you run this program, a new line is added to the text file; this line is the string Me again!.

Deleting a file

Deleting a file couldn't be easier. In fact, it's so easy I almost hesitate to create an entire section for this lonely, little topic. But it's an important topic, so here goes. All you do is this:

```
unlink("/tmp/a.txt");
```

Yes, you use the unlink subroutine. This doesn't make a lot of sense other than the fact that Unix uses an unlink command, which in itself isn't very sensible. But we live with what we are given.

Checking if a file exists and obtaining file information

Perl includes several bizarre functions whose names start with a minus sign and are followed by a single letter. These don't look like functions, but they are. To use these functions, follow them with a string. Here are four important functions:

✦ -e determines whether the named file exists.

✦ -d determines if the string represents an existing directory.

✦ -r determines whether you can read from the named file.

✦ -w determines whether you can write to the named file.

Here's a sample program that tests out all these functions:

```
if (-e "/tmp/a.txt") {
    print "Yuppers, good old a.txt is there!\n";
}

if (-d "/tmp/subdir2") {
    print "Oh boy, it's true: It's a directory!\n";
}

if (-r "/tmp/a.txt") {
    print "Oh yeah, I can read the file!\n";
}

if (-w "/tmp/a.txt") {
    print "Yessir, I can write to the file!\n";
}
```

The first if block tests whether the file /tmp/a.txt exists. To call the function, I first typed -e, and then I put the name of the file in quotes. If the file exists, the function returns true, and the program drops down into the code block and prints out a nice message.

The next if block determines whether /tmp/subdir2 exists and is a directory. If so, the program drops into the code block and prints out an exciting message.

The third if block determines whether it can read from the file /tmp/a.txt. If so, I print out a friendly message. And finally, the fourth if block determines whether it can write to the file. If so — you guessed it — the program prints out a message.

If you're familiar with Windows, you may be surprised that there's a distinction between a file's existence and the fact that you may or may not be able to *read* that file. The Unix operating system has a nice permission set that allows you to specify who has rights to read a file, write to a file, and execute a file. You can turn off any or all of these permissions. If you turn off the read permission for a group of users, those users can see that the file exists, but they can't read its contents.

**Book III
Chapter 5**

Processing Text
Files and
Directories

Chapter 6: Advanced Perl Coding

In This Chapter

✔ **Accessing data through references**

✔ **Building objects**

✔ **Manipulating dates and times**

In this chapter, I cover some miscellaneous advanced Perl topics. These are all important topics that you will want to become familiar with. I talk about references (which let you build lists that contain other lists and hashes, and hashes that contain other hashes and lists), object-oriented programming in Perl, and manipulating dates and times. Come along for the ride.

Accessing Data through References

Prior to Perl version 5.0, you could not create lists that contained other lists and hashes, or hashes that contained other hashes and lists. The best you could do was combine two lists into a single list, whereby the members of the inner list became additional members of the outer list; in the end, you just had one list containing scalars.

The Perl designers realized this shortcoming, so they added a feature known as *references*. References are scalar variables that refer to other variables — scalars, lists, or hashes. At first glance, references may seem to have little in common with the notion of lists of lists and hashes of hashes; however, references are a fundamental framework that is necessary. And with this fundamental framework, you can do much more than just put lists and hashes inside other lists and hashes.

Creating references

To understand what a reference is, remember the distinction between a list and an array: The array is the variable, and the list is the contents of that array. In other words, an array variable holds a list.

Seeing the need for references

Suppose you have a set of classes and each class has an associated list of students. How can you store this in Perl? In versions of Perl prior to 5.0, you really couldn't store it at all, at least not without a lot of data acrobatics. The reason was that hashes could contain only scalars. The various Perl manuals talk about ways you may work around this, and I won't go into them here, because you no longer need to work around the former shortcoming. Let me just say it was messy.

Today, with version 5.0 and later, you still store only scalars inside lists and arrays; however, the difference is that a scalar now can *refer* to a list or hash. And so by adding a special type of scalar called a *reference,* the Perl designers quickly solved the problem of not being able to put lists and hashes inside other lists and hashes.

Now think about this: First, I will create an array that holds a list. Next, I will create a variable that refers to the array. The variable that refers to the array is called a reference, and I can access the members of the list by using the array or the reference.

Here's some sample code that does this:

```
@tunes = ('Yankee Doodle', 'Rhapsody in Blue',
    'Bohemian Rhapsody');

$myref = \@tunes;

print $myref->[0];
print "\n";
print $myref->[1];
print "\n";
print $myref->[2];
print "\n";
```

This code first creates an array called @tunes and stores a list in the array. This list contains the titles of three songs. Next, the code creates a reference to the @tunes array (by putting a backslash before the name @tunes). The code stores this reference inside the scalar variable called $myref. Now $myref contains a reference to the array. However, $myref is not itself an array; $myref is still a scalar in that it contains a single item, a reference.

Next the code accesses the elements of the array referred to by $myref, one by one. Here's how you access the first element of the array referred to by $myref:

```
$myref->[0]
```

The technique I just showed you for accessing the elements in an array reference is a shorthand way to do it. To understand the longhand way, you must first note that to get to the original array through the reference, you use this:

```
@{$myref}
```

@{$myref} is the same as @tunes. Now remember, the first element of @tunes is as follows:

```
$tunes[0]
```

To use the longhand notation, you replace tunes with {$myref}, like so:

```
${$myref}[0]
```

But that's pretty complex, and thus I (and most sane people) use the shorthand notation, $myref->[0].

Looping with references

To access the array that a reference refers to, you can use @{$myref}. Thus, if you want to loop through the items in an array using a reference variable, you can use code such as the following:

```
@tunes = ('Yankee Doodle', 'Rhapsody in Blue',
    'Bohemian Rhapsody');

$myref = \@tunes;

foreach (@{$myref}) {
    print "$_\n";
}
```

Because $myref refers to @tunes, the line

```
foreach (@{$myref}) {
```

is equivalent to

```
foreach (@tunes) {
```

Building anonymous references

You can create a list and then create a reference to the list, all without storing the list in an array variable. Look at it this way: When you create a list and store it in an array, and then create a reference to the array, you're creating a reference to the list itself, not the array variable. References to lists that aren't stored in an array are called *anonymous arrays* because the list is floating out there in memory somewhere, and you have a reference to the list, but the list is not stored in an array variable. When you do this, you can access the elements of the list using the reference just as you can with any other reference.

As discussed in "Storing lists and hashes inside lists and hashes," later in this chapter, an ideal time for creating an anonymous array (or an anonymous hash) is when you want to put a list or array inside another list or array.

Perl 5.0 and later provides a handy syntax for creating an anonymous array or an anonymous hash, which you can then build a reference to.

The term *anonymous array* is official nomenclature, included in the Perl manuals, even though it's a bit of a misnomer. Remember, the array is the variable, and the list is the thing that the array holds. Because no array variable is present, we're really talking about an anonymous *list,* not an array. But because the Perl manuals use the term *anonymous array,* I will too.

Here's some sample code that creates an anonymous array, builds a reference to the array (or list, really), and then accesses the list through the reference:

```
$dogs = ['Chihuahua','poodle','big-bad-barking-thing'];
foreach (@{$dogs}) {
    print "The $_ barks a lot\n";
}
```

Here's the output from this code:

```
The Chihuahua barks a lot
The poodle barks a lot
The big-bad-barking-thing barks a lot
```

The first line of the code creates an anonymous array (or list) using brackets. If you surround a list of items with brackets (instead of parentheses, which are what you use for creating regular arrays), you get a reference to an anonymous array. You can then store this reference in a scalar variable; I stored my reference in this code in the $dogs variable.

Then I loop through the anonymous array using the reference, as in @{$dogs}.

Recall that if you have a reference, you can access the array that the reference refers to by putting the reference name inside braces and then plopping an @ character in front of it all, as in @{$dogs}. But in the preceding sample code, I don't have an array variable; I bypassed the array variable and created an anonymous array, and then got back a reference to the anonymous array. Nevertheless, Perl is smart enough to use @{$dogs} to access the array, as if the array really existed. In this sense, the term *anonymous array* is a bit less of a misnomer.

Storing lists and hashes inside lists and hashes

After you understand how to create a reference to an array or a reference to a hash, you can start storing those references inside other arrays and hashes. Remember, an array and hash can only hold scalars. But a reference is a scalar, so you are free to put a reference to an array or hash inside another array or hash. That's the magic key for creating lists of lists, lists of hashes, hashes of lists, and hashes of hashes.

First, I'll show you how to create a list containing two other lists. Remember that to create a reference, you precede the array or hash name with a backslash. Now, here's the code:

```
@fruit = ('apple', 'orange', 'banana');
@veggies = ('peas', 'carrots', 'corn');
@food = ( \@fruit, \@veggies );

foreach (@food) {
    foreach (@{$_}) {
        print "$_\n";
    }
    print "======\n";
}
```

The first two lines create two arrays. (I'm told corn is not technically a vegetable, but I just ignore that fact when I eat corn so I can say I'm getting my veggies.)

The third line is the magical line that creates a list holding another list. Notice how I do it: The list itself contains two scalar variables, and each scalar variable is a reference to an array. Thus, I haven't broken any rules: The list still contains only scalars. I then store the list inside the @food array variable.

And just to show that it worked, I step through the items in the @food array using the foreach word. But because each element in the list is itself a list, I need to do a bit of finagling. I want to step through each element in these inner lists, but all I have is a reference stored in the default scalar variable, $_. To step through the items in the list referred to by $_, I need to access the array variable. To do that, I type @{$_} as in the following line:

```
foreach (@{$_}) {
```

When you run the program, you can see that I did step through the outer list and the two inner lists. Here's the output:

```
apple
orange
banana
======
peas
carrots
corn
======
```

Building Objects

In the following sections, I talk about the wonderful world of objects and what they are. Then I show how you can implement objects and classes in Perl.

If you're already familiar with objects and object-oriented programming, you can skip to the later section, "Building classes and objects in Perl."

Introducing objects

Simply put, an object is an item that has both attributes and capabilities. The example I like to use when teaching about objects is the pen. Consider the attributes of a single pen: It has a length, an ink color, and an amount of ink. And what are the capabilities of a pen? You can write with it, and you can replace the ink cartridge. (Of course, you can't replace the ink cartridge in all pens, but for this example, I assume you can.)

Suppose you want to create a new *type* in the computer program, a type called Pen. I'm not talking about a variable here; I'm talking about a type, like an *array* is a type. Just as you can create variables that are arrays, you can create variables that belong to your new type called Pen.

But unlike an array, which just holds data, variables of the type Pen hold data (which are attributes) and also have capabilities. Each variable of type Pen has a data member representing the length of the pen (which is called Length), a data member representing the color of the ink (which is called Color), and a data member representing the amount of the ink (which is called InkAmount). Each variable of type Pen also has the ability to write and the ability to have its ink cartridge replaced.

Okay, I know, that sounds bizarre: How can a variable have abilities? These abilities are really just functions that operate on the data. One function may be called Write, and it may take a set of coordinates and draw a line on the screen in the color specified in the variable's Color data member. Another function may be ReplaceInkCartridge, which takes the InkAmount data member and restores it to some value, such as 100.

Now for some terms. The new type you created is called a *class*. The word class is just another name for the word *type*. And when you create a variable of your new type (or class), you are creating an *object*. This object is an *instance* of your new class.

These three terms — class, object, and instance — should be familiar to you from real life. For example, one day when I was teaching an object-oriented programming course, to prove a point I grabbed a pen and brought in the receptionist, who had no programming background. I asked her (slowly, now), "This object is an instance of what class of thing?" She pondered that for a moment, piecing together the somewhat complex sentence, and then responded, "Pen." That proves beyond a shadow of a doubt (okay, so it may not hold up in court, but close enough) that these words are the same as their English equivalents.

To recap, a class is a type of thing. When you build a class, you can provide member data (such as the Length in the Pen class), and you can also include member functions (such as Write in the Pen class).

Think about this: One pen may have a length of 4 inches and a color of black. Another pen has a different length, say 5 inches, and a different color, say red. Think about the situation of an array: One array may have the numbers 10, 20, and 30 in it. Another array may have the strings Hello and There in it. I have two different arrays, each with its own data.

The same is true with classes. I may have one pen with `Length` equal to `4` and `Color` equal to the string `Black`. I may have another pen with `Length` equal to `5` and `Color` equal to the string `Red`. This shows that two different instances of the same class can have different values for the data members.

The member functions, however, don't change between instances. The `Write` function operates the same way regardless of which `Pen` you're dealing with. It uses whatever values are in the member data for the particular pen (the pen having `Color` equal to `Red` draws a red line, and the pen having `Color` equal to `Black` draws a black line).

That's a quick background to the notion of objects. In the later section "Building classes and objects in Perl," I show you how to use this information to create some classes in Perl and then create objects, which are instances of these classes.

Before moving on, think about the following points to gain a better understanding of object-oriented principles:

✦ An object belongs to a class. This class is the object's type.

✦ An object has specific values for the member data. A class provides the member data names, but not the values.

✦ Each instance of a class has the same names of data elements, but can have different values for those data elements.

✦ Each instance of a class has the same member functions, but the member functions use the data for the particular instance.

✦ Think of a member function of an object as an object's capability. You ask the object to perform the behavior associated with the capability: You tell the pen to `Write`, and you tell the pen to `ReplaceInkCartridge`.

The final point isn't particularly vital in understanding objects; however, I simply want you to know that typically you think of the object as performing the work, and you simply ask the object to do the work. You don't do the work for the object; the object does the work itself.

Understanding constructors and destructors

Typically when you program objects, you include two special functions in your classes:

+ **Constructor:** You call this function when you want to create a new instance of the class. The constructor creates the object, and in this function, you include code to initialize any of the data members.

+ **Destructor:** You call this function when you're ready to get rid of the object. Inside the destructor, you include code to clean up any data if necessary.

Building classes and objects in Perl

In Perl, classes exist as packages. A *package* is a set of Perl instructions that you put in a file and then make available to other Perl programs.

Unlike other languages, Perl has a limited syntax devoted to objects and classes, which makes heavy use of the existing data structures. In particular, when you create an object, you store the data members in a hash.

To create a Pen class, type the code in Listing 6-1 and save it in a file called Pen.pm (note the .pm filename extension).

Listing 6-1: The Pen.pm File

```perl
package Pen;

# Constructor
sub new {
    my $class = shift;
    my $self  = {};
    $self->{'Length'} = 4;
    $self->{'Color'} = "red";
    $self->{'InkAmount'} = 100;
    bless($self, $class);
    return $self;
};

sub getLength {
    my $self = shift;
    return $self->{'Length'};
}

sub getColor {
    my $self = shift;
    return $self->{'Color'};
}
```

(continued)

Listing 6-1 *(continued)*

```
sub getInkAmount {
    my $self = shift;
    return $self->{'InkAmount'};
}

sub Write {
    my $self = shift;
    my $words = shift;
    print $words;
    $self->{'InkAmount'} -= length($words);
}

sub ReplaceInkCartridge {
    my $self = shift;
    $self->{'InkAmount'} = 100;
}

return 1;
```

Listing 6-1 is the code for the class. To try out the class, type in Listing 6-2, which uses the class. Save Listing 6-2 as filename testpen.pl (this time you use the filename extension .pl, as usual) and put the file in the same directory as the Pen.pm file.

Listing 6-2: A File That Demonstrates Using the Pen.pm Class

```
use Pen;

$redpen = Pen->new();
print $redpen->getInkAmount();
print "\n";
$redpen->Write("Hello\n");
print $redpen->getInkAmount();
print "\n";
```

To try this out, type the following:

```
perl testpen.pl
```

Here's the output:

```
100
Hello
94
```

And now here's a breakdown of the different parts of Listing 6-1. At the beginning of the file is the name of the package; this matches the filename. Next comes the constructor for the class. Technically, you can call this function anything you want; however, by convention most people call it new. This function creates the instance of the class.

The first line in new extracts the first parameter passed into the subroutine. (The shift function does this quite nicely because you can call shift several times, each time getting the next parameter.) This first parameter is saved in the variable called $class, which represents the class of object you're creating.

The next line creates an anonymous hash reference (remember, anonymous hash references use curly braces, as in {}) and saves the hash in the reference variable called $self. This $self hash holds the data members of the class.

The next three lines put some good initial values in the $self hash. The keys for the hashes are the three data member names: Length, Color, and InkAmount.

The next line is strange; here it is:

```perl
bless($self, $class);
```

This line lets the Perl system know that the $self hash is an instance of the class. That's all. Don't worry too much about this line; just remember to include it. Finally, the new subroutine returns the $self hash, which is now officially an instance of the class.

The next several subroutines are the member functions. Each one is pretty simple, and if you understand one, you understand them all. I'll walk you through the longest one, Write.

The Write subroutine takes a single parameter, a string. You call it like this (taken from Listing 6-2):

```perl
$redpen->Write("Hello\n");
```

However, each member function has a "secret" first parameter that is the object. The first line inside the Write subroutine extracts the first parameter by using the shift keyword, like so:

```perl
my $self = shift;
```

After this line runs, the `$self` variable contains the same hash that was returned by the `new` subroutine. Thus, `$self` is the object itself. The next line in the `Write` subroutine extracts the string passed into the function. The subsequent line prints out the string to represent the writing aspect of the member function. And just to make things interesting, the last line subtracts some ink from the `InkLevel` member, based on the length of the string passed in.

Notice that I access the `InkLevel` member through the `$self` object (or hash). I put the name inside curly brackets, as in `$self->{'InkAmount'}`.

Always access the data members of the hash by using curly brackets as in `$self->{'InkAmount'}`. If you accidentally use parentheses instead of curly brackets, you see this error:

```
Not a subroutine reference at Pen.pm line 33.
```

The final line of Listing 6-1 is as follows:

```
return 1;
```

This line serves little purpose beyond making the Perl interpreter happy. This line is necessary because when you create a package in Perl, the package must return a *true* value. Otherwise, Perl won't load the package.

The thinking behind this is that your package may do some work and if the package encounters any problems, the package can return a false value (such as `return 0;`) to notify Perl of the problem. But for just creating classes, you really won't be doing much initialization, so you can just type `return 1;` to make the Perl interpreter happy.

Listing 6-2 uses the class created by Listing 6-1. The first line tells Perl to use the package from Listing 6-1. Next, the code creates the new instance of the object by calling the `new` function from within the `Pen` package. I do this by using the `->` notation, like so:

```
$redpen = Pen->new();
```

The `new` function returns a new instance of the object (remember, the function transforms the hash into an object using the `bless` function), and then this code saves that object in the `$redpen` variable.

Next, I call some members of the object. The first line calls `getInkAmount()` and prints out the results. The next line prints a carriage return. Then the code calls the `Write` function like so:

```
$redpen->Write("Hello\n");
```

The next line again calls `getInkAmount` to show that the value did indeed go down after the `Write` call. (Remember, the `Write` subroutine decremented the value in the `InkAmount` member.) Finally, the last line prints a carriage return.

Modifying data members and creating multiple instances

Listing 6-1 isn't useful because every pen gets the color red, the length 4, and the ink level 100. Listing 6-3, an enhanced version of Listing 6-1, enables you to go to the next level by specifying the color, length, and ink level for different instances. This listing includes three additional member functions that let you set the different data values.

Listing 6-3: A Modified Pen.pm File That Lets You Set the Data Members

```
package Pen;

# Constructor
sub new {
    my $class = shift;
    my $self  = {};
    $self->{'Length'} = 4;
    $self->{'Color'} = "black";
    $self->{'InkAmount'} = 100;
    bless($self, $class);
    return $self;
};

sub getLength {
    my $self = shift;
    return $self->{'Length'};
}

sub getColor {
    my $self = shift;
    return $self->{'Color'};
}
```

(continued)

Listing 6-3 *(continued)*

```perl
sub getInkAmount {
    my $self = shift;
    return $self->{'InkAmount'};
}

sub setLength {
    my $self = shift;
    $self->{'Length'} = shift;
}

sub setColor {
    my $self = shift;
    $self->{'Color'} = shift;
}

sub setInkAmount {
    my $self = shift;
    $self->{'InkAmount'} = shift;
}

sub Write {
    my $self = shift;
    my $words = shift;
    print $words;
    $self->{'InkAmount'} -= length($words);
}

sub ReplaceInkCartridge {
    my $self = shift;
    $self->{'InkAmount'} = 100;
}

return 1;
```

The important parts to Listing 6-3 are formatted in bold. Listing 6-4, the testpen2.pl file, demonstrates how to use these new subroutines.

Listing 6-4: A File That Sets the Data Members

```perl
use Pen;

$redpen = Pen->new();
$redpen->setLength(4);
$redpen->setColor('red');
$redpen->setInkAmount(100);
```

```
$bluepen = Pen->new();
$bluepen->setLength(5);
$bluepen->setColor('blue');
$bluepen->setInkAmount(100);

$redpen->Write("Hi\n");
$bluepen->Write("Goodbye\n");

print $redpen->getInkAmount();
print "\n";
print $bluepen->getInkAmount();
print "\n";
```

In Listing 6-4, I create two different instances of the Pen, and I store one in the $redpen variable and one in the $bluepen variable. I set the length, color, and ink amount for each by calling the setLength, setColor, and setInkAmount member functions, respectively.

Then I call Write for each. The output shows that I am indeed working with two different instances, each with its own member variables. Look at the output:

```
Hi
Goodbye
97
92
```

The first two lines of the output are the output from the calls to Write. Now look at the next two lines. The first of these lines is 97, which is the value of the InkAmount member for the $redpen instance. The next line is 92, which is the value of the InkAmount member for the other instance, $bluepen. The values are different because each instance has its own InkAmount instance, which can be different values.

Do you see why they're different? The $redpen instance's InkAmount went down by 3 because I printed only three characters, H, I, and \n. The $bluepen instance's InkAmount went down by 8 because I printed a longer string of characters, G, o, o, d, b, y, e, and \n.

Manipulating Dates and Times

Perl is often used for processing files for the Web, and with that, you often need to calculate and format the current date and time.

**Book III
Chapter 6**

**Advanced Perl
Coding**

Historically, the Unix system and its original programming language, C, had decent functions for processing times; however, using these functions was a nightmare. They worked well, but they were difficult to use. Many newer languages have good support for processing dates and times. Unfortunately, Perl is not one of these languages (even though it's newer). Perl bases its date and time handling on the original C functions that are still present on most computers, including Windows and Unix.

The standard way of calculating a time in a computer (at least the Unix way of doing it) is to note the number of seconds since January 1, 1970. (This is called the *epoch.*) But beware: Windows XP and the Mac OS prior to OS-X use different starting times from Unix. So don't copy numbers between different computers without first converting them to an actual time (Year, Month, Date, Hours, Minutes, Seconds).

Here's a list of the date and time functions built into Perl; I discuss each of these in the following sections:

✦ gmtime: Converts a time in seconds to a list containing several members such as year, month, and date. This function uses Greenwich mean time for its time zone (hence the gm in the name).

✦ localtime: Same as gmtime, except this function uses the local time zone.

✦ time: Returns the current time in number of seconds since the epoch.

You can find another function called strftime in a module called POSIX. Also, in the Perl docs, you will find a function called times. This is related to the current process and doesn't have much to do with processing dates and times.

Obtaining the current time

To obtain the current time, use the time function. This function returns the number of seconds since the epoch (January 1, 1970, for Unix systems). The function returns a scalar as an integer:

```
$now = time();
print "$now\n";
```

Here's some sample output:

```
1060191022
```

But a big ol' number like that isn't particularly useful for most of us mere humans. To convert this number to something more interesting, try the `localtime` function:

```
$now = time();
@nowinfo = localtime($now);
foreach (@nowinfo) {
    print "$_\n";
}
```

Here's some sample output from this code:

```
49
31
10
6
7
103
3
217
1
```

That output is much clearer, right? Okay, maybe not. But each of these numbers has significance, more so than the giant 1060191022 number. Here's how this breaks down:

✦ 49 is the seconds part of the current time.

✦ 31 is the minutes part.

✦ 10 is the hours.

✦ 6 is the date of the month.

✦ 7, or August, is the month number (; January starts at 0).

✦ 103 — which is the Y2K adjusted version of 2003 — is the year.

Thus, so far you have August 6, 2003, at 10:31:49.

The final three numbers are extra information for helping you process the current date and time:

✦ 3 is the day of the week. Monday is 1, so 3 is Wednesday.

✦ 217 is the number of the day in the year. This is the 217th day of the year.

✦ 1 means the current date is in daylight savings time; otherwise, a 0 is used.

TIP

If two people in different time zones run the preceding sample code at the same time, they will see different values, depending on their time zone. If you want the two people to see the same values given in Greenwich mean time, use the function gmtime in place of localtime. It operates the same, except the information is adjusted to GMT.

TIP

If you have a time stored in a database in seconds format (as in 1060191022), and you want to convert that time rather than the current time, pass the number as the parameter to the localtime or gmtime function, like so:

```
@nowinfo = gmtime(1060191022);
foreach (@nowinfo) {
    print "$_\n";
}
```

Formatting a time

If you want to format a time (for example, transform 1060191022 into Wed Aug 06 10:30:22 2003), you use a special function called strftime. This function is not built into Perl, however. To use it, you have to use the module called POSIX. Using POSIX is easy; you just put this line at the beginning of your program:

```
use POSIX "strftime";
```

The strftime function uses what's called a *format string* to format the date. (If you're familiar with the C function printf, you've seen format strings before.)

The format string is a string containing some special characters that ultimately get replaced with things like Mon or Monday or Feb or February or 2003, for example. Take a look at this code:

```
use POSIX "strftime";
@now = localtime(1060191022);
$now_string = strftime("%a %b %d %H:%M:%S %Y", @now);
print "$now_string\n";
```

The first line uses the strftime function found in the POSIX module. The next line converts the strange number 1060191022 to a time list using the localtime function. The next line is where the fun begins: The strftime function takes the time list and transforms it into a nicely formatted string. The final line prints out the nicely formatted string. Here's the output:

```
Wed Aug 06 10:30:22 2003
```

Look closely at the format string:

```
"%a %b %d %H:%M:%S %Y"
```

The `strftime` function makes the following replacements:

✦ `%a` with the day of the week in three-letter format, `Wed`.

✦ `%b` with the name of the month, `Aug`.

✦ `%d` with the number of the day, `06`.

✦ `%H` with the hour, `10`. The colon stays put.

✦ `%M` with the minute, `30`. The colon stays put.

✦ `%S` with the seconds of the time, `22`.

✦ `%Y` with the year, `2003`.

Like magic, `%a %b %d %H:%M:%S %Y` becomes `Wed Aug 06 10:30:22 2003`.

You can rearrange items in the string if you don't like the format. Or you can leave parts out. What do you think this code will do, using the same `@now` variable?

```
$now_string = strftime("%Y", @now);
```

Because the format string has only `%Y` in it, `strftime` replaces that with just the year. Thus, this line puts the string `2003` in the variable `$now_string`. Here's another example:

```
$now_string = strftime("%a, %B %d", @now);
```

If you look closely, I'm using a capital `B` instead of a lowercase `b` in the format string, and I haven't told you what the capital `B` does. It gets replaced by the fully spelled-out month, as in `August`, instead of just three letters, as in `Aug`. Thus, this code puts the following string inside `$now_string`:

```
Wed, August 06
```

Notice that I put a comma inside the string; the comma gets left as is. In fact, you can put any characters you want inside the string, as in this example:

```
$now_string = strftime("The current time is %H:%M.", @now);
```

This code puts the following string inside `$now_string`:

```
The current time is 10:30.
```

The percent symbol is the special character that tells `strftime` to look at the following character to figure out a replacement. But what if you want a percent character to appear in the string? Then use %%, like so:

```
$now_string = strftime("%% %% %% %H:%M %% %% %%", @now);
```

This yields the following output:

```
% % % 10:30 % % %
```

Here is a list of the more useful characters you can use:

- ✦ `%a`: Weekday name in three letters.
- ✦ `%A`: Full weekday name.
- ✦ `%b`: Month name in three letters.
- ✦ `%B`: Full month name.
- ✦ `%c`: A general format for the entire time. (Try it.)
- ✦ `%C`: The century number. I'm not sure why you'd use this, but it's available if you need it.
- ✦ `%d`: The number of the day in the month, ranging from 01 to 31. (Single digits start with a leading zero.)
- ✦ `%e`: The number of the day in the month, ranging from 1 to 31. (Single digits have no leading zero.)
- ✦ `%H`: The hour in a 24-hour range, with a leading zero on single digits (00 to 23).
- ✦ `%I`: The hour in a 12-hour range, with a leading zero on single digits (00 to 11).
- ✦ `%j`: The number of the day within the year (range 001 to 366).
- ✦ `%k`: The hour in a 24-hour range, without a leading zero on single digits (0 to 23).
- ✦ `%l`: The hour in a 12-hour range, without a leading zero on the single digits (0 to 11).
- ✦ `%m`: The number of the month (0 to 11). Remember that January is 0, not 1.

✦ %M: The minute, ranging from 00 to 59, with a leading zero on single digits.

✦ %p: The characters AM or PM, for morning or afternoon. The function assumes noon is PM and midnight is AM.

✦ %P: The characters am or pm, for morning or afternoon.

✦ %r: The characters a.m. or p.m. for morning or afternoon.

✦ %S: The seconds ranging from 00 to 61, with a leading zero on single digits.

✦ %u: The day of the week. For some reason, Monday is 1, and Sunday is 7; the week starts on Monday, and there is no 0.

✦ %U: The number of the week within the year. The first week is 0. Single digits do not get a leading 0.

✦ %w: The day of the week, but this time Sunday is 0, Monday is 1, and so on.

✦ %W: A special form of the week within the year. The first week starts with the first Monday of the year, and that week gets the number 01. The single digits get a leading zero.

✦ %x: A shorthand way of formatting the current day, month, and year using the format preferred by the people living in the same location where the computer is running. Americans, for example, see the messy 8/6/03, meaning August 6, 2003.

✦ %X: A shorthand way of formatting the current time using whatever is preferred by the people in the current location. Americans, for example, see 3:30:15 PM.

✦ %y: The year in two-digit format, as in 03 for 2003. As you can see, that's not very Y2K friendly.

✦ %Y: The year, as in 2003.

✦ %z: The current time zone printed out in longhand, as in Pacific Daylight Time.

Not all of these characters are available on all operating systems. Try them out, and if you just see the character printed, the conversion isn't available on your computer. Try a different one in that case.

Chapter 7: Perl and CGI Scripts

In This Chapter

✓ Configuring Apache for CGI

✓ Adding more cgi-bin directories

✓ Writing a simple CGI script

✓ Reading data from a form

✓ Using CGI.pm

✓ Displaying errors and warnings

*O*ne of Perl's most important uses is in CGI scripts. CGI (Common Gateway Interface) refers to the running of programs in response to Web page requests. These programs generate HTML output, which is sent to the Web browser. This is different from the normal way of dishing out Web pages, where the Web server just grabs an .html file and sends it to the browser. A CGI program runs in response to a request and generates the HTML dynamically. You've probably seen CGI scripts before; you can recognize them by looking for the word cgi-bin in the Web address.

In this chapter, I assume you know where your CGI directory is on your Web server. The location varies from server to server; however, if you're using the Apache server on your own system, the default is in the cgi-bin directory under the main Apache installation. If you're using a third-party hosting service, ask the service where to put your CGI scripts. (Most likely you'll have a cgi-bin directory in your main directory, but I can't make any promises.)

The best way to understand how a CGI script works is to try one. First, make sure you know where your Perl executable is installed on your server. For example, on Linux, it might be at /usr/bin/perl. On Windows, it might be C:\perl\bin\perl.exe, which translates in Unix-ese to /perl/bin/perl (use forward slashes and leave off the .exe, and you can probably leave off the C: if that's where Apache is installed).

For you Unix folks, try this:

```
#!/usr/bin/perl
print "Content-type: text/html\n\n";
print "Hi, Dummies Readers!";
```

If you're a Unix or Linux user, and you want to locate your Perl program, simply type:

```
which perl
```

The result of this command (such as /usr/bin/perl) is exactly the term that you would put after the #! character.

For you Windows fans, try this:

```
#!/perl/bin/perl
print "Content-type: text/html\n\n";
print "Hi, Dummies Readers!";
```

Save this file as first.pl in your cgi-bin directory. (For more details on where the cgi-bin directory is, see the next section.) Next, if you're using Linux or Unix, go to the cgi-bin directory and type the following:

```
chmod a+x first.pl
```

Then you can open the file in your browser, going through the Web server, using this address: http://localhost/cgi-bin/first.pl.

If all goes well, you see the message Hi, Dummies Readers!. If you don't, fear not; the next section helps you get everything installed and set up correctly. Read on.

Configuring Apache for CGI

By default, Apache comes set up with a certain directory ready to go for CGI scripts. By default, this is /usr/local/apache/cgi-bin on Unix and Linux, and the cgi-bin directory under the main Apache directory on Windows. (If you're on Unix or Linux, and you don't see a /usr/local/apache/cgi-bin directory, then you'll probably instead have a /var/www/cgi-bin directory.) If you plop a file in this directory, Apache tries to execute it.

Remember the following two points about your cgi-bin directory:

✦ The files in the cgi-bin directory must have executable permissions. (In Windows, this isn't an issue.)

✦ You can set up other cgi-bin directories on your server by modifying the `httpd.conf` file.

In Linux and Unix, the Apache server does not run under the username of the person creating the CGI scripts (even if you have multiple users on the Web server, each with their own cgi-bin directories). Therefore, when you create a CGI script, you need to set execute permissions for *all*. To do this, switch to your cgi-bin directory and enter the following command, replacing *myscript.pl* with the name of your script file:

```
chmod a+x myscript.pl
```

The `chmod` command, which stands for "change mode," sets the permissions for the file, and the `a+x` option adds execute permission for all.

In Windows, you don't need to set the permissions. However, the execution issues might not work as you would expect. Normally for a file that's not a program, Windows looks up the file association and runs the program associated with the file's type (which is based on the file's extension, such as `.doc` or `.xls`). So if you try to execute a file that has a `.doc` extension and you have Microsoft Word installed, Windows looks up the association, finds that Word is the association, and runs Word, passing the name of your file as a parameter. Word then opens the file passed as a parameter. (The program that runs can do whatever it wants with the parameter or outright ignore it, based on how the programmers coded the product; Word, however, does open the file.)

I've just described the normal way of executing things. Apache, however, handles things a bit differently with the script files in the cgi-bin directory. Apache looks at the beginning of the file for the pound-bang (#!) line, which I talk about in the next section; Apache runs the program given in the pound-bang line and passes the script file as a parameter.

Specifying a pound-bang (#!) line

Under Linux/Unix and Windows, you need to specify a pound-bang line at the beginning of your script files. (Some people call it a shebang line.) This line tells Apache what program to run to execute the script. (Technically speaking, the Linux and Unix versions of Apache let the shell system determine how to run the program.)

**Book III
Chapter 7**

Perl and CGI Scripts

Take a look at this simple Perl script for Linux or Unix:

```
#!/usr/bin/perl
print "Content-type: text/html\n\n";
print "Hello from Perl";
```

Here's a sample script for Windows:

```
#!/perl/bin/perl
print "Content-type: text/html\n\n";
print "Hello from Perl";
```

Each sample script starts with a line that begins with a pound character (#) and a character that the programming world calls a *bang*, which is an exclamation point (!). Then comes the path and filename of an executable file. For the Linux/Unix version, the path and filename is /usr/bin/perl. For the Windows version, it's /perl/bin/perl, which corresponds to \perl\bin\perl.exe. This first line tells Apache (or the Unix/Linux shell) which program to run to process the script. In both cases, it's the Perl program, so Apache will run Perl to run the script.

Make sure that you include the first pound-bang line. If you forget it, Apache won't know how to run the script, and you will get an Internal Server Error message in the browser. In this chapter, I use the Unix/Linux form of the pound-bang, with the usual default path of /usr/bin/perl. Modify the pound-bang line accordingly for your system.

Adding more cgi-bin directories

You may want more than one cgi-bin directory. For example, if you're running a server that has multiple users, you may want to give each user his or her own cgi-bin directory. To do this, add ScriptAlias directives to the http.conf file and specify a directory.

Suppose you have a directory in your file system that's not accessible as a Web directory. (The directory isn't under the DocumentRoot directory or under an Alias directory.) But you want to put CGI scripts in the directory, so you must include a ScriptAlias directive in your http.conf file.

For example, suppose you want the directory /home/jeff/myscripts to have CGI scripts in it. You also want the directory name to look like this in a URL:

```
http://www.somedomain.com/myscripts/somescript.pl
```

Replace *somedomain* with your domain name. Then include this line inside your `http.conf` file:

```
ScriptAlias /myscripts/ "/home/jeff/myscripts/"
```

Always add a trailing slash after both the alias name and the directory name in the `ScriptAlias` line. (If you don't, Apache won't correctly locate the directory.) Also, you must restart Apache before changes to `http.conf` will take effect.

Writing a Simple CGI Script

Earlier in the chapter, I show you a simple CGI script that was written in Perl. The idea is that when you request the Web page, Apache runs the Perl program, which writes out the HTML that is sent to the browser. Here's the script again (remember to adjust the pound-bang line accordingly):

```
#!/usr/bin/perl
print "Content-type: text/html\n\n";
print "Hi, Dummies Readers!";
```

The first line writes out required header information that the browser receives but doesn't write out as part of the `.html` file. The next line prints out the lines that become the `.html` file.

Every CGI script that generates HTML must write out this line of text before writing any HTML:

```
Content-type: text/html
```

This line is followed by two newlines. This line is a header line that the browser interprets and decides what type of file it is receiving; it's part of the HTTP protocol, and if you don't include it, the browser won't know the file type and will either issue an error or will just prompt you with a Save As dialog box.

From Perl, you would write out the header line and HTML code like so:

```
#!/usr/bin/perl
print "Content-type: text/html\n\n";
print "<html><head><title>";
print "This is my web page!";
print "</title></head>\n";
```

```perl
print "<body>\n";
print "<h1>Welcome!</h1>\n";
print "<table border=\"1\">\n";
for ($i=0; $i<10; $i++) {
    print "<tr><td>$i</td><td>$i</td></tr>\n";
}
print "</table>";
print "</body></html>";
```

In this example, I'm writing more than just static HTML; I'm using Perl to generate the HTML. If you save this file in your cgi-bin directory as complex.pl, you can load it by using http://localhost/cgi-bin/complex.pl. Here's the resulting HTML:

```
<html><head><title>This is my web page!</title></head>
<body>
<h1>Welcome!</h1>
<table border="1">
<tr><td>0</td><td>0</td></tr>
<tr><td>1</td><td>1</td></tr>
<tr><td>2</td><td>2</td></tr>
<tr><td>3</td><td>3</td></tr>
<tr><td>4</td><td>4</td></tr>
<tr><td>5</td><td>5</td></tr>
<tr><td>6</td><td>6</td></tr>
<tr><td>7</td><td>7</td></tr>
<tr><td>8</td><td>8</td></tr>
<tr><td>9</td><td>9</td></tr>
</table></body></html>
```

This example isn't particularly interesting; it's just a table. But you can see how I used Perl to generate the table. Further, you can see that the Content-type line did not appear in the output. Now really, your program is writing out that line, but the browser interprets it separately and doesn't display it in the browser window, and if you view the HTML source in the browser you won't see the line. Now here's a more interesting example:

```perl
#!/usr/bin/perl
use POSIX;
print "Content-type: text/html\n\n";
print "<html><head><title>";
print "This is my web page!";
print "</title></head>\n";
print "<body>\n";
@now = localtime(time);
$now_string = strftime("%a %b %d %H:%M:%S %Y", @now);
print "The time is $now_string<br>\n";
print "</body></html>";
```

This example uses the POSIX module for the `strftime` function, figures out the current time, formats it with `strftime`, and then prints out the formatted time. (The local time is the time for the Web server, not the Web browser.)

Reading Information Passed to the CGI Script

When a browser requests a Web page from a Web server, the browser sends an HTTP-GET request, which is a set of data requesting a particular Web page. Included in this data is a Web address such as `http://www.dummies.com/`. When you fill in a Web form, the form can send the data in two different ways, depending on a parameter inside the `<form>` tag.

The first method is to append the information to the URL and request the page because the data is part of the URL. Here's an example:

```
http://www.jeffcogswell.com/cgi-bin/getresp.pl?
name=George+Washington&email=president@whitehouse.gov
```

(This will all be on one line, however.) Here, the data is encoded into the URL and therefore part of the GET request. For this reason, this method of sending data is called an *HTTP-GET*.

The HTTP-GET method is sometimes not the best method because the information shows up in the Address bar of the browser in the resulting page. You may not want this information transferred so visibly.

If that's a problem, an alternative is to use the *HTTP-POST* method. With this method, instead of sending the data as part of the URL, the browser sends the data separately from the URL, almost like an attachment.

The CGI script can receive the data either as a result of the HTTP-GET or as a result of the HTTP-POST. For an HTTP-GET, the CGI script reads an environment variable to obtain the data. For an HTTP-POST, the CGI script reads from the standard input. In the sections that follow, I demonstrate each of these methods.

Although reading form data is easy using the techniques I describe in the following two sections, the biggest headache is tearing apart the resulting string to get at the data. The method I describe here is best for simple forms that contain only one data item. For everything else, I recommend using the CGI.pm module, which I describe in the section, "Writing CGI scripts with CGI.pm," later in this chapter.

Reading from an HTTP-GET

Suppose you have an HTML form consisting of this code:

```
<html>

<body>
<form method="get" action="/cgi-bin/getresp.pl">
Name: <input type="text" name="name"><br>
E-mail Address: <input type="text" name="email"><br>
<input type="submit" value="Send">
</form>

</body>
</html>
```

This is a simple form that includes a text box for a name and a text box for an e-mail address. The parameter inside the `<form>` tag specifies the HTTP-GET method, like so:

```
method="get"
```

The form code is requesting the `/cgi-bin/getresp.pl` file, which is a CGI script. Here's the `getresp.pl` file:

```
#!/usr/bin/perl
print "Content-type: text/html\n\n";
print "Hello from Perl<br>\n";
print "ENV:<br>\n";
print $ENV{QUERY_STRING};
```

This code consists of several print statements. The final line is the key because the `$ENV{QUERY_STRING}` variable extracts the data from the form. Suppose that I type the string `George Washington` for the name, and `president@whitehouse.gov` for the e-mail address. Here's the output:

```
Hello from Perl
ENV:
name=George+Washington&email=president@whitehouse.gov
```

(Note that depending on your system, you might instead see HTTP characters in place of the special characters, as in `name=fred+bloggs&amp;` `email=fbloggs%40spammesenseless.org`.) If you try out these two files — the HTML file and the CGI script — you will see that the data in the URL matches the final line of the output. The data is divided into portions separated by an ampersand character, &. Each data item consists of a key, an equal sign, and then a value, like this:

```
name=George+Washington
```

A space is indicated by a plus sign. How do you indicate a plus sign, you ask? Good question, my friend: You indicate it with a set of characters denoting a hex value: %2B, which is the ASCII value for a plus character.

Reading from an HTTP-POST

Suppose you have this HTML form, which uses a POST method to send the data to the Web server, as shown in the method="post" parameter of the <form> tag:

```
<html>

<body>
<form method="post" action="/cgi-bin/postresp.pl">
Name: <input type="text" name="name"><br>
E-mail Address: <input type="text" name="email"><br>
<input type="submit" value="Send">
</form>

</body>
</html>
```

This form requests the postresp.pl CGI script, which is as follows:

```
#!/usr/bin/perl
print "Content-type: text/html\n\n";
print "Hello from Perl<br>\n";
$line = readline(*STDIN);
print $line;
```

This code obtains the data from the POST by reading a single line of text from the standard input.

The standard input is the stuff you type into the console if you run a program from the console. Therefore, if you run this Perl program from the console rather than as a CGI script, it lets you type something in at the prompt, and what you type in is read by the $line = readline(*STDIN); line, which stores the line of text in the $line variable. However, when this program runs as a CGI script, the standard input is not anything that anybody types into a command prompt; the standard input is the data sent by the form.

For example, if you type `George Washington` and `president@whitehouse.gov` into the form and click the button, you see the following output in your browser:

```
Hello from Perl
name=George+Washington&email=president@whitehouse.gov
```

If you read the previous section, "Reading from an HTTP-GET," you will see that the data is the same whether you read it via an HTTP-POST or HTTP-GET operation. The difference is in how you obtain the data: For HTTP-GET, you obtain the value in `$ENV{QUERY_STRING}`. For HTTP-POST, you obtain the value in the first line of the standard input.

Writing CGI Scripts with CGI.pm

If you're writing anything beyond a simple CGI script, I encourage you to use a module that ships standard with Perl called *CGI.pm*. This is the CGI module, which will make your life considerably easier. That can be beneficial in areas such as good health and preventing hair loss (speaking as a long time computer programmer with premature hair loss; dare I admit this in a book that will be read by millions?).

The CGI module includes functions that write out text in various HTML formats, without requiring you to write out the HTML tags yourself. The module also has a method for sending the introductory line `Content-type: text/html` (not that the line is all that difficult to write yourself, but the function call is easier to remember). Best of all, the module has some functions that read the HTTP-GET and HTTP-POST data sent from a form so you don't have to tear it apart yourself, manually.

To use the CGI module, start with this line after your pound-bang line:

```
use CGI qw(:standard);
```

This line imports the standard section of the CGI module, which contains the more common HTML features.

The `qw` thingy in the preceding Perl line looks strange to a lot of people. The `qw` function is a built-in Perl operator that creates a list containing strings. If you put multiple words inside the parentheses separated by whitespace, each word becomes a separate item in the list.

After you've included the preceding `use` line, you can use the functions inside the module. Here's an example:

```perl
#!/usr/bin/perl
use CGI qw(:standard);
print header;
print start_html("Welcome!\n");
print h1("My Page");
print h2("Page 1...");
print end_html;
```

When you run this code as a CGI script, the following HTML is sent to the browser:

```
<?xml version="1.0" encoding="iso-8859-1"?>
<!DOCTYPE html
  PUBLIC "-//W3C//DTD XHTML 1.0 Transitional//EN"
  "http://www.w3.org/TR/xhtml1/DTD/xhtml1-transitional.dtd">
<html xmlns="http://www.w3.org/1999/xhtml"
  lang="en-US">
<head><title>Welcome!</title>
</head>
<body>
<h1>My Page</h1>
<h2>Page 1...</h2>
</body>
</html>
```

(I reformatted this code a bit so it looks better on the printed page.) This code includes all the extra high-tech junk at the beginning that the HTML gurus tell us we *should* include in our `.html` files to make an HTML file that's XML compatible. That's fine. But what matters the most is that the Perl script is simple and you don't need to write a bunch of HTML code in your strings.

Here are some of the functions available; these have the same names as their HTML equivalents:

✦ `head`, `title`: For HTML head content

✦ `h1`, `h2`, `h3`, `h4`, `h5`, `h6`: HTML headers

✦ `p`, `br`: New paragraph and soft return (line break)

✦ `a`, `img`: Link (anchor) and image

✦ `table`, `tr`, `td`: Table, table row, and table data

Writing HTML using the object form of CGI.pm

Although you can simply call the function in CGI.pm — h1("hello"); for example — you can also use a CGI class available from the CGI.pm module. In this case, you include a simpler form of the use statement. Here's an example:

```
#!/usr/bin/perl
use CGI;
$c = new CGI;
```

```
print $c->header;
print $c->start_html("Welcome!\n");
print $c->h1("My Page");
print $c->h2("Page 2...");
print $c->end_html;
```

This isn't all that different from the non-object (or *functional*) approach, but the option is available if you prefer a more object-oriented approach.

If you want to see all the functions available, take a look at the source code for the CGI.pm module. You can normally find the CGI.pm file in the lib directory of the main installation directory. After you open the file, scroll down (or search) until you find %EXPORT_TAGS. This is the list of functions that are available to users of the CGI.pm file.

The CGI.pm module is huge and has much more functionality than I have room to describe here. In fact, it's so huge that the guy who wrote CGI.pm, Lincoln Stein, has written a book that you might want to pick up called the *Official Guide to Programming with CGI.pm* (Wiley Publishing, Inc.). Although the book came out in 1998, the information is still relevant. You can also visit the module's official site at stein.cshl.org/WWW/software/CGI/.

Specifying HTML parameters

Often in HTML code, you need to specify parameters deep down inside the inner sanctums of the HTML tags. For example, an <img> tag isn't that useful without the src parameter, which specifies the image file. Take a look at this example:

```
#!/usr/bin/perl
use CGI qw(:standard);
print header;
print start_html("Welcome!\n");
print img({-src=>"/mypic.jpg"});
print end_html;
```

The primary line here is the `img` tag. Notice how I set the parameters:

```
img({-src=>"/mypic.jpg"})
```

I put the parameters inside curly braces; curly braces are how you create an anonymous reference to a hash. I then put the name of the parameter preceded by a minus sign (in this case, `-src`), an equal sign, and the greater than sign (to make an arrow-looking thing), and then the data. Thus, I have `-src=>"/mypic.jpg"`, which results in this HTML:

```
<img src="/mypic.jpg" />
```

This tag follows the XML standard of putting a closing forward slash to indicate that no closing tag, such as `</img>`, is present.

If you want to have multiple parameters, separate them with commas, as in the following line:

```
print img({-src=>"/mypic.jpg", -alt=>"mypic"});
```

This line results in the following HTML:

```
<img src="/mypic.jpg" alt="mypic" />
```

Reading form data

The CGI.pm module is great for reading data. Although you can easily write your own HTML, reading CGI form data is difficult without the help of an extra library.

Here's a CGI script that accesses the parameters:

```perl
#!/usr/bin/perl
use CGI::Carp qw(fatalsToBrowser);
use CGI qw(:standard);
use CGI qw(:cgi-lib);
print header;
print start_html("Welcome!\n");
$params = Vars;
print "All params:<br>\n";
while (($key,$value) = each %{$params}) {
    print "$key=$value<br>\n";
}
print "Individual Params:<br>\n";
print $params->{'name'};
```

```
print br;
print $params->{'email'};
print end_html;
```

Vars is a function that returns a reference to a hash. I save this reference in the $params variable. Then I iterate through the hash using the while construct. (The each function returns the next key and value pair from the hash each time I call it.) Next, I print out the key and value pair.

Then I access the items individually. Remember, $params is a reference to a hash; it's not a hash itself. I have to use $params->{'name'}; (not $params['name']) to access the individual elements.

The preceding example works with both the HTTP-GET and HTTP-POST methods of sending data from a form. Suppose you save the preceding code as cgipm4.pl (which is what I call it on the accompanying CD-ROM). Then you can use this script in response to either of the forms in the sections "Reading from an HTTP-GET" and "Reading from an HTTP-POST," earlier in this chapter. In both cases, change the action parameter of the form tag to action="/cgi-bin/cgipm4.pl".

Displaying Errors and Warnings

If you write a CGI script that has errors in it, you receive a rather foreboding message such as this:

```
Internal Server Error

The server encountered an internal error or
misconfiguration and was unable to complete your request.

Please contact the server administrator,
webmaster@cogswell.biz and inform them of the time the
error occurred, and anything you might have done that
may have caused the error.

More information about this error may be available in
the server error log.
```

When you see this error, you can look in the error.log file found in the logs directory under the main Apache installation. But I have a better way of finding out the errors.

First, to display errors right on the Web page, add this code to the beginning of your CGI script, after the pound-bang line:

```
use CGI::Carp qw(fatalsToBrowser);
```

This mysterious line, which uses a module called CGI::Carp, causes syntax problems and other errors to display right in the browser window. Here's an example of a bad script:

```
#!/usr/bin/perl
use CGI::Carp qw(fatalsToBrowser);
print "Content-type: text/html\n\n";
asdf3893333&&
```

(Hopefully that last line isn't your e-mail name because I don't have a disclaimer at the beginning of the book that all names are fictitious.) If you save this script in your cgi-bin directory and try to run it, here's what you see in the browser:

```
Software error:
syntax error at cgi-bin/error.pl line 4, at EOF

Execution of cgi-bin/error.pl aborted due to
compilation errors.

For help, please send mail to the webmaster
(webmaster@cogswell.biz), giving this error message and
the time and date of the error.
```

This method of finding errors is better than looking in the error.log file because it shows you the error message. Of course, you generally don't want visitors to your site to see an error message, but for your own debugging, this can be pretty handy.

You can also have Perl's built-in warning mechanism write its errors to the HTML as well. To turn on Perl's warnings, add a -w parameter at the end of your pound-bang line, like so:

```
#!/usr/bin/perl -w
```

This line causes Perl to generate warning messages if you do something it doesn't like in your code. To see these messages, add this line after the pound-bang line:

```
use CGI::Carp qw(warningsToBrowser);
```

Or, if you want both errors and warnings, add this line:

```
use CGI::Carp qw(fatalsToBrowser warningsToBrowser);
```

Next, include this line:

```
warningsToBrowser(1);
```

Here's a sample script that generates a warning:

```
#!/usr/bin/perl -w
use CGI::Carp qw(warningsToBrowser);
warningsToBrowser(1);
print "Content-type: text/html\n\n";
print $a;
```

Warnings don't appear in the browser window; they appear as comments in the resulting HTML. If you save the preceding script as `warning.pl` in your cgi-bin directory and then open it in the browser, you see nothing in the browser window. But if you then view the source, here's what you see:

```
<!-- warning: Use of uninitialized value in print
at cgi_bin/warning.pl line 5. -->
```

The CGI::Carp module slows down your script a bit. Therefore, I recommend using the module only during your own debugging. After you've worked out the bugs and you go live with the script, remove (or comment out) the `use CGI::Carp` line.

Chapter 8: Ten Useful Perl Functions

In This Chapter

✔ Sorting and reversing arrays

✔ Obtaining the length of an array

✔ Treating an array as a stack or queue structure

✔ Converting hex to decimal

✔ Obtaining a random number

✔ Searching and replacing substrings

✔ Converting a string to uppercase or lowercase

I n this chapter, I show you ten important functions in Perl that will make your job easier. These include functions on dealing with arrays, such as sorting and reversing arrays, and obtaining the length of an array. Additionally, I've included a couple ways that you can treat an array as a stack or queue, giving you more power in your data structures. I also include information on random numbers, converting between hex and decimal, and manipulating strings.

Sorting an Array

If you want to sort an array, you can do so by simply calling `sort`:

```
@names = ("John", "Jerry", "Jeff", "Julia", "Jessica");
@newarray = sort @names;
foreach (@newarray) {
    print "$_\n";
}
```

As you can see from this code, `sort` doesn't actually modify the array; instead, it creates a new array with the members sorted.

The sort function is useful for sorting numbers, as well. Here's an example:

```
@nums = (5,3,4,1,2);
@newnums = sort @nums;
foreach (@newnums) {
    print "$_\n";
}
```

This code sorts the numbers in ascending order and prints out 1, then 2, then 3, and so on.

You can also sort in reverse order. To do so, you need to explicitly provide a *comparison routine*. By default, sort uses the standard ascending approach to sorting, where the letter a comes before b, and the number 10 comes before 11.

If you want, you can provide your own routine that reverses this sort mechanism. To do this, you follow the word sort with an open brace, a short routine, and a close brace, like so:

```
@newarray = sort {$b cmp $a} @names;
```

If you replace the sort line in the first program of this section with this line, your program prints out the items in descending order: Julia, John, Jessica, Jerry, Jeff. Remember, cmp is an operator that compares strings. The comparison routine inside braces is what sort uses when it compares the items in the list one by one, sorting them into place. The two items come into the comparison routine with the names $a and $b. But by flipping them in the cmp operator, you reverse the operation.

You can do the same with numbers, like so:

```
@newnums = sort {$b <=> $a} @nums;
```

This time I'm using the <=> operator, which is to numbers as cmp is to strings. And again, I'm flipping $a and $b by putting $b first. And it works!

Reversing an Array

To reverse the members of an array, use the reverse subroutine. Note that reverse doesn't actually modify the array; instead, it returns a new array with the elements reversed. Here's an example:

```
@names = ("John", "Jerry", "Jeff", "Julia", "Jessica");
@newarray = reverse @names;
foreach (@newarray) {
    print "$_\n";
}
```

Obtaining the Length of an Array

Obtaining the length of an array is a common task, and beginning Perl programmers often struggle to figure out how to do this. However, it's quite simple. All you need to do is replace the @ sign in the array name with $#, like so:

```
@names = ("John", "Jerry", "Jeff", "Julia", "Jessica");
print $#names;
```

This prints the value 4. Why 4 and not 5? Because the "length" that $# gives you is the maximum index in the array. Because the first index is 0, the final index is 4. If you want the size of the array, just add 1 to $#names.

If the array has no members in it, the maximum index is given as -1. In other words, $# returns -1, meaning the array is empty.

Treating an Array as a Stack Structure

A *stack* is a useful data structure. It's an array that operates under the principle "last in, first out," or LIFO for short (pronounced "lie-foe"). Think of a stack like a stack of papers on your desk: You can keep adding more papers to the stack and periodically take a paper off the top. But unlike a real stack of papers, a computer stack only lets you take papers off the top. And instead of holding papers, a stack can hold any data item you want, be it numbers, strings, whatever.

A stack is, arguably, the single most-used data structure in existence. The computer uses a stack structure to keep track of all the function calls it makes as it's running programs — not just your programs, but Perl itself and even the operating system. Whenever you call a function, the computer "pushes" the function's address onto its internal stack. Then when you call another function, it pushes that function. It does this each time you call a function. Then when you return from a function, the computer pops the top off the stack and then peeks at what's left on top to see where to return to after the function is finished.

You can use stacks for many purposes, such as solving mazes and processing HTML, among others. Perl includes two handy functions for treating an array as a stack:

+ `push` adds an element to the end of the array.

+ `pop` removes an element from the end of the array, returning the element.

Here's a sample program:

```
@names = ();

push @names, "John";
push @names, "Jessica";
push @names, "Julia";

$name = pop @names;
print "$name\n";

$name = pop @names;
print "$name\n";

$name = pop @names;
print "$name\n";

print $#name;
```

This program generates the following output:

```
Julia
Jessica
John
-1
```

I included the final line of code to show that all the calls to `pop` did indeed empty the array.

Treating an Array as a Queue Structure

A *queue* is a special structure. It's an array that operates under the principle "first in, first out," abbreviated FIFO and pronounced "fie-foe." The queue structure is much the same as people standing in a line. The first person to get there gets to go first, and as more people show up, they have to wait their turn. After the person in front goes, the next person in line gets to go.

In the computer world, you've seen a queue in action with print servers. If you're at work and you print a document, you may discover that ten print jobs are ahead of yours. Sorry, you have to wait in line. One by one, the print server prints whatever print job is at the front of the line. As the server prints each job, it removes the job from the queue, revealing another print job. You typically use a queue when you're processing incoming data of any sort; if you're processing telephone calls, for example, you process them one by one as they come in. As more calls come in, they're added to the queue.

If you want to treat the lowest index in the list as the front, use these two functions:

✦ `shift` to remove a person — er, I mean value — from the front of the list

✦ `push` to add a person to the end of the line

Here's an example:

```
@names = ();

push @names, "John";
push @names, "Jessica";
push @names, "Julia";

$name = shift @names;
print "$name\n";

$name = shift @names;
print "$name\n";

$name = shift @names;
print "$name\n";

print $#name;
```

Here's the output. Note the order of the names; John arrived first and got to go first:

```
John
Jessica
Julia
-1
```

If you want to treat the highest index in the list as the front of the line, use these two functions instead:

✦ pop to remove a person from the front of the line

✦ unshift to add a person (or data element) to the end of the line

Here's the same example as the preceding one, except this time you're treating the highest index of the list as the front of the line:

```
@names = ();

unshift @names, "John";
unshift @names, "Jessica";
unshift @names, "Julia";

$name = pop @names;
print "$name\n";

$name = pop @names;
print "$name\n";

$name = pop @names;
print "$name\n";

print $#name;
```

Both of the two sample programs in this section produce the same output:

```
John
Jessica
Julia
-1
```

The two programs behave the same, even though they effectively have stored the items in the list in opposite order from each other. Which one is better? Neither. Which one should you use? Either one. It's a matter of personal preference. (The people who developed Perl like to say, "There's more than one way." That's true here, too.)

Converting Hex to Decimal

Perl has a handy function for converting hexadecimal data to decimal data. The function is called hex:

```
$string = "EA10";
$decnum = hex $string;
print $decnum;
```

If you want to type hex numbers into your program, don't use the hex function. The hex function is useful if you're reading data from a file or from the Internet and you get a string containing a hexadecimal number that you want to convert to a decimal. (This is true even though the preceding example has the hex number hardcoded into the string; I did that to show an example of a variable that may contain a hex string.) If you want to type hex numbers right into your program, simply do this:

```
$mynum = 0xEA10;
print $mynum;
```

Obtaining a Random Number

Perl has two functions for working with random numbers:

+ srand seeds the random-number generator.

+ rand returns the next random number as a floating point number between 0 and 1.

Here's an example:

```
srand time;
print rand;
print "\n";
print rand;
```

**Book III
Chapter 8**

In this example, I pass the result of the time function (that is, the number of seconds since the epoch) to the seed to help ensure that I'll get a different sequence of random values each time the program runs. Then I grab two random numbers. Here's some sample output:

```
0.34429931640625
0.44195556640625
```

Why did I use the time function? To ensure that you will generate a different set of random numbers than I do, because the chances of you and I running our programs at exactly the same time is highly unlikely. (Most programs use the time to get the random-number generator going.) The default maximum value for a random number is 1. However, you can specify a maximum value that rand will return by using this statement:

```
print rand 500;
```

Ten Useful Perl
Functions

This prints out a random floating point value somewhere between 0 and 500. (Theoretically, it may print out 0.0, or it may print out 500.0, although the chances are slim.) Here's the number I saw when I ran it:

```
253.204345703125
```

If you're trying to debug a program that uses a random-number generator, you can try this little trick: seeding the random-number generator with a constant value. Debugging is difficult when dealing with random situations because you might not have the same sequence of events happen each time you run your program. For example, suppose you're writing a card game that will shuffle the cards using a random-number generator. The cards will be shuffled differently each time you run the program (if you use the `time` function to start out the random-number generator). But what if while debugging you want the cards to be shuffled the same each time? You can start the random-number generator with a fixed number of your choice, rather than the time, like so:

```
srand 10000;
```

The first number you get won't be 10000; instead, it will be a floating point number within the range you specify. Each time you run the program, that first random number will be the same. When you're finished debugging, you can replace the `10000` with the `time` function.

Starting with version 5.004 of Perl (no, that doesn't include version 5.0), you don't need to call `srand` because Perl automatically calls it the first time you call `rand`. But the earlier versions of Perl don't call `srand` automatically, so you won't get a new seed each time. Personally, I like to always call `srand` when my program starts (if I'll be using random numbers, that is), just to be on the safe side.

Searching and Replace Substrings

Perl has three functions for searching for a substring within a string:

+ `substr`

+ `index`

+ `rindex`

The first of these functions, `substr`, is multifaceted. You can use it to extract a substring from a string based on position; and you can use it to replace a substring. Here's an example:

```
$name = "Thomas Jefferson";
$part = substr($name, 7, 4);
print "$part\n";
substr($name,7,4) = "JEFF";
print "$name\n";
```

In this example, the first call to substr finds what characters are in the $name variable starting at the seventh index for four characters. (Remember, the seventh index is the eighth position because the first index is 0.) Then the code prints out what it finds:

```
Jeff
```

The second call to substr replaces the characters starting at the seventh position for four characters with the string JEFF. Then the code prints out the value in $name to show that it has changed:

```
Thomas JEFFerson
```

You can also use the index and rindex functions to locate a substring within a string. The index function returns a number of the first occurrence of the substring starting from the left of the string. The rindex function finds the substring starting from the right:

```
$string = "I am a pearl; a pearl am I.";
print index($string, "pearl");
print "\n";
print rindex($string, "pearl");
```

This prints out the following:

```
7
16
```

Converting a String to Uppercase or Lowercase

Perl offers four functions that modify the case of a string:

✦ lc returns a new string that's an uppercase version of the original string.

✦ lcfirst returns a new string with the first letter converted to lowercase. The remaining characters stay the same.

✦ uc returns a new string in all uppercase.

✦ ucfirst returns a new string with the first letter converted to uppercase. The remaining characters stay the same.

Here's some sample code:

```
$test = "HELLO";
$result = lc $test;
print "$result\n";

$test = "HelLO";
$result = lcfirst $test;
print "$result\n";

$test = "hello";
$result = uc $test;
print "$result\n";

$test = "helLO";
$result = ucfirst $test;
print "$result\n";
```

Book IV

Tcl/Tk Front End Development

MARKETING MIS-STEPS:
The Magic-Eye GUI

I don't see it.

It looks like File Manager to me.

I see the opening screen for "DOOM."

I'm getting a headache.

Contents at a Glance

Chapter 1: What Are Tcl and Tk?

In This Chapter

✔ Trying out Tcl

✔ Creating a simple Tcl program

✔ Adding comments to a Tcl program

✔ Breaking up long lines in a Tcl program

*W*hen most people think of LAMP, they think of Linux, Apache, MySQL, Perl, and PHP. However, many large businesses have adopted another language for in-house development: Tcl. Tcl stands for Tool Command Language and is pronounced (don't laugh) "tickle." I'm not going to lie to you; Tcl is a strange language. The syntax is unusual. But once you start to understand the language, you'll find that it's very powerful, useful, and even object-oriented.

Along with Tcl is an interesting library for creating graphical user interfaces (GUIs) called Tk. Tk stands for Toolkit (nothing fancy, I know, but then again, neither is Tool Command Language). Although the name Tk may be boring, the library is not. Tk is a rich library that includes objects for creating windows and controls and for processing events. Tk can be used with other languages besides Tcl. Most languages have a Tk interface so you can create rich GUIs in Tk using the language of your choice.

If you're interested in using Tk with a language other than Tcl (many people use Tk with the Python language, for example), the information in this part of the book is still relevant. Although this part focuses on Tk from within Tcl, the functions are the same regardless of what language you use.

Trying Out Tcl

The easiest way to become familiar with the strange behavior of Tcl is to try out a few examples. If you already know another language, remember that what you're about to see is quite different from most other languages.

Start up the Tcl command-line interpreter. The usual way to start it is by typing `tclsh` at the prompt. You see a percent sign for the prompt:

```
%
```

Type in the following line (you don't type the percent sign):

```
% set a 100
```

You see the following output appear on the screen:

```
100
```

You just did two things: You stored the number 100 in a variable called a by using the `set` command. In doing so, the interpreter also gave you back the value you just put in the variable, which is 100, and the shell printed out the value for you.

Now try this:

```
% puts $a
```

Again, you see this result:

```
100
```

The `puts` command prints out what follows. What follows the word `puts`? Well, you typed in the characters $a. When the Tcl interpreter sees a dollar character, it looks at the variable name that follows (in this case, a) and then replaces the dollar character and variable name with the variable's value (in this case, 100). Thus,

```
puts $a
```

gets replaced by

```
puts 100
```

The Tcl interpreter then runs this command, which prints out the value 100.

Tcl behaves very differently from other languages. The statement % `puts` $a doesn't mean print out the value stored in the variable called a. The difference is very subtle; instead, the Tcl interpreter replaces the $a with the value stored in a, which for now is 100, and then runs the `puts` command along with the characters 100. Thus, the Tcl interpreter performs a *substitution* before running the command.

Remember that when you stored a value in the variable a, the shell printed out the value after the interpreter stored the value, like so:

```
% set a 100
100
```

The shell did this because the interpreter sent back the value to the shell. But you can use this value that was returned by the interpreter. Take a look at this strange statement:

```
% set b [set a 100]23
```

When you press Enter, here's what you see:

```
10023
```

The variable b gets the value 10023. What happened? The Tcl interpreter performed another substitution, thanks to the square brackets. When you have square brackets in a line, the Tcl interpreter runs those lines first. Then when the interpreter gets back a value, it replaces the stuff inside brackets with the value.

In this example, the stuff in brackets looks like this:

```
set a 100
```

This command stores 100 in the variable a. But it also returns the value 100. So everything inside the brackets is replaced with 100. Thus, the line

```
set b [set a 100]23
```

gets replaced with

```
set b 10023
```

Then the Tcl interpreter runs this new line, which stores 10023 in the variable b. Here's what you see when you print out the value stored in b:

```
% puts $b
10023
```

Here's the value stored in a:

```
% puts $a
100
```

Whew! How's that for a bizarre programming language? As you can see, you can perform substitutions in Tcl two ways:

✦ You can type a $ to substitute a variable name with its value.

✦ You can put a command in brackets to substitute the command with its result.

But substitution, unfortunately, isn't always as clear as it might seem. Try typing in this interesting example:

```
% set c [puts $b]60
10023
60
```

This example printed out two lines. But what goes inside the variable c? You might think that the variable gets 1002360, but it doesn't. Try this:

```
% puts $c
60
```

The 10023 part (the value of the b variable) never made it into the c variable. The reason is that the puts command prints something out to the shell but doesn't return anything. Remember, the set command returns something, which the shell then prints out. The puts command, on the other hand, prints something directly to the shell but doesn't return anything. Because the puts command doesn't return anything, it gets replaced with emptiness. That means

```
set c [puts $b]60
```

gets replaced by

```
set c 60
```

This statement stores 60 in the variable c. Yikes. That can be confusing, but after you think it through a few times, it will make more sense.

You can also print out strings. Try this example:

```
% puts "Hello everybody"
```

When you press Enter, you see the words Hello everybody appear on the console.

You can also intermix variables. Remember how the interpreter performs the substitution: If you put a dollar sign followed by your variable name, the interpreter replaces the dollar sign and variable with the variable's value (unless you put these characters inside curly braces). So you can probably guess what this example will do:

```
% set x 100
100
% puts "My favorite number is $x"
```

After pressing Enter at the end of the final line, you see this:

```
My favorite number is 100
```

Creating a Simple Tcl Program

To create a simple Tcl program, you type the code into a text editor as you would any other programming language. You then save the file to a directory, giving the file a `.tcl` filename extension. To run the program, you type the following line, replacing *myprogram.tcl* with the name of your file:

```
tclsh myprogram.tcl
```

Alternatively, if you're using Unix, you can make your Tcl file executable by setting the following permission:

```
chmod u+x myprogram.tcl
```

Then you can put a pound-bang (`#!`) line at the beginning of the file that specifies the Tcl interpreter. The line looks like this:

```
#!/usr/local/bin/tclsh
```

(If you installed the Tcl binaries in a different location, such as `/usr/bin`, type `#!/usr/bin/tclsh` instead.) Then you can run your program by typing the name of the file, like so:

```
myprogram.tcl
```

The Unix shell looks at the first line and runs the program `/usr/local/bin/tclsh`, passing your file as a command-line parameter.

This pound-bang business, unfortunately, doesn't work on Windows. You still have to type `tclsh` and then your filename to run your program on a Windows computer. Oh well.

Open up your favorite text editor and type in the following example:

```
set x 100
puts "Hello there, my value is $x"
```

Then save this file as `simple.tcl`. Next, exit the editor and run the program like so:

```
tclsh simple.tcl
```

You see the following output:

```
Hello there, my value is 100
```

If you're using Unix, you can also type your program like this:

```
#!/usr/local/bin/tclsh
set x 100
puts "Hello there, my value is $x"
```

Then you can make the file executable with this:

```
chmod u+x simple.tcl
```

And you can run the program directly with this:

```
simple.tcl
```

In the remainder of this book, I leave out the pound-bang line, to save space. You are free, however, to add the line, and then set the permissions on your file and run your programs directly without having to type `tclsh`.

Adding comments to a Tcl program

If you want to add a comment to a Tcl program, use the # character, like so:

```
# this is a comment
```

You are free to indent the # character using tabs and spaces. However, you can't put the # character after a command as you can in other languages. For example, the following line won't work right:

```
set x 100 # This is wrong; can't have a comment here.
```

Instead, put the comment on a line before or after the command you're discussing:

```
# Store 100 in the variable x
set x 100
```

Breaking up long lines

Tcl is picky about its format. Although some languages let you break up a statement among multiple lines, Tcl does this only if it's looking for a terminator to a bracket or curly brace. But you can divide up a command elsewhere, provided you end the first line with a space followed by a backslash.

For example, suppose you have a command like this:

```
label .mylabel -text .
```

You can break up this command into multiple lines like this:

```
label \
.mylabel \
-text
.
```

When the Tcl interpreter sees a line ending with a space and a backslash, the interpreter continues reading what's on the next line as if the text is still on the previous line. In other words, Tcl fuses all the lines together into a single line.

Chapter 2: Processing Variables and Expressions

In This Chapter

✔ Evaluating expressions

✔ Processing strings

✔ Storing data in lists

Tcl provides you with the ability to evaluate mathematical and string-based expressions, a fundamental part of any language. Tcl also offers excellent string features and list-processing features. This chapter gives you the lowdown on how to use all these features.

Evaluating Expressions

A computer isn't much of a computer if it can't do calculations. I know I'd hate to go back to the dark ages of having to do long division on paper. To do calculations in Tcl, you use the expr command, which stands for *expression*. The reason for the term *expression* is that you can do more than just calculations; you can evaluate expressions including variables.

In the sections that follow, I show you how to evaluate expressions and how to manage the substitutions of the variables in the expressions.

Evaluating numerical expressions

To evaluate an expression, you use the expr command. Here's an example from inside the Tcl shell; remember that the % is the prompt, which you don't type:

```
% expr 2 + 5
```

When press Enter, you see this answer:

7

Here's a log of five samples showing addition, subtraction, multiplication, and division of both integers and floating point numbers; notice my liberal use of spaces, which is allowed:

```
% expr 15424 + 54782
70206
% expr 70206  -  15424
54782
% expr 542 * 253
137126
% expr 137126 / 542
253
% expr 10000.0 / 26.0
384.615384615
```

The first four expressions involve integers and are pretty straightforward. The final expression involves two floating point numbers. To tell the expr command that I want the numbers treated as floating point numbers rather than integers, I tacked on a .0 after each number. Without the .0, the expr command would assume the numbers are integers and would print the answer as a truncated integer, like so:

```
% expr 10000 / 26
384
```

If you use both an integer and a floating point, the expr command shows the results as a floating point number, as in the following two examples:

```
% expr 10000 / 26.0
384.615384615
% expr 50 / 24.35
2.05338809035
```

You can figure out a remainder by using the % operator, which is common in many programming languages:

```
% expr 17 % 5
2
```

In other words, when you divide 17 by 5, you get a remainder of 2.

Evaluating mathematical expressions

The expr command supports numerous mathematical functions. For example, if you want to calculate the cosine of a number, you can use the cos function:

```
% expr cos(3.1415926)
-1.0
```

Because the `expr` command claims the cosine of 3.1415926 (pi) is `-1.0`, that means the cosine is using radians, not degrees. If you want to use degrees, multiply the number in degrees by pi and then divide by 180, like so:

```
% expr cos(45 * 3.1415926 / 180)
0.70710679066
```

This means the cosine of 45 degrees is about 0.7071.

Here's a list of the mathematical functions available in the `expr` function:

✦ `abs(x)`: The absolute value of a number, either integer or floating point.

✦ `acos(x)`: The inverse (or *arc*) cosine. The argument must be between –1 and 1, inclusive.

✦ `asin(x)`: The inverse (or arc) sine. The argument must be between –1 and 1, inclusive.

✦ `atan(x)`: The inverse (or arc) tangent. The argument should be between –1 and 1, inclusive.

✦ `atan2(y, x)`: The arc tangent of y divided by x. Why would you want this? Because that tangent is the quotient of opposite divided by adjacent. You can just plug in the sizes of the right triangle, and this function provides you with the angle of the triangle. Pretty cool, eh? Here's an example:

```
% expr atan2(5,5)
0.785398163397
% expr atan2(100,100)
0.785398163397
```

✦ `ceil(x)`: If you pass a floating point number to this function, you get back the next higher integer (expressed as a floating point value), or the same number if you pass an integer value. For example, `ceil(3.5)` returns `4.0`, `ceil(4.0)` returns `4.0`, and `ceil(-2.5)` returns `-2.0`.

✦ `cos(x)`: The cosine of x.

✦ `cosh(x)`: The hyperbolic cosine of x, if you know what a hyperbolic cosine is. (Most calc classes skip this for some reason. It has to do with the shape of a line hanging from two poles — really!)

✦ `double(x)`: Converts an integer to a floating point.

✦ `exp(x)`: The exponential of x, which is the reverse of the natural log. In other words, it returns *e* raised to the power of x.

✦ `floor(x)`: If you pass a floating point value to this function, you get back the next lower integer, expressed as a floating point value, or the same number if you pass an integer value. For example, `floor(3.5)` returns `3.0`, `floor(4.0)` returns `4.0`, and `floor(-2.5)` returns `-3.0`.

Book IV Chapter 2

Processing Variables and Expressions

◆ fmod(x, y): The remainder when dividing x by y. The result is given as a floating point number, even though it will always have an integer value.

◆ hypot(x, y): Returns the answer to the Pythagorean formula, the square root of x squared plus y squared. That's the length of the hypotenuse of a right triangle with sides of lengths x and y. Here's an example:

```
% expr hypot(3,4)
5.0
```

◆ int(x): Converts a floating point number to an integer by truncating the number.

◆ log(x): The natural logarithm of x. The value x must be positive.

◆ log10(x): The base-10 logarithm of x. The value x must be positive.

◆ pow(x, y): Raises x to the power of y.

◆ rand(): A random number between 0 and 1, not including 0 and 1. (Note that the Tcl online manual points out that rand is not cryptographically secure.) The first time you call rand, the random-number generator is seeded using the computer's system clock.

◆ round(x): Rounds off a floating point to the closest integer. A value of 0.5 gets rounded up. Here are some examples:

```
% expr round(3.6)
4
% expr round(-3.6)
-4
% expr round(3.3)
3
```

◆ sin(x): The sine of x in radians.

◆ sinh(arg): The hyperbolic sine of x. Few people really know what these secretive hyperbolic functions are all about. Bridge designers use them, so I've heard.

◆ sqrt(x): The square root of x. This function doesn't do complex numbers, so x must be positive.

◆ srand(x): Resets the random-number generator, using x to seed the generator, and returns the first random number.

◆ tan(x): The tangent of x.

◆ tanh(x): The hyperbolic tangent of x. Many people live in wonder as they ponder the use of hyperbolic functions. Civil engineers use them on occasion, so I've heard.

◆ wide(x): Creates a 64-bit integer equal in value to x.

Controlling substitution with braces

If you don't want the interpreter to substitute variables for you, you can surround an expression with braces: { and }. When the interpreter encounters braces, it knows not to do any substitution. Instead, it just passes what's inside braces to the command. The command can then do whatever it wants with the items passed. The expr command does its usual work of evaluating whatever it receives.

Here's an example that illustrates the use of braces. Open up the Tcl shell and type in the following line:

```
% set x {$q}
```

Without the braces, x would get whatever value is stored in q. If q didn't have a value, you'd see an error message. The braces prevent the interpreter from substituting $q for its value. This means x gets the value $q, with no substitutions.

Next try this:

```
% puts $x
$q
```

If you print out the value in x, you get the characters $q.

Now, what if you want to use x in an expression? Try this:

```
% expr $x
can't read "q": no such variable
```

The interpreter substitutes $x for its value, $q, and passes $q on to expr. The expr command then tries to evaluate $q, which doesn't exist, resulting in the error that you see.

What if you want to evaluate $x? Put braces around it like this:

```
% expr {$x}
$q
```

Did you see what happened? With the braces, the interpreter doesn't replace $x with $q. Instead, it just passes the character $x on to the expr command. In the earlier example without the braces, the interpreter replaces $x with its value, $q, and passes on $q to the expr command. The expr command can't evaluate $q because the variable called q doesn't exist.

If you include the braces, the interpreter does no substitution and passes the text on to the command. Without the braces, the interpreter does the substitution first and then passes the results on to the command.

Processing Strings

Tcl lets you store and process strings. If you've worked in other languages, you're probably not the least bit surprised. What would a language be without strings? A very boring language at best. Not to mention nearly useless.

Here's an example of storing a string in a variable called `name`:

```
set name "George Washington"
```

That's pretty simple. Just type `set`, the name of the variable, and then put the string inside double quotes. If you're doing this interactively, you can then print out the string like so:

```
% puts $name
George Washington
```

You can see from the output that the double quotes are not part of the string.

If you want to combine and concatenate strings, you can do this:

```
set firstname "George"
set lastname "Washington"
set fullname "$firstname $lastname"
puts $fullname
```

When you run this code, the name is printed out:

```
George Washington
```

But you can do even more with strings with Tcl. In the following sections, I show you many of the possibilities.

To use the string-processing features in Tcl, you use various string commands. You precede the names of these string commands with the command name `string`.

Determining information about a string

Tcl includes two commands for finding out information about a string: `length` and `is`.

TIP

Processing strings without double quotes

In Tcl, you don't have to put double quotes around your strings. If you don't have any spaces in your string, you can just type the strings, like so:

```
% set word hello
hello
```

```
% puts $word
hello
```

But I usually put double quotes around my strings to keep the code clear so people reading it will know I'm typing a string and not, for example, a command name.

The length command

The length command determines the length of a string. Here's an example:

```
% set name "George Washington"
George Washington
% string length $name
17
```

This example, of course, is in the interactive mode. Here's an example of the length command in a program:

```
set name "George Washington"
set L [string length $name]
puts $L
```

Do you see the difference? The string length command returns a value, which in interactive mode is fine because the shell prints out the returned value. But in program mode, Tcl doesn't print out the return value. Instead, I save that to a variable. Remember that the brackets group items and the Tcl interpreter runs those first. The bracketed part returns a value — in this case, 17 — and then the interpreter does a substitution to make this command:

```
set L 17
```

This command stores 17 inside the L variable. Then I print out the value in L.

The is command

The is command determines if the characters comprising a string match a certain set of possible strings. For example, you might want to know if the characters in the string are all digits and could qualify as an integer. Or you might want to know if the string contains only spaces — or only uppercase characters. Here are some examples in the interactive Tcl shell:

```
% set sample "abc123"
abc123
% string is integer $sample
0
% set sample "123"
123
% string is integer $sample
1
% set sample "    "

% string is space $sample
1
% set sample "abcABC"
abcABC
% string is upper $sample
0
% set sample "ABCDEF"
ABCDEF
% string is upper $sample
1
```

The first line stores the string abc123 in the sample variable. The next line checks whether the string contains digits that qualify as an integer. Here's the format of this line:

```
string is integer $sample
```

As usual, you start with the string command. Then you follow with the is subcommand, the integer subcommand, and finally, the name of the variable whose value you want to substitute. (For more on the subcommands available with is, see the end of this section.) This line returns 0 (which means false) because abc123 is not an integer.

Then the string 123 is stored in the variable. It is then tested again with the same string is integer $sample command, and this time, it returns a 1, which means true.

The is command returns 1 if the test is true. If the test fails, the is command returns a 0. A 1 means true; a 0 means false.

Continuing with the sample code, you then store a string of spaces in the sample variable. You test whether the string contains only spaces with the command string is space $sample. Because the string does contain only spaces, you get back a 1.

Next, you store the string abcABC in the variable sample and test whether the string contains only uppercase letters with the command string is upper $sample. Because this string doesn't contain only uppercase letters, you get back a 0, which means false. Then you store ABCDEF in the sample variable. Again, you test whether this string contains only uppercase letters, and this time, you get back a 1, which means true.

Here's a list of all the subcommands available to the is command:

+ alnum: This tells you whether the string contains only letters and digits.

+ alpha: This tells you if the string contains only letters.

+ ascii: This tells you if the string contains only characters whose ASCII value is less than 128. (If you aren't familiar with ASCII values, you probably don't have any use for this subcommand.)

+ boolean: This returns 0 if the string contains the characters 0, false, no, or off. It returns 1 if the string contains the characters 1, true, yes, or on. You can also mix the case; for example, On returns 1, and oFF returns 0.

+ control: This returns 1 if the string contains control characters.

+ digit: This returns 1 if the string contains only digits.

+ double: This returns 1 if the string contains characters that can be interpreted as a valid double-size floating point value. (Surrounding spaces are acceptable.) For example, the following two lines both return true:

```
string is double "  1.23e05"
string is double "1.234"
```

+ false: This returns true if the string is 0, false, no, or off. As with the boolean command, you can mix the case; Off is acceptable, as is n0.

+ graph: This returns true if the string contains only printable characters excluding spaces.

+ integer: This returns true if the string contains a set of characters that can be interpreted as an integer.

+ lower: This returns true if the string contains only lowercase letters.

+ print: This returns true if the string contains only printable characters or spaces.

+ punct: This returns true if the string contains only punctuation.

+ space: This returns true if the string contains only spaces.

+ true: This returns true if the string contains 1, true, yes, or on. You can change the case, too; for example, you get back a true with yES or On.

✦ upper: This returns true if the string contains only uppercase letters.

✦ wordchar: This returns true if the string contains only alphanumeric characters or an underscore.

✦ xdigit: This returns true if the string contains only hexadecimal digits, which are 0, 2, 3, 4, 5, 6, 7, 8, 9, A, B, C, D, E, F, a, b, c, d, e, and f.

Searching and obtaining parts of a string

The abilities to extract portions of a string and to search strings are important features in a language or string library. Tcl makes this pretty easy. Here are six string subcommands that you can use:

✦ first: Find one string inside another.

✦ last: Find the last occurrence of a string inside another string.

✦ index: Obtain a single character within a string based on position (also called *index*).

✦ range: Obtain a piece of a string by specifying the position and length.

✦ wordstart: Find the start of a word containing a position.

✦ wordend: Find the end of a word containing a position.

The final two items in this list, wordstart and wordend, are particularly useful for processing text containing sentences divided up into words.

Here's an example of all the subcommands in a single program:

```
set sentence "Hi other computers, I'm a computer too."
puts $sentence

puts [string first "compu" $sentence]
puts [string first "compu" $sentence 20]
puts [string last "compu" $sentence]
puts [string last "compu" $sentence 15]
puts [string index $sentence 5]
puts [string range $sentence 5 6]

set wstart [string wordstart $sentence 5]
set wend [string wordend $sentence 5]
puts [string range $sentence $wstart $wend]
```

Here's the output from this program:

```
Hi other computers, I'm a computer too.
9
26
```

```
26
9
h
he
other
```

Here's a closer look at this example:

+ **Lines 1 and 2:** Create the string and print it out.

+ **Line 3:** Locates the first occurrence of the string `compu` within the string. You can see from the output that the answer is 9. (The first character has index 0; thus, the c in `compu` is in the ninth position in the string.)

+ **Line 4:** Again looks for the string `compu` but starts looking at the 20th position. Thus, the output shows position 26 as the first location.

+ **Lines 5 and 6:** Demonstrate the `last` command. Line 5 looks for the last instance of `compu` in the string, which you can see from the output is 26. Line 6 again looks for the last instance of `compu`, but starts looking backwards from the 15th character position, ignoring anything after that. The output is 9.

+ **Line 7:** Returns the character at index 5 in the string (which is really the 6th position because these crazy computers like to call the first position index 0). The character at index 5 is the letter h.

+ **Line 8:** Obtains a range of characters from the string. If you've worked in other programming languages, the way this one works might seem a bit different: You specify the start index and the end index, not a length. So this string command, `string range $sentence 5 6`, obtains the characters starting with index 5 and ending with index 6. That's just two characters, which are `he`.

+ **Lines 9, 10, and 11:** These lines are particularly interesting. I purposely wrote an interesting sentence (okay, so maybe not so interesting, but it is a sentence) and stored it in the string. This sentence is divided up into several words. The last thing I do in my program is I take an index, in this case 5, and I ask Tcl to figure out which word index 5 sits inside of and to give me the index of that word's first character. Remember, index 5 is the sixth position. That's the letter h within the word `other`. Thus, the `wordstart` command gives me the index of the letter o in `other`.

  Next, I find the index of the final character in the word containing index 5. The word is still `other`, so I'm talking about the index of the letter r.

I store the index of the first letter, o, in the variable wstart, and I store the index of the final letter, r, in the variable wend. Then I print out the range of characters, like so:

```
puts [string range $sentence $wstart $wend]
```

And what do I see in the output? I see the word other! Very cool.

Comparing strings

In Tcl, you can compare strings three ways:

✦ compare: Compares two strings and returns 0 if they match

✦ equal: Another way to compare strings, returning 1 if they match

✦ match: Matches a string to a regular expression

The final item, match, deals with regular expressions, and I don't discuss it in this chapter. You can find out more about regular expressions throughout Book VII.

The compare command returns a 0 if the two strings match. If the strings are different, it returns either -1 or 1, depending on whether the internal codes of the characters in the first string are greater or less than the second string. (That's kind of bizarre, and I've only met one person in my life who actually used the -1 versus 1 result of a comparison such as this. Most people write code that checks whether compare returns 0.)

The equal command doesn't return -1, 0, or 1 as compare does. It's simpler; it returns 1 (representing true) if the strings match, or 0 if they don't. For that reason, I prefer to use equal instead of compare.

Here are some examples in a single program. Note that in some of these examples I use options to modify how the command behaves. (An *option* is simply a word [or group of characters] preceded by a hyphen that changes how the command behaves.)

```
set str1 "Hello"
set str2 "Hello"
set str3 "Goodbye"
set str4 "GoodBYE"

puts [string compare $str1 $str2]
puts [string compare $str3 $str4]
puts [string compare -nocase $str3 $str4]
```

```
puts ""

puts [string equal $str1 $str2]
puts [string equal $str3 $str4]
puts [string equal -nocase $str3 $str4]
```

Here's the output from the program:

```
0
1
0

1
0
1
```

I know, the output isn't very exciting. But the concepts are. Look at the first three lines of output. The first of these lines compares the strings in the two variables str1 and str2. Those two variables both contain the string Hello, so they match. Thus, you see a number 0, which is what the compare command returns in the event of a match.

The second line of output is the result of comparing str3 to str4. These variables don't match: One has lowercase bye in it, and the other has uppercase BYE in it. So the compare command returns a 1, which means the strings are different.

The third line again compares str3 and str4, but this time adds the option -nocase, which tells compare to ignore case. In this case, bye and BYE match, so the output is 0.

Next I write a blank line to keep the output somewhat neat. And then I do the same comparisons, but this time, I use the equal command. I get the same results, too, except this time, I get a 1 when the two strings match, and a 0 when they don't match.

Which is better, compare or equal? Take your pick. They're both great.

Creating and modifying strings

In this section, I share some words of wisdom on how to create and modify strings. It's nothing too philosophical. Here are the commands you can use:

✦ map

✦ replace

- ✦ repeat

- ✦ tolower, toupper, totitle

- ✦ trim, trimleft, trimright

map

The map command replaces characters and strings with other characters and strings. Here's an interactive example:

```
% string map {a A b B} "There's a bear in my house"
There's A BeAr in my house
```

You enter the information you want to replace inside curly braces and use spaces to divide each item. In this example, each a gets replaced with an A, and each b gets replaced with a B. You can see in the output that those characters did get replaced.

Here's an example that's a bit more interesting:

```
set mymap {Monday Montag Tuesday Dienstag Wednesday Mittwoch}
set mystring "Today is Monday, tomorrow is Tuesday!"
set result [string map $mymap $mystring]
puts $result
set mystring2 "And then comes Wednesday!"
set result2 [string map $mymap $mystring2]
puts $result2
```

This example replaces three English words with their German counterparts. The first line sets up a map, which is really just a list. The first item in the list is Monday, and that maps to the second item, which is Montag (the German word for Monday). Next I create a string, map it, and print it out. And just for good measure, I do the same process on another string. Here's the output:

```
Today is Montag, tomorrow is Dienstag!
And then comes Mittwoch!
```

replace

The replace command replaces characters based on position. Here's an example:

```
set mystring  "Eat at Joe's"
set result [string replace $mystring 7 9 "Frank"]
puts $result
```

This example replaces the characters starting at index 7 and ending at index 9 (which are the characters `Joe`) with the characters `Frank`. Here's the output:

```
Eat at Frank's
```

Although the various string commands in this section seem like they modify a string, the reality is that they create a new string. For example, when I say the `replace` command replaces characters, it doesn't really replace the characters in the original string; instead, it creates a new string and replaces those characters, leaving the original string unchanged.

repeat

The `repeat` command is pretty simple; it creates a new string and repeats it a certain number of times. Here's an interactive example:

```
% string repeat hello 5
hellohellohellohellohello
```

One use for the `replace` command is if you want to create long strings filled with spaces for padding purposes, such as in reports and other output. Here's an example:

```
set a "Hello"
set b "Goodbye world"
set alength [expr 15 - [string length $a]]
set blength [expr 15 - [string length $b]]
puts [string repeat " " $alength]$a
puts [string repeat " " $blength]$b
```

In this example, I calculate the length of each string — `Hello` and `Goodbye world` — and subtract the result from 15 to obtain an indentation amount. Then I print out a space that's repeated the number of times of the indentation amount and then print out the string. Here's the output:

```
          Hello
  Goodbye world
```

The text is now right-aligned. Pretty good, eh?

You can write some really complex code with Tcl. If you're so inclined, you can shorten the preceding example to just these four lines:

```
set a "Hello"
set b "Goodbye world"
puts [string repeat " " [expr 15 - [string length $a]]]$a
puts [string repeat " " [expr 15 - [string length $b]]]$b
```

Tcl does a substitution with each set of brackets, starting with the innermost ones. If you get carried away with this kind of code, you're likely to create code that's hard to read and even harder to debug. Therefore, I recommend keeping your code as simple as possible and stretching it onto multiple lines if necessary.

tolower, toupper, and totitle

The tolower, toupper, and totitle commands change the case of a string. Here's an interactive example:

```
% set words "Hi i am SAM. who are you?"
Hi i am SAM. who are you?
%
% string tolower $words
hi i am sam. who are you?
%
% string toupper $words
HI I AM SAM. WHO ARE YOU?
%
% string totitle $words
Hi i am sam. who are you?
```

The tolower command converts all the letters to lowercase. The toupper command converts all the letters to uppercase. And the totitle command converts the first character to uppercase and all the other letters to lowercase. Why would you use totitle? I don't know. BUT I'm suRE somEboDY CAN coMe Up wITH a gOOd ExamplE.

trim, trimleft, and trimright

The trim, trimleft, and trimright commands remove spaces from a string. trim removes spaces from both the right and left side; trimleft removes spaces from the left; and trimright removes spaces from the right. Here's a short interactive example:

```
% set words "   \t   Hi   \t "
          Hi
% string trim $words
Hi
% string trimleft $words
Hi
% string trimright $words
          Hi
```

Because I'm showing this example in a book, you can't really see that space was trimmed from the right side, but trust me that it was. You can see that the tab character, \t, was also trimmed from the left side. Tabs count as space.

Storing and Manipulating Lists of Data

At times, you may want to store lists of data inside a single variable. For example, you might be reading a sequence of data from a user — such as first name, last name, and e-mail address — and want to store all that data in a single variable.

To create a list in Tcl, put curly braces around the data, like so:

```
% set info {George Washington george@whitehouse.gov}
```

This line creates a list of three elements:

✦ George

✦ Washington

✦ george@whitehouse.gov

You can also mix numbers and strings in a list:

```
% set stuff {1 2 yes no}
1 2 yes no
```

The problem with using the curly braces, however, is that no substitution takes place. Therefore, you can also create a list using the list command. Take a look at the following example to see what I'm talking about:

```
% set fruit1 apple
apple
% set fruit2 pear
pear
% set fruit3 banana
banana
% set fruits { $fruit1 $fruit2 $fruit3 }
$fruit1 $fruit2 $fruit3
% set fruits [ list $fruit1 $fruit2 $fruit3 ]
apple pear banana
%
```

In this example, you can see that I save three words in different variables. Then I create a list using the brace notation. Unfortunately, instead of ending up with the words apple, pear, and banana in the list, I end up with exactly what I typed into the list, $fruit1, $fruit2, and $fruit3. If I want to get the names of the fruit into the list, I can use the list command, as the final command demonstrates.

If you need to store a variable in a list, you can use the list command, which allows for substitution:

```
% set name Jeff
Jeff
% set names [list $name Sally Frank]
Jeff Sally Frank
```

The next few sections demonstrate all sorts of amazing feats you can perform with lists.

Finding the length of a list

If you want to know how many elements are in the list, use the llength command. Here's an interactive example:

```
% set info {George Washington george@whitehouse.gov}
George Washington george@whitehouse.gov
%
% puts [llength $info]
3
```

The llength command tells you how many elements, not characters, are in the list. In this example, the list contains three elements. Each element in the list has several characters (George, for example, has six characters), and the number of characters is independent of the number of elements in the list.

Searching and sorting a list

If you want to retrieve an element from a list, use the lindex command:

```
% set food [list apple orange banana]
apple orange banana
% lindex $food 2
banana
```

As you can see in this example, you type lindex, then the list (or variable containing the list), and then the index number. Remember that the first index is 0:

```
% lindex $food 0
apple
```

You can also extract a range of items from a list by using the lrange command:

```
% lrange $food 1 2
orange banana
```

The first number is the starting index and the second number is the ending index of the range you want to extract. Thus, in this example, the range is from index 1 to index 2.

The result of lrange is also a list, which you can then store in a variable and manipulate as a list, like so:

```
% set somefood [lrange $food 1 2]
orange banana
% puts somefood
somefood
% lindex $somefood 1
banana
```

Tcl also lets you use the word end as the final argument to lrange; this word end denotes the end of the list, as in the following:

```
set somefood [ lrange $fruit 1 end ]
```

Here, the word end gets replaced by 2, because the list in $fruit has a final index of 2.

Want to locate an item in a list? Use the lsearch command:

```
% lsearch $food banana
2
```

This output means banana is in the list under index 2, which is the third position. If the item you're searching for doesn't exist, you get back the index -1, as in this example:

```
% lsearch $food grapes
-1
```

Finally, you can easily sort a list by using the lsort command. The lsort command doesn't actually change the list; instead, it gives you back a new list just like the original except sorted:

```
% lsort $food
apple banana orange
% puts $food
apple orange banana
```

Here I called `lsort` and then printed out the original list to show that it didn't change. But that's not particularly useful; here's how you save the sorted list in a new variable:

```
% set newfood [lsort $food]
```

Or you can save the sorted list back in the original list:

```
% set food [lsort $food]
```

The Tcl interpreter doesn't get confused when you try to put the sorted list back in the original variable, thanks to the substitution that takes place. Remember the steps that the preceding lines of code go through. First, the variable `$food` gets replaced with its variable, yielding this statement:

```
set food [lsort {apple banana orange}]
```

Then the stuff in brackets is run, yielding this:

```
set food {apple banana orange}
```

This statement stores the sorted list {apple banana orange} in the variable `food`.

Modifying a list (sort of)

Tcl offers three commands for modifying a list:

+ `lappend` lets you add on to the end of a list.
+ `linsert` lets you insert items into a list.
+ `lreplace` lets you replace items within a list.

If you're wondering why there's no command to delete items from a list, you use `lreplace` to do so. I show you how in a minute.

Here's a sample session showing you how to use `lappend`:

```
% set food {apple orange banana}
apple orange banana
% lappend food pear
apple orange banana pear
% puts $food
apple orange banana pear
```

This code first stores a list of three elements in the `food` variable: `apple`, `orange`, and `banana`. Then the code appends the variable `pear` to the list, and finally, the code prints out the items in the list.

Did you notice anything strange about this code? When I call `lappend`, I don't put a dollar sign in front of `food`. That is, I don't ask the Tcl interpreter to do a substitution. The reason is that `lappend` takes a list variable and actually modifies the variable. Thus, I also didn't have to save the results into another variable.

Now here's a demonstration of the `linsert` command, continuing with the preceding code:

```
% puts $food
apple orange banana pear
% linsert $food 2 peach grapefruit
apple orange peach grapefruit banana pear
% puts $food
apple orange banana pear
```

In this example, first I print out the current list in the `food` variable, just to be sure everything is in order. Then I call `linsert`, inserting the items into index 2 of the list. Unfortunately, `linsert` doesn't modify a list as `lappend` does; instead, it creates a new list. So I pass `$food` (with a dollar sign) instead of just `food` (without the dollar sign).

You can see the results of the insert, and that the two new items, `peach` and `grapefruit`, ended up starting in the third position, which is index 2.

Then I print out the value in `food` to confirm that the variable did not change. Thus, you can save the results either in a new variable or in the original variable:

```
% set food [linsert $food 2 peach grapefruit]
apple orange peach grapefruit banana pear
% puts $food
apple orange peach grapefruit banana pear
```

That was easy as pie — or grapefruit as the case may be.

Finally, here's a sample session showing you how to use `lreplace` (which, like `linsert`, doesn't modify the list):

```
% puts $food
apple orange peach grapefruit banana pear
% set food [lreplace $food 1 3 asparagus broccoli]
apple asparagus broccoli banana pear
```

The two numbers in the `lreplace` command are the starting and ending indexes of what you want to replace. In this example, I'm replacing indexes 1 through 3, which are the `orange`, `peach`, and `grapefruit` elements. I'm replacing these three elements with only two elements, `asparagus` and `broccoli`, and I'm saving the results back in the `food` variable. You can see in the output that the three items did get replaced by the new two new items.

Earlier, I mentioned you can use `lreplace` to remove items from a list. Here's how you can remove the two new foods you just added, `asparagus` and `broccoli`, in case you don't like them:

```
% set food [lreplace $food 1 2]
apple banana pear
```

And now you're down to just `apple`, `banana`, and `pear` — sounds tasty to me.

Chapter 3: Controlling the Structure

In This Chapter

✔ **Building if statements**

✔ **Comparing strings**

✔ **Selecting with a switch command**

✔ **Looping with for and foreach commands**

✔ **Looping with while**

✔ **Breaking out of a loop and continuing with another iteration**

*T*cl includes the usual control structures you would expect to find in any good programming language. However, the syntax of these structures fits into the usual Tcl way of doing things, which may seem a bit strange if you're familiar with other programming languages.

A *control structure* is a command that causes lines of code to run multiple times, over and over, either until a certain condition is met, or while something is true. In this chapter, I show you how to program control structures in Tcl.

If you've explored the Tcl manuals, you probably quickly found that they're not very good, to be quite frank. Often they don't give solid examples and instead rely on your ability to decode cryptic syntax rules. But rest assured; thanks to this book, you don't need to go overboard in learning geekspeak. I've provided solid examples right here for you.

Choosing Conditions

Tcl includes two incredibly powerful commands for making comparisons and testing conditions:

✦ The `if` command

✦ The `switch` command

In the sections that follow, I demonstrate how to harness the power of these mighty commands.

Doing this or that with an if command

Tcl is picky — almost too picky at times. But part of this pickiness has to do with the fact that Tcl is a *command* language. Every line starts with a command. If Tcl thinks the line is finished, it won't read the next line, even if you intended for the next line to be a continuation of the previous line. Yikes. Other languages don't work this way, but once you understand Tcl's basic approach to processing commands, this shortcoming will make more sense. Maybe. I guess.

Suppose you have a variable and you want to execute one block of code if the variable contains a certain value and another block of code otherwise. You can do this with an if command. Here's a sample program; save this as if.tcl:

```
gets stdin a
if {$a > 50} {
    puts "a > 50"
} else {
    puts "a <= 50"
}
```

This program uses the gets command to read data from the console. (The console is called *stdin* when you're reading from it, which is shorthand for *standard input*. I usually pronounce stdin as "standard in.") When you run this program, the data you enter gets put in the variable a, thanks to the a at the end of the gets command line.

Next comes the if command. Notice that I put an expression inside curly braces. The expression is $a > 50. This if command tests whether the value in the a variable is greater than 50. If it is, Tcl executes the line inside curly braces after the expression:

```
puts "a > 50"
```

But if the value of a is not greater than 50, Tcl executes the code in braces following the else command:

```
puts "a <= 50"
```

For Tcl to discover the else block, you must have the word else on the same line as the closing brace from the main if block, like so:

```
} else {
```

Otherwise, if you put the else on the next line like so:

```
}
else {
```

you get an error like this:

```
invalid command name "else"
    while executing
"else {
    puts "a <= 50"
}"
    (file "if.tcl" line 5)
```

The else block is *optional*. If you want to run some code only if a certain block is true and don't want to do anything else, you can leave out the else block altogether.

Here's a sample session from my own console window:

```
$ tclsh if.tcl
25
a <= 50

$ tclsh if.tcl
50
a <= 50

$ tclsh if.tcl
100
a > 50

$ tclsh if.tcl
abc
a > 50
```

For the final run, I purposely typed in something that's not a number, just to see what would happen. Tcl somehow interpreted abc as a number greater than 50.

Here's a list of the ways to compare numbers in Tcl. You already know that <= is the "less than or equal to" comparison. Here's the complete list:

✦ < means less than.

✦ > means greater than.

✦ <= means less than or equal to.

✦ >= means greater than or equal to.

✦ == means equal to. (Yes, that's two equal signs in a row.)

✦ != means not equal to.

These operators are all used for comparing numbers. In a later section, "Comparing strings," I show you how to — you guessed it — compare strings.

Evaluating conditions inside an if block

If you read Book II, Chapter 2, you know that you can test whether a string is a valid integer. When you read text from the command line, it comes in as a string. Thus, say that you have a line like this:

```
gets stdin a
```

Your variable a can contain anything the user might type in, not just numbers. What if you want to just get numbers? Then you can use a fancy if statement in conjunction with some of the string-processing commands. Here's the string command you want to use here:

```
[string is integer $a]
```

If you remember how substitution works, you can logically figure out that you can put this string command inside an if block like so:

```
gets stdin a
if {[string is integer $a]} {
    if {$a > 50} {
        puts "a > 50"
    } else {
        puts "a <= 50"
    }
} else {
    puts "Sorry, that's not a number"
}
```

See how I put the string command right inside the if statement's expression area? And it works! Here's a sample session of this program; I typed in the abc part when I ran the program:

```
$tclsh if2.tcl
abc
Sorry, that's not a number
```

When I typed in `abc`, the first `if` statement checked whether my input was a number. Because I didn't type in a number, the code inside the `else` block ran, printing the `Sorry` message.

You can also use the `expr` command for more complex expressions, again using the brackets for substitution. Here's a pretty cool numerical analysis program:

```
gets stdin a
set pi [expr acos(-1)]
set a [expr $a * $pi / 180]
if {abs(cos($a)) < 1e-5} {
    puts "That's a good angle!"
} else {
    puts "No good..."
}
```

This program figures out a good value for pi, then converts an angle from degrees to radians, and then tests if the angle's cosine is within a certain error level around the value 0. If so, the angle is either plus or minus 90 degrees. Here are some sample sessions:

```
$tclsh if3.tcl
90
That's a good angle!

$tclsh if3.tcl
-90
That's a good angle!

$tclsh if3.tcl
180
No good...

$tclsh if3.tcl
45
No good...
```

Comparing strings

If you are using Tcl version 8.4 or above, and if you want to compare strings in an `if` command, don't use the comparison operators ($<$, $>$, and so on) that you use for numbers. Instead, use the following commands:

+ `eq` to test if two strings are equal

+ `ne` to test if two strings are not equal

Here's a sample program:

```
gets stdin word
if {$word eq "hello"} {
    puts "Hello back atcha!"
}
```

This simple program tests whether the string stored in the variable word is equal to the string hello. Here's a sample session:

```
tclsh ifstring1.tcl
hello
Hello back atcha!
```

If you want, you can also use ne for testing whether two strings are not equal. Try changing the eq to ne in the preceding example to see how it works.

If you want to do a case-insensitive comparison (where hello is considered equal to Hello, for example), use the string equal command with the -nocase option, like so:

```
gets stdin word
if {[string equal -nocase $word "hello"]} {
    puts "Hello back atcha!"
}
```

Here's a sample session:

```
$tclsh ifstring2.tcl
HeLLo
Hello back atcha!
```

Evaluating multiple conditions at once

Tcl supports logical operators that let you perform multiple tests simultaneously. For example, you might want to test whether a book's author is a certain name, and the price is below a certain number. In English, your expression might look like this:

> If the book is written by Jeff Cogswell and the price is under $500, I will definitely buy the book.

An and operator, such as what I used in this important statement, translates easily into Tcl. Here's a sample program. To show the and, I use two ampersands in a row, &&, like so:

```
gets stdin author
gets stdin price
if {$author == "Jeff Cogswell" && $price < 500} {
    puts "Sounds like a bargain!"
} else {
    puts "I cannot vouch for the book's accuracy"
}
```

I separated two conditions with the characters &&, which means both conditions must be met for the main if block to run; otherwise the else block runs. Here's a sample session:

```
$tclsh and.tcl
Jeff Cogswell
34.95
Sounds like a bargain!

$tclsh and.tcl
Ernest Hemingway
15.95
I cannot vouch for the book's accuracy
```

Instead of the logical and operator, you can try out a logical or operator. With the or operator, you run the block if either condition is true; both conditions don't need to be true. Here's an example; notice I simply changed the && (which means *and*) to || (that is, two vertical bar characters, which means *or*):

```
gets stdin author
gets stdin price
if {$author == "Jeff Cogswell" || $price < 500} {
    puts "Sounds like a bargain!"
} else {
    puts "I cannot vouch for the book's accuracy"
}
```

Here's a sample session. Note that only one condition must be met for the main if block to run: Either the author must be me (er, I mean Jeff Cogswell), or the price must be less than 500:

```
$tclsh or.tcl
Jeff Cogswell
6523.35
Sounds like a bargain!

$tclsh or.tcl
Ernest Hemingway
```

**Book IV
Chapter 3**

**Controlling the
Structure**

```
8000.25
I cannot vouch for the book's accuracy

$tclsh or.tcl
Ernest Hemingway
.05
Sounds like a bargain!
```

Using many ifs and elses

If you want to test for more than one condition, you can pile a bunch of if and else statements within a single giant if block. Here's an example that shows how this works:

```
gets stdin a
if {$a > 50} {
    puts "a > 50"
} elseif {$a == 50} {
    puts "a == 50"
} else {
    puts "a <= 50"
}
```

I put the command elseif after the closing brace of the initial if block, and I added the expression $a == 50. This big block of code reads data from the console and stores it in the variable a. Then the code tests if a is greater than 50, and if so, it writes out a message. Otherwise, the code tests if a equals 50, and if so, it writes out a message. But if neither condition is true, the code writes out a final message.

Here are some sample sessions:

```
$tclsh ifelseif.tcl
25
a <= 50

$tclsh ifelseif.tcl
50
a == 50

$tclsh ifelseif.tcl
60
a > 50
```

Selecting from many conditions with switch

If you want to compare a single variable or expression to several possibilities, instead of piling a bunch of if and elseif statements together, you can use a switch statement.

Here's a program that reads in a string from the console, saves the string to the variable name, and then compares name to various strings, printing out a message if name equals the particular string:

```
gets stdin name
switch $name {
    "Jeff" { puts "Hi Jeff" }
    "Sally" { puts "Hi Sally" }
    "Bill" { puts "Hi Bill" }
    "Jessica" { puts "Hi Jessica" }
    default { puts "Hi you" }
}
```

If the name contains the string Jeff, the program prints out Hi Jeff. If the name contains the string Sally, it prints out Hi Sally, and so on. As you can see, this switch statement is just like a big if command followed by a bunch of elseif commands and a final default command.

From here to the end of this section is a more sophisticated example of the switch statement. If you're familiar with other programming languages, this one might surprise you a bit because you can put strings in switch statements in Tcl:

```
gets stdin name
set greeting { "Hello there $name" }
switch $name {
    "Jeff" {
        puts [expr $greeting]
        puts "You look sharp today!"
    }
    "Sally" {
        puts [expr $greeting]
        puts "Great outfit!"
    }
    "Bill" {
        puts [expr $greeting]
        puts "Good to see you!"
    }
    "Jessica" {
        puts [expr $greeting]
        puts "Thanks for stopping by!"
    }
    default { puts "I don't know you" }
}
```

Look carefully at the second line:

```
set greeting { "Hello there $name" }
```

Because I have curly braces in the `set` command, the interpreter doesn't substitute the `name` variable (which is good, because at this point, the `name` variable doesn't exist). Instead, the string gets the exact value `Hello there $name`.

Now look inside each section in the `switch` statement. Under each section, I have this statement:

```
puts [expr $greeting]
```

Tcl does several substitutions here. First, Tcl substitutes `$greeting` for the `greeting` variable's value, which is `Hello there $name`. Then this value gets passed to the `expr` command, which evaluates the expression `Hello there $name`. In the case where `name` is `Jeff`, the expression `Hello there $name` evaluates to `Hello there Jeff`. This whole `expr` command is inside brackets, so the brackets get replaced by what the expression evaluated to, turning the line into this:

```
puts Hello there Jeff
```

This statement prints out the line `Hello there Jeff`. Here's a sample run of this program:

```
$tclsh switch2.tcl
Sally
Hello there Sally
Great outfit!

$tclsh switch2.tcl
Jessica
Hello there Jessica
Thanks for stopping by!

$tclsh switch2.tcl
Frank
I don't know you
```

Of course, you might wonder why you can't just do this for each block:

```
"Jessica" {
    puts "Hello there $name"
    puts "Thanks for stopping by!"
}
```

Well, you *can* do that. But the cool thing about the way I did it is that you can change the greeting in one place. Okay, so I guess you can also do this:

```
puts "$newgreeting $name"
```

I admit that this will work too. But I thought my solution was pretty cool because it demonstrates an interesting feature in Tcl.

Looping with Various Commands

Tcl lets you loop sections of code over and over for a certain number of iterations or while a certain condition is true. In the following sections, I show you how to do this.

Looping for each number

The most common method of looping (one that dates back to the 1960s in various ancient programming languages) is the `for` loop. The `for` loop is a way of looping through a set of numbers. Here's an example:

```
for {set i 0} {$i <= 10} {incr i} {
    puts $i
}
```

Before dissecting this program, take a look at the output so you know what to expect:

```
0
1
2
3
4
5
6
7
8
9
10
```

The program wrote out the numbers 0 through 10. How did it do this? It ran the following line over and over while the variable `i` looped from 0 through 10:

```
puts $i
```

Now look back at the first line of the code. The key is in the `for` command. The `for` command gets four sets of braces after it.

```
for {set i 0} {$i <= 10} {incr i} {
```

Book IV
Chapter 3

Controlling the
Structure

The first brace set contains an initialization. Typically, you do what I did here and store a number in a variable: `set i 0`. (This stores the number 0 in the variable i.)

The second brace set contains a condition that the `for` loop tests for at the beginning of each iteration of the loop. If the condition is true (that is, if the variable i is less than or equal to 10), the `for` command again runs the code inside it, the `puts $i` line.

The third brace set is a command that the `for` command executes after each iteration of the loop. In this case, after each iteration is done, the `for` loop increments the i variable thanks to the `incr i` command. And the result, in this case, is that you get a loop that counts from 0 to 10.

Looping for each item in a list

Many newer languages like Tcl have a construct called `foreach`. The `foreach` construct loops through the elements in a list. Here's an example:

```
set stuff {1 2 3 "hello" "goodbye"}
foreach item $stuff {
    puts $item
}
```

This code first creates a list variable and stores the items 1, 2, 3, hello, and goodbye in the list. Then the code runs the `foreach` command, which loops through each item in the list, storing the item in the variable called item. The first time the loop runs, the item variable has the value 1. When the loop runs again, the item variable has the value 2. The next time item has the value 3, then hello, and finally goodbye. And with each iteration, the code runs the `puts $item` command, which prints out the value in item.

Here's the output from the program:

```
1
2
3
hello
goodbye
```

Instead of using a list variable, you can create a list right in the `foreach` command like this:

```
foreach item {5 10 25 500} {
    puts $item
}
```

In the first iteration, the item variable gets the value 5. In the next iteration, the item variable gets the value 10, then 25, and then 500. Here's the output:

```
5
10
25
500
```

If you want to count a range of numbers — such as 0, 1, 2, 3, up to, for example, 100 — use a regular for loop. But if you want to count a particular set of numbers — such as 5, 10, 25, and 500 — the foreach loop is better, as demonstrated in the preceding example.

Tcl also has an interesting feature that enables you to move through a list but store the list in pairs. Take a look at this example:

```
foreach {item1 item2} {5 10 25 500} {
    puts "item1=$item1 item2=$item2"
}
```

The first line is just like the previous example, but this time, I added two counter variables, item1 and item2. (Don't use a comma between any of these variables, or you'll get strange errors that are almost impossible to figure out. I speak — ahem — from experience.)

In the first iteration of this loop, item1 gets 5, and item2 gets 10; these are the first two items in the loop. In the next iteration, item1 gets 25, and item2 gets 500; these are the next two items in the list. In other words, you move through the list in groups of two rather than one. Here's the output:

```
item1=5 item2=10
item1=25 item2=500
```

But notice I have an even number of items in the list, and that works out nice and neat. What if you try to fake out the loop and put an odd number of items in the list? What will happen? Here's an example:

```
foreach {item1 item2} {5 10 25 500 600} {
    puts "item1=$item1 item2=$item2"
}
```

In the first iteration, you have 5 and 10 in item1 and item2, respectively. Then you get 25 and 500. But what about the third iteration? The loop has only one number left, 600. Here's the output so you can see what happens:

```
item1=5 item2=10
item1=25 item2=500
item1=600 item2=
```

Book IV
Chapter 3

Controlling the
Structure

In the final iteration, the 600 goes in the first variable, item1. The other variable, item2, simply gets an empty value, which prints as nothing.

Sometimes putting all the elements in a single list can be confusing because you might forget which item goes with which variable. Here's an alternative form:

```
foreach item1 {1 2 3} item2 {10 20 30} {
    puts "item1=$item1 item2=$item2"
}
```

This loop runs through three iterations. In the first iteration, item1 gets 1 (taken from the first list, {1 2 3}), and item2 gets 10 (taken from the second list, {10 20 30}). In the second iteration, item1 gets 2, and item2 gets 20. And in the third and final iteration, item1 gets 3, and item2 gets 30.

Looping while something is true

The simplest way to loop is to simply loop while something is true. In other words, you set up some initial conditions, and you run a loop over and over while a certain condition is true. Here's an example using the while loop:

```
set num 2
while {$num < 65537} {
    puts $num
    set num [expr $num * 2]
}
```

This code first stores 2 in the variable num. Then the code keeps running over and over as long as num is less than 65537. When num is not less than 65537, the loop ends.

Each iteration of this loop first prints out the value in num. Then the code stores twice the value of num in num by calling the expr command. (I know, that's kind of a complex way to do it. Other languages might use something simple like num = num * 2, but alas that isn't possible with Tcl.)

Breaking out and continuing again

Regardless of the kind of loop you use (for, foreach, or while), you may want to write some code where if something happens, you want to break out of the loop and continue with code that follows the loop. Or you might want to stop in the middle of the current iteration and immediately continue with the next iteration. For these situations, you use the break command and continue command, respectively.

Here's an example of the continue statement:

```
set num 2
while {$num < 65537} {
    set num [expr $num * 2]
    if {$num == 4096} {
        continue
    }
    puts $num
}
```

```
4
8
16
32
64
128
256
512
1024
2048
8192
16384
32768
65536
131072
```

Notice that 4096 (which normally would have shown up) isn't in the list. That's because in the program I compare the `num` variable to 4096, and if it matches, I skip the rest of the iteration and go on to the next one.

A common mistake with the `continue` command is to forget to do whatever is necessary to move on to the next iteration. For example, in the preceding program, I made sure to multiply the `num` variable by 2 before continuing with the next iteration. If I first checked for 4096 and didn't multiply by 2, the next iteration would also be 4096, and the next iteration would be 4096, and so on, and the program would just keep running forever (or least until you interrupted it).

Here's an example of the `break` command:

```
set num 2
while {$num < 65537} {
    puts $num
    gets stdin choice
    if {$choice == "n"} {
        break
    }
    set num [expr $num * 2]
}
```

In this example, you have the option to continue with the rest of the loop or break out of it, depending on what you type into the console. I call the `gets` command to read a string from the console, and then I compare the input to the string n. If it matches, I break out of the loop. Here's some sample output:

```
2
y
4
y
8
y
16
n
```

The y and n letters are what I typed in; the program wrote out the numbers. Remember, however, that I didn't have to type y to continue; I could have typed anything except an n. That's because the program only tests whether I typed in an n, and if so, it breaks out of the loop.

Chapter 4: Building Procedures

In This Chapter

✔ Creating a procedure

✔ Passing a parameter to a procedure

✔ Returning a value from a procedure

✔ Creating local and global variables

✔ Passing multiple parameters to a procedure

*T*cl provides you with a whole set of commands, but you can also make your own commands with the proc command. By using proc, you can make your own procedures, which become commands within your program.

 If you're familiar with other languages such as Perl or PHP, what I'm describing here are simply procedures and functions. However, Tcl programmers think in terms of commands, so creating a new procedure is akin to creating a new command. In this chapter, I refer to the process as creating a procedure, not a command, because the command is called proc, which stands for (drum roll) *procedure*.

Creating a Simple Procedure

To create a procedure, you use the proc command, as I do in this example program:

```
proc MyProc {} {
    puts "Hi!"
}

MyProc
MyProc
MyProc
```

When you run this program, here's the output you see:

```
Hi!
Hi!
Hi!
```

The first line of the program declares a new procedure called `MyProc`; notice the word `proc` followed by the name, `MyProc`. Don't worry yet about the empty braces that follow. Then comes an open brace, some more code, and finally a closing brace. The code inside the braces makes up the new procedure called `MyProc`.

Then on the following lines, I test out the new procedure by *calling* it three times. Each time the program runs a `MyProc` line, the program instead runs the code inside the `MyProc` procedure, which is this line:

```
puts "Hi!"
```

Thus, this `puts` line runs three times, resulting in the output of three lines of `Hi!`.

Here's another example:

```
proc MyProc {} {
    puts "Hi!"
    puts "Goodbye"
}

MyProc
MyProc
```

This time the `MyProc` procedure has two lines of code in it. I call the procedure twice, and I get the following output:

```
Hi!
Goodbye
Hi!
Goodbye
```

The first two lines of output are from the first call to `MyProc`. The final two lines of output are from the second call to `MyProc`. If you're curious about the two empty braces in the `proc` line, I take that up in the next section.

Passing Parameters to a Procedure

A procedure isn't particularly useful unless you can supply the procedure with information. For example, suppose you want a procedure that takes a temperature in Fahrenheit (thank goodness for spell-checkers) and writes out the same temperature in Celsius. (But don't say centigrade. That's a holdover from when the U.S. government tried to convert the country to the metric system.) To create a procedure that converts a Fahrenheit number to a

Celsius number, you have to tell the procedure the Fahrenheit number you want it to convert. To do that, you need to *pass a parameter* to the procedure.

Here's a sample program that does that:

```
proc Celsius {degree} {
    puts [expr ($degree - 32) * 5 / 9]
}

puts "Here are some samples"
Celsius 32
Celsius 212
Celsius 72
puts "Now type your own number"
gets stdin temp
Celsius $temp
```

This procedure takes a temperature and stores that temperature in a variable called `degree`. This `degree` variable is accessible throughout the procedure but not outside the procedure. (If you create a variable outside the procedure and call `degree`, that `degree` variable will be a different variable from the one inside the procedure, so be careful.)

Inside the procedure, I run the value of the `degree` variable through the famous equation to convert the temperature in Fahrenheit to a temperature in Celsius, and I print out the answer.

Outside the procedure, I print out an introductory message and then call the procedure three times, trying out a different number each time. The format for calling a procedure is just like the format for typing a command: You type the name of the procedure, a space, and then the parameters. In other words, the format `Celsius 32` is very similar to the format `puts "Hello"`.

Next I type out another message, read a number from the console, save the number in the variable called `temp` (for temperature), and call `Celsius` again. This time when I call `Celsius`, I pass the value stored in `temp`, not a number that's hardcoded in the program. Here is a sample session; I typed the 75 line.

```
$tclsh parameter.tcl
Here are some samples
0
100
22
Now type your own number
75
23
```

Book IV Chapter 4

Building Procedures

Although most people (myself included) just say parameters, technically there's a subtle difference between the term *parameter* and another term, *argument*. Simply put, the items in the top line of the `proc` command that define the procedure are parameters, shown in bold here:

```
proc Celsius {degree} {
```

The numbers that follow when you call the command are arguments, shown in bold here:

```
Celsius 32
```

However, these days most people just say *parameters* for both. Incidentally, I'm saying these terms in the plural because you can pass multiple parameters, as I show you later in this chapter in "Passing Multiple Parameters."

Returning a Value from a Procedure

A procedure is useful if it can read data, but it's even more useful if it can return data. For example, think about the `expr` command. If you use `expr` in the command shell, you get your answers right away:

```
% expr 5 + 2
7
```

But if you use `expr` in a program, nothing appears in the console. That's because you might not want anything to appear in the console. For example, you may want to store the answer in a variable, like so:

```
set answer [expr 5 + 2]
```

In other words, when you put the command inside brackets, you get back an answer that gets substituted for the stuff inside brackets. How does this happen? The `expr` command *returns* the answer.

You can create a procedure yourself that also returns an answer. If you try out the program in the preceding section, "Passing Parameters to a Procedure," and try to save the number like so, it won't work:

```
set answer [Celsius 212]
puts "My answer is"
puts $answer
puts "and I'm sticking to it"
```

Keeping variables local

Like functions in most languages, if you create a variable inside a procedure, that variable exists only within the procedure itself. In other words, the variable has *local* scope. For example, suppose you have a line such as this inside a procedure:

```
set x 100
```

The variable x is not available outside the procedure. (If you have a variable called x outside the procedure, it's a different variable.)

Similarly, if you're in a procedure and try to access a variable that lives outside the procedure, you won't be able to until you declare the variable as global. Here's a simple program that demonstrates this:

```
proc testproc {y} {
    global g
    set x 100
    puts $x
    puts $g
    puts $y
}
set g 200
testproc 1
```

The variable g is global, but to access it inside the function, I had to declare it as global using the global command. Inside the function, the variable x is local. Similarly, the variable y is local, and its value was passed into the function.

You just get a blank line in response to printing $answer, because answer doesn't contain the answer. (Yes, your number prints out, but that happens inside the Celsius procedure.)

Instead you need to return a value. Here's a modified form of the Celsius procedure that returns a number and doesn't print out anything:

```
proc Celsius {degree} {
    set result [expr ($degree - 32) * 5 / 9]
    return $result
}

set answer [Celsius 212]
puts "My answer is"
puts $answer
puts "and I'm sticking to it"
```

This time everything works as expected, as this output shows:

```
$tclsh return.tcl
My answer is
100
and I'm sticking to it
```

What happened? The `Celsius` procedure returns a value. First, it calculates the temperature in Celsius, and then it returns the number to a caller. When you type

```
[Celsius 212]
```

inside another line, Tcl calls the `Celsius` procedure, passing 212 as a parameter, and substitutes the stuff in brackets for the answer that Celsius returns, which happens to be 100.

Passing Multiple Parameters

Sometimes you want to create a procedure that can have multiple items passed to it, not just a single item. You can do this two ways:

✦ You can write your procedure to accept a single list as a parameter; this list can contain multiple items.

✦ You can include multiple parameters in your procedure.

You can also combine these two approaches. First, here's an example where I pass a list to a procedure:

```
proc ListNames {names} {
    foreach name $names {
        puts "Hello $name, good to see you"
    }
}

ListNames {"Tom" "Dick" "Harry" "Suzy"}
```

The `ListNames` procedure takes a single list as a parameter. Here's the output from this program:

```
Hello Tom, good to see you
Hello Dick, good to see you
Hello Harry, good to see you
Hello Suzy, good to see you
```

Typically, you would pass a list to a procedure if you're working with various list items and want to process items as a list. You wouldn't do this as a way to collect variables and pass them into a procedure. Here is how you pass multiple separate variables:

```
proc ShowInfo {name age} {
    puts "Hello $name, you are $age years old."
}

ShowInfo "Tom" 25
ShowInfo "Sally" 30
```

This procedure takes two parameters: name and age. It then prints out a message using both of them. The calls to ShowInfo pass the two parameters separately, not as a single list. Here's the output from this program:

```
Hello Tom, you are 25 years old.
Hello Sally, you are 30 years old.
```

You can also mix multiple parameters with lists, because passing a list is just passing a single parameter that happens to be a list. Here's an example:

```
proc NameInfo {name inf} {
    puts "Hello $name, here is your information."
    foreach item $inf {
        puts $item
    }
}

NameInfo Tom {1 2 3}
NameInfo Sally {5 6 7}
```

Passing a variable number of parameters

For you experienced technical folks out there, you may be interested to know that you can create a procedure that expects a variable number of parameters, much like the ellipsis (...) in C and C++ or the general argument in Perl. To use multiple parameters in Tcl, name the final parameter in the proc command args, like so:

```
proc Multiples {a b args} {
    puts $a
    puts $b
    puts $args
}

Multiples 10 20 30 40 50
```

```
puts ""
Multiples 1 2 3
```

The additional arguments all come into the procedure as a list in the args variable. You can see this in the output from the program:

```
10
20
30 40 50

1
2
3
```

This procedure takes two parameters, and uses the second parameter as a list. To call the procedure, I pass a name and then a list, as in the final two lines of the program. Here's the output from this program:

```
Hello Tom, here is your information.
1
2
3
Hello Sally, here is your information.
5
6
7
```

Chapter 5: Manipulating Files

In This Chapter

✔ **Creating a new file and writing to the file**

✔ **Opening a file and reading from the file**

✔ **Appending to an existing file**

✔ **Finding out information about a file**

✔ **Managing files and directories**

*I*f you're interested in opening and closing files, and reading and writing from files, Tcl can do all of these things. This chapter focuses on how to manipulate files. I also show you how to find out such information as whether a file exists, whether a filename is a file or directory, and much more.

Creating a New File and Writing to It

To create and open a new file for writing, you use the open command. What you're about to read is a holdover from the ancient days of C programming, and if I had my way, things would be different. But I don't, at least not in Tcl. Thus, you have to use a command that's nothing more than a copy of the old C way of doing things.

The open command takes two parameters: the name of a file (which can also contain a path to the file) and a cryptic string that describes how you want to open the file. Suppose that you want to create a new file so that you can write to it; for that, you use a letter w (which stands for *write*). Here's the command:

```
open "/tmp/data.txt" "w"
```

This command creates and opens a file in the /tmp directory called data.txt and returns a value that represents the file. But you also need to store that value in a variable. Therefore, you typically put the open command inside brackets and save the results like this:

```
set myfile [open "/tmp/data.txt" "w"]
```

This saves the result of the open command in a variable called myfile, which you can then use in subsequent operations, such as a command to write to the file and a command to close the file. Here's a complete program that demonstrates this:

```
set myfile [open "/tmp/data.txt" "w"]
puts $myfile "Hello"
puts $myfile "Goodbye"
close $myfile
```

This program creates and opens the file and then writes two lines of text to the file. The command close closes the file.

Here's what the file looks like after you run this program:

```
Hello
Goodbye
```

I used the puts command to write these two lines to the file. But unlike the usual use of the puts command, I included the myfile variable, which, as I mentioned, is the result of the open command.

Save the result of the open command to a variable and put that variable name after the puts command. That way the puts command knows to write to the file rather than the console.

Opening a File and Reading from It

If you already have a file, you can use the open command in Tcl to open the file for reading. Then you can begin reading data from the file. Suppose you have a file in the /tmp directory called data.txt, and it contains two lines of text like this:

```
Hello
Goodbye
```

(If you read the previous section, this is the same file I created in that section.) To read this data, you use the open command, passing the letter r for the second parameter (which stands for *read*).

Here's a sample program:

```
set myfile [open "/tmp/data.txt" "r"]
gets $myfile a
puts "The first line is: $a"
```

```
gets $myfile a
puts "The second line is: $a"
close $myfile
```

In this example, first I call the `open` command and pass the name of the file (with its directory) that I want to open, along with a string consisting of the letter `r`, for read. I save the results of the `open` command to the variable called `myfile`, which I will use in subsequent file commands. The next line reads from the file. Here's how I did it:

```
gets $myfile a
```

The `gets` command reads a string and is usually used to read data from the console like so:

```
gets stdin a
```

But this time, instead of using `stdin` for the second parameter, I used `$myfile`. The `gets` command will read a line and save it as a string in the variable specified, in this case `a`. The next line of the program prints out the contents of the `a` variable along with a friendly message. Then I do the same two lines again for another line of text from the file.

Finally, I close the file. Here's the output:

```
The first line is: Hello
The second line is: Goodbye
```

Typically, when you open a file for reading, you want to make sure you don't encounter any errors before just barreling forward, trying to read the data from the file. For example, if the file doesn't exist, the `open` command will fail with an error like this:

```
couldn't open "/tmp/databb.txt": no such file or directory
    while executing
"open "/tmp/databb.txt" "r""
    invoked from within
"set myfile [open "/tmp/databb.txt" "r"]"
    (file "read.tcl" line 1)
```

Therefore, you should first check if the file exists before opening it. I talk about testing whether a file exists in "Finding Out Information about a File," later in this chapter. Here's a quick preview:

```
if {[file exists "/tmp/data.txt"]} {
    set myfile [open "/tmp/data.txt" "r"]
    gets $myfile a
```

```
      puts "The first line is: $a"
      gets $myfile a
      puts "The second line is: $a"
      close $myfile
} else {
      puts "Sorry, the file doesn't exist."
}
```

Appending to an Existing File

You may have a file that already has information in it, and you want to write more information to the end of the file. Normally, if you type the following line in your program, you overwrite any data already in the file:

```
open "/tmp/data.txt" "w"
```

If you want to *append* to the file, replace the w with an a, like so:

```
open "/tmp/append.txt" "a"
```

The next `puts` command will add onto (that is, append to) the file. To see this in action, try the following short program:

```
set myfile [open "/tmp/append.txt" "a"]
puts $myfile [clock seconds]
close $myfile
```

Save this program as `append.tcl` and run it like this:

```
$ tclsh append.tcl
```

Then wait a moment and enter this again:

```
$ tclsh append.tcl
```

Do this a few times. The contents of the file should look similar to this:

```
more \tmp\append.txt
1062372095
1062372146
1062372226
1062372229
```

Each time you run the program, you append another line onto the file instead of overwriting the existing file. (Incidentally, the `clock seconds` command grabs the current system time in seconds.)

Finding Out Information about a File

Tcl includes a huge number of commands for finding out information about a file. These commands all live as subcommands under the `file` command. To try out some of these, I recommend that you pick a file that you know exists on your computer. One way is to create a file in the current directory. On Linux or on Windows in the command shell, you can type this line to create a simple file:

```
echo hi > test.txt
```

Then you can open up the Tcl command shell and try out some of these commands.

It would be silly for me to just list all the commands available to you when you can look them up for yourself in the online help. Therefore, I'm going to focus on the more useful commands. You can find other commands in the Tcl online help under the file entry, here:

```
www.scriptics.com/man/tcl8.4/TclCmd/file.htm
```

Here's an interactive session (on Linux) demonstrating some of the commands (remember to create the `test.txt` file first):

```
% # This will show the time the file was last accessed:
% file atime test.txt
1062382720
% # Now format the time as a string
% clock format [file atime test.txt]
Sun Aug 31 19:18:40 PDT 2003
%
% # Here's the time the file was last modified:
% file mtime test.txt
1062382719
% # Format it:
% clock format [file mtime test.txt]
Sun Aug 31 19:18:39 PDT 2003
%
% # Get the file attributes
% file attribute test.txt
-group users -owner jeffcogs -permissions 00644
%
% # Find out if the file exists
% file exists test.txt
1
%
% # Is it a directory?
% file isdirectory test.txt
```

```
0
% # Nope, got back 0
%
% # Is it a file?
% file isfile test.txt
1
% # Yup, got back 1
%
% # How big is the file?
% file size test.txt
3
% # Only three bytes...
```

Managing Files and Directories

If you want to delete a file, rename a file, move a file, create a directory, or remove a directory, you can use subcommands of the file command. These are strange operations in that none of them involve opening and reading a file. They are operations that act on a file itself, not the contents of the file.

Here's a summary of the commands you need to use:

✦ copy: As you might expect, this command copies a file. If the file you're trying to create already exists, however, the copy will fail unless you include an option called force.

✦ delete: This command deletes a file or directory. Sometimes, however, a file or directory may not have the right permissions to allow a delete; if you include an option called force, Tcl will try to override that permission.

✦ mkdir: This command creates a directory.

✦ rename: This command renames a file or directory. If the file permissions don't allow a rename, you can include the force option, and Tcl will try to override the permissions.

Here's an interactive session of the copy command; remember to precede the command with the file command as I do here:

```
% file copy myfile.txt myfile2.txt
% file copy myfile.txt myfile2.txt
  error copying "myfile.txt" to "myfile2.txt": file
    already exists
% file copy -force myfile.txt myfile2.txt
```

Prior to this example, I created a file called `myfile.txt`. Then in this example, I copied the file to `myfile2.txt`. Then I tried copying the file again, but because the `myfile2.txt` file already exists, I received an error message. So I tried again, but this time, I added the `-force` option, which did the trick.

Here's an example of `delete`. When I created the `myfile.txt` file, I gave it read-only permissions, meaning it can't be deleted without overriding the permissions:

```
% file delete myfile.txt
%
```

Oops; Tcl deleted the file without regard for permissions. For this reason, you need to be careful with the `delete` command. But this "deleting without regard for permission" isn't the case with directories because that's where the `-force` option applies. If you have a directory with files in it, `delete` won't delete the directory:

```
% file delete mydir
error deleting "mydir": directory not empty
% file delete -force mydir
%
```

At first, `delete` refused to delete `mydir` because I put some files in `mydir`. Instead, I received an error message. But then I tried again with the `-force` option, and this time `delete` deleted the directory for me.

The `mkdir` and `rename` commands are easy to use:

```
% mkdir newdirectory
% file rename test.txt newfilename.txt
```

Be careful using the `-force` option with directories because it will delete everything in them. Also, be careful with `delete` in general because a read-only permission won't prevent `delete` from deleting a file.

Additionally, you can use the following commands with files and directories; these are not subcommands of the `file` command:

✦ cd: This command changes the directory.

✦ pwd: This command prints the working directory.

Here's a short example program that demonstrates these two commands:

```
cd /tmp
puts [pwd]
```

The `cd` command takes as a single parameter the directory you want to switch to. (On both Linux and Windows, you can use the forward slash, as usual.) The `pwd` command returns a string representing the current directory; it doesn't actually print out the string. To print out the string, put the `pwd` command in quotes and print it with `puts`. Or save it to a variable like this:

```
set mydir [pwd]
```

In interactive mode (but not in a program), you can also use many of the usual shell commands, depending on your operating system. Here are some examples:

✦ `dir`: This command displays a directory listing. (Windows)

✦ `ls`: This command displays a directory listing. (Linux)

✦ `copy`: This command copies a file. (Windows)

✦ `cp`: This command copies a file. (Linux)

You can include all the usual options, such as `dir /s` on Windows or `ls -ltr` on Linux. Because all these commands are present, you can use `tcl` as your shell, rather than the usual shell, if you prefer.

Creating File Links

For you advanced users, Tcl includes a `link` command that lets you inspect or create a symbolic or hard link. This is something most Linux users are aware of; however, most people don't realize that links also exist on Windows 2000 and XP. But on these Windows operating systems, you can have only symbolic links for directories and hard links for files.

On Linux, to create a link called `file2` to an existing file called `file1`, use this line:

```
file link file2 file1
```

This results in a symbolic link, where the new file effectively points to the original file. The default is to create a symbolic link; however, you can be redundant and specify `-symbolic` as an option like so:

```
file link -symbolic file2 file1
```

Or, you can create a hard link, whereby you have two separate filenames aliased to the same file structure on the disk, like so:

```
file link -hard test2.txt test.txt
```

You can use these two techniques on either files or directories.

On Windows XP and 2000, you can create a hard link only for a file, like so, assuming `file1.txt` already exists:

```
file link -hard file2.txt file1.txt
```

After you run this command, you see what appears to be a copy of `file1.txt`. However, if you modify the contents of `file2.txt`, you also modify the contents of `file1.txt`, and vice versa. Amazing, no? Most people don't know this exists in Windows. (If you get an error message, it means you're not using an NTFS drive, even if you have Windows 2000 or XP. The error message you see is `could not create new link 'file2.txt' pointing to 'file.txt': invalid argument`.)

Directory links are interesting because you get to see something you might never have seen on Windows. For directories, you must specify the `-symbolic` option, even though on Linux that's the default. If you have a directory called `testdir1`, you can create a link like so:

```
file link -symbolic testdir2 testdir1
```

You then have two names for the same directory. In the DOS window, you see this, containing a rather interesting `JUNCTION` item (because Microsoft uses the term *junction* for a linked directory):

```
C:\temp\more>dir
 Volume in drive C has no label.
 Volume Serial Number is 9090-6698

 Directory of C:\temp\more

08/31/2003  06:08 PM    <DIR>          .
08/31/2003  06:08 PM    <DIR>          ..
08/31/2003  06:08 PM                12 test.txt
08/31/2003  06:08 PM                12 test2.txt
08/31/2003  06:12 PM    <DIR>          testdir1
08/31/2003  06:01 PM    <JUNCTION>     testdir2
               4 File(s)             34 bytes
               4 Dir(s)  12,648,849,408 bytes free
```

Anything you put in `testdir1`, you also see in `testdir2` and vice versa; they are effectively the same directory just with different names. (But remember, this works only on an NTFS drive, not FAT or FAT32.)

Chapter 6: Programming with the Tcl Packages

In This Chapter

✔ **Accessing files on the Web**

✔ **Manipulating text**

✔ **Building advanced data structures: queues, stacks, and records**

Tcl comes standard with several extra packages that provide extended functionality. A *package* is a Tcl program that is stored inside a subdirectory under the special directory called lib.

Several of the main packages available with Tcl are collectively known as tcllib, which is supposed to stand for Standard Tcl Library. If you want to see a list of all the packages available and view the online docs, visit www.tcl.tk/software/tcllib/. Additionally Tcl ships with some other packages that aren't technically part of the Standard Tcl Library. In this chapter, I look at some of these available packages.

Accessing Files on the Web

Tcl includes a handy package for accessing data on the Web. (This package isn't part of tcllib.) The following program accesses the Web site www.dummies.com and prints out the contents to the console:

```
package require http
set tok [http::geturl "www.dummies.com"]
set res [http::data $tok]
puts $res
```

Amazing: only four lines of code! This program first opens the package called http, which allows you to access the Web. Then the program calls http::geturl, which makes the connection to the site. The http::data command grabs the Web page, and I save the results to the res variable. Then I print out the variable.

However, this program gets stuck if the server sends back a redirection. If you try the preceding program on www.dummies.com, you won't see anything. Here, then is a more sophisticated program that checks the error code. If the error code is between 300 and 399, then the response is a redirection request. In that case, I grab the redirection and try again. (This only works for redirections on the same server, however.)

```
package require http
set url "www.dummies.com"
set tok [http::geturl $url]
set ncode [http::ncode $tok]
puts $ncode
if {$ncode >= 300 && $ncode <=399} {
    # Redirect
    upvar #0 $tok state
    array set meta $state(meta)
    puts "Redirecting to $meta(Location)"
    http::cleanup $tok
    set tok [http::geturl "$url$meta(Location)"]
}

set res [http::data $tok]
puts $res
```

Now you can try this program on www.dummies.com, as I did here.

Manipulating Text

The tcllib library includes a handy package called textutil. This package has several commands for manipulating text. Typically, it works like this: First you read all the text from a file into a single string; then you use textutil to manipulate the string, as I do in the following sections. Note also that in order to use the textutil library, you need the following command in your .tcl file prior to any textutil commands:

```
package require textutil
```

You then access the commands by typing two colons, textutil, two colons again, and the command. For example, if a command is indent, you type ::textutil::indent to specify this command.

Adjusting indentation level

Want to change the indentation level of a text file (such as a file containing Tcl source)? Use the indent command found in the textutil package. Suppose this is a file called indenttest.txt:

```
set x 100
if {$x == 100} {
    set y 200
    if {$y == 200} {
        puts "Works!"
    }
}
```

The following program reads the indenttest.txt file, indents each line four spaces, and prints out the results. Then it reduces the indention of each line a couple spaces and prints out the new results:

```
package require textutil
set f [open "indenttest.txt"]
set t [read $f]
close $f
set res [::textutil::indent $t "    "]
puts $res
puts ""
set res2 [::textutil::indent $res "  "]
puts $res2
```

Notice how I make use of the textutil package and then access the indent command using ::textutil::indent. First, I open a file and read in the file's contents into the t variable. Then I try indenting the whole file with several spaces and printing out the results. Next, I try indenting again, but with fewer spaces, and again print out the results. Here's the output; notice that the second block is indented less than the first block:

```
    set x 100
    if {$x == 100} {
        set y 200
        if {$y == 200} {
            puts "Works!"
        }
    }

  set x 100
      if {$x == 100} {
          set y 200
          if {$y == 200} {
              puts "Works!"
          }
      }
```

Reformatting text

Often when working with online text you need to reformat text to fit within a certain width. Many e-mail programs perform this function, and the textutil package includes a command called adjust that squeezes down the text. (If the text is already narrow, no changes are made, even if the text is extremely narrow.) In the following example, I have included a long string with no newlines; I then call the adjust function with a parameter of 60 to reformat the text. This adds newlines where necessary to fit each line within 60 characters. Then I try the same thing again but with a parameter of 40, limiting each line to 40 characters. Here's the code:

```
package require textutil

set address "Four score and seven years ago our fathers
    brought \
forth on this continent a new nation, conceived in \
liberty and dedicated to the proposition that all men \
are created equal. Now we are engaged in a \
great civil war, testing whether that nation or any \
nation so conceived and so dedicated can long endure. \
We are met on a great battlefield of that war. We have \
come to dedicate a portion of that field as a final \
resting place for those who here gave their lives that \
that nation might live..."

set formatted [::textutil::adjust $address -length 60]
puts $formatted
puts ""
set formatted [::textutil::adjust $address -length 40]
puts $formatted
puts ""
```

Building Advanced Data Structures

The tcllib includes several handy data structures for advanced data processing. The three that I look at here are common structures used in many programs:

+ **queue:** Implements a first-in-first-out (FIFO) data structure. This is a list that behaves much like people waiting in line.

+ **stack:** Implements a last-in-first-out (LIFO) data structure. This is a list that behaves much like a stack of papers.

+ **record:** Allows you to build data types consisting of several parts. (This is much like struct in C and C++ and record in Pascal.)

To use these data structures, you need to include the following line near the beginning of your program:

```
package require struct
```

You then access a command by typing two colons, the word `struct`, two more colons, and then the command name. Here are two examples: `::struct::queue` and `::struct::stack`.

Standing in line with a queue

A *queue* is a data structure that behaves like people standing in line. You can keep adding more and more to the data, and this data goes at the end of the line. You can then take data off one by one, and the data comes from the front of the line. For example, if you put a 100 in a queue, then a 200 in the queue, then a 300 in the queue, the queue will look like this:

(front of the line) 100 200 300 (back of the line)

If you take off an item, you'll have to take the first in the queue. The first item you take off, then, is a 100, leaving the queue like this:

(front of the line) 200 300 (back of the line)

The next item you take off is a 200, leaving the queue like this:

(front of the line) 300 (back of the line)

. . . and so on. A queue is commonly used in situations where you have several data items trying to access a single device. What kind of device? A printer is an example. The program running the printer can take several print jobs, but then puts them all in a queue, printing them one by one. The following program demonstrates a queue. This approach is usually called FIFO, which stands for First In, First Out.

```
package require struct

::struct::queue myqueue
myqueue put 50
myqueue put 60
myqueue put "Hello"
set x [myqueue get]
puts $x
set x [myqueue get]
puts $x
```

Notice the strange syntax here. You first create the queue using the `::struct::queue` command, passing a name for your queue. Oddly, this name then becomes a command, which you can use to manipulate your new queue, by passing a subcommand (in this first case, the subcommand is `put`). First I call `put` to add a 50 to the queue. Then I `put` a 60, and then I `put` the string `Hello`.

**Book IV
Chapter 6**

**Programming with
the Tcl Packages**

Next, I take something off the queue using the `get` subcommand and print it out; then I take something else off the queue and print that out. Here's the output, verifying that the first item I put in was the first item I got back:

```
50
60
```

Gathering papers with a stack

A *stack* is a data structure that works like a stack of papers on your desk: The most recent addition to the list is the first item you can retrieve from it. Let's say you put something on the stack, say a 1. Then you put something else on it, say a 2. And then you put a 3. Now, because this is a stack, when you take items off, you can take them only off the top. Thus, you first take the 3 off the stack, leaving the 1 and 2 behind. Next, you take off the 2 from the stack, leaving the 1 behind. Finally, you can take off the 1, leaving an empty stack.

A common use of a stack is in how the computer keeps track of your function calls: Each time you call a function, the computer saves the function on a stack. Then when your program returns from the function, the computer pops the top off the stack, and whatever is underneath is the function to return to. This is usually called First In, Last Out, or FILO. Or, sometimes Last In, First Out, or LIFO.

Here's a sample program that creates and manipulates a stack:

```
package require struct

::struct::stack mystack
mystack push 100
mystack push "Hi"
mystack push 250
set x [mystack pop]
puts $x
set x [mystack pop]
puts $x
```

This code creates a new stack using the `::struct::stack` command. Then the code pushes a 100 onto the stack using the `push` command. (*Push* is the correct term for putting something on the stack.) Next, I push a string `Hi` on the stack, and then I push 250. Now I have a 100 at the bottom, a `Hi` string in the middle, and a 250 on top.

To retrieve an item from the top of the stack, you use the `pop` command. So, next I use the `pop` command to pop something off the stack. What will I pop off? The item on top, which is 250. Then if I pop something else off the stack, I'll get the string Hi. Here's the output:

```
250
Hi
```

Grouping data in a record

A *record* is a handy way to collect data that's divided up into subdata, so to speak, thereby allowing you to group related data together. For example, I may want to create a data structure that's made up of a *name,* an *e-mail address,* and a *company.* Using the record structure, I can group those three items together into a single entity that I will call emailinfo.

After the record is defined, I can create a new instance of my emailinfo structure; I can set the *name* for the instance, the *e-mail* for the instance, and the *company.* Using this definition, I can create unlimited instances of the emailinfo structure, and again set the name, e-mail, and company. Here's an example:

```
package require struct

::struct::record define emailinfo {
    name
    email
    company
}

emailinfo friend
friend config -name "Jeff" -email "jeff@me.com" \
    -company "Me, Inc."
emailinfo friend2
friend2 config -name "Suzy" -email "suzy@me.com" \
    -company "Me, Inc."

puts [friend cget -name]
puts [friend cget -email]
puts [friend cget -company]

puts [friend2 cget -name]
puts [friend2 cget -email]
puts [friend2 cget -company]
```

Notice how I specify the structure; I use the ::struct::record command and the define subcommand. Then I provide the name for my structure. And then inside braces I give the names of the items making up the structure.

To create a new instance of the structure, I type the name of my structure type followed by a name for the instance. Thus, `emailinfo friend` creates a new structure called `friend` of type `emailinfo`.

Next, I set the members of my new structure called `friend`. To do so, I type the name of the structure as a command, in this case `friend`. Then I type the subcommand `config`. And finally, I type each item name as an option followed by a value, as in `-name "Jeff"`.

To access the members of the structure, I again type my structure name (such as `friend`) and then use the `cget` subcommand, followed by the name of the item as an option, as in `friend cget -name`. Here's the output from this program:

```
Jeff
jeff@me.com
Me, Inc.
Suzy
suzy@me.com
Me, Inc.
```

Chapter 7: Designing GUIs with Tk

In This Chapter

✔ **Creating a hierarchy of widget names**

✔ **Constructing a simple window**

✔ **Adding a button to a window**

✔ **Creating a listbox and working with the pack and bind commands**

✔ **Creating a second window**

✔ **Attaching a menu to a button**

✔ **Building a scale slider**

✔ **Changing a control's settings**

*W*hen you install Tcl, you get an additional product called Tk. Tk, which simply stands for Toolkit (how's that for creativity), is a library for creating graphical user interfaces, or GUIs. Originally Tk was built specifically for use with Tcl, but over time, people have written libraries that let you use Tk from nearly any language. Examples of such languages are Python, Perl, and C++.

If you've ever struggled with a complex GUI library such as Microsoft Foundation Classes, Tk will be a welcome addition to your world of programming. It's extremely simple to use. Yes, occasionally some of the code gets a little strange, but nevertheless, Tk is *easy*.

But Tk has another strong point: It's operating-system-independent! Yes, that's correct. You can develop a program in Tcl/Tk on a Linux computer, and hand the program to somebody with either a Windows PC or a Mac and he or she will be able to run the program. It's true, and you can't say that about many other languages (especially C++). And even better, the windows and controls you create will look "native," meaning the Windows controls will look like Windows controls, and the Mac OS controls will look like Mac OS controls.

In this chapter, I show you how to get up and running with Tk using the Tcl programming language. But first, let me share with you an important lesson I recently learned.

When you save your Tcl/Tk programs to a file, don't name the file the same as one of the built-in widget commands! For example, don't name your file `button.tcl` or `canvas.tcl`. If you do, you'll get some very strange error messages because Tcl will get confused over the names. These errors will be a bit nonsensical, and you could pull your hair out trying to interpret them.

Although a *For Dummies* book is a reference guide and you're not required to read the thing from cover to cover (especially a huge book like this one), I do ask that you read the following two sections, "A Hierarchy of Widgets and Names" and "Creating a Simple Window," before proceeding with any other sections or chapters in this book on Tk. In those sections, I provide you with some important information about Tk.

A Hierarchy of Widgets and Names

When you create a GUI with Tk, everything you create gets built in a hierarchical manner. At the very top of this hierarchy is your main window. Inside the main window, you have controls known in the Tk world as *widgets*. Then inside these various widgets you might have more widgets. And inside some of those widgets you might have even more widgets. (This is starting to sound like a scene from *Alice in Wonderland*.)

In order to keep everything in your wonderland clean and neat, Tk requires that you give a name to your widget that shows the hierarchy. First, remember this rule:

The main window's name is simply . (a period or dot).

That's hard to spell out in written text without getting lost in a morass of punctuation, but the main window's name is just a period or dot. Next, every widget owned by the main window has a name that starts with a period, as in these examples:

✦ `.mybutton1`

✦ `.greatbiglistbox`

✦ `.textentry`

✦ `.canvas1`

These names reflect not only the name of the widget, but also the name of the widget's owner — the main window. Why is that necessary? Because some widgets can have other widgets inside of them. For example, one important widget type is called a frame. A *frame* is simply a holder of other widgets, allowing you to organize your widgets neatly inside a window. You could name a frame that's owned by the main window something like `.bigframe`. And if another frame is owned by `.bigframe`, you might call it `.bigframe.smallerframe`.

Then, inside `.bigframe`, you may have two buttons and a listbox with the following names, respectively:

✦ `.bigframe.button1`

✦ `.bigframe.button2`

✦ `.bigframe.listbox1`

Notice how each of these names starts with a dot (representing the main window) and is followed by the name of the frame, then a dot, and finally the control's own unique name. But don't be fooled: *The name of the first button is not simply* `button1`. The name of the first button is the whole she-bang, `.bigframe.button1`. Never try to abbreviate the name; you need the whole name to make sense.

Sometimes people like to store their widget names in variables, and you can too, if you like. I don't do so in any of the examples in this book so that the names are clearly visible. But suppose you store your `.bigframe` widget's name in a variable called `f`, like so:

`set f .bigframe`

Then, thanks to the magic of substitution, you're free to refer to the `.bigframe.button1` widget like so:

`$f.button1`

Because `$f` gets replaced with `.bigframe`, the interpreter changes `$f.button1` into `.bigframe.button1`, which is the button's full name.

What if you have more than one window? That doesn't change anything about the names: Your main window is still the head honcho, the owner of all the other widgets *including the additional windows*. In the section, "Creating a Second Window," later in this chapter, I show you how to make additional windows. There you'll see that you still need to name your additional windows as if they're owned by the main window (because they are!) starting with a dot, as in `.secondwindow` or `.auxilliaryinformation`, for example. If you have a button on the second window, then that button may be called, for example, `.secondwindow.coolclicker`.

Creating a Simple Window

When you run a Tcl program, you run it under the auspices of the `tclsh` program, which passes the Tcl commands on to the Tcl interpreter. When you run a Tcl program that contains Tk commands, you don't use `tclsh`. Instead, you use a program called `wish`, which stands for *windowing shell*. (The designers of Tcl/Tk are so filled with verbal creativity that I can't stand it.)

This means that if you're using the pound-bang thingy at the beginning of a script in Linux or Unix, you'll want to reference the `wish` program, not the `tclsh` program. In other words, I recommend adding the following line at the very beginning of your Tcl/Tk programs if you want them to run as executables:

```
#!/usr/local/bin/wish
```

(This is assuming, of course, that `wish` is found in the directory called `/usr/local/bin`. If you installed it elsewhere, adjust the path accordingly, please.)

Or, you can run your programs like so:

```
wish myprogram.tcl
```

In Windows, you can set up a file association so that `.tcl` programs open with `wish.exe`. Then you can just run the file like so:

```
myprogram.tcl
```

And `wish` will launch, running your script.

When you run `wish`, you automatically get an initial main window. Isn't that great? I'll say it again: You automatically get a main window, which means you don't have to *create* a main window! Life is good, sometimes.

Instead of creating a main window, all you have to do is provide some information about the main window. Therefore, here's about the simplest Tk program you can imagine:

```
wm title . "Hello"
```

This just sets the title of the main window. Try storing this in a file called `basicwindow.tcl` and run it directly as follows:

```
wish basicwindow.tcl
```

(Or, if you're on Linux, you can include the pound-bang line, set the executable permission on the file, and run the file directly by simply typing `basicwindow.tcl`. On Windows, if you set up a file association, you can also run the file by simply typing `basicwindow.tcl`.)

You will see a simple window open. Figure 7-1 shows an example on a Windows system.

Figure 7-1:
The simple window you see here consisted of just one line of code!

In case you're curious, I'm doing the screenshots for this chapter in Windows for two reasons: First, I'm required to use Microsoft Word to write this book, which runs on Windows; and second, the truth of the matter is that although you may develop your Tk programs on a Linux box, most end users will run them on Windows. But that's okay. Remember, one of the great things about Tk is that your Tcl/Tk programs will run on any operating system that includes a Tcl/Tk system.

Adding a Button to a Window

If you want to put a button on a window, you can use the `button` command, which is part of the Tk library. Remember, in Tcl everything starts with a command. When you use Tk, you still follow this rule. Take a look at this program:

```
button .mybutton -text Hello
pack .mybutton
```

Save this program as `simplewin.tcl` and run it using this line:

```
wish simplewin.tcl
```

You see a tiny window like the one shown in Figure 7-2.

Figure 7-2:
This tiny
window has
a single
button on it.

As you can see, the code for this tiny window is pretty simple. The first line creates a button by calling the `button` command. The first parameter to the `button` command (and all widget commands in general, for that matter) is the name of the button.

Remember, you have to name your widgets starting with a dot. From there, you specify whether the widget is contained in another widget. This button isn't, so I just follow the dot with the final part of the name: `.mybutton`.

Then I specify an option, which in this case is `-text`. That option is the text that appears on the button. I chose `Hello` to appear on the button, as you can see in Figure 7-2.

But just because you create a widget doesn't mean Tk automatically plops the widget on the window for you. To add the widget to a window, you need to use the `pack` command:

```
pack .mybutton
```

The format of the `pack` command is simple; you simply type `pack` followed by the name of the widget.

The word *pack* may seem like a strange choice for a command that adds a widget to a window. However, in reality, *pack* refers to the way the widgets get positioned in a window. The `pack` command is a *geometry manager* that organizes the widgets. Tk offers three different geometry managers called `pack`, `grid`, and `place`. The `pack` command is a special one that squishes your controls all together as much as possible. You can also include some options in the `pack` command; these are present in many of the examples in this chapter. If you want to find out more about geometry managers, see Book IV, Chapter 8.

The preceding program is really cool and all, but I must admit it doesn't do much. If you click the button, *nothing happens*. A good button is one that rolls up his sleeves and actually does something rather than sit around on the couch all day eating potato chips.

Remember that `button` is a command, and like most commands in Tcl, you can provide options. The `button` command includes an option called `-command`. If you type this option, you follow it with a set of braces, inside of which you can include code that runs when the user clicks the button.

Here's a new program that you can try out:

```
button .mybutton -text Hello -command {
    tk_messageBox -icon info -message \
      "Hello, thank you for stopping by!"
}
pack .mybutton
```

I saved this as `buttoncmd.tcl`. When you run it using `wish buttoncmd.tcl`, you see a window with a button on it, just like the one from the program shown in Figure 7-2. But this time, when you click the button, it actually does something: The code inside the `-command` option runs.

That code calls a command called `tk_messageBox`, which displays a message box. The message box shows the message `Hello, thank you for stopping by!` Try clicking the button and see for yourself.

Creating a Listbox (And More on the Pack and Bind Commands)

You've seen listboxes before, and I'm sure you'll agree they're quite useful. Here's a quick little program that puts a listbox on a window:

```
wm title . "Simple Listbox"
listbox .lb -width 10 -height 10
pack .lb
```

This creates a listbox called `.lb`. Notice the `listbox` command has some options after it, `width` and `height`. *These are in terms of characters, not pixels.* That is, the listbox defined in this program can display approximately ten characters across, and can hold ten lines of text. I say *approximately*, because all major operating systems today use proportionally spaced fonts, meaning you won't necessarily see exactly ten characters fit in the allotted space.

If you run the preceding example, you won't see much. It would be nice if you had a few items appear in the listbox, and it would be nice if you could double-click those items. Here's a more sophisticated example that does all that and more:

```
wm title . "Listbox Demo 2"
pack propagate . off

frame .buttonbar
pack .buttonbar -side top

button .buttonbar.bt1 -text "Add" -command {
    .lb insert end grapes kiwi
}
button .buttonbar.bt2 -text "Del" -command {
    .lb delete 1 3
}

pack .buttonbar.bt1 .buttonbar.bt2 \
    -side left -padx 5 -pady 5

listbox .lb -width 250 -height 250
pack .lb -side bottom

.lb insert end apple banana orange

# Create a handler to catch double-clicks from the listbox
# Note: This is a digit 1 after the word Double!
bind .lb <Double-1> {
    tk_messageBox -icon info -message [selection get]
}
```

In this program, you'll first notice that I have included more than one button. But these buttons are inside a frame. A frame is nothing more than a holder for other widgets. The pack command requires you to use a great deal of -side parameters for some complex layouts, and I find that if I want a row of buttons across the top of my window, it's easier to just put a frame at the top, and then fill the frame with my buttons. Thus, in this example program I created a frame, and then created some buttons. Notice how I named the buttons by starting with the frame, as in .buttonbar.bt1.

Also notice that I included two extra parameters in the pack command, -padx and -pady. These just specify some blank space to include around the buttons that I'm packing. And you probably also noticed that I was able to include two buttons in a single pack command; that's not a big deal.

The first button's command inserts items into the listbox. Notice how I do this: I treat the listbox's name as a command, and I follow with a subcommand. The subcommand in the first button is insert, and the one in the second button is delete. The insert command takes an index, which can be either a number or the word end, and then several strings that I want to put in the listbox (in this case, it's the strings grapes and kiwi). The `delete` command takes two indexes, which represent the start and end of a range that I want to delete. In this case, I'm deleting the items that have index 1, 2, and 3. (The first item in the listbox gets index 0.)

But you might notice something bizarre: If you read the program from top to bottom, you'll see that I used `.lb` as a command before the code where I created the `.lb` control. But that's okay, because the place where I use `.lb` as a command (in a button command) runs after I create the `.lb` control; the `.lb` control gets created when the program first starts, and the button command runs only when the user of the program clicks the button.

After the buttons, I make the listbox. Notice the `pack` command that follows this `listbox` command and compare it to the previous `pack` command, the one that followed the `frame` statement. The one for the `frame` statement includes the option `-side top`. The one for the `listbox` statement includes the option `-side bottom`. The `pack` command positions controls relative to a side of the window. Thus, the first `pack` command will position the frame at the top of the window, and the second `pack` command will position the listbox at the bottom. (But positioning items in windows is a bit more complex than it seems, so be sure to read Book IV, Chapter 8, where it is explained more fully.)

The final part of the program is probably the most interesting. If you want to write code that responds to mouse clicks and such, you use the `bind` command. Although some widgets have mouse capabilities built right in (like the button, which has its `-command` option), other widgets require that you *bind* a function to the widget. The listbox is an example of the latter type of widget.

Although the concept may seem strange, in practice this is quite easy: You just choose the widget and which type of event you want to respond to; in this case, I want it to respond to a double-click of the left mouse button. Tk has a name for each type of event, and the name for a double-click of the left button is `Double-1`. (Yes, that's the numeral *1*.) You can see, then, the format of the command; it's much like a `proc` command, and it starts with the word `bind`. Then comes the name of the widget you're binding to (in this case, the listbox) and the event name inside angled brackets. And finally, you have a set of curly braces containing the commands to run.

For a really detailed explanation of the different events available, take a look at `www.scriptics.com/man/tcl8.4/TkCmd/bind.htm`. Or, for the short version, read on.

Think of the event name as having multiple parts separated by hyphens. The event `Double-1` has two parts. The first part, `Double`, in this case refers to the number of clicks. The second part, 1, refers to button 1, which is the left button (or the right if the system is configured for left-handed use).

Want to instead respond to a double-click while the Control key is held down? Then instead of `Double-1` use `Control-Double-1`. That's easy. Or you can require the Shift key using `Shift-Double-1`. Want both keys? Then it's `Control-Shift-Double-1` or `Shift-Control-Double-1`; either works with the same effect. Want just a single click while holding down Shift and Control? Then just use `Control-Shift-1`. You can also use `Alt` for the Alt key in all these combinations. (If you're on a Mac, just test out different combinations of these to see which corresponds to the Apple key, and so on.)

Creating a Second Window

Tk lets you create additional windows besides the main window. But remember: These additional windows are still owned by the main window. Thus, their names still start with a dot. And further, if you close the main window, the additional windows will close as well, and your program will end.

Try out this example:

```
wm title . "First Window"
button .mybutton -text Hello
pack .mybutton
toplevel .win2 -width 300 -height 300
wm title .win2 "Second Window"
button .win2.button2 -text Click
pack .win2.button2
```

The key here is the `toplevel` command, which creates a new window. In this case, the new window is called `.win2`, and it has a width and a height of 300. I then give the new window a title using the `wm title` command. Notice that in the `wm title` command I provide the name of my window (`.win2`), and then I put the title in double quotes. Thus, the new window will include the words `Second Window` in the title bar.

And then you can see how I add a button (or any widget, for that matter) to the new window: I create the button as usual, and I give it a name that starts with the name of my new window. In this case, my button's name is `.win2.button2`. Because that name starts with `.win2`, the button will automatically show up on the `.win2` window (the second window, that is) when I add the button using the `pack` command.

Adding a Menu Bar to a Window

Over the years, I've used lots of GUI systems for lots of different languages, and I have to say that creating a menu bar is usually the most cumbersome task in any system. Tk is no different. The problem is not that menus are inherently complex; the problem is that you typically have lots of menus, and they're arranged hierarchically.

The following example creates a window and adds a menu bar to the window. The menu bar consists of two menus, a File menu and an Edit menu.

```
wm title . "Menu demo"

# Declare the main menu bar
menu .mymenus

# Declare the file menu item
menu .mymenus.filemenu
.mymenus add cascade -label "File" -menu .mymenus.filemenu
.mymenus.filemenu add command -label "Exit" -command { exit }

# Declare the edit menu item
menu .mymenus.editmenu
.mymenus add cascade -label "Edit" -menu .mymenus.editmenu
.mymenus.editmenu add command -label "Stuff" -command \
    { exit }

# Add the menu to the window
. configure -menu .mymenus
```

Look carefully at this code because it contains some gotchas. First, I declare the menu widget, and I call it .mymenus. That's not a problem. But next, I must declare *another* menu widget for each of the menus on the menu bar.

However, I don't create a menu widget for each menu item; just the menus themselves. That's confusing and an important point to remember. Also, notice that the widgets for the menus are children of the main menu widget; thus in my example, I named them .mymenus.filemenu and .mymenus.editmenu.

After declaring the .mymenus.filemenu widget, I call the add cascade command for .mymenus, which creates the menu. I provide the text that appears at the top of the menu, in this case File, using the -label option. Then comes another gotcha: I have to specify which widget I'm adding this menu for. Yes, I know, that's not particularly sensible, but it's the way Tk does it. So I include the -menu option with the .mymenus.filemenu widget.

I want to add some menu items that go under this File menu. In this case, I want an Exit menu item underneath the File menu. To do that, I put the menu name and use the `add command` command. I provide a label for the menu item (`"Exit"`), and then, just like I did when I created a button, I use a `-command` option to specify the Tcl commands to run. For this example, I'm just using the `exit` command, which closes the program.

Then I repeat all this for the Edit menu (and any more menus I may want to add). Yes, it's a lot of work, but that's just because programs tend to have a lot of menus. But it works! And finally, when I've created all the menus I need, I need to attach the whole menu bar to the window. I don't use the `pack` command for this. Instead, I put the window's name (in this case a dot) followed by the `configure` command, then `-menu`, and the name of my main menu.

(What you're really doing is reconfiguring the window's options. The option you want to reconfigure is the `menu` option; to do this, you add `-menu` followed by the name of your main menu widget.)

When you run the program, your window will have a menu bar like the one shown in Figure 7-3.

Figure 7-3:
Adding a menu bar is a bit involved but well worth the effort.

Attaching a Menu to a Button

Tk includes some interesting widgets that you may or may not have seen before. If you use X Windows or KDE (the Linux or Unix windowing systems), then you've likely seen buttons that you can click that result in a menu opening up. Microsoft Windows doesn't include a control like that, but Tk does. Here's a sample program that does just that:

```
wm title . "Menu button demo"

# Create the menu button, specifying the menu
menubutton .menubtn -text "Click me" \
    -menu .menubtn.mymenus -relief raised

# Declare the menu itself; it must be a
```

```
# child of the menu button.
menu .menubtn.mymenus

# Declare the file menu item
menu .menubtn.mymenus.menu1
.menubtn.mymenus add cascade -label "File" \
    -menu .menubtn.mymenus.menu1
.menubtn.mymenus.menu1 add command -label "Exit" \
    -command { exit }

# Declare the edit menu item
menu .menubtn.mymenus.editmenu
.menubtn.mymenus add cascade -label "Edit" -menu \
    .menubtn.mymenus.editmenu
.menubtn.mymenus.editmenu add command -label "Stuff" \
    -command { exit }

pack .menubtn
```

If you read the previous section, "Adding a Menu Bar to a Window," this code may seem a bit familiar. The process of creating a set of menus is the same for both menu buttons and window menu bars. But, when you create a menu button, instead of starting with a menu widget, you start with a menubutton widget. Further, the -relief option is available; this option describes how the button looks — that is, whether the button is a regular raised button, an inset button, or any of several types. Here are the types you can try out; their names are rather self-explanatory. Feel free to try them out to see what they look like:

✦ raised

✦ sunken

✦ flat

✦ ridge

✦ solid

✦ groove

When you run the preceding program, you see a window similar to Figure 7-4.

**Book IV
Chapter 7**

**Designing GUIs
with Tk**

Figure 7-4:
A menu
button
provides
your user
with easy
access to
various
commands.

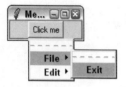

Sliding Across the Numbers with a Scale

A slider control is found on most operating systems; Tk includes an interesting-looking slider control that you can use. This slider control doesn't make use of any native slider controls, but that's okay; it looks cool. (And isn't that all that matters anyway?)

Here's a sample program; you'll notice the slider control is called a *scale* widget.

```
set curx 0
set cury 0

proc drawH {x} {
    global curx
    global cury
    .mycanvas create line $curx $cury $x $cury
    set curx $x
}

proc drawV {y} {
    global curx
    global cury
    .mycanvas create line $curx $cury $curx $y
    set cury $y
}

scale .myHscale -orient horizontal -length 284 \
    -from 0 -to 250 \
    -command "drawH" -tickinterval 50
grid .myHscale -row 1 -column 0
scale .myVscale -orient vertical -length 300 \
```

```
      -from 0 -to 300 \
      -command "drawV" -tickinterval 50
grid .myVscale -row 0 -column 1
canvas .mycanvas -width 300 -height 300
grid .mycanvas -row 0 -column 0 -pady 5

.myHscale set 5
.myVscale set 5
```

The key to this program is in the two `scale` declarations. You can choose whether the slider control is a horizontal or vertical control; you can choose the size of the slider control (I chose 300 pixels); and you can choose the range. I'm using a range of 0 to 300, which matches the size of the scale.

You can also specify a `-command` option. However, this `-command` option is a bit different from the `-command` option in a button! For this command option, you specify a procedure that the slider will call when the user moves the slider. Further, the slider will pass a parameter to the procedure that's an integer representing the position of the slider. Thus, you'll notice that I only put the name of the procedure (`drawH` and `drawV`), but my procedures each take a parameter.

And what does this program do? If you move the sliders up and down, a little line moves. You can use this to draw like an Etch A Sketch drawing toy. Pretty cool, wouldn't you say? Check it out in Figure 7-5.

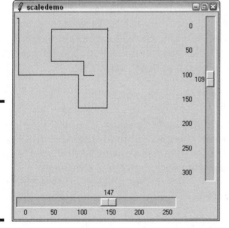

Figure 7-5:
The slider controls let the user select a number on a range.

**Book IV
Chapter 7**

Designing GUIs with Tk

Changing a Control Such as a Label's Text

In this section, I show you how to use a label control, but the main point of this section is how to modify an existing widget. First, a label control simply holds some text. If you want some text on your window, you can use a label control.

Here's an example of a label control:

```
wm title . "Configure label demo"
label .mylabel -text "This is a label!"
pack .mylabel
```

This code will simply write the words "This is a label!" on a window. Nothing special. But what if you want to modify the existing label? Take a look at this modified version of the preceding program:

```
wm title . "Configure label demo"
label .mylabel -text "This is a label!"
pack .mylabel

button .mybutton -text "Change" -command {
    .mylabel configure -text "New label!"
}
pack .mybutton
```

The first three lines are the same; plus I've added a button. In the button's command section, I want to modify the label's text. How do I do that? When I originally created the label, I specified the text using the `-text` option so it would seem logical that I should somehow modify that option. To modify an option, you use the `configure` command. This is standard on all the widgets, not just the label. Take a look at how I do it:

```
.mylabel configure -text "New label!"
```

I specify the name of the widget, and then I use the `configure` command. And then I put the option and the new value for the option. This explains something earlier in this chapter, in the section, "Adding a Menu Bar to a Window." Here's a line from the program in that section:

```
. configure -menu .mymenus
```

The first item in this line is the name of the main window, a dot. Then comes the `configure` command. Next is the `-menu` option. That means I'm modifying the `-menu` option of the window. What am I doing? I'm specifying a new menu bar. Of course in that program, I didn't already have a menu bar, so really I'm adding a new one. But that doesn't matter; I'm still reconfiguring the existing window. That's what the `configure` command is for.

If you use the `configure` command and you cause a change in the size of a widget, the parent window will resize if necessary. This occurs only if you're using the grid or pack managers. (See Book IV, Chapter 8, for more information.)

Book IV
Chapter 7

Designing GUIs with Tk

Chapter 8: Arranging Controls, Drawing Pictures, and Handling Text

When programming in Tk, the placement of controls on a window becomes a vital issue. Nobody wants to spend hours tweaking pixel locations just to get a decent-looking GUI.

Additionally, the ability to work with graphics is a useful tool for your Tk tool belt, as is the ability to process text. In this chapter, I talk about all three of these topics.

Arranging Controls with Geometry Managers

Programmers either spend hours trying to carefully position the controls on their windows, tweaking them pixel by pixel, or spend big bucks for design tools that let them visually position their controls.

I, for one, love the design tools; for years, I've been an addict of programs such as Delphi and Borland C++ Builder. On the other hand, if I'm building a simple program in Tk, it is much easier to let Tk manage the layout for me, leaving me with time to focus on getting the program right.

Tk provides three different *geometry managers* (which some people — particularly those experienced in Java — call *layout managers*). These geometry managers handle the layout of the controls on your window automatically for you. Here are the three different managers:

+ pack: This manager carefully packs together your controls so they take up the minimal amount of space needed on the form. You have a certain amount of control — but not total control — over where the controls are positioned.

+ grid: This manager lays out the controls in a managed grid fashion. I find this useful if I want my controls to be aligned.

+ place: This manager gives you complete pixel-by-pixel control over the exact location of the controls.

These three approaches are common in layout managers in other languages, too. When I was first exposed to this kind of layout management in the Java language back in the mid-1990s, I was skeptical of the pack and grid approaches, mainly because I didn't trust the managers to do a good job. And so I stuck to the place approach. But I quickly realized something: First, the pack and grid approaches work extremely well; and, second, they make cross-platform development much more reliable. If I specified absolute pixel positions with the place approach, my programs didn't always look the best when run on another operating system. But with the pack and grid approaches, they always looked great, regardless of the operating system.

Nevertheless, I do at times find a need for the place approach; sometimes I do want complete control. So, these days I use all three approaches. In the following three sections, I describe each of them.

Squeezing controls with pack

Of the three geometry managers, pack is probably the most confusing to understand, primarily because it performs a lot of behind-the-scenes "magic" to lay out your widgets. However, after you understand pack, it's actually easy to use.

Before I show you some examples, let me say this: The most important aspect to understanding pack is to recognize that pack positions controls around the four sides of the window.

pack also "squeezes down" the window, minimizing the space between the controls, so getting your head around this four-sided aspect of pack can sometimes be difficult; at times, it may even seem counterintuitive.

The following example turns off this squeezing-down feature so you can see how the controls naturally gather around the sides of the window. Try this out to see what I mean:

```
wm title . "Pack demo 1"
pack propagate . off

button .bt1 -text "One"
button .bt2 -text "Two"
button .bt3 -text "Three"

pack .bt1 .bt2 .bt3 -side left

button .bt4 -text "Four"
pack .bt4 -side bottom

button .bt5 -text "Five"
pack .bt5 -side bottom

button .bt6 -text "Six"
pack .bt6 -side bottom
```

Figure 8-1 shows what this code looks like when it runs. The special line
`pack propagate . off` turns off the squeezing effect for the window
named dot (.), which is the main window. Notice in the figure that the three
buttons labeled One, Two, and Three are all gathered up against the left side.
And also notice that they move inward. First, the button called One was
placed against the left side. Then the button called Two was placed as far left
as it could, which was up against the existing button called One, and so on.
Notice also that I called `pack` with all three of these buttons listed and an
option `-side` set to `left`.

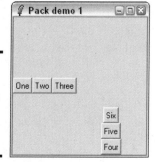

Figure 8-1:
With `pack`,
the controls
gather
around the
edges.

Next, the button called Four was pushed against the bottom side. Then, when
I packed button Five, that button appeared as far towards the bottom as it
could, which is just on top of button Four. Similarly, button Six appeared

above button Five. This time I called pack separately for each of these buttons, using the option -side bottom each time. Calling pack separately three times in a row with the same -side option value has the same effect as calling it once and including all three widgets together.

Now try removing the pack propagate . off line in the preceding program and then run the program again. Your window will look like that shown in Figure 8-2.

Figure 8-2:
With the squeeze effect turned on, the controls are all squished together.

This time, the controls are all squished together, although they have the same relative positions as before. Notice, however, that if you entered this code and got the results in Figure 8-2 and didn't know what was going on, you may be a bit troubled. You typed this:

```
button .bt6 -text "Six"
pack .bt6 -side bottom
```

And even though you set the -side option to bottom, button Six ended up at the *top*. See where the confusion arises? Sometimes, even though pack is doing the layouts correctly, they just *seem* wrong. At first.

If you're using pack and struggling to get the layout right, remember the way it works: Controls are piled up relative to a side, working inward, and the controls are then squished together.

Creating a default vertical column of controls

The pack command can also be used to create a vertical row of controls. By default, pack uses the option -side top. If you leave that off, you can get a vertical row, like so:

```
wm title . "Pack demo 2"
button .bt1 -text "One"
button .bt2 -text "Two"
button .bt3 -text "Three"

pack .bt1 .bt2 .bt3
```

Figure 8-3 shows what this window looks like.

Figure 8-3:
By default,
pack uses
the top side.

Creating a horizontal toolbar

If you know the way pack works, you can make some sophisticated layouts by adding a frame and then putting controls inside the frame. For example, a common look is to have a row of buttons across the top of a window, and a main widget taking up the rest of the window.

To do this kind of look, create a frame and put the frame at the top. Then add buttons to the frame, packing the buttons inside the frame from the frame's left. Finally, add the main control at the bottom. In the following example, I have commented out some lines — I will discuss these shortly. Also, the control I add at the bottom is a canvas control, which you can draw images on.

```
wm title . "Pack demo 3"
pack propagate . off

frame .buttonbar
pack .buttonbar -side top

button .buttonbar.bt1 -text "One"
button .buttonbar.bt2 -text "Two"
button .buttonbar.bt3 -text "Three"

pack .buttonbar.bt1 .buttonbar.bt2 .buttonbar.bt3 \
    -side left -padx 5 -pady 5

#try each of these two instead of the above
#pack .buttonbar.bt1 .buttonbar.bt2 .buttonbar.bt3 \
```

```
#     -anchor e -side top -padx 5 -pady 5
#pack .buttonbar.bt1 .buttonbar.bt2 .buttonbar.bt3 \
#     -anchor w -side top -padx 5 -pady 5


canvas .drawingboard -width 250 -height 250 -bg azure
pack .drawingboard -side bottom
```

When you run this program, you'll see a nice-looking layout like that shown in Figure 8-4. (The canvas is the empty area under the buttons which is blank for now.)

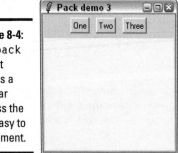

Figure 8-4: The pack layout makes a toolbar across the top easy to implement.

Aligning controls with e and w

To find out even more about the pack command, try replacing this command in the preceding code:

```
pack .buttonbar.bt1 .buttonbar.bt2 .buttonbar.bt3 \
    -side left -padx 5 -pady 5
```

with the first of the commented-out commands:

```
pack .buttonbar.bt1 .buttonbar.bt2 .buttonbar.bt3 \
    -anchor e -side top -padx 5 -pady 5
```

This stacks the buttons instead of arranging them from left to right. But notice how the buttons are aligned; their right sides all line up. That's because I included the -anchor e option. The e stands for *East*, which is the right side. Now instead try the next commented-out line:

```
pack .buttonbar.bt1 .buttonbar.bt2 .buttonbar.bt3 \
    -anchor w -side top -padx 5 -pady 5
```

This is the same as the previous line, except I replaced w with w, which stands for *West*. This time the buttons are still stacked, but their left sides are all lined up. The align option can be useful if you want various alignment features such as this.

Arranging controls with grid

The grid command is easier to understand than the pack command. When you lay out controls with the grid command, you must imagine a large grid. You choose where inside the grid you want the commands to be placed. However, the grid command squeezes the controls together so your grid won't be uniform with each row the same height and each column the same width. Here's an example of grid:

```
wm title . "Grid demo"

button .bt1 -text "One"
button .bt2 -text "Two"
button .bt3 -text "Three"

grid .bt1 -row 0 -column 0 -padx 5 -pady 5
grid .bt2 -row 0 -column 1 -padx 5 -pady 5
grid .bt3 -row 0 -column 2 -padx 5 -pady 5

canvas .drawingboard -width 250 -height 250 -bg azure

# Try taking out the -columnspan 3 part to
# see what happens...
#grid .drawingboard -row 1 -column 0
grid .drawingboard -row 1 -column 0 -columnspan 3
```

This creates a nicely organized layout, as shown in Figure 8-5.

Notice the format of the grid command in each of the buttons midway through the code: First comes a row number and then a column number. Finally, so that everything isn't squished too tightly, I add some padding between the controls. The -padx option puts space on the right and left (in this case, 5 pixels), and the -pady option puts space on the top and bottom (again, in this case, 5 pixels).

But look at the grid command for drawingboard, and you'll see that it has an option called -columnspan with parameter 3. Because the column is defined as 0 in this case, columnspan tells the control to take up three columns in the grid, columns 0, 1, and 2. Well, the earlier buttons took up their own columns; the first was in column 0, the next was in column 1, and the third was in column 2. Thus, this canvas widget will be aligned underneath all three buttons, as you can see in Figure 8-5.

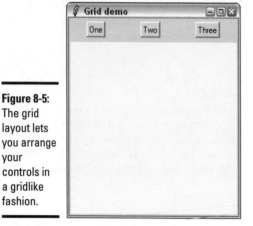

Figure 8-5:
The grid layout lets you arrange your controls in a gridlike fashion.

To really see what this means, try taking out the `-columnspan 3` option, as I suggest in the comments in the code, and then see what the layout looks like. When you run the program, the leftmost button and the canvas take up the first column, with the middle button and rightmost button floating off to the right, which is probably not what you wanted the layout to look like.

Positioning controls with place

The most specific way to position controls on a window is by using the `place` geometry manager. With `place`, you state the absolute position, in pixels, of each control. The problem with `place`, however, is that the main window doesn't get resized to accommodate the controls. That means you also have to choose the size of the main window; otherwise, some of the controls may be floating off the window and will be invisible.

To set the size of the window, you must create a `frame` widget, choose its size, and then position it on the window. From there, I usually use the `pack` command to position the frame. This forces the window to be the size of the frame.

Next, I use `place` to position all my widgets on the frame rather than the window. Here's an example that does this:

```
wm title . "Place demo"

# To size the main window, start with a frame that is packed
frame .mainframe -width 300 -height 350
```

```
pack .mainframe

button .mainframe.bt1 -text "One"
button .mainframe.bt2 -text "Two"
button .mainframe.bt3 -text "Three"

place .mainframe.bt1 -x 10 -y 10
place .mainframe.bt2 -x 50 -y 10
place .mainframe.bt3 -x 100 -y 10

canvas .drawingboard -width 250 -height 250 -bg azure

place .drawingboard -x 10 -y 50
```

You can see the results of this code in Figure 8-6.

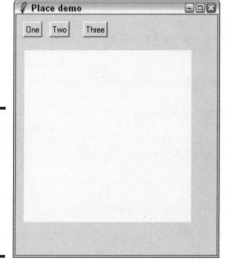

Figure 8-6:
The place
command
lets you
choose a
specific
position
for each
control.

Notice the format of the place command. You specify the widget you want
to place, and then you choose an *x* value (the horizontal position) and a *y*
value (the vertical position) in pixels. That's it. Nice and simple.

Drawing on a Canvas

The canvas widget is an all-purpose widget for performing drawing operations. Using the canvas widget, you can draw rectangles, lines, arcs, curves,
text, and much more.

The following steps outline the basic way to use a `canvas`:

1. **Create the** `canvas` **widget and give it a name like any other widget.**

2. **Position the** `canvas` **widget on your window.**

3. **Call your** `canvas` **widget's set of commands.** The general format is the name of your `canvas` followed by the word *create* followed by a command such as `rectangle` or `arc`.

In the following sections, I show you how to do all this. For starters, however, I show how you can specify colors in your drawings.

Colors

The Tk system supports a huge variety of colors, each with a unique name. Examples are `azure2`, `blueviolet`, `DarkOrchid4`, `LemonChiffon`, `purple`, `wheat4`, `firebrick1`, `DarkSeaGreen1`, and `chocolate`. I'm not making this up. If you want to see a list of all the colors, visit `www.tcl.tk/man/tcl8.4/TkCmd/colors.htm`. There you'll find hundreds of colors (and hundreds of unique names).

Here's an example that demonstrates several of these colors by drawing a colored bar of each. I won't bother with a screenshot, because this book is in black and white, but try out this example to see the color output. And feel free to try adding some more colors to the `colorlist` variable in this code:

```
canvas .mycanvas -width 300 -height 300
pack .mycanvas

set top 0
set colorlist {azure2 blueviolet DarkOrchid4 \
    LemonChiffon purple wheat4 \
    firebrick1 DarkSeaGreen1 chocolate}
foreach mycolor $colorlist {
    set bottom [expr $top + \
        [expr 300 / [llength $colorlist]]]
    .mycanvas create rectangle 0 $top 300 $bottom \
        -fill $mycolor
    set top $bottom
}
```

Arcs

Creating arcs is easy in Tk. The key is in understanding that an arc is a portion of a circle, where you specify two angles: where on the circle to begin the arc, and a length of the arc in degrees. Additionally, you have three different arc styles to choose from: a filled-in pie slice, a single arc of a circle (just a curve, nothing filled in), and a filled-in chord, which is sort of a "pie crust" part. Here's an example that demonstrates these styles:

```
canvas .mycanvas -width 600 -height 300
pack .mycanvas

.mycanvas create arc 10 10 290 290 -fill blue
.mycanvas create arc 10 10 290 290 -start 190 \
    -extent 30 -fill green

.mycanvas create arc 310 10 590 290 -fill blue \
    -style chord
.mycanvas create arc 310 10 590 290 -start 190 \
    -extent 30 -fill green -style arc
```

This code creates the window shown in Figure 8-7.

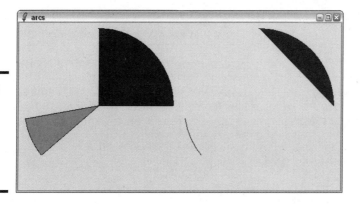

Figure 8-7:
The `arc` command allows for three different styles.

To see how arcs are positioned, look carefully at the first two `arc` commands. Each occupies the same circle that fits inside the square 10, 10 through 290, 290. The difference, however, is in the angles. In the first `arc` example, I don't specify any angles, so by default, I get an angle from 0 degrees to 90 degrees (which ranges from due East to due North on the circle). That's in the upper-right quadrant. In the next `arc` command, I do specify an angle, from 190 degrees extending a distance of 30 degrees. That's in the lower-left quadrant. (190 degrees is slightly more than 180; 180 would be due West.) Notice that the two arcs are aligned at their centers.

That can be confusing: Each of the two `arc` commands so far takes up a position 10,10 through 290,290, and yet the two commands don't totally fill that rectangular area. Instead, they fill only the quadrant where they belong.

The default style is a pie shape, and you can specify the color of the pie using the -fill option. To show the other two styles, I draw two more arcs in the right side of the window. The first is a chord, which is like the pie crust of a pie shape: It's surrounded by the arc on the circle and a line connecting the two points (in this case, the two points are the default points: 0 degrees and 90 degrees). The second is an arc, which is just a curve along the perimeter of the imaginary circle.

Lines and curves

Here's a cool thing: With the canvas widget, you can draw a sequence of lines and then, by setting a single option, you can generate a curve that fits the lines you drew. The line command is easy; you just specify a sequence of numbers representing points as I do in the following code:

```
canvas .mycanvas -width 300 -height 350
pack .mycanvas

.mycanvas create line \
    10 10 75 100 125 50 250 200 40 200 \
    -smooth off -width 1 -fill black -width 10 \
    -joinstyle round

.mycanvas create line \
    10 40 75 130 125 80 250 230 40 230 \
    -smooth off -width 1 -fill black -width 10 \
    -joinstyle miter -cap round

.mycanvas create line \
    10 70 75 160 125 110 250 260 40 260 \
    -smooth off -width 1 -fill black -width 10 \
    -joinstyle bevel -arrow last
```

In the first line command, I have a bunch of line segments. The first starts at point 10,10 and goes to point 75,100. The next starts at that point — 75,100 — and goes to 125,50. The next starts there at 125,50 and goes to 250,200. And the final one starts there at 250,200 and goes to 40,200. Easy. The window for this code is shown in Figure 8-8.

With the line command, you also have several options. You can specify the width of the line; in the preceding code, all my lines are really fat, measuring in at 10 pixels. You can also specify a color (mine are all black, but you can use other colors like bisque3, whatever that is, or OliveDrab2).

You can also specify a cap style for the end of each line. Your choices are bevel, miter, and round. You can try out these different types and see what they look like.

Figure 8-8:
Lines can take on different styles.

You can also specify an arrow shape at the end of your line. I do this in the third `line` command, shown in Figure 8-8. In this case, I put an arrow at the end of the line sequence. You can also put one at the beginning by using `-arrow first`. Or if you want one on both ends, use `-arrow both`.

And you can specify a joint style connecting each line. This is subtle, but if you look at each of the three line sequences in the current example (and in Figure 8-8), you'll see I used a slightly different join style for each. This style is the `-joinstyle` option, and the choices are `bevel`, `miter`, and `round`.

Notice also that I added the option `-smooth off` for each line. This is the default, so I was just being clear (although redundant) by using this option. In the next example, however, I turn on this option. Almost like magic, I get a curve that carefully fits the endpoints of the line sequence. Just to show how this curve fits, I also draw the same line sequence with the curve option off so you can compare the two. Here's the example code:

```
canvas .mycanvas -width 600 -height 300
pack .mycanvas

.mycanvas create line \
    10 10 75 100 125 50 250 200 0 200 \
    -smooth off -width 1 -fill black
.mycanvas create line \
    10 10 75 100 125 50 250 200 0 200 \
    -smooth on -width 5 -fill red -capstyle round
```

```
.mycanvas create line \
    310 10 375 100 425 50 550 200 300 200 \
    -smooth off -width 1 -fill black
.mycanvas create line \
    310 10 375 100 425 50 550 200 300 200 \
    -smooth on -width 5 -fill red -capstyle round \
    -splinesteps 3
```

The window for this code is shown in Figure 8-9. In this code and in the figure, I also had some fun with the -splinestep option. This option controls how smooth the line is. In my code, I used a value of 3. If you look closely at the right half of Figure 8-9, you can see that the line command used three smaller segments (shown in bold) in place of each original segment (shown as narrow). (The bottom line really does have three segments; two of the three are in the same direction, appearing as one long segment.) The higher the number you specify in the -splinesteps option, the more segments you'll get.

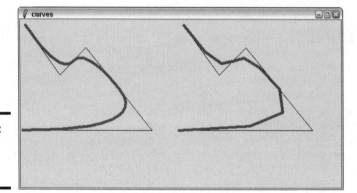

Figure 8-9:
Lines can
also be
curved.

Polygons

A polygon is just like a line sequence, except the polygon adds a final line connecting the endpoint and the start point, closing up the polygon. The canvas widget then fills the polygon with your color of choice. Here's an example:

```
canvas .mycanvas -width 600 -height 300
pack .mycanvas

.mycanvas create polygon 10 10 210 50 130 290 -fill blue
.mycanvas create polygon 300 50 510 290 550 60 350 280 \
    -fill red
```

This example creates two polygons. The first is a simple triangle, and the second is a bit more complex, as shown in Figure 8-10.

Figure 8-10:
Polygons
are line
sequences
that are
closed and
filled.

The basic format of the `polygon` statement is simple: Specify your sequence of points and then specify a color with the `-fill` option. Here's a fun example you can try out that creates a bunch of random polygons:

```
canvas .mycanvas -width 300 -height 300 -bg lightgray
pack .mycanvas

set colorlist {red green blue \
    orange purple yellow4 \
    darkcyan DodgerBlue2 chocolate}

for {set x 0} {$x < 5} {incr x} {
    set pointcount [expr 2 * (int(rand() * 5) + 1)]
    set mylist {}
    for {set y 0} {$y < $pointcount} {incr y} {
        set newpoint [expr int(rand() * 300)]
        set mylist [concat $mylist $newpoint]
    }
    set colorindex [expr int(rand() * 8)]
    set color [lindex $colorlist $colorindex]
    .mycanvas create polygon $mylist -fill $color
}
```

Rectangles and text

To wrap up this section on the canvas, I thought I'd show you how to draw rectangles and text on a canvas. These are both easy. For a rectangle, you specify the coordinates of the upper-left corner and lower-right corner of the rectangle.

**Book IV
Chapter 8**

Arranging Controls,
Drawing Pictures,
and Handling Text

Text is easy, too: You specify the text you want to display and a position. You can choose a font and size for the text, as well as a fill color in which the text is drawn. The following example code shows how to add both a rectangle and some text to the canvas:

```
canvas .mycanvas -width 600 -height 300
pack .mycanvas

.mycanvas create rectangle \
    10 10 290 290 -fill cyan

.mycanvas create text \
    100 100 -text "Hi there" \
    -font {Helvetica 32 italic} -fill brown

.mycanvas create text \
    400 75 -text "Tcl is great!" \
    -font {"Comic Sans MS" 28} -fill darkgreen
```

In this example, I use a Helvetica font of point size 32, and a Comic Sans MS font of point size 28. The results of this program are shown in Figure 8-11.

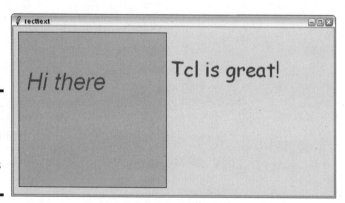

Figure 8-11: Rectangles and text are easy with the canvas widget.

Be careful with the font you choose in the `text` command. In the current example, I specified a font called Comic Sans MS. This is a Microsoft font available on Windows. Lately I've seen it on other operating systems, too, such as the Mac; however, you can't be sure the font will be available on all systems. Fortunately, however, if the font isn't present, Tk will assign a default system font as a substitute.

Processing Text with a Text Widget

The text widget is one of the more sophisticated widgets in Tk. The latest version includes a whole slew of features, such as the ability to specify different font sizes and shapes at different locations within the text widget, as well as the ability to embed other widgets within the text control.

In the following sections, I show you several great ways to work with the text widget.

Reading and writing with a text widget

A text control isn't particularly useful unless your program can read the text widget's contents and, possibly, modify the text in the widget. The following example shows you how to do this:

```
frame .myframe
pack .myframe
button .myframe.mybutton -text "Read sel" -command {
    tk_messageBox -icon info -message \
      [selection get]
}
pack .myframe.mybutton -side left
button .myframe.mybutton2 -text "Read all" -command {
    tk_messageBox -icon info -message \
      [.mytext get 1.0 end]
}
pack .myframe.mybutton2 -side left
button .myframe.mybutton3 -text "Write start" -command {
    # Insert text at the 1st line (1), first column (0)
    .mytext insert 1.0 "**Inserted text**"
}
pack .myframe.mybutton3 -side left
button .myframe.mybutton4 -text "Write" -command {
    # Insert text at the current position
    .mytext insert insert "**Current position**"
}
pack .myframe.mybutton4 -side left

# With the text widget, width and height
# are in terms of characters not pixels.
text .mytext -width 40 -height 15
pack .mytext
```

In this example, I have three buttons and a `text` widget. The first button reads the contents of the widget and displays the contents in a message box. You can see that to access the `text` widget's contents, I use the `get` command. But notice what follows the `get` command in the statement: The first term is `1.0`, and the next is `end`. The `1.0` is a position in the text. The `1` refers to the 1st line, and the `0` refers to position 0 within that line. In other words, 1.0 is the first character in the `text` control. (Yes, lines are numbered starting with 1, although positions within a line are numbered starting with 0.) Thus, `2.5`, for example, would refer to the *6th* character on the *2nd* line. Following the 1.0 is the word `end`, which simply refers to the end of the text. Thus, `[.mytext get 1.0 end]` retrieves the text from the first line, first character through the end of the text — in other words, the entire text in the widget.

The next two buttons insert text into the widget. The first of these buttons inserts text at the beginning of the widget:

```
.mytext insert 1.0 "**Inserted text**"
```

Again, there's that `1.0`. The next button inserts text at the current insertion point of the text:

```
.mytext insert insert "**Current position**"
```

Yes, that's the word `insert` twice. The first `insert` is the command; the second refers to the current insertion point.

At the end of the code is where I actually create the `text` widget. All I need to say here is that the size of the widget doesn't refer to pixels; instead, the size refers to point size. This `text` widget is 15 lines tall (the height) and holds approximately 40 characters in width.

Remember, this 40 won't be exact because you're dealing with proportionally spaced fonts. Of course, you're free to specify a fixed-width font if you want, like so:

```
text .mytext -width 40 -height 15 -font {"Courier New" 14}
pack .mytext
```

Then you'll get an exact number of characters in the control.

Choosing text with tags

A *tag* is a two-fold feature in a `text` widget that refers to a particular font style (color, font name, size, and so on), and then to various locations within the `text` widget's text. At these locations, the text is displayed in the tag's font style. This lets you have different font styles within a single `text` widget. And the cool thing is that as you type text into the control, the text maintains the same formatting.

To create a tag, first you specify the information about the tag. You can see in the following code that I do this through the `tag configure` command. First, you provide a name for the style (in this case, I chose the name `highlight`; these style names don't start with a dot as widget names do). Next you specify various information for the style. Then you choose text that has the particular style. For the style in this example, I want a red font that's underlined:

```
text .mytext -width 30 -height 15
pack .mytext

.mytext insert 1.0 "Hello there, everybody"

.mytext tag configure highlight -foreground red -underline 1
.mytext tag add highlight 1.0 1.5
.mytext tag add highlight 1.13 1.18
```

The final two lines choose the text to hold the particular style. In each, I specify the style I want by name (in this case, `highlight`). Next I specify two points in the text, a starting point (`1.0` for the first example, and `1.13` for the second example) and an ending point (`1.5` for the first example, and `1.18` for the second example). However, remember that the ending point itself doesn't take on the style. Thus, the characters at `1.5` and `1.18` do not get the style specified in the `highlight` tag.

When you run this program, you see the window shown in Figure 8-12.

Figure 8-12:
You can choose styles for different portions of the text.

In the following example, you create two styles and a button; when you click the button, the text changes to those styles:

```
button .mybutton -text "Highlight" -command {
    .mytext tag add big 1.0 1.5
    .mytext tag add fun 1.6 1.9
}
text .mytext -width 30 -height 15
.mytext insert 1.0 "Hello there, everybody"
.mytext tag configure big -foreground red \
    -underline 1 -font {Helvetica 18}
.mytext tag configure fun -foreground blue \
    -underline 1 -background red
pack .mybutton .mytext
```

Embedding widgets

One really cool feature with the text control is that you can embed other widgets right inside the text — and those widgets will move when the text moves. The text and the widget will move to accommodate any new text you add before it.

Embedding a widget is easy; you just create the widget as you normally would and then call the text widget's window create command, specifying a location and the name of the widget to embed. In the following example, I use the word insert for the location; this means "insert at the current insertion point":

```
text .mytext -width 30 -height 15
pack .mytext

.mytext insert 0.1 "Hello "

button .mytext.bt1 -bitmap questhead -command {exit}
.mytext window create insert -window .mytext.bt1

.mytext insert end " there"
```

When you run this example, a button appears right inside the text. Try typing some text on either side of the button, and you'll see how the button can move.

When you run this program, you'll see the window shown in Figure 8-13.

Figure 8-13:
You can
embed
widgets
right inside
a text
control.

Searching

An important feature of any good text control is searching. The following
example shows you how easy it is to search for text. When you run this
example, type a string inside the entry box (which is just a scaled-down
single-line text box) and click the Find button, and you'll see the next
instance of the found text highlighted. Very easy indeed. (You don't have to
type in the whole *Gettysburg Address* as I do here; you can enter whatever
you want in the text box.)

```
wm title . "Text Search"

text .textbox -width 40 -height 15 -font {Helvetica 12} \
    -wrap word
pack .textbox -side bottom
entry .word -textvariable whattofind
pack .word -side left
button .findbtn -text "Find" -command "FindText"
pack .findbtn -side left

proc FindText {} {
    global whattofind
    set res [.textbox search -count foundsize \
        $whattofind insert]
    if {$res != ""} {
        .textbox tag delete sel 0.0 end
        # See the text for an explanation of
        # the following strange lines!
        .textbox mark set insert "$res + $foundsize chars"
        .textbox tag add sel $res "$res + $foundsize chars"
        focus .textbox
    }
}

.textbox insert 1.0 \
```

**Book IV
Chapter 8**

**Arranging Controls,
Drawing Pictures,
and Handling Text**

```
{Four score and seven years ago our fathers brought \
forth on this continent a new nation, conceived in \
liberty and dedicated to the proposition that all men \
are created equal. Now we are engaged in a \
great civil war, testing whether that nation or any \
nation so conceived and so dedicated can long endure. \
We are met on a great battlefield of that war. We have \
come to dedicate a portion of that field as a final \
resting place for those who here gave their lives that \
that nation might live. It is altogether fitting and \
proper that we should do this. But in a larger sense, \
we cannot dedicate, we cannot consecrate, we cannot \
hallow this ground. The brave men, living and dead who \
struggled here have consecrated it far above our poor \
power to add or detract. The world will little note nor \
long remember what we say here, but it can never forget \
what they did here. It is for us the living rather to be \
dedicated here to the unfinished work which they who \
fought here have thus far so nobly advanced. It is rather \
for us to be here dedicated to the great task remaining \
before us--that from these honored dead we take increased \
devotion to that cause for which they gave the last full \
measure of devotion--that we here highly resolve that \
these dead shall not have died in vain, that this nation \
under God shall have a new birth of freedom, and that \
government of the people, by the people, for the people \
shall not perish from the earth.}
```

The key to all this is in the `FindText` procedure, which runs in response to the button. This procedure calls `.textbox search`, which performs the search. This command returns the position of the search, which I store in the `res` variable; the command starts looking at the current insertion location. Further, in this command you can optionally include the name of a variable that will receive the length of the found text; I chose to call this variable `foundsize`.

After the search, I move the insertion point to the start of the found text. To do so, I use the following line:

```
.textbox mark set insert "$res + $foundsize chars"
```

This line and the next have a strange syntax in them, which I describe shortly. The next line is where I select the text. To select text, simply use the tag called `sel`. You don't need to create this tag; it exists automatically, unlike other tags. But notice how I highlight the text:

```
.textbox tag add sel $res "$res + $foundsize chars"
```

Here I make use of a special syntax that gives you the end of the located text. The search command returned the found position, and I stored that in the res variable. For the end position, I use this line:

```
"$res + $foundsize chars"
```

This is a special way of specifying text later in the text widget. Don't worry too much about the mechanics here, because it only makes a little bit of sense; the chars word is a built-in keyword that you must use here. The key here is that $res is the start position and $foundsize is the length of the selection.

And finally, I call the focus command, which is a special command that moves the focus to the requested widget, in this case the text box. (Otherwise focus stays on the button that you clicked.)

Loading and saving a file

In this final section of this chapter, I want to show you how to load a file into a text widget and save the contents of a text widget to a file. Here's one way:

```
proc LoadFile {atextbox filename} {
    if {[file exists $filename]} {
        set myfile [open $filename "r"]
        while {![eof $myfile]} {
            set buf [read $myfile 10000]
            $atextbox insert end $buf
        }
        close $myfile
    } else {
        tk_messageBox -icon info -message \
            "Sorry, I couldn't find the file."
    }
}

proc SaveFile {atextbox filename} {
    set myfile [open $filename "w"]
    puts -nonewline $myfile [$atextbox get 1.0 end]
    close $myfile
}

text .textbox -width 40 -height 15
pack .textbox
LoadFile .textbox "address.txt"
SaveFile .textbox "address2.txt"
```

Book IV
Chapter 8

Arranging Controls, Drawing Pictures, and Handling Text

This loads a file called address.txt (containing our favorite, *The Gettysburg Address*) that I created earlier, and then resaves text to a new file called address2.txt. The LoadFile procedure that I have included here checks if the file exists, and if so, opens the file and begins reading in it. I don't read the file in line by line, however, using the gets command. That's because I want to copy the exact contents and paste it byte-for-byte into the text widget. (When I tried this with the gets command, the newlines got lost.) So instead I use the read command, which reads text into a buffer. I keep reading more and more text, adding it to the end of the text widget, until I reach the end of the file.

The save is even easier. In my SaveFile procedure, I open a file, grab the whole text from the widget, and write it all out in one swoop using the puts command. (Notice that I included an option in puts called nonewline, which makes sure not to add an extra newline at the end that wasn't already there.) Then I close the file. Easy!

Chapter 9: Displaying Standard Dialog Boxes in Tk

In This Chapter

✓ **Getting input from a message box**

✓ **Selecting a directory**

✓ **Choosing a file to open**

✓ **Picking a filename to save**

✓ **Grabbing a color**

✓ **Creating a generic dialog box**

Some time back, designers of the various operating systems figured out that certain tasks required certain dialog boxes that came up again and again. And rather than force programmers to reinvent the wheel every time they wanted to create these dialog boxes, the designers decided to give them some standard dialog boxes instead.

You're probably very familiar with the standard dialog boxes on your operating system of choice. These include, among others, a dialog box for File Open, and a dialog box for File Save. Tk lets you access these standard dialog boxes. In addition, Tk has a special generic dialog box that you can use for special situations where you want the user to select from a set of buttons. In the following sections, I give you the whole scoop and nothing but the scoop on these dialog boxes.

Getting Input from a Message Box

The simplest type of stock dialog box is the message box. Here's a sample program that you can try out:

```
wm title . "Message box demo"
tk_messageBox -icon info -message \
    "Greetings from a message box!"

set res [tk_messageBox -icon warning -message \
    "Now go away, please." -type yesno]
```

```
if {$res == "no"} {
    tk_messageBox -icon info -message \
        "Okay, I guess you can stay. We're having a party."
}
```

This program opens a message box using the `tk_messageBox` function. The message box that opens has a message (`Greetings from a message box!`) and an OK button. After the user clicks OK, the program opens a second message box, but this one requires the user to click either Yes or No. The user makes a choice, and the program saves the result in the `res` variable.

If the user clicks the No button (that is, if `res` equals `"No"`), the program opens up another dialog box (just for fun). Figure 9-1 shows the sequence of message boxes that I just described.

Figure 9-1:
The `tk_`
`message`
`Box`
function
opens up a
message
box.

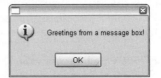

The main differences in the message boxes in the preceding program are in the choice of buttons and the choice of an icon. I selected the buttons using the `-type` option, and I selected the icon using the `-icon` option. Here are the choices for the `-type` option:

✦ `abortretryignore`: Please don't use this one. It's outdated, and users cringe when they see it. (At least *this* user does.)

✦ `ok`: This is the default, so if you leave off the `-type` option, you'll just get an OK button.

✦ `okcancel`: This gives you an OK and a Cancel button.

✦ `retrycancel`: If you want your program to try an action again and again at the user's request, you can use this type.

✦ `yesno`: Hopefully your users will be able to make up their minds between yes and no.

✦ `yesnocancel`: But, if they can't choose between yes and no, you can also include a Cancel button. Yes no?

Displaying the standard bitmaps

Tk includes a few standard bitmap icons you can use in the `tk_messageBox` call and the `tk_dialog` call. Here are some examples you can try out to see what they look like:

```
tk_messageBox -message "error" -icon
        error
tk_messageBox -message "info" -icon info
tk_messageBox -message "question" -icon
        question
tk_messageBox -message "warning" -icon
        warning

tk_dialog .mydialog "Important" "error"
        error 0 "OK"
tk_dialog .mydialog "Important" "info"
        info 0 "OK"
```

```
tk_dialog .mydialog "Important"
        "question" question 0 "OK"
tk_dialog .mydialog "Important" "warning"
        warning 0 "OK"
```

If you try these out on a Windows computer, you'll see that the `tk_messageBox` call ends up using the built-in bitmaps you're used to seeing in message boxes, while the `tk_dialog` calls use bitmaps unique to Tk. (Apparently, `tk_messageBox` makes use of the built-in message box capabilities of Windows, which use built-in Windows bitmaps, thereby preventing Tk from choosing its own images.)

Selecting a Directory

Many programs allow the user to pick a directory. For example, you may be storing several configuration files for your program, and you want the user to specify where to store the files. In this case, the user doesn't pick a file-name; instead, the user simply chooses a directory. Tk includes a directory-choosing dialog box, shown in Figure 9-2.

Figure 9-2: The directory chooser lets the user, well, choose a directory.

Here's the code that I used to put up the dialog box for Figure 9-2:

```
wm title . "Directory chooser demo"

label .mylabel -text .
pack .mylabel -side top

button .mybtn -text "Directory..." -command {
    set result [tk_chooseDirectory -mustexist on -initialdir
        "/"]
    if {$result != ""} {
        .mylabel configure -text $result
    }
}
pack .mybtn -side top
```

This program opens a window with a button on it. When the user clicks the button, the directory chooser opens. Notice how I opened the directory chooser inside the button's command code: I called tk_chooseDirectory, passing a few options.

Set the -mustexist option to on to make sure that the directory the user selects actually exists. (This option is commonly set; you don't want the user wasting time typing in a nonexistent directory.) The -initialdir option lets you choose a starting point. (Just a tip: If you're on a Windows system, please don't start the directory out in the Windows directory. Really now, how often do end users need to access that directory? And while I'm on that topic, please be careful not to hardcode Windows-specific directories into a Tk program that may be run on a Linux system.)

The tk_chooseDirectory function returns a string containing the directory that the user chose. In my example, I save that string in the result variable. (If the user clicks Cancel, tk_chooseDirectory will return an empty string.) Then, just to prove I got the directory name, I make sure it's not an empty string, and then set the label's text to the directory name.

Choosing a File to Open

The File Open dialog box is one of the most common dialog boxes that a user sees (next to, possibly, one that begins with, "This program has performed an illegal operation...") . The following code demonstrates how to display the File Open dialog box:

```
wm title . "Open file dialog demo"

label .mylabel -text .
pack .mylabel -side top

set filetypes {
    {"some files" {"*.txt" "*.abc"} }
    {"other files" {"*.def" "*.123"} }
}

button .mybtn -text "File..." -command {
    set result [tk_getOpenFile \
        -filetypes $filetypes \
        -defaultextension ".txt" -initialdir "/"]
    if {$result != ""} {
        .mylabel configure -text $result
    }
}
pack .mybtn -side top
```

This code creates a button; when the user clicks the button, the File Open dialog box appears. To do this, I call getOpenFile. I choose an initial directory for the dialog box using the -initialdir option. Look at the list called filetypes after the first pack command. That's a list of lists; notice how I have a left brace, {, denoting the start of a list, followed by another left brace, {, denoting another list inside the first list. Each sublist contains a string and yet another list containing the file extensions available for that type. These items will show up in the drop-down list box called "Files of Type." Then, to use this list in the tk_getOpenFile function, I pass the list to the -filetypes option. And to get the ball rolling, I pick the default file type that appears in the list, in this case .txt.

Remember, this dialog box doesn't actually *open* a file. Instead, it simply lets the user choose a file to open, and it returns the name of the file. Your program must then take it upon itself to open the file using the usual open command; then it can process the file accordingly.

Picking a Filename to Save

The File Save dialog box ranks as #3 in the Most Important Dialog Boxes list. Or maybe #2. I'm not sure. Either way, here's an example of how to show this ubiquitous dialog box:

```
wm title . "Save file dialog demo"

label .mylabel -text .
pack .mylabel -side top

set filetypes {
    {"some files" {"*.txt" "*.abc"} }
    {"other files" {"*.def" "*.123"} }
}

button .mybtn -text "File..." -command {
    set result [tk_getSaveFile \
        -filetypes $filetypes \
        -defaultextension ".txt" -initialdir "/"]
    if {$result != ""} {
        .mylabel configure -text $result
    }
}
pack .mybtn -side top
```

This dialog box works the same way as the Open File dialog box; if you haven't done so already, take a look at the previous section, "Choosing a File to Open," to see how the different options work.

The tk_getSaveFile command doesn't actually save a file; it simply lets the user pick a filename. It's up to your program to then save the file. You can save a file using the open command and the puts command.

Grabbing a Color

A color chooser is a handy dialog box. Those of us who used the early Macintosh computers remember how this dialog box was by far the coolest dialog box on the Mac, because it showed a gazillion colors at once on the old color screens. That dialog box alone probably sold 10,000 Macintosh computers. And now other operating systems feature a similar dialog box as well. Not to be left behind, the designers of Tk have given you access to this dialog box. Here's an example:

```
wm title . "Color box demo"

canvas .mycanvas -width 300 -height 300
pack .mycanvas -side bottom

label .mylabel -text Color
pack .mylabel -side top
```

```
button .mybtn -text "Set color..." -command {
    set result [tk_chooseColor]
    if {$result != ""} {
        tk_messageBox -icon info -message $result
        .mycanvas create rectangle 10 10 280 280 -fill
            $result
        .mylabel configure -text $result
    }
}
pack .mybtn -side top
```

This program is simple; it creates a button, and when the user clicks the button, the color chooser opens up. When the user clicks OK, the `tk_chooseColor` function returns the color, which I save in the `result` variable. Then I show the `result` value in a message box, draw a rectangle in that color, and set a label's text to show the color value.

Making a Lifesaving Decision (Or Just Getting Information)

In this final section of this chapter, I show you how you can create a custom dialog box. You're kind of limited on your options, however; if you want to create a sophisticated window with lots of controls, see Book IV, Chapter 7.

With the `tk_dialog` function, you create a window where you specify a title bar, a text message, and several buttons with your choice of text. The user chooses one of the buttons, and the `tk_dialog` function returns a number representing the button's index. Here's an example:

```
wm title . "Modal dialog demo"

label .mylabel -text 1
pack .mylabel -side top

button .mybtn -text "Important..." -command {
    set result [
        tk_dialog .mydialog "Important" \
            "The computer has died. What to do?" \
            warning \
            2 \
            "Sleep" "Read" "Quit" "Eat" "Celebrate"
    ]
    if {$result != ""} {
        .mylabel configure -text $result
```

```
        }
}
pack .mybtn -side top
```

Here's how it works:

1. The button's command calls the `tk_dialog` function, passing first a name for the dialog box (why, I don't know, but it's required, even though you don't use it again).

2. Next you pass a string that will appear in the title bar of the dialog box.

3. Then you pass the name of an icon bitmap. (Feel free to use one of the pre packaged bitmaps. See the sidebar "Displaying the standard bitmaps" in this chapter for more information on the pre packaged bitmaps.)

4. Next you add a number that's the default value returned by the dialog box in case the user closes the dialog box without choosing one of the buttons.

5. And finally, you include all the strings you want to display on the different buttons. Just list them one after the other.

You can see how this all looks in Figure 9-3.

Figure 9-3:
The generic
dialog box
is rather
generic.

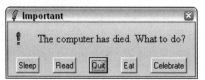

Chapter 10: Ten Useful Tcl/Tk Tools

In This Chapter

✔ Komodo

✔ Visual Tcl

✔ VisualGIPSY

✔ SpecTcl

✔ tkBuilder

✔ FastBase MySQL + Tcl Interface

✔ mysqltcl

✔ [incr Widgets]

✔ Tcl Dev Kit (with plug-in for Web browsers)

✔ Tcl Developer Xchange

The great thing about Tcl and Tk is that because they're both free, you can also find a lot of great tools for them that are also free. If you're willing to spend some money, though, you can find even more great tools. In this chapter, I talk about several tools that can help your Tcl/Tk development, some free, some not.

Tk GUI Designers

Because Tk is so popular, many people have created visual designers to help you graphically lay out the controls on your windows. In this section, I list five such designers. The first of these is actually an entire development tool created by ActiveState.

The remaining four are all free and very similar in nature: Each includes a complete IDE for typing in your Tcl code and also provides a way to lay out widgets visually, generating Tcl code for you. Therefore, for each of these four I simply point you to the appropriate Web site where you can download the tools and try them out yourself and figure out which one you like best.

Komodo

(Not free.) This is a powerful tool that lets you develop and debug your programs. It includes a really nice text editor that colors your code based on the syntax. (This is called *syntax highlighting*.) It also includes a project window allowing you to quickly navigate between the files in your application. Among its remaining features is a complete debugger, allowing you to trace through your code and track down problems. You can purchase this from ActiveState at `www.activestate.com/Products/Komodo/`.

Visual Tcl

Free! This is an incredibly powerful tool that makes laying out controls and adding code to the controls incredibly easy. It features a toolbar filled with common widgets such as frames, buttons, and so on. Additionally, it includes an attribute editor that allows you to customize each control in a window; with it you can set each control's properties, such as width, height, and color. Find this at `vtcl.sourceforge.net/`.

VisualGIPSY

Free! This tool lets you easily drop controls on a form and then set the control's properties using an Object Inspector window. Additionally, among many other features, it includes a tree view that lets you see how your controls are arranged hierarchically. (Remember, a frame can hold other controls, including other frames that can themselves hold controls.) Find this at `www.prs.de/int/products/vg/index.html`.

SpecTcl

Free! This is a nice program that includes some very fancy icons (check out the Web page to see what I'm talking about). It lets you create a new window and then drag and drop widgets on the window, generating valid Tcl/Tck code. Find this at `spectcl.sourceforge.net/`.

tkBuilder

Free! I've used this one a great deal for a previous job I had. With this tool you can create a window, and easily drag and drop controls onto the window. The program then generates valid Tcl/Tk code for you automatically. You can find it at `sawpit.iwarp.com/`.

Developer Tools

Here are some general developer tools that can help you with your Tcl programming. Note that in the previous section, "Tk GUI Designers," I mentioned Komodo from ActiveState. That tool could be in this category as well.

FastBase MySQL + Tcl Interface

Free! This is a tool that provides an interface to MySQL. You can find it at `www.fastbase.co.nz/fbsql/index.html`.

mysqltcl

Free! This is another tool that provides an interface to MySQL. This is also the one that is mentioned in the official MySQL docs, although the other one I mention here (FastBase) is at least as good as this one. You can find it at `www.xdobry.de/mysqltcl/`.

[incr Widgets]

Free! This is a huge collection of additional Tk widgets. I encourage you to take a look at it. The library ships with many Tcl installations, including the one by ActiveState. Additionally, you can locate it online at `www.tcltk.com/iwidgets/`.

Tcl Dev Kit (with plug-in for Web browsers)

(Not free) ActiveState is one of the frontrunners in the Tcl world. In addition to the Komodo tool, it offers a nice Tcl development tool called Tcl Dev Kit, which includes a feature that lets you package up your Tcl programs into standalone executable binaries; a browser plug-in that lets you run Tcl inside your browser; and more. Check it out at `www.activestate.com/Products/Tcl_Dev_Kit/`.

Tcl Developer Xchange

Finally, this isn't a tool, but rather a site for Tcl tools. It's part of the official Tcl site. Here you can find a huge repository filled with various tools for Tcl, including applications written in Tcl, additional libraries, GUI designers, and so on. Check it out at `www.tcl.tk/software/`.

Book V

PHP Web Pages for Dynamic Content

"Before I go on to explain more advanced procedures like the 'Zap-Rowdy-Students-who-Don't-Pay-Attention' function, we'll begin with some basics."

Contents at a Glance

Chapter 1: What You Can Do with PHP

In This Chapter

✓ Examining the advantages and drawbacks of PHP

✓ Discovering PHP function libraries

✓ Taking a look at applications of PHP

In this chapter, I talk about some of the possible applications of PHP. When considering the potential of PHP — as well as when you should use it — keep in mind that PHP is a server-side scripting language. All PHP processing takes place on the side of the Web server, which dishes out Web pages. Unless someone runs a PHP processor on his or her own client computer and manually sends files through it, all PHP processing takes place on the server side.

Using a server-side scripting language can have complications. For example, if you're writing a script that does a lot of processing (like grinding through hundreds of files and millions of calculations), your Web server performance may suffer if thousands of clients are accessing it each day. If that's the case, strongly consider moving the processing to the individual users' machines by using a client-side script or program.

However, by running the program on the server side, you have complete control over the computer that's doing the processing and over the libraries available to it. You don't, for example, have to require users to first download an entire "language runtime" (as you do in Java) and expect them to run it on their computers. Therefore, users with even the most basic machines — such as a 486 running Windows 95 and Internet Explorer 3.0 — can, potentially, still access your site if the pages your Web server sends out after the PHP processing are simple enough. Additionally, you don't have to worry about different versions of PHP floating around. Regardless of what browser and what computer connects to your Web server, your PHP code runs on your Web server, and you control which version of PHP runs on the Web server. This results in what the gurus call *platform independence*.

Introducing PHP Function Libraries

One reason PHP is such a powerful language is that it includes many different *modules* (which are additions to the language that exist as a separate file that PHP loads when it begins), each serving a different purpose. Visit www.php.net/manual/en/funcref.php to view the categories of functions, which are grouped into modules. (For the lowdown on functions, see Book V, Chapter 4.) In the online documentation, these function categories are numbered with Roman numerals. I'm proud to say my brain can easily convert Roman numerals to the more standard Arabic numeral (at least, um, using the help of an online conversion program I found). The PHP function list has 113 categories of functions. (That's CXIII for you Roman readers out there.)

These functions include the following:

✦ Database access functions

✦ String conversion and processing functions

✦ FTP functions for file transfer

✦ Arbitrary-precision mathematical functions

✦ File and database functions

✦ PDF functions for creating PDF files

✦ Graphics functions for creating graphical images

PHP programs can use the PDF and graphics functions to create PDF files or GIF images, for example, and send those files or images to the client computer. With GIF images, this means you can create graphics on the fly by having your program generate the graphic rather than having a graphic file stored on the Web server. For example, you can create a bar graph showing current statistics, such as the results of an online poll. A program that creates a PDF file can customize the PDF with the name of the person who downloaded the file and the time the file was created.

In using these various functions, however, there is a small catch: Some of them require an external piece of software (called a *library*) that must be present on your Web server. For example, although the GIF functions are a standard part of the PHP installation, the PDF generation routines require the presence of PDFLib, which is a commercial library. Check with the online manual to see which libraries must be present, if any, to run the functions in any particular category.

If you want to explore the PDF features of PHP, you can visit www.php.net/
manual/en/ref.pdf.php. This page includes several examples as well as a
link to the page describing the PDFLib library.

In this book, I cover only the function categories that don't require a special
library. (The exception is in Book VI, where I discuss PHP in conjunction
with MySQL. To use MySQL functions in PHP, you need to have MySQL
installed, which is a separate installation.) If you're interested in using the
additional libraries, the PHP online manual (www.php.net/docs.php) provides the information you're looking for.

Adding Dynamic Content

The most important application of PHP is *dynamic content*. Using PHP, you
can create Web sites that give out customized pages based on different criteria, such as who the user is or what information the user is looking for.

For example, suppose you're writing a page that lets users of your Web
server write an e-mail message. The user types the e-mail message into an
edit box and then clicks Send. Now suppose another page opens showing
the name of the recipient of the e-mail and a friendly confirmation that the
message has been sent. How can you generate a page that shows the recipient's name? When you create the site, you can't create millions of Web
pages, each with a different recipient name and then just pick the correct
one later on when a user types in a message. That's akin to leaving a million
monkeys alone at a typewriter for a million years to see if they accidentally
write a Shakespearean play. Instead, you want to dynamically generate a
Web page that prints out the recipient's name.

Instead, you want to create a Web site that dynamically builds each Web
page, filling it with pertinent information, such as the current e-mail message the user is viewing. How do you do that? Through PHP!

When you write PHP code, you are writing a program that runs within a Web
page, and that program can modify the page, customizing it as needed. This
is what dynamic content is all about.

For example, take a look at the todaysdate.php file that follows:

```
<html>
    <head>
        <title>Today's Date</title>
    </head>
```

```
<body>
        Greetings! Today is
    <?php
        $today = getdate();
        $month = $today['month'];
        $mday = $today['mday'];
        $year = $today['year'];
        print "    $month $mday, $year\n";
    ?>
    </body>
</html>
```

This file uses some advanced PHP techniques — calling functions — which I cover in Book V, Chapter 4. This PHP program first figures out what the current date is (that's the part that says getdate()) and stores it in a storage bin called $today. Then the next three lines separate the date information stored in the $today storage bin, saving the month portion in a storage bin called $month, the day in a storage bin called $mday, and the year in a storage bin called $year. These storage bins are called *variables,* which I explain in detail in Book V, Chapter 3. If you want to find out more about the getdate function, which is built into PHP, check out www.php.net/getdate.

After separating the date information, the program prints the date. To do this, I use a special technique that enables you to print variables by putting their names inside the string. When the program runs, instead of printing $month, it prints the information that's stored in the $month variable.

When you process this script, you get the following HTML file:

```
<html>
    <head>
        <title>Today's Date</title>
    </head>
    <body>
            Greetings! Today is
            December 31, 2003
    </body>
</html>
```

Although this date says December 31, 2003, you'll see whatever the current date is when you run the PHP code.

Now consider this for a moment: The HTML file that gets sent to the client is a *static* (nonchanging) file with the date hardcoded in it. If you run it again tomorrow, you'll get a different HTML file with tomorrow's date hardcoded into it. In other words, this single PHP program causes the Web server to dish out a different HTML page that's customized for the current date. This is dynamic content.

Running Types of Applications

The idea of dynamic content opens a world of possibilities. No longer do you have to type in every last HTML page and say, "That's it! This is what you get!" Instead, you can build Web pages on the fly, customized for the current situation. In the sections that follow, I provide a general idea of just a few of the many things you can do with PHP.

Creating math and engineering applications

The PHP language includes a set of functions serving mathematical purposes. These functions include the BCMath category of functions, which provide arbitrary-precision mathematics. If you're a scientist or an engineer, or if you work with such people, you can appreciate the importance of this. Normally when you use a computer to perform math, you end up with size limitations. For example, an integer has a limit on how big it can be, and floating point numbers (which are numbers containing a decimal point) have a limit on how many significant digits they can contain. But using the BCMath library, you have unlimited precision. (Well, okay, theoretically you could have a number with so many millions of digits that you eat up all the memory in the computer, but for most work, you shouldn't have any problems or limitations.)

You can find out more about the BCMath library by visiting `www.php.net/bc`.

PHP includes a set of more traditional mathematical functions in its Math category. This category includes too many functions for me to list here, but these functions include such familiar items as `cos` (cosine), `sin` (sine), `sinh` (hyperbolic sine — those elusive things that most calc classes skip), `log` (natural logarithm), `min` and `max` (for minimum and maximum), `rand` (for random numbers), and so on.

You can explore the traditional math routines by visiting `www.php.net/math`.

For scientific and engineering (and other) applications, you also have a library of graphics routines that I mention earlier in this chapter. In addition, you have access to various third-party libraries (some free, some not) that provide additional mathematical features. For example, one free library called PEAR (which is standard on many PHP installations) includes a library that handles complex numbers.

Designing database applications

One powerful aspect of PHP is its ability to interface with various databases. Most people who use PHP use the MySQL database, which is the database I focus on throughout this book.

Using a database, you can store large volumes of information, and using PHP, you can give your Web site users access to this data. For example, you may have a database containing user preferences for the Web site, such as content layout or font colors. You store this information in the database. Then when a user connects to your Web site and logs in with a username, PHP looks up the user's preferences in the database.

PHP dynamically generates Web pages, so if you want to provide customized font colors, for example, you would include PHP code that writes out a FONT tag in HTML, containing the colors chosen in the user preferences. Then when the client computer receives the Web page, it contains the color information already hardcoded into it.

Similarly, you can retrieve more complex information from a database. For example, suppose a university wants to include an office directory on its Web site. It wants users to be able to type a last name into the online directory and then see a Web page displaying a list of professors with that last name, along with e-mail addresses and office locations. You can easily do this with PHP: You take the requested last name, perform a database search, and retrieve all the *rows* in the table (a *row* is the preferred term for a *record*) where the last name column contains the requested value.

Then the dynamic content begins. In your PHP code, you display an HTML line containing the professor's name, e-mail address, and office location that the program found in the database. You might use an HTML table to carefully format the data. And you might even include an anchor tag <A that contains mailto: HREF around the e-mail address so the user can click the link to send an e-mail to that address. All this dynamic HTML is up to your PHP code, which displays the formatted HTML; the data in the database doesn't contain any HTML code — just data. Again, that's what dynamic content is all about.

Chapter 2: Writing Server-Side Scripts

In This Chapter

✔ **Exploring the PHP processor**

✔ **Creating PHP scripts**

✔ **Using appropriate filename extensions**

✔ **Embedding HTML in a PHP script**

✔ **Dealing with errors in your PHP code**

*W*hen you're surfing the Web in your free time, you occasionally come to Web sites that request that you first log in. If you look at the HTML source for such Web sites, you might expect to see a silly little JavaScript program with a password hardcoded right in the script. But the truth is that most (better!) Web sites don't use such a simple script.

A simple JavaScript program is a *client-based script,* meaning the code runs on the user's computer — the client computer. These scripts are freely readable by Web surfers. The alternative to running scripts on the client computer is to use a server-side script. A *server-side script* is a program that runs on the server, the computer that dishes out Web pages to users. When you log into a server, the server runs its own scripts, including those that test for a password.

Many languages are available for server-side scripts, but at least only one language allows you to write scripts right into the HTML files. This language is called PHP, which is an acronym for PHP: Hypertext Preprocessor. Yup, the letter *P* stands for PHP, which is an acronym whose first letter stands for PHP, which . . . well, you get the idea. Bizarre? Yes. True? Still yes.

PHP is a *preprocessor* because it processes an HTML file before the Web server dishes out the HTML page. Typically, without the presence of PHP, the Web server receives a request from the client computer (the Web surfer's computer) for a particular file, and the server then happily sends back the page as is. But with PHP present, first the PHP preprocessor reads the HTML file, looking for statements written in the PHP language. It then executes these statements and spits out a possibly different-looking, final HTML page. The Web server then happily sends this page to the client machine. Figure 2-1 shows you this process. (Note that in this minibook I refer to the PHP "processor" simply because it's a bit shorter than "preprocessor.")

As you study PHP, remember that you're writing a file that is processed by the PHP preprocessor and that the output from the processor is a valid HTML file. Keeping this in mind will help you stay sane during your development, because at times you will start to feel like you're working on some abstracted level several steps away from the actual HTML files. That's because you are, and it can get a little mind-numbing at times. But fear not; I'm here to help you get through it.

When you're doing a lot of PHP development, you should have access to the online PHP manual. This manual is an excellent supplement to the *For Dummies* book in your hands. You can find it at `www.php.net/docs.php`. From there, you can access the manual in many different languages in various file formats. For an English version in online HTML format, you can go right to `www.php.net/manual/en/`. And incidentally, you probably already noticed from these URLs that the main PHP home page is `www.php.net`.

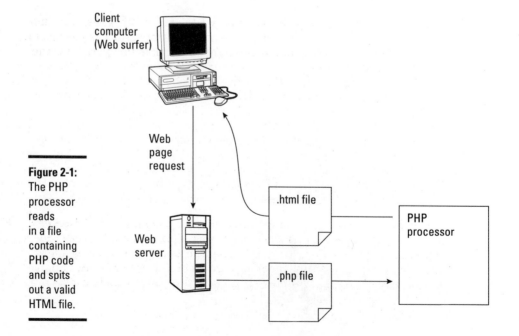

Figure 2-1:
The PHP processor reads in a file containing PHP code and spits out a valid HTML file.

Client computer (Web surfer)

Web page request

Web server

.html file

.php file

PHP processor

Referencing self-referential references

The idea of an acronym, *PHP*, referring to itself, *PHP: Hypertext Preprocessor,* may seem a little bizarre. People call this a *self-referential* or *recursive* acronym. Really, it doesn't make much sense. You could just as easily call it *ZHP* and claim it stands for *ZHP: Hypertext Preprocessor*. But the truth is, the acronym PHP originally stood for Personal Home Page. But as the language advanced, people realized the name Personal Home Page wasn't very descriptive. So they decided to change the name to something more meaningful. The HP part was easy, Hypertext Preprocessor. But oh, what to do with that first letter P? Apparently they couldn't think of a good name, so they made it a recursive acronym. The P now stands for nothing at all!

Exploring the PHP Processor

The PHP processor is a stand-alone program that runs on the Web server, independently from the Web server software. When a Web browser requests from the server a file ending in .php, the Web server software calls the PHP processor and passes to the processor the HTML file containing the PHP code.

The PHP processor takes as input the name of a file, and it writes out a new file. It writes the file to the standard output, which means that if you run the PHP program from a command line (such as in Unix or Linux), you see the output right on the screen.

Because PHP is a stand-alone program, nothing is stopping you from running it from the command prompt, passing in a file with PHP code, and checking out the resulting HTML. Here's a quick PHP session. Using my favorite text editor, I created a file that looks like this:

```
<?php
    print "Hi\n";
?>
```

This is a simple PHP program that prints out a Hi message. The first line tells the PHP processor that PHP code follows. The next line tells the PHP processor to print something, in this case, the word Hi followed by a new-line. The line ends with a semicolon, as do all PHP lines inside the <?php and ?> tags. Finally, ?> tells the PHP process that the PHP code ends.

I saved this file as `myfile.php`. Next, I type the following line at the Linux command prompt:

```
php myfile.php
```

The PHP processor reads the `myfile.php` file and displays the following output on-screen (you might see different numbers if you're using a different version of PHP):

```
X-Powered-By: PHP/4.1.2
Content-type: text/html
```

```
Hi
```

You can see that the processor output the word `Hi`. It also output a carriage return, which is the `\n` inside the double quotes. (The `\n` stands for *newline*.)

But what's all that junk that appears at the beginning of the output? These "junk" lines at the beginning of the output tell the browser what type of information follows. In this case, HTML follows, which is what `text/html` means. The other part, `X-Powered-By`, tells how the HTML was generated, in case the browser wants this information.

Say you take the `myfile.php` file and put it on a Web server, and then go to a client computer and browse to the `.php` file like so:

```
www.jeffcogswell.com/myfile.php
```

You see the word `Hi` appear in your Web browser. Now when you view the source for the file in the Web browser, you see this:

```
Hi
```

The output includes a newline at the end, exactly as the PHP program requested. This is getting pretty nifty!

For a `.php` file to get processed, the PHP processor must be present on the Web server. The Web server also must be configured to send `.php` files through the PHP processor.

You can't simply open a `.php` file in your browser. If you store a local `.php` file on your computer and open it in the browser, the browser treats it as an `.html` file and ignores all your PHP code.

If you want to try out some PHP at home, you can use one of the following two methods:

✦ Manually run the `.php` file through the PHP processor and save the resulting code to an `.html` file. Then you can open the `.html` file in your Web browser.

or

✦ Make sure that you have a Web server installed on your local computer, and then connect to the Web server by using, for example, `http://localhost/myfile.php`.

Starting and Ending PHP Code

Take a look at the sample PHP script called `myfile.php` in the preceding section. Notice that the first line is `<?php` and the final line is `?>`. These are the beginning and ending of an HTML tag that the PHP processor looks for to recognize where valid PHP code begins. This way you can create an `.html` file that may contain some PHP code in addition to the HTML code. If no PHP code is present, the PHP processor copies the file as is and sends it on to the Web server, which in turn sends the file to the client. Normally such a PHP-less file is simply an `.html` file, complete with HTML tags. However, if the file contains any PHP code, the code is placed inside an HTML tag. This tag starts with `<?php` and ends with `?>`.

Although in this book I start my PHP code with `<?php`, you can do so other ways as well. The PHP processor figures out where the PHP code starts and ends depending on how the processor is configured. Some people just use `<?` and `?>` (no `php`) for the opening and closing tags. I do this on my own Web site because I know that the PHP processor is configured to allow just `<?` and `?>`, which makes my coding a bit faster. (Hey, those extra three characters add up over time.) PHP provides four possible ways to start and end your PHP code:

✦ `<?php . . . ?>`

✦ `<script language = "php"> . . . </script>`

✦ `<? . . . ?>`

✦ `<% . . . %>`

The first two techniques always work. The second item takes a little longer to write than the first, but it's more in line with the HTML standards. The third one works only if configured (and I prefer it). (To configure it, you must set an option in the `php.ini` file; see the sidebar "Configuring the configuration file.") The final technique is a bit awkward, but its presence conforms with servers that are also running Microsoft Active Server Pages (ASP or ASP.NET), which you usually use in conjunction with Microsoft FrontPage.

Configuring the configuration file

PHP includes a configuration file called `php.ini`. This file includes a list of options for the PHP processor. The file is a text file and therefore easy to edit using any text editor. The file consists of several lines, each specifying an option. (The best way to get acquainted with the file is to open it in a text editor and look it over. It's filled with documentation explaining what all the lines do.) You can find `php.ini` in these locations:

🗸 **Unix/Linux:** The file is in `/usr/local/lib` or under the lib directory of your base installation directory.

🗸 **Windows:** The file is in the Windows directory. However, if you have Apache running, you can move the configuration file to the main Apache directory, `c:\program files\apache group\apache`.

One useful option is to specify whether the tags `<?` and `?>` can be used to begin and end PHP code. I like being able to quickly type `<?` rather than `<?php`, so I turn this option on. Here's the line you need to include in your `php.ini` file:

```
short_open_tag = On
```

To "uninclude" a line without deleting the line, put a semicolon at the beginning of the line; the PHP processor will ignore the line. To turn off the short tag option, for example, change the line to this:

```
;short_open_tag = On
```

Why would you turn off this option? Because the tags `<?` and `?>` are not compatible with true XML (if you care about that).

You can use whichever techniques are available to you on your PHP installation, and of those, use whichever is most comfortable to you. Remember that the PHP code is processed on the server side, and the output is always HTML. Ultimately just an `.html` file goes to the client computer. This means you don't need to worry about what type of browser the client is running.

Using Appropriate Filename Extensions

When you save a PHP script, you provide the file with a `.php` extension. This extension is important because it tells the Web server software that the file contains PHP code. When the Web server sees this extension, the server passes the file to the PHP processor for preprocessing and then sends out the results over the Internet.

A common mistake programmers often make is to forget the `.php` extension and instead use one of the standard HTML extensions such as `.html` or `.htm`. This is a problem because if the Web server sees one of these two extensions, it does not send the file to the PHP processor. Instead, it just sends out the file as is.

For example, suppose you have a file called `phoops.html`, which looks like the following. (Notice I gave it an `.html` extension rather than a `.php` extension.)

```php
<?php
    print "Hi\n";
?>
```

Then you point your browser to this file by typing in an address such as `www.jeffcogswell.com/phoops.html`.

Incidentally, this is a real site. I uploaded this file to my `jeffcogswell.com` site if you want to check it out.

When the browser opens the page, you see . . . nothing! That's because when the browser sees the tag starting with `<?php` and ending with `?>`, the browser doesn't recognize the tag and simply ignores what's inside. And what is left? Nothing! So nothing appears in the browser window.

Notice also that if you view the source for the page in the browser, you see the same `phoops.html` file; the PHP code is still present in the file because the PHP processor didn't run.

If you fix the filename extension by changing it to `.php` — for example, `phixed.php` — the file gets processed by the PHP processor, and you see the single line `Hi` for the HTML source in the browser. You can see this happen at `www.jeffcogswell.com/phixed.php`.

One reason for using PHP is to provide server-side code that people surfing the Web can't see. If you forget to use the `.php` extension and instead use `.html` or `.htm`, all your (possibly secret) code goes to the Web surfers' computers, allowing them to see every line of it if they're viewing the source for the HTML. So remember to use the `.php` extension!

Converting PHP to HTML

Because the purpose of a PHP script is to generate an `.html` file readable by a browser, ensure that your PHP output is as readable as possible — by you and by the browser. Makes sense, no?

Because a `.php` file contains PHP code embedded in a tag starting with `<?php` and ending with `?>`, the PHP code can be considered a simple HTML tag; it starts with `<` and ends with `>`. But what does the PHP processor do with the other parts of the file that are outside the `<?php ?>` tag? The answer is nothing. The PHP processor simply does not modify those parts.

Take a look at this file, which I'm calling `myfile2.php`:

```
<html>
    <head>
        <title>Better Example</title>
    </head>
    <body>
        <?php
            print "Hi";
        ?>
        <br>
    </body>
</html>
```

This is a valid `.html` file, with a PHP program embedded in it. The PHP program is in the middle, inside the `<?php` and `?>` tags. The rest of the file is basic HTML. Notice two things about this file:

✦ The `print` statement in the PHP code doesn't have a `\n` in it.

✦ The PHP code is followed by a `<br>` tag, which represents a newline in HTML.

Now think about this carefully: The PHP processor reads this file and sends out a file that is valid HTML. Each part of the file that is not part of the PHP code remains as is. But the PHP portion executes as a script, and in this case, that script prints out the word `Hi`. After processing, the PHP code in the HTML file is replaced by this output.

After the PHP processor runs, the resulting HTML file looks like this:

```
<html>
    <head>
        <title>Better Example</title>
    </head>
    <body>
        Hi          <br>
    </body>
</html>
```

The part that previously contained the PHP code was replaced by the output from the PHP code. The output is the word `Hi`.

But something might look a little odd here. Notice that the `<br>` tag, which was part of the original `.html` file and not part of the PHP code, is on the same line as the word `Hi` and spaced out a bit. Why is that? It's because

I didn't put a newline in my PHP code. So the PHP code was replaced by the PHP code's output, which was simply the two characters Hi. These two characters don't include any indentation and don't include any newlines.

The word Hi starts exactly where the <?php was in the .php file. And immediately after the word Hi is a set of spaces, which were on the original <br> line.

If you're really sharp, you may notice a flaw in what I just said. Technically, there *is* a newline — an HTML newline — in the original myfile2.php file after the end of the PHP code, right after ?>, which didn't appear in the output. Why wasn't this included in the final output? Frankly, I have no idea. Apparently the PHP processor considers that newline to also be part of the PHP code. Go figure.

Now what happens when you open this file in a Web browser? As you probably realize at this point, the easiest way to view the file is to point your browser to the myfile2.php file on a Web server hosting a PHP processor. Here's one: www.jeffcogswell.com/myfile2.php.

If you view the source for the file the Web browser sees, you see the preceding .html file. Further, inside the browser, you see a simple word: Hi. The title of the browser window is Better Example, which is what's defined in the <title> tag.

Working with newlines in PHP and HTML

To see how the newlines work in a PHP program, take a look at the following newlinedemo.php file:

```
<html>
    <head>
        <title>Newline Demo</title>
    </head>
    <body>
        <?php
            print "Hi\n\n\n\n";
        ?>
        there<br>everybody
    </body>
</html>
```

When you point your browser at this file (at www.jeffcogswell.com/newlinedemo.php, for example), the PHP processor reads the newlinedemo.php file and writes the following file, which is sent to your browser:

```
<html>
    <head>
        <title>Newline Demo</title>
    </head>
    <body>
        Hi



        there<br>everybody
    </body>
</html>
```

Notice the blank lines that appeared after the word `Hi`. These are the new-lines resulting from the `\n` in the `print` string. The next line, `there<br>everybody`, is left intact as it was in the original `newlinedemo.php` file.

Here's what you see in the browser:

```
Hi there
everybody
```

The `<br>` did its thing: A newline appears between the words `there` and `everybody`. But what about all the newlines after the word `Hi`? To answer this question, you need to know that a browser always shows whitespace as a single space. By *whitespace,* I mean spaces, tabs, and newlines, as many as you want, inside the HTML file. Although the browser saw four newlines in the HTML file, the browser displays only a single space. And thus, the words `Hi` and `there` are separated not by any newlines but rather a single space.

Here are the rules for newlines:

✦ When you put a `\n` in a `print` statement in your PHP code, you get a newline in the resulting `.html` file. The purpose of including such new-lines is usually to make the resulting HTML code look cleaner.

✦ Multiple newlines in the `.html` file result in a single space in the browser window.

✦ If you want a newline to appear in the browser window, use the `<br>` tag.

Embedding HTML in PHP scripts

If you want to get fancy, you can consider one more option when working with newlines. You can put a `<br>` tag inside your `print` statement. Here's another newline example demonstrating this, which I'm calling `newlinedemo2.php`:

```
<html>
    <head>
        <title>Newline Demo 2</title>
    </head>
    <body>
        <?php
            print "Hi<br>";
        ?>
        there<br>everybody
    </body>
</html>
```

I put a `<br>` tag inside the string in the `print` statement. Remember, you can print out anything you want in a string, but what you put in the string is what appears in the resulting HTML file. Here's the resulting HTML:

```
<html>
    <head>
        <title>Newline Demo 2</title>
    </head>
    <body>
        Hi<br>          there<br>everybody
    </body>
</html>
```

Notice the `Hi<br>` portion, which is the string that the PHP code printed. (Of course, the `<br>` is followed by more whitespace. Yuck. How does the browser interpret that? It ignores the whitespace because it follows a `<br>`.) Here's what you see in the browser:

```
Hi
there
everybody
```

This time, a newline appears after the word `Hi` in the browser, thanks to the `<br>` tag in the file.

The resulting HTML isn't as clean as it could be. It would be nice if the word `there` were on the next line and indented evenly with the word `Hi` so it's easier for humans to read it.

Cleaning up converted PHP scripts

By making the HTML code look nicer, you can more easily find problems that may exist in it. Here is a modified version of the `newlinedemo2.php` file, called `newlinedemo3.php`; this program simply has a `\n` added to the end of the `print` statement. This file produces a slightly cleaner `.html` file, although this cleaner `.html` file doesn't look any different in the browser than the `newlinedemo2.php` file in the preceding section.

```
<html>
    <head>
        <title>Newline Demo 3</title>
    </head>
    <body>
        <?php
            print "Hi<br>\n";
        ?>
        there<br>everybody
    </body>
</html>
```

Here's the resulting `.html` file for `newlinedemo3.php`:

```
<html>
    <head>
        <title>Newline Demo 3</title>
    </head>
    <body>
        Hi<br>
        there<br>everybody
    </body>
</html>
```

I suppose you could make further arguments for cleaning this up even more, such as putting a newline in the original HTML before the word `everybody`. But the point is that it's up to you to write your `.php` files so that the PHP is easy to read and the resulting HTML is clear and easy to understand.

Why use PHP if you can do it with HTML?

At this point, you may be asking a valid question: Why would you use PHP to generate an `.html` file if you can just write the HTML file yourself? With the examples in this chapter, you certainly could save yourself a lot of work by just typing in the HTML and ignoring the PHP. But that's because in these simple examples, each PHP file always results in the same HTML file no matter how many times you load it. However, you can do much more with PHP than just what

the `print` statement offers. Your PHP programs can open up databases, read information, and print out the information to the resulting `.html` file; process numbers and print out the results; or any number of possibilities. I provide some examples of what you can do in Book V, Chapter 2. As you work through the more advanced examples, remember that your PHP code is ultimately writing out HTML code to an `.html` file that will be interpreted by a Web browser.

Dealing with Errors in Your PHP Code

Because PHP is a script processor that lets you generate HTML pages, you may wonder about errors. If you make a mistake in your PHP code, what happens?

The answer is a frightening one: The error messages appear in the generated HTML page. This means that the users who connect to your site see the error messages in all their glory right on their Web browser screens.

Suppose this is your PHP file:

```
<html>
    <head>
        <title>Error Demo!</title>
    </head>
    <body>
        <?php
            (as=*#a!@#
        ?>
        there<br>everybody
    </body>
</html>
```

The PHP code in this file consists of several random characters, which, as luck would have it, do not happen to create a valid PHP program. If you try to open this file in your browser, you (and any visitors to your site) see the following:

```
Parse error: parse error in
            /home/jeffcogs/public_html/errordemo.php on line 7
```

This error message appears right in the browser.

Therefore, as with any other program, always test out your PHP code by putting it on your Web server and requesting it through a browser. You can then see your errors and go back and fix them in the code.

Exploring Some PHP Ground Rules

To conclude this chapter, here are a few quick ground rules for the PHP language:

✦ **End your statements with semicolons.** You can see how I did this in the examples throughout this chapter.

✦ Remember that the PHP processor is case-sensitive. This means that if you mean `print`, you can't say `PRINT`.

✦ You can have more than one `<?php ?>` tag in a single `.php` file, putting code inside each tag.

✦ Remember that PHP is not compiled; it is interpreted. This means that any changes you make to a `.php` file are immediately available. Unlike C++, for example, you don't need to compile the program to see the changes.

✦ You can provide comments in the following three ways:

• You can start a comment with a pound sign, #, as in Unix scripts.

• You can start a comment with two forward slashes, //, as in C++.

• You can surround the comments in /* and */ as in C and C++.

The following code demonstrates the three kinds of comments:

```php
<?php
    print "Hello<br>";  // This is a comment
    print "Hi"; # And this is a comment, too
    /* And this is also a comment */
?>
```

Getting Help with PHP

The main PHP Web site is an excellent source for information on PHP. The site includes the entire PHP documentation, which is continually updated. You can view the documentation online, or you can download the documentation in various formats. (For my Windows system, I like the `.chm` format, which is a Windows help file.) The main PHP site is `www.php.net`. The documentation is available at `www.php.net/docs.php`.

As you work with PHP, you will discover that tons of built-in functions are available to you. If you want to find online information on a particular function, point your Web browser to `www.php.net/functionname`, where `functionname` is the name of the function. For example, for help on the `echo` function, visit `www.php.net/echo`.

Chapter 3: Storing Information

In This Chapter

✔ **Naming your variables and storing information in them**

✔ **Determining whether your variables exist**

✔ **Working with expressions**

✔ **Handling bits and types**

✔ **Programming strings**

A s with any language, PHP allows you to store information. What would a computer be if it couldn't remember things? (Answer: a forgetful computer!) The most basic way to store information is through variables.

Note: In this chapter, I'm assuming you have a basic understanding of what variables are, and I provide you with the necessary knowledge for using variables in PHP. If you're not sure what variables are, check out Book III, Chapter 2, where I introduce the concept of variables. Although Book III deals with the Perl language, the information in question applies to pretty much any language.

Naming Variables

In PHP, a variable name starts with a dollar sign, $. This is similar to the way languages such as Perl handle variables and unlike the way languages such as C++ deal with them. After the dollar sign, you can have a letter or underscore, and after that, you can have any number of letters, numbers, or underscores. PHP doesn't have a limit on the length of variables' names.

In PHP, variable names are case-sensitive. That means the variable $MyName is a separate variable from $myname. If you've worked in languages such as BASIC, Pascal, or SQL, this is new to you, but if you're coming from C++ or Perl, you're probably used to this.

Technically speaking, the dollar sign is *not* part of the variable name in PHP. The dollar sign merely tells the PHP processor that a variable name follows. However, throughout this book when I refer to variables in the text, I put the dollar sign in as a reminder that you need it in the code.

The following are examples of valid variable names in PHP:

- ✦ `$abc`
- ✦ `$abc1`
- ✦ `$ABC`
- ✦ `$LotsOfMoney`
- ✦ `$_name`
- ✦ `$my_name_its_a_great_name`

And the following are examples of names you're not allowed to use in PHP:

- ✦ `$2abc` isn't valid because it starts with a number.
- ✦ `$123` isn't valid because it starts with a number.
- ✦ `$T(x` isn't valid because it contains a parenthesis. You can use only letters, numbers, and underscores.
- ✦ `$` by itself isn't valid because the dollar sign isn't part of the variable name, and therefore, there is no variable name here.

Although you're allowed to use built-in PHP names, such as `$print`, as variables, I strongly discourage you from doing so. Although this won't cause the PHP processor trouble, it can make your program more complicated for us mere humans to read.

One common mistake that programmers who are coming from other languages make is to forget the dollar sign when typing in a variable name. If you leave off the dollar sign, the PHP processor thinks you're trying to use a function name and gets confused.

Storing Information in Variables

The purpose of a variable is to hold information. A variable is a storage bin that has a name and some piece of information inside it. The information that you put in a variable normally has a type associated with it, such as `integer` or `string` (which is a sequence of letters, numbers, or other characters).

PHP is what the computer scientists call a *loosely typed* language. This means that when you create a variable, you don't have to specify what type of data the variable holds. Many other languages require you to assign data types to your variables. A variable for the balance in a bank account, for example, would be assigned a numeric data type. For better or worse, this assignment would prevent any type of data other than numbers from being stored in the variable. However, PHP isn't so picky; you don't specify a type, and you don't declare your variables upfront. You can put a number in it and, later, a string of characters. It doesn't matter.

Here's a sample line of PHP that stores the number 42 inside a variable called $universe:

```
$universe = 42;
```

In other words, this line creates a variable called $universe and then puts the number 42 inside the variable. The left side of the equal sign specifies the name of the variable, $universe, and the right side of the equal sign specifies the value that you're putting in the variable.

Although I say that this line creates a variable called $universe, keep in mind that this is just one line inside a complete program. When the PHP processor is running your program, the first time it encounters the variable name $universe it creates that variable. After that, the variable $universe exists, and in further encounters with the variable name, the PHP processor won't create a new one.

Here's a complete .php file containing this $universe line:

```
<?php
    $universe = 42;
    print $universe;
?>
```

When the PHP processor goes through this code, you end up with HTML containing the single number 42.

I know I've said this before, but it's extremely important to understand: This PHP program doesn't simply print out the number 42! Rather, this PHP program creates an .html file containing the single number 42. If you want to use the language "prints out the number 42," think of the program as "printing out the number 42 to the .html file."

Understanding Data Types

The PHP language includes four basic types of information that you can store in a variable:

✦ **Boolean:** This is a simple type that can be either true or false.

✦ **Integer:** This is a type for whole numbers, including negative numbers, 0, and positive numbers.

✦ **Float:** This is a type for floating point numbers that include a decimal point.

✦ **String:** This is a type for strings of characters.

(Remember that a single variable can hold any type. You can store an integer in a variable and later put a string in the same variable.) Here's an example that demonstrates each of the four types:

```
<html><body>
<?php

    $myiq = 206;
    $myname = "Wiley";
    $mytemp = 98.6;
    $AmICool = true;

    print $myiq."<br>";
    print $myname."<br>";
    print $mytemp."<br>";
    print $AmICool."<br>";

?>
</body></html>
```

After the PHP processor gets its hands on this code, you end up with the following output in your browser window:

```
206
Wiley
98.6
1
```

This output probably is what you expect, although the last item may seem a little strange. The `print` statement prints Boolean variables as either 0 for false or 1 for true.

Note that in the preceding PHP code, I'm using a little trick called the *concatenation operator,* which is the dot or period. You can see this in each of the print lines, such as `print $myiq."<br>";`. This is the way you print multiple items — in this case `$myiq` and the `"<br>"` string — with a single `print` statement. I talk more about this concatenation operator in the section, "Concatenating and squishing together strings," later in this chapter.

The `integer` type in PHP is a 32-bit signed integer. If you need more precision than 32 bits, use the BCMath library. (Note that the documentation states that this type is platform dependent, although these days you can pretty much always expect it to be signed 32 bits.) The floating point numbers are 64 bits. (Again, this is platform dependent, but unless you're using a bizarre computer, you can expect 64 bits.)

Determining Whether a Variable Exists

Like making sure you have money in your bank account before spending it, you probably want to make sure a variable exists before using it. You can do this by using the isset keyword.

Note: In the following example, I use an if statement to make a comparison. I cover if statements for PHP in Book V, Chapter 4.

Here's an example of how to check for a variable's existence:

```php
<?php
    $a = "hello";
    if (isset($a)) {
        print "a is set and contains $a<br>";
    }
    if (isset($b)) {
        print "b is set and contains $b<br>";
    }
?>
```

As you can see, I typed isset and put the name of the variable I'm testing for inside parentheses: isset($a).

This code results in the following output in the browser:

```
a is set and contains hello
```

If you have experience with only compiled languages, the notion of determining whether a variable exists may seem strange. However, remember that PHP is interpreted, and you can put a variable name in your code and test whether it exists, without it actually existing. In most compiled languages, you can refer to a variable only after you have declared it, meaning a test for a variable's existence is a moot point.

Removing Variables

After you're sick and tired of a certain variable (or just don't need it anymore), you can use the unset function to remove it from existence, like so:

```php
<?php
    $reader = "Jeff";
    $author = "Me";
    if (isset($reader)) {
        print "The reader exists!<br>";
    }
    unset($author);
```

```
    if (isset($author)) {
        print "The author exists! (whew)<br>";
    }
?>
```

This results in the following output in the browser:

```
The reader exists!
```

Apparently the author — I — was obliterated!

Expressing Your Variables and Other Expressions

You can easily manipulate your variables by using basic mathematical operations such as addition, subtraction, and so on. How these operations work depends on the type inside the variable. Take a look at this simple example:

```
<?php
    $a = 10;
    $b = 20;
    print $a + $b;
?>
```

This code is pretty straightforward. You can probably see that the number 30 will appear in your browser. As far as operators go, with integers, you have everything you expect, including the following:

- ✦ + (addition)
- ✦ - (subtraction)
- ✦ * (multiplication)
- ✦ / (division)
- ✦ % (modulus)

This last operator may be unfamiliar to you. The *modulus* operator gives you the remainder in a division problem. For example, 54 % 10 yields 4, because 50 divided by 10 is 5 with a remainder of 4.

These operators also work for floating point numbers; however, the modulus (%) operator works only with integers. (The PHP processor doesn't complain if you attempt to use modulus with floating point numbers; instead, it just gives a result of 0.)

The division operator always does floating-point division; even when you use integers, it yields a float. Consider this example:

```php
<?php
    $a = 5;
    $b = 2;
    print $a / $b;
?>
```

Although $a and $b are both integers, the result of $a / $b is not a rounded form of 2.5 — say, 3. Rather, the result *is* 2.5, which is a float. That's because with division, the PHP processor treats both variables involved as floats, even if they're integers. If you need an integer version of a floating-point answer, you have two options. You can simply truncate it, as follows:

```php
print floor($a / $b);
```

Or you can round it:

```php
print round($a / $b);
```

The difference is that rounding approximates floating-point numbers to the nearest integer (less than 0.5 rounds down; 0.5 and higher rounds up). Thus, 2.5 rounds to 3. Floor, on the other hand, just chops off the decimal, meaning 2.5 truncates to 2. In other words, round($a) gives you the same as floor($x + 0.5).

There has been lots of discussion online about the potential problems with the lack of a true division operator. Because the division operator uses floating points, and because floating points are known for not being absolutely accurate, people worry about losing information in their integral division problems. However, my advice is this: If you're writing a software package that requires absolute precision with integers, please use the BCMath library and don't rely on the built-in integer types. Here's a short example of the BCMath library's integral division function:

```php
$bca = "5";
$bcb = "2";
print bcdiv($bca, $bcb);
```

These statements output the result of dividing integer $bca by integer $bcb. In this case, the result is 2, which is the expected answer. If you had used a slash (as in $bca / $bcb), you would get 2.5, which is not an integer.

Some languages let you use the basic operators (such as +) on strings to build a new string containing two strings squished together. But in PHP, you can't use the arithmetic operators on strings; if you do, you'll always get the number 0 for a result. However, you can combine strings in PHP by using the *dot operator,* which is just a fancy name for a period. See "Stringing Up Characters with Strings," later in this chapter, for information on how to use this operator.

Assigning in more ways than one

In PHP, you can assign values to your variables simply by using an equal sign. However, you can assign values other ways as well.

If you want to add something to or subtract something from the value in a variable, you can use the += and -= operators. For example, suppose you have a variable called $LA_smog and this variable contains the value 15354, like so:

```
$LA_smog = 15354;
```

Next, you want to add 3,000 to this value and store the results back in LA_smog. You can do this by using the traditional + operator, as in the following statement:

```
$LA_smog = $LA_smog + 3000;
```

Or you can do it by using the += operator, as in the following statement:

```
$LA_smog += 3000;
```

Each of the two preceding statements causes $LA_smog to contain the value 18354.

If you're concatenating strings (as I describe in the section "Concatenating and squishing together strings" later in this chapter), you can use the dot-equal operator, like so:

```
$name = "Thomas";
$name .= " A. Edison";
print $name;
```

The second line uses the dot-equal operator, which takes the existing string in $name and adds on the string " A. Edison". After the first two lines run, $name contains "Thomas A. Edison".

And finally, if you're into bit-switching (see the next section, "Flipping the bits"), you can assign values with any of the bitwise operations. You do this by preceding the operator character with an equal sign, as in this example:

```
$mybits = 10;
$mybits &= 3;
```

This example takes the value 10, "ands" it with the value 3, and stores the result, 2, back in $mybits.

Flipping the bits

If you're into manipulating individual bits of your numbers, PHP provides the *bitwise* operators. Table 3-1 lists these operators.

Table 3-1	Use the Bitwise Operators to Manipulate Individual Bits		
Operator	*Description*	*Example*	*Result*
<<	Shift Left	10 << 2	40
>>	Shift Right	10 >> 2	2
&	And	11 & 7	3
|	Or	11 | 7	15
^	XOr	11 ^ 7	12
~	Not	~7	-8

Note that the *Not* operator on the value 7 returns a negative number, –8. This is because the PHP processor uses *signed* integers.

In some languages, you can use the caret symbol, ^, for exponents. In PHP, however, the caret symbol is used for the *exclusive-or* bitwise operation. Be careful not to mistake it for an exponent. To perform powers, use the pow function, found in the Math library:

```
$result = pow(3, 4);
```

This yields 81, which is 3 to the 4th power.

Mixing and matching types

In PHP, after you create a variable and store data of a particular type in it, you're not restricted to that type. You're free to later put data of some other type inside the variable. Take a look at this example:

```
<?php
    $yourbossincome = 2000000;
    print $yourbossincome."<br>";
    $yourbossincome = "way too much for so little work";
    print $yourbossincome."<br>";
?>
```

This code results in the following output in your Web browser:

```
2000000
way too much for so little work
```

You can see that I used the same variable. First, I put the number 2000000 in it, and then I put the string "way too much for so little work" in it. PHP can handle this change in type just fine, unlike strongly-typed languages such as C++ and Pascal.

But be careful, though, because by doing this, strange things can happen (in addition to your getting fired for complaining about your boss). For example, look carefully at the following code:

```
$yourbossincome = 2000000;
print $yourbossincome - 1000000;
print "\n<br>\n";
$yourbossincome = "way too much for so little work";
print $yourbossincome - 1000000;
```

Hexing and "octing" your numbers

If you want to use hexadecimal and octal numbers in your PHP program, you can. (If you're not familiar with hexadecimal and octal numbers, you can skip this sidebar.) To store the hexadecimal number 3C in a variable, for example, simply precede the number with a 0x, as in the following statement:

```
$number = 0x3c;
```

Remember, however, that if you print out this variable with a print statement, you'll see the decimal equivalent, in this case, 60.

You can also store octal numbers. You do this by preceding the number with a 0, as in the following statement:

```
$number = 012;
```

Make sure that you don't precede base-10 integers with a 0. The number 012 is *not* the *decimal* number 12; it's the *octal* number 12, which corresponds to the decimal number 10.

Remember: Do not put a 0 at the beginning of your numbers. Do not try to write a 10 as 010, or the PHP processor will store a different number entirely. Be careful!

This strange code results in the following output in your browser:

```
1000000
-1000000
```

You get this result because when you attempt to do a numerical operation on a string (such as subtracting 1000000), the PHP processor understands the string to have the numeric value 0. Thus, 0 minus 1000000 is -1000000, which is what you see in the output.

Stringing Up Characters with Strings

A *string* is a sequence of characters. One great feature of PHP (especially if you're coming from the world of C programming) is its support for strings. In the sections that follow, I provide you with lots of fun information about strings and how to work with them.

Specifying a string

PHP allows you to specify strings in three different ways:

✦ By using single quotes

✦ By using double quotes

✦ By using a format known as *heredoc*

Each method has a slightly different result. The following sections provide the details.

Specifying with quotes

First, you can simply surround your string with single quotes, as in the following statement:

```
print 'Where did all the time go?<BR>';
```

Or you can surround it in double quotes, like this:

```
print "Where did all the time go?<BR>";
```

These two lines of code have the same result; however, the two methods are slightly different. You may have noticed that throughout this minibook, I embed some of my strings with a \n, which is called an *escape character*.

This particular escape character denotes a newline. Now, to illustrate the difference between the single- and double-quote methods of specifying strings, try rewriting each of the two preceding lines of code with a \n at the end, followed by a few more characters:

```
print 'Where did all the time go?<BR>\n...';
print "Where did all the time go?<BR>\n...";
```

These two lines of code look similar, but they produce different output in the resulting HTML. Running these two lines produces the following output:

```
Where did all the time go?<BR>\n...Where did all the time
    go?<BR>
...
```

See what happened? The \n inside the *single quotes* resulted in the literal characters \n appearing in the output. However, the *double quotes* caused the PHP processor to convert the \n to a newline.

If you plan to use escape characters in your strings, or if you plan to embed variables (described in the section, "Embedding variables [and printing them, too]," later in this chapter), you must use double quotes. These characters and variables are then converted properly. However, if you want your text to print exactly as is — backslashes, dollar signs, and all — then use single quotes.

You're rolling along, having a great day, and suddenly you're hit with a major bug where you're seeing a bunch of \n's appear in your Web browser. Most likely the problem is that you accidentally used single quotes when you should have used double quotes. I speak, ahem, from experience. (Yup.)

If you're running a Web site that receives lots of hits, and you're looking for every possible way to maximize the speed, always use the single-quote style strings except when you need to embed either an escape sequence or a variable in the string. The PHP processor grinds though a single-quote string a bit faster than through a double-quote string.

Specifying with heredocs

The third way to specify strings may look a little odd if you're coming from the perspective of a traditional programming language, such as C++ or Pascal. You can use a string-specifying method called *heredoc*. The idea with heredoc is that you type into the code file exactly what you want your lines of strings to look like. Here's an example:

```
<?php
    $tome =
<<<EOT
Well hello there, everybody! I'm your speaker here at the
PHP for Life conference, where you'll be immersed in all
the PHP you can handle now and in subsequent lives.
Let us all hold hands and recite the PHP mantra.
EOT;

    print "<p>";
    print $tome;
    print "<p>";
?>
```

Here's how I created the string: I wrote a line that is not indented, starting with three less-than ($<$) signs, followed by an identifier of my choice. I chose EOT (which, in my own crazy head means either End of Text, or perhaps Eat Only Truffles, depending on my mood). The string then begins at the beginning of the next line. (If you indent, the indentation becomes part of your string!) To note the end of the string, I repeat the identifier I chose, which in this case is EOT. And because this is a variable assignment, like all variable assignments I end with a semicolon.

This results in the following HTML:

```
<p>Well hello there, everybody! I'm your speaker here at the
PHP for Life conference, where you'll be immersed in all
the PHP you can handle now and in subsequent lives.
Let us all hold hands and recite the PHP mantra.<p>
```

You can use whatever identifier you want to start your heredoc string, provided that the identifier follows the same rules as valid PHP variables (starts with a letter and can include numbers and underscores) and that you use the same identifier at the end of your heredoc string. If you want to call your identifier HEREDOC, that's fine. Or if you prefer something a little more personal and dear to your heart like PIZZA or ANDROMEDAGALAXY, that's great too. However, I do encourage you to be consistent and use the same identifier in all your code. Oh yes, and you don't have to use all uppercase letters, although I encourage you to do so, because it helps the identifier stand out.

The line ending the string must consist of only your chosen identifier followed by a semicolon, if a semicolon is required as part of the statement. If you put anything else on the line, the PHP processor assumes this line isn't the ending identifier, and the processor keeps rolling along, line by line, making that big ol' string get even bigger. That's an error, and your program won't work correctly. Also, make sure that you don't put anything after the closing identifier (which, remember, must be in the left-most column), and possibly a semicolon (if needed).

Although I didn't show it in the preceding heredoc sample, a heredoc string has the same feature as the double-quote strings, in that you can embed escape sequences and variable names. Here's an example:

```php
<?php
    $name = "Perseus Harold Pock (but call me PHP)";
    $tome2 =
<<<EOT
Greetings, Earthlings! I am $name.
\tIt is my pleasure to welcome you to my own galaxy,
\tthe Andromeda galaxy. I own it.
EOT;

    print "<p>";
    print $tome2;
    print "<p>";
?>
```

The first line of the heredoc string contains the variable $name, which the PHP processor replaces with the value of $name. The second and third lines of the string start with a \t, which is the escape character for a tab. So when you run this program, the resulting HTML contains:

```
<p>Greetings, Earthlings! I am Perseus Harold Pock (but call
    me PHP).
            It is my pleasure to welcome you to my own galaxy,
            the Andromeda galaxy. I own it.<p>
```

The heredoc approach also has a particularly useful application. If you use the <pre> tag in HTML, heredoc is handy for that. A common use of the <pre> tag is for displaying program code in a browser. The word *pre* stands for preformatted. By using preformatted text in an HTML file, the browser won't mess up the output by treating all whitespace as just a single space. This is the case in the preceding example about Perseus Harold Pock: My HTML tabs, a result of the \t's in my PHP code, and newlines won't appear in the browser — they'll be replaced by whitespace.

Here's an example of using heredoc with the <pre> tag:

```
<html><head><title>Your Program</title></title>
<body>
Your code is:<p>
```

```
<pre>

<?php
    $myname = "Perseus of Andromeda";

    $code =
<<<EOT
#include <iostream.h>

int main() {
    cout << "$myname" << endl;
    return 0;
}
EOT;

    print $code;
?>

</pre>
Please review it carefully and check for errors.<P> Thanks!
</body>
</html>
```

I put the PHP portion of this example in bold to help you sort it out from the
rest of the code. Placed before the PHP section is a section of HTML code
that ends with an opening <pre> tag. Then comes the PHP, which includes a
heredoc statement that writes out another tome, which in this case is C++
code. (You don't have to know C++ to understand this example; I just wanted
to use a different language for the output. As far as PHP is concerned, it's just
text. The PHP processor does not attempt to run the C++ code. To PHP, the
C++ garbage is just a string.)

But look! Inside this string, I've embedded a PHP variable, $myname. If you
were reading a value into the $myname variable from a database, rather than
hardcoding the string Perseus of Andromeda as I have here, you could
seriously customize the output. Here's what the final HTML looks like after
the PHP processor gets ahold of the code:

```
<html><head><title>Your Program</title></title>
<body>
Your code is:<p>
<pre>

#include <iostream.h>

int main() {
    cout << "Perseus of Andromeda" << endl;
    return 0;
```

```
}
</pre>
Please review it carefully and check for errors.<P> Thanks!
</body>
</html>
```

When you open this HTML in a browser, this is what you see:

```
Your code is:


#include

int main() {
    cout << "Perseus of Andromeda" << endl;
    return 0;
}

Please review it carefully and check for errors.
Thanks!
```

Escaping from a string

When you're using a double-quote style string or a heredoc style string (but not a single-quote style string), you can embed within the string various *escape sequences* that denote specialized information that would otherwise be hard to put into a string. PHP includes only a few of these escape sequences, which are described in the following list:

+ \n This is the usual way for denoting a newline. See the paragraph following this list for some notes about using \n.

+ \t This is a tab character.

+ \r This is another way to do a newline, called a carriage return. See the paragraph following this list for some notes about using \r.

+ \\ This is just a good old backslash. Because a backslash denotes a special character, this enables you to actually specify the backslash itself!

+ \" This is a double quote. Inside heredoc strings, you don't need to use the backslash before it, but inside double-quote strings, you need the backslash so the PHP processor doesn't think the string ends here.

+ \$ Because variables start with a dollar sign, this gives you a way to denote an actual dollar sign in your strings.

And now for those notes about the linefeed and carriage return. Which should you use, \r or \n? Most people use \n. However, without taking pages to go into the gory details, suffice to say that Windows computers use a combination of \r followed by \n to denote a newline, and Unix and Linux computers use just \n. The Macintosh uses just \r. Go figure. But the truth is, browsers don't really care because they treat all whitespace (including linefeeds) as a single space. So I just always use \n.

Embedding variables (and printing them, too)

If you're using the heredoc style strings or the double-quote style strings, you can use a cool technique for embedding your variables right in the strings. Why would you do that? Take a look at the following code:

```php
<?php
    $myname = "me";
    print "Hello, $myname! It's a fine name and my name
    too!";
?>
```

This code results in the following HTML:

```
Hello, me! It's a fine name and my name too!
```

This output is just as if you printed "Hello," and then the value stored in $myname, and then "! It's a fine name and my name too!".

The PHP processor doesn't always know exactly where the variable name ends, resulting in confusion. Look at these two lines:

```
$word = "apple";
print "$words are my favorite food";
```

The PHP processor doesn't know that the variable you're attempting to use in the string is $word. Instead, it looks for a variable called $words. To fix this, you can surround the variable name with braces, like so:

```
$word = "apple";
print "{$word}s are my favorite food";
```

Or you can put the dollar sign outside the braces and just surround the name itself with braces, as in ${word}.

Concatenating and squishing together strings

Concatenation is one of those words that no one outside the computer world seems to know, yet each person inside the computer world, after learning what it is, uses the technique almost daily. If you're new to concatenation, you can be sure to start using it at the beginning of your day, just after your morning cup of coffee.

To concatenate or embed?

At this point, you may wonder which choice is better when writing out strings and variables. Suppose $a contains the string "Hello" and $b contains the string "there". Now have a gander at these two lines of code:

```
print $a."<br>".$b;
print "$a<br>$b";
```

Both of these lines produce the same output. Which one is better? It's really up to you. Personally, most people find the second version easier to type and understand. However, remember that when you're using arrays and objects, if you plan to use the embedded format, you must surround the variable names with braces so the PHP processor doesn't get confused. (For more information on arrays, see Book V, Chapter 5; for objects, see Book V, Chapter 7.) Here's an example; note that in the final line I'm putting braces, { and }, around the variables inside the strings.

```
class MyClass {
    var $name;
}
$obj = new MyClass();
$obj->name = array("George",
    "Washington");
print "{$obj-
    >name[0]}<br>{$obj-
    >name[1]}";
```

This code produces the following HTML output:

```
George<br>Washington
```

Concatenation simply means putting two strings together to form one big string. To concatenate strings in PHP, you can use the . (dot) operator, as in the following example:

```
$a = "php is ";
$b = "great";
$c = "as everybody knows";
print $a.$b."<br>".$c;
```

This results in the following HTML:

```
php is great<br>as everybody knows
```

When this HTML is opened in the browser, it looks like this:

```
php is great
as everybody knows
```

As you can see, in my string I'm including a
 HTML tag, which outputs a newline on the browser screen.

Chapter 4: Controlling the Program Flow

In This Chapter

✔ Using `if` statements

✔ Looping with `while`

✔ Taking a look at `for` loops

✔ Examining `switch` statements

✔ Breaking and continuing loops

✔ Building HTML tables with loops

An important feature in programming languages is the capability to jump around within a program, rather than just execute the statements line by line. Earlier scripting languages lacked control structures like `while` loops and `for` loops. However, over time, programmers have realized the importance of control structures even in scripting languages. Thus, PHP includes the usual gamut of control structures: `if` statements, `while` loops, `for` loops, and `case` or `switch` statements. I discuss these control structures in this chapter.

If you're familiar with C++ or with languages I cover in this book (Perl, for example), you'll discover that many PHP control structures are similar to those in C++. Knowing this will save you some time in exploring these control structures. However, PHP does have some differences; for instance, PHP has an `elseif` keyword.

Comparing with if Statements

The simplest form of a control structure is the `if` statement. The `if` statement allows the flow of your program to be changed based on a comparison: One block of code is performed if the comparison evaluates to true, and another is performed if the comparison evaluates to false.

Here's an example of an `if` statement in PHP:

```
<html><title>Car System</title>
<body>
```

```
<?php
    $CarIsBrokenDown = true;
    if ($CarIsBrokenDown) {
        print ("Click here for the bus schedule");
    }
?>
</body>
</html>
```

The preceding example is a complete .php file including an if statement that checks whether $CarIsBrokenDown evaluates to true. Notice that I used the simplest form of an expression: a Boolean variable. I simply used the variable name, $CarIsBrokenDown. If this expression evaluates to true (in other words, if $CarIsBrokenDown contains true), the PHP processor executes the code inside the braces.

This if statement isn't very useful as is, considering I immediately set the variable to true and then test whether it's true. Here's an example that has more power:

```
<html><title>Expired Hot Dogs</title>
<body>
    <h2>Welcome to the hot dog web page!
    Let's see if they're still good...</h2>
<?php

    $today = getdate();
    $todayastime = mktime($today);
    print "Today is {$today['weekday']}, {$today['month']}".
        " {$today['mday']}, {$today['year']}.<br>\n";
    $expiration = mktime(0, 0, 0, 12, 31, 2003);
    $expstring = date("F j, Y", $expiration);

    if ($todayastime == $expiration) {
        print "They expire, like, NOW, so you better
            hurry!<br>";
    }
    elseif ($todayastime > $expiration) {
        print "They expired on $expstring. Better not risk
            it.<br>";
    }
    else {
        print "They're perfectly good! Enjoy!<br>";
    }
?>

</body>
</html>
```

This example uses the more complex forms of the if statement. First, I call into some of the internal PHP functions that let me get information about the date. The first line calls the getdate() function, which gets the current date in the form of an array keyed by various words such as month and weekday. The second line calls the mktime($today) function to convert the date to a *Unix time,* which is the number of seconds since January 1, 1970. The third line prints out the date information. The line setting the $expiration variable calls mktime for December 31, 2003, which is when the hot dogs I'm selling expire. The next line converts that date to a string.

Then the fun begins. In the expressions in the if statements, I use only the Unix times, because comparing them is easy. First, I check if today's date and time match the expiration date and time. (Notice how I compared these two numbers: I used two equal signs in a row, as in ==.) If so, I print a message stating the food is about to expire.

But if this first evaluation *fails* (meaning the expression evaluated to false), then I use the elseif statement, which performs another comparison. (The PHP processor performs this second comparison only if the first comparison failed.) This second comparison checks if the current date and time are greater than the expiration date and time. If so, the PHP program prints a message stating the food is expired.

Finally, if the second comparison also fails, I use an else block, which the PHP processor runs only if the previous comparisons all failed. From a logical standpoint, if the expression ($todayastime == $expiration) failed (that is, if it evaluated to false), and the expression ($todayastime >= $expiration) also failed, the only possibility left is that $todaysdate < $expiration; that is, today is before the expiration date. Thus, if today is before the expiration date, the PHP processor will make it to the final else block.

In summary, this if-elseif-else block of code works like so:

1. If the expiration date and time is right now, print a message telling the person to hurry up and eat the hot dogs . . .

2. . . . else if the expiration date has passed, print a message warning the person not to eat the hot dogs . . .

3. . . . else the expiration has not passed, tell the person to enjoy the hot dogs.

I uploaded this sample if statement to my server. If you want to see it in action, visit www.jeffcogswell.com/hotdog.php.

If you have an expression that tests for equality, use two equal signs, as in if ($a == $b). This is different from a variable assignment, where you always use a single equal sign, as in $a = 10;. But if you want to test for inequality, use an exclamation point (called a bang) followed by an equal sign, as in if ($a != $b). Other languages (including Perl and C++) use this same syntax.

Looping with while

If you have some code that you want repeated over and over while a certain condition is true, and want the code to stop after the condition is no longer true, you can use a while loop.

Here's a quick example of a while loop:

```
<html><title>While Your Power Bill Runs</title>
<body>
    Welcome to your power bill. The following
    numbers represent your expected bill for
    the next several months. Be sure to pay
    up or we'll shut it off.<br>
<?php
    $power = 2;
    while ($power < 10000) {
        print "\$".$power.".00<br>\n";
        $power *= 2;
    }
?>
</body>
</html>
```

This example initializes the variable $power to 2 and then begins calculating powers of 2, representing . . . your power bill! The loop runs as long as $power is less than 10,000. First, it prints out the value, formatted to look like a dollar amount, and then it multiplies the value by 2. It then repeats the process — printing and then multiplying — as long as the value is less than 10,000.

If the condition in a while loop is never true, the code inside the while loop never executes. Thus, in the following code, the print statement never runs:

```
$x = 10;
while ($x < 5) {
    print "phoops\n";
}
```

For example, suppose you're reading weather data and you want to print out data as long as the temperature is below 95 degrees. If the temperature is 95 degrees or higher, you don't want to print out any data. In that case, you can be assured that the code in your while loop will not execute the first time. (This is not true in some languages and can be a concern among programmers.)

If you have a situation where you always want the code inside the loop to execute at least once, and then to check the condition *after* each iteration, you can use a slightly modified form of the while loop, called the do-while loop.

The do-while loop looks like this:

```
<html><title></title>
<?php

    $number = 20;
    do {
        print "$number<br>\n";
        $number++;
    } while ($number < 30);

?>
</html>
```

This example starts a counter called $number at 20, and continues counting up to, but not including, 30. Now look at the following code, where I changed the final while condition:

```
<html><title></title>
<?php

    $number = 20;
    do {
        print "$number<br>\n";
        $number++;
    } while ($number < 0);

?>
</html>
```

The value in $number will never be less than 0. If this were a standard while loop, the code inside the curly braces would never execute. But because I used the do-while loop, the code executes once. Here's the resulting HTML:

```
<html><title></title>
20<br>
</html>
```

Doing for Loops

If you have a block of code and you know the exact number of times you want to execute the block of code, or if you know specific beginning and ending conditions, you can use a for loop.

Here is a simple example of a for loop:

```
<?php
    for ($counter = 10; $counter<20; $counter++) {
        print "$counter<br>\n";
    }
?>
```

The for statement contains three expressions inside parentheses. The first expression, $counter = 10, sets the initial conditions. Before the code inside the curly brackets starts, the PHP processor stores 10 in the variable called $counter. (If the variable doesn't already exist, PHP creates it at this time.)

Next, the PHP processor tests whether the second expression inside the if line is true. If so, the PHP processor runs the code inside the curly brackets. After the code is finished, the PHP processor performs the code in the third expression, $counter++. That is, the PHP processor adds 1 to $counter.

If, at the end of any iteration, after incrementing $counter, the middle expression $counter < 20 is no longer true, the for loop finishes.

Think of the parts like this:

✦ The first expression is the initial condition.

✦ The middle expression is the while condition.

✦ The final expression is what the PHP processor does at the end of each iteration.

Thus, this for loop runs a counter that changes like this: 10, 11, 12, 13, 14, 15, 16, 17, 18, and 19.

If you prefer the syntax of the while loop, you can code the preceding for loop by using a while loop as follows:

```php
<?php
    $counter = 10;
    while ($counter < 20) {
        print "$counter<br>\n";
        $counter++;
    }
?>
```

Looping with concurrent expressions

The syntax of the `for` loop in PHP allows you to include multiple expressions for each of the three parts of a `for` loop. Take a peek at the following code:

```php
<?php
    for ($height = 10, $width=20; $height < 20; $height++,
        $weight++) {
        $area = $height * $width;
        print "$area<br>\n";
    }
?>
```

Look carefully at the three parts of the `for` statement, and you'll see that some of them have more than one expression:

✦ `$height = 10, $width=20` These are the initial conditions. Before executing the `for` loop, PHP sets both of these initial conditions: `$height` is set to 10, and `$width` is set to 20.

✦ `$height < 20` This is the while condition for the `for` loop. Note that you can have only one expression here. If you want multiple expressions, use a logical operator, such as `$height < 20 && $width < 25`. Because logical operators are common to most languages, I talk about logical operators in the book about Perl; see Book III, Chapter 3, for details. (However, you often find redundancies in doubled-up conditions. For example, this "and" condition has the same effect as simply using `$width < 25`, because `width` will reach 25 before `height` reaches 20.)

✦ `$height++, $weight++` This is the statement that the `for` loop executes prior to each iteration. `$height` increases by 1, and `$weight` increases by 1.

If you think about it, you could break up the final part — `$height++, $weight++` — and put one or both of these expressions inside the loop; whether you do so is personal preference. Thus, you could transform your `for` loop like so:

```php
for ($height = 10, $width=20; $height < 20; $height++) {
    $area = $height * $width;
    print "$area<br>\n";
    $weight++;
}
```

Or even like this:

```
for ($height = 10, $width=20; $height < 20; ) {
    $area = $height * $width;
    print "$area<br>\n";
    $height++;
    $weight++;
}
```

You can leave out parts of the for loop, but you still need the two semicolons.

This brings up a strange point. If you're so inclined, you can even do this, which has the same result as the preceding code:

```
for ($height = 10, $width=20; $height < 20; $height++,
        $weight++,
    $area = $height * $width, print "$area<br>\n") {}
```

I had to break up this code to fit within the margins of this book, but in a text editor, these two lines of code would be squeezed onto a single line. Notice I put everything inside parentheses and nothing in the curly brackets. This code performs the same thing as the previous code; however, the present code is harder to read.

You sometimes see code like this, where everything is stuffed into the for loop expressions. The online PHP manual even has a similar example. My thoughts? Don't do it. Code like this is difficult to read, confusing to beginners, and, in general, bad practice. In fact, I prefer to have only one expression in each part of the for loop, although occasionally I'll need to use more than one.

Speeding up your for loops

If you're concerned about getting the most speed out of your for loops (which is important if you have PHP code on a high-traffic Web site), you'll want to consider the biggest bottlenecks in your code. Take a look at the following code:

```
for ($loop = 1; $loop < GetSize(); $loop++) {
    print ("$loop<br>\n");
}
```

This code calls a function called GetSize(), which is some function that you might write. Now suppose GetSize does something processor-intensive, such as looking up something in a database.

The PHP processor executes the test condition (the middle part of the `for` statement) *every time* the loop runs, at the beginning of the loop. Thus, if you have a call to a function as I do in the preceding example, and that function does something intensive like search a database, you end up doing that intensive operation with every iteration. Add to that the fact that this PHP code executes with every hit on the Web site, and you're in for some serious bandwidth trouble.

The fix is deceptively simple: Put the call to `GetSize` outside the loop and save it in a variable, like so:

```
$size = GetSize();
for ($loop = 1; $loop < $size; $loop++) {
    print ("$loop<br>\n");
}
```

Comparing with switch Statements

The `if-elseif-else` block of code is handy, but can be tedious if you have a large list of items to compare. PHP includes a `switch` block (sometimes called a `case` statement in other languages such as Pascal) that lets you do multiple comparisons quickly and easily. Here's an example:

```
<?php
    $today = getdate();
    $day = $today['weekday'];
    switch ($day) {
        case "Sunday":
            print "One day left before work<br>\n";
            break;
        case "Monday":
            print "I know, it's Monday...<br>\n";
            break;
        case "Tuesday":
            print "Hey, you survived Monday!<br>\n";
            break;
        case "Wednesday":
            print "Midweek!<br>\n";
            break;
        case "Thursday":
            print "Only one day left!<br>\n";
            break;
        case "Friday";
            print "Friday!<br>\n";
            break;
```

```
        default:
            print "Saturday!<br>\n";
            break;
    }
?>
```

This code grabs the current date in the form of an array by calling getdate(). Then the code extracts from the date the name of the current day (such as Thursday) and saves it in the $day variable. Then the switch statement begins. Basically, this code compares the $day variable first to Sunday, and if the variables match, the code runs the following line:

```
print "One day left before work<br>\n";
```

Otherwise, the code continues, comparing the variable to each string following the word case. If the PHP processor gets to the last case (Friday) and still doesn't find a match, the processor runs the code in the default section:

```
print "Saturday!<br>\n";
```

The default section is optional. If you don't include it, and none of the cases matches up, the PHP processor does not run any of the code following the case statements.

Notice that each case ends with the word break. This tells the PHP processor to jump out of the switch statement at that point. In the next section, "Tearing apart a switch statement," I provide you with the details of how break works and how you can use it to make more complex switch statements.

For the C++ programmers out there, you might notice something interesting about the preceding switch example: You can't do this in C++, but you can do it in PHP! In C++, you can't use strings in a switch statement; you can use only so-called ordinal values, meaning integers and characters. But PHP doesn't have this limitation. You're free to use strings in your switch statements.

Tearing apart a switch statement

When you put the word break after a case line in a switch statement, the PHP processor breaks out of the switch statement. If you don't include the word break, the processor continues into the *next* case, running the statements there, until the processor encounters a break statement or until the switch statement ends. Look at the following example:

```php
<?php
    $today = getdate();
    $day = $today['weekday'];
    switch ($day) {
        case "Sunday":
            print "Starting out...<br>\n";
        case "Monday":
        case "Tuesday":
            print "First half!<br>\n";
            break;
        case "Wednesday":
        case "Thursday";
        case "Friday";
            print "Second half!<br>\n";
            break;
        default:
            print "Saturday!<br>\n";
            break;
    }
?>
```

Suppose the $day variable contains Sunday. You can trace the switch state-
ment through and see how it will work. First, the PHP processor compares
$day to Sunday. It matches, so the PHP processor runs the line after the case
line, which is print "Starting out...
\n";. But there's no break
statement, so the PHP processor continues running the lines that are not
case lines. The next line is the one after Tuesday. Even though it's Sunday,
the PHP processor runs the line print "First half!
\n";. After this,
the word break is present, so the processor breaks out of the switch statement. Thus, for Sunday, the processor prints the following two lines:

```
Starting out...<br>
First half!<br>
```

Following this same logic, you can see that if today is Monday or Tuesday,
the processor prints only the following line:

```
First half!<br>
```

Then it breaks out of the switch statement.

But if today is Wednesday, Thursday, or Friday, the processor runs only
this line:

```
 print "Second half!<br>\n";
```

Then it breaks out. Finally, if today is `Saturday`, no cases match. The processor runs the `default` section, which says to print the string `"Saturday!<br>\n"`.

Understanding switch statements and objects

The PHP `switch` statement is incredibly powerful. We're talking amazing here. If you've explored classes and objects in PHP (see Book V, Chapter 7, for more information), you'll be delighted to know that you can use the `switch` statement with objects. And if you're coming from another language such as C++, you'll be overjoyed. Hang on to your seat. Look at this example:

```php
<?php

    class Test {
        var $name;
    };

    $mine = new Test;
    $mine->$name = 1;

    $one = new Test;
    $one->$name = 1;
    $two = new Test;
    $two->$name = 2;

    switch ($mine) {
        case $one:
            print "one\n";
            break;
        case $two:
            print "two\n";
            break;
        default:
            print "None of the above\n";
            break;
    };
?>
```

This example creates a simple class called `Test` and then an instance of `Test` (which is a shorter way of saying an object of class `Test`). Then the example creates two more instances of `Test` that will be compared to the first instance. Typically, in a more complex program, you would create these two comparison objects elsewhere, give them global scope, and allow the functions to access them.

Now look at the switch statement. The first case compares the $mine variable to the one called $one. The second case compares the $mine variable to the one called $two. Then I've provided a default case. And when you open this .php file in a browser, *voila!* The comparison succeeds, and you see the word one appear in your browser. Amazing. I'm going to go tell my friends about this; C++, for example, doesn't let you use strings in a switch statement.

Breaking and Continuing Your Loops

If you're inside a loop, whether it's a for loop, a while loop, or a do-while loop, you may occasionally need to include a special situation where the loop ends early. A realistic example of this is if you're writing a program that's looking up data in a database and you encounter an error.

You can abort a loop early by using a break statement. Here's a rather contrived example:

```php
<?php
    $number = 0;
    while ($number < 10) {
        print "$number<br>\n";
        if ($number == 5) {
            break;
        }
        $number++;
    }
?>
```

Instead of looking up data in a database and seeing if the lookup failed, I just test if the number is 5. But you can get the idea from this code: If the number is 5, I call the break statement, which breaks me out of the while loop prematurely. Here's the HTML output:

```
0<br>
1<br>
2<br>
3<br>
4<br>
5<br>
```

You also may need to stop the current iteration but continue executing the loop with the next iteration. To do that, use the continue keyword. Here's an example:

```php
<?php
    $number = 0;
    while ($number < 10) {
        if ($number == 5) {
            $number += 2;
            continue;
        }
        print "$number<br>\n";
        $number++;
    }
?>
```

In this example, if the number is 5, I want to skip over the print statement. Further, I want to add 2 to the current number. And so I do a special situation for 5 in the form of an if statement, and then I do a continue to skip over the rest of the code and go right to the next iteration. In the next iteration, the value of $number is 7, because I added 2 to $number. Of course, you can also implement this with an else statement and no continue, like in the following example:

```php
<?php
    $number = 0;
    while ($number < 10) {
        if ($number == 5) {
            $number += 2;
        }
        else {
            print "$number<br>\n";
            $number++;
        }
    }
?>
```

It's up to you whether you want to use a continue statement or an if-else block. However, I find that often the continue statement is more convenient when if-else blocks make for messier, more complex code.

Building HTML Tables with Loops

One cool thing you can do with some of these control structures is to build HTML tables. Remember that PHP is a scripting language for creating dynamic HTML pages.

Typically, you want to read your data from a database (such as MySQL) and then display the data in the form of a table on an HTML page. However, to keep things simple, in this example I'll skip the MySQL stuff and just use some hardcoded data that I put in an array. (For more on arrays, see Book V, Chapter 5; for more on MySQL, see Book VI.) Here goes:

```
<html><title>Houses For Sale</title>
<body>
The following houses are for sale. They are all next to each
            other.
Please make your decision fast, because they are going
            quickly.
<table border="1">
    <tr>
        <td><b>Address</b></td>
        <td><b>Hauntings</b></td>
        <td><b>Termite Count</b></td>
    </tr>
    <?php
    // Initialize the data
    $Houses[1]['address'] = '123 Main St.';
    $Houses[1]['hauntings'] = 5;
    $Houses[1]['termites'] = 6920;
    $Houses[2]['address'] = '125 Main St.';
    $Houses[2]['hauntings'] = 10;
    $Houses[2]['termites'] = 9563225;
    $Houses[3]['address'] = '124 Main St.';
    $Houses[3]['hauntings'] = 2;
    $Houses[3]['termites'] = 4279;
    $fields =
            array(1=>'address',2=>'hauntings',3=>'termites');
        for ($housenum=1; $housenum<=3; $housenum++) {
            print "<tr>\n";
            for ($fieldnum=1; $fieldnum<=3; $fieldnum++) {
                $fieldname = $fields[$fieldnum];
                print
            "<td>".$Houses[$housenum][$fieldname]."</td>\n";
            }
            print "</tr>\n";
        }
    ?>
</table>
</body></html>
```

This code is pretty self-explanatory. You can see the HTML (before the PHP code) that sets up the table with the `<table>` tag. Then the code includes some HTML tags that create a row in the table. Next comes the PHP code, which traverses through a two-dimensional array, using two `for` loops, an outer one and an inner one. The outer loop traverses through the houses; the inner loop moves through the data for the particular house.

When you open this `.php` file in a browser, you see a table containing the data, as shown in Figure 4-1. (Hmmm . . . looks like the house in the middle is the source of the trouble.)

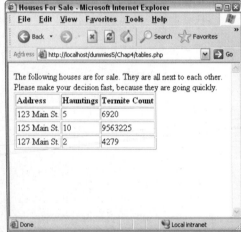

Figure 4-1:
You can use PHP to build a table. But I don't recommend buying the houses.

Chapter 5: Arrays and Functions

In This Chapter

✔ Gathering data into arrays

✔ Looping through arrays

✔ Copying arrays

✔ Working with multidimensional arrays

✔ Writing your own functions

Like most reputable languages, PHP allows you to store large amounts of data inside arrays and to divide up your programs into functions. PHP implements these two features a little differently from other languages, which provides you with some extra power over what some other languages offer. In this chapter, I show you how you can make arrays and functions work not just for you, but also with you.

Gathering Data into Arrays

An *array* is a variable that contains multiple storage slots, as opposed to a simple variable (sometimes called a *scalar*), which stores only a single data item. (If you want to find out more about arrays, I provide a quick introduction in Book III, Chapter 4.)

PHP arrays are a little different from those in some other languages in that you can index the array based on any value, not just a number starting at 0. For example, if you want an array to store the names of the lead actors in various movies, you can use the movie name as the index of the array. Here's an example:

```php
<?php
    $movies = array(
        "The Matrix" => "Keanu Reeves",
        "Raiders of the Lost Ark" => "Harrison Ford",
        "Forrest Gump" => "Tom Hanks",
        "Men in Black" => "Will Smith"
    );
    print $movies["The Matrix"];
?>
```

This example uses the language construct `array()` to create an array and store it in the `$movies` variable. The first array item's index is `The Matrix`, and its value is `Keanu Reeves`. The second array item's index is `Raiders of the Lost Ark`, and its value is `Harrison Ford`. After declaring the array, I print to the HTML the value in the array's first item. Notice that I reference it by its index, which is `The Matrix`.

You're not limited to using just strings for the indexes; the indexes can be either strings or integers. If you want your indexes to be integers — in which case, the first item in the array has index 0, the next one has index 1, the next has index 2, and so on — you can leave out the indexes in the declaration:

```php
<?php
    $names = array("Suzy", "Carousel", "Jennifer", "Jeff"
    );
    print $names[1];
?>
```

In this example, the first item — the one with the value `Suzy` — has index 0. The second has index 1, and so on. I then print to the HTML the item with index 1, which has the value `Carousel`.

If you attempt to create an array whose indexes are floating point numbers, you will find that it *almost* works. At first glance, it may appear that the process is working fine. However, in reality, the PHP processor truncates any float indexes to integers. Thus, `$myarray[1.5]` is the same as `$myarray[1]`.

PHP lets you intermix specifying and not specifying an index when you initialize an array. Doing so isn't the best programming style, but you might have a situation where you need it. Look at the following example:

```php
<?php
    $nums = array(
        1 => 2,   2 => 4,
        5 => 10,  6 => 12,
        14,  16,  18
    );
    print "1,{$nums[1]}<br>\n";
    print "2,{$nums[2]}<br>\n";
    print "3,{$nums[3]}<br>\n";
    print "4,{$nums[4]}<br>\n";
    print "5,{$nums[5]}<br>\n";
    print "6,{$nums[6]}<br>\n";
    print "7,{$nums[7]}<br>\n";
    print "8,{$nums[8]}<br>\n";
    print "9,{$nums[9]}<br>\n";
?>
```

In this example, I specified indexes for four of the elements; these indexes are 1, 2, 5, and 6. I didn't specify any indexes after that. In such situations, the PHP processor determines which index is numerically the highest, adds 1, and uses that for the next index. Because 6 is the highest, the next index is 7, then 8, and then 9.

When you open this PHP code in the browser, you see the following output:

```
1,2
2,4
3,
4,
5,10
6,12
7,14
8,16
9,18
```

You can see the indexes that were used: 1, 2, 5, 6, as I explicitly specified, and then 7, 8, and 9 as specified automatically by the PHP processor. I skipped the indexes 3 and 4, so the PHP processor didn't put anything in these indexes.

Be careful if you assign some indexes and let the PHP processor assign others. You may inadvertently overwrite an element. Look at the following example:

```php
<?php
    $names = array(0=>"Suzy", 1=>"Carousel",
        "Jennifer", 2=>"Jeff" );
    print $names[0]."<br>";
    print $names[1]."<br>";
    print $names[2]."<br>";
    print $names[3]."<br>";
    print $names[4]."<br>";
?>
```

The processor gets to the value Jennifer and assigns the index 2 automatically, because the processor only considers elements that it has encountered so far. Then when it gets to the next element, it sees that the element is also 2, and the processor then overwrites the previous element. Thus, the name Jennifer gets overwritten by the name Jeff, and in the end, you have three elements, not four! So be careful!

If you need to embed an array's value in a string, and the indexes are themselves strings, your best bet is to use angled brackets for clarity. But doing so can get messy because how do you notate a string inside a string? One way is to use double quotes for the main string, and single quotes for the index, like so:

```
print "{$movies['The Matrix']} was in The Matrix.<br>";
```

In this line of code, the array is called $movies, and the index is The Matrix. For the main string, I used double quotes, and for the index, I used single quotes.

Although it might seem bizarre and hard to believe (and I admit I was surprised), using double quotes throughout also works:

```
print "{$movies["The Matrix"]} was in The Matrix.<br>";
```

This works because the *parser* (the mechanism in the PHP processor that breaks the line of code apart and figures out what the different parts are) is smart enough to know that the stuff inside the curly brackets is special and might have double quotes in it.

So which one should you use? Like so many times in programming, the choice is yours. Personally, I prefer the single quotes inside double quotes, because that's a bit easier for us humans to read.

You can't use single quotes for the outer string because you can't embed variables inside single quotes. The PHP processor treats the entire thing as the actual string. Thus, if you do this:

```
print '{$movies["The Matrix"]} was in The Matrix.<br>';
```

you see the following output in your browser window:

```
{$movies["The Matrix"]} was in The Matrix.
```

This is probably not what you were hoping for.

Intermixing types of indexes

Occasionally, you may want some of your indexes to be integers and some to be strings. PHP allows you to do this; all you have to do is mix and match the indexes, as shown in the following example:

```php
<?php
    $nums = array(
        "a" => "b",
        1 => 2,
        "x" => "y"
    );
    print "a,{$nums['a']}<br>\n";
    print "1,{$nums['1']}<br>\n";
    print "x,{$nums['x']}<br>\n";
?>
```

In this code, I created an index a and stored the value b in it. Then I created an index 1 and stored the value 2 in it. Finally, I created an index x and stored the value y in it. And the program worked just fine.

The PHP processor allows you to mix types of indexes and will let the processor pick some indexes for you, all within the same code. This can get confusing. Here's an example of some potentially confusing code:

```php
<?php
    $funs = array(
        1=>2,
        "a"=>"b",
        3,
        "x"=>"y"
    );
    print "1,{$funs[1]}<br>\n";
    print "2,{$funs[2]}<br>\n";
    print "a,{$funs['a']}<br>\n";
    print "x,{$funs['x']}<br>\n";
?>
```

In this example, the third item in the array doesn't have an index. To assign an index, the PHP processor follows the usual rules and looks at whatever *numbered* indexes are present, finds the highest one, and adds 1. This example includes only one numbered index, which is 1, so this item gets the index 2. Thus, $funs[2] gets the value 3. You can see that this is correct when the print statements run.

In traditional languages such as C++, arrays always have integers for an index and always start at either 0 or 1, depending on the language. However, other languages, such as Python and Perl, allow you to use strings for indexes.

Storing values in an array

If you've already declared a particular array, you can add values to the array or modify the values that are already in it.

If you're familiar with other languages such as C++, you'll be happy to know that in PHP you can add new elements to the end of an array on the fly, even after you've created the array, thereby making the array longer. In C++, you can't do that.

After you create an array, you can change the value in one of its elements by simply assigning something new to the element. Suppose you have an array called `$nums`, and you initialized element 2 to have the value 4. You now want this element to have the value 10. Here's how you can change the value:

```
$nums[2] = 10;
```

This statement replaces whatever value element 2 previously had with the value 10.

In PHP, a variable doesn't have a fixed type. Therefore, you can write code such as this:

```
$nums[2] = 10;
```

Then later, you can change it to this:

```
$nums[2] = 'hello';
```

You can also add new values to an array, simply by assigning them with an index. Here's an example:

```
<?php
    $needmore = array(
        "icecream" => "chocolate",
        "pizza" => "pepperoni",
        "sandwich" => "turkey" );
    $needmore["snacks"] = "potato chips";
    print $needmore["pizza"]."<br>\n";
    print $needmore["snacks"];
?>
```

Here, I created the `$needmore` array and put three items in it. Then I added another item to the array, the value `potato chips` for the index `snacks`.

Removing a value from an array

To remove an item from an array, use the `unset` keyword. (Yes, the name is a little strange, but this is the world of computers.) Here's an example:

```php
<?php
    $movies = array(
        "The Matrix" => "Keanu Reeves",
        "Raiders of the Lost Ark" => "Harrison Ford",
        "Forrest Gump" => "Tom Hanks",
        "Men in Black" => "Will Smith" );
    unset ($movies["The Matrix"]);
    print $movies["The Matrix"];
?>
```

This code removes from the array the entry whose key is `The Matrix`. When you run this code, you see nothing in the output because `$movies["The Matrix"]` no longer has a value.

Because an array in PHP holds a set of values grouped by keys, the arrays don't have an order to them. This means you can remove an item from the array without leaving an empty slot in the array, as would be the case with other languages.

You might be curious why you would want to remove an item from an array. After all, can't you just ignore the item if you don't need it? Yes, you could, but sometimes you may want to loop through all the elements of the array. And if you have extra elements, it would be hard to simply skip over them. To find out how to loop through an array, check out the next section.

Looping through an array

If you need to perform an operation (such as printing out each member name; not removing a gall bladder) on every member of an array, PHP provides several ways to do so. Here's an example:

```php
<?php
    $missingbodyparts = array( "Jim" => "spleen", "Sally" =>
        "gall bladder",
        "Hank" => "appendix", "Jill" => "tonsils" );
    foreach ($missingbodyparts as $part) {
        print $part."<br>";
    }
?>
```

Here's the HTML output from this program:

```
spleen<br>gall bladder<br>appendix<br>tonsils<br>
```

This code fills the array `$missingbodyparts` with various body parts, keyed by a human's name. (Fortunately, nobody is missing his or her head.)

In this code, after I fill the array, I loop through each value in the array with the `foreach` keyword, printing each value. Notice the format of the `foreach` keyword; it's followed by a set of parentheses containing first the array name, then the keyword `as`, and then a temporary variable name that contains the value.

While the preceding code loops through the values of the array, you have no way to determine the index of each value. If you want both the index and value, modify the `foreach` construct slightly, adding a temporary variable for the index like so:

```
foreach ($missingbodyparts as $name=>$part)
```

At first, this syntax might seem strange, but notice that `$name=>$part` follows the same format as when you initialize the array, as in `"Jim" => "spleen"`. Here's an example:

```php
<?php
    $missingbodyparts = array( "Jim" => "spleen", "Sally" =>
        "gall bladder",
        "Hank" => "appendix", "Jill" => "tonsils" );
    foreach ($missingbodyparts as $name=>$part) {
        print "$name $part <br>";
    }
?>
```

Here's the HTML output from this program:

```
Jim spleen <br>Sally gall bladder <br>Hank appendix
<br>Jill tonsils <br>
```

This time inside the loop, you have access to both the index and the value.

The `foreach` keyword was introduced with PHP 4.0. Prior to PHP 4.0, you had access to a slightly different keyword, `each`, that let you loop through an array. This `each` keyword is still available, and you're welcome to use it with newer versions of PHP, although I find `foreach` much easier to use. If you want to find out more about the `each` keyword, please visit `www.php.net/each`.

Copying arrays

PHP provides two ways to copy arrays. One way is simply to assign the array to another array, as in the following code:

```php
<?php
    $music = array("Beatles" => "Let It Be",
        "Guess Who" => "No Time",
        "Led Zeppelin" => "Going to California",
        "David Bowie" => "Space Oddity");
    $moremusic = $music;
    $moremusic["David Bowie"] = "Changes";
    print $music["David Bowie"];
    print "<br>\n";
    print $moremusic["David Bowie"];
?>
```

In this example, I put together an array, filling it with various song titles. I then copy the array, which is the line shown in bold. When PHP copies the array this way, it also copies the individual elements; this means you now have two separate arrays, $music and $moremusic. To demonstrate this, I then change the song title of the David Bowie entry in the second array to Changes. I print out the song title for the David Bowie entry of the original array and then in the new array, yielding the following output:

```
Space Oddity<br>
Changes
```

The original array ($music) still has the original song, meaning the two arrays are entirely separate.

The other way to copy arrays is to create a new array and move through it, setting its members to those in the original array, like so:

```php
<?php
    $music = array( "Beatles" => "Let It Be",
        "Guess Who" => "No Time",
        "Led Zeppelin" => "Going to California",
        "David Bowie" => "Space Oddity" );
    foreach ($music as $artist => $title) {
        $music2[$artist] = $title;
    }
    foreach ($music2 as $artist => $title) {
        print "$artist $title<br>";
    }
?>
```

This example initializes the $music array and then moves through the array with the foreach keyword, adding elements to the $music2 array. You might notice that I didn't actually create the $music2 array. Because PHP is an interpreted language, the PHP processor lets you create variables on the fly. So when the processor came to the first $music2[$artist] = $title; line, the processor created the $music2 array for me, putting a single element in it, the current $artist and $title.

 You might wonder, if you can use a single copy statement such as $music = $music2, why bother looping through the array? Because while looping through the array, you can do any extra processing and modifications you want, such as adding spaces or other formatting to the strings, or anything necessary for your particular program.

Dimensioning with multidimensional arrays

To create a multidimensional array in PHP, use double-bracket notation, like in the following example:

```
$day["January"][1] = "Monday";
$day["January"][2] = "Tuesday";
$day["January"][3] = "Wednesday";
$day["February"][1] = "Thursday";
$day["February"][2] = "Friday";
$day["February"][3] = "Saturday";
```

Or you can create a multidimensional array like this:

```
$day2 = array (
    "January" => array(1=>"Monday", 2=>"Tuesday",
        3=>"Wednesday"),
    "February" => array(1=>"Thursday", 2=>"Friday",
        3=>"Saturday"));
```

Each example puts together a two-dimensional array, where the first index is a month, the second is a date, and the value is a day of the week. The first form takes up more lines, although it's easier to read. The second form takes fewer lines of code, but it is more confusing to read. The choice is yours.

Sorting arrays (and other fun)

You have at your disposal a list of built-in PHP functions that operate on arrays. These functions let you do fun things like sort the arrays by value or key, sort them in reverse order, count the elements in the array, and shuffle the arrays.

For a complete list of these fun features, check out www.php.net/manual/en/ref.array.php.

Extracting elements from functions returning an array

Some functions return an array. Many scripting languages, PHP included, have a handy feature that enables you to save the separate portions of the array into individual variables. In PHP, you use the list keyword. The syntax is a little bizarre, and I demonstrate it in the following, equally bizarre example:

```php
<?php
    function food() {
        $stuff = array("Goopabluck", "542789", "Yacklblob");
        return $stuff;
    }
    list($martianname, $martianyear, $martianfood) = food();
    print $martianname."<br>".$martianyear.
        "<br>".$martianfood;
?>
```

In this example, I use a function declaration, which is a topic I discuss in "Calling Code with Functions," later in this chapter.

The function called food returns an array that contains the values Goopabluck, 542789, Yacklblob. (Yes, I said it was bizarre.) Later, I call the function. I could just save the results in my own array, say $martianstuff or something. However, when I call the food function, I know that the function returns an array, and I know how many values the array contains, *and* I want to put these values in separate variables. The way to do this is with the list keyword.

The syntax for the list keyword looks similar to a function but doesn't treat it like a function. Think of it as simply a way to pull out the parts of an array and put them in the individual variables. When the food function returns the array to me, I place the array's first value in the $martianname variable, the second value in the $martianyear variable, and the third value in the $martianfood variable. In the end, I have three variables rather than an array.

The list keyword works only with arrays whose keys are integers, and the list keyword assumes that the first element has the key 0. If you use list with an array that does not start at 0, the first variable in the list keyword will be empty. For example, suppose you modified the food function to include the following line:

```php
$stuff = array(1=>"Goopabluck", 2=>"542789", 3=>"Yacklblob");
```

The first variable in the list statement, $martianname, will be empty; the
second variable, $martianyear, will be Goopabluck; and the third variable,
$martianfood, will be 542789.

The list keyword also enables you to extract only the first members of an
array. For example, if I wanted the food function to return only the first two
members of the array, I could use this statement:

```
list($martianname, $martianyear) = food();
```

Calling Code with Functions

What would a programming language be without functions? Well, other than
a language without functions, it would be one that's not particularly useful.
And so, the designers of PHP, being of the levelheaded sort, have given us
the ability to write functions in PHP code.

I'm assuming in this chapter that you have a basic understanding of functions. If you're not sure what functions are, please check out Book III,
Chapter 3. (Perl uses the term *subroutine,* which is essentially the same
thing as a function in PHP.)

Here's an example of defining and then using a function in PHP:

```
<html><head><title>Dummies Library</title></head>
<body>
    <h1>Welcome to the Dummies Library!</h1>
    Your book is overdue! Here is your fine:
<?php
    function OverdueBookAmount() {
        return time() * 100;
    }
    print OverdueBookAmount();
?>
    If you're unable to pay this fine, please use a credit
            card.
</body></html>
```

I've shown the function OverdueBookAmount in bold. Further, as a reminder
of the purpose of PHP, I included some HTML so that this code generates a
complete Web page, which looks like this:

```
Welcome to the Dummies Library!
Your book is overdue! Here is your fine: 105476132900 If
            you're
unable to pay this fine, please use a credit card.
```

(Make sure you don't have any overdue books at this library!) The function returns a number, which when I ran it was 105476132900. The calling code takes the results and does what it wants with it; in this case, `print OverdueBookAmount();` causes the results to be printed to the .html file. To call the function, you simply type the function's name, followed by open and closed parentheses.

You can also pass parameters into a function, like so:

```php
<?php
    function OverdueBookAmount($forgive) {
        if ($forgive == true) {
            return 0;
        }
        else {
            return time() * 100;
        }
    }
    print OverdueBookAmount(false);
?>
```

This time the function `OverdueBookAmount` takes a single parameter called `$forgive`. This variable is then a local variable that can be used throughout the function. The `$forgive` variable is used in an `if` statement, and later, the function is called, passing a value into the function. The value passed in this case is `false`, which is a Boolean value.

In PHP, because you do not specify a type when you create a variable, you also do not specify types for the parameters in a function. Be careful because that means any code calling your function can pass any value, not just those of a certain type. In my `OverdueBookAmount` function, for example, I could pass the string value `GoAway` rather than simply `true` or `false`. If I do that, the PHP processor will convert the value if necessary when I use it in an expression. In my example, however, the PHP processor does not need to do any conversions. If I pass `GoAway`, my code compares this value to `true`, which will have strange results; the comparison will succeed (because PHP treats empty strings as false in comparisons such as this, and PHP treats strings that contain something as true), causing the `if` block to execute.

Although PHP variables are case-sensitive — meaning the variable name `$CornOnTheCob` is a separate variable from `$CORNONTHECOB` — the same is not true for functions. When you create a function called `GetYeTheToaster`, you can later make a call to the function with `GETYETHETOASTER`. However, I don't recommend doing so because it can create confusing code.

A function doesn't have to return anything. In the eyes of the most staunch computer scientists, however, a function by definition must return something, and if it doesn't, it's instead called a *procedure* or *subroutine*. In PHP as in the C++ language, regardless of whether the piece of code returns something, it's still called a function. If you write a function that doesn't return anything, just don't call return. Or, if you must call return to exit the function, don't put anything after it, like so:

```
return;
```

Declaring local and global variables

In addition to passing variables into functions as parameters, you can also create variables within a function that are local to the function. These variables exist only inside the function; they go away when the function is over. When you call the function a second time, the variables get re-created from scratch. Creating a local variable within a function is easy; you simply create a variable inside the function as you would any other variable. Because you create it inside the function, the variable is automatically local to the function.

Global variables are different from locals and also different from many other languages. If you want to create a variable that is global, meaning all functions have access to the variable, simply create the variable outside of any other function. But then, inside the function, you have to type the keyword global, followed by the global variable's name. The following code demonstrates both a local and a global variable:

```php
<?php
    $globalvar = 10;
    function HasLocals() {
        global $globalvar;
        $globalvar = $globalvar + 1;
        $localvar = 20;
        print "Inside function: $globalvar<br>$localvar<br>";
    }
    print "Before function: $globalvar<br>";
    HasLocals();
    print "After function: $globalvar<br>";
?>
```

Note that you can put several variables on a single global statement, like so:

```
global $globalvar, $globalvar2;
```

In PHP 4.0 and later, you can call a function even if you declare it later in your code. Therefore, you don't need what other languages call forward declarations. However, if you're using PHP 3.0 (in which case, I encourage you to upgrade), make sure your function declarations appear only before you call them.

However, there is an exception to the rule for PHP 4.0 and beyond. In Book V, Chapter 7, I discuss how you can divide up your code into multiple files. If you put a function in another PHP file, the include or require statement must precede any calls to any functions in the file you're including or requiring. See Book V, Chapter 7, for details.

Creating advanced functions

Because PHP is an interpreted language, you can do some strange things that are not allowed in traditional, compiled languages such as C++. For example, you can declare a function *inside* an if statement. You can then have different forms of the function, and the PHP processor will use a different form based on the condition.

Here's an example of this unusual feature:

```php
<?php
    $username = $_GET['username'];
    if ($username == "Jeff") {
        function Calc($a) {
            return $a * $a;
        }
    }
    else {
        function Calc($a) {
            return $a + $a;
        }
    }
    for ($i = 0; $i<10; $i++) {
        print Calc($i)."<br>\n";
    }

?>
```

This example uses the $_GET array, which requires an HTML form; I discuss these in Book V, Chapter 6. Here's an HTML form that you can use for this example:

```
<html><head><title>Advanced Function Demo</title></head>
<body>
<h1>Welcome to my site!</h1>
```

```
<form name="form1" method="get" action="advancedfunc.php">
    Your name please?
    <input type="text" name="username">
    <br>
    <input type="submit">
  </form>
</body>
</html>
```

When you open this form and subsequently run the PHP program (by clicking the submit button), you see these numbers in the browser if you enter the name Jeff (each number will appear on a separate line):

```
0 1 4 9 16 25 36 49 64 81
```

Otherwise, you see these numbers:

```
0 2 4 6 8 10 12 14 16 18
```

You can see how this conditional function works; The program defines the Calc function one way if the username is Jeff and another way if the username is not Jeff.

If you're an advanced programmer, you have at your disposal many of these advanced function features that most people probably wouldn't have much use for, such as variable-length argument lists and variable functions. If you're interested in exploring these two topics, you can find them on the PHP site at these three addresses:

✦ www.php.net/functions for conditional functions

✦ www.php.net/manual/en/functions.arguments.php for variable-length functions

✦ www.php.net/manual/en/functions.variable-functions.php for variable functions, which refers to calling a function by name when that name is stored as a string in a variable

Chapter 6: Interacting with HTML

In This Chapter

✔ Getting data from an HTML form

✔ Sending headers and redirecting HTML pages

✔ Setting and retrieving cookies

✔ Providing user authentication

*P*robably the most powerful aspect of PHP is its capability to allow for dynamic, interactive HTML. Although HTML already allows you to create forms through which users can enter data, such processing takes place on the client end. Wouldn't it be nice to be able to process that data on the server end? You can with PHP. On the server end, you have at your disposal many features such as CGI programs and Perl scripts. Or, you can work your server-side processing right into the PHP files. In this chapter, I show you how to accomplish this so that you can create dynamic Web pages complete with user interaction.

Getting Data from an HTML Form

To get data from an HTML form, the first thing you need to do is create an HTML form. You put this form in a separate file from the .php file that processes the form. For example, you may create a file called userentry.html that looks like Listing 6-1.

Listing 6-1: A File That Provides the User Input Form

```
<html><head><title>User Information</title></head>
<body>
<h1>Welcome to my site!</h1>
<form name="form1" method="get" action="processinput.php">
  <p>Least Favorite Food:
    <select name="food">
      <option>Anchovies</option>
      <option>Asparagus</option>
      <option>Brussels Sprouts</option>
      <option>Seaweed</option>
    </select>
```

```
      <br>
      Favorite Actor:
      <input type="text" name="actor">
      <br>
      <input type="submit">
   </p>
   </form>
</body>
</html>
```

This is a basic form in an HTML page. Figure 6-1 shows you what the form looks like when a client opens it in Internet Explorer.

Figure 6-1:
This is what the form looks like on the client computer in Internet Explorer.

After you have the form, you can put together the .php file that reads the data from the form. The process of the user filling in the data and the PHP program retrieving the form data goes like this:

1. The user receives the .html file containing the form.

2. The user enters data and clicks the Submit button.

3. The client browser sends a request for a PHP file and sends the entered data along with the request.

4. The server receives the request and sends it to the PHP processor, which accesses the data, processes the data, and builds a Web page.

5. The server sends the built Web page back to the client.

Before I show you a .php file that can process the data, I want to say a few words about these steps. When the user enters the data in a form and clicks the Submit button, the browser sends the data to the server by appending the data to the end of the `.php` filename. For example, say that you use the preceding form, choose Asparagus, and enter Ingrid Bergman. When you click Submit, the browser treats this as if you entered the following URL into the Address bar of the browser:

```
http://www.jeffcogswell.com/processinput.php?food=Anchovies&a
          ctor=Ingrid+Bergman
```

Note that for the domain name I'm using my own, `jeffcogswell.com`. Because I didn't specify a domain name in the action parameter of the form tag, the browser will use whatever domain is hosting your `userentry.html` file, not `www.jeffcogswell.com`.

In Listing 6-1, I provided names for the two form fields:

✦ `"food"`: The drop-down list box (a select object)

✦ `"actor"`: The text field

Now look at the preceding URL. After the `processinput.php` filename, the URL consists of a question mark and the following two parts, separated by an ampersand, `&`:

✦ `food=Anchovies`

✦ `actor=Ingrid+Bergman`

In other words, the value of `"food"` is `Anchovies`, and the value of `"actor"` is `Ingrid+Bergman`. The Web browser replaced the space between Ingrid and Bergman with a plus sign; that way, no spaces need to be passed in the URL, which otherwise could be confusing.

If you actually typed in Ingrid+Bergman, with a plus sign, the URL would replace the plus sign with the characters %2B, the hexadecimal form of the code for a plus sign. Remember when life was simple before computers, automated teller machines, and, heaven forbid, talking cars?

Writing the server-side script

Back at the ranch (or the server side, anyway), the Web server receives the URL, tears it apart, and feeds the `.php` file to the PHP processor, along with the parameters, `food=Anchovies` and `actor=Ingrid+Bergman`. The PHP processor stores the parameters in an array called `_GET`.

The `_GET` array is *superglobal,* meaning you can access it from anywhere, including any functions, without having to declare it with the `global` keyword.

When your PHP program starts, the _GET array has the following keys and values:

✦ _GET['food'] = "Anchovies"

✦ _GET['actor'] = "Ingrid Bergman"

Notice that by the time your PHP program gets the parameters, the space between Ingrid and Bergman has returned; the plus sign was only used in the URL.

Knowing that PHP does these automatic conversions for you, you can put together the simple .php file in Listing 6-2 and save it as processinput. php.

The name processinput.php must be the same name you used in the action parameter of the form tag in the original .html file, which is what I did in Listing 6-1.

Listing 6-2: A PHP File That Reads the Parameters Passed in from the Form

```
<html><title>Results</title>
<body>
<?php
    $food = $_GET["food"];
    $actor = $_GET["actor"];
    print "$food<br>\n$actor\n";
?>
</body>
</html>
```

Now you're ready to try this out. Don't simply open the processinput.php file, or nothing will happen. Instead, open userentry.html. Then choose a food, type in an actor name, and click Submit. If you uploaded the files correctly to your server, you see a page that lists what you chose:

```
Anchovies
Ingrid Bergman
```

Sharing data between HTML pages

In the preceding section, you discover how the Web server and PHP system process the URLs by stripping out the parameters that follow a question mark and that are separated by ampersands. Now, you can write .php files and .html files that interact with each other through such parameters.

For example, you can have an .html file that looks like this:

```
<html><title>Not particularly useful yet</title>
<body>
    <a
    href="processinput.php?food=Anchovies&actor=Ingrid+
        Bergman">
    Click here</a> for the results!
</body>
</html>
```

Try putting this file on your server, and alongside it, put the file shown earlier in Listing 6-2. Then open this .html file in a client computer and click the <u>Click here</u> link. When you do, you get the results from the .php file, just as if the data were passed in through a form:

```
Anchovies
Ingrid Bergman
```

Of course, as in the preceding .html file, this isn't particularly useful because the data is hardcoded. However, imagine if this .html file were simply the result of a .php file after processing? Now you're onto something, Watson.

Try this one on for size. Update your processinput.php file so that it looks like Listing 6-3.

Listing 6-3: A File That Sends Parameters to Another .php File

```
<html><title>Results</title>
<body>
<?php
    $food = $_GET["food"];
    $actor = $_GET["actor"];
    $foodHTML = urlencode($food);
    $actorHTML = urlencode($actor);
    print "$food<br>\n$actor<p>\n";
    print "<a href=formattedresults.php?".
        "food=$foodHTML&actor=$actorHTML>";
    print "Click here</a> for formatted results!";
?>
</body>
</html>
```

Notice two main changes from the original processinput.php shown in Listing 6-2:

✦ I added two calls to the urlencode function. This is a built-in function that replaces the space in the actor name with a + (plus); then this program stores the results of urlencode in variables called $foodHTML and $actorHTML. That's required for sending the name as a parameter in a URL.

✦ I added a link to another .php file, called formattedresults.php. Look closely at the link: I embedded within the string the $foodHTML and $actorHTML variables. Sneaky, no?

The second .php file, formattedresults.php, is shown in Listing 6-4.

Listing 6-4: A File That Reads Parameters Passed to It and Sends Them Back

```
<html><title>Formatted Results</title>
<body>
<table border="1">
    <tr>
        <td>Food</td>
        <td>Actor</td>
    </tr>
    <tr>
        <?php
            $food = $_GET["food"];
            $actor = $_GET["actor"];
            $actorHTML = urlencode($actor);
            $foodHTML = urlencode($food);
            print "<td>$food</td>\n";
            print "<td>$actor</td>\n";
        ?>
    </tr>
</table>
    <?php
        print
        "<a href=processinput.php?".
        "food=$foodHTML&actor=$actorHTML>";
    ?>
    Click here</a> for unformatted results.
</body>
</html>
```

The .php file in Listing 6-4 is similar to that in Listing 6-3, except that it formats the data in a table. And like Listing 6-3, Listing 6-4 also includes a link to get back to the original data.

Here are the three files that you need on your server to try out Listing 6-4:

✦ `userentry.html`, shown in Listing 6-1. This is the file you start out with by viewing it in your client browser.

✦ The updated `processinput.php`, shown in Listing 6-3. The `userentry.html` file links to this.

✦ The `formattedresults.php` file, shown in Listing 6-4.

After you've uploaded these files, you can test the whole program by following these steps:

1. **Visit the** `userentry.html` **page.**

2. **Choose a least-favorite food, type a favorite actor's name, and then click Submit.**

   You go to the results of the `processinput.php` page, which includes a link.

3. **Click the link.**

   You go to the `formattedresults.php` page. If you typed the code in correctly, the results of `formattedresults.php` will also have your chosen food and actor, even though you did not come to the `formattedresults.php` file by way of a form. It works — get out the anchovies and celebrate!

When you're choosing the names of the form elements that will be passed as parameters into the `.php` files (such as `food` and `actor`), be careful that you don't use *HTML entities* for your names. HTML entities are the codes HTML uses for special characters. For example, suppose you have the following HTML file:

```
<html>
&amp
</html>
```

When you open this file in a browser, you see only an ampersand, &, not the characters &amp. The reason is that & (with a semicolon after it) is a special HTML entity for ampersand. Even if you leave the semicolon off (as I did in the preceding HTML), the browser still interprets it as an ampersand.

You may run into trouble if you have a form and you name one of your elements `amp`. If you pass this element in a form to a PHP file, all is fine . . . at first. You may, for example, pass the following URL to the server after filling out the form:

```
http://www.mydomain.com/processsomething.php?name=Harold&amp=
         100
```

At this stage, there is no problem. Your `processsomething.php` file extracts the variables just fine. `_GET['name']` yields `Harold`, and `_GET['amp']` yields `100`.

But suppose your `processsomething.php` file wants to include a clickable link, passing these two values to another `.php` file (just like Listings 6-3 and 6-4 do earlier in this chapter). You can include in `processsomething.php` a line like this:

```
print "<a href=dosomething.php?name=$me&amp=$size>Click</a>";
```

This line yields the following HTML code after the PHP processor has its way:

```
<a href=dosomething.php?name=harold&amp=100>Click</a>
```

Again, this works fine so far. If you open the resulting HTML file in your browser, and you look at your source for the HTML, you see `&amp=100` at the end of the `a` tag, which is not a problem. However, the browser will get confused. If you move your mouse over the link from this line of code, you see the following line in the status bar of the browser:

```
href=dosomething.php?name=harold&=100
```

Look closely at this line. The letters `amp` are gone. Yes, the browser got confused by the `&amp` and insisted on changing it to an ampersand. Oops! (That's actually by design; the browser is *supposed* to change `&amp` to an ampersand.)

TIP

A handy newline converter

If you have several strings that end with newline characters (shown as `\n` in the string) and you want to display these lines in the resulting HTML as a newline, you can easily convert the `\n` characters to `<br>` tags, like so:

```
print nl2br("Hello\nEverybody\n");
```

The key here is the `nl2br` function. It takes a string and replaces `\n` with a `<br>` tag and another `\n`. This results in the following HTML:

```
Hello<br />
Everybody<br />
```

Yes, the `<br>` tags show up as `<br />`, but that's really the XHTML and XML–standardized version of the `<br>` tag. The browsers treat the `<br />` tag the same as a `<br>` tag.

What do you do to avoid this problem? The answer is simple: Avoid using form field names that are HTML entities such as `amp`. How do you know if you're using an HTML entity? You can find several tables on the Web that list them. Here's a pretty good one:

```
www.htmlgoodies.com/tutors/&command.html
```

Yes, there's an ampersand in the URL here; be sure to type it.

Sending Headers and Redirecting HTML Pages

If you've done a lot of Web surfing, you've undoubtedly come to a page that automatically redirects you to another page, sending you off to another realm from where you started. (Sounds exciting, eh.) If you want to redirect users from your own Web page, you can accomplish this several ways, including with PHP.

When you have a `.php` file and the PHP processor is building an `.html` file, the processor creates a set of *HTTP response headers* (or just *headers* for short) that the Web server sends to the client first. These headers direct the browser in various ways. For example, have you ever wondered how the Web browser knows to start up Adobe Acrobat when you point to a `.pdf` file on the Internet? At first, it may seem that the browser just looks at the `.pdf` extension. But that's not the case. For example, suppose you create a simple file like this:

```
<html><body>
    Hi! This is just an HTML file!
</body></html>
```

If you save this file on your Web server with filename `fooldya.pdf` and point your browser to the file, different things might happen depending on which browser you're using. For Internet Explorer, the file displays as a regular `.html` file inside the browser. Acrobat doesn't open, even though the file has a `.pdf` extension. (However, if you bypass the Web server and just save this file on a Windows client computer, for example, and choose Internet Explorer's File⇨Open menu, Acrobat *will* launch because in such cases Internet Explorer does use the filename extension.) If you're using the Mozilla browser on a Linux box, you'll likely see a prompt to download the file or open it.

When you load the file from a Web server, how does the browser know to launch Acrobat? Before the browser receives the HTML data, the browser receives a set of HTTP response headers. One of these headers is called Content-Type and looks like this:

```
Content-Type: application/pdf
```

Getting the headers straight

PHP enables you to control which HTTP response headers the Web server sends to the client browser. Remember, however, that the HTTP response headers must go to the browser before the first line of HTML code. Therefore, after you start sending the HTML code, you can no longer send any more headers for that .html file. How do you know if you've sent HTML yet? You know by the position of the HTML in your .php file. If you put your calls to header() in PHP code that's at the beginning of the file, before any HTML tags, like so, you'll be fine:

```
<?php
    header("Content-type:
        application/pdf");
```

```
?>
<html>
    // . . . some HTML code
</html>
```

You run into trouble if you do something like the following because the <html> tag comes before the call to header():

```
<html>
<?php
    header("Content-type:
        application/pdf");
?>
```

This header, which comes from the Web server, instructs the browser to open Acrobat to view the PDF file. How does the server know that the file is a PDF file? Often the server simply looks at the filename extension. So we're back to the filename extension.

However, PHP does have some powerful header tools. If you have some documents on your Web site that you want to force to be a certain type (such as PDF), you can use PHP to control the type. You can also control many other aspects of the files by using the headers, which I discuss in the following sections.

Controlling the application type

Suppose you have a file on your Web server that does not have a standard filename extension (and for whatever reason, you don't want to rename it), but you want to specify to the client browser what type of application to use when it encounters the file. For example, I uploaded to my Web site a file called AnotherRealPDF (with no filename extension). Suppose I were contractually not allowed to change the filename, or the file was put up by somebody else and I don't have rights on the server to change the filename. Then I can write this PHP file, which I'll call openpdf.php:

```php
<?php
    header("Content-type: application/pdf");
    readfile("AnotherRealPDF");
?>
```

I upload the file to my site, and when users access it as `http://
www.jeffcogswell.com/openpdf.php`, the actual PDF file — called
`AnotherRealPDF` — downloads to their computers and opens in Acrobat.
(The `readfile` function simply opens the specified file and sends it to the
client computer. Note that some browsers, notably Mozilla and Netscape,
substitute a different default filename, `openpdf.php`.)

You can also use this header approach in conjunction with the techniques
I describe in the section "Providing User Authentication," later in this
chapter. For example, you can put your PDF file in a private part of the file
system (outside of the public HTML directories) and then allow only certain
users to see the file:

```php
<?php
    if (!isset($_SERVER['PHP_AUTH_USER'])) {
        header('WWW-Authenticate: Basic realm="Please Login
            to My Site"');
        header('HTTP/1.0 401 Unauthorized');
        print 'Sorry, you are not authorized to view this
            page.';
        exit;
    } else {
        $username = $_SERVER['PHP_AUTH_USER'];
        $password = $_SERVER['PHP_AUTH_PW'];
        if ($username == "me" && $password == "me") {
            header("Content-type: application/pdf");
            readfile("AnotherRealPDF");
        }
        else {
            print 'Sorry, you are not authorized to view this
                page.';
        }
    }
?>
```

Redirecting to a different page

You may want to set up an automatic redirector that sends visitors of a certain page to a different page. In this section, just to make life interesting,
I explain how to dynamically construct the redirector. Here's a serious
example: On my Web site, I have a "causes" page, which includes a link to

missingkids.org, the Web site for the National Center for Missing and Exploited Children. But I provide more than just a link: I have a form that includes a drop-down list of all the states. If you click your state and then click Submit, you are taken to the missingkids.org site, showing the cases for your state. How did I do this? I did it all in PHP, using a combination of forms and redirects.

First, the form was simple: It's just a list of values containing the two-letter code for each state. The form's action looks like this: /kidsredir.php. Nothing fancy there. The value for the state is passed as a parameter named state. Now the magic is in the kidsredir.php file; here's the entire file:

```php
<?php
    $state = $_GET["state"];
    header("location:
            http://www.missingkids.org/precreate/".$state.
            ".html");
?>
```

This file extracts the state into the $state variable and constructs a URL based on that state. And then the magic begins: This file contains no HTML code, making it safe to send headers. This file sends a header called location, which forces the browser to redirect to the given site. Thus, if you choose California in the list, you first go here:

http://www.jeffcogswell.com/kidsredir.php?state=CA

which, in turn, redirects you here:

http://www.missingkids.org/precreate/CA.html

. . . all thanks to the magic of the headers.

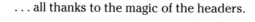

Printing your page headers

If you want to print your page's headers and you're using PHP with Apache, you can use a handy function called apache_request_ headers. Here's a sample:

```php
<?php
$headers = apache_request_headers();
foreach ($headers as $header => $value) {
    echo "$header: $value <br />\n";
}
?>
```

If you're using a version of PHP earlier than 4.3.0, you need to use the function getallheaders in place of apache_ request_headers.

Setting and Retrieving Cookies

A cookie is a simple storage mechanism on the browser side, which is the client side. Therefore, it may seem a little strange to be dealing with cookies in a book that covers a server-side language like PHP. But fear not, all strangeness shall go away, and you will soon be using PHP to read and write cookies on browsers.

The setting and unsetting of cookies takes place when the browser processes the headers. Therefore, you can set cookies only at the beginning of your .php files, before you have any HTML code.

Setting a cookie

To set a cookie, call the setcookie() function. Pass the name of the cookie and a value for the cookie. Listing 6-5 demonstrates this.

Listing 6-5: setcookie.php

```php
<?php
    // This code must come before the HTML, since
    // cookies are part of the headers!
    setcookie('dummies1000', 'hello');
?>

<html><title>Set a Cookie! Yum yum!</title>
<body>
    This file will store a temporary cookie in the browser.
        The cookie
    will be a session-only cookie, and will go away when you
        shut
    down your browser.<p>
    The cookie information is as follows:<p>
<pre>
    name: dummies1000
    value: 'hello'
</pre>
</body>
```

Notice that I set the cookie prior to any HTML code. The cookie is called dummies1000 (think of that name as a variable name), and its value is the string 'hello'.

Having a cookie

Listing 6-6, called getcookie.php, shows you how to retrieve the value of a cookie.

Listing 6-6: getcookie.php

```
<html><title>Have a cookie! Yum yum!</title>
<body>
    This file reads the temporary cookie that was set
    in the <a href="setcookie.php">setcookie.php</a>
    file.<p>
<pre>
    name: dummies1000<br>
    The value according to the PHP code is...
    <?php
        print $_COOKIE['dummies1000'];
    ?>
</pre>
</body>
```

When you open the setcookie.php page, the cookie is set for the duration of the session, which simply means the cookie is (dare I say it?) *eaten* (groan) after you shut down the browser. But if you keep the browser open and then visit getcookie.php, you will see that the cookie's value is indeed still set.

When you set a cookie, the cookie's value is not available to the page where you set it. It's true and a bit of a bummer. So if you write a PHP program where you set a cookie value, don't attempt to access the _COOKIE array inside that same .php file, hoping to access the value. Instead, just hard-code the cookie's value or store it in another variable.

Storing cookies for the long term

The setcookie() function includes some optional parameters that give you more control over your jar of cookies. (Ahh, so many cookie jokes.) One crunchy and useful parameter is the expiration parameter. This is a date that the cookie is removed from the system. Prior to that date, the cookie lives on the user's system in the cookie cache.

To specify the date, you have to give it in a Unix time, which is the number of seconds since January 1, 1970.

If you want, for example, to see that your cookie rots and expires 60 days from the date the page is loaded, determine the current Unix time and add the number of seconds corresponding to 60 days, which is $60 \times 60 \times 60 \times 24$. Thus, to set a cookie that will stay on the user's system for 60 days, use this:

```
<?php
    $expiredate = time()+60*60*60*24;
    setcookie('dummies1001', 'goodbye', $expiredate);
?>
```

```
<html><title>60-day Cookie! What a concept!</title>
<body>
    I just set a cookie called dummies1001, containing
    the value "goodbye", which will last for 60 days, until
    <?php
        print date("F j, Y", $expiredate);
    ?>
</body>
```

Then to read the cookie, access it as you would any other cookie:

```
<html><title>Have a 60-day cookie! Woohoo!</title>
<body>
    The cookie for dummies1001 is set to:
    <?php print $_COOKIE['dummies1001']; ?>
</pre></body>
```

Providing User Authentication

Some Web sites display a dialog box requesting that users enter a username
and password before they can enter the site. These dialog boxes are not
HTML pages; they're created by the browser. If you have some top-secret
Web pages that you want to guard, PHP gives you the ability to notify the
browser to open such a dialog box. This is called *HTTP authentication*.

You can use PHP's HTTP authentication features only if you're running PHP
as an Apache module, not as a CGI. For more information on this and other
features, refer to *PHP 5 For Dummies,* by Janet Valade (Wiley Publishing, Inc.).

The HTTP authentication dialog box is not part of PHP; it's controlled by the
HTTP response headers that the Web server sends just prior to the HTML
code. PHP simply provides you with a means for specifying the necessary
headers that tell the browser to display the dialog box.

The process goes like this:

1. The PHP program sends the header requesting a username and
   password.

2. The user enters the username and password, which gets sent back to
   the server.

   If the user clicks Cancel, the process aborts, and the PHP program can
   print an invalid user message or whatever message you wants to show.

3. The Web server reloads and restarts the `.php` file from the beginning.

This time, the username and password are set, and no headers are sent to the browser. The PHP program can now verify the username and password.

The idea of reloading and restarting the `.php` file seems a bit awkward at first, but the reasoning is sound: To authenticate the page, the Web server must first send a header asking for a username and password. The browser sends back the username and password, and the authentication header is no longer needed. Instead the server can send a new set of headers. But the authentication header has already been sent, so there's no bringing it back. How do you fix this? Restart the page. This seems strange, but it works.

Here's a simple `.php` file that requests authentication; remember that the system restarts this page after authentication:

```php
<?php
    $username = $_SERVER['PHP_AUTH_USER'];
    $password = $_SERVER['PHP_AUTH_PW'];
    if (!isset($_SERVER['PHP_AUTH_USER'])
    || $username != "me" || $password != "me") {
        header('WWW-Authenticate: Basic realm="Please Login
            to My Site"');
        header('HTTP/1.0 401 Unauthorized');
        print 'Sorry, you are not authorized to view this
            page.';
        exit;
    }
?>
<html><title>Top Secret Page</title>
<body>
    <h1>This is a top secret page!</h1>
    Welcome! Here you can discover all my deepest secrets!
            You have been warned!
</body></html>
```

When you open this page in the browser through the Web server, you're presented with a dialog box asking for your username and password. If you type the username and password correctly (they're both me in this case), you see the secret members-only page. If you type the username and password incorrectly, you see the dialog box again, until you press Cancel or get it right. If you later return to the page without exiting your browser, your browser will remember the login information and not prompt you again.

The header WWW-Authenticate includes a parameter called Basic realm. The text you follow this with appears as a message at the top of the login dialog box. In theory, you could use the realm to organize sections of your site; however, PHP doesn't provide much support for this, because it only uses one PHP_AUTH_USER variable and one PHP_AUTH_PW variable.

The Basic realm text must be in double quotes. Therefore, you need to surround your WWW-Authenticate header with either single quotes or double quotes. If you use double quotes, you need to escape the double quotes for the basic realm, like so: header("WWW-Authenticate: Basic realm=\"Please Login to My Site\"");.

In this authentication example, I hardcoded the values to compare the username and password against. For simple security, this works fine. But for advanced security, I have the following recommendations:

✦ Always encrypt passwords in the browser (using, for example, JavaScript) and send the encrypted passwords to the server.

✦ If you have multiple usernames, store them in a MySQL database. I discuss how to do this in Book VI, Chapter 3.

Chapter 7: Advanced Programming with PHP

In This Chapter

✔ Including and requiring other PHP files

✔ Converting between types

✔ Referring to reference variables

✔ Processing strings

In this chapter, I cover some of the more advanced topics that can help turn you into an ace PHP programmer. For example, I show you how you can divide up your PHP programs into multiple files or how you can include PHP files that other people have written. I also talk about converting types, creating reference variables, and processing strings. These are all important topics that will help you get the most out of PHP.

Including and Requiring Other PHP Files

To better organize your programming, you can divide your source code into multiple files. In PHP, you can put some code in a file and then allow another .php file to access the file by either *requiring* or *including* the file.

Requiring files

Suppose you have a function called GetDateString that you want to use in many of your .php files. Instead of rewriting the same function in each file, you can put the function in its own file and then require it.

Here's a file called myfunctions.php:

```php
<?php
    function GetDateString() {
        return date("l, F j, Y", time());
    }
?>
```

And now here's a file called `userequire.php` that uses the function `GetDateString` in the `myfunctions.php` file:

```
<html><title>Today!</title>
<body>
Greetings! Today is
<?php
    require "myfunctions.php";
    print GetDateString();
?>
</body></html>
```

When you view this `userequire.php` file in a browser, you see something like this:

```
Greetings! Today is Tuesday, June 8, 2010
```

Hopefully by 2010, computers will be so powerful we won't need to write code in PHP or any other language.

I started the `myfunctions.php` file with `<?php` and ended it with `?>`, even though I already had a `<?php` and `?>` in the `userequire.php` file and I called `require` inside the `<?php` and `?>` tag. I did this because the PHP rules require that every `.php` file must enclose the code inside the `<?php` and `?>`, even if the `require` keyword is inside such delimiters.

Including files

You can use the `include` keyword rather than the `require` keyword by simply changing the keyword `require` to `include`:

```
include "myfunctions.php";
```

The two keywords are interchangeable in functionality and syntax, with this single difference: If the PHP processor can't find the file you're trying to require or include, and you use a `require` statement, you get a fatal error, and the processor stops processing your file, displaying an error message in the resulting HTML. But if you use an `include` statement and the processor can't find the file, the processor only issues a warning (and prints it to the HTML) and continues processing the rest of the file. For most situations, I use `require`, and if I do my homework and actually test my software, I shouldn't have to worry about it — the files I include or require should be present. (Okay, if you're a true hacker, you might write code that intentionally attempts to include a file that may or may not be present, and then handle the situation accordingly, but I prefer not to write such complex code. It's hard to maintain.)

Setting the include path

To find the file that you include (or require), you must either put the file in the same directory as the file doing the including, or provide a full path to the file, as in /home/jezebel/html_files/myphpstuff.php. However, if you move your site to a different host with a differently organized file system, coding an absolute path can be a problem.

A better way than coding absolute paths into your files is to use the PHP system include path. PHP maintains a set of directories that it looks in for the included files. If you add your directory to this path, you don't need to use any paths in the names of the files you include. How do you set this secret wonder known as an include path? You can do it two ways. If you have access to the php.ini file (which you might not if you're using a third-party hosting service), you can set it in the php.ini file. Open the php.ini file and search for a line that starts with include_path =. (It might start with a semicolon, which means it's commented out. Remove the semicolon.) The line might look like this for Linux/Unix:

```
include_path = ".:/php/includes"
```

Or look like this for Windows:

```
include_path = ".;c:\php\includes"
```

For the Linux/Unix one, add your path inside the string, separating the items with a colon, like so:

```
include_path = ".:/php/includes:/home/
        jezebel/html_files"
```

For Windows, separate the items with a semicolon and use backslashes:

```
include_path = ".;c:\php\includes;c:\
        phpfiles\jezebel"
```

(Notice that you don't double up the backslashes.)

Finally, if you don't have access to the php.ini file, you can add a line to your .php file that sets the include path, like so:

```
ini_set('include_path','/home/ jezebel/
        html_files ');
```

You can also use variable names in your require and include statements:

```
$headerfile = "myfunctions.php";
require $headerfile;
```

This means that if you're really brave and writing some seriously complex code, you can construct different filenames based on different situations. For example, say that you're writing a set of "helper" functions that do some database work for you, and you write different forms of these functions for different database systems. You can construct the name of the correct file to include or require on the fly, store the name in a variable, and then require or include the file using the variable name. Or, you can conditionally include or require your files, as I discuss in the section "Conditionally requiring and including," later in this chapter.

Be careful when declaring variables and using the variable names as the file to include (or require). Don't, under any circumstances, let the clients of your site specify the name of the include file (through a form, for example). If they do, they can specify a remote include file that can issue operating system commands (using the PHP `system` keyword), giving them full access to your site. I've seen suggestions on message boards that you can also use the `_GET` array to extract the name of the file and include or require the file. But doing so is dangerous. By supplying the name of a malicious file in a URL, hackers can easily mess up your system. *Don't do it!* I can't overemphasize the importance of this security issue.

Including files using URLs

If you have a PHP file on a remote system that you want to include or require, you can simply use the fully qualified URL for the file, like so:

```
include "http://www.jeffcogswell.com/URLFile.php";
```

But there's a catch to using the file this way, because of how the remote server processes the PHP file. Basically, the PHP processor on the remote server might get in the way and muck things up for you, making your life difficult.

Suppose you have a file on the remote system. The file is called `URLFile.php` and looks like this:

```
<?php
    print "This is text printed out by the remote
    system!<br>\n";
    function TestRemote() {
        print "This is text printed out by the remote".
            "system in the TestRemote function!<br>\n";
    }
?>
```

This file is nothing fancy; it's just a `print` statement and then a function called `TestRemote` that itself has a `print` statement. Now suppose you upload this file to a remote server (such as `http://www.jeffcogswell.com/URLFile.php`). Then on your own server, you have a file called `requireURL.php` that looks like this:

```
<?php
    require "http://www.jeffcogswell.com/URLfile.php"
    TestRemote();
?>
```

Requiring and including only once

If you include a file and later on include another file that re-includes the first file, you may run into some problems. For example, you may have some code in an included file that you want to execute only once. But if that file gets included multiple times for whatever reason, your code will get executed multiple times.

PHP provides a simple way to prevent this. Instead of using the include or require keyword, you can use the keywords include_once or require_once. You use these two words the same way as the include and require counterparts, except PHP will

carefully check whether the file already has been included and, if so, skip over it.

Be careful that you do not mix the case of the filenames, especially if PHP is running on a Windows system. To Windows, the file a.php is the same as A.php because filenames in Windows are not case sensitive. But to PHP, a.php is different from A.php. Thus, if you call include_once first for a.php and later for A.php, PHP thinks they're two different files and includes A.php. The solution here is to be consistent in your filenames and not change their case in different places in your program.

This file seems sound, but it won't work. The reason is that the require statement will ask the remote system to send back the file. But the remote system is (presumably) running a PHP server. So what does the server get back from the remote system? Not the PHP code. Oops. Instead, the server gets back the resulting .html file. Ouch. Here's the resulting .html file with no PHP code:

```
This is text printed out by the remote system!<br>
```

The PHP processor on your server won't totally freak out and try to parse this text as PHP (fortunately) because the PHP processor drops back to HTML when including or requiring a file. (That's why you still need the <?php and ?> inside the included or required file.) But all is not good, because this resulting .html file does not have your TestRemote function. Not good. When you open the requireURL.php file on your server, here's what you see in the browser:

```
This is text printed out by the remote system!
Fatal error: Call to undefined function: testremote() in
E:\LAMP\dev\Book5\Chap7\requireURL.php on line 3
```

The TestRemote function is gone. (Remember that unlike other places in PHP, function names are not case sensitive. You can see this by noting that the error message says the PHP processor was looking for testremote and not TestRemote. No biggie; that's not what's causing the problem.)

The way to fix this problem is to coerce the remote system to give you back the actual .php file, not the HTML results of the processed .php file. The easiest way to do this is by changing the filename extension to either .html or .txt. Then make the change accordingly in your own PHP file:

```php
<?php
    #works!
    require "http://www.jeffcogswell.com/URLfile.txt";
    TestRemote();
?>
```

When you do this, the file travels from the remote server to your server unchanged, and then your PHP processor can have at it, treating the file as if it's your own local file.

Including remote files can be dangerous. For example, suppose one computer has a file that millions of other computers use, and somebody hacks into that one computer's system, replacing the file with a new file containing malicious code. Or suppose that the people maintaining the remote file modify the file and introduce bugs, causing your program to mess up. Both of these examples are reasons why you may not want to include remote files.

In order for your PHP processor to open remote files for the use of an include or require statement, make sure that you're using PHP 4.3.0 or above and that the PHP processor is configured to accept URL files. Allowing URL files is the default, but you can explicitly control the processor by using the php.ini file with a line like this:

```
allow_url_fopen = On
```

This allows the use of HTTP in the include and require files.

To not allow it, use this line:

```
allow_url_fopen = Off
```

Passing variables to an included file

If you include (or require) a file that exists on the same server as the .php file doing the including, the included file automatically picks up the global variables and other scoped entities as the file doing the including. The following code segments demonstrate this. First, here's a file called global.php:

```php
<?php
    require "globalstuff.php";
    $myglobal = 10;
    printglobal();
?>
```

And here's the file called `globalstuff.php`:

```php
<?php
    function printglobal() {
        global $myglobal;
        print "Today's incredible global value is
    $myglobal<br>\n";
    }
?>
```

I declared the `$myglobal` variable in the `global.php` file, and I used the variable in the `globalstuff.php` file. I didn't have to make any special provisions to pass the variable or anything like that.

Be careful about sharing global variables. Most people feel global variables are a bad idea; however, my feeling is that a few situations do require global variables, and you can use them sparingly. If you start mixing modules together, all sharing global variables, things can easily get out of hand. So be careful.

Conditionally requiring and including

If you want to include (or require) a file only during certain situations, PHP allows you to do *conditional* requiring and including. Really, there's no magic to this. You just put the `require` or `include` statement inside a plain old `if` block. First, here's a sample file you can include or require; I called it `condrequired.php`:

```php
<?php
    function phoo() {
        print "Thank you for calling the Phoo
    Phunction!<br>";
    }
?>
```

Just a simple phunction, called `phoo`, that's all. Now here's a file that includes `condrequired.php` and calls `phoo`:

```php
<?php
    $today = getdate();
    $weekday = $today['weekday'];
    print "Today is $weekday!<br>\n";
    if ($weekday == 'Wednesday') {
        require('condrequired.php');
        phoo();
    }
?>
```

I call `require` only inside the `if` block. Thus, the PHP processor opens
and processes `condrequired.php` only if the `$weekday` variable is set to
`Wednesday`. If not, the PHP processor doesn't require `condrequired.php`.
You can do this type of thing if you have a file that you need to require or
include only in special situations.

Typically, you'll be using PHP on a Web server that dishes out Web pages. If
you have a page that gets lots of hits, conditionally including or requiring
other `.php` files can help speed up your PHP programs because you're not
including or requiring files when they're not needed.

You may be tempted to do something like the following, where I include a
file only under a certain condition and then later call one of its functions:

```php
<?php
    // This won't work!!!
    function doCond() {
        $today = getdate();
        $weekday = $today['weekday'];
        print "Today is $weekday!<br>\n";
        if ($weekday == 'Wednesday') {
            require('condrequired.php');
            return true;
        }
        return false;
    }

    // This won't work!!!
    $special = doCond();
    if ($special) {
        phoo();
    }
?>
```

Here, I put the `require` inside a function called `doCond()`, and that function
returns either true or false. Alas, this approach does not work. The problem
is that the `require` takes place inside the function, and anything defined

inside the `required` file (such as the `phoo` function), ends up in the scope of the `doCond` function where the `require` statement is. Outside of the `doCond` function the `phoo` name doesn't exist.

Therefore, don't call `include` or `require` from within a function unless you're okay with the items in the included or required file being available only within the function.

If you run the preceding PHP code, you get a "Today is" message and then an error message like this:

```
Fatal error: Call to undefined function: phoo() in
conditional-bad.php on line 16
```

Advanced Coding with Variables

Variables can be boring if you use them only at their most basic level. But thanks to some advanced features in PHP, you can get more out of your variables and keep your coding exciting, making your day go by quicker. Or something like that.

In this section, I talk about two particularly useful topics in the Wonderful World of Variables: converting between variables and working with reference variables.

Converting between data types

In general, PHP takes care of a great deal of the conversion headaches, and you rarely have to convert between types. For example, look at this somewhat mysterious code:

```php
<?php
    $a1 = '1';
    $a2 = '2';
    $combined = $a1 + $a2;
    print "$combined<br>\n";
?>
```

The first two lines store the strings `'1'` and `'2'` in the variables `$a1` and `$a2`, respectively. But what does the next line do? It adds the strings `'1'` and `'2'`, but what does that mean? Here's the output in the browser, which may or may not surprise you:

3

That's it, just a 3. But that's the sum of 1 and 2. Here's what happened: The + operator is not available for strings, only numbers. So when PHP encountered the plus sign, it automatically converted the strings on either side of the plus sign to the numbers 1 and 2. Then the processor added the two numbers to get 3 and stored that in `$combined`. And note that `$combined` is an integer. You can verify this by adding the following line after the `print` statement:

```
var_dump($combined);
```

This line produces the following output:

```
int(3)
```

This output means that the variable is of type `int` (meaning integer) and contains the value 3. In other words, PHP did the conversions for you automatically.

Suppose that you didn't have numbers inside the strings, and instead added the strings `ham` and `sandwich` like so:

```
<?
    $a = "ham";
    $b = "sandwich";
    print $a + $b;
?>
```

PHP converts each string to the number 0 before adding the two together. Again, the + sign is only for numbers; the best that PHP can do is convert these two strings to some number, so it chooses 0. Thus this example prints 0.

Of course, if what you really wanted was a string "12" rather than the integer 3, you can use the dot operator:

```
$reallywanted = $a1 . $a2;
```

This creates the string 12, which you can verify through `var_dump`, like so:

```
    print "$reallywanted<br>\n";
    var_dump($reallywanted);
```

In this output, you see the string "12" and the `var_dump` results of `string(2) "12"`.

But what if you wanted the string "3"? Then you can do this:

```php
$wantedastring = "$combined";
```

I simply put the $combined variable inside quotes, which writes the value of $combined into the string. Here's the full program:

```php
<?php
    $a1 = '1';
    $a2 = '2';
    $combined = $a1 + $a2;
    print "$combined<br>\n";
    var_dump($combined);
    print "<br>\n";
    $reallywanted = $a1 . $a2;
    print "$reallywanted<br>\n";
    var_dump($reallywanted);
    print "<br>\n";
    $wantedastring = "$combined";
    print "$wantedastring<br>\n";
    var_dump($wantedastring);
?>
```

The final var_dump verifies that wantedastring is a string:

```
string(1) "3"
```

Or, if you prefer, the following example shows two more ways to convert a number to a string:

```php
<?php
    $a1 = '1';
    $a2 = '2';
    $combined = $a1 + $a2;
    $anotherstring = strval($combined);
    var_dump($anotherstring);
    print "<br>\n";

    $yetanotherstring = (string)$combined;
    var_dump($yetanotherstring);
?>
```

The first way is to call strval. The second way is to use a cast. For a cast, you put the type name in parentheses before the name of the variable you want to convert. Here's the output from this latest and greatest program:

```
string(1) "3"
string(1) "3"
```

You can cast a number to a string three ways:

✦ Put it in quotes, as in `"$combined"`.

✦ Call `strval`, as in `strval($combined)`.

✦ Cast it directly, as in `(string)$combined`.

You can also take the road back home and cast your strings into numbers, provided the strings contain valid numbers. This time, you have just two ways to do it, because the quoting thing only builds strings. Here's some sample code:

```php
<?php
    $somestring = "123";
    $wantnumber1 = intval($somestring);
    $wantnumber2 = (int)$somestring;

    var_dump($wantnumber1);
    print "<br>\n";
    var_dump($wantnumber2);
    print "<br>\n";
?>
```

Here's a breakdown of this code:

✦ The first line stores the string `"123"`.

✦ The second line converts the string to an integer by using a function called `intval`.

✦ The third line converts the string to an integer by a direct cast. (Interestingly, you can use either the word `int` or `integer` in the cast; either works fine.)

✦ The final set of lines dumps information about the variables proving (beyond a reasonable doubt) that the two variables are, in fact, integers.

And so you can convert a string to an integer two ways:

✦ Call `intval`, as in `intval($somestring)`.

✦ Cast it directly, as in `(int)$somestring`.

In addition to converting between strings and integers, you can add floats to the list. Rather than discussing all the possibilities (converting floats to integers, strings to floats, platypuses to, well, you get the idea), I'll just show you some sample code in the following list. Here's the lowdown on how to do particular conversions:

- ✦ **A float to an integer:** Use `intval($myfloat)`, passing the float to the function. Or cast, as in `(int)$myfloat`.

- ✦ **An integer to a float:** Use `floatval($myint)`, passing the integer to the function. Or cast, as in `(float)$myfloat`.

- ✦ **A string to a float:** Use `floatval($mystring)`, passing the string to the function. Or cast the string to the float, as in `(float)$mystring`.

- ✦ **A float to a string:** Use `strval($myfloat)`, passing the float to the function.

The function `floatval` is available starting with PHP version 4.2.0. If you're using an earlier version, you don't have access to this function. In that case, simply use a cast.

On the CD-ROM, look in the `Book5/Chap7` directory in the source code directory at the file `convertfloats.php` for a full sample of all these conversions. Or just go to www.jeffcogswell.com/dummies/convertfloats.php.

Referring to reference variables

Before I start talking about reference variables, I want to warn that if you're familiar with reference variables in a certain other language (hint: C++), forget what you know, at least while programming in PHP.

A *reference variable* is an alias to another variable. A reference variable is simply another name for a variable. For example, say that you have a variable called `$platypus`. Then you set up a reference to this variable called `$duckbill`. This means you have two names for the same variable. Typically you would want to do this inside a function if you have, for example, a global variable, and you want to give the variable a name more appropriate to the function's usage.

If you're a C++ programmer, you might be saying, "Well isn't that the same thing as a reference in C++?" Trust me when I say this: No. A reference in C++ is a pointer to another variable. But when you create a reference in PHP, you get a new symbol that refers to the same variable. So for my mammal example (yes, a platypus is a mammal), you have two symbols, `$platypus` and `$duckbill`, that refer to the same variable. (If you have a strong Unix background, the PHP manuals compare references to hard links.) In other words, you have one variable with two distinct names: `$platypus` and `$duckbill`. In C++, a reference variable refers to another variable. In PHP, two names refer to the same variable; they are aliases to one another.

So how do you create a reference variable? Like this:

```
$platypus = 10;
$duckbill =& $platypus;
```

This code first creates a variable called $platypus and stores 10 in it. Next, the code creates a variable called $duckbill and makes it an alias or reference to $platypus using the =& notation.

To create a reference, type the name of the reference variable and then the =& operator, followed by the name of the variable that the new variable will be an alias for. (Make sure that you use an equal sign followed by an ampersand, not the other way around. If you type $x &= $y, you'll modify $x by performing a logical *and* operator with the value currently in $x and the value in $y.)

Now here's more code that shows the implications of the platypus who was billed for having a duck:

```
<?php
    $platypus = 10;
    $duckbill =& $platypus;

    $platypus = 20;
    print "$duckbill<br>\n";

    $duckbill = 30;
    print "$platypus<br>\n";

?>
```

Look closely at this code. The first two lines are the same as the previous code. Then I store 20 in $platypus and print out the other variable, $duckbill. What do you see? 20. Next, I store 30 in $duckbill, and I print out the other variable, $platypus. What do you see? 30. As the example shows, the two variable names are aliases to the same variable.

After you've set up a variable name as a reference to another variable, you can later make it refer to a different variable. Here's a sample program:

```
<?
    $platypus = 20;
    $manatee = 50;

    $coolmammal =& $platypus;
    $coolmammal = 30;
    print "$platypus<br>\n";
```

```
$coolmammal =& $manatee;
$coolmammal = 70;
print "$manatee<br>\n";

?>
```

Look at the third set of lines. I changed what $coolmammal refers to. Previously, it referred to $platypus. But when the PHP processor runs the line $coolmammal =& $manatee;, $coolmammal will then be an alias for $manatee.

In C++, you're not allowed to *unseat* a reference variable — that is, make the reference refer to another variable — at least not by the ANSII C++ standard. (Some older compilers allowed you to do so.) In PHP, you can unseat a variable name and have it refer to a different variable. Just run another &= line.

Processing Strings

The PHP language includes excellent support for strings. But even better is the set of additional string-processing functions.

The PHP string library includes many string functions, some of them very specialized. Check out www.php.net/strings for the whole list. (In the sections that follow, I discuss some of the more useful ones.)

Doin' the C-style printf thing

If you're either an old C-hack like myself, or if you just like to format strings during your free time, you'll appreciate the PHP printf function. I will assume that you're familiar with printf in other languages here. If not, take a look at www.php.net/sprintf for more information (yes, this is sprintf with an s, which is a slightly different version, but the same rules apply). The printf in PHP has all the usual goodies. Here's an example:

```
<?php
    $mynum = 100;
    $mystr = "Greetings Planet Earth";
    $myfloat = 3.1415926;
    printf ("%s from 0x%x on behalf of %f<br>\n",
        $mystr, $mynum, $myfloat);
?>
```

Here's the output from this program:

```
Greetings Planet Earth from 0x64 on behalf of 3.141593<br>
```

Obtaining information about a string

The following list shows some useful functions for gaining information about a string, so you can look deep into its soul and see what characters make it tick:

- ✦ `strlen`: Gives you the length of a string.
- ✦ `strpos`: Looks for a substring.
- ✦ `stripos`: Looks for a substring, but in a case-insensitive manner.
- ✦ `ord`: Gives you the ASCII code for the first character in a string.
- ✦ `strcmp`: Passes two strings to this function. You get back a 0 if the strings are the same.
- ✦ `strcasecmp`: Same as `strcmp`, but this function does a case-insensitive comparison.

Regarding the `strcmp` function, if you're into advanced programming, keep in mind that you'll get back a negative number if the first string is less than the other. You'll get back a positive if the first is greater. (Some people spend days deciphering what it means for one string to be less than the other. I'd rather use my meditation time for more important things, like levitating. And with `strcasecmp`, the notion of *less than* and *greater than* becomes even more complicated. Personally, I don't bother with it.)

Having more stringy fun

If you need to split up a string into smaller strings (such as breaking up the words separated by spaces), you can use the intriguingly named functions `explode` and `implode`. (Those PHP folks are so much fun.)

```php
<?php
    $bag_o_candy = "raisins nuts chocolates";
    $bigmess = explode(" ", $bag_o_candy);
    var_dump($bigmess);

    $another_bag = implode(" ", $bigmess);
    print "<br>\n$another_bag<br>\n";
?>
```

The first string in the call to `explode` is the delimiter by which you either pick apart the string into an array or piece the array back together. I used a single space because the words in my string were separated by single spaces. Here's the output from this code in a browser:

```
array(3) { [0]=> string(7) "raisins" [1]=> string(4) "nuts"
[2]=> string(10) "chocolates" }
raisins nuts chocolates
```

The `explode` function in PHP works much like the `split` function that you find in Tcl and Perl, languages I discuss elsewhere in this book.

Here are a few more fun functions for strings:

✦ `ltrim` and `rtrime`: These two functions strip away whitespace from the left side of a string and the right side of the string, respectively.

✦ `wordwrap`: This interesting function inserts newline (\n) characters into a string to break up the string into multiple lines. You specify the maximum length of each line. Note that this function inserts \n and not `<br>`. Use the `nl2br` function to add in the `<br>` HTML tags.

✦ `strrev`: This function reverses a string.

Here's an example of these functions:

```php
<?php
    $paragraph = "    .rb2ln yltneuqesbus dna ".
        "parwdrow llac I retfa senil elpitlum ".
        "otni pu nekorb eb lliw taht ecnetnes ".
        "a si sihT    ";
    $paragraph = strrev($paragraph);
    $paragraph = ltrim(rtrim($paragraph));
    print nl2br(wordwrap($paragraph, 20));
?>
```

After you type all that in, here's what you see in the browser:

```
This is a sentence
that will be broken
up into multiple
lines after I call
wordwrap and
subsequently nl2br.
```

And finally, remember that you can get a single character out of a string just by treating the string as an array, like so:

```
$a = "abc";
print $a[1];
```

I mention this because some languages lack this seemingly fundamental feature. Also, remember that `$a[1]` gives you the letter `b`. The first index is 0, so `$a[0]` gives you the letter `a`.

Chapter 8: Creating Graphics

In This Chapter

✓ **Creating bars and graphs without using extra libraries**

✓ **Creating graphics files**

✓ **Creating thumbnail images**

*W*ith PHP, you can create graphics on the fly. Remember, graphics creation takes place on the server side; the server then sends the graphics to the client browser.

In this chapter, I show you two different ways to create graphics:

✦ Manipulating the HTML to display bars and other graphs, without using extra libraries

✦ Using the graphics libraries available on most PHP installations (or optionally available with older PHP versions)

Creating Bars and Graphs without Using Extra Libraries

A common and simple way to display bars and other types of graphs is to use a small graphic file containing just a single pixel of a particular color. Then, using the magic of HTML, you can stretch the single pixel into a larger rectangular area, effectively drawing a rectangle on the browser screen in the color of the single pixel. Isn't that cool? Of course, PHP fits into all this by supplying the dynamic HTML.

Here's an example:

```
<html><title>High Temperatures</title>
<body>
<h1>Temperatures for this week!</h1>
<?php
    $temps = array(110, 130, 160, 165, 32, 164, 163);
    $days = array("Mon", "Tue", "Wed", "Thur", "Fri", "Sat",
    "Sun");
    print "<table>";
    for ($day = 0; $day<7; $day++) {
        print "<tr>";
```

```
                    print "<td>{$days[$day]}: {$temps[$day]}</td>";
                    print "<td><img src=\"greenpixel.gif\"
                        width=\"{$temps[$day]}\" height=\"30\"></td>";
                    print "</tr>";
                }
            print "</table>";
        ?>
        </body>
        </html>
```

To use this example, you need a graphic image file that contains a single pixel (I used green). The file is called greenpixel.gif, and you can easily create it with one of your own graphics programs or download my version from www.jeffcogswell.com/dummies/greenpixel.gif. You can see the actual example by going to www.jeffcogswell.com/dummies/stretch-pixel1.php.

In the preceding PHP code, the key part is the fourth print statement. This print statement prints out a complete img tag, including width and height. With HTML's img tag, if you leave off the width and height parameters, the browser displays the image in its original width and height, as specified by the image file. But if you *add* a width or height parameter, the browser stretches or compresses the image accordingly. In the preceding code, I specified the width to be the temperature and the height to be 30. When you stretch a single-pixel image, you get a rectangle of the same color as the pixel. Thus, the PHP generates HTML that shows a bar graph of the temperatures for the week. (Oh my, what strange weather we've been having!) Figure 8-1 shows you what the page will look like if a user visits the Web page using Microsoft Internet Explorer.

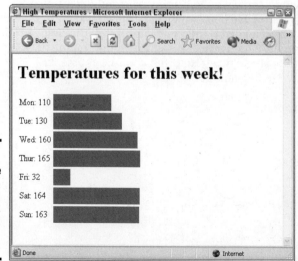

Figure 8-1: The bars are generated by stretching a single-pixel .gif file.

In addition to drawing bar graphs, you can also use preexisting graphics files (that is, files that the PHP program doesn't generate) to create tables and other graphics. The next example uses two graphics files: `blueempty.gif` (a blue square that's 30 pixels by 30 pixels) and `box.gif` (a 30 x 30 square with an X in it). You can either create these two 30 x 30 graphic files yourself or use mine. If you want to use mine, you can get the files from `www.jeffcogswell.com/dummies/box.gif` and `www.jeffcogswell.com/dummies/blueempty.gif`.

The following example draws a table listing the names of the participants in a tennis tournament, fills in the table showing who is playing in each match, and uses CSS (Cascading Style Sheet) styles to draw the text:

```
<html><head>
<title>This Week's Tennis Matchups</title>
<style type="text/css">
<!--.text {  font-family: Arial, Helvetica, sans-serif; font-
    size: 11px}-->
</style></head>
<body>
    <table border="0" cellspacing="0" cellpadding="0">
<?php
    $names = array ("bill","suzie","julie","hank", "jim",
    "jen");
    $matches = array(
        "bill.suzie", "bill.hank", "suzie.jim", "julie.jim",
    "julie.jen"
    );
    print '<tr height="30"><td></td>';
    foreach ($names as $topname) {
        print "<td><span class=\"text\"><center>".
            "$topname</center></span></td>";
        print "\n";
    }
    print "</tr>";
    foreach ($names as $leftname) {
        print '<tr height="30">';
        print "<td><span
    class=\"text\">$leftname</span></td>";
        foreach ($names as $topname) {
            if (in_array("$leftname.$topname", $matches) ||
            in_array("$topname.$leftname", $matches)) {
                print "<td><img src=\"box.gif\"></td>";
            }
            else {
                print "<td><img src=\"blueempty.gif\"></td>";
            }
        }
        print "</tr>\n";
    }
?>
```

```
        </table>
</body>
</html>
```

This example is a little more sophisticated than the previous one. Figure 8-2 shows what the example looks like in a browser. In this example, the current matches are hardcoded in an array; in real life, you would probably read the matches from a database or file. If you want to see this example without having to type it in, visit www.jeffcogswell.com/dummies/grid.php.

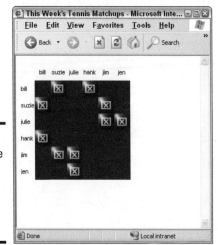

Figure 8-2:
You can use
a table to
carefully
position
your
graphics.

Creating Graphics Files

In the preceding section, you find out how to use existing graphics and carefully draw them with HTML to get different results. Although that's fun, you're pretty much limited to basic rectangular drawings with HTML. In this section, I show you how to create new graphics files on the fly and how to manipulate existing graphics files.

The functions I discuss in this section fall under the category of image functions in the PHP manual. If you want to explore the entire list of functions, check out www.php.net/image.

To do the examples in this section, make sure that your PHP system is configured to use the *GD library,* which is a general-purpose graphics library that takes care of all the behind-the-scenes graphics processing. (Because PHP is a server-side language, visitors to your Web site do *not* need to have the GD library installed on their local machines.) The GD library is a standard part of PHP as of version 4.3, but you need to make sure PHP is configured to use it.

To configure the library on a Linux computer, you need to go through the standard configuration process, including a —with-gd option. You can find out more about this process at www.php.net/manual/en/installation.php.

To configure the library on a Windows computer with a prebuilt PHP installation, you need to edit the php.ini file, found in the C:\Windows directory. (If the file isn't there, you can copy the php.ini-dist file found in the PHP installation directory to the Windows directory, renaming it C:\Windows\php.ini.) Then you need to modify the extension_dir line as follows:

```
extension_dir = C:/Program Files/PHP/php-4.3.0-Win32/
    extensions/
```

Or use whatever path contains your PHP installation. In this entry, the extensions/ directory follows the PHP installation path.

Then remove the semicolon on the following line:

```
;extension=php_gd.dll
```

to get

```
extension=php_gd.dll
```

Then restart the Apache server.

The creator of the GD graphics library, Boutell.Com, is continually revising the product and issuing new versions at www.boutell.com/gd/. The latest version as of this writing is version 2.0, which includes a significant number of new features. The online manual for the PHP image library at www.php.net/image includes many functions that rely on GD version 2.0. If your PHP installation has an older version of GD, check whether the functions you want to use require the newest version. Functions that require 2.0 will display a message such as the following on their Web documentation page (www.php.net/imagecopyresampled is the Web documentation page for the imagecopyresampled function, for example):

```
Note: This function was added in PHP 4.0.6 and
requires GD 2.0.1
```

GIF files and PHP images

The most recent versions of the GD library do not handle GIF images. The reason is that for a long time, a company called Unisys owned the patent on a certain compression routine (called LZW) needed to read and write GIF files. Unisys expected people to pay royalties for using GIF file algorithms in their software. To avoid licensing fees, GD developers removed GIF support. Such removal has been common in the last few years among Web programmers, primarily as a political stand. Instead of GIF files, GD supports PNG files. (The PNG format was also created to avoid legal issues with using GIF files.) For the longest time, however, the main browsers found on client computers — Internet Explorer and Netscape, both running on Windows — did not support PNG, making the use of PNG more of an oddity, and barely useful. (Interestingly, Internet Explorer on the Macintosh had better support for PNG before Internet Explorer for Windows did.) Today, both Internet Explorer and Netscape support PNG files (although not perfectly). If you want to know the details, check out the Current Status of PNG page at `www.libpng.org/pub/png/pngstatus.html`, as well as the PNG-Supporting Browsers page at `www.libpng.org/pub/png/pngapbr.html`.

The whole issue that brought about PNG files — the patents — is mostly history, because the original patent protecting the compression in GIF, patent number 4,558,302, filed on June 20, 1982, expired on June 20, 2003, according to some legal analysts. (But talk to an attorney before embarking on an LZW fest in your software, because I'm not offering legal advice or suggestions here. Moreover, Unisys has patents outside the United States that don't expire until 2004.) For an interesting take on all this, check out `burnallgifs.org`. And for Unisys' take on it, visit `www.unisys.com/about__unisys/lzw/`.

The message isn't consistent on all the pages, but it usually looks something like this one. If you need these newer functions (which are quite useful), I recommend upgrading your version of PHP. If you're relying on a hosting service and it's using an older version of PHP, either encourage the service to upgrade or find a different host. Many professional hosting services stay current with the latest versions.

To determine if the version of PHP you're using has a 1.0 or 2.0 version of GD, use the following PHP program:

```
<?php
    phpinfo();
?>
```

Run this program on the server in question and then scroll down to the "gd" section. (If no gd section is present, GD isn't even available on the server.) Inside the gd section, you will see a row that says "GD Version" followed by the version number.

Setting the file type

When you create a PNG file, JPG file, or any other kind of graphic file, and you want your PHP program to send the file to the browser, your program needs to tell the browser what type of graphic file it is. To specify the file type, you set a header by calling the `header` function.

PHP headers must be set before any HTML code in your PHP program. Therefore, make sure that you specify the file type before the HTML code.

For PNG files, you can set a header by using this line:

```
header('Content-type:image/png');
```

And for JPG files, you can use this line:

```
header('Content-type:image/jpeg');
```

This line of code uses the full `jpeg` name, not the three-letter abbreviated form, `jpg`.

Drawing a polygon

The graphics library has numerous functions for drawing shapes such as lines, rectangles, and ellipses. You can explore the different functions in the PHP documentation by visiting `www.php.net/image`. To get you started, here's a PHP program that draws a simple polygon:

```php
<?php
    $pic = imagecreate(400, 400);
    $bgcolor = imagecolorallocate($pic, 255, 255, 255);
    $mycolor = imagecolorallocate($pic, 255, 0, 0);
    $points = array(
        200, 0, # point 1
        0, 200, # point 2
        400, 200, #point 3
        0, 400, #point 4
    );
    imagefilledpolygon($pic, $points, 4, $mycolor);
    header('Content-type:image/jpeg');
    imagejpeg($pic);
?>
```

Here are the individual lines of this program:

✦ First, I create a blank image of size 400 width by 400 height by calling `imagecreate`.

✦ Next, I set the background color. (The first time you call `imagecolor allocate`, you set the background color.) I wanted a white background, which translates to a Red-Green-Blue setting of 255, 255, 255.

✦ Next, I create another color, which I'll use later. This color is red, with RGB 255, 0, 0.

✦ I then create a set of points for my polygon. For these points, you create an array of all the points. The first point is (200, 0), the second is (0, 200), the third is (400, 200), and finally, the fourth is (0, 400). (The filled polygon will assume a final point that is the same as the first point 200,0, thereby closing the polygon.)

✦ Next, I draw the polygon by calling `imagefilledpolygon`. I pass to this function the image I'm drawing to, the array of points, the number of points (this array has four points, taking up eight numbers, so I pass 4), and the color.

✦ Then the magic part begins: I set the header specifying — in this case — the jpeg type by calling `header`. Finally, I send the image to the browser by calling `imagejpeg`, passing the image variable.

If I wanted to instead send a PNG file, I would change the final two lines to this:

```
header('Content-type:image/png');
imagepng($pic);
```

Regardless of whether you use png or jpg, you see the same image, a red bow-tie-shaped thing on its side; you can see it online at `www.jeffcogswell.com/dummies/createjpg.php`.

For some reason, all the image function names are shown in the online reference as having all lowercase letters, as in `imagefilledpolygon`. I prefer to capitalize the distinct words in such functions, as in `ImageFilledPolygon`. PHP's function names are case-insensitive, so you can use `ImageFilled Polygon` instead of `imagefilledpolygon` if you prefer. However, for this book, I'm sticking with the official names, which are all lowercase. I will not rebel; I will not resist. I am a machine, a computer. I will do as I'm told.

Creating dynamic images

As an example of what you can do with the powerful image-editing functions in PHP, in this section I show you how you to read a preexisting graphics file and enhance the images based on user data, before sending the images to the user's client browser.

For the following example, you need four images. The first is a map of the United States. I made my own simple (okay, *slightly goofy*) map, which you can download and use; it's available at `www.jeffcogswell.com/dummies/usmap.png`.

The second file is a basic `.html` file containing a form. I called this file `usmaplookup.html`. This is the file the people visiting your Web site will load. Here's the code:

```
<html>
<title>Latitude and Longitude Lookup</title>
<form name="form1" method="get" action="drawmap.php">
    Latitude: <input type="text" name="latitude"> N <br>
    Longitude <input type="text" name="longitude"> W<br>
    <input type="submit" name="Submit" value="Submit">
</form>
```

This code displays a simple form that lets the user enter in a latitude and longitude. This HTML code then opens the `drawmap.php` file, passing the latitude and longitude. Here's the `drawmap.php` file:

```
<html><title>Latitude and Longitude Results</title>
<?php
    $latitude = $_GET['latitude'];
    $longitude = $_GET['longitude'];
    print "You chose latitude $latitude<br>";
    print "and longitude $longitude.<p>";
    print '<img src="buildmapimage.php?latitude='.$latitude.
        '&longitude='.$longitude.'">';
?>
```

This simple `.php` file obtains the latitude and longitude numbers and creates HTML code that displays a short message and an image. The image is the key. Whereas an `<img>` tag normally would reference an image file ending with, for example, `.jpg`, `.gif`, or `.png`, this "image" file is called `buildmapimage` and ends in a `.php` extension. The extension doesn't matter; the browser doesn't care what it is. The browser just happily sends the URL to the Web server and waits for an image to come. The server, in turn, runs the `.php` file that generates the image file. In this example, the URL also has some parameters after it, a latitude and longitude. The `buildmapimage.php` file can extract this information and use it to dynamically create an image. Now we're getting somewhere!

Here's the `buildmapimage.php` file:

```php
<?php
    $pic = imagecreatefrompng("usmap.png");
    $mycolor = imagecolorresolve($pic, 192, 0, 0);

    // Calculate the location
    $latitude = $_GET['latitude'];
    $longitude = $_GET['longitude'];
    $width = 557;
    $height = 306;
    $x = $width - (($longitude - 67) * ($width / 58));
    $y = $height - (($latitude - 25) * ($height / 24));

    imagefilledrectangle($pic, $x-2, $y - 2, $x+2, $y+2,
            $mycolor);
    header('Content-type:image/png');
    imagepng($pic);
?>
```

This file first loads an existing image, `usmap.png`, with a function called `imagecreatefrompng`. Next, the program sets a color (red) that will be used later on for drawing a point on the map. Then the program extracts the latitude and longitude data and does a *linear transformation* (geek speak for *adjusts the data*) to fit the data points on the map. The map I made is 557 pixels wide by 306 pixels tall. The calculations that follow translate the latitude and longitude into pixels on the map.

Then the code draws a small box on the map at the calculated position in the color I defined earlier and, finally, sends the resulting graphic image to the browser.

The `drawmap.php` file shows up in the browser just like any other `.html` file; it contains text and images, like you would expect. What the users visiting the page don't realize is that the map was created dynamically.

If you want to see what this program will look like on-screen, hop over to `www.jeffcogswell.com/dummies/usmaplookup.html`. For the Latitude, enter any integer between 25 and 49. For the Longitude, enter any integer between 67 and 125.

Creating Thumbnail Images

Here's a handy little trick. Why take up space on your server with thumbnail images, when you can generate them dynamically? And why go through the headache of manually creating thumbnails for all the pictures from your trip to the Wisconsin Dells? Although thumbnail images don't have a huge impact on server space, you can have PHP generate them dynamically if you want.

I don't recommend the procedure I'm about to show you if you have a seri-ously high-traffic site because this procedure requires some computation time. If you have, for example, a Brad Pitt and Jennifer Aniston worship page filled with a gazillion pictures that gets a bazillion hits a day, I suggest creat-ing the thumbnails yourself and storing them on the server rather than rely-ing on PHP.

To use this demo, make sure you have the latest and greatest GD library. You need version 2.0 or greater for it to work. If you're stuck with an earlier version, all is not lost. In the following program, replace `imagecreatetrue color` with `imagecreate`. The difference is that `imagecreatetruecolor` can generate full-color images, whereas `imagecreate` is limited to 256 colors.

Here's a `.php` file that generates thumbnails; save this as `getthumbnail.php`:

```php
<?php
    $imagefilename = $_GET['imagefilename'];
    $height = $_GET['thumbheight'];
    $width = $_GET['thumbwidth'];
    $pic = imagecreatefromjpeg($imagefilename);
    $thumb = imagecreatetruecolor($width, $height);
    $white = imagecolorallocate($thumb, 255, 255, 255);
    imagefilledrectangle($thumb, 0, 0, $width, $height,
        $white);

    // Calculate the relative width or height so the image
    // doesn't get distorted.
    $origwidth = imagesx($pic);
    $origheight = imagesy($pic);
    if ($origheight > $origwidth) {
        $thumbwidth = $origwidth * $height / $origheight;
        $thumbheight = $height;
    }
    else {
        $thumbheight = $origheight * $width / $origwidth;
        $thumbwidth = $width;
    }
    imagecopyresized($thumb, $pic,
        0, 0, // thumb position
        0, 0, // original position
        $thumbwidth, $thumbheight, // thumb size
        $origwidth, $origheight // original size
    );
    header('Content-type:image/jpg');
    imagejpeg($thumb);
?>
```

Here's a rundown of this program:

✦ This `.php` file receives three parameters: The name of the original graphic file (used to build a thumbnail), the thumbnail width, and the thumbnail height.

✦ The code then opens the original file, creates a second graphic file to hold the thumbnail, and fills the graphic file with white to provide a blank background.

✦ Next, the program calculates the size of the thumbnail, making the image just big enough to fit inside the thumbnail, but without distorting the image.

✦ Then this code calls `imagecopyresized`, which is the routine that shrinks the file. I carefully labeled the numeric parameters so you can see what they do.

✦ Finally, this code sends the image.

Here's a sample that uses the preceding code to generate a list of thumbnails. For the `img` tag, I'm not specifying an image file but rather a PHP file — the `getthumbnail.php` file you just created.

```
<html><title>Thumbnails!</title>
<body>
    <?php
        $pics = array('rocks1.jpg', 'rocks2.jpg',
            'rocks3.jpg',
            'rocks4.jpg', 'rocks5.jpg', 'rocks6.jpg');
        foreach ($pics as $pic) {
            print "<a href=$pic>\n";
            print "    <img src=\"getthumbnail.php?".
                "imagefilename=$pic".
                "&thumbheight=128&thumbwidth=128\"".
                "border=\"0\">"; // Don't put a \n here!
            print "</a>\n";
        }
    ?>
</body>
</html>
```

This code assumes you have on your server files called `rocks1.jpg` through `rocks6.jpg`. I used these filenames because I have several sample files with these names on my server. You can try out the preceding two scripts by going to `www.jeffcogswell.com/dummies/thumbnails.php` (and you'll get to see some great pictures of a recent vacation of mine!).

Chapter 9: Modeling Data with Classes

In This Chapter

✓ Building classes

✓ Declaring constructors and implementing destructors

✓ Understanding dynamic binding

✓ Inheriting and deriving objects

✓ Obtaining information about your classes

*P*HP supports object-oriented programming, which means you can build classes and objects. Classes enable you to effectively organize and model your data, and PHP is no stranger to this kind of advanced programming. (If you're not familiar with classes and object-oriented programming in general, and terms such as *member,* head on over to Book III, Chapter 6.)

In this chapter, I show you how to build classes in PHP. This includes all the usual goodies that come with classes: adding constructors and destructors, and inheriting and deriving. Additionally, I talk about dynamic binding and obtaining information about your classes. Are you ready for some real programming?

Building Classes

In addition to having a full procedural-based syntax, PHP also offers object-oriented programming through classes. The syntax for classes is simple, as you can see in the following code:

```php
<?php
    class Pumpernickel {
        var $ounces;
        function tell_all() {
            print "Today's pumpernickel bread has only
    {$this->ounces} ounces remaining!<br>";
        }
    }
```

```
$bread = new Pumpernickel;
$bread->ounces = 10;
$bread->tell_all();

?>
```

This code defines a new class called `Pumpernickel`. The `Pumpernickel` class has two members, a variable called `$ounces` and a function called `tell_all`. Next, the code creates a new instance of `Pumpernickel` and saves it in the variable called `$bread`. The code then sets the new `Pumpernickel` instance's `ounces` member to 10 and calls the instance's `tell_all` function. Here's the output from this code:

```
Today's pumpernickel bread has only 10 ounces remaining!<br>
```

As you can see, creating classes is pretty easy in PHP. Here are some key points to remember:

✦ To access a member, type the name of the variable holding the object, followed by `->`, and the name of the member. Do not put a dollar sign before the name of the member. `$bread->ounces` is correct, whereas `$bread->$ounces` is incorrect.

✦ The member functions access the member variables by preceding variable names with `$this->`.

✦ Use the `var` keyword to declare member variables in a class, as I did in the preceding code.

✦ Do not end your class with a semicolon. This is different from the C++ language, so if you're coming from that world, keep this in mind.

Why is this feature missing in PHP?

People in PHP online discussion groups sometimes complain that the language is missing "vital" object-oriented (OO) features, such as public and private access, function overloading, and all sorts of other fun stuff. True, PHP doesn't have these advanced OO features like other languages such as Java, Python, C++, and so on. But does it matter? No. As you code in PHP, remember the purpose of the language. PHP is not an extensive language meant to build gigantic, super-powered, stand-alone applications. PHP is a server-side scripting language. The designers purposely kept its language features simple — shunning such things as public and private access — and kept its function library rich. This way, the language can remain simple, fast, and easy so that you can use it to generate powerful Web sites.

Constructing and Destructing Objects

If you want to put initialization code in your classes, you can use a *constructor*. A constructor is a member function that has the same name as the class and runs when you create a new instance of a class. Here's an example:

```php
<?php
    class Bulldozer {
        function Bulldozer() {
            print "Constructing something";
        }
    }
    $obj = new Bulldozer();
?>
```

When you create a new instance of `Bulldozer`, you will see that construction is indeed taking place. (Would you expect anything else from a well-tempered bulldozer?) Here's the output, which is nothing fancy:

```
Constructing something
```

You can also include parameters in the constructor, like so:

```php
<?php
    class Bulldozer2 {
        var $year;
        function Bulldozer2($ayear) {
            $this->year = $ayear;
            print "<p>\n";
            print "This bulldozer was built in ".
                "{$this->year}.\n";
        }
    }

    $obj2 = new Bulldozer2(1968);
?>
```

When this code creates the new instance of `Bulldozer2`, the code passes the number 1968 to the constructor. The constructor then saves the number in the `$year` member variable.

When you define a set of parameters for a constructor, as I did in the preceding code, you must pass those parameters when you create an instance. If you then attempt something like this:

```
$obj3 = new Bulldozer2();
```

you get a warning like this:

```
Warning: Missing argument 1 for bulldozer2() in
constructor.php on line 11
```

To avoid this problem, you can provide default values for the parameters. Here's a revised `Bulldozer2` constructor function that handles default values:

```
function Bulldozer2($ayear=1970) {
    $this->year = $ayear;
    print "<p>\n";
    print "This bulldozer was built in ".
        "{$this->year}.\n";
}
```

What if you want to add a destructor to your class? Technically speaking, PHP does not support destructors of objects (at least not at the time of this writing; however, version 5.0 will include destructor support). Meanwhile, you can simulate destructors rather easily. Have a gander at this code:

```
<?php
    class Destructionizer {
        function Destructionizer() {
            print "Starting!\n";
        }
        function Destroy() {
            print "Destroying!\n";
        }
        function Test() {
            print "Test!\n";
        }
    }
    $myobj = new Destructionizer;
    $myobj->Destroy();
    unset($myobj);
    // $myobj->Test();   # This will generate
                         # an error if uncommented!
?>
```

This code defines a simple class called `Destructionizer`. (If exclamation points were allowed in class names, you can be assured I would have included one!) In this code, after defining the class, I do the following:

+ I create a new instance of `Destructionizer`.

+ Then I call `Destroy()`, which is *not* a destructor. It is a member function that I chose to give an appropriate name; you might put some cleanup code in this function.

✦ Then I get rid of the object by calling `unset`. The `unset` keyword destroys the object but does *not* call any member functions. Therefore, if I want a destructor, my job is to include a function that performs some cleanup work, and then I have to call the function manually before I delete the object with the `unset` keyword. That's what I do in the preceding sample, and it works.

Here's the output from this code in a browser:

```
Starting! Destroying!
```

Notice also that I included a commented-out line. If you uncomment the line, you will see that the object is indeed gone because trying to use it results in a runtime error:

```
Fatal error: Call to a member function on a non-object in
destructor.php on line 16
```

Coding for Dynamic Binding

PHP, like many interpreted languages, has powerful support for something called *dynamic binding*. (If you're an OOP — Object-Oriented Purist — you'll know this as *polymorphism*.) Take a look at the following code:

```php
<?php
    class A {
        function foo() {
            print "This is foo for class A!<br>\n";
        }
    }

    class B {
        function foo() {
            print "This is foo for class B!<br>\n";
        }
    }

    function Process($obj) {
        $obj->foo();
    }

    $objA = new A();
    $objB = new B();
    Process($objA);
    Process($objB);
?>
```

This code does the following:

✦ It defines two classes, A and B, each having a member function called foo.

✦ Then it declares a function called Process, which takes an object as a parameter and calls the object's foo function.

✦ Finally, it creates an instance of A and of B, and calls Process for each instance.

When you put this code on a Web server and open it in a browser, here's what you see:

```
This is foo for class A!
This is foo for class B!
```

The Process function doesn't care what type of object it receives as a parameter. When the program runs, the Process function tries to call foo() on whatever object it receives, whether the object is of class A, class B, class Snooty, class No, or whatever. In other words, while the program is running, the variable $obj inside the Process function binds to the function called foo() for whatever object $obj holds. The program is performing *dynamic binding*.

If you frequent the PHP online forums, you're likely to find somebody complaining that PHP doesn't support dynamic binding as a "true object-oriented language should." Well, good news! PHP *does* support dynamic binding. So why the complaints? Usually the people posting the complaints are referring to a slightly different topic called *function overloading*. If you're familiar with C++, you know that you can have two functions by the same name within a single class, but with different parameters. The compiler can figure out which function to call based on the parameters, and such figuring takes place at compile time (called *static binding*). PHP does not support function overloading, but it does support dynamic binding. Hurray!

Inheriting and Deriving Objects

PHP allows you to derive new classes from existing classes. When you do so, you are defining a new class that includes all the members of the original class, plus any other members you add. Take a look at this example:

```php
<?php
    class FrozenFood {
        var $price;
        function Describe() {
            print "This food's price is ".
```

```
                    "{$this->price}.<br>\n";
        }
    };

    class FrozenPizza extends FrozenFood {
        var $toppings;
        function DescribeToppings() {
            print "This pizza has {$this->toppings}";
            print " on it.<br>\n";
        }
    }

    $pizza = new FrozenPizza();
    $pizza->price = 4.53;
    $pizza->toppings =
        "pepperoni sausage anchovies";
    $pizza->Describe();
    $pizza->DescribeToppings();
?>
```

This example creates a class called `FrozenFood`, which contains two
members — one variable called `$price` and one function called `Describe`.
Next, this code creates a new class called `FrozenPizza`, derived from
`FrozenFood` using the `extend` keyword. Because `FrozenPizza` is derived
from `FrozenFood`, `FrozenPizza` gets the same members as `FrozenFood`
(`$price` and `Describe`), plus any members that `FrozenFood` defines for
itself (`$toppings` and `DescribeToppings`.) You can see in the code that follows that the object `$pizza` of class `FrozenPizza` does indeed have all four
members: `$price`, `$toppings`, `Describe`, and `DescribeToppings`.

When you derive a new class, you are free to override any of the base class's
member functions. For example, I can add a new `Describe` function to the
`FrozenPizza` class, like so:

```
class FrozenPizza extends FrozenFood {
    var $toppings;
    function DescribeToppings() {
        print "This pizza has {$this->toppings}";
        print " on it.<br>\n";
    }
    function Describe() {
        print "This is a pizza!<br>\n";
        FrozenFood::Describe();
        $this->DescribeToppings();
    }
}
```

This class now has its own `Describe` function, and the base class, `FrozenFood`, also provides a `Describe` function. Suppose you have code like this:

```
$pizza = new FrozenPizza();
$pizza->price = 4.53;
$pizza->toppings =
    "pepperoni sausage anchovies";
$pizza->Describe();
```

Which version of `Describe` will the PHP processor run? It will run the one in the `FrozenPizza` class because the object is of type `FrozenPizza`.

You can see in the code for `Describe` in the `FrozenPizza` class that I used an interesting construct:

```
FrozenFood::Describe();
```

This line calls the base class version of `Describe`, which is in the `FrozenFood` class.

Getting Information on Classes

The PHP library includes a set of handy functions that help you get information about objects and classes. The following list describes some of the more useful functions:

- ✦ `get_object_vars`: This function returns an associative array of the variables in an object. The keys are the names of the variables, and the array values are the variable values. To use this function, pass the variable name of an object.

- ✦ `get_class`: This returns a string containing the class name. To use this function, pass the variable name of an object.

- ✦ `get_parent_class`: This returns a string containing the base class name. To use this function, pass either an object or the name of a class. (To pass the name of the class, *do not* put the name in quotes.)

- ✦ `get_class_methods`: This returns an array of the member functions for a class. Some people prefer to call member functions *methods,* thus the name of this function.

- ✦ `get_declared_classes`: This function returns an array of the names of all the classes the PHP processor knows about. This array contains any classes you declared, plus any built-in classes.

You can explore the other class and object functions by visiting `www.php.net/classobj`.

Here's a sample program that demonstrates how to use these functions:

```php
<?php
    class Base {
        var $basevar;
        function BaseFunc() {
            print "Hello!<br>\n";
        }
    }
    class Derived extends Base{
        var $derivedvar;
        function DerivedFun() {
            print "Greetings!<br>\n";
        }
    }
    $obj = new Derived();
    $obj->basevar = 10;
    $obj->derivedvar = 20;
    $objvars = get_object_vars($obj);
    print "The object belongs to class <b>";
    print get_class($obj)."</b><br>\n";
    print "The base class is <b>";
    print get_parent_class($obj)."</b><br>\n";
    print "Object's Variables<br>\n";
    foreach ($objvars as $name=>$var) {
        print " * $name = $var<br>\n";
    }
    print "Base class has these functions<br>\n";
    $basemethods = get_class_methods(Base);
    foreach ($basemethods as $method) {
        print " * $method<br>\n";
    }
    print "Here are all the classes defined:<br>\n";
    $allclasses = get_declared_classes();
    foreach ($allclasses as $classname) {
        print " * $classname<br>\n";
    }
?>
```

Here's the output from this program:

```
The object belongs to class <b>derived</b><br>
The base class is <b>base</b><br>
Object's Variables<br>
 * basevar = 10<br>
 * derivedvar = 20<br>
```

```
Base class has these functions<br>
 * basefunc<br>
Here are all the classes defined:<br>
 * stdClass<br>
 * __PHP_Incomplete_Class<br>
 * Directory<br>
 * COM<br>
 * VARIANT<br>
 * base<br>
 * derived<br>
```

As you can see, PHP also has some classes defined within its inner workings in addition to the classes you created.

Chapter 10: Ten Ways to Enhance Your Web Site

In This Chapter

✔ **Redirect** `index.html` **to** `index.php`

✔ **Dynamically generate style sheets**

✔ **Allow file uploads**

✔ **Use POST when appropriate**

✔ **Randomly generate picture-of-the-day images**

✔ **Write text from a file**

✔ **Determine which browser is running**

✔ **Determining host names from IP addresses**

*I*n this chapter, I provide you with ten great ways you can use PHP to enhance your Web site. Hang on and keep reading!

Redirect index.html to index.php

The filename `index.html` is often the default file in a Web server. If visitors to your site use just the site name (`www.dummies.com`, for example), the server, by default, dishes out `index.html`. However, what if you have PHP code in your index file? You may want to use `index.php` instead.

The easiest way to redirect `index.html` to `index.php` is to configure Apache to send out the `index.php` file by default. If you have access to the root `httpd.conf` file, you can set the configuration for the whole server. If you're using a third-party hosting service, your domain maps to a directory on the file system (most likely the directory is your own `public_html` directory). In that case, you need to use an `.htaccess` file.

Whether you use the `.htaccess` or root `httpd.conf` file, you can type the following directive into either the `.htaccess` or `httpd.conf` file itself:

```
DirectoryIndex index.php
```

Remember that some visitors may continue to manually type `index.html` (if they've been using the Internet a long time). Those people will get frustrated if they see a `404: File not found` error message for typing in something as obvious as `index.html`. And the preceding redirection won't help because visitors didn't just type the name of the domain; they also typed `index.html`. Therefore, I also recommend that you include an `index.html` file that has a redirect. The only catch is that you can't do this redirect in PHP because `index.html` has an `.html` extension and therefore won't go through the PHP processor. (Thus back to your original desire to use `index.php`. Oops.) Here's the entire `index.html` file you need:

```
<html><head><title>Redirect!</title>
<meta http-equiv="Refresh" content="0; URL=index.php">
</head></html>
```

The HTML `Refresh` meta tag causes the browser to immediately load the `index.php` file.

If you're a Unix-head, you might have heard that you can use a symbolic link to accomplish a redirect. I tried it with the following code:

```
ln -s index.php index.html
```

My fear was affirmed: Although the redirect works, the file does *not* go through the PHP processor. The Apache server has no idea that the file it's really reading is `index.php`. Apache simply opens `index.html`, and the operating system secretly gives Apache the data in `index.php`; Apache has no idea this is a symbolic link. Apache sends the file to the browser as an `.html` file because that's the extension on `index.html`. And what goes to the browser? All your PHP code. So don't use a symbolic link because it doesn't work the way you might want it to.

Display the Current Time

Some people like to put the current time on their Web pages. However, if you have a static HTML page, any time that you type in will quickly be outdated. To avoid this problem, you can use PHP.

Here's a quick little `.php` file that displays the current time:

```
<html><head><title>Welcome</title></head>
<body>
Welcome to my Web page!
It is
```

```
<?php
    print date("l, F dS, Y \a\\t h:i:s A T");
?>
</body></html>
```

This file uses the date function to format the current date. Each letter in this string means a different date format; you can see a list of these letters and their formats at www.php.net/date.

The only thing I want to add about this date string concerns the strange \a\\t. If you have a letter that's a format specifier but want that letter to appear as is, precede it with a backslash. Because a is a format specifier, and I want the letter a to appear, I use \a. The letter t is also a format specifier, but \t is a tab. To just print a t, I use two backslashes. Thus \a\\t prints the happy little word at.

The preceding code generates server-side code (which is why I included the T, which prints the time zone), which can be a problem if the client is in a different time zone and you want the page to show the *local* time. The solution to this problem is to use a client-side language, such as JavaScript, and skip PHP altogether. Here's an .html file that prints the local time using JavaScript:

```
<html><head><title>Welcome</title></head>
<body>
Welcome to my Web page!
It is
<SCRIPT LANGUAGE="JavaScript" TYPE="text/javascript">
document.write(Date())
</SCRIPT>
</body></html>
```

Dynamically Generate Style Sheets

Style sheets are fun to play with, and they can add much fancier formatting to your Web pages than is available with plain old HTML. Style sheets enable you to specify text size, color, font, borders, shading, and all sorts of good stuff. Most people like to put their style sheet in a separate file and then have each Web page connect to that style sheet. Then whenever you add a new Web page, you don't need to reenter all the style information. And if you want to make a change to a style, you only need to modify it in the one place.

The cool thing about adding PHP to your Web site is that you can have multiple style sheets and then dynamically choose which style sheet to use. You could have a user log in by specifying a username and then look up the user's preferred style sheet in a MySQL database. Or you might change the style sheet based on the season (for example, yellow and brown colors for autumn).

Here's a single .php file that demonstrates two different style sheets based on the time:

```
<html><head><title>Changing Styles</title>
<style type="text/css">
<!--
<?php
    if (time() % 2 == 0) {
        print 'body {  font-family: Georgia, '.
        '"Times New Roman", Times, serif; '.
        'font-size: 14px; font-weight: bold; '.
        'color: #000099}';
    }
    else {
        print 'body {  font-family: '.
        'Arial, Helvetica, sans-serif; '.
        'font-size: 16px; font-weight: bold; '.
        'color: #006666}';
    }
?>
-->
</style></head>
<body bgcolor="#FFFFFF" text="#000000">
This is some basic text!
</body></html>
```

This file chooses the style for the body text based on the current Unix time. (I recommend, however, that you let the users have some say over the style.) I put the styles in the same .php file; if you want these styles available across the site, simply put them in their own .php file and either include or require that file.

If you try out this example yourself, remember that the program will pick a style sheet based on whether the current time in seconds is even or odd. Therefore, you may have to refresh the page a few times before you see a change.

Allow File Uploads

Some Web sites enable users to upload files. A good example is a Web e-mail service that lets users attach files to outgoing e-mail messages.

To handle uploads, you create a form in HTML and create a separate `.php` file that receives the uploaded file. Here's a sample `.html` file:

```
<html><head><title>File Upload Form</title></head>
<body>
<form enctype="multipart/form-data"
action="upload2.php" method="post">
<input type="hidden" name="MAX_FILE_SIZE" value="30000">
Filename: <input name="filename1" type="file"><br>
<input type="submit" value="Submit">
</form>
</body></html>
```

The two key parts are the `enctype` parameter in the `form` tag and the `file` input box. The `enctype` parameter and its value of `"multipart/form-data"` are required to tell the browser to send out a file. The input box of type `file` causes a text box and a browse button to appear in the browser. The browse button opens a File Open dialog box, and when the user selects a file, the filename appears in the text box.

You can support multiple file uploads by having multiple `file` type form objects; just make sure that you give each one a different `name` value. Notice that the `name` value I have provided in the preceding example is `filename1`; you could name the others `filename2`, `filename3`, and so on.

The hidden form object called `MAX_FILE_SIZE` tells the browser not to upload files that are larger than the specified number of bytes, in this case 30,000. (However, people have reported instances where their browsers ignored this, so in your PHP code, you may want to double-check the size of the file received.)

On the receiving end, your `.php` file gets an array called `$_FILES` that contains the information about the uploaded files (but not the files themselves). The `$_FILES` array has an entry for each file that was uploaded, and the keys are the names used in the file type input box in the HTML form. (Thus, if the files came from the preceding `.html` file sample, the `$_FILES` array would have a single key, a string containing `filename1`.) The value of each item in the array is itself an array. Here's the `.php` file that processes the uploads:

```
<?php
    $uploads_dir = '/home/me/uploads';
    foreach ($_FILES as $myfile) {
        $filename = $myfile['name'];
        switch ($myfile['error']) {
```

```
                case UPLOAD_ERR_NO_FILE:
                    continue 2; // continue for loop
                case UPLOAD_ERR_INI_SIZE:
                case UPLOAD_ERR_FORM_SIZE:
                    print "Sorry, $filename ".
                        "is too big.<p>";
                    continue 2;
                case UPLOAD_ERR_PARTIAL:
                    print "The upload of file ".
                        "$filename was broken. ".
                        "Please try again!<p>";
                    continue 2;
            }
            print "Thank you for the file $filename.";
            print "This file is of type ".
                $myfile['type'].".<br>";
            move_uploaded_file(
                $myfile['tmp_name'],
                $uploads_dir.$myfile['name']);
        }
    ?>
```

Here's a rundown of this code:

✦ The `foreach` loop runs for each uploaded file.

✦ The `$myfile` variable (specified in the loop header) contains the information about each file.

✦ `$myfile['name']` is the name of the file.

✦ If something goes wrong, `myfile['error']` is set to one of the four
  values I list in the `switch` statement.

✦ `$myfile['type']` is the MIME type of the file. (JPEG images, for example, will have `"image/pjpeg"` for this value.)

✦ And `$myfile['tmp_name']` is the complete path and filename where
  PHP stored the uploaded file. Typically, the file will be stored in a temporary directory; therefore, you will want to move the file as I did in the
  preceding sample using the `move_uploaded_file` function.

In the preceding code, I used the constants UPLOAD_ERR_NO_FILE,
UPLOAD_ERR_INI_SIZE, UPLOAD_ERR_FORM_SIZE, and UPLOAD_ERR_
PARTIAL, which are built into the PHP language. However, they only
appeared as of PHP version 4.2. If you're using an earlier version, you
need to use numbers instead. Replace UPLOAD_ERR_INI_SIZE with the
number 1; UPLOAD_ERR_FORM_SIZE with the number 2; UPLOAD_ERR_
PARTIAL with the number 3; and UPLOAD_ERR_NO_FILE with the number 4.
(Be careful — I didn't do these in numerical order in the preceding example;
the order will be 4, 1, 2, 3.)

In this example, I use a strange construct, the `continue 2` construct. This tells PHP to break out of the current loop and then continue with the next outer loop.

The only value in the `$myfile` array I didn't demonstrate in this code is `$myfile['size']`. This contains the size of the uploaded file.

After I get the uploaded file with this code, I move the file out of the temporary directory into my uploads directory by using the `move_uploaded_file` function. Be sure to use this function rather than the standard `copy` function because this function has various intrusion protections built in.

If you're using a PHP version earlier than 4.1.0, you can't use the `$_FILES` variable. Instead, use `$HTTP_POST_FILES`. However, before using it you have to access it as a global like this:

```
global $HTTP_POST_FILES;
```

Use POST When Appropriate

An HTML form that uses the `GET` method of sending data back to the Web server adds the data to the URL. This may not be the best method for sending the following types of information:

✦ **Passwords or other sensitive data:** If a user enters a password, the password is sent through the URL and thus is visible to anyone standing by. And anybody can look at the history or the drop-down list of the address box to see the data in the URL and, thereby, obtain the password.

✦ **Large amounts of data:** You may have data that's too big for a URL. If you have an edit box on a form that allows large amounts of text (such as the kind you see in a typical Web-based e-mail system), you can't use the `GET` form of sending data.

In these cases, the `POST` method works better. Switching to the `POST` method of sending data is easy; all you do is specify the `POST` method in the HTML `form` tag, like so:

```
<form name="form1" method="post" action="welcome.php">
```

On the PHP side, the receiving file (in this case, `welcome.php`) can extract the data by using the `$_POST` array rather than the `$_GET` array, like so:

```
$password = $_POST['password'];
```

As you can see, this is identical to the way you send and extract data with the GET method, except that you use the word POST instead of GET. So why would you ever use GET? The advantage to GET is that by carefully constructing a URL, you can "fake out" a .php file and let the PHP code think the data came from a form. This URL can be a direct link in an <a> tag, or it can be in the print statement of a PHP program, or wherever. Here's an example:

```
print '<a href="mydata.php?info=hi&name=jeff">click</a>';
```

Randomly Generate Picture-of-the-Day Images

Some people who have Web sites (especially if they're "official" sites for movie stars and other famous people) like to have picture-of-the-day images, which are random images from a directory.

Here's an example that generates a picture of the day. First, I created a directory called picoftheday, and I put three images in that directory, pic1.gif, pic2.gif, and pic3.gif. Then I created a file one directory up called picoftheday.php. Here's the file:

```
<html><head><title>Pic of the day!</title></head>
<body>
Here's today's picture!<p>
<?php
    $num = (time() % 3) + 1;
    $filename = "pic$num.gif";
    print "<img src=\"picoftheday/$filename\">";
?>
</body></html>
```

I take the remainder of the current time divided by 3 (yielding the value 0, 1, or 2) and add 1 (to get 1, 2, or 3). Then I build the filename, and finally, I print out an HTML <img> tag. Easy!

Just for fun, I chose to make my selection based on the current time. Alternatively, you can use the rand function, as I do in the section "Create a Random Link," later in this chapter.

Write Text from a File

Occasionally, you may have some text files you want to write out somewhere inside a Web page. For example, I have a directory on my server called news, where I keep all my latest notes; these notes are simple text files that appear as "News!" on my main Web page. This latest note is the contents of the most recent file in the news directory. Here's the code that makes this happen:

```
<html><head><title>Latest notes!</title></head><body>
<h1>Welcome to my site!</h1>
<?
if ($dir = @opendir("news")) {
    $curmaxtime = 0;
    $mostrecentfile = "";
    while (($file = readdir($dir)) !== false) {
        $fullfile = "news/$file";
        if (!is_dir($fullfile)) {
            $mystats = stat($fullfile);
            if ($mystats[9] > $curmaxtime) {
            $curmaxtime = $mystats[9];
            $mostrecentfile = $fullfile;
            }
        }
    }
    closedir($dir);
    if ($curmaxtime > 0) {
        print "Last updated: ".
            date("F j, Y, g:i a",$curmaxtime)."<p>";
        readfile($fullfile);
    }
}

?>
</body></html>
```

The while loop scans through all the files in the directory and locates the newest one. The if statement prints out a note about when the note was last updated and then dumps out the contents of the note.

Determine Which Browser Is Running

If parts of your site require a certain browser, you can determine a Web site visitor's browser type by calling the function get_browser.

The get_browser function returns an array filled with amazing information about the browser. Here's an example that you can try out:

```
<html><head><title>I know all about you!</title>
</head>
<body>
<h1>Here's your browser info as I see it!</h1>
```

```php
<?php
    $info = get_browser();
    foreach ($info as $key=>$value) {
        print "$key: $value<br>\n";
    }
?>
</body></html>
```

For the `get_browser` function to work, your PHP installation must be configured with browser capabilities turned on. To do this, you need to include a line in your Apache configuration file that points to a browser capabilities file. Here's the line:

```
php_value browscap "/browscap.ini"
```

Substitute the / for the full path to the location of your `browscap.ini` file. Where do you get the `browscap.ini` file? You can download it from `www.php.net/get_browser`. On that page, you will see a link for downloading the latest browser capabilities file. If you don't do this, you will see the following warning:

```
Invalid argument supplied for foreach()
in /var/www/html/ch5_10_6.php on line 7
```

Create a Random Link

Sometimes it's fun to have a random link on your page. If you have a set of links, you can easily do this with an array and a random number. Here's a quick example; if you want to try this, keep refreshing your browser to see a different link:

```php
<html><head><title>Link-o-the-day</title></head>
<body>
<?php
    $links = array(
        "http://www.dummies.com",
        "http://www.php.net",
        "http://www.jeffcogswell.com",
        "http://www.wiley.com",
        "http://www.whitehouse.gov");
    $linknum = rand(0, count($links) - 1);
    print '<a href="'.
        $links[$linknum].
        '">click here!</a>';
?>
</body></html>
```

Determine Host Names from IP Addresses

If you have an IP address and need to convert it to its full name (such as if you're inspecting the $_SERVER array and looking at the REMOTE_ADDR value), then you can call gethostbyaddr to convert the IP address to a name using a DNS server.

Here's a quick example:

```
<html><head><title>Who are you?</title></head>
<body>
<?php
    print "You are ";
    print gethostbyaddr($_SERVER['REMOTE_ADDR']);
?>
</body></html>
```

And you can go the other way. (If there's a will, there's a way, after all.) If you have a host name, you can obtain the IP address by using the gethost bynamel function. This function returns an array because some site names are set up to use multiple IP addresses for distribution purposes. Here's a code snippet:

```
<?php
    $ips = gethostbynamel('www.yahoo.com');
    foreach ($ips as $ip) {
        print "$ip<br>\n";
    }
?>
```

The server I use in this example is a good one because it has many IP addresses. If you know that you'll need only one, though, you can instead use gethostbyname (no letter *l* at the end). This returns a scalar, not an array.

Book VI

MySQL Databases on the Web

"I STARTED DESIGNING DATABASE SOFTWARE SYSTEMS AFTER SEEING HOW EASY IT WAS TO DESIGN OFFICE FURNITURE."

Contents at a Glance

Chapter 1: What Is MySQL?

In This Chapter

✔ Introducing MySQL

✔ Connecting MySQL and PHP on the Web

✔ Starting the MySQL daemon

✔ Setting up MySQL users

✔ Controlling access

*W*hen you want to store data on a Web server, you can easily put the data in a file, but simple files only get you so far. If you have complex data to store, you're better off using a database. Further, when you use a file, if you have lots of users requesting Web pages and those Web pages contain PHP code that accesses the files, you can quickly run into some problems: One user may be uploading data and writing to the file, and another may be downloading data from the same file, making for a serious mess. A database works best in such situations.

MySQL is a popular database system that many people use for their Web databases. The PHP and MySQL development teams work closely together to ensure that the two products interact with grace and ease. (Now doesn't that sound nice?)

Here are some of the features of the MySQL database system:

✦ **It's free.** MySQL ships with the GNU Public License, so you can use it without forking over big bucks. (Although, if you prefer, you can purchase a commercial license, which includes various support plans.)

✦ **It's widely available.** Most third-party host providers include MySQL as part of the standard package.

✦ **It works well with friends.** The MySQL database system includes interfaces from numerous languages, including C++, Perl, Tcl, and PHP.

✦ **It's a fully relational database management system (RDBMS).** MySQL includes a full Structured Query Language (SQL) implementation, which enables you to access your data the same way other large database systems do using *relational* methods, whereby you can connect data from different tables.

For users of third-party hosting services

If you're using a third-party hosting service, most likely MySQL is already installed and ready for you to use. Usually, a hosting service provides you with a single database you can access, and a single username and password for accessing that database. You can change the password, but you probably can't change the username or the database name and can't create new databases. In general, you do have a significant amount of power because you can store many tables of information within the single database. If you're using a third-party hosting service, I encourage you to read this chapter because doing so greatly enhances your general understanding of MySQL, and also I specifically address your situation throughout the chapter.

These features make MySQL a great choice for a Web server database. In this chapter, I provide you with information on configuring MySQL.

You can find information about MySQL at the main MySQL site at www.mysql.com. You can find the online manual at www.mysql.com/doc/en/index.html.

Connecting MySQL and PHP on the Web

When you create a Web site that requires database access, you typically use PHP code to access the data. Remember, PHP is a server-side scripting language, and the PHP processor takes a .php file, grinds through it, and generates a resulting .html file. The Web server then sends the resulting .html file to the client browser on the Web user's computer. (You can find out more about PHP in Book V.)

For example, suppose your company wants to create a Web page that lists the company directory on its internal corporate Web site. To tackle this problem, you create a .php file that connects to a MySQL database, retrieves the data for the phone list, and then writes out an HTML table showing the names, e-mail addresses, and phone extensions.

You also include a Web form that allows certain users to modify the data in the company directory. This Web form is guarded with an HTTP authentication (using PHP), requiring users to log in before gaining access to the form. Users make updates using the HTML form and then click a submit button. The submit button connects to a .php file that again requires HTTP authentication. (But because users already entered their information, they don't have to reenter it.) This .php file connects to the database and updates the directory information accordingly.

MySQL stores its data in a database. You can have multiple databases on your system, but often people have only a single database containing many tables of information. MySQL also maintains a list of passwords and usernames, including a *root* username, which is the administrator. You can set up your MySQL system so that each user has certain rights. For example, you may authorize one user to read certain databases and another user to modify certain databases. When you write a PHP program to connect to a MySQL database, you supply this username and password. However, these usernames and passwords are separate from the username and password you would require in HTTP authentication (although you can make them the same if you want).

Often when using a third-party hosting service, you are given only a single database and a single username (often the same as the database). This single username can modify and read the data in your database. You can set up HTTP authentication on the Web pages that modify the data. Further, you can store your data within the single database in separate tables of information, so you're not limited to storing only a tiny bit of data.

Figure 1-1 shows a typical process for reading data from a MySQL database using PHP; in this diagram, an "SQL query" simply refers to a program requesting data from a MySQL database.

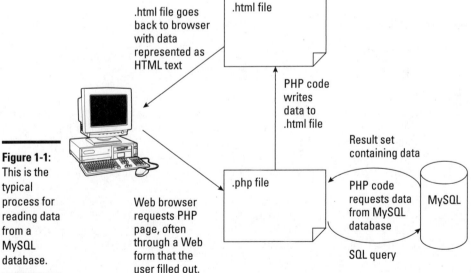

Figure 1-1: This is the typical process for reading data from a MySQL database.

Figure 1-2 shows a typical process for writing data to a MySQL database using PHP.

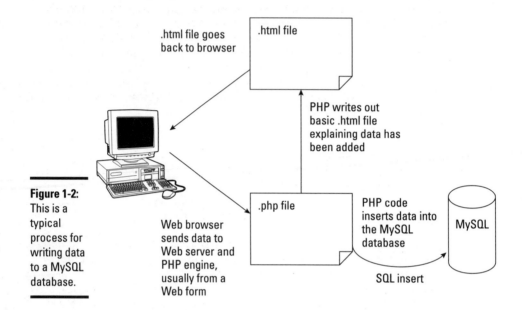

.html file goes back to browser

.html file

PHP writes out basic .html file explaining data has been added

Figure 1-2:
This is a typical process for writing data to a MySQL database.

Web browser sends data to Web server and PHP engine, usually from a Web form

.php file

PHP code inserts data into the MySQL database

MySQL

SQL insert

Starting MySQL

The MySQL web site includes easy, clear instructions for installing MySQL; you can find the instructions at `www.mysql.com/doc/en/Installing.html`.

If you follow these instructions, you should be ready to go. The Linux version starts up the daemon automatically. (A *daemon* is a program that runs all the time on your computer, often supplying some sort of service, such as MySQL database handling. As for who in the computer world came up with this term — which is really just a variant of *demon* — and why they use it, frankly, I don't have a clue. It must have been somebody having a really bad day.)

If you're using Red Hat Linux 8.0 and higher, you can configure the MySQL daemon (called mysqld) to start up automatically upon reboot by selecting Server Settings from the Gnome menu, and then selecting Services. In the window that opens, click mysqld, and then choose Start. Then check the box beside mysqld on the menu.

If you're working on a Windows system, you may need to start MySQL as a service. (Services can run only on the NT, 2000, and XP versions of Windows. If you're using Windows 95, 98, or Me, you need to upgrade anyway because they're not very secure as Web servers.) You can easily find out if the service is running by making sure the `mysql\bin` directory is in your path. Then from the command prompt, type the following:

```
mysqlshow
```

If the server is running, you will see a list of tables similar to this:

```
+-----------+
| Databases |
+-----------+
| mysql     |
| test      |
+-----------+
```

If the server is not running, you'll see this error message:

```
mysqlshow: Can't connect to MySQL server on 'localhost'
    (10061)
```

If you see this error message, you need to start up the MySQL service. To do so, follow these steps. (If you have the Apache server running on your Windows computer, instead of following Steps 1, 2, and 3, you can right-click the Apache icon in the tray on the lower-right corner of your screen and, in the pop-up menu that appears, choose Open Services.)

1. On the Windows desktop, right-click My Computer and, in the pop-up menu, choose Manage.

The Computer Management window opens, as shown in Figure 1-3.

2. Expand the Services and Applications tree, which you can see in the left pane of the window in Figure 1-3.

3. Under Services and Applications, click Services.

The Services list appears in the right pane, as shown in Figure 1-4.

4. In the Services pane, scroll down to MySQL, right-click the name MySQL, and in the pop-up menu, choose Start.

The MySQL service starts, and the word Started appears under the Status column beside the word MySQL.

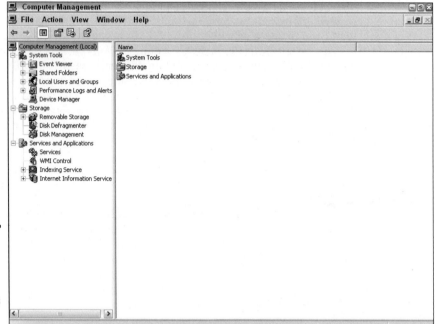

Figure 1-3:
Expand the
Services
and
Applications
tree.

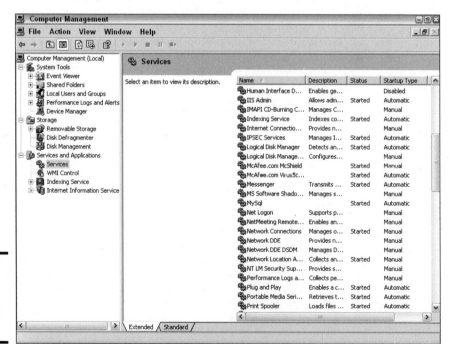

Figure 1-4:
The list of
services is
in the right
pane.

Now close the Computer Management window, return to the command prompt, and try the `mysqlshow` command again.

The MySQL system also includes a handy command-line utility called mysql (in all lowercase). This command-line utility lets you make changes to your database and tables. Typically when you create Web pages that access the MySQL databases, those pages use a programming language such as PHP to access the databases. But when you're logged into your own system and want to make changes to the databases, you will likely use the mysql command-line utility.

Don't confuse the mysql command-line utility with the MySQL service or daemon. The MySQL service or daemon is the heart of MySQL. The service or daemon listens to data requests and then manipulates the data on the hard drive. The mysql command-line utility is just that: a command-line utility that lets you manipulate your data. People often like to think of the mysql command-line utility as MySQL itself, while in fact, the command-line utility is nothing more than a user interface to MySQL.

Adding MySQL Users

In this section I show you how to add users to your MySQL system. You can have these users log into MySQL and perform database processes.

If you're using a third-party hosting service, usually you will have received a username and password and won't have access to the root, in which case you can skip this section and use that username and password in the sample PHP programs throughout this text.

To add users to your MySQL system, you must be logged in either as the administrator under username `root`, or as a user who has administrator rights.

The easiest way to add a user to the MySQL system is by logging into the command-line utility. To start the command-line utility, make sure the `mysql/bin` directory is in your path and, from the command line, type the following:

```
mysql -u root -p
```

If you enter `mysql` immediately, then you're logged in, in which case you need to add a root password (because presently your system is wide open). To find out how to set a root password, check out the nearby sidebar "Creating a root password."

Removing the anonymous user on Windows

If you discover that you can connect to MySQL simply by typing `mysql` with nothing after it, your system is set up to allow anonymous users. Bad news: This anonymous user has full root privileges! Very bad indeed. This is the default with many Windows installations, but fortunately you can fix the problem. (In fact, *please* fix the problem. You don't want hackers getting into your site.) First, enter `mysql` from the command prompt. Then select a database by typing this line:

```
use mysql
```

You see the message `Database changed.` Now type this line (note that those things before the semicolon are two consecutive single quotes with no space between them):

```
delete from user where user='';
```

You probably also have a default root user that allows anyone to log in from anywhere using the username root with no password. (Big time yikes!) To remove that major security hole, type this:

```
delete from user where host = '%' and
          user = 'root';
```

Then type this command:

```
quit
```

After you're outside the `mysql` command-line utility, type this line:

```
mysqladmin -u root -p reload
```

You are prompted for the root password, which you may enter. Now you won't be able to get into mysql by simply typing `mysql`. Whew!

If you don't get in right away, you're presented with a password prompt:

```
Enter password:
```

Type in your root password and press Enter.

If you've forgotten your root password (or never knew it), please check out the following Web page for information on how to reset your root password:

`www.mysql.com/doc/en/Resetting_permissions.html`

After you have created your user password and are inside the mysql command-line utility, you can add your first user. In this section, I show you how to create a user with username `phpuser` and password `phppass`. I encourage you to find a different password other than the one I've written here in this big thick book that over 100 million people will purchase and read. You may also consider picking a different username. However, in the samples throughout this book, I use the username `phpuser` and password `phppass`. You need to substitute your own username and password for the examples.

Creating a root password

If you don't have a root password, you will want to add one so that your system isn't left wide open for just anybody to climb into and muck things up. Here's how you set a root password:

First, if you're on Linux or Unix, make sure you're logged in as root.

Next, regardless of your operating system, start mysql without a password by using either

```
mysql
```

or

```
mysql -u root
```

Then type the following, substituting your own secret password for *somepassword*:

```
set password for root@localhost=
          password('somepassword');
```

The word `password` after the equal sign is vital: This function takes the following string and encrypts it. Thus, you're not storing your password in the database; you're storing an encrypted form of your password. Then, when you log in, mysql automatically encrypts the password you type and compares it to the encrypted password stored in the database. If the two match, mysql lets you in. Otherwise, you get an error message.

After you type this preceding `set` command, you can exit out of mysql and then start it back up, using the password:

```
mysql -u root -p
```

You are then prompted for the password, which you may now enter. Then you'll get into the newly password-protected mysql command-line utility. Yay!

Here's how you add the user. Make sure you're inside the mysql utility and then enter the following:

```
grant all privileges on *.* to phpuser@localhost
identified by 'phppass';
```

Then press Enter. You see a message stating the query worked. (Although, really, the message isn't particularly clear. It is as follows.)

```
Query OK, 0 rows affected (0.00 sec)
```

(Yes, it worked, even though the message says that zero rows were affected.) You now have a user called `phppass` with full privileges. You can exit out of the mysql program by typing `quit`. Then you can sign back in by using this new username:

```
mysql -u phpuser -p
```

You are then prompted for the password:

```
Enter password:
```

After you enter the password, you will be logged in under the new username.

Managing domain access

If you peruse the MySQL online documentation, you will see references to both `username` and `username@localhost`. The `@localhost` thing seems to crop up a lot. The idea behind `username` and `username@localhost` is you are specifying where the user can be when logging into MySQL. By simply specifying `username`, you're saying the user can log in from any computer. By specifying `username@localhost`, you're saying the user must be logged into the same computer running MySQL, and from there, log into MySQL. In other words, these two choices allow people to log in remotely to your MySQL system.

Like most things in this great big world of ours, tradeoffs exist. Here are some points to consider when deciding whether to allow outside access:

✦ **Disadvantage:** It can create a security risk. You don't want people from across the globe trying to log in to your database through their own remote connections. (You'd probably prefer they log in through your `.php` files, which run on your server.)

✦ **Advantage:** Allowing for such remote connections lets you create some rather powerful, distributed software.

Here's my rule of thumb: I don't allow outside access on my server because all my access takes place from within the server. If I want to use the mysql program, I first telnet into my server and then run mysql. If I want to access the MySQL databases from my Web pages, I use PHP, which runs on the server side and does not require outside access. Thus, I have no need for outside access. Unless you're planning to run client-side database software that will make remote connections to your server, thereby creating a distributed system, you should also turn off any access from the outside. (If you're not sure what all this mumbo jumbo means, most likely you won't need the outside access, and you can just do away with it once and for all!)

Preventing outside access

By default, your system should be set up to prevent outside access. Here's how you can check whether your system allows outside access. Log into the mysql program as the root and then carefully type these commands:

```
use mysql
select host, user from user;
```

In case you're curious, this is an SQL `select` statement that retrieves all the rows from the user table, showing only the user and host columns. I talk all about SQL in Book VI, Chapter 5.

Here's some sample output (yours will be similar but not necessarily the same):

```
+---------------+---------+
| host          | user    |
+---------------+---------+
| %             | guest   |
| 192.168.1.103 | jeff    |
| localhost     | phpuser |
| localhost     | root    |
+---------------+---------+
```

This is a list of users allowed to access your system. The `user` column is the username, and the `host` column is the name of the host from which the user is connecting. And look: This output is saying that the user named `jeff` (that's me!) can log in from the computer on IP address `192.168.1.103`, which is a separate computer. In other words, `jeff` can log in remotely. (However, `192.168.1.103` is an IP address on the local network and not a computer from outside the network.)

Now look at the first line: The host is simply `%`, which in SQL is a wildcard. That means if you see a line like this, somebody can log into the system with username `guest` from *any* computer on the Internet. If you don't want guest logging in from anywhere on the Internet, change the entry's host to local-host, like so:

```
update user set host = 'localhost' where user = 'guest' and
    host = '%';
```

Or, if you prefer to remove the guest user altogether, you can type this:

```
delete from user where user = 'guest';
```

Logging in remotely

If you want to allow outside access, you can specify an IP address (or computer name on a local network) when you create a user; you'll then be able to log in from the computer with that IP address. I have installed MySQL on both my desktop and laptop computers. On the MySQL system running on the desktop, I created a user called `jeff@192.168.1.100`. (The IP address

192.168.1.100 is for the laptop.) To create this user, I sit down at my desktop, start the mysql program, and type the following:

```
grant all privileges on *.* to jeff@192.168.1.100;
```

This creates a user called `jeff` who can log in from the computer having IP address `192.168.1.100`.

Next, to log into the desktop from the laptop, I first make sure the daemon is running on my desktop computer, and from the Windows laptop, I type the following:

```
mysql -h 192.168.1.102 -u jeff -p
```

The `-h` option specifies the computer running the MySQL server; in this case, `192.168.1.102` is the IP address of my desktop. I am then prompted for the password, and I can log in using the mysql utility. In this case, I'm running the mysql utility on my laptop while looking at data on the desktop computer.

Technically speaking, the users `jeff@localhost` and `jeff@192.168.1.100` are distinct users as far as MySQL is concerned. However, if you grant the same privileges to both users, the client program will be able to use a single username, `jeff`, whether the client runs on the localhost or on the `192.168.1.100` computer.

You can also use a mixture of wildcards and numbers in the host, like so:

```
grant all privileges on *.* to jeff@"192.168.1.%"
identified by 'mypass';
```

Now you can log in from any computer on the network, provided the computer you're using has an IP address starting with 192.168.1. You can then log in as username `jeff` with password `mypass`. (However, you still can't log in from `localhost`, even if your local machine has an IP address starting with 196.168.1. The mysql program will grab your host as `localhost`, not by its IP address.)

Changing your user password

After you're logged into MySQL, perhaps using the mysql program, you can change your password if you want. (If you're using a third-party hosting service, I encourage you to change your password from the one the service originally gave you.)

The easiest way to change your password is from within the mysql program. Just follow these steps:

1. **Start mysql, logging in with your username, like so:**

   ```
   mysql -u username -p
   ```

   Be sure to substitute *username* with your own username, whether it's `phpuser`, or whatever. After this, you are prompted for your password.

2. **Enter your password and log in.**

3. **After you're logged in, you can set your password with this command:**

   ```
   set password for username = password('newpassword');
   ```

   Substitute *username* with your own username and *newpassword* with whatever you want the new password to be.

Restricting access

If you have created a MySQL username (such as `phpuser`), you will want to limit the type of access available to the user. The instructions in the earlier section, "Adding MySQL Users," show you how to create a username that has full administrative rights, including the ability to modify the root password. For most users, you don't want them having the ability to modify the root password.

Here's how you can limit the rights of what this user can do. The general guideline is to give a MySQL user only those rights that are absolutely necessary. For example, hosting services typically create a database for each Unix user, and then for that database, assign a MySQL username and password that has access only to that database and nothing more.

If you're reading this chapter straight through and following the examples, you probably don't yet have a database or table that the PHP programs can access. Thus, you can't limit the `phpuser` access to those tables. But because this book is a reference guide, here's what I encourage you to do: Peruse this section, and then after you've read Book VI, Chapter 4, and set up your databases (or, after you've set up your databases on your own), follow the instructions in this section step by step.

In these instructions, I'm assuming you have a database called `phpbase`. This database contains all the tables that you want your `.php` files to have access to.

If you want to add an extra level of security, you can create additional MySQL usernames that the PHP programs will access depending on who is accessing the `.php` files through the Web; such usernames would have only the rights you want the Web page to have. (You can determine who is accessing the `.php` files by using HTTP authentication.) You may have a MySQL username that can read only the data in the `phpbase` database. You may also have a MySQL username that can modify the data. Therefore, the `.php` files that can modify the data would use the MySQL username that can modify the data, and so on.

Follow these steps to set the privileges for the `phpuser` user:

1. **Start the mysql command-line program, logged in as root.**

2. **Revoke all privileges by typing this command:**

```
revoke all on *.* from phpuser@localhost;
```

3. **Next, add only the rights you want.**

This example lets the user insert data into the tables (but not create new tables or databases), delete data, retrieve data, and modify data for only the `phpbase` database:

```
grant insert, delete, select, update on phpbase.*
to phpuser@localhost;
```

Here are the specific privileges I granted and what they mean:

+ `insert`: The user can add data to the tables in the `phpbase` **database.**

+ `delete`: The user can delete data from the tables in the `phpbase` database.

+ `select`: The user can read data in the tables in the `phpbase` **database.**

+ `update`: The user can modify existing data in the `phpbase` **database.** (Note that modifying existing data is a separate process and privilege from adding new data to a table.)

If you're already familiar with SQL, you will recognize these privileges as respective SQL keywords. If you want to see all the privileges that are available, check out the MySQL manual's entry at `www.mysql.com/doc/en/GRANT.html`.

Here are a few clarifications about this example:

+ Because I already created this user and gave this user a password, I don't need to include the `identified by 'phppass'` clause as I did elsewhere in this chapter.

✦ I specified the database name, phpbase, but I had to put .* after the name, meaning I'm granting these privileges to all tables inside the phpbase database. And yes, in this case you use the * wildcard rather than the % wildcard as you do elsewhere. It's just an annoying rule to follow; that's all. (You can't leave off the .*, or mysql will think you're referring to a table called phpbase, which you're not, and you'll get an error.)

Now you can test the restrictions. Exit mysql by typing quit and then log back in as the phpuser user:

```
mysql -u phpuser -p
```

You will be prompted for a password; go ahead and enter it. Then, after you're inside mysql, you should be limited on what you can do as the phpuser user. For example, try accessing the system database:

```
use mysql
```

If the restrictions are working, you will see an error message:

```
ERROR 1044: Access denied for user: 'phpuser@localhost'
to database 'mysql'
```

However, you can access the phpbase database:

```
use phpbase
```

which results in this message:

```
Database changed
```

But you can't create a new table from this username. Generally that's fine, because you probably don't want your .php files creating a new table. Instead, you'll create the table while logged into mysql as root, and then later, your .php files will modify the table only by adding data, removing data, or modifying the data in the table.

In this section, I showed you how to set the privileges. Now, you'll be able to perform the basic access typically required by a PHP program, as I explain in Book VI, Chapter 4.

Chapter 2: Managing Databases and Tables

In This Chapter

✔ **Finding out what databases are available**

✔ **Creating, deleting, backing up, and moving a database**

✔ **Setting user privileges for a database**

✔ **Creating a table and dropping (or deleting) a table**

✔ **Adding data to a table and looking at the data in a table**

✔ **Getting information about a table**

✔ **Seeing what tables are in a database**

*B*efore going any further, I want to clear up some definitions. In the world of databases, people have different definitions for the same words. (Isn't that just like a bunch of computer people?) However, most companies that develop database products all agree on the definitions of these terms. I want to share these definitions with you so you, me, and all the other database people on the planet can see eye to eye (or at least computer-interface-to-computer-interface, as the case may be).

The following are informal definitions that most people agree on:

✦ **Table:** A set of data organized into rows and columns.

✦ **Database:** A collection of tables. In MySQL, you can have several distinct databases.

✦ **Row:** A single record within a database. The term *record* has become nonstandard, and today, people prefer the term *row*.

✦ **Column:** A single field within a database. A row (or record) is made up of several columns (or fields) such as name, email_address, and phone_number. As with *record,* the term *field* has become nonstandard; these days people prefer the term *column.*

In this chapter, I talk about various issues involved in setting up databases and tables in MySQL, along with such important topics as how to back up your databases and how to automate various tasks.

A note about how databases are stored

Unlike some database systems, the MySQL database system uses an open approach to its data. If you've ever looked at, for example, a Microsoft Outlook file on a Windows computer, you know that all the e-mail, calendar entries, attachments, notes, and so on are stored in a single file. I've seen some such files that are an unwieldy 200+ megabytes in size. Fortunately, MySQL's file management is more simple: For each database, MySQL creates a new directory. Inside that directory, for each table, MySQL creates a set of files.

Throughout the discussions in this chapter, remember that an alternative method exists to managing databases: You can go to the directory containing your databases and simply work with the files. You can back up these files to a CD-ROM, copy them, move them to another computer, and so on. MySQL is perfectly fine with all this.

However, be sure that you don't copy the files while some process is busily writing data to the files because you could end up with a mess.

Managing a Database

In this section, I talk about how to manage your databases, including creating, deleting, and backing up databases. I also include a section on usernames and privileges pertaining to databases.

Finding out what databases exist

The easiest way to find out what databases exist is to start up the mysql command-line utility and type the following:

```
show databases;
```

When you press Enter, you see something similar to this:

```
+-----------+
| Database  |
+-----------+
| menagerie |
| mysql     |
| phpbase   |
| test      |
+-----------+
```

This output shows that my system has four databases present: menagerie, mysql, phpbase, and test.

Creating a database

Use the mysql command-line program to create a database. Creating a database is something you just do once, and you don't want to have a Web page create a database, at least not a page that the general public accesses. A database contains tables that contain your data, and most people prefer to have just one or two databases on their system. If every user came along and added a database, you could end up with a very messy system. (You might, however, have such a Web page for your own own personal work.)

A database holds the tables that store the information that the Web pages access through the PHP code. (That's a pretty good explanation of how a database works, so you may want to tear out this page and paste it on your monitor.) Normally, you will create a database, create some tables, and then write the code (in PHP or Perl or any language of your choice) to access the data. With PHP, you write your `.php` files to access the data in the tables through a Web interface.

Creating a database is easy. Just perform the following steps:

1. **Choose the name for your database.**

2. **Start up mysql with the root password.**

You always need root privileges to create a database, although you can use another username as long as it has root privileges

3. **Type the following line:**

```
create database databasename
```

Replace *databasename* with the name for your new database — phpbase, for example. When you press Enter, the mysql utility instructs MySQL to create the database called *databasename*. If the database already exists, you get an error message similar to this:

```
ERROR 1007: Can't create database 'databasename'.
    Database exists.
```

Deleting a database

If you want to delete a database, you can use the following procedure from within the mysql utility.

When you delete a database, remember that you are also deleting *all the data* inside the database. You won't be able to retrieve the data unless you previously backed it up. (I recommend doing regular backups of your data. See the section "Backing up a database [or table]," later in this chapter, for details.) For Unix gurus, if you have set up a symbolic link to a database and then delete the symbolic-linked database, you lose not only the symbolic link but the actual database as well.

Here's how you delete an entire database (and all its contents):

```
drop database databasename;
```

Substitute the poor, unlucky database's name for the word *databasename*, and the poor, unlucky database will be gone. The mysql utility won't issue an "Are you sure?" message or anything. It simply instructs the MySQL daemon or server to delete the database, and you get back a strange message such as `Query OK, 3 rows affected (0.00 sec)`.

The databases are stored in files in their own directories. For example, the `menagerie` database is stored in a directory called `menagerie`. If you delete a database, the entire directory is deleted.

Backing up a database (or table)

Generally, you will want to make regular backups of your database in case disaster strikes, such as a meteor spinning towards Earth at 0.8 times the speed of light. If the meteor hits, you'll be glad that you backed up the data on a CD-ROM because everything else will be gone. How often should you back up your data? That depends on how active your database is. If the data changes only a little bit every week, then maybe once a month is good. If you have massive amounts of data coming in and getting modified every day, then a nightly backup is probably a good idea.

Backing up a database is a bit touchier than it may seem at first. Suppose you have a Web site running and people are accessing your database through the Web site, reading data, changing data, and adding data. When you back up the database, make sure that the files aren't in a temporary, inconsistent state. Otherwise, your backup will not be valid.

The best way to ensure your data is safe before backing up is to shut down the daemon or server and then back it up. Or you can go into the mysql utility as user `root` and type the following:

```
flush tables with read lock;
```

This code writes all outstanding data to the tables and then temporarily *locks* the tables so they can't be changed. At this point, the data in the tables can be read by other MySQL programs, but no changes are allowed. (I show you how to unlock the tables at the end of this section.)

Because a database is simply a collection of tables, the easiest way to back up a database is to back up the tables inside the database, which encompass all the data in the entire database. You can use the mysql utility to back up the tables. (Unfortunately, the mysql utility doesn't include a command for backing up an entire database. The MySQL package, however, does come with some utilities that can assist you with backing up a database. You can read about them at `www.mysql.com/doc/en/Backup.html`.)

Here's how you back up the tables in the database on Unix or Linux:

1. **Create a directory to hold the backed-up files, such as** `/home/harold/backups/phpbase`.

2. **Start the mysql utility and enter these commands:**

   ```
   backup table pet to '/home/harold/backups/phpbase;
   ```

Here's how you back up the tables on a Windows system:

1. **Create a directory to hold the backed-up files.**

   The backup procedure will not create a directory for you. For example, you might create the directory `c:\temp\phpbase`.

2. **Start the mysql utility and enter these commands:**

   ```
   use phpbase
   backup table pet,pet2 to 'c:/temp/phpbase';
   ```

   Substitute the name of your database for `phpbase`. Also notice that you must use forward slashes, not backslashes in the backup command. (In a more perfect world, all computers would agree on the forward slash/backward slash business.)

After you've finished backing up the database, you can unlock the tables with this command:

```
unlock tables;
```

Setting user privileges for a database

In Book VI, Chapter 1, I talk about assigning limited privileges for a user. The idea in that section is to create a user that can only read rows, delete rows, change rows, and add rows to any table in a particular database. But you may want to create a user that has full access to a particular database and no access to another database.

If you're running an ISP, granting a user full access to only one database is a common approach for managing your MySQL installation. Most hosting services create a single username and give that user a single database. In this section, I show you how to ensure that the user can access only his or her assigned database, assuming the user doesn't have somebody else's password.

To assign these privileges, follow these steps:

1. **First, create the** `jessica` **database if you haven't done so already.**

To do this, go into the mysql utility and type the following:

```
create database jessica;
```

2. **If you have not yet created the** `jessica` **username for MySQL, create the username and set the privileges all at once, as follows:**

```
grant all privileges on jessica.* to jessica@localhost
identified by 'jessicapass';
```

Or if you have already created the `jessica` **username for MySQL, you can follow these steps to limit the privileges:**

a. Revoke the rights for the main system:

```
revoke all on *.* from jessica@localhost;
```

b. If you previously gave Jessica rights to some other database, such as the phpbase database, you can revoke those rights too, as follows:

```
revoke all on phpbase.* from jessica@localhost;
```

c. Now grant Jessica permission to use the jessica database:

```
grant all privileges on jessica.* to
jessica@localhost;
```

Here's a sample session with username `jessica` demonstrating that she can access only the database called `jessica`:

```
mysql -u jessica -p
Enter password: ***********
Welcome to the MySQL monitor.
mysql> show databases;
+-----------+
| Database  |
+-----------+
| jessica   |
| mysql     |
| phpbase   |
+-----------+
3 rows in set (0.02 sec)
mysql> use menagerie;
ERROR 1044: Access denied for user: 'jessica@localhost'
    to database 'menagerie'
mysql> use jessica;
Database changed
```

Moving a database to another computer

If you want to move a database to another computer, I suggest simply copying the files. That's by far the easiest way. The following are the different methods of moving databases, depending on your operating system:

✦ **In Linux:** Go to the mysql installation and look under the `data` directory. You will see a directory called `data` that contains a separate subdirectory for each database. You can copy that subdirectory to a shared file system, allowing you to copy it to another computer. If you don't see a data directory, try looking in `/var/lib/mysql`, which is another common place to find your database subdirectories.

✦ **In Windows:** Go to the directory `c:\mysql\data` (or wherever you put mysql; for me, the data directory is `C:\Program Files\mysql\data`). In the directory, look for a subdirectory with the same name as your database. Copy that subdirectory and all its contents to a disk, CD-ROM, or shared drive, or onto the Interplanetary Photon-wave Network Connection (when they invent that). Then switch to the other computer, go to that computer's same `mysql\data` directory, and copy the database directory into the data directory. Make sure that as you copy, the database directory is created (or that you create it manually).

Managing Tables

To create a table, you need a database. In this database, you can create as many tables as you want.

A table is a collection of data stored in the form of *rows,* which some people call *records.* Each record is made up of a set of *columns,* which some people call *fields.* Here's an example of a description for a table called `candy`:

✦ `name` is a `varchar(30)`.

✦ `weight` is a `double`.

✦ `price` is an `int`.

✦ `quantity` is an `int`.

Each row of information in the `candy` table has a name, weight, price, and quantity. The name is of type `varchar(30)` (`varchar(30)` means a character string up to 30 characters long). The weight is a double (which is a double-precision floating point number). The price is an integer given in cents (never use floating point variables for dollars; instead, use integers for cents because integer math is more accurate than floating point math), and the quantity is an integer.

In the sections that follow, I show you how to create this table inside MySQL, get information about the table inside MySQL, delete the table, and see what other tables are available.

For the following sections, you will use the database called `phpbase`. To use this database, first log into mysql as `root` and then type the following:

```
use phpbase
```

Now you can precede with the examples.

Although the following examples use the mysql command-line utility, keep in mind that the statements you are typing are SQL language statements, and you can use these statements in your programs that run independently from the mysql utility.

Creating a table

Creating a table is simple. Here's a rundown of the process:

+ You use a specialized SQL keyword called `create table`. (Okay, that's two keywords.)

+ You give the table name and, in parentheses, a description of the columns in the table.

+ You end with a semicolon.

Assuming you started the mysql utility and are using the database `phpbase`, you can type the following lines into the mysql prompt:

```
create table candy (
    name varchar(30),
    weight double,
    price int,
    quantity int
);
```

As you type each line and press Enter, the mysql utility recognizes that you haven't yet typed a semicolon, so it starts the next line with the following characters:

```
    ->
```

These characters indicate that you can continue typing the command. (The `create table` command you see here is stretched over multiple lines.)

After you run this command, you see the happy, friendly (albeit nearly meaningless) message:

```
Query OK, 0 rows affected (0.01 sec)
```

This message means that you successfully created the table.

Adding rows to a table

If you have a table, you probably don't want to leave it sitting around bored doing nothing. Instead, you want to put some data in it. (Hey, you made the thing — you may as well use it.) In Book VI, Chapter 3, I talk about the types of data you can put in your tables and how you can relate your tables to one another. For now, I stick with the table called candy that I created in the preceding section, "Creating a table."

The candy table holds rows that each consist of a name in the form of a string, a weight in the form of a double-precision floating-point variable, and a price and quantity, both as integers. Here's how you add a row of data to this table from the mysql utility (make sure you're using the phpbase database):

```
insert into candy values(
'OozingPeanutbutterExplosion',
6.95,
275,
100
);
```

This code adds a new row to the candy table consisting of the name 'OozingPeanutbutterExplosion' (yum), the weight 6.95 (I suppose that's ounces, which is still a lot), the price $2.75 shown as 275 cents, and the quantity 100, representing the number that will soon to be in my stomach.

This code added only one row, or record. You can add more rows by using different names and values. And you don't need to break up the line into multiple lines if you don't want to:

```
insert into candy values('ChunkableChrunchableChocolate', 2.80, 75, 50);
```

Viewing the data in a table

If you have a table (such as one called candy) that has data in it, you can use the mysql command-line utility to look at the data in the table. To do so, you use the select statement. (The word select is a part of the SQL language that I talk about in Book VI, Chapter 5.)

Make sure you're running the mysql utility and using the `phpbase` database. Then look at the `candy` table by typing the following command:

```
select * from candy;
```

The data is printed out in a nice, neat table, like so:

```
+----------------------------------+--------+-------+----------+
| name                             | weight | price | quantity |
+----------------------------------+--------+-------+----------+
| OozingPeanutbutterExplosion      |   6.95 |   275 |      100 |
| ChunkableChrunchableChocolate    |    2.8 |    75 |       50 |
+----------------------------------+--------+-------+----------+
2 rows in set (0.00 sec)
```

This table contains two rows, one for the Oozing something or other, and the next for the Chunkable Chocolate whatever.

If you want, you can look at only a few columns by replacing the asterisk in the preceding `select` statement with the names of the columns, separated by commas:

```
select quantity, weight from candy;
```

The statement results in this output:

```
+----------+--------+
| quantity | weight |
+----------+--------+
|      100 |   6.95 |
|       50 |    2.8 |
+----------+--------+
2 rows in set (0.00 sec)
```

Here I'm only looking at the `quantity` and `weight` columns. Note that they appear in the list in the order I entered them in my `select` statement: I typed `quantity` before `weight`, even though the table stores `weight` before `quantity`.

Here's a quick way to sort the information. Put the words `order by` in the statement, like so:

```
select price, weight, quantity
from candy
order by price;
```

The rows you list are sorted by the column in the order by clause. Here's the output:

```
+-------+--------+----------+
| price | weight | quantity |
+-------+--------+----------+
|    75 |    2.8 |       50 |
|   275 |   6.95 |      100 |
+-------+--------+----------+
2 rows in set (0.00 sec)
```

The select statement is the most important statement in the SQL language. It's at the heart of any data lookup. You can use select to do complex data lookups that involve pulling data from multiple tables and organizing the data in special ways. You can also use the select statement to do things like count how many records are in a table. In Book VI, Chapter 5, I give you a rundown of what you can do with the select statement, along with examples from various languages such as PHP and Perl, which run separately from the mysql command-line utility.

Getting information about a table

Sometimes while using the mysql program, you may want to obtain information about a table, such as what columns are in the table. In this section, I show you how to access such information. But remember, this information pertains to the structure of the table (which primarily means the columns of the table) and not the data in the table (which refers to the rows).

The easiest way to obtain information from a table is by going into the mysql utility and typing this statement:

```
describe candy;
```

You see output like this:

```
+----------+-------------+------+-----+---------+-------+
| Field    | Type        | Null | Key | Default | Extra |
+----------+-------------+------+-----+---------+-------+
| name     | varchar(30) | YES  |     | NULL    |       |
| weight   | double      | YES  |     | NULL    |       |
| price    | int(11)     | YES  |     | NULL    |       |
| quantity | int(11)     | YES  |     | NULL    |       |
+----------+-------------+------+-----+---------+-------+
4 rows in set (0.00 sec)
```

This list of columns is arranged in, well, rows. Each row in this table represents a column. The first row pertains to the name column, and its type is varchar(30). The second row shows that the candy table's second column is weight, its type is double, and so on.

This list also shows you additional information about the table. The item called `Null` will be set to `YES` if the column is allowed to contain *no data*. (The idea of *no data* is separate from the value 0 or the empty string. The value 0 is a value, and the empty string is a value. No data means no value is present at all.)

If the column is a keyed column, the type of key appears under the word `Key` in the list. If the column has a default value, that value appears under the word `Default`. And if this column is a counter that automatically increments each time you add a new row to the table, you see the word `auto_increment` under the word `Extra`.

For information on how to specify whether a column can or can't be Null, or how to create a key, add a default value, or use `auto_increment` columns, see Book VI, Chapter 3.

The statement `describe candy;` is a shorthand version of an equivalent statement, which goes like this:

```
show columns from candy;
```

You are free to use either `describe` or `show columns from`.

Dropping (or deleting) a table

In SQL terminology, when you delete a table, you say you are *dropping* the table. Dropping a table is easy to do (but breaking up a table is hard to do . . . *groan*). Go into the mysql utility, make sure you're using the database containing the table, and then type the following:

```
drop table candy;
```

But you don't have to do that right now if you want to keep the scrumptious `candy` table.

Seeing what tables are in a database

If you want to see what tables are inside the database, just go into mysql, use the database in question, and type this:

```
show tables;
```

You will see something like this:

```
+------------------+
| Tables_in_phpbase |
+------------------+
| candy            |
+------------------+
```

Only one table is present, the one called `candy`. If you had more than one table, the additional tables would be listed underneath the word `candy`.

Automating your work with command files

Sometimes you may need to retype the same information over and over. For example, if you enter a long `create table` statement and then get an error message telling you you've typed something wrong, the preferred choice between retyping it or quitting and going to the beach will quickly become apparent. To avoid unnecessary trips to the beach (and unnecessary typing), you can store your statements in a file. Most people give the file an `.sql` filename extension, although you're free to use whatever extension you like.

For example, suppose you create a file called `morecandy.sql` that contains these lines:

```
use phpbase;
create table morecandy (
    name varchar(30),
    weight double,
    price int,
    quantity int
);
```

Rather than typing these same lines directly into the mysql utility, you can exit out of the mysql utility and do this:

```
mysql -u root -p <
    morecandy.sql
```

This runs the mysql utility, logging in as user `root`. You are then prompted for the password as per the `-p` option. The mysql utility then runs in script mode, reading the lines from the `morecandy.sql` file and running them just as if you typed them in. (You advanced readers will recognize that you're really just redirecting `stdin` to make this happen.)

If you're doing this in Windows, you can also select all the text in your `morecandy.sql` file, start up the mysql utility, and paste the text into the command-line (sometimes called DOS) window.

Chapter 3: Relating Your Data

In This Chapter

✔ **Dividing data into tables and tables into columns**

✔ **Creating indexes and keys so your data can be searched and sorted**

✔ **Dealing with different data types**

*I*n this chapter, I talk about what to consider when building the data that your programs use. You find out how to divide up your data, order and arrange it, and connect data found in multiple tables.

Remember four key points that are at the heart of all these ideas:

✦ You use SQL (Structured Query Language) to manipulate data.

✦ The database server is called MySQL, and it interprets the SQL for you.

✦ Your database programs run on the server side.

✦ A server-side language such as PHP or Perl uses SQL to access the data.

Dividing Your Data into Tables

Large corporations often hire people skilled in data analysis to come up with plans to organize the companies' data. If you're interested in that field, or if you simply need to do data analysis, this section will help you find your way through the piles of data and then figure out how to organize it. Although you can apply the principles outlined here to many areas of data analysis, I focus on the data that a Web site uses.

Suppose you're building a Web site that manages for-sale ads. Consumers can post their ads, selling everything from lawn mowers to cars, pianos, the neighbor's cat, whatever. Well, better not sell Fluffy.

You could just throw together one giant table, filled with whatever columns you can think of, and then move on to the fun part of designing the HTML and PHP. But if you don't spend time planning out how to organize your Web site data, your site will not be a success. So instead, slow down, take a deep breath, and spend some time designing the data. You will be a much happier camper (and Web entrepreneur) in the end.

Determining what tables to create

The first thing you want to do is get an idea of what information you'll need on the site. In this first brainstorming session, don't worry too much about organization. Focus on writing down some ideas.

Your site organizes ads, so you need to include a data item consisting of an *ad*. That's good. Not a bad start. But what else? You have people posting the ads. So there's another thing. Call that data item *customer,* because these people are your customers.

The people buying the items for sale are the seller's customers. However, these people may pay to use your site (or at least need to register with your site), so they may be customers, too. So you have two kinds of customers: sellers and buyers.

Of course, one person may sell something, and that same person may also do some buying. In that case, the customer is both a buyer and a seller. Therefore, it's probably best not to distinguish two types of customers. Instead, you'll maintain only one type of customer and allow the customer to buy and sell.

How do customers buy something? They respond to an ad. How do they respond? Via an e-mail address. In this first version of your Web site, you want the seller to include an e-mail address in the ad, and the buyer is free to contact the seller directly, without using your site. However, the buyer must register with your site before he or she can see the ads. In future versions of the site, you may want to create a more complex system that includes e-mail messages on your site. But start out small, or you'll never get the thing off the ground and investors will be screaming at you. That's not fun.

Here are two types of data you have, so far:

+ Customer

+ Ad

One customer can have zero ads, one ad, or more than one ad. But a single person can be only a single customer. And one ad cannot belong to more than one customer.

Data analysts call this type of relationship *one to many,* as in "one customer to many ads." In another universe (or at least another Web site), you may have a need for *many to many,* or perhaps *one to one,* but not here.

These data types become your tables: the Customer table and the Ad table. Later on in your analysis, you may need to divide up the customer information into more than one table. Or you may need to divide up the ad information into more than one table. You'll have to wait and see.

Dividing the tables into columns

What information is important to include in the `Customer` table? In this high-tech world, the first thing to consider, even before the customer's name, is almost always the customer's *e-mail address*. The reason is that you want to have a way to contact the customer. For example, if the customer forgets her password, you want your system to be able to e-mail a new password to her. And wait, that's another item for the `Customer` table: a password.

Now it's time to brainstorm. Here are some initial thoughts for information to include in the `Customer` table:

✦ Name

✦ E-mail address

✦ Phone number

✦ Password

Of course, the customer also needs an ad. But if the customer has multiple ads, how can you list them all here? And because you have a separate `Ad` table, how do you know which ad goes with which customer?

Hold that thought for a moment and move on to the `Ad` table. The problem here is figuring out a way to connect or relate the two tables. (Hint: The term *relational* database is key here because you're trying to *relate* the two tables.)

Here's some information you may want to include in the `Ad` table:

✦ Category

✦ Item name

✦ Headline

✦ Full description

✦ Price

And, of course, you need the e-mail address of the customer posting the ad, and more customer information . . . and, well, you're back to the relating problem. Leave that out for now.

So far, you have two pretty good tables. The `Customer` table fully describes a customer, and the `Ad` table fully describes an ad. Now you need to figure out a way to relate the two. The way to do that is to assign each customer a number (or ID). You will use this number internally to relate the tables.

Then you have some choices about a unique identifier. Here are two possibilities:

✦ Include a customer number in the Ad table. Then, each ad will indirectly have a number that specifies which customer the ad goes with.

✦ Have a unique ID for the ad. Then you would create a third table containing two IDs that you use to match up an ad with a customer.

Database purists (which I'm not) would probably say the second approach is best, because it pulls apart the data as much as possible and makes it easy to search for all ads by customer or all customers that go with a single ad. But remember, you have only one customer per ad. So the notion of searching for all customers that go with a single ad really doesn't apply here. So I suggest that you go with the first approach, simply putting a customer ID in the Ad table. And because each customer has an ID, you would put that ID in the Customer table, too, meaning it's in *both* tables.

Before you start building the two tables, review the data carefully. Does the data have everything you need? From my experience, I can say it probably doesn't. Four more items may be important:

✦ The date the customer signed up

✦ The date the customer last signed in

✦ The date the ad ran

✦ The date the ad expires and goes away

And speaking of which, after an ad goes away, should it stay on the system so that the customer who made the ad can go back and review what ads he or she created? That sounds like a good idea, and in that case, you will want the ad to have a "finished" item.

Now look at the phone number item in the Customer table. Is that important? And if the phone number is, what about the address? My feeling is that at this point, in the first generation of your amazing online ad service, you have no reason for the phone number. So just drop that one.

To credit card or not?

When it comes to the credit card issue, I prefer to stay on the safe side and not risk legal troubles. Suppose one of your .php files gets messed up and one day some unsuspecting (yet unscrupulous) customer logs into your site and his browser suddenly displays a giant table listing all your customers' credit card numbers, expiration dates, and associated zip codes. (The zip codes are important for verifying authenticity.) Then suppose that customer goes on a serious shopping spree.

Or what if a hacker downloads the entire table and also goes on a shopping spree? If this happened, would you be held liable? You may say, "No way!" but the local district attorney's office may disagree and file charges nevertheless. It's best to not risk it.

I prefer not to handle credit card charges on my system and therefore not have any credit card information in my hands. If I need to charge a customer for something, I rely on a third-party credit card service that takes care of it for me. Further, if you're really serious, I suggest you talk to an attorney or an accountant or both to get the straight scoop on the legal issues of credit card processing. I'm not an attorney and can't give you advice here (or I'll lose the law license that I don't even have). You have lots of options for credit card services. I prefer to make a choice based on a recommendation — ask your associates what they're using and whether they're happy with it. For more options, you can also do a Yahoo! search on credit card services.

And here's a hotly debated topic: If the customers have to pay to post an ad (you do want to make a living), do you store the customer's credit card information here? Take a look at the sidebar "To credit card or not?" for more on this topic.

The data items you've identified become columns in your tables. Table 3-1 shows you the columns you've come up with for the Customer table and what types to assign to them.

Table 3-1	Columns for the Customer Table
Column	*Type*
ID	integer
Name	varchar(30)
E-mail address	varchar(50)
Sign-up date	date
Last access date	date

Table 3-2 shows you the columns you came up with for the Ad table.

Table 3-2	Columns for the Ad Table
Column	*Type*
Category (or Category ID?)	Refer to the text at the end of this section for details.
Item Name	varchar(50)
Headline	varchar(100)
Description	text
Price	integer
Expiration Date	date
Status	integer
CustomerID	integer

While designing the Ad table, you decide that instead of using the word "finished" to specify whether an ad is completed, you'll use a column called Status. That way, a customer can assign one of many statuses to an ad. For example, one status may be Draft, meaning the ad is in draft form and not yet ready to be published. The customer can return to edit the draft into a final ad. Then other statuses may be Active, Expired, and Canceled.

For the other types, you are rather arbitrary in choosing the lengths. But the varchar type is flexible because you're specifying the *maximum* length with varchar. When you use varchar in a MySQL table, the MySQL system uses up only as much space as the string needs and no more. So the string "hushbuckle" takes up less space in a varchar than the string "flumbiddylottaquash". But varchar is limited; you can only have up to 255 characters. If you want anything more than that, use a special type called text, as I did for Description.

For Price, choose an integer. Never ever use floating points for prices, because floating points are not exact due to the way they store their data. Instead, use an integer and store the amount in pennies. You can always format the amount 122 as $1.22 in your PHP programs.

The Category column may make you think a bit more. How will you implement categories? You have a couple choices:

✦ You can assign a number, and then your PHP programs will know the different categories and have maybe an array of category names. This category would be an integer.

✦ You can store a string in the category, containing the category name. I prefer to stay clear of this approach because strings aren't the best items to search on due to their length. Numbers are always easiest.

Here's the approach that I suggest: Make the `Category` a number, and instead of calling the column `Category`, call it `CategoryID`. Then create a table called `Categories`. That table will contain a list of category names and IDs. This has the added benefit that you can update the category list without having to modify your PHP programs. In general, modifying the data is a better alternative to modifying the programs, because when you modify the programs you introduce the possibility of those evil things called *bugs*. Modifying the data can cause bugs but is less likely to than modifying programs.

A purist may say you should have thought of this `Category` issue sooner, but like any kind of software engineering, you keep refining the analysis until you have your project complete. So forget the purists; the only real problem will be if you don't discover these problems until after the site goes live (or until this book goes to print).

Table 3-3 is what you'll use for the `Category` table.

**Book VI
Chapter 3**

Relating Your Data

Table 3-3	Columns for the Category Table
Column	*Type*
Category ID	`integer`
Category Name	`varchar(30)`

Allowing your data to be searched and sorted

MySQL and other SQL implementations are pretty flexible when it comes to searching and sorting. You can search for records that match criteria you supply for any column. For example, you can search the `Customer` table for all customers whose names contain the word `"Van"`. If you want to search for all ads within a certain price range, you can do that, too.

To do custom searches, such as a search for all rows in the `Customer` table where the customer name contains the word `"Van"`, you can use the SQL `select` statement in various forms. In Book VI, Chapter 5, I show you how to use MySQL and the SQL language to perform complex `select` statements. In this chapter, I briefly discuss searching and demonstrate some simpler forms of the `select` statement.

The default file format used by MySQL is called *MyISAM*, which stands for MySQL Indexed Sequential Access Method. MyISAM enables you to specify that certain columns in your table are *keys*. When you specify a key, MySQL creates an *index* for that column. The index is similar to the index you find in a book, in that it keeps a list of all the values for the row that the key goes with, and it keeps track of which rows have what data for the keyed column. Then when you want to search for a row where the key equals a certain value, MySQL looks in the index and quickly gives you the results. Here are the types of keys you can specify:

+ **Simple key:** MySQL builds an index for the keyed column. (In SQL terminology, this is just a key, but for clarity, in the rest of this book, I call this kind of key a simple key.)

+ **Unique key:** MySQL builds an index, and the keyed column for a row must either be empty (that is, contain NULL) or contain a value that's distinct from all the other rows in the table.

+ **Primary key:** MySQL builds an index, and each row must contain a distinct value for the keyed column, which can never be NULL.

For example, think of an `Orders` table that contains customer orders. The Order table may contain a customer name, the product the customer ordered, and an order number, stored as a `Customer` column, a `Product` column, and an `OrderNumber` column, respectively. Every time a customer orders a product, your computer adds another row to the `Order` table describing the customer's order.

Now let's say you have a product called the Banarooza 9000. (It's a lot better than the old, outdated Banarooza 8000.) Lots of customers have ordered this product, so if you look at all the rows in the `Orders` table, you'll see many rows with `Banarooza 9000` in the Product column. Clearly, this column isn't unique, since `Banarooza 9000` appears in many orders. To speed up your searching, however, you can create a simple key on this column. MySQL will then build an index for this column; then MySQL can very quickly tell you the names of all the customers who ordered the Banarooza 9000.

But now look at the `OrderNumber` column. Every order has a unique number. To ensure that MySQL prevents any program that accesses the table from adding a row using an order number already present, you can set up your table such that `OrderNumber` is a unique key, meaning no two rows can have the same value in this column.

With unique keys, you can choose whether to allow a row to leave that column empty, or insist each row must have data in this column. For example, suppose you have some very old orders in the system that don't have order numbers. For these orders, you would leave the `OrderNumber` column blank (or NULL), in which case you can use a unique key. On the other hand, if you want to ensure that every order must have a number (and as such the column can never be blank or NULL), then you would use a primary key.

You can still search on columns that don't have keys. These are called non-keyed rows. When you search on a non-keyed row, MySQL must search through every row in the table, checking whether the row satisfies your match. For enormous tables, this *linear* search (linear because the search goes one by one through the rows) can be extremely time consuming.

You will often design better tables if you use a primary key rather than a unique key. A primary key forces you to put data for the keyed column in every row.

In order for MySQL to look up data in two tables at once by relating the data, you must use primary keys. For example, if you have a CustomerID column in your order table and you want MySQL to use that to find information from a Customer table that also contains a CustomerID column, then the CustomerID column in the *Customer* table must be a primary key.

Coding the keys

Here are three `create table` statements, each specifying a different type of key. First, here's a simple key:

```
create table key1 (
    num integer,
    name varchar(30),
    key(num)
);
```

Notice that you specify the key *after* you specify the columns. You do so by using the word `key`, followed by the name of the column in parentheses.

Here's a unique key:

```
create table key2 (
    num integer,
    name varchar(30),
    unique key(num)
);
```

This is the same as the simple key example, except that you add the word `unique` **prior to the word** `key`.

And now here's a primary key:

```
create table key3 (
    num integer NOT NULL,
    name varchar(30),
    primary key(num)
);
```

For the primary key, I added the words `NOT NULL` after the column name that I'm keying. The rest of the statement is just like a simple key, except that I add the word `primary` before the word `key`.

Studying the key rules

When you work with keys, MySQL has some rules you need to follow. I know, I hate rules too (that's what I told Officer Friendly the other day when he pulled me over), but unlike traffic rules, these rules have a good reason for existing. (I told Officer Friendly that, too, but for some reason, he turned into Officer Angry.)

Here are the most important rules pertaining to keys:

✦ You can have as many simple keys and unique keys as you want in a single table.

✦ You can combine rows into a single key. MySQL uses the combined rows to create a single index. To combine rows, put them together inside parentheses for the key phrase, like so:

```
key(num, name)
```

✦ You may have only one primary key in a single table, although that single key can combine multiple columns using a line of code as in the following example:

```
create table key5 (
    num integer NOT NULL,
    name varchar(30) NOT NULL,
    primary key(num, name)
);
```

Notice I added NOT NULL to each row in the primary key.

For some more esoteric rules, check out the page for the `create table` syntax in the MySQL online documentation. The page is located at `www.mysql.com/doc/en/CREATE_TABLE.html`.

Typing the Data in a Table

MySQL includes a rich set of data types that you can use for the rows in your table. The following list describe the more useful types:

✦ `tinyint` (or `bit` or `bool`): This integer ranges from –128 to 127. A column of this type takes up a single byte of storage.

✦ `tinyint unsigned` (or `bit unsigned` or `bool unsigned`): This integer ranges from 0 to 255. This is a single byte of storage.

✦ `smallint`: This integer ranges from –32768 to 32767. This type takes up 2 bytes of storage.

✦ `smallint` unsigned: This integer ranges from 0 to 65535. This type takes up 2 bytes of storage.

✦ `int` (or `integer`): This integer ranges from –2147483648 to 2147483647. Columns of this type take up 4 bytes of storage.

✦ `int unsigned` (or `integer unsigned`): This integer ranges from 0 to 4294967295. This type takes up 2 bytes of storage.

✦ `float` and `double`: A floating-point value. Columns of type `float` take up 4 bytes. Columns of type `double` have greater precision and take up 8 bytes.

✦ `date`, `time`, `datetime`: A single date, time, or combination date and time, respectively. A `date` is 3 bytes; a `time` is 3 bytes; a `datetime` is 8 bytes. (The SQL `select` statement can retrieve dates, times, and timestamps in various formats. See Book VI, Chapter 5, for more information.)

✦ `blob`: This stands for *b*inary *l*arge *ob*ject and can hold varying sizes of data in binary format. This type is useful for storing graphics and other data. You can store up to 65536 bytes. However, MySQL uses up only as much space as is required for the data, plus 2 bytes, leaving no wasted space.

✦ `text`: This is just like a `blob` but is useful for storing text. The only difference between a `blob` and a `text` is that if you put text (instead of binary data) in a blob and do a search, the search is case-sensitive. If you put the text in a `text` column and do a search, the search is case-insensitive. As with the `blob` type, you can store up to 65536 bytes, again without wasted space.

✦ `mediumblob` and `mediumtext`: These are just like `blob` and `text` respectively, except that they can hold up to 16,777,216 bytes (that's 2 to the 24th power, or 16 megabytes).

✦ `longblob` and `longtext`: These are just like `blob` and `text` respectively, except they can hold up to 4,294,967,296 bytes, which is 2 to the 32nd power, or 4 gigabytes. It's hard to imagine what you would need to put in a table such that each row might require 4 gigabytes, but a hundred years from now, they'll laugh at me for saying that as they place the entire genome structure for each human being in a giant table, each one requiring 4,294,967,292 bytes, which will just fit in a MySQL `longblob` column (with 4 bytes to spare).

Finally, you can use an exciting type called `auto_increment`, which you use in conjunction with one of the integer types (`int`, `tinyint`, and so on) but only on a keyed column. When you add a new row of data to the table, the column automatically gets a number that's one higher than the highest number currently in the column. (You can also manually specify a number for the column when you add a row, if you don't want MySQL to automatically pick a number for you.) Here's an example of a `create table` statement:

```
create table autoinc (
    autonum integer auto_increment,
    name varchar(30),
    key (autonum)
);
```

Then you can add a row like this:

```
insert into autoinc (name) values ('jim');
insert into autoinc (name) values ('susan');
insert into autoinc (autonum, name) values (100, 'floyd');
insert into autoinc (name) values ('frank');
```

And then you type this:

```
select * from autoinc;
```

Which gives you these results:

```
+----------+--------+
| autonum  | name   |
+----------+--------+
|       1  | jim    |
|       2  | susan  |
|     100  | floyd  |
|     101  | frank  |
+----------+--------+
```

Now you can see how the one time I specified a number (100), MySQL used that new max to determine that the next `auto_increment` number is 101.

Creating the Databases and Tables

If you don't already have a database called `phpbase`, log into MySQL as `root`, and type the following statement:

```
create database phpbase;
```

Then press Enter. For information on creating the `phpuser` user, see Book VI, Chapter 1.

You can easily create these tables in MySQL from the MySQL prompt. Create a file called `tables.sql` and enter the following:

```
use phpbase;
create table customer (
    ID integer auto_increment,
    name varchar(30),
    email varchar(30),
    signup date,
    last_access date,
    primary key (ID)
);
create table ad (
    adID integer auto_increment,
    categoryID integer,
    item_name varchar(50),
    headline varchar(100),
    description text,
    price integer,
    expiration_date date,
    status integer,
    CustomerID integer,
    key (CustomerID, expiration_date),
    primary key(adID)
);
create table category (
    categoryID integer auto_increment,
    category_name varchar(30),
    primary key (categoryID)
);
create table status (
    statusID integer auto_increment,
    description varchar(10),
    primary key(statusID)
);
```

Save this file as `tables.sql`, and then type the following statement at the command prompt:

```
mysql -u root -p < tables.sql
```

Enter the `root` password, and MySQL creates the three tables.

Dealing with errors in the creation process

If you get an error, make sure you typed the `tables.sql` file properly. If the error is, for example, in the creation of the `ad` table, that means MySQL succeeded in creating the `customer` table. Thus, when you try running this `.sql` script file again, you'll get an error in the `create table customer` section because that table already exists.

If your script fails (for whatever reason), I recommend that you log into mysql as `root` and remove any of the three tables that already exist, by entering the following statements:

```
mysql> use phpbase;
Database changed

mysql> drop table customer;
Query OK, 0 rows affected (0.00 sec)

mysql> drop table ad;
Query OK, 0 rows affected (0.00 sec)

mysql> drop table category;
Query OK, 0 rows affected (0.00 sec)

mysql> drop table status;
Query OK, 0 rows affected (0.00 sec)
```

Run all of these statements; it doesn't matter if some of the tables you're "removing" don't exist. You may get some errors on the statements that refer to nonexistent tables, but that's okay.

When you've finished this cleanup and fixed the typos in the `tables.sql` file, try the file again by entering the following statement:

```
mysql -u root -p < tables.sql
```

Adding data to your tables with text files

In this section, you find out how to add some initial data to your tables. Then later in this chapter, I show you how to enter data into these tables through a Web form.

The normal way to add a row to a table is by using the `insert` statement. However, if you need to add several rows, using the `insert` statement can become annoying because you have to type those same crazy statements over and over. Instead, I recommend creating a text file and then using a handy statement called `load data`. First, I'll show you how to do this with the `category` table. Create a text file called `categories.txt` and put the following text into it:

```
appliances
autos
books
CDs and cassettes
computer equipment
lawn equipment
musical instruments
```

Now log into mysql as `root`. Then type this statement:

```
use phpbase;
```

If you created the `category.txt` file using an editor in Windows, carefully type the following:

```
load data local infile 'categories.txt'
into table category
lines terminated by '\r\n'
(category_name);
```

Or if you created the `category.txt` file using an editor in Linux or Unix, replace the `lines terminated by` line in the preceding statements with this:

```
lines terminated by '\n'
```

Or if you created the `category.txt` file using a Macintosh, replace the `lines terminated by` line in the preceding statements with this:

```
lines terminated by '\r'
```

(The reason for these annoying differences is that due to some unknown — but probably political — reasons, Microsoft and Apple chose to use different ways of ending their lines compared to the way Unix has since its beginnings somewhere around 1970. And today we pay the price.)

If you see the following error message, the `load data` command is disabled with MySQL:

```
ERROR 1148: The used command is not allowed with
this MySQL version
```

If this is the case, you can turn on the `load data` command temporarily by exiting out of MySQL and restarting MySQL using a special parameter like this:

```
mysql -u root -p --local-infile=1
```

You should now be able to use the `load data` command (until you restart MySQL again without the `local-infile` parameter).

Here's a breakdown of the statement for adding data to the `category` table with the text file `category.txt`:

✦ The `load data local infile` statement reads the data from a local data file and stores the data in the table automatically.

✦ The string at the end of the first line is the name of the file to read.

✦ The `into table category` clause specifies which table to use.

✦ The `lines terminated by` clause specifies how to interpret the file, as I just described.

✦ The last line contains the list of columns in the table to populate. (Because I have an `auto_increment` column in this table, I don't include a value for the `auto_increment` column. Instead, I let MySQL fill that column.)

Testing and debugging the data-insertion process

After you type the lines in the preceding section, you can check that the information went in correctly by typing a `select` statement like so:

```
select * from category;
```

Your data should look like this:

```
+------------+---------------------+
| categoryID | category_name       |
+------------+---------------------+
|          1 | appliances          |
|          2 | autos               |
|          3 | books               |
|          4 | CDs and Cassettes   |
|          5 | computer equipment  |
|          6 | lawn equipment      |
|          7 | musical instruments |
+------------+---------------------+
7 rows in set (0.00 sec)
```

If your data looks strange (for example, you have missing characters, only one row, and so on), delete your data and try again. Enter the following statement to delete the data from the `category` table:

```
delete from category;
```

Then try altering the form of the `lines terminated by` clause by using one of the other two I describe in the preceding section. Ugh.

If you encounter problems during this process, please accept my apology for suggesting that this way is *easier* than using an `insert` statement. But after you have figured out the correct process for your computer and operating system, this process really is a time saver, and you can use it for other projects. Please make a mental note of which form of the `lines terminated by` clause is correct for your computer. And remember, what matters is not necessarily which type of computer you're using, but what type of text editor you're using, and how the editor writes out its line terminators.

Now you can create data for the status table as well. Here's the data you will want in the table:

```
+----------+--------------+
| statusID | description  |
+----------+--------------+
|        1 | draft        |
|        2 | active       |
|        3 | canceled     |
|        4 | expired      |
+----------+--------------+
```

Chapter 4: Accessing MySQL from PHP

In this chapter, I show you how to write PHP code that connects to a MySQL database. You can create rather powerful Web sites in this manner; your PHP code can access data from a MySQL table and use that data to customize the Web page. Online retailers, for example, can create a .php file to look up product information from a database and build a product page. The Web user sees a different page for each product without even realizing the pages were built dynamically.

For the examples in this chapter, I'm using the following database, tables, and user information:

✦ The database name is phpbase.

✦ The username is phpuser, and the password is phppass.

✦ The table names are customer, ad, category, and status.

For details on creating these tables, see Book VI, Chapter 3.

Connecting to MySQL from PHP

Before discussing how to connect to MySQL from PHP, I want to remind you that because PHP is a server-side language, all the MySQL access takes place on the side of the server. When you access MySQL through PHP, the end user's client computer does not access MySQL. PHP is a preprocessor that receives .php files from the Web server, processes the PHP code inside the .php files (code that can include MySQL calls), generates a resulting .html file, and sends the .html file back to the Web server, which sends it to the client browser.

End users simply see a Web page in their browsers. They do not see the PHP code access the MySQL database. In fact, they probably don't even know whether the database you're using is MySQL, and they probably don't know that you're using a database system. (The PHP part is a bit of a giveaway because the .php filename extension is in the URL.)

Here is a short example of a .php file that connects to a database. (For this example I'm using the database, username, password, and tables described at the beginning of this chapter.) This example uses a select statement to retrieve a row from the category table:

```
<html><title>Categories!</title>
<body>
<?php
    mysql_connect("localhost", "phpuser", "phppass");
    $result = mysql_query(
        "select * from phpbase.category
        where categoryID = 3"
    );
    if ($result) {
        if (mysql_num_rows($result) > 0) {
            $row = mysql_fetch_assoc($result);
            $id = $row["categoryID"];
            $name = $row["category_name"];
            print "$id $name<br>\n";
        }
        mysql_free_result($result);
    }
    mysql_close();
?>
</body></html>
```

When you open this file in the browser, you see the following output:

```
3 books
```

The output is nothing fancy, but this example shows you how to connect to a database. This first line inside the PHP code does the connecting:

```
mysql_connect("localhost", "phpuser", "phppass");
```

The first parameter is the name of the host you want to connect to; this will almost always be localhost. Remember, the PHP processor runs on the same computer as the Web server and normally that's where you'll find the MySQL installation as well. Thus, "localhost" refers to the computer where PHP is running.

The PHP and MySQL password dilemma

You will quickly discover a minor security flaw in the PHP/MySQL world — one that doesn't have a good solution. When you write a PHP program that accesses MySQL, you have to put the MySQL password in the PHP program. But how can you hide the password? Unfortunately, PHP doesn't really offer many good ways to hide it. Thus, anyone who can log into the system and look at your PHP code will see your MySQL password. Although they won't be able to access the root through this and therefore can't do anything like adding MySQL users and changing MySQL passwords, they can wreak havoc by wiping out the data in your database.

However, remember that the people visiting your Web page don't see the .php files or the PHP code. Instead, they see the generated .html files built by the PHP processor, and no PHP code goes to their systems. The problem is that Unix, although very secure, is very open on letting people logged into the system move from directory to directory.

So here's a pretty good trick: Put any PHP code that contains the MySQL username and password in its own special .php file. Put that special .php file in a directory that the Web server doesn't have access to. (For example, if your Web pages sit in a web_files directory or public_html directory or whatever, put the special .php file in some *other* directory.) Then in your main .php files, include or require the special .php file, using a full path to the special .php file. Finally, make sure the directory containing that .php file is secure. Use the Unix chmod command to block read and write access from anybody but yourself (you want to be able to change the files in the directory, of course) and whatever Unix username the PHP processor runs under (usually the name nobody). If you're using a third-party hosting service and you're not allowed to set the permissions, put the file off the Web server directory, away from the web_files or public_html directory or whatever it's called on your system.

Book VI Chapter 4

Accessing MySQL from PHP

If you're using a distributed system and your Web server and PHP processor lie on a different computer from the MySQL installation, put for the first parameter the name of the computer housing the MySQL software.

The call to mysql_query performs the database query. Inside this line, you put a complete SQL statement, but without a semicolon at the end of the SQL statement. (You do put a semicolon at the end of the PHP statement, as I do after the closing parentheses.) The SQL statement I'm using is as follows:

```
select * from phpbase.category
where categoryID = 3
```

(Notice that I'm not including the quotes that were in the program. The quotes are part of the PHP program; the SQL statement is what's inside quotes.)

This statement selects rows from the `category` table found in the database called `phpbase`. The statement retrieves only those rows where `categoryID` is 3. In this case, only one row has `categoryID` equal to 3, the row where `category_name` is books.

Next, I make sure that the `mysql_query` call succeeded by checking its result. If so, I call `mysql_num_rows`, passing the result of `mysql_query`. This function tells me how many rows are in the *result set*. (A result set is a set of rows that you get back from a `select` statement.) If at least one row is present in the result set, I grab the first row by calling `mysql_fetch_assoc`. This function is really cool: It returns an array where the keys are the names of the columns in the table. Thus, I can check the columns in this particular row by inspecting the values of `$row["categoryID"]` and `$row["category_name"]`. And, in fact, that's what I do, and I print out the values of these two columns.

Finally, I call `mysql_free_result`, which releases the memory held in the result from the query, and I call `mysql_close`, which closes the connection.

In the following sections, I give you more detail on how to work with the `mysql_query` function, the `mysql_fetch_assoc` function, and many others. For now, remember the two following points:

✦ Call `mysql_connect` to connect to the MySQL system, passing the host name, the username, and the password.

✦ Call `mysql_close` to end your connection with the MySQL system.

Adding MySQL Data with PHP

The `mysql_query` function in PHP is a general-purpose statement for performing SQL statements on a MySQL database. Although the name contains the word *query*, which usually implies looking up data, you can use this function for all your SQL work, not just queries.

Here's a simple `.php` file that adds a row to the `customer` table in the `phpbase` database:

```
<html><title>Simple Insert...</title>
<body>
<?php
    mysql_connect("localhost", "phpuser", "phppass");
    $result = mysql_query(
        "insert into phpbase.customer
        (name, email, signup, last_access) values
        ('Jeff', 'me@domain.com', '2003-06-21',
            '2003-06-21')"
    );
    if ($result) {
```

```
        print "Succeeded!\n";
    }
    else {
        print "Something went awry with the awful SQL!";
    }
    mysql_close();
?>
</body></html>
```

This code first connects to the MySQL system using the `mysql_connect` function. Next, the code calls `mysql_query`, simply passing an SQL statement. Here's the SQL statement by itself:

```
insert into phpbase.customer
(name, email, signup, last_access) values
('Jeff', 'me@domain.com', '2003-06-21', '2003-06-21')
```

Book VI
Chapter 4

Accessing MySQL from PHP

This is a basic SQL `insert` statement, which adds data to the `customer` table. Notice that I specified the database name followed by a dot, before the table name, as in `phpbase.customer`.

The MySQL functions in PHP include an older function, `mysql_db_query`, in which you specify the database as a parameter rather than in the SQL statement. However, this function has been *deprecated,* meaning the PHP folks are phasing it out. Therefore, be sure to use `mysql_query` instead of `mysql_db_query`.

Notice that in the SQL statement I passed to `mysql_query`, I did not include a semicolon (not inside the double quotes, that is). I did end the `mysql_query` function call itself with a semicolon — just not inside the double quotes.

If you open this page in a Web browser, you simply see the word `Succeeded!`, meaning the `mysql_query` statement succeeded. But this script is only the beginning. As is, it's not very useful because the new data is hardcoded right into the script. In the next two sections, I show you how to create a Web form that allows users to enter data and how to use JavaScript to validate the data before sending it out.

Entering data with PHP and a form

If you want to allow users of your site to add data to your tables, the easiest way is to set up a form in an `.html` file and have the form submit its data to a `.php` file, at which point the `.php` file submits the data to the database, and the world submits to your Web site and becomes yours. Whooohahaha.

But seriously, folks, start with a form like the one shown in Listing 4-1. This is the `newcustomer.html` file.

Listing 4-1: A Form That Allows New Customers to Sign Up

```html
<html><head><title>New Customer Form</title></head>
<body bgcolor="#FFFFFF" text="#000000">
    Welcome new customer! We're so glad you
    headed our way.<p>
    Our motto is: <i>If we can't sell your stuff,
    then you're stuck with it!</i><p>
    Please fill out this-here form to getcha
    started:<p>

    <form name="form1" method="get"
    action="newcustomer.php">
    Name: <input type="text" name="name"><p>
    Email address:
    <input type="text" name="email"><p>
    <input type="submit" name="Submit"
    value="This is me, I swear!">
    </form>

</body>
</html>
```

Listing 4-1 presents a simple form requesting a username and e-mail address. The form passes the data on to the newcustomer.php file, shown in Listing 4-2.

Listing 4-2: A .php File That Enters the Username and E-mail Address into the Database

```php
<html><title>Simple Insert...</title>
<body>
<?php

    $name = $_GET["name"];
    $email = $_GET["email"];
    $now = date("Y-m-d");
    print "Name is $name<br>\n";
    print "Email is $email<br>\n";

    mysql_connect("localhost", "phpuser", "phppass");

    $result = mysql_query(
        "insert into phpbase.customer
        (name, email, signup, last_access) values
        ('$name', '$email', '$now', '$now')"
    );
    if ($result) {
        print <<<EOT
```

```
       <h1>Thank you.</h1>
       Your signup is highly appreciated. To show our
       appreciation, we will send you something that
       you, in turn, will appreciate. <p>
       Remember our motto: If we can't sell it,
       then it must really be the junk you
       always thought it was!
EOT;
       }
       else {
           print "Something went awry with the awful SQL!";
       }
       mysql_close();
?>
</body></html>
```

If you look closely at this form, you can see the SQL `insert` statement inside the `mysql_query` function. Instead of hardcoding the username and e-mail address, I embedded the variable names inside the string containing the SQL `insert` statement, along with the current date for the `signup` and `last_access` columns. (Thus, I used double quotes around the string.)

Speaking of quotes, look closely at the quotes in the string I'm passing to the `mysql_query` function. Although PHP is easy to use, sometimes you can get lost in all the quotes and end up with a royal mess. Remember these rules:

+ If you're going to embed variables in the string containing the SQL statement, PHP requires you to surround the string with double quotes.

+ SQL normally uses single quotes. But remember to include the single quotes. Notice in Listing 4-2 that I surrounded the variables' names with single quotes in the SQL statement, as in `'$name'`. These single quotes are part of the string itself and are not modified by PHP. Thus, if `$name` contains `jeff`, the string `"abc'$name'def"` translates to `abc'jeff'def`.

If you put the `newcustomer.html` file on your Web browser running PHP, you first see a friendly form allowing you to enter a username and e-mail address. Then when you click the "This is me, I swear!" button, you receive a friendly response stating that the data has been added to the table.

After running the form, you probably want to make sure the data went into the table. To find out, start up the mysql command-line utility. Log in either as `root` or as `phpuser`. From the `mysql` prompt, type the following:

```
select * from phpbase.customer;
```

Notice that instead of typing `use phpbase` beforehand, I simply specify the database right in the `select` statement, which is allowed.

You then see your results. Here's a sample output:

```
+----+----------------+-------------------------+------------+-------------+
| ID | name           | email                   | signup     | last_access |
+----+----------------+-------------------------+------------+-------------+
|  1 | Abraham Lincoln | president@whitehouse.gov | 2003-06-22 | 2003-06-22 |
+----+----------------+-------------------------+------------+-------------+
1 row in set (0.00 sec)
```

But what if you reenter the same username and e-mail address? As is, you'll end up with a duplicate record. And what if you enter a nonsensical e-mail address? Nothing in Listings 4-1 and 4-2 stops you from doing so. I explain how to handle these two situations in the next two sections, "Validating the data with JavaScript" and "Validating the data with PHP."

Validating the data with JavaScript

Many books written on PHP and MySQL have readers go through a bunch of hoops just to make sure the user typed a legitimate e-mail address. The problem is that the authors who write these, ahem, *other* books usually forget that you have other tools and languages at your disposal. JavaScript is one such language.

For doing quick checks, such as making sure that the e-mail address is in the correct format and that the user typed the same password or e-mail address in two different text boxes, I recommend using JavaScript, not PHP.

When you use JavaScript to validate the date, you put the JavaScript code in the same `.html` file containing the form, not in the `.php` file called by the form.

To make this work, I employ a little JavaScript trick whereby the data of the form is first passed to a JavaScript program. If the script function returns true, the browser proceeds by sending the data through a URL as is the usual case with forms. But if the script function returns false, the browser does not send out the data.

Listing 4-3, the `newcust.html` file, is a modified version of Listing 4-1. It is an `.html` file that contains a form. The form is different in that it contains two boxes for the e-mail address, requiring the user to type the e-mail address twice to (hopefully) reduce typos. The code includes two JavaScript functions, one that compares the values of the two e-mail edit controls to make sure they match, and one that uses a regular expression to make sure the e-mail address is in a valid form.

The JavaScript in Listing 4-3 doesn't check that the e-mail address is a real address. The code simply makes sure the address has the proper form, such as me@domain.com. Typically, if you want to verify an e-mail address, you use a PHP program that sends an e-mail to the address and waits for a response. If the response comes, you know the e-mail address is valid. I show you how to send out a verification e-mail in Book VI, Chapter 7.

Listing 4-3: A File That Uses JavaScript to Prevent Basic Entry Problems

```
<html><head><title>New Customer Form</title>
<script language="JavaScript">
function IsNotNull(){
    if (document.form1.name == null ||
        document.form1.email == null ||
        document.form1.remail == null) {
        alert("Please fill out all the fields.");
        return false;
    }

        if (document.form1.name.value.length == 0 ||
        document.form1.email.value.length == 0 ||
        document.form1.remail.value.length == 0) {
        alert("Please fill out all the fields.");
        return false;
    }
    return true;
}

function IsValidEmail(){
    var email = document.form1.email.value;
    var myreg
        = /^[^@\s]+@([-a-z0-9]+\.)+[a-z]{2,}$/
    if (myreg.test(email)) {
        return true;
    }
    else {
        alert("The email address is invalid.");
        return false;
    }
}
function CheckForMatch() {
    if (document.form1.email.value !=
    document.form1.remail.value) {
        alert("The email addresses do not match.\n"+
            "Please re-check them. Thanks!");
        return false;
    }
    return true;
}
```

```
function checkfields() {
    if (IsNotNull() == false) {
        return false;
    }
    if (IsValidEmail() == false) {
        return false;
    }
    if (CheckForMatch() == false) {
        return false;
    }
    return true;
}
</script></head>
<body bgcolor="#FFFFFF" text="#000000">
    Welcome new customer! We're so glad you
    headed our way.<p>
    Our motto is: <i>If we can't sell your stuff,
    then you're stuck with it!</i><p>
    Please fill out this-here form to getcha
    started:<p>

    <form name="form1" method="get"
    action="newcustomer.php"
    onSubmit='return checkfields();'>
    Name: <input type="text" name="name"><p>
    Email address:
    <input type="text" name="email"><p>
    Retype email address:
    <input type="text" name="remail"><p>
    <input type="submit" name="Submit"
    value="This is me, I swear!">
    </form>
</body></html>
```

Look at the form tag in the body of the HTML. I use the JavaScript event onSubmit, and in the code that follows, I call my own checkfields function. Earlier in the file, you can see the checkfields function, which calls the following functions:

✦ IsNotNull to make sure the user typed something into all the fields

✦ IsValidEmail to make sure the user typed a proper e-mail address

✦ CheckForMatch to make sure the user typed the same thing into both e-mail fields

In the `IsNotNull` function, I cover two cases. The first is that the fields themselves are null, and the second is that the fields contain no characters. The reason I use both cases is to cover situations of browser incompatibility.

The `IsValidEmail` function is a doozy. This function tests the e-mail address against a regular expression. The Internet has lots of pages showing various regular expressions to test for a proper e-mail address. I drew on several and, from there, built my own.

The regular expression I use in Listing 4-3 isn't perfect; for example, if the user types `me@something.xyz`, the test will pass, even though this is not a real e-mail address.

Finally, `CheckForMatch` simply makes sure the two e-mail addresses match to hopefully prevent typos.

Validating the data with PHP

When you submit the data to a PHP file for processing, you will want to check for various problems, such as whether the user already exists.

Listing 4-4 shows a modified version of Listing 4-2, adding in a test to make sure the name or e-mail doesn't already exist. (I also shortened some of the messages to save book space. I want you to get your money's worth.)

Regarding indexes and speed

To keep the examples throughout this chapter simple, I chose not to index the `customer` table based on the name and e-mail fields. You can still search the table based on these two fields; however, the search will be slower than it would be if you had an index for the two fields. The tradeoff is that if you do create an index for these two fields, MySQL must update the index every time you add a user.

When trying to decide whether to add an index, compare how many times you'll be adding a user to how many times you'll be looking up a

user. If your users occasionally return after adding themselves, clearly you'll be looking up users more often than creating users. Therefore, you want to make the lookups faster, even if this means the process of adding users is slower. Therefore, it is in your best interest to add an index for the username and e-mail fields. The only reason I don't show you how to do that in this book is that I prefer to keep the examples simple. For your *real* online system, however, please look at the tradeoffs and comparisons to make your decision.

To use the code in Listing 4-4, which I'm naming `newcust2.php`, you need to update your `newcustomer.html` to access `newcust2.php` instead of the older `newcustomer.php` file. To do this, change the following line:

```
action="newcustomer.php"
```

to this:

```
action="newcust2.php"
```

(and then click your browser's reload button when you open `newcustomer.html` to see the change).

Listing 4-4: A File That Makes Sure the Username or E-mail Address Doesn't Already Exist in the Table

```
<html><title>Simple Insert...</title>
<body>
<?php
    $name = $_GET["name"];
    $email = $_GET["email"];
    $now = date("Y-m-d");
    mysql_connect("localhost", "phpuser",
        "phppass");
    $result = mysql_query(
        "select * from phpbase.customer
        where name = '$name'
        or email = '$email'"); // Watch the quotes!
    $found = false;
    if ($result) {
        if (mysql_num_rows($result) > 0) {
            print "It looks like you're already signed
                up with us!";
            $found = true;
        }
    }
    if ($found == false) {
        $result = mysql_query(
            "insert into phpbase.customer
            (name, email, signup, last_access) values
            ('$name', '$email', '$now', '$now')"
        );
        if ($result) {
            print "<h1>Thank you!</ht>";
        }
        else {
            print "Something went awry
                with the awful SQL!";
        }
    }
```

```
        mysql_close();
?>
</body></html>
```

Displaying MySQL Data on a Web Page

Thanks to the magic of SQL, you can perform complex queries and retrieve some great data from your tables and display the results on a web page. In this section, I assume that you either used the forms in the earlier section, "Entering data with PHP and a form," to enter some data into your tables, or you used a `load data` command to get the data in. First, I'm assuming you set up the `category` and `status` tables as I described at the beginning of this chapter. Table 4-1 shows some data for the `customer` table.

Book VI
Chapter 4

Accessing MySQL
from PHP

Table 4-1		Sample Data for the Customer Table		
ID	*Name*	*e-mail*	*signup*	*last_access*
1	Hank Harshigan	hank@harshigan.com	2004-06-01	2004-06-11
2	Floyd Flabbergaps	floyd@flabbergaps.com	2004-06-02	2004-06-02
3	Erica Exagabule	erica@exagabule.com	2004-06-03	2004-06-05
4	Jessica Jamboliable	jessica@jamboliable.com	2004-06-04	2004-06-04
5	Julia Julianopolis	julia@julianopolis.com	2004-06-05	2004-06-11

To get this data into the table, you can use the form from Listings 4-3 and 4-4, earlier in this chapter.

Getting some sample ads is a bit tricky because the `ad` table has lots of columns. In Book VI, Chapter 5, I take you through the process of creating a form for entering ads. For now, type in the following two SQL statements to enter some ads (I recommend saving these statements in a file called `ads.sql` and then running `mysql -u root -p < ads.sql`):

```
insert into phpbase.ad values
(1, 3, 'PHP & MySQL For Dummies',
'Great new book! Must sell!',
'This is a great book that I purchased while '
'in college and now I don\'t need it because '
'I know everything in it.',
15700, '2004-08-01', 2, 4);

insert into phpbase.ad values
(2, 5, '386 Computer',
'Fantastic computer! Runs great!',
'This was my very first computer '
```

```
'that I bought back in the mid 1980s.'
'It works great! Includes WordStar.',
2385, '2004-09-01', 2, 2);
```

If a string spans multiple lines, I end the string with a single quote and then don't follow with a comma; next, I continue the string on the next line by starting with a single quote again. The MySQL interpreter will fuse these lines into a single string.

In Book VI, Chapter 5, I show you how to do complex queries, and how to build an HTML form whereby visitors to your Web page can look up information based on their criteria and even modify the data. You've seen this kind of thing everywhere; online bookstores are a common example.

For the remainder of this section, I show you how to query a database for records that match a criteria. Please do not confuse this with a full-text search like you might find on a newspaper site. Typically a newspaper site will have all its newspapers online, and you can search any paper for a word or phrase such as "Bill Clinton" or "George Bush." Although such sites probably use some kind of indexing mechanism, many of the sites don't use a database to store the text. Instead, they search the text files directly.

Here's a `.php` file named `simplelookup.php` that lists the ads:

```php
<html><title>Ads!</title>
<body>
<?php
    mysql_connect("localhost", "phpuser", "phppass");
    $result = mysql_query(
        "select * from phpbase.ad");
    if ($result) {
        if (mysql_num_rows($result) > 0) {
            while ($row = mysql_fetch_assoc($result)) {
                print "<h2>{$row['headline']}</h2>\n";
                print "<b>item:</b>";
                print "{$row['item_name']}<br>\n";
                print "<b>description:</b>";
                print "{$row['description']}<br>\n";
                print "<b>price:</b>";
                $price = $row['price'] / 100;
                print "\$$price<br>\n";
            }
        }
        mysql_free_result($result);
    }
    mysql_close();
?>
</body></html>
```

Notice that I embedded a bunch of HTML in the print statements. Also, I divided the price by 100 because the price is stored in cents rather than dollars.

To show the records, I call mysql_query, passing a simple select statement. The select statement returns multiple rows. To get the individual rows, I repeatedly call mysql_fetch_assoc, passing the result from the call to mysql_query, until I get back a NULL value.

Unless I get a NULL value, mysql_fetch_assoc returns an entire row stored in an array. I access the values in the array by using the table's column names as keys to the array. Then when I'm finished with one row, I retrieve another row, and so on. Nice and simple.

If you prefer, you can retrieve a record in a numeric array rather than an associative array, which means the array's keys will be 0, 1, 2, and so on rather than the names of the columns. (I generally prefer to use the names of the columns, although using the numeric approach may be a bit faster.) To retrieve the row as a numeric array, use a line like this instead of calling mysql_fetch_assoc:

```
$row = mysql_fetch_array($result, MYSQL_NUM);
```

To retrieve an associative array, you can instead use mysql_fetch_array, passing MYSQL_ASSOC for the second parameter, as in mysql_fetch_array($result, MYSQL_ASSOC). The result is the same as if you called mysql_fetch_assoc.

Chapter 5: Querying with SQL and PHP

In this chapter, I show how you can use PHP to create Web forms that allow Web site visitors to interact with your MySQL tables. Although showing data from the tables is useful, in some cases you want to give the visitors the ability to add data to your site or to look up information in the databases. Either way, you interact with the user through the use of HTML forms. This shows you how to do just that.

In the examples in this chapter, I use the tables described at the beginning of Book VI, Chapter 4.

Creating a Lookup Form

If you want to give your Web site visitors the ability to look up data, first you need to decide what type of search criteria to make available to them. In this section, I show you how to do searches based on exact values in the columns. For example, the users may want to look up all ads of a particular category. Later in this chapter, in "Viewing a customer's ads," I show you how to provide forms that allow for more flexible searches.

Looking up by category number

The following example shows a form that lets you search based on a category number. In the example in the next section, I show you how to modify this form to retrieve the category names rather than just use a number.

The `categorynumber.html` file in Listing 5-1 shows the form in HTML.

Listing 5-1: A Form That Allows the User to Browse by Category Number

```
<html><head><title>Untitled Document</title></head>
<body bgcolor="#FFFFFF" text="#000000">
    <h1>Browse by category!</h1>
    <form name="form1" method="get"
    action="browsecategory.php">
    Category Number:
        <input type="text" name="categorynum"><br>
    <input type="submit" name="Submit"
    value="Show All">
</form>
</body></html>
```

The form in Listing 5-1 requires the `browsecategory.php` file in Listing 5-2.

Listing 5-2: The PHP File for Browsing by Category

```
<html><head><title>Untitled Document</title></head>
<body bgcolor="#FFFFFF" text="#000000">
<?php
    $categorynum = $_GET['categorynum'];
    mysql_connect("localhost", "phpuser", "phppass");
    $result = mysql_query(
        "select * from phpbase.ad where ". // watch the space
        "categoryID = $categorynum");
    if ($result) {
        if (mysql_num_rows($result) > 0) {
            while ($row = mysql_fetch_assoc($result)){
                print "<h2>{$row['headline']}</h2>\n";
                print "<b>item:</b>";
                print "{$row['item_name']}<br>\n";
                print "<b>description:</b>";
                print "{$row['description']}<br>\n";
                print "<b>price:</b>";
                $price = $row['price'] / 100;
                print "\$$price<br>\n";
            }
        }
        mysql_free_result($result);
    }
    mysql_close();
?>
</body>
```

Take a look at the `select` statement in Listing 5-2. Here's the same `select` statement by itself:

```
select * from phpbase.ad where
categoryID = $categorynum
```

Be sure to put a space at the end of the string containing the first line of the `select` statement — after the word `where` — so that the `select` statement is correct (otherwise you'll have words running together and MySQL won't know what you're trying to say).

The PHP processor replaces `categorID` with the value in `$categorynum`, building a `select` statement such as this:

```
select * from phpbase.ad where categoryID = 3;
```

Then the code following the `mysql_query` function call processes the results of the `select` statement.

Looking up by category name

Because the category number isn't very intuitive, and because you have a table giving a name for each category, why not let the users look up the data by category name instead? To do this, you create a new form that you can use in place of the one in Listing 5-1. The file that the form calls — shown earlier in Listing 5-2 — is the same.

To obtain the category names, include some PHP code inside the file that has the form. Therefore, this will be a `.php` file instead of an `.html` file. (Remember that this PHP code operates on the side of the server.) The `categoryname.php` file in Listing 5-3 contains the new form.

Listing 5-3: A Form That Includes a Category Name, Not Just a Number

```
<html><head><title>Untitled Document</title></head>
<?php
    mysql_connect("localhost", "phpuser", "phppass");
    $result = mysql_query(
        "select * from phpbase.category");
    if ($result) {
        if (mysql_num_rows($result) > 0) {
            while ($row = mysql_fetch_assoc($result)){
                $name = $row["category_name"];
                $num = $row["categoryID"];
                $catByNum[$num] = $name;
            }
        }
        mysql_free_result($result);
    }
    mysql_close();
?>
<body bgcolor="#FFFFFF" text="#000000">
    <h1>Browse by category!</h1>
    <form name="form1" method="get"
    action="browsecategory.php">
```

```
Category Number:
<select name="categorynum">
<?php
    foreach ($catByNum as $num=>$name) {
        print "<option value=\"$num\">$name</option>\n";
    }
?>
  </select>
  <br>
    <input type="submit" name="Submit"
    value="Show All">
</form>
</body></html>
```

If you open Listing 5-3, `categoryname.php`, in a browser on a client computer, you see something like Figure 5-1.

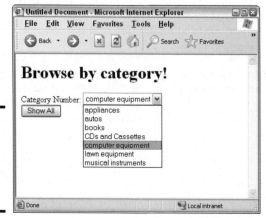

Figure 5-1:
The client browser shows a list of categories.

In Listing 5-3, the PHP code simply does a query on the entire `category` table. Here's the `select` statement:

```
select * from phpbase.category
```

The PHP code then loops through every row, saving the category names in an associative array keyed by `categoryID`, which is a number. By the time the code reaches the `mysql_close` function, the `catByNum` array contains all the categories as values, with the category numbers as keys.

Later, inside the HTML form, the PHP processor kicks back in for a second round of PHP fun. This time, the PHP code constructs a set of HTML `option value` statements for the combo box control (which is called a "select" object in the HTML world). The cool thing about the `option value` statements is that you can set up a list of words to display in the combo box and, for each word, provide a value that gets sent out in the URL to the server. Bingo! That's where you can put the category numbers. Thus, one option value that results from this code is as follows:

```
<option value="1">appliances</option>
```

This means that the combo box will show the word *appliances,* but if I choose *appliances,* the browser will send the value 1, not the word *appliances.* The value 1, in turn, is the `categoryID` associated with appliances. It works!

At this point, you may realize that you could just as easily hardcode the category values in your HTML file rather than look them up in the table. However, the idea is that if you modify your table by changing the category names, removing categories, or adding new categories, using the `option value` method means you don't have to change the `categoryname.php` file. If you hardcode the values, after changing the table in the database you would also have to change the HTML, which is extra work.

Having said that, I can think of at least two instances when you may want to skip the PHP and hardcode the categories in the HTML. First, if you don't expect to change the categories very often; and second, if you're running a very large server and need to keep your database lookups to a minimum. Both cases would justify hardcoding the categories in the HTML.

Modifying Data with a Web Page

Although allowing users to look up data is great, letting them change the data (in certain situations) is even better. For example, you may want to give users the ability to modify an ad by fixing spelling errors or changing the ad's status, for example.

Typically, you allow users to modify a row in a table by first looking up the row and determining all the information about the row. Then you display the row in an HTML form, allowing the user to change the data. The HTML form sends the data back to the server, where a `.php` file updates the row with any new values. That doesn't sound too hard — and it's not.

In this section, I show you how to allow users to modify an ad. The catch is that *anybody* can modify *any* ad. If this were a real classified ad system, you would want to add some security measures, such as a login section. By using the techniques I show you in Book VI, Chapter 7, you can add a login section. To make this work, you must modify the `customer` table to include an encrypted password. When the user logs in, you encrypt the user's password and compare it to the one in the `customer` table. Then that customer can modify only the ads "owned" by that customer, which means the ads containing a `customerID` value matching the `customerID` for the logged in customer.

Contending with add, search, and update

The designers of online database systems tend to want to use the same form for the add, search, and update interfaces. This is a bad idea because it can confuse people. For example, I once helped work on a database system for an oil change center back in the mid-1980s. The single form contained all the fields, you could type in any field, and you could use this form to add, search, and update. After typing the data, you could click a search button to get the rest of the columns for the row, and from there, you could change them and make a really big mess. Confusing? Absolutely! Instead, have one form for adding new data. Then have another form for searching for data. Finally, if the user searches for data and obtains a row, you may want to include a link on the page that lets the user go to a different page to modify the data. Use different forms, and life will be much easier for all involved. Users will thank you in the end.

In the spirit of the "Contending with add, search, and update" sidebar, I use three forms for this example. This example includes a form for adding an ad, a form for looking up an ad (based on the examples earlier in this chapter), and a form for updating the data.

Creating a new ad

The techniques I show you here are not new. Everything I show you here I describe in Book VI, Chapter 4. Further, this form includes a category search using the techniques I explained in the earlier section, "Looking up by category name." The createAd1.html file in Listing 5-4 is the form that serves as the starting point for creating an ad. This is an .html file with no PHP code in it, and it simply contains a form asking for the user's e-mail address. When the user clicks Submit, the Web server moves on to the file createAd2.php in Listing 5-5.

Listing 5-4: The Form That Asks for the User's E-mail Address

```
<html><head><title>Locate Customer</title></head>
<body bgcolor="#FFFFFF" text="#000000">

<h2>Please enter your email address
so I can find you in the system.</h2>

<form name="form1" method="get"
action="createAd2.php">
   <input type="text" name="email">
   <input type="submit" value="Submit">
</form></body></html>
```

After obtaining the user's e-mail address, the ad system is ready for the user to enter an ad. The `createAd2.php` file in Listing 5-5 enables you to do this. The first thing that this PHP program does is make sure that the e-mail address is for a legitimate user of the system. If not, the code prints out the message `Sorry, you are not a known user.`

To demonstrate the techniques of entering data into a MySQL server via the Web, I purposely left out a part that would probably be important to any online classified ad system: a password system. As it is, anybody can access this system and place ads for anybody else. The point here, however, is to show you how to enter data through HTML forms. In Book VI, Chapter 7, I take you through the creation of an example Web site that allows users to register with the site and log in. To make a successful classified ad system, combine the information in that chapter with the information in the present chapter.

Listing 5-5: The Form That Allows the User to Enter an Ad

```
<html><head><title>Create New Ad</title></head>

<body bgcolor="#FFFFFF" text="#000000">
<?php
    $CustomerOkay = false;
    mysql_connect("localhost", "phpuser", "phppass");
        $email = $_GET['email'];
    $result = mysql_query(
        "select ID, name from phpbase.customer ". // space!
        "where email = '$email'");
    if ($result) {
        if (mysql_num_rows($result) > 0) {
            $row = mysql_fetch_assoc($result);
            $CustomerOkay = true;
            $CustName = $row['name'];
            $CustID = $row['ID'];
        }
    }
    if ($CustomerOkay == false) {
        print "<h1>Sorry, you are not ".
            "a known customer.</h1>";
    }
    else {
        print "<h1>Welcome, $CustName!</h2>";
        // Categories
        $result = mysql_query(
            "select * from phpbase.category");
        if ($result) {
            if (mysql_num_rows($result) > 0) {
                while ($row =
                mysql_fetch_assoc($result)){
                    $name = $row["category_name"];
                    $num = $row["categoryID"];
```

```php
                                $catByNum[$num] = $name;
                        }
                }
                mysql_free_result($result);
        }


        // status
        $result = mysql_query(
            "select * from phpbase.status");
        if ($result) {
            if (mysql_num_rows($result) > 0) {
                while ($row =
                mysql_fetch_assoc($result)){
                    $name = $row["description"];
                    $num = $row["statusID"];
                    $statusByNum[$num] = $name;
                }
            }
            mysql_free_result($result);
        }


        // This else block ends AFTER
        // the following HTML code!
?>
Please enter your ad here. Click Submit when finished!<p>
<form name="form1" method="get" action="createAd3.php">
  Headline:
    <input type="text" name="headline" size="50"
    maxlength="100"><br>
  Category:
    <select name="category">
<?php
    foreach ($catByNum as $num=>$name) {
        print "<option value=\"$num\">$name</option>\n";
    }
?>
    </select><br>
  Item Name:
    <input type="text" name="itemname" size="50"
    maxlength="50"><br>
  Description:<br>
    <textarea name="description" cols="50"
    rows="10"></textarea><br>
  Price: $
    <input type="text" name="price"><br>
  Ad Expiration Date:
    <input type="text" name="expiration"><br>
  Initial status:
    <select name="status">
<?php
```

```
    foreach ($statusByNum as $num=>$name) {
        print "<option value=\"$num\">$name</option>\n";
    }
    print "</select>";
    print "<input type=\"hidden\" ";
    print "name=\"customerID\" value=\"$CustID\">";
    print "<input type=\"hidden\" ";
    print "name=\"email\" value=\"$email\">";
?>
    <input type="submit" value="Submit">
</form>
<?php
        mysql_close();
    } // This is the end of the else block!
?>
</body>
</html>
```

After Listing 5-5 checks that the e-mail address is valid, the HTML portion kicks in and creates a Web form for the user to enter in the classified ad. But I do something cool here: Although the ad table contains a category number (as opposed to a name), I knew that a number would be meaningless to the user posting an ad. Instead, I wanted to list the categories. Therefore, I use the technique described earlier in this chapter in the section, "Looking up by category name." I also do the same thing for the Status column of the ad table. As with categories, I didn't want the user to have to pick a status based on number. So I looked up the status names from the status table and used these to populate a drop-down list box.

After the user fills out the form, the form sends the data to the Web server and requests createAd3.php, which is shown in Listing 5-6. This file inserts the ad into the table. This insertion is, in fact, quite easy: I just collect all the data that came over (using the $_GET array) and then construct an SQL insert statement, which puts the data into the Ad table.

In these examples, I use the GET method of sending data from a form. This requires that I look at the $_GET array in PHP. Using GET has two drawbacks: All the data is visible in the Web address, and you have a limit on how much data you can send out.

For this reason, in Book VI, Chapter 7, I use the POST method instead of the GET method. From the perspective of PHP, little difference exists between the two: You either check the $_GET array or the $_POST array. The advantage to POST is that if you're entering a password, for example, the password doesn't appear in the address bar after the user clicks Send. Further, you can send much larger data with POST. For the ads here, which are small, GET can handle it. But if you want to allow much larger ads, I recommend using POST instead.

Listing 5-6: The Final .php File That Inserts the Ad into the Table

```php
<html><head><title>Results</title></head>
<body bgcolor="#FFFFFF" text="#000000">
<?php
    $headline = $_GET['headline'];
    $category = $_GET['category'];
    $itemname = $_GET['itemname'];
    $description = $_GET['description'];
    $price1 = $_GET['price'];
    $price = $price1 * 100; // Convert to cents
    $expirationstr = $_GET['expiration'];
    $expirationnum = strtotime($expirationstr);
    $expiration = date("Y-m-d", $expirationnum);
    $status = $_GET['status'];
    $customerID = $_GET['customerID'];
    $email = $_GET['email'];

    mysql_connect("localhost", "phpuser", "phppass");
    $result = mysql_query(
        "insert into phpbase.ad
        (categoryID, item_name, headline,
        description, price, expiration_date,
        status, CustomerID)
        values
        ('$category', '$headline',
        '$itemname', '$description',
        '$price', '$expiration', '$status',
        '$customerID')"
    );

    if ($result) {
        print "<h2>Thank you for your ad!</h2>\n";
        print "When you browse your ads now,<br>\n";
        print "you should see your new ad!<p>\n";
        print "<a href=\"viewAd2.php?email=$email\">";
        print "Click here to browse your ads!";
        print "</a>";
    }
    else {
        print "The SQL failed. Here's why:<br>\n";
        print mysql_errno().": ".mysql_error()."<br>";
    }
    mysql_close();
?>
</body></html>
```

If you want to carefully compare the MySQL calls in Listing 5-6 to other MySQL calls, you may notice something missing. In Listing 5-6, I don't call `mysql_free_result` as I normally do. The reason is that when you perform an SQL `insert` statement with `mysql_query`, the result is a simple Boolean value rather than a result set. (An SQL select statement, on the other hand, returns a result that you use in subsequent fetch calls.)

The mysql_free_result is only for use when you get back a result set, not a Boolean variable. Therefore, don't call mysql_free_result after an SQL insert statement, or you'll get an error.

I want to mention one more exciting thing about Listing 5-6. This Web form has the unusual feature that users can use a wide variety of formats to type in an expiration date. This is possible through the strtotime function, which takes a date in string format and converts it to a Unix time. (I then reformat the Unix time using the date function in Listing 5-6.) For example, all the following formats are valid:

**Book VI
Chapter 5**

**Querying with
SQL and PHP**

✦ September 1, 2005 You can enter dates with month name, day number, a comma, and then the year.

✦ 9/1/2005 You can enter month-day-year in all numbers separated by slashes.

✦ tomorrow You can enter the words tomorrow or yesterday (although an ad that expires yesterday isn't particularly useful).

You can also use the word *next* as in next Thursday or next Year, but these results may not give you what you expect. And further, the PHP people changed the way the system handles the word *next* starting in version 4.3.0. Apparently to the PHP people, next Sunday means "two Sundays from now," whereas I personally disagree with that. It's best to avoid the issue altogether.

If you want to explore the engine behind the date processing function, check out the official GNU date processing page at www.gnu.org/manual/tar-1.12/html_chapter/tar_7.html.

Viewing a customer's ads

When a customer has multiple ads, viewing all the customer's ads is easy. All you do is call an SQL select statement, searching on the customer's ID.

The viewAd1.html file in Listing 5-7 contains a basic form for entering the customer's e-mail address. This form in turn calls viewAd2.php, which is shown in Listing 5-8.

Listing 5-7: The Entry Point for Viewing a Customer's Ads

```
<html><head><title>Locate Customer</title></head>
<body bgcolor="#FFFFFF" text="#000000">

<h2>Please enter your email address
```

```
so I can find you in the system.</h2>

<form name="form1" method="get"
action="viewAd2.php">
   <input type="text" name="email">
   <input type="submit" value="Submit">
</form></body></html>
```

The code in Listing 5-8 retrieves the customer's ads and then formats them in a list for the Web browser. But I do something interesting in this ad: I perform an *SQL join*. A *join* simply means I retrieve data from two tables. In this case, I want to retrieve each ad from the `ad` table, but with that, I also want to retrieve the category name and status name, rather than just the category number and status number. But the `ad` table contains a number, not a name.

One way you could do this is by retrieving the numbers for the category and status and then using a separate SQL `select` statement to retrieve the names. But instead, I chose to get fancy and do it all with one `select` statement using a join. Take a close look at the SQL select statement in Listing 5-8. Instead of asking for individual columns, I tack on a table name (and the database name to be complete) — `phpbase.category.category_name` and `phpbase.ad.price`. Then, rather than search a single table, I search three tables:

```
from phpbase.ad, phpbase.status, phpbase.category
```

But which records do I retrieve? To specify records, you use a `where` clause. First, I want all the records in the `ad` table that match a particular customer ID. So that goes first in my `where` clause, like so:

```
where phpbase.ad.customerID = $CustID
```

But with these records, I want to join the data from the `category` and `status` tables, retrieving a name, not just a number. For the `Status` table, I use this condition:

```
phpbase.status.statusID =  phpbase.ad.status
```

The MySQL engine looks at the `status` value in the row found in the `phpbase.ad` table (that's to the right of the equal sign), and then finds the row in the `status` table having a `statusID` matching the ad's `statusID` (this is to the left side of the equal sign). This row includes a status name, which I specify back in the beginning of the `select` statement when I select `phpbase.status.description`.

This works for joining to both the `status` table and the `category` table. But joining to the `status` table has a slight problem. The `status` table has a column called `description` and so does the `ad` table. In the end, PHP builds the associative array with only one `description` index, and one of the values will be lost. So I tack on the word *as* in the first part of the `select` statement:

```
phpbase.status.description as status_desc
```

When I get my data back, the status table's `description` column will instead have the column name `status_desc`. When I access the associative array in PHP, I can get the status description using the name `status_desc`. To get the ad description I can use the name `description`. Thus, I have both columns, and one has been renamed.

Listing 5-8: The Heart of the Ad Viewing System

```
<html><head><title>View Your Ads</title></head>
<body bgcolor="#FFFFFF" text="#000000">
<?php
    $CustomerOkay = false;
    mysql_connect("localhost", "phpuser", "phppass");
        $email = $_GET['email'];
    $result = mysql_query(
        "select ID, name from phpbase.customer ". // space!
        "where email = '$email'");
    if ($result) {
        if (mysql_num_rows($result) > 0) {
            $row = mysql_fetch_assoc($result);
            $CustomerOkay = true;
            $CustName = $row['name'];
            $CustID = $row['ID'];
        }
    }
    if ($CustomerOkay == false) {
        print "<h1>Sorry, you are not ".
            "a known customer.</h1>";
    }
    else {
        print "<h1>Welcome, $CustName!</h2>";
        print "Here are your ads!<p>\n";
        print "<hr>";
        $result = mysql_query(
            "select phpbase.ad.headline,
                phpbase.category.category_name,
                phpbase.ad.item_name,
                phpbase.ad.description,
                phpbase.ad.expiration_date,
                phpbase.ad.price,
                phpbase.status.description
                    as status_desc
```

```
                from phpbase.ad, phpbase.status,
                    phpbase.category
                where phpbase.ad.customerID = $CustID and
                    phpbase.status.statusID =
                    phpbase.ad.status and
                    phpbase.category.categoryID =
                    phpbase.ad.categoryID;");

        if ($result) {
            if (mysql_num_rows($result) > 0) {
                while ($row = mysql_fetch_assoc($result)){
                    print "<h2>{$row['headline']}</h2>\n";
                    print "<b>Category:</b> ";
                    print "{$row['category_name']}<br>\n";
                    print "<b>item:</b> ";
                    print "{$row['item_name']}<br>\n";
                    print "<b>description:</b> ";
                    print "{$row['description']}<br>\n";
                    print "<b>expires on:</b> ";
                    print "{$row['expiration_date']}<br>\n";
                    print "<b>price:</b> ";
                    $price = $row['price'] / 100;
                    print "\$$price<br>\n";
                    print "<b>Status:</b> ";
                    print "{$row['status_desc']}<p>\n";
                    print "<hr>";
                }
            }
            mysql_free_result($result);
        }
    }
    mysql_close();
?>
</body>
</html>
```

Chapter 6: Accessing MySQL from Perl

In This Chapter

✔ Obtaining the DBI and MySQL packages

✔ Connecting to a database

✔ Querying a database

✔ Modifying a database

*I*n this chapter, I show you how to get going with MySQL under the Perl programming language. When you work with MySQL from Perl, all the MySQL concepts apply. If you're new to MySQL, I encourage you to read the first three chapters of this minibook, Book VI, to get acquainted with MySQL. In this chapter, I assume you're familiar with the basics covered in those chapters.

If you installed Perl on a Linux system, you should be all set with the Perl DBI package (that's the main database package) and the MySQL package. If you're using Windows, you need to install the two packages manually. In the first section of this chapter, I show you how to install the packages on Windows. If you're using Linux, you can skip this first section.

If you have Linux and the Perl DBI and MySQL packages aren't present, or if you're using Windows and you have problems with the installation I describe in the next section, check out the main Perl/MySQL installation page in the MySQL manual at www.mysql.com/doc/en/Perl_support.html.

Obtaining the Perl DBI and MySQL Components on Windows

Unlike most of what I discuss in this book, DBI and MySQL components are not automatically installed with most Perl distributions for Windows. The following installation procedure works with the ActiveState distribution of Perl.

To install Perl DBI and MySQL, you don't need to download anything before-hand. Just follow these steps:

1. **Make sure that you're connected to the Internet, and then start ppm (the Programmer's Package Manual for Perl) by typing the following command from the command prompt:**

   ```
   ppm
   ```

   You see an introductory message followed by a ppm> prompt. Make sure that you're connected to the Internet because ppm will download the modules for you.

2. **At the ppm> prompt, type this:**

   ```
   install DBI
   ```

   You see something like this, followed by several lines beginning with the word Installing:

   ```
   =====================
   Install 'DBI' version 1.37 in ActivePerl 5.8.0.804.
   =====================
   Downloaded 435317 bytes.
   Extracting 61/61: blib/arch/auto/DBI/Driver_xst.h
   ```

   When the installation is finished, you see a message that the DBI was successfully installed.

3. **At the ppm> prompt, type this:**

   ```
   install DBD-mysql
   ```

   Again, you see something like this, followed by several lines beginning with the word Installing:

   ```
   =====================
   Install 'DBD-mysql' version 2.9002 in ActivePerl
       5.8.0.804.
   =====================
   Downloaded 178800 bytes.
   Extracting 17/17: blib/arch/auto/DBD/mysql/mysql.lib
   ```

   You then see a message that DBD-mysql was successfully installed.

4. **Type** quit **to exit the** ppm **program.**

That's it; you're done. If any of this didn't work as planned, please check out the MySQL docs at www.mysql.com/doc/en/Perl_support.html.

Connecting to a Database and Performing a Simple Query

The Perl DBI is remarkably easy to use. Listing 6-1 shows a sample program that connects to the `phpbase` database on MySQL with username `phpuser` and password `phppass`. The program then performs an SQL query against the `customer` table, prints out the results, and ends the connection.

The focus in this section is on the connection aspect of this program. In the sections that follow, I give you more details on how to set up a query, execute a query, and retrieve rows from the result set.

Book VI
Chapter 6

Accessing MySQL
from Perl

**Listing 6-1: A Program That Connects to a Database,
Queries a Table, Prints the Results, and Disconnects**

```
use DBI;
$database = "phpbase";
$user = "phpuser";
$password = "phppass";
$dbh = DBI->connect("DBI:mysql:$database", $user, $password);

$statement = "SELECT * FROM phpbase.customer";
$sth = $dbh->prepare($statement);
$rv = $sth->execute;
while(@row = $sth->fetchrow_array) {
        print "$row[0]    $row[1]  $row[2] ".
              "$row[3]   $row[4]\n";
}
$rc = $sth->finish;
$rc = $dbh->disconnect;
```

Here's the sample output in my `phpbase.customer` table:

```
1    Hank Harshigan   hank@harshigan.com 2003-06-23  2003-06-23
2    Floyd Flabbergaps  floyd@flabbergaps.com 2003-06-23  2003-06-23
3    Erica Exagabule   erica@exagabule.com 2003-06-23  2003-06-23
4    Jessica Jamboliable  jessica@jamboliable.com  2003-06-23   2003-06-23
5    Julia Julianopolis  julia@julianopolis.com  2003-06-23   2003-06-23
```

The first line of this program uses the DBI package. You don't need to specify the MySQL package because the DBI package locates the MySQL package when DBI sees the `connect` statement requesting MySQL.

The next three lines save the database, username, and password in variables.

Then comes the connection line, which is a call to the `connect` function in the DBI package. Here's the line:

```
$dbh = DBI->connect("DBI:mysql:$database", $user, $password);
```

The first parameter of the `connect` function is the database name preceded by the *driver*. The driver is the underlying package that connects to the database. In Perl, you use DBI for your database work, and DBI talks to a driver specific to the database system you're using. That means you can use DBI to talk to many different database systems, not just MySQL. Thus, in the `connect` statement, you specify not only your database but also the driver that you want. You do that by embedding all the information in a single string like this:

```
DBI:mysql:$database
```

`$database` is the variable containing your database name. This string is the first parameter to `connect`. The next parameter is the username, and the final parameter is the password.

The `connect` function returns a *handle* to the database connection. In computer terms, a handle is a number that represents some object. Here, the handle is a number representing the database connection. You use this handle in subsequent database calls; this handle identifies which connection you're referring to. (Yes, that implies you can open up multiple connections at once to different databases.)

After you have a handle, you can query the database and make changes to it. In the sample program in Listing 6-1, I query the `customer` table in the database. (See the next section for details on querying the database.)

When you're finished with your work, you need to close the connection. You do so by calling the `disconnect` function, as I do in the final line of the sample program.

Querying the Database

To query the MySQL database using Perl, you need to perform two steps, which is a common approach in database systems:

✦ Prepare the SQL `select` statement.

✦ Execute the SQL `select` statement.

After you execute the SQL statement, you receive a result set, from which you can obtain information. You have several options for fetching data from the result set. In the two following sections, I show you how to prepare and execute your SQL statement, and the different ways to fetch data from the result set.

Preparing and executing the SQL statement

Often the system wants to first prepare the SQL statement, which simply means you call a function called prepare, passing as a string your SQL statement. (Yes, you'll prepare the statement yourself, but MySQL wants to prepare it as well when you're finished preparing it.) After MySQL prepares the statement, you can execute it. These two steps take two separate functions. Here's an example from the program in Listing 6-1:

```
$statement = "SELECT * FROM phpbase.customer";
$sth = $dbh->prepare($statement);
$rv = $sth->execute;
```

In this example, before calling the two functions, you save your SQL statement in a variable called statement. (That way you can print it out to the console if you want to look at it, without having to retype it.) Then you call prepare, passing your SQL statement. The prepare function gives you back a *statement handle*. That means the DBI now knows about your statement, and you can reference it using this handle.

Next, you call execute, which is part of the statement handle's object. The execute function returns a result set.

Fetching data from the result set

You can call various fetch functions to obtain the rows in the result set. The Perl DBI provides four functions for fetching data:

✦ fetchrow_array: Fetches into an array

✦ fetchrow_arrayref: Fetches into a reference to an array

✦ fetchrow_hashref: Fetches into a reference to a hash

✦ fetchall_arrayref: Fetches all into a reference to an array

These functions live as members of the statement handle's object. The first three functions in the list fetch the next row in the result set; they simply differ on the type of data they return. The fetchrow_array function returns a simple list; fetchrow_arrayref returns a reference to an array; and fetchrow_hashref returns a reference to a hash organized by column name.

The fourth function — `fetchall_arrayref` — differs from the others in that it fetches all the rows into one big reference to an array. In Perl, the term *reference to an array* can simply mean an array holding other arrays — that's what it means here.

If you want to fetch all the rows at once, use the `fetchall_arrayref` function. You can then loop through the data inside the resulting reference to an array. If you'd rather loop through, retrieving one row at a time, use any of the other three functions.

In Listing 6-1 earlier in the chapter, I use the `fetchrow_array` function. Here's the line from the program:

```
@row = $sth->fetchrow_array
```

The `fetchrow_array` function is a member of `$sth`, which is the statement handle object. The results of this call are saved in the `@row` array. You can easily loop through the array using the built-in Perl functions.

The `fetchrow_array` function returns a single row; or, it returns a false value if no more rows exist in the result set. By wrapping the call inside the comparison of a `while` loop, you can loop through all the rows in the result set.

Alternatively, you can try the `fetchrow_arrayref` function. Doing so is similar to using the `fetchrow_array` function. Here's the `while` loop in Listing 6-1 recoded to use the `fetchrow_array` function:

```
while($row = $sth->fetchrow_arrayref) {
        print "$row->[0]    $row->[1]  $row->[2] ".
              "$row->[3]  $row->[4]\n";
}
```

You save the results in a scalar value, rather than an array variable, because you're getting back a reference. You access the array by dereferencing the reference as in `$row->[0]`. Other than those two differences along with the different function name, this code is the same as Listing 6-1.

When dealing with functions that return a reference, always save the result of the function in a scalar variable, not an array or hash. If you use an array or hash, you'll get some bizarre errors from the database engine.

Here's the same example recoded using the hash reference style of access:

```
while($row = $sth->fetchrow_hashref) {
        print "$row->{'ID'}    $row->{'name'}   "
              "$row->{'email'} ".
              "$row->{'signup'}  $row->{'last_access'}\n";
}
```

This example saves the reference into a scalar, not an array. To access the items, you use the column name of the table, and you dereference the reference, as in $row->{'email'}.

Here's the example recoded using the method that retrieves the entire result set into a single array:

```
$table = $sth->fetchall_arrayref;
$numrows = $#{$table};
$numcols = $#{$table->[$i]};
for $row (0 .. $numrows) {
        for $col (0 .. $numcols) {
                print "$table->[$row][$col]   ";
        }
        print "\n";
}
```

This is more complex than the previous examples. With large result sets, this method is not a good idea because it consumes a lot of memory. But the method works well if you like to pull out all the data at once. Notice that as usual, fetchall_arrayref returns a reference, so you save the value into a scalar variable.

Next, you figure out the size of the array. To do so, you must dereference the array variable using {$table} and then use the $# construct to get the size. That gives you the number of rows. To figure out the number of columns, look at the first row in the table, using the same procedure used for figuring the number of columns.

Then you have two loops to go through both dimensions of the table. You gather each item using $table->[$row][$col].

Modifying the Database

For SQL statements that don't return a result set (that is, pretty much any statement but a select statement), you can use the do function. Whereas select statements require that you first call prepare and then execute, you can skip the prepare and execute functions and instead call do for statements such as insert, update, and delete. Here's an example that inserts data into a table, modifies some data, and then deletes some data.

First, here's the insert statement:

```
use DBI;
$database = "phpbase";
$user = "phpuser";
$password = "phppass";
```

```
$dbh = DBI->connect("DBI:mysql:$database", $user, $password);

$statement = "
insert into phpbase.customer
(name, email, signup, last_access)
values
('Sally Salmoneater', 'sally\@salmoneating.com',
'2003-09-03', '2003-09-03')
";

$dbh->do($statement);

$rc = $dbh->disconnect;
```

You simply put the SQL `insert` statement inside a string and call `$dbh->do`, passing your statement. (Notice that I put a backslash before the @ symbol; otherwise, Perl will think that @salmoneating was a variable name. The backslash prevents the incorrect substitution.)

You can do an update by changing the statement variable assignment to this:

```
$statement = "update phpbase.customer
set email = 'sally\@salmoneater.com'
where name = 'Sally Salmoneater'
";
```

You can perform a delete by changing the `select` statement:

```
$statement =
    "delete from phpbase.customer
    where email like '%sally%'";
```

Checking for errors

Checking for errors is always a good idea. The DBI package has an `err` variable and an `errstr` variable, which you can access via `$dbh->err` and `$dbh->errstr`. These are the same numbers returned by the MySQL engine.

However, if the DBI package encounters an error, depending on how the DBI is configured, your program might automatically die, and the Perl interpreter will issue an error message. Typically, that's a bad thing: You don't want your program choking simply because it can't connect to the database server.

You can turn off this default behavior by modifying your `connect` function parameters. Then you can inspect two variables for errors. One is an error number, which is the error code returned by MySQL. The other is the error string, which is the string returned by MySQL.

Here's a sample program that demonstrates how to turn off the auto-death problem and how to inspect the two error variables. (This program purposely uses a bad password, thereby causing MySQL to issue an error.)

```
use DBI;
$database = "phpbase";
$user = "phpuser";
$password = "incorrect";
$dbh = DBI-
        >connect("DBI:mysql:$database",
        $user, $password,
    {RaiseError => 0, PrintError => 0}
);
print DBI::err;
print "\n";
print DBI::errstr;
print "\n";
```

Chapter 7: Creating a Username System for Your Web Site

In This Chapter

✔ Creating the login tables

✔ Building a registration system

✔ Designing the login forms and private pages

✔ Coding access routines

✔ Helping users who forget their passwords

*T*his chapter is a hands-on example of what you can do with MySQL when it's combined with the power of a server-side language such as PHP. I chose PHP for the example simply because that's what I used on my site. You can also do all this using Perl or any number of languages.

In this chapter, you find out how to create a set of pages that allows a user to register with your site and choose a password and a site theme. (For this example, the theme is a background color.) Then the user can log in later, or even click a Remember Me check box, allowing the client computer to remember the username and password. I also show you how you can have private pages that require the user to log in. If the user is presently logged in, the page appears; otherwise, a login screen appears.

These pages and files are only the beginning. From here, you can add more private pages, more theme material such as graphics and images, and so on, as far as your imagination can take you.

Each section of this chapter is devoted to a particular file or two, in standard reference-guide format. However, I do encourage you to read the entire chapter through to get the full picture.

The whole system I create in this chapter is a bit complex. For that reason I've put together a line diagram to help you see how the different parts of the program interact, shown in Figure 7-1. As you work through the sections of this chapter, you might want to refer to this diagram periodically to help you keep everything straight.

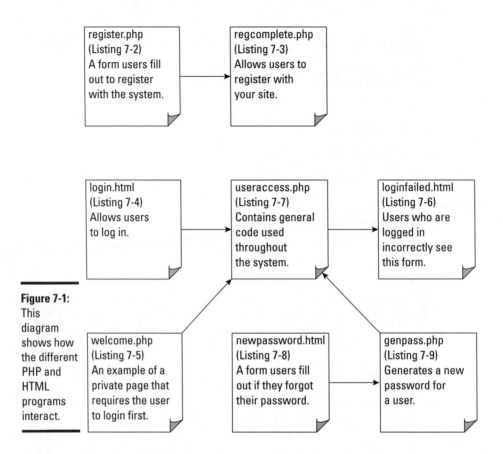

Figure 7-1:
This
diagram
shows how
the different
PHP and
HTML
programs
interact.

Creating the Login Tables

When you set up your user login system, first you need to set up the MySQL tables. As usual, I recommend that you type the SQL in a file by itself and then run the file using a line such as the following:

```
mysql -u root -p < tables.sql
```

The `tables.sql` file in Listing 7-1 contains the data for the tables. When you make your own tables, remember to include the `use phpbase` line at the top of the file.

Listing 7-1: The Tables for Use in MySQL

```
use phpbase;
create table login (
    loginID integer NOT NULL auto_increment,
```

```
        email varchar(50) unique,
        password char(34),
        lastaccess date,
        signup date,
        themeID integer,
        key(email),
        primary key(loginID)
    );

    create table usertheme (
        themeID integer NOT NULL,
        name varchar(15),
        backgroundcolor char(6),
        primary key(themeID)
    );

    insert into usertheme
    values (1, 'pink', 'FFCCFF');

    insert into usertheme
    values (2, 'blue', 'CCFFFF');

    insert into usertheme
    values (3, 'yellow', 'FFFFCC');

    insert into usertheme
    values (4, 'salmon', 'FFCCCC');

    insert into usertheme
    values (5, 'green', 'CCFFCC');

    insert into usertheme
    values (6,'purple', 'CCCCFF');
```

The login table consists of a unique loginID, an e-mail address, a password (which will be encrypted), the signup date, the last access date, and the user-selected theme.

For the table creation, I chose to include a loginID, even though I don't use it much in the examples in this chapter. As your system grows, you may want to allow users to know their unique IDs for quick lookups and such.

After the table creation, Listing 7-1 includes six entries for the usertheme table. In this simple example, the themes consist of six possible colors, and the theme name is the name of the color. You can put other information in this file, such as the filename of a graphic to display at the top of each page or the name of graphics set for use in navigating the site. Then each user sees a color and graphics set depending on the chosen theme.

Building the Registration System

After you create the tables (as described in the preceding section), you can create a page that allows users to register with your Web site. I recommend that you give users multiple ways to get to this page. Here's the usual way to do this: The users access the system through a central page, where they are presented with a login form. Somewhere on that page is a link where they can register if they haven't already done so. This is a common method that Web e-mail sites use.

The idea is that users need to access the registration page only once, and they'll need to use the login page often (hopefully). Thus, the login page should be more readily accessible.

For this set of samples, I have a page called login.html, which I think of as the main access point, and I describe that page in the next section, "Designing a Login Form."

Figure 7-2 shows the signup form running on a client Windows browser.

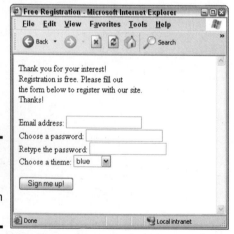

Figure 7-2:
Visitors use this form to register with the site.

Listing 7-2 is the register.php file for the signup form. For the sake of brevity, I purposely didn't include a set of JavaScript functions that validate the data. However, I recommend that you include such a system. I describe how to do this in Book VI, Chapter 4.

Listing 7-2: The File That Allows Users to Register with Your Site

```php
<?php
    require "useraccess.php";
    $themeByNum = GetThemeNames();

    // You probably want to add some JavaScript
    // validation. See Book 6, Chapter 4!
?>
<html>
<head>
<title>Free Registration</title>
</head>

<body bgcolor="#FFFFFF" text="#000000">
  Thank you for your interest! <br>
  Registration is free. Please fill out<br>
  the form below to register with our site.<br>
  Thanks!<p>
<form name="form1" method="post"
action="regcomplete.php">
  <p>Email address:
    <input type="text" name="email">
    <br>
    Choose a password:
    <input type="password" name="password">
    <br>
    Retype the password:
    <input type="password" name="password2">
    <br>
    Choose a theme:
    <select name="themeID">
<?php
    foreach ($themeByNum as $num=>$name) {
        print
            "<option value=\"$num\">$name</option>\n";
    }
?>
    </select>
  </p>
  <p>
    <input type="submit" name="Submit"
    value="Sign me up!">
    <br>
  </p>
</form>
</body>
</html>
```

Although I could have used an .html file to accomplish much of what Listing 7-2 does, I wanted to include a list of the available themes. Therefore, I made the signup form a .php file that includes a section that accesses the database and retrieves the theme names.

In all the forms in this chapter, I use the Post method rather than the Get method. I chose Post because Get displays the user information in the URL. When the user logs in using a Get method form, his or her password is displayed in the Web browser's address box, where onlookers can easily see it. That's probably a bad idea. The Post method, however, doesn't do this; the data is sent behind the scenes and doesn't appear in the URL.

After the user fills out the registration form and clicks the Submit button, the browser accesses the regcomplete.php file, shown in Listing 7-3. This file processes the user login.

Listing 7-3: The File That Processes a User Registration

```
<html><head>
<title>Registration Complete</title></head>
<body>
<?php
    require "useraccess.php";
    // Use POST so password isn't shown in URL!
    $email = $_POST['email'];
    $password = $_POST['password'];
    $themeID = $_POST['themeID'];
    $result = signup($email, $password, $themeID);
    if ($result) {
?>
    Thank you for your registration!
<?php
    }
    else {
?>
    Sorry, there was a problem signing you up.
    Perhaps you have already registered with us?
<?php
    }
?>
</body></html>
```

In Listing 7-3, the PHP code accesses the e-mail, password, and theme choice, and calls into a function called signup. This signup function is my own creation and lives in a file called useraccess.php, which I require at the beginning of Listing 7-3. I describe the useraccess.php file and its functions in the "Coding the Access Routines in a Single .php File" section, later in this chapter.

In Listing 7-3, I employ a little PHP trick: You can intersperse blocks of HTML with blocks of PHP, and the PHP processor is smart enough to sort through it all. Thus, the processor prints the HTML text, Thank you for your registration!, only if the $result value is true. After that HTML text, I include an else statement, and then I again close the PHP code, after which I have more HTML text (starting with Sorry, there was a problem . . .). This HTML text appears only if the $result value is false. That PHP processor is pretty smart.

Designing a Login Form

I consider the login.html file to be the central starting point for users. The idea is that from this page the user can perform the following operations:

Book VI
Chapter 7

Creating a
Username System
for Your Web Site

✦ Log in

✦ Sign up for access (registration) by clicking a link

✦ Click a link if he or she forgot a password

Using this one-stop approach, users don't need to remember all sorts of links and have multiple bookmarks. They need to bookmark only this one page to access your system.

Figure 7-3 shows the login form.

The login.html file is simple; it's just a bunch of HTML code, with no PHP code. (Thus, it has an .html filename extension.) Listing 7-4 shows the login.html file.

Listing 7-4: The Login Form

```
<html><head><title>Login Please</title></head>
<body bgcolor="#FFFFFF" text="#000000">
<h2>Please sign in! </h2>
New member?
<a href="register.php">Click here to register</a>.
<form name="form1" method="post" action="welcome.php">
   <p>Email address:
     <input type="text" name="email">
     <br>
     Password:
     <input type="password" name="password">
     <br>
     <input type="checkbox" name="remember" value="1">
     remember me!<p>
```

```
        <input type="submit" name="Submit" value="Login">
</form>
<p><a href="newpassword.html">Click here<a>
if you forgot your password.
</body>
</html>
```

Figure 7-3: Users access this form to log in to the site. It serves as an entry point to the system.

Designing a private page

After the user clicks the Login button, the browser goes to the welcome.php page. The welcome.php page does the logging in. I wanted to make this system as robust as possible, so I incorporated the following points into the program:

✦ If users go directly to welcome.php, the system checks whether they are already logged in. If not, the system presents a message that they are not logged in and gives them the option of logging in.

✦ If users come to the welcome.php file by way of the login.html file, the welcome.php file logs them in using the information they entered in the login.html file's form.

These two points seem almost circular in nature, but the logic really does make sense. And even better, the welcome.php file is nothing special. I broke out the PHP code and put it in the useraccess.php file, leaving nothing in the welcome.php file beyond the word *welcome.*

Listing 7-5 shows the `welcome.php` file. The idea is that you can use this file as a boilerplate for all your private files. The key is the PHP code that I put at the top of this file. This PHP code calls the `checkAccess()` function, which does the bulk of the work. The `checkAccess` function checks whether the user is currently logged in and, if not, takes the user back to the `login.html` file.

If you put this PHP code at the start of all your private files, each file is protected. If a Web user comes to the page directly without going through the `login.html` form, the PHP code automatically takes the user to the `login.html` form. However, if the user is already logged in, the file is simply displayed as you created it.

Listing 7-5: The welcome.php File

```php
<?php
    require "useraccess.php";
    $themeID = checkAccess();
    $theme = getTheme($themeID);
?>
<html>
<?php
    print "<body bgcolor=\"#{$theme->bgcolor}\">\n";
?>
    <h1>Welcome!</h1>
</body>
</html>
```

For details on how the `checkAccess` function works, see the section "Coding the Access Routines in a Single .php File," later in this chapter.

Applying themes

Notice that the `checkAccess` function in Listing 7-5 returns data into the variable called `$theme`. This data is an instance of a class defined in the `useraccess.php` file called `ThemeInfo`. You can see how I actually use the theme. Look at the following code from Listing 7-5:

```php
print "<body bgcolor=\"#{$theme->bgcolor}\">\n";
```

This code takes whatever background color is stored in the `bgcolor` member of `$theme` and writes it out for the HTML `<body>` tag.

Dealing with login failure

If the user tries to access one of the private pages or types incorrect login information into the `login.html` form, the user gets taken to the `loginfailed.html` file, shown in Listing 7-6.

Listing 7-6: The File That Users See if They Incorrectly Access the System

```
<html><head><title>Login failed</title></head>
<body bgcolor="#FFFFFF" text="#000000">
Sorry! Could not log you in. Please
<a href="login.html">click here</a>
to try again!<br>
</body>
</html>
```

Coding the Access Routines in a Single .php File

In this section, I go through the functions in the `useraccess.php` file. My idea was to pull together most of my PHP code into a single file, making the code easier to maintain. The `useraccess.php` file in Listing 7-7 shows the code. I describe the individual functions in the next few sections.

Listing 7-7: A File That Contains Most of the PHP Code for the System

```
<?php
    // Remember, this might be called whether
    // there was a POST or not!
    function checkAccess() {
        // First check for a POST.
        $email = $_POST['email'];
        $password = $_POST['password'];
        $remember = $_POST['remember'];

        // If no POST, check for a cookie
        if ($email == NULL) {
            $email = $_COOKIE['dummiesemail'];
            $password = $_COOKIE['dummiespassword'];
        }
        elseif (!$remember) {
            // If there was a POST, save the cookie
            // This will wipe out any long-term
            // cookies by this same name. See
            // text for explanation.
            setcookie('dummiesemail', $email);
```

```
            setcookie('dummiespassword', $password);
    }

    $okay = false;
    if ($email && $password) {
        mysql_connect("localhost", "phpuser",
            "phppass");
        $result = mysql_query(
            "select loginID, password, themeID ".
            "from phpbase.login where ".
            "email = '$email'" //watch the quotes!
        );
        if ($result) {
            if (mysql_num_rows($result) > 0) {
                $row = mysql_fetch_assoc($result);
                $pass = $row['password'];
                $userid = $row['loginID'];
                $theme = $row['themeID'];

                // This is for when MD5 is used...
                // Need to use the same salt that
                // was used originally.
                $passcrypt = crypt($password,
                    substr($pass, 0, 12));
                // If DES is used, just use
                // $passcrypt = crypt($password);
                if ($pass == $passcrypt) {
                    $okay = true;
                }
            }
        }
        mysql_close();
    }
    if (!$okay) {
        header("location: loginfailed.html");
    }
    // If $remember is set, store in
    // long-term cookie.
    if ($remember) {
        // Remember until May 17, 2033.
        // That's close enough to forever. :-)
        setcookie('dummiesemail', $email,
            2000000000);
        setcookie('dummiespassword', $password,
            2000000000);
    }
    return $theme;
}

function signup($email, $password, $themeID) {
    mysql_connect("localhost", "phpuser",
        "phppass");
```

```php
    $passcrypt = crypt($password);
    $now = date("Y-m-d");
    $result = mysql_query(
        "insert into phpbase.login
        (email, password, lastaccess,
        signup, themeID) values
        ('$email', '$passcrypt', '$now',
        '$now', '$themeID')"
    );
    mysql_close();
    return $result;
}

class ThemeInfo {
    var $bgcolor;
}
function getTheme($themeID) {
    mysql_connect("localhost", "phpuser",
        "phppass");
    $newtheme = new ThemeInfo;
    $newtheme->bgcolor = "FFFFFF"; // white bg

    $result = mysql_query(
        "select backgroundcolor from ".
        "phpbase.usertheme ".
        "where themeID = '$themeID'"
        // watch the quotes!
    );
    if ($result) {
        if (mysql_num_rows($result) > 0) {
            $row = mysql_fetch_assoc($result);
            $newtheme->bgcolor =
                $row['backgroundcolor'];
        }
    }
    mysql_close();
    return $newtheme;
}

function GetThemeNames() {
    mysql_connect("localhost", "phpuser",
        "phppass");
    $result = mysql_query(
        "select * from phpbase.usertheme");
    if ($result) {
        if (mysql_num_rows($result) > 0) {
            while ($row =
            mysql_fetch_assoc($result)){
                $name = $row["name"];
                $num = $row["themeID"];
                $themeByNum[$num] = $name;
            }
```

```
        }
        mysql_free_result($result);
    }
    mysql_close();
    return $themeByNum;
}

function GeneratePassword() {
    // skip the L's since they look like 1's!
    $wordlist = array("apple", "array", "book",
    "bold", "catalog", "cook", "door", "down",
    "echo", "eat", "flag", "funny", "garage",
    "going", "house", "heavy", "inside",
    "icecream", "jump", "jack", "kludge", "keep",
    "merry", "making", "need", "next", "other",
    "open", "perfect", "place", "quite", "quick",
    "rest", "read", "taking", "tophat", "under",
    "upside", "video", "vanish", "wane", "wipe");
    $firstword = $wordlist[rand(0,
        count($wordlist) - 1)];
    $secondword = $wordlist[rand(0,
        count($wordlist) - 1)];
    $number = rand(10,99);
    $newpass = $firstword.$number.$secondword;
    return $newpass;
}
// Important: Do not put any blank lines
// After the closing > in this file!
?>
```

If you're not careful when entering Listing 7-7, you could easily run into a problem that is a nightmare to track down. *Don't put any blank lines at the end of your* useraccess.php *file.* Make sure there are no newlines after the closing ?>. The reason for this is that when these blank lines are included they are sent to the browser as text. But this useraccess.php file gets processed during the HTML headers. If you send blank text lines, the browser gets very confused. Therefore, don't let any blank lines creep into this file!

Logging in with the checkAccess function

The checkAccess function is a multipurpose function that performs the following operations:

✦ Checks whether a user is already logged in

✦ Logs the user in if he or she isn't logged in already

✦ Uses the results of the login.html form if present for the login; otherwise, uses cookies so the user doesn't have to keep logging in

✦ Saves the user login information for the entire session (or long term if the user chose the Remember Me check box in the login form)

✦ Sends the user to the `loginfailed.html` page if the user provides incorrect login information

The goal behind this function is to allow you to put a call in to this function at the beginning of any private page, and PHP will take care of the rest. You can see how I did that earlier in this chapter in Listing 7-5, which is the `welcome.php` page.

The first thing this function does is look for the e-mail and password in the `$_POST` array. If the page that calls this function (`welcome.php`, for example) was arrived at via the `login.html` page, the `$_POST` array will contain the information the user typed into the form.

If the `$_POST` array doesn't have the e-mail and password information, this function checks the user's cookies for the information.

If an e-mail address and password are located (and if the user got here via the `login.html` page and did *not* check the Remember Me box), the e-mail address and password are saved in a *session cookie*. That way, if the user visits other protected pages without closing the Web browser, he or she doesn't have to go through the login process again. (How is this possible? More semicircular reasoning is required here: Because the e-mail address and password were saved to a session cookie, the next time this `checkAccess` function gets called, the cookies will be set, and the part that checks the cookies for e-mail and password information will work.)

Also if an e-mail address and password are located, the page verifies the information against the login table within MySQL. This gives the illusion of being logged into the system, when, in fact, each time the user accesses a private page, the system simply verifies that the user is allowed to see the page. There is no "logging in" taking place, even though the user feels like there is.

If the login cannot be verified, or if no e-mail address and password are present, the code sends the user to the `loginfailed.html` page, by setting a header as follows:

```
header("location: loginfailed.html");
```

Because you're calling a header function, you can only use this `checkAccess` function at the beginning of a `.php` file, before the initial `<html>` tag and before calling any PHP `print` or `echo` statements. You can see that I followed this rule in the `welcome.php` page earlier in Listing 7-5.

Dealing with encryption troubles

I tested the sample system in this chapter on a Windows XP system and a Linux system, both running Apache. And I found something bizarre: The `crypt` function behaved differently on each computer. As it turns out, this difference is related to how Apache was configured for each operating system.

The problem is that the `crypt` function has different ways of choosing which encryption technique to use. (The two most common encryption techniques are DES, which stands for Data Encryption Standard, and MD5, which stands for Message Digest version 5.)

Two factors are important here: how big you make the password field of your login table and how you handle password comparisons after the user types in the password. Both factors are related to what type of encryption is used.

Here's a test program you can use to find out which encryption technique you're using:

```php
<?php
    print crypt("test");
    print "\n";
?>
```

Follow these steps to find your encryption technique:

1. **Save this file as** `crypttest.php` **and run it several times at the prompt on your Web server using** `php crypttest.php`.

If you see the same output each time you run it, your system is using DES encryption. If you see a different output each time, your system is using MD5 encryption. (It's not that MD5 encrypts differently each time; rather with MD5, the PHP system randomly generates a *salt* each time. Different salts cause the MD5 algorithm to behave differently, resulting in a different encryption.)

2. **Next, look at the output and count the number of characters in the random string.**

This is how long you need to make the `password` column of your `login` table.

3. **If the output from the little test program showed the same value each time, then use this line to encrypt your passwords:**

```php
$passcrypt = crypt($password);
```

4. **If the output from the little test program showed different values each time, then use this line to encrypt your passwords, which extracts the salt that was used when the user registered, and forces the MD5 algorithm to use that same salt.**

```php
$passcrypt = crypt($password,
        substr($pass, 0, 12));
$passcrypt = crypt($password,
        substr($pass, 0, 12));
```

Finally, if the user came to this page via the `login.html` page, and that user checked the Remember Me box, the e-mail address and password are saved in a long-term cookie. The expiration date is set to Unix date 2000000000, which corresponds to sometime on May 17, 2033, less than 30 years from the publication of this book. (If you're reading this on May 18, 2033, too bad — although for me, it would be cool if this book were still going strong after 30 years.)

Now here are some final points about the cookies. If you save the long-term cookie, you may realize that the cookie will get rewritten the next time the user logs in. This is not a problem for a couple reasons:

✦ If it's the same user logging in, the cookie's expiration date will not change because the data in the cookie doesn't change.

✦ If a different user logs in, that user's information is saved as a session cookie (not long term unless the user checks the Remember Me box), and that new cookie information overwrites the previous cookie. In other words, everything works out as you want it to.

In addition to using cookies, PHP includes a sophisticated mechanism for handling *sessions*. This mechanism keeps track of user information during a single browser session using cookies and other devices, much like I do in these examples. If you want to explore the PHP session-handling mechanism, check out `www.php.net/session`.

Signing up with the signup function

The `signup` function is simple. It doesn't do any checking; it just enters the user information into the login table.

This function takes an unencrypted password as a parameter and encrypts the password before saving it to the database. You want to make sure, however, that you use the correct encryption approach for your particular PHP installation. Take a look at the sidebar, "Dealing with encryption troubles" for more information on this.

Obtaining theme info

The `useraccess.php` file (refer to Listing 7-7) contains three items dealing with themes:

✦ The `ThemeInfo` class
✦ The `getTheme` function
✦ The `getThemeNames` function

The `ThemeInfo` class for now has only one member, `$bgcolor`. For this example, I could just use a background color and not bother creating a `ThemeInfo` class. However, I want to provide you with a starting point whereby you can add additional theme information beyond just a background color. Thus, I create the `ThemeInfo` class.

The getTheme function takes a themeID, which is just a number, and looks up the theme information, filling in the ThemeInfo class. To do so, the code uses MySQL and looks in the usertheme table. The idea is that when a user logs in, the checkAccess function obtains the themeID stored for that user in the login table. The checkAccess function doesn't look up all the theme information at that point; instead, it just returns a theme number. Then, later, a .php file can call getTheme, pass this theme number, and obtain a ThemeInfo structure filled with the theme information. (If you prefer, you could have the checkAccess function fill in the ThemeInfo object and return it instead of a theme number. The choice is yours.)

The GetThemeNames function (used by the register.php file) grabs all the theme names and numbers from the usertheme table and fills them into an array. It then returns the array. The register.php file uses this to populate a drop-down list box so the user can pick a theme by name rather than number, which would be pretty meaningless to the user.

Generating a new password with the GeneratePassword function

The GeneratePassword function is fun. The idea is that when a user forgets a password, this function generates a new one for the user. However, we all have had experience with automatically generated passwords like "89gq35jhpw," which are difficult to remember. So instead, the GeneratePassword function uses a popular approach of generating a password by picking two words from a word list and then putting them together with a two-digit number in between them. Because this list has 42 words, and there are 90 possible two-digit numbers, this list can generate 158,760 different passwords.

It's true that if somebody is determined, that person could write a program that would go through all the possibilities and break into your system. For online systems that deal with newsletters and such, this isn't a huge cause for concern. But with systems that deal in e-commerce, 158,760 password combinations does not provide adequate security.

However, the real idea is that in an actual system, the user obtains this generated password simply for the purpose of getting into the system the first time. After that, the user can change the password to something else.

The GeneratePassword function is used by the genpass.php file, which is called from the form in the newpassword.html file. I discuss these two files in the next section, "Helping Users Who Forgot Their Passwords."

Improvements to the useraccess.php file

To keep these examples simple, the last-access field is updated only when the user logs in. However, you may want to add some PHP code that updates the lastaccess field in the checkAccess() function, which I describe in the section, "Coding the Access Routines in a Single .php File," earlier in this chapter. That way you can easily keep track of when the user last logged in. You may want to display this information after a user is logged in as a check for the user. If the user says, "Hey! I didn't log in that day!" he or she can promptly change his or her password (which I show you how to do in the section, "Helping Users Who Forgot Their Passwords").

Helping Users Who Forgot Their Passwords

People have different ideas on how to handle a lost password. Do you e-mail the user the original password or generate a new one? The problem with e-mailing the user the original password is that if you're storing the passwords using one-way encryption (as in the samples in this chapter), you can't retrieve the original password even if you wanted to.

Some users prefer that you just e-mail them their passwords, and lots of systems do this without any problem. Other people believe this is a security risk because it requires that you store your passwords in the database.

It's up to you to decide whether you want to encrypt a password. In this section, I show you a page that the user can fill out to request a new password. The form, shown in Figure 7-4, allows the user to type in the e-mail address to which the new password should be sent.

Listing 7-8 is the newpassword.html file for the form. This file contains an HTML form that gets the user's e-mail address and sends it to the genpass.php file.

Listing 7-8: A File That Contains a Form the User Can Fill Out to Request a New Password

```
<html><head><title>New Password</title></head>
<body bgcolor="#FFFFFF" text="#000000">
<h2>New Password Request</h2>
<p>Forgot your password? I'm here to help! Since the
    passwords are encrypted, I'm unable to figure out
    what your old password was, so instead I'll assign
    you a new password and email it to you. Please fill
    out the form below and click the button and a new
```

```
    password will be on its way! </p>
<form name="form1" method="post" action="genpass.php">
    Email address:
        <input type="text" name="email"><p>
        <input type="submit" name="Submit"
            value="Send me one!">
</form>
</body>
</html>
```

**Book VI
Chapter 7**

Creating a
Username System
for Your Web Site

Figure 7-4:
Users fill out
this form if
they forgot
their
passwords.

The `genpass.php` file, shown in Listing 7-9, does the work by first checking whether the e-mail address is in the system. If it is, the code calls the `GeneratePassword` function in the `useraccess.php` file, updates the login table with an encrypted form of the password, and then e-mails the new password to the user. To e-mail the password, the mail function takes an e-mail address as the first parameter, a subject as the second parameter, and the e-mail body as the third parameter.

The process I'm describing here is a reasonably secure approach because you can assume that only the user has access to his or her own e-mail.

Listing 7-9: A File That Generates a New Password and E-mails It to the User

```
<html><head><title>New Password</title></head>
<body bgcolor="#FFFFFF" text="#000000">
<h2>New Password Request</h2>
<?php
    require "useraccess.php";
```

```
$email = $_POST['email'];
mysql_connect("localhost", "phpuser", "phppass");
$result = mysql_query(
    "select *  from phpbase.login where ".
    "email = '$email'" //watch the quotes!
);
$found = false;
if ($result) {
    if (mysql_num_rows($result) > 0) {
        $found = true;
    }
}

if (!$found) {
    print "Sorry, that email address is not in";
    print "our records.<p>";
    print '<a href="newpassword.html">Click here'.
        '</a> to try again!';
}
else {
    // Generate a new password
    $newpass = GeneratePassword();
    $newpasscrypt = crypt($newpass);

    $result = mysql_query(
        "update phpbase.login ".
        "set password = '$newpasscrypt' ".
        "where ".
        "email = '$email'" //watch the quotes!
    );

    mail($email, "Password request",
        "Your new password is\n".
        "$newpass\n".
        "Please remember it.");

    print "A new password has been mailed to ";
    print "you! Please check your email!<p>";
    print '<a href="login.html">Click here'.
        '</a> to log in!';
}
    mysql_close();

?>
</body></html>
```

Improvements to the password system

The password system I present in this chapter is a good starting point. However, if you want to improve the system, here are some ideas. First, you probably want to add a form whereby the user can change his or her password. The form should include at a minimum these four fields: the e-mail address, the old password, the new password, and the new password typed a second time. Within these fields, you want to include some JavaScript that ensures that the two new passwords match to help avoid typos. The form passes these four items to a `.php` file that checks whether the old password is correct for the e-mail address. If so, the code encrypts the new password and saves it in the login table. That's pretty easy.

In the case of e-mailing the user a forgotten password, the user may get pretty annoyed if somebody typed his or her name into the form in the `newpassword.html` file and clicked send just as a means of harassment. Then the unsuspecting user would suddenly get an e-mail announcing that his or her password has changed, and here it is. The user may also be concerned that the e-mail is a fake.

A better approach is to send the user an e-mail saying something like, "We received a request from you (or somebody else) for a new password. If this is not correct, please ignore this e-mail. If it is, click this link to obtain your new password."

The link should include some sort of random security code generated at the time the original form was filled out. The user then clicks the link, which is a PHP file that does the same work shown in Listing 7-9.

Chapter 8: Ten Ways to Enhance a Web Site with Databases

In This Chapter

✔ Programming an online user poll

✔ Adding a hit counter

✔ Performing advanced queries

✔ Creating databases that support transactions

✔ Building a forum or message board

✔ Creating a journal or daily note

✔ Building a distributed database

✔ Tracking usage information

In this final chapter in the MySQL minibook, I give you some suggestions on ways you can use MySQL to make a great Web site.

Programming an Online User Poll

I like to put polls on my site that allow visitors to vote on various things. For some time, I've been running a poll asking people what C++ compiler they use.

I didn't write the poll myself because I wanted to get it up immediately when I launched my site and didn't have time to write one. However, I now realize that writing a poll isn't that complex.

Here's what you need to do to write a poll:

✦ Create a Web form whereby users can choose their answers to the poll.

✦ Create a PHP page that updates the results in a MySQL table.

✦ Write a PHP (or Perl or any other) program that reads the data in the results table and writes out an HTML page showing the results of the poll. If you're using PHP, I recommend taking a look at Book V, Chapter 8, to discover ways that you can present data in the form of a bar graph.

Adding a Hit Counter

Many Web pages include a hit counter, which is simply a little box at the bottom of the page that shows how many people have accessed the page since the hit counter was created.

Services exist that provide hit counters (some for free, some not). But you can use MySQL to create your own hit counter. Here's how:

✦ Create a table that includes, for example, a page name and a hit count.

✦ Write PHP code that makes calls to MySQL to increment the value stored in the hit count for that page. (You would use the SQL update statement for this.)

You have the option of making the hit counter private or displaying it on your page for users to see. If you're using PHP, you can print the value as plain text, or you can create an image using the PHP graphics functions and write the number on the image.

If you're interested in noting page hits in the hopes of selling ads on your Web page, you may not want to write your own hit counter. Because you made the data, all you have to do is change the value in the table to 1,000,000 and claim you had 1 million hits since you created the page six hours ago. People buying ads don't fall for this. If you're trying to sell ads or perform some other financial venture that requires that you prove how many people have visited your page, don't write your own hit counter. Pay for one of the premium third-party hit counter services because advertisers and others will trust their data.

Performing Advanced Queries

In Book VI, Chapter 5, I show you how to perform complex queries using a join. You can also modify your queries by using two other useful SQL features:

✦ The like keyword and % wildcard character

✦ The order by statement for sorting results

Here's an example of a select statement that uses both features:

```
select * from customers
where e-mail like '%hotmail.com'
order by name;
```

Order, order in the table!

Question: How can I retrieve the data in my table in the order it's stored in? Answer: You can't. MySQL may give you back the data in the order it's stored in (or it may not), but by the SQL standards, MySQL is under no obligation to do so. The reason is that tables do not have a specific order to them, and the database system can store the rows in whatever order it sees fit. When you retrieve data from a `select` statement and get back multiple rows, the SQL standard makes no guarantees or promises on what order the data is in. Instead, if you need a particular order, add the `order by` clause to your `select` statement.

This retrieves all the data from the `customers` table where the e-mail address ends with the string `hotmail.com`. In that way, you can find everybody in your table who has an e-mail address at a particular domain, which in this case is `hotmail.com`. Notice that I use the word `like`, and inside the string, I put a % character, which is a wildcard, accepting any number of characters. Thus, `me@hotmail.com` matches the `%hotmail.com` pattern.

The `order by` clause takes the resulting records and sorts them by the `name` field. Thus, you can get all the records in a particular order.

If your web site is going to do a lot of order-by processing, I recommend that you create an index on the field that you're ordering by. That way, MySQL won't have to work as hard on its sorting.

Creating Databases That Support Transactions

If you're a database guru, you know what *transactions* are. Basically, a transaction is a series of SQL commands that you perform on a database. When you finish all these SQL commands, you have the option of either *committing* the data, which means making the changes permanent, or *rolling back* the data, which means undoing the batch of SQL commands, returning the table to its previous state. This is useful during error situations or if you're doing large batches of changes that you want to have take effect only after you're done entering them all in.

Using the default data formats, MySQL is unable to perform transactions. By default, MySQL stores individual tables in a format called MyISAM. This file format is a tried-and-tested variation of a popular database format called ISAM, which stands for Indexed Sequential Access Method. The MyISAM format does *not* support transactions. Two other MySQL-supported formats do not support transactions. They are ISAM, which is an older version of MyISAM and one that may not be present when MySQL version 5.0 ships; and HEAP, which is a highly optimized form stored strictly in memory (and not on the hard drive) that's useful for temporary data.

However, MySQL supports other formats that *do* allow for transactions. You are also free to mix table types within a single database. These transaction-supporting formats are InnoDB and BerekelyDB:

✦ **InnoDB** is a separate product from MySQL, which was built primarily to work along with MySQL. You can find out more about InnoDB, a free (GNU Public License) and extremely powerful database system at `www.innodb.com` and at `www.mysql.com/doc/en/InnoDB.html`.

✦ **Berkeley DB** (BDB for short) is also a separate database engine, but was built specifically for MySQL by Sleepycat Software. BDB is free and has its own licensing program. You can find out more about BDB at `www.sleepycat.com` and in the MySQL documentation at `www.mysql.com/doc/en/BDB.html`.

Building a Forum or Message Board

Many Web sites these days include special forum areas. In years past, you either had to hope that your Web host had a forum or had to provide a link to a third-party forum site.

Although linking to a third-party forum site is still a good idea if you're anticipating heavy forum usage, you can also store your own forums in your MySQL databases. (The forum messages themselves are stored as memo fields.)

Here are some things you can include in your forum:

✦ Forms for filling out the messages.

✦ `.php` files that sort the messages by thread and print them in fancy ways.

✦ The ability for users to enter special symbols like smilies. You can save the smilies as their actual text as in :-) and then parse through the messages to display them, replacing the text :-) with an `<img>` HTML tag pointing to a graphics file containing the smiley picture.

✦ A username and password system.

If you want to see a good example of a forum written in MySQL with Perl, running on Apache, take a look at the SlashDot site, `http://www.slashdot.org`. You can read about their code (which is open source and freely available) at `http://slashcode.com/faq.shtml#Slashcodecom0`.

Creating a Journal or Daily Note

You may want to keep a journal on your site for everyone to read. Or you may want to periodically upload a new file and have the text in the file appear on the main page of your site.

Using MySQL, you can enter these journal notes into a form (guarded by HTTP authentication so only you can access it) and store the notes in a column of type `memo`. (Or, if you prefer, you can save the notes to a file instead of a table.)

Then you can write a PHP or Perl program that gathers the notes and posts them all in the form of a journal, or posts only the most recent in the form of a daily note.

With PHP, you can embed the note in an existing page (like the main `index.html` page); this way, you can add updated notes on your page without having to modify the `index.html` page every time.

Adding an Administrator-Only Section

Most likely, you will want to restrict access to various tables or even databases so that only you can access them. To do so, you can create an administrator-only section of your site, which contains pages that only you have access to.

To protect these pages, you can either use a username and password encoded in a MySQL table or use HTTP authentication. The username-and-password method is handy if you want to allow multiple people to access the administrator sections. You can even include access levels, which provide people with different levels of access across pages. Each page may have an access level code in its PHP code; the user table in a MySQL database would then need to contain an access level column.

Building a Distributed Database

MySQL is surprisingly powerful and allows you to connect to multiple databases simultaneously, thereby creating a *distributed database*. If you write Perl or PHP code, you can specify a database server to connect to. (Remember, in the connecting string, you usually typed `localhost`, but you can alternatively specify a server such as `www.somedomain.com`.) Often, you just use `localhost`. However, you can also connect to remote servers by using their domain names in place of `localhost`.

To connect to a remote server, make sure that the server running the PHP or Perl installation has access to the remote database server.

From there, you can even connect to other servers simultaneously, and do some queries on one server and send the data to other servers. If you're doing distributed systems programming, what I'm saying here will probably turn on some light bulbs for you and give you some cool ideas.

Tracking Scores for Games

If you write computer games, a nice feature to add to your Web site is a place where registered users can enter their high scores.

Here are some tips for creating this feature:

+ In the form for entering the data, users should enter their user ID or registration code; this ensures that you get registered users only.

+ Users can upload a data file created by your game containing high scores. Then you can use Perl or Tcl to extract the score from the data file.

These simple ideas should help validate the information that users provide. Although savvy users may be able to hack into the file and fake their scores, most people won't be able to. Then you can be assured that the people are entering in their actual high scores.

Tracking Usage Information

You can find what connections have been made to your server if you're using PHP and you look at the $_SERVER global array. From here, you can extract information and store it in a MySQL database, allowing you to track complex usage information.

Here's a short PHP program that dumps out everything in the $_SERVER array:

```
<html><head><title>Who are you?</title><head>
<body>
<?php
    print "<hr>";
    foreach ($_SERVER as $key=>$value) {
        print "$key: $value<br>\n";
    }
?>
```

When I run this program on my system, one item of interest is the array value whose key is REMOTE_ADDR. This tells you the IP address of the computer that connected to your Web server. That way you know who has been connecting to your computer, and at least you know their IP address.

Book VII

Processing Web Files with Regular Expressions

The 5th Wave   By Rich Tennant

"I'LL BE WITH YOU AS SOON AS I EXECUTE A FEW MORE COMMANDS."

Contents at a Glance

Chapter 1: Why Use Regular Expressions?

In This Chapter

✔ Introducing regular expressions

✔ Matching single characters

✔ Matching multiple characters

✔ Trying out regular expressions in Tcl

✔ Trying out regular expressions in PHP

Since the beginning of modern computers, a few topics have emerged that have had a certain mystique about them. These are topics that most computer folks have heard of but don't actually explore; later, when asked during a job interview if they're familiar with these topics, these same people are often forced to lie and say, "Yes."

Compiler design — and the tools that accompany it (things called parsers and lexers, for example) — is an example of such a black box topic. For a while, the C++ programming language was the same way, but these days loads of people know it.

Another such topic is *regular expressions,* which is the subject of this and the next several chapters. A *regular expression* is a pattern that you can compare strings against. In the sections that follow, I explain what regular expressions are and why you would use them.

Getting to Know Regular Expressions

Because you're studying Apache, PHP, Perl, MySQL, and all that good stuff (by reading this very book), chances are high you've worked at the command-line a good bit.

If you're familiar with old DOS, you may have seen something like this:

```
dir *.*
```

or maybe this:

```
dir *.ex?
```

And if you're familiar with Unix or Linux, you've probably seen this:

```
ls *.php
```

or maybe this:

```
ls *.ph?
```

If you haven't seen any of these, don't worry. Instead, if you've ever opened a file on a Windows computer, you've probably seen a dialog box similar to Figure 7-1.

Figure 7-1:
The Open dialog box in Windows uses the * symbol in its file types.

If you're familiar only with the Mac, you may not have encountered pattern matching like this. But continue reading, and you'll get the idea of what I'm talking about here.

The notation `*.doc` (regardless of your operating system) means all files that end with the characters `.doc`. That is, the * means any set of characters. I won't list them all here (that would fill at least a few pages), but you can see that `document1.doc`, `LetterToThePresident.doc`, and `HappyResignation.doc` all match `*.doc`.

The sequence `*.doc` is an example of a *pattern*. The * character is called a *wildcard* character. Although the * character means something different in the world of regular expressions, this idea of *pattern matching* is what the topic of regular expressions is all about.

In the world of filenames, although the * character matches any number of any characters, the ? character matches only one character. Thus, the following are examples of filenames that match `*.ph?`:

✦ `myfile.php`

✦ `another.phd`

Because the ? can match only a single character, here are examples that don't match:

✦ `myfile.phood`

✦ `myfile.phun`

✦ `myfile.phrivolous`

However, the pattern `*.ph*` *would* match the three files I just listed.

If you're on a Windows computer and at the command prompt, you may get a surprise if you create a file called `myfile.phrivolous` and then type the following statement:

`dir *.ph?`

Book VII
Chapter 1

The filename `myfile.phrivolous` appears in the list. Why does that happen? It's a long story (and no, the ? doesn't match multiple characters on Windows), but suffice to say that every file in the Windows operating system has an *alternate filename* consisting of up to eight characters followed by a dot, followed by exactly three characters. (This is called an 8.3 filename.) The filename `myfile.phrivolous` will have an alternate 8.3 filename of something like `MYFILE~1.PHR`. When you do a directory listing, Windows checks the wildcard pattern against both the regular long file name and the old 8.3 filename. But don't worry; this has nothing to do with regular expressions, and you don't need to concern yourself with it. Call it an archeological oddity. I won't say anything else about it (other than that I think it's annoying and there was little reason for old DOS computers to *ever* have 8.3 filenames, and why we should have to still live with the remnants is beyond me).

And so, you can see that you've been dealing with a form of regular expressions for some time. Here's a good starting definition:

> A regular expression is a pattern to which you can compare other strings.

Of course, you can do a whole lot more with regular expressions than check whether a string matches a pattern, which you'll see over the course of the next 70 or so pages. (For example, you can search for all substrings that match a particular pattern, and you can replace them with something else if you want.) But at the heart of the matter, that's what regular expressions are all about: pattern matching.

A quick example

Here's an example of where regular expressions can come into play, and this will give you a taste of what a regular expression is.

Today, I pulled a list of words from one of my Web sites in progress. This list was in the form of option values in a drop-down combo box for an HTML form. Here's an example of a line from the list:

```
<option value="MyPage">My Page</option>
```

The list of items kept getting longer and longer as I worked on the page. I finally decided that these items belonged in a MySQL database. Many of us programming nerds have encountered the situation where we have a text file filled with data of a certain format, and we want to quickly do a bunch of editing on the document and change the lines to a different format. In my case, I wanted to transform the preceding line into this line:

```
insert into mytable (name) values ('My Page');
```

This is, of course, an SQL statement. I was going to change the file containing HTML option values into an .sql file that I could pull into MySQL and populate a table.

Oh, what to do, what to do? Thanks to my flying fingers and many years of piano playing, I've mastered the ability to press cursor keys, Shift keys, Backspace keys, Home keys, and Delete keys at an almost alarming rate. I can do this. I know I can.

But why bother editing this manually? The Great Gurus of Computers have presented us with an easier method: regular expressions. And, as it happens, the editor I was using supported regular expressions.

If you're on Unix, almost every editor supports regular expressions. If you're on Windows, such editors are becoming more common but are still rare. However, if you're going to master regular expressions, and you're using Windows, you'll want an editor that has great *regex* capabilities. (The word *regex* is what we often call regular expressions.) One great editor I've found for Windows is called Scintilla. Scintilla is really a library that provides an editor, and somebody wrote an entire program around Scintilla called SciTE, short for Scintilla Text Editor. You can find this gem at www.scintilla. org. And, of course, Windows versions of the old Unix classics such as emacs and vi are available. (You can find emacs at `http://www.gnu.org/software/emacs/emacs.html`. For vi, I would start with the vi FAQ at `http://www.faqs.org/faqs/editor-faq/vi/part1/`, which includes links for downloading.)

This particular day I was on my Windows machine, so I used the Scintilla editor. But I'll show you how to do the same thing in the vi editor, which is what I usually use on Unix.

Using the Windows-based editor, I opened the Search and Replace dialog box, shown in Figure 7-2. I made sure to select the Regular Expression check box. Without it, all would fail, and I'd be baffled why my carefully constructed regular expression didn't work.

For the Find What box, I carefully typed this seemingly cryptic set of characters:

```
<o.*>\(.*\)<.*$
```

For the Replace With box, I typed the following:

```
insert into mytable (name) values ('\1');
```

I clicked the Replace All button, and instantly, everything changed from the HTML `option value` format to the SQL `insert into` format! Like magic!

Book VII
Chapter 1

Why Use Regular
Expressions?

Figure 7-2:
Using
regular
expressions
in the
Search and
Replace
dialog box.

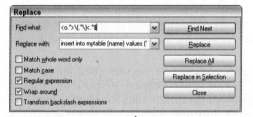

You may be thinking that instead of going through the trouble of figuring out the regular expression, it may have been easier to use brute force and manually edit the file. But that's not the case. After you're familiar with regular expressions, expressions like the preceding ones are easy to understand and come up with — really!

As for what all these cryptic letters and symbols mean, well, that's the point of this minibook. In the chapters that follow, you discover what the different pieces mean. For now, here's what you need to know: The stuff I typed in the Find What box extracts a string from each line and saves it in a variable of sorts called \1. This string is the name in the middle of the line; for example, the \1 string in the line `<option value="MyPage">My Page</option>` would be `My Page`. In the Replace With box, I use that \1 variable; you can see the \1 in it. Thus, the line containing `My Page` will become `insert into mytable (name) values ('My Page');`.

If you're a little familiar with regular expressions, you may want to know more about the cryptic expression used earlier. The first part — `<o.*>` — searches for the initial option tag. Here's a closer look:

✦ The `<o` represents the start of the option tag.

✦ The `.*` means any number of any characters.

✦ The `">` is the closing part of the tag.

Continuing with the technical stuff, the last part — `<.*$` — finds the closing `</option>` tag. In this part, the expression starts with the final `<` and goes to the end of the line. Here's a breakdown:

✦ The `<` represents the final `<`.

✦ `$` means the end of the line.

✦ The middle part — `\(.*\)` — grabs everything in between and saves it in a variable that you can access in the replace string as \1. The reason everything gets saved is thanks to the parentheses. (However, some editors, such as the one I'm using, require you to put backslashes before each parenthesis.)

Now I want to show you how you can do this same thing in the ancient but beloved vi editor. (Please don't tell anybody I use it. I have a reputation to uphold.) This technique will work in other Unix editors as well, because they tend to use this same format. The only difference is that for those editors, you will type a different set of keystrokes to get to the search and replace feature. (Check your docs for the route to the land of Search and Replace if you're not sure.)

Here's the command for the vi editor:

```
:g/<o.*>\(.*\)<.*$/s//insert into mytable (name) values ('\1');/g
```

Again, if you're somewhat familiar with regular expressions and want to try out this command, here are the parts in the vi string:

✦ The : is what you type to get to command mode.

✦ The g/ means global replace.

✦ The search string follows.

✦ The s// means replace with what follows.

✦ The /g at the end signifies the end of the global replacement, which in my mind is a bit redundant, but required nevertheless.

Practicing with regular expressions

Most (better) languages include direct support for regular expressions or, at the very least, optional libraries that provide regex support.

Perl, Tcl, and PHP, which I discuss in this book, all have excellent regular expression support:

✦ Perl's support for regular expressions is so complete in terms of features that it has become a standard for regular expressions.

✦ PHP supports the same kind of regular expressions Perl does through a set of Perl-compatible regular expression functions. PHP also supports another kind called Posix regular expressions, which I ignore in this book because I find them highly inferior and, these days, nonstandard.

✦ Tcl has great support for Perl regular expressions and full support for Posix, although Tcl has its own specialized regex engine that is about the most powerful (and fastest) around. The regex gurus of the world are, in fact, trying to get the developers of the other languages to follow suit with the Tcl engine. (However, as you'll see in the examples throughout this minibook, the Tcl engine has some of its own features that are nonstandard, and the engine isn't always compatible with the de facto standard of Perl regular expressions.)

Other languages that include support for regular expressions are Python (as a standard module), JavaScript (regular expressions are built in), and even the newer Microsoft languages VB.NET and C#. One notable (and unfortunate) exception is C++. To this day, I don't understand why the standard C++ library doesn't have support for regular expressions. However, if you're a C++ programmer and want to use regular expressions, you can download the PCRE library (Perl Compatible Regular Expressions library), which has become the standard regular expressions library. You can find out more about it at www.pcre.org.

**Book VII
Chapter 1**

**Why Use Regular
Expressions?**

If you want to practice using regular expressions, what do you do? Here are some of the options I use:

✦ I write a small Perl or PHP program. (You can use any language that supports regex, of course.)

✦ I run Tcl's command-line utility, tclsh. This is one of the easiest ways to quickly test a regular expression.

✦ I run Perl in command-line mode. I start Perl, type Perl commands in at the prompt, and when finished, I press Ctrl+D, which signifies the end of the file.

Note, however, that this is not a command-line interpreter. Instead, I'm actually typing in the lines of a Perl program. I can't go back and edit the lines, meaning I have to be careful to type everything correctly the first time. As you can imagine, this method is for very short, maybe two-line Perl programs.

✦ I start the Python command-line interpreter. Although this book isn't about Python, you may want to take a look at it at www.python.org. From there, I can try things out on the fly without having to write a test program.

A quick note to the Python users reading this: Use raw strings when entering your regexes, by putting an r before the opening quotes, as in r"expression". That way \t, for example, will remain as a backslash followed by a t and won't get converted to a tab character. See my Python Regular Expressions page at www.jeffcogswell.com/python/regex.html for more information.

✦ I try out a quick regular expression using one of the text editors I mention at the beginning of this chapter.

✦ I use my own invention, The Amazing Regex Tester, which tests a regular expression in several languages (JavaScript, PHP, Perl, and Tcl). This is a Web form where you type in a regular expression and a string, and a PHP program tests the regular expression and then calls into both Perl and Tcl (as CGI scripts) to test the regular expression. It's pretty handy; you can find it at www.jeffcogswell.com/regex.html.

In the following section, "Matching any character," I explain how to test a regular expression, and I show you how to do this in Perl, PHP, and Tcl.

I use Perl to demonstrate most of the examples in this chapter simply because Perl's flavor of regular expressions has become an industry standard of sorts. Although the syntax to these examples is specific to Perl, the regular expressions are not specific to Perl. All these concepts apply to all the languages that support Perl-style regular expressions. Further, in many cases in this chapter and throughout this minibook, I offer examples in other languages as well. Tcl, for instance, has become a favorite of mine for quickly testing out a regular expression.

Matching any character

When working with regular expressions, temporarily forget what you know about filename patterns. (I say "temporarily" because I assume you'll be working with filenames at some point in the future away from this book.) The characters * and ? do not mean the same thing in regular expressions as they do in filenames.

Here's a regular expression that matches a single character:

.

In case you can't see that, it's just a single dot, or period. The period matches any single character.

Here's a simple Perl program to get you started with this basic regular expression:

```
print "Testing 'a' against /./ \n";
if ("a" =~ /./) {
    print "It matches!\n";
}
```

The first line prints out a message. The second line compares the string "a" against a regular expression. In Perl, the regular expression goes inside forward slashes. In Perl, you can do a regex comparison with the =~ operator. This is just like any other comparison operator in that it returns either true or false. (Regular expressions are such an important part of Perl that the designers of the language have devoted a syntax to regular expression, including the forward slashes and the =~ comparison operator.)

When you run the preceding code, you see this output:

```
Testing 'a' against /./
It matches!
```

Here's another example:

```
print "Testing 'b' against /b/ \n";
if ("b" =~ /b/) {
    print "It matches!\n";
}
```

This regular expression, b, just means find the letter b. Whereas the dot character matches any character, the b pattern matches only the letter b.

(And the a pattern matches only the letter a, the q pattern matches only the letter q, and so on.)

Thus, the preceding print statement prints It matches! because "b" =~ /b/ evaluates to true.

Now try this example:

```
print "Testing 'a' against /b/ \n";
if ("a" =~ /b/) {
    print "It matches!\n";
}
```

In this case, the output is as follows:

```
Testing 'a' against /b/
```

This output does not include It matches! because the comparison failed. The string "a" does not match the regular expression /b/.

Incidentally, if you want to test for a match that fails, use the "doesn't match" operator, !~, like so:

```
print "Testing 'a' against /b/ \n";
if ("a" !~ /b/) {
    print "It doesn't match!\n";
}
```

This prints It doesn't match! because "a" doesn't match the pattern b. (Think of ~= as being analogous to "equal", and !~ as being analogous to "not equal." In Perl and many other languages, the syntax makes sense, because equal is == [two equal signs], and not equal is !=.)

Here's another example:

```
print "Testing 'abc' against /b/ \n";
if ("abc" =~ /b/) {
    print "It matches!\n";
}
```

This comparison also evaluates to true, so the code prints It matches!. The regular expression engine doesn't care if there are characters to the left of the matching string (in this case, an a) or to the right of the matching string (in this case, a c). Because the engine found something inside the string that matches the pattern (the b), the engine returns true. Thus, you can be assured that abc matches b.

Finally, here's one you can try for yourself: What happens if you test abc against . (dot)? It will match. Try it and see.

To summarize, here are the rules so far:

✦ The . (dot) character is a wildcard character and will match any single character.

✦ If you want to match a specific character, simply specify that character (unless that character is a special character, which I discuss in Book VII, Chapter 2).

✦ The regex engine will search for the pattern anywhere within the string.

✦ If you're using Perl, you can use ~= to test if a string matches a pattern, and != to test if a string doesn't match a pattern.

What if you want to match the single dot character, and you don't want the dot to be a wildcard? In that case, put a backslash before the dot, like so:

```
print "Testing '.' against /\./ \n";
if ("." =~ /\./) {
    print "Yupperoos!\n";
}
```

Although you may need to perform some finger acrobatics to type this code, you can see that the regular expression inside the forward slashes is simply a backslash and then a dot. This will print the happy phrase Yupperoos!

Thus, here is another rule: To match against the actual dot character, precede the dot character with a backslash.

Matching multiple characters

The regular expression engine lets you put multiple characters in your pattern, not just a single character or a dot. Here's an example in Perl:

```
if ("abc" =~ /abc/) {
    print "Good job!\n";
}
```

You can probably see that this comparison will be true and the encouraging message Good job! will print out. The regular expression is simply abc, and you're testing that against the string abc, which matches.

If you read the preceding section, "Matching any character," you know that the engine doesn't care if you have characters before or after the matching section of the string. All the regex engine cares about is finding the pattern within your string. Take a look at this example:

```
if ("123abcdef" =~ /abc/) {
    print "Cool beans!\n";
}
```

Because the string 123abcdef contains the pattern abc, the test succeeds, and the enlightened message Cool beans! appears.

You can probably see that the following example will fail:

```
if ("123aaadef" =~ /abc/) {
    print "Wudduh yaknow!\n";
}
```

This will print nothing because the result of the comparison is false. The string 123aaadef does not match the pattern abc because the character string abc is nowhere to be found in 123aaadef, no matter how hard you look — and I looked for a very long time.

So far this is boring, wouldn't you say? How about something a little more interesting? Regular expressions can have wildcards, so consider this comparison:

```
if ("pup" =~ /p.p/) {
```

The pattern p.p will match the letter p, followed by any character, followed by another letter p. Thus, pup matches. And php will also match:

```
if ("php" =~ /p.p/) {
```

But phd will not:

```
if ("phd" =~ /p.p/) {
```

Although the first p matches the p in the pattern, and the h matches the dot in the pattern (because the dot is a wildcard), the d in the string does not match the p in the string, so the match fails.

Here's a goodie:

```
if ("The php language is great" =~ /php/) {
    print "It's so true!\n"
}
```

This, again, will match, because the pattern, php, can be found somewhere in the string; thus, the agreeable message It's so true! prints out.

Consider this comparison:

```
if ("The PHP language is great" =~ /php/) {
    print "Once again?\n"
}
```

This comparison will fail, and nothing will print. The reason is that the letters php are not in the string. Yes, the letters PHP are in the string, but regular expressions are, by default, case sensitive.

To summarize, here are some rules:

✦ You can have expressions containing several characters.

✦ Your expressions of several characters can contain the dot wildcard.

✦ By default, your expressions are case sensitive.

Trying Out Regexes in Tcl and PHP

Because most of the examples in this chapter use Perl, in this section I give you some tips on getting started with regular expressions in Tcl and PHP, the two other languages I cover in this book.

Regexing in tcl

Tcl's shell tool, `tclsh`, makes testing regular expressions incredibly easy. In fact, this is probably the easiest way to test a regular expression. However, remember that Tcl is only *mostly* Perl-compatible with its regex engine and completely Posix-compatible.

For example, start the `tclsh` engine. (I show you how to do this in Book IV, Chapter 1.) After you're inside the engine, type the following:

```
% regexp {abc} abc
```

(The % symbol is the prompt, and you don't type it.) Press Enter, and you see the following answer:

```
1
```

But if 1 is the answer, what is the question? (Life, the universe, and everything?) The question is whether the pattern abc (inside curly brackets { }) matches the string abc (at the end). The answer is true, which Tcl prints out as 1. Now try one that doesn't match:

```
% regexp {abc} def
```

The pattern abc doesn't match the string def, so the answer is as follows:

```
0
```

And, finally, try this one:

```
% regexp {p.p} php
```

Because the regular expression p.p matches php, this prints the value 1, for true.

Regexing in PHP

The PHP language uses the PCRE library for its regular expressions, making it essentially Perl-compatible. However, PHP doesn't have the =~ operator as Perl does for testing for a match. Instead, PHP has a function called preg_match, which takes two parameters, a pattern (stored as a string), and a string to compare the pattern with.

This function has an odd quirk: Your pattern must start and end with a slash delimiter *inside the string*, like so:

```
<?php
    if (preg_match("/ph./", "php is cool")) {
        print "It matches!\n";
    }
?>
```

The pattern in this program is ph.. The slashes inside the string "/ph./" are not part of the pattern. They are simply required; that's all. They don't do anything other than add some extra work in the form of keystrokes. Make sure that you include them; otherwise, you will get an error such as this:

```
Warning:  Delimiter must not be alphanumeric or backslash
```

The preg_match function thinks the p and the . in ph. are delimiters. So don't forget the real delimiters: / at the beginning and / at the end.

I'm almost inclined to say "Just like in Perl, you need to put slashes around the expression." But this isn't just like Perl. The Perl interpreter recognizes regular expressions when they are inside slashes. Here, the PHP interpreter doesn't recognize this as a regular expression because the PHP language doesn't have regex-specific syntax. This is just a string as far as the PHP interpreter is concerned. So why do you need two slashes? I have no idea. Just remember to put them in.

Chapter 2: Following the Syntax of Regular Expressions

In This Chapter
- ✔ Matching multiple characters with quantifiers
- ✔ Matching special characters
- ✔ Matching whitespace
- ✔ Using the delimiter characters as part of an expression
- ✔ Matching specific sets of characters

Do you remember when you first learned to ride a bike? Prior to riding one, you would look at the big kids in envy, that they could somehow balance themselves on just two tires, shooting along at speeds that reached the level of parental heart attacks.

Riding a bike seemed daunting, but after you finally learned how to do it, you discovered how easy it was, what a useful skill it was (nothing like being able to breeze over to the convenience store to get a peanut butter cup without your parents knowing), and how natural it was.

Regular expressions are the same way. Not too many years ago, I looked at regular expressions as something mysterious that I had little use for. Today, I wonder how I lived so long without them.

The syntax of regular expressions may seem daunting at first. But if you read this chapter carefully, you'll begin to see that they really are a natural way of describing patterns. In this chapter, I describe regular expression syntax, and I use Tcl for many of the examples simply because doing so is incredibly easy. Use Tcl wisely, my friend, and don't tell your mother if you sneak off to the 7-Eleven to get a peanut butter cup. What she doesn't know won't scare her.

A typical use of regular expressions

If you read Book VII, Chapter 1, you may still be wondering in what instances you would use regular expressions. Here are a few examples:

✔ You're reading text typed into an edit control on a Web form and want to make sure the text matches a certain format. An e-mail address is a good example of a format that you can use a regular expression for.

✔ You want to scan a file for a list of words that match a certain format and extract certain words. For example, you may want to create a list of functions in a PHP file. To do so, you can scan a file containing PHP code for the word *function* and, from there, grab the word following the word *function*. Accumulating these terms builds a list of functions.

True, you can do these same operations without regular expressions. For example, you can split up every line of a PHP file by whitespace and carefully compare each resulting word to the string `"function"`, and then take the next word. But using a regular expression to do this is easier and provides greater flexibility.

For an example of a regular expression that verifies e-mail addresses, check out Book VI, Chapter 4.

Matching Multiple Characters Using Quantifiers

The most basic way to use a pattern is to specify the characters you want to match. The regular expression a matches the character a. The regular expression B matches the character B. Suppose, however, that you want to match the letter d, and you want to allow multiple instances of it. For example, you may want to allow the strings cdr, cddr, and cdddr to all match, or any number of d's. (If you're a self-professed language nut like I am, you may recognize these as words from the LISP programming language. And yes, the LISP community makes it a rule that its programmers must know how to *pronounce* these words, cdr ("coulder"), cddr ("couldider"), and, well, I have no idea. But I'm not making this up.)

Here are a few handy rules for matching multiple characters:

✦ If you want to match one or more instances of a character, follow the character with a plus sign, +. The plus sign means *at least one.*

✦ If you want to match any number of instances of a character (or no instances at all), follow it with a star, *. The star symbol means *any number including zero,* or, as the computer people often say, *zero or more.*

✦ If you want to specify that a character is optional (that is, it can appear 0 or 1 times — either there, or not at all, but not repeated), follow the character with a question mark, ?.

✦ If you want to specify an exact number of times (or a range of exact numbers) that a character can appear, follow the character with the number in braces, as in {3}, or a range as in {2,5}, which means 2 to 5 times.

The plus symbol requires that you have at least one instance of the character. The star symbol allows you to have no instances of the character, or as many as you want. The plus and star symbols are both examples of *quantifiers*.

Consider the regular expression cd+r. The following four examples are in the Tcl Shell program, tclsh. The % sign is the prompt; I typed what was to the right of the %. The regular expression is inside curly braces (it's cd+r in these examples), and the word I'm testing against the regular expression follows. The result prints on the next line: 1 means it matches; 0 means it doesn't match. (All four examples match, which you can see because they're each followed by the output of 1.)

```
% regexp {cd+r} cdr
1
% regexp {cd+r} cddr
1
% regexp {cd+r} cdddr
1
% regexp {cd+r} cddddddddr
1
```

But the following example does *not* match because the + sign requires that you have at least one instance of the character:

```
% regexp {cd+r} cr
0
```

If you want the string cr to match (as well as the others, cdr, cddr, and so on), use the star character, *. The star means that you can have 0 or more matches; thus, all of the following examples match, including the final one, cr:

```
% regexp {cd*r} cdr
1
% regexp {cd*r} cddr
1
```

```
% regexp {cd*r} cdddr
1
% regexp {cd*r} cdddddddddr
1
% regexp {cd*r} cr
1
```

Here's a Perl example that demonstrates the use of braces for providing an exact number or range of numbers:

```
if ("aaabc" =~ /a{2,5}bc/) {
    print "...aaand we haaave a maaatch!\n";
}
```

This pattern says that you must have two, three, four, or five a characters in a row, followed by bc to match. Thus, the preceding string matches, and you see the drawn out message. But the following example will not result in a message:

```
if ("abc" =~ /a{2,5}bc/) {
    print "...aaand we haaave a maaatch!\n";
}
```

In this example, you have only one a, and the expression requires that 2 to 5 a's match. This expression also works in Tcl:

```
% regexp {a{2,5}bc} aaabc
1
%
```

Matching Special Characters

If you read Book VII, Chapter 1, you know that the dot (or what we used to call a period or decimal point) is a special character, and that to match the dot itself you must precede the dot with a backslash.

Here's an example in Perl:

```
if ("abc" =~ /a\.c/) {
    print "match!\n";
}
```

And here's the same example in Tcl:

```
% regexp {a\.c} abc
0
```

This match fails in both cases because the string abc does not match the pattern a\.c. The string a.c, however, does match the pattern. (Please note that I almost wrote, "*Only* the string a.c will match the pattern." However, that's not the case. Do you know why? Because the pattern 1234a.c5678, for example, will also match the pattern because 1234a.c5678 contains the substring a.c.)

In regular expressions, you have several special characters besides dots that you can match. Each special character uses a character that has special meaning just like the dot. In the sections that follow, I show you many characters that have special meaning, such as brackets [and], the caret ^, and the dollar sign $. If you ever need to match these characters and don't want to make use of their special meaning, put a backslash in front of the character, like so:

/a\[c/

This regular expression will match an a, followed by a bracket, [, followed by a c.

Here's a Perl example that will either print 1 for true (in the case of a match), or nothing for false (in the case of no match):

```
print "a[c" =~ /a\[c/;
```

This example prints a 1, meaning the string and regular expression match.

Here's a list of the standard special characters in regular expressions; each character has a special meaning that I describe in the following sections:

◆ . (dot) is a wildcard and means any character.

◆ $ matches the end of a line. I talk about why this character is important in Book VII, Chapter 3.

◆ ^ (caret) matches the beginning of the line. Again, I discuss this character in Book VII, Chapter 3. The caret also has meaning when placed inside brackets; see the section "Matching a specific set of characters" for details.

◆ [and] deal with matching a specific set of characters called *classes*. I talk about this in the section "Matching a specific set of characters."

◆ + and * specifies that the preceding character can be matched 1 or more times, or 0 or more times, respectively.

One minor annoyance of regular expressions is that some patterns have special meaning and, as such, use special characters such as [or $, or, as you have already seen, the dot character. To actually match these characters in a pattern, as explained earlier, you precede them with a backslash as in \[or \$, or \..

But other patterns are the reverse: To use these patterns that have special meaning, you use a backslash followed by a character. For example, if you just put an s in a regular expression, you will match the character s. But if you precede the s with a backslash as \s, you will match *whitespace*. (This is a rule I discuss in the next section, "Matching whitespace.") In other words, these are opposite rules: Sometimes a backslash gives you the actual character you want to match, and sometimes a backslash turns a plain old character into a pattern of special meaning. Be careful!

A couple paragraphs back I listed some characters that have special meaning and require backslashes if you want to use them as plain old characters. Here's the opposite — a list of some of the more common patterns that have special meaning when you *do* include a backslash. I talk about these patterns in the sections that follow.

✦ \s matches whitespace. Without the backslash, s matches the character s.

✦ \t matches a tab (as in most programming languages). Without the backslash, t simply matches the character t.

✦ \S matches anything that is not whitespace. Without the backslash, S matches the characters S.

✦ \d matches any digit, as in 0, 1, 2, 3, 4, 5, 6, 7, 8, and 9. Without the backslash, d matches the character d.

✦ \w matches a word. Without the backslash, w matches the character w.

Matching whitespace

What is whitespace? Although it sounds like a term out of astrophysics, whitespace is any combination of the space bar and the Tab key (even on pages that are blue or yellow). Every word in this sentence is separated by whitespace. When you write code, you typically indent your lines using whitespace, consisting of either a few space characters or a few tabs. (Or, in the case of many old code editors — and this is one of my pet peeves — you may get a *combination* of spaces and tabs. Yuck.)

How do you match whitespace? By using the whitespace character, \s. (This is one of the cases where you need the backslash to get the special meaning.) Consider the pattern abc\sdef. The string abc followed by a space followed by def matches this pattern. And so does the string abc followed by a tab, followed by def.

I want to show you a line of Perl code that demonstrates how to match whitespace. This is going to get a little ugly, though, because you'll recall that to put a tab in a string, you use \t. (Not *more* backslashes!) First, here's a basic example using a space:

```
print "abc def" =~ /abc\sdef/;
```

This prints 1 because the space matches the \s, or whitespace character.

Here's the ugly tab example I alluded to:

```
print "abc\tdef" =~ /abc\sdef/;
```

The string inside quotes is abc, followed by a tab, followed by def. This matches the pattern because the tab character matches the \s, or whitespace character.

Try the example with multiple spaces:

```
print "abc    def" =~ /abc\sdef/;
```

(That's several spaces — not a tab — between abc and def.) This does *not* match. The reason is that the \s pattern matches a single whitespace character, meaning a single space or a single tab. I have four spaces, so it doesn't match.

Usually when people want to match whitespace, they don't want to just match a single space or a single tab. Instead, they usually want to match any combination and any number of spaces and tabs, all collectively constituting *whitespace*. To match multiple spaces and tabs, add the + sign after the space, as in abc\s+def. This will match one or more whitespace characters, meaning any amount of space between the words. However, make sure that you use the + sign and not the * if you want *at least one* space character. Thus, all the following comparisons will yield a true in Perl:

✦ if ("abc\t def" =~ /abc\s+def/) {

✦ if ("abc   def" =~ /abc\s+def/) {

✦ if ("abc   def" =~ /abc\s+def/) {

The following Tcl examples, both of which print 1, represent yet another successful match for two lucky pairs.

```
% regexp {abc\s+def} "abc\t    \tdef"
```

and

```
% regexp {abc\s+def} abc\t\t\tdef
```

Note that for the first of these two Tcl examples I had to delimit the string with quotes so the tclsh program would know that the big space is part of the string. Without the quotes, the program thinks the stuff past the spaces is some other word and ignores it. With the second example, I have no whitespace, so Tcl knows that this is all one string.

TIP

You may want to match only a single space character or a single tab character. In these cases, you don't use the `\s` whitespace character because that will match either the space or tab.

To match a space character specifically, use a space in your regular expression, as in the following lines. First, here's a Perl example:

```
if ("Hi there" =~ /Hi there/) {
    print "I need space!\n";
}
```

And next is a Tcl example:

```
% regexp {Hi there} "Hi\tthere"
0
```

The first line matches and prints a 1. The second line doesn't match because a tab character doesn't match a space. Thus, the second line prints nothing.

Similarly, for a tab, put `\t` in your regular expression, as in `Hi\tthere`.

Matching digits and numbers

A common need in regular expressions is to match digits and numbers. If you want to match a single digit, use the `\d` expression. Here's a Tcl example:

```
% regexp {\d} 3
1
```

If you need to match a whole string of digits (that is, a number), use `\d+`. The + means "1 or more," so `\d+` means 1 or more digits. But what if you want an optional minus sign? Use a minus sign, followed by a question mark, `-?`. (The question mark means 0 or 1, meaning *optional*.) Thus, a regex for a whole number could be this:

```
-?\d+
```

In Perl, you may use this expression like so:

```
if ("-500" =~ /-?\d+/) {
    print "This is a whole
    number.\n";
}
```

But if you want to use this regular expression in Tcl, the - symbol is a special character, so you need to put a backslash in front of it. (Rules, rules, rules. . . .) Here's an example:

```
% regexp {\-?\d+} -100
1
```

Matching the delimiters

When you specify a regular expression in a particular language, you need to tell the language parser where your regular expression starts and where it finishes. To do this, you usually use delimiters. Here's a simple Perl sample:

```
if ($mystring =~ /abc/) {
```

The Perl processor knows that the regular expression is abc because of the presence of the two forward slashes, /.

Here's a sample in Tcl:

```
regexp {abc} abc
```

Here, the delimiters are { and }. The Tcl processor knows the regular expression starts at the { and ends at the }. But what if you want to use the delimiter inside a regular expression? Although some languages let you switch to a different set of delimiters, I prefer to use this rule:

> If you need to specify a regular expression delimiter in a regular expression, put a backslash before the delimiter.

As for switching to a different set of delimiters, I *usually* discourage that practice because it can make code more confusing. However, if you're writing a regular expression that uses lots of the delimiters in it, you may consider switching delimiters.

If you're a Tcl guru, you might see a problem with this: By using braces, { and }, you are preventing any variable substitution inside the regular expression. Therefore, if you want to substitute variables inside your regular expression, go ahead and use double quotes as your delimiter.

Book VII Chapter 2

Following the Syntax of Regular Expressions

Matching a specific set of characters

When you build a regular expression, if you put a character by itself (as in a or B, for example) you will match just that character. And if you want to match any character, you include a dot. But what if you want to match one of a certain set of characters?

Here's an example: Suppose you want to see if a string matches the pattern William or william. For the first character, you want to match the lowercase w or the uppercase W. To accomplish this, you can use a *character class* as in the following pattern:

```
[Ww]illiam
```

This pattern matches either a W or a w for the first character, and then a lowercase i, a lowercase l, and so on.

Here are a few Perl examples:

```
print "William" =~ /[Ww]illiam/;
print "william" =~ /[Ww]illiam/;
print "illiam" =~ /[Ww]illiam/;
```

The first two examples match because the first character can be either W or w. The third one, however, doesn't match because [Ww] means you must have either W or w, and illiam doesn't have either.

[Ww] will match only a single character. For example, suppose this is your pattern:

```
[Tt]homas\s[Jj]efferson
```

All the following strings match this pattern:

```
Thomas Jefferson
thomas jefferson
Thomas jefferson
thomas Jefferson
```

But the string thomas Jjefferson does *not* match the pattern because [Jj] matches only a single character. If you want to match any number of instances of w and W, use one of the usual quantifiers, like so:

```
print "Tttththomas JjjJJJjJJJjJJJefferson" =~
    /[Tt]+homas\s[Jj]+efferson/;
```

This stuttering mess matches. The [Tt] has a + after it, meaning you can use one or more instance of T or t (or any combination thereof). Similarly, [Jj] has a + after it, meaning any number and combination of J and j works, as long as you have at least one J or j. So for this bizarre pattern, the good old string Thomas Jefferson also matches.

Here are the rules for matching characters in a set:

✦ For a specific set of characters in a pattern, list the characters inside square brackets, as in [Ww]. But remember that this matches only a single W or a single w, not two characters.

✦ If you want multiple characters, follow the bracket with +, *, or any of the other quantifiers.

Matching every character except those in a set

If you have numerous characters you want to allow to match, and only a couple that you don't want to match, you can specify the *negation* of a character class. That just means you're saying, "Match all characters *except* these characters."

Look at this short regular expression:

```
[^abc]
```

Because this regular expression is surrounded by brackets, it's a set, or character class. If the caret ^ (or "hat") weren't present, this would mean "match either a, or b, or c and nothing more." But because the caret is there, it means "match anything *but* a or b or c."

Look at this Tcl example:

```
% regexp {[^abc]} x
1
```

The x matches [^abc] because x is not a, b, or c. But look at this example:

```
% regexp {[^abc]} a
0
```

This match fails because a does not match the expression. The expression is that of any character *other than* a, b, or c.

Specifying the caret character in a set

What if you have a character class and you want to include the caret in the set? For example, what if you want to match ^, !, @, a, b, and c? Then you put the caret inside the brackets with the other characters, but don't put it *first*. Thus, for the six characters I just mentioned, you can do this:

```
[!^@abc]
```

This regular expression will match a single character to any of !, ^, @, a, b, or c.

Here's a useful example. Suppose you want to find out if a string is a valid arithmetic expression of positive whole numbers, such as any of the following:

✦ 1 + 5 for addition

✦ 5 - 2 for subtraction

✦ 10 / 2 for division

✦ 5 * 5 for multiplication

✦ 2 ^ 3 for exponent or power

The middle character can be +, -, /, *, or ^. So you would put all those inside brackets, but don't put the power symbol (the caret) first. For the numbers, you can have any number of digits. I'll build this regular expression in parts. First, here's the number at the beginning:

\d+

The \d means digit, and + means one or more. Thus, \d+ allows one or more digits. Then add this:

\s*

This means optional whitespace. Because you can type 10 / 2 or 10/2, you want to allow space after the digit and before the arithmetic character. And because this space is optional, you add the *, meaning you can skip the whitespace, or you can put as much whitespace as you want. Now comes the arithmetic character:

[+-/*^]

Notice I didn't put the caret first. In fact, I put it all the way at the end. Now add more optional whitespace:

\s*

Finally, add another number, consisting of one or more digits, again:

\d+

Put all the parts together to get this regular expression:

\d+\s*[+-/*^]\s*\d+

When you see a regular expression such as \d+\s*[+-/*^]\s*\d+, break it down into parts, as I just did. Otherwise, this long string of characters may give you a serious headache. (This is why regular expressions have a mystique about them. Do your friends know what \d+\s*[+-/*^]\s*\d+ means? I didn't think so.)

Here's some Tcl fun:

```
% regexp {\d+\s*[+-/*^]\s*\d+} "2 / 5"
1
% regexp {\d+\s*[+-/*^]\s*\d+} "5    *    10"
1
```

```
% regexp {\d+\s*[+-/*^]\s*\d+} 2^8
1
```

All of these patterns match.

Here are some Perl samples:

```
print "5 / 10" =~ /\d+\s*[+-\/*^]\s*\d+/;
print "2^ 12" =~ /\d+\s*[+-\/*^]\s*\d+/;
```

Both of these match. However, if you look closely at the pattern, you'll notice a slight difference from what I just described. Look inside the character class, and you'll notice I put a backslash in front of the division sign represented by a forward slash, /. The forward slash is the default delimiter in Perl. Thus, I put the backslash in front of the forward slash so the Perl interpreter knows it's part of the regular expression.

If you want to use the arithmetic pattern I just gave you, I suggest a couple improvements:

✦ You may want to make sure you can't have characters before or after the string that don't match the regular expression. To do this, put a ^ at the beginning and a $ at the end of the expression.

✦ If you want this expression to appear inside a sentence or other text, you can also put word boundaries around the expression by starting with \b and ending with \b.

At this point, you'll want to try to start remembering all the different uses of the ^ character:

✦ If you use it as the first character inside a character set, as in [^abc], it means *all characters except those in the set.*

✦ If you use the ^ anywhere else inside the character set, as in [ab^], then it actually becomes a part of the character set. (Thus [ab^] means the set of characters a, b, and ^.)

✦ If you use the ^ outside of a character set, it means the beginning of a line.

✦ If you want to match the actual character, ^, like any other special character, put a backslash in front of it, as in \^.

Matching a range of characters

Characters have ASCII values associated with them. For the letters and the digits, the ordering that results from these values is as you would expect: a is before b, which is before c, and so on, and similarly with A, B, C, and so on. For the digits, the ordering is 0, 1, 2, 3, 4, 5, 6, 7, 8, 9.

If you want to allow a range of characters, list them all inside brackets as in this example (which matches any lowercase letter):

```
[abcdefghijklmnopqrstuvwxyz]
```

You can use a range, like so:

```
[a-z]
```

This range also matches any lowercase letter. Here's an example of it in use:

```
if ("c" =~ /[a-z]/) {
    print "Lowercase!\n";
}
```

Here are some common ranges:

+ `[a-zA-Z]` matches any letter, uppercase or lowercase
+ `[0-9]` matches any digit
+ `[0-9a-zA-Z]` matches any digit or letter

The hyphen, like the caret, is also a special character inside a character class. If you actually want a hyphen as part of your character class, put it *first* in the list, as in `[-ab]`. This example will match the character - or the character a, or the character b:

```
if ("-" =~ /[-ab]/) {
    print "Yeeeup!\n";
}
```

But what if you want both a hyphen and a caret? Put the hyphen first, and then put the caret somewhere else in the class, but not first. (Remember, putting the caret first will match any character except what's inside the class.) Here's an example:

```
if ("^" =~ /[-^]/) {
    print "Caret or hyphen!\n";
}
```

When you run this, you will see this output:

```
Caret or hyphen!
```

Chapter 3: Customizing, Searching, and Replacing

In This Chapter

✔ **Preventing characters from preceding or following the pattern**

✔ **Making a regular expression case insensitive**

✔ **Preventing (or allowing) "greediness"**

✔ **Searching and replacing**

One of the great features of regular expressions is that you can search for text that is either a single string or a set of lines like you would find in a text file. When you search for a pattern, you can note that the text was found or obtain the text that matched the pattern. Further, you can replace the text in the original string. This is all about searching and replacing. But before I discuss this exciting concept, I want to share two important topics with you: The first deals with extra characters in a match (that is, preventing /abc/ from matching with the string "123abcdef"), and the second is a pair of customizing options, called "greediness" and case insensitivity.

Preventing Extra Characters at the Beginning and End

Because a regular expression can match the characters in the middle of a string, what do you do if you want to *exactly* match a string to a regular expression? For example, look at this code in Perl:

```
$a = "123abcdef";
if ($a =~ /abc/) {
    print "This string matches abc.\n";
}
```

If you run this code, you'll see the message This string matches abc. The regular expression engine found abc inside the string 123abcdef and, therefore, declared it a match. But suppose you want to ensure that only the string abc will match. You can do this two ways: You can use start-of-line and end-of-line expressions; or, you can use the word boundary expression. Because you're dealing with a string (and not really lines of text, at least not in the case of the preceding code), the term *start of line* refers to the start of the string, and the term *end of line* refers to the end of the string.

Here are two more rules to keep in mind:

✦ If you start your regular expression with a caret, ^, the regular expression will match only at the beginning of the string.

✦ If you end your regular expression with a dollar sign, $, the regular expression will match only at the end of the string.

Taken together, if you start with a ^ and end with a $, the match will succeed only if the entire string matches. Try out the preceding Perl code with a couple changes:

```
$a = "123abcdef";
if ($a =~ /^abc$/) {
    print "The first string matches abc.\n";
}

$b = "abc";
if ($b =~ /^abc$/) {
    print "The second string matches abc.\n";
}
```

When you run this code, you see only the message `The second string matches abc`. This time, the string `123abcdef` didn't match the regular expression.

What was that crazy thing I said about word boundaries? A *word boundary* is basically where a word is adjacent to the start of a string (or line), whitespace, the end of a line, or a punctuation character. (The only exception is the underscore, which is considered part of a word.) Understanding word boundaries is handy for looking for words inside a regular expression.

A more technical definition of *word boundary* is where a word character and a non-word character meet. What is a word character? A letter, a digit, or an underscore. A non-word character is everything else, including a start of a line or the end of a line. Thus, consider this sentence:

```
Hi everyone, how are you?
```

The word boundaries are where you would think of them as being: between the start of the line and the letter *H*, between the letter *i* and the space, between the space and the letter *e*, between the *e* and the comma, between the space and the *h*, between the *w* and the space, between the space and the *a*, between the *e* and the space, between the space and the *y*, and between the *u* and the question mark. That's it. (A word boundary does not appear between the comma and the space, or between the question mark and the end of the line, because these are not word characters.)

Here's a good rule, along with the rule for the word boundary notation:

✦ Think of word boundaries as where the words start or end. But remember that underscores are considered word characters.

✦ To specify a word boundary in a regular expression, use \b (unless you're using Tcl, which I discuss at the end of this section).

All this means that if you want to, you can change your abc expression in the preceding examples to use the word boundary characters. This makes for some interesting results. Look at these truly interesting, if not astounding, examples:

```
$a = "123abcdef";
if ($a =~ /\babc\b/) {
    print "The first string matches abc.\n";
}

$b = "abc";
if ($b =~ /\babc\b/) {
    print "The second string matches abc.\n";
}

$b = "Hi, abc is here";
if ($b =~ /\babc\b/) {
    print "The third string matches abc.\n";
}
```

Notice that the regular expression is \babc\b. In English with some hand-waving gestures for emphasis, that means "word boundary – abc – word boundary." (You have to pronounce the hyphens somehow. Yeah.)

When you run this Perl code, you see the following output:

```
The second string matches abc.
The third string matches abc.
```

The first string still doesn't match, thankfully. The second one still does, which is also a good thing. But the third one matches as well. The word boundary sees abc surrounded by word boundaries in the sentence, Hi, abc is here. Thus, abc matches there as well.

For some reason, the word boundary expression \b isn't always present in some regular expression engines, particularly in some older editors that don't use full Perl-style regular expressions. (The editor in Microsoft Visual Studio 6.0 is an example.) If you're using an editor's search features, test out the \b expression to find out if it's available.

If you're using Tcl, instead of using \b to look for the word boundaries, use these bizarre sequences of characters:

✦ [[:<:]] for the beginning of a word

✦ [[:>:]] for the end of a word

Here's a quick example:

```
% regex {[[:<:]]abc[[:>:]]} {Hi, abc is here!}
1
```

(Here's something strange: If you try to use \b inside a regular expression in Tcl, Tcl will interpret it as a Ctrl+b character sequence.)

Customizing the Regex Engine While Matching

When you compare a string and a pattern, sometimes you may want to provide additional information about how you want the regular expression to do the comparison. Most languages let you specify various options when testing against a regular expression. Here are two particularly useful options, which are covered in the next few sections:

✦ Whether to do a case-sensitive or case-insensitive comparison.

✦ Whether to take the first character that matches or go as far as you can to the end, taking the very last instance of the character that matches. (These are called *non-greedy* and *greedy,* respectively.)

Regarding case (or not)

If you're matching words from a human language (such as English, or maybe Quersbugual, which is my top-secret language) rather than a computer language (such as C++), you may want to allow matches irrespective of case. For example, you may want to allow the pattern hello to match HELLO or hELLO or Hello.

Although you could build a regular expression to do this using something like [Hh][Ee][Ll][Ll][Oo], doing so is cumbersome and, frankly, hard on the eyes. (My vision is bad enough as it is.) The easier way is to turn on the *case-insensitive option.*

Although different languages offer different methods for setting regex options outside of a regular expression, one universal way is to put the string (?i) inside your regular expression. Perl, Tcl, and PHP all accept this. (The i stands for insensitive. It's a very insensitive thing to do, after all. But it works.)

Here's an example from Tcl:

```
% regexp {(?i)hello} HeLLO
1
% regexp {(?i)hello} hELLO
1
```

Here's a Perl example:

```
$str = "hELLo";
if ($str =~ /(?i)hello/) {
    print "Welcome!\n";
}
```

This example prints the string Welcome!, meaning the pattern matched. And here's an example in PHP, which also prints the welcoming string, Welcome!

```
<?php
    $str = "hELLo";
    if (preg_match("/(?i)hello/", $str)) {
        print "Welcome!\n";
    }
?>
```

Getting greedy (or not)

Suppose you're using a regular expression to look for HTML img tags in a string such as this:

```
<body><img src="pic.jpg">This is me!</body>
```

If you just want to find out if this string contains an img tag, you can simply match this string against the regular expression <img\b. However, if you're trying to obtain the information that follows the <img characters and goes up to the closing > character, you may run into a problem. Consider this regular expression:

```
<img .*>
```

Suppose you test this regular expression against the preceding line of HTML code. The <img in the regex matches the <img in the HTML string. The space matches the space right after the img tag in the HTML. But what does the .* match? It matches up to the character >. But which > character? After the <img in the HTML code, I see two > characters.

By default, the regular expression engine goes as far as it can in the string. Therefore, it matches the > character in the regex with the final > in the string, which is part of the closing body tag. That means the .* matches with the following (including the space just before src):

```
src="pic.jpg">This is me!</body
```

In other words, the regex engine is *greedy* and goes as far as it can. But this is not what I wanted in this particular case; I only wanted to go up to the first > character. So to make that happen, I turn off the greediness.

To turn off the greediness, add a question mark, ?, just before the > character, turning your regular expression into this:

```
<img\b.*?>
```

However, although what I said sort of makes sense (put the ? before the >), in reality, the rule is that you put the ? character immediately after the quantifier. The quantifier here is the * character, and although this rule doesn't change anything in this particular expression (the ? is still wedged between the * and >), it will elsewhere, especially if you're grouping.

In the following example, you'll see that the ? character goes inside the parentheses. This is a Perl program that demonstrates greediness and "ungreediness" with grouping:

```
$_ ='<body><img src="pic.jpg">This is me!</body>';

# Greedy
/<img\b(.*)>/;
print "$1\n";

# Not greedy
/<img\b(.*?)>/;
print "$1\n";
```

As I describe in the next section, "Searching and Replacing," I'm using the default variable in conjunction with the regular expression because doing so makes it easier for my brain to process the regular expression. (Your brain may vary.)

The first `print` statement in this code prints out the full greedy version, showing you that the code grabbed more than I wanted:

```
src="pic.jpg">This is me!</body
```

(This includes a space at the beginning.) The second `print` statement shows the non-greedy version, which grabbed just what I wanted:

```
src="pic.jpg"
```

(Again, this has a space at the beginning.)

Searching and Replacing

With regular expressions, you have the powerful capability to not only match text against a pattern, but also to search for a pattern within some text and replace the text. To replace text, you have to go beyond the regular expression — the regular expression that you use for finding the text to be replaced. After you find the text, you can replace it with some other text.

Due to the overlapping of topics in regular expressions, presenting the material in a strictly linear matter is somewhat difficult. The book in your hand is a reference guide, and as such, the following sections draw on material from Book VII, Chapter 4. I recommend that you read both sections carefully because they are interrelated.

In the following two sections, I talk about two important ways to replace text:

✦ Replacing the text that matched the pattern with literal text.

✦ Replacing the text with text that consists of some of the text itself. It sounds messy, but you can do some pretty powerful text manipulations with it.

The next two sections deal with these replacement techniques.

Replacing with straight text

The simplest way to do a replacement is to replace the text matching a pattern with some other text. For example, suppose you have comment blocks in a code file that looks like this:

```
#======================
#======================
# Myfunction()
#======================
#======================
```

And suppose you want to replace the lines that don't have the function name with a simpler form, resulting in this:

```
#
#
# MyFunction()
#
#
```

To make this example more interesting, say that the person who wrote the original code was careless and used different numbers of = characters throughout the code. How do you replace these lines with the simpler comment line consisting of just the # character?

**Book VII
Chapter 3**

Customizing,
Searching, and
Replacing

First, figure out the regular expression to identify the lines you want to replace. The pattern is simple: a # character followed by a bunch of = characters. That pattern looks like this:

#=+

When coming up with this pattern, I hesitated whether to go with the * or the + for the quantifier. My first impulse was to use the *, making the = characters optional, but then it occurred to me that if the # is followed by no = characters, that line is already in the correct format, and I have no reason to change it. So instead I went with the +, meaning the pattern has to have at least one = character.

I want to replace only those lines where the comment is by itself on the line, rather than at the end of a line with legitimate code. So I'll add the ^ character at the beginning of the expression and the $ character at the end. (Will these represent start-of-line and end-of-line respectively, or start-of-string and end-of-string respectively? At first, you may say *line,* but in fact, I'll probably read in the text file line by line, rather than as an entire file into a single string. So in that case, the ^ and $ characters will refer to the start and end of string.)

Now that you have the regular expression, think about the replacement string. That's easy: It's just a single # character. That means you're ready to code. I'll show you the code, and then I'll explain what the parts mean. Here's the code in Perl:

```perl
foreach (<>) {
    s/#=+/#/;
    print $_;
}
```

That's it! That's the whole thing. The first line opens the file whose name is passed in as a command-line parameter, reads the file's lines into an array, and loops through each line. With each iteration, the program puts the line in the default variable, which you can access with $_.

Next is the good part. This is a search and replace pattern in Perl. It starts with the letter s (which stands for search). Slashes divide up the two parts to this statement. First comes a slash and then the pattern you're searching for, which is #=+. Then comes another slash and the text you're replacing the matching text with. Then comes a final slash to wrap up the operation. And you end with a semicolon as always.

The search and replace that takes place modifies the default variable. The third line prints out the modified line. And that's it! Save this program as comments.pl and create a text file called commentinput.txt that looks like this:

```
#=====================
#==================
# My Function
#=====================
#=================
MyFunction() {
    Ooh ooh yeah!
}
```

Then you can run your program like so:

```
perl comments.pl commentinput.txt
```

And here's the result:

```
#
#
# My Function
#
#
MyFunction() {
    Ooh ooh yeah!
}
```

 If you want to do a search and replace on a variable other than the default variable, you can use the =~ operator. Here's the same comments.pl program, modified to use a different variable:

```
foreach $line (<>) {
    $line =~ s/#=+/#/;
    print $line;
}
```

The $line variable, rather than the default, gets used in and modified by the search and replacement.

Manipulating and replacing

When you search and replace text, often you will want to use the text that you find in the replacement string.

For example, suppose you want to find all the instances in a file where two words, separated only by a space, each start with a capital letter. You can assume that such words make up a person's name. You want to, in turn, replace these with the name in reverse format, separated with a comma. Thus,

```
Ingelbert Inguishable
```

will become

```
Inguishable, Ingelbert
```

To make a replacement such as this, you need to not only search for a pattern, but also make note of what text you find. This is easy with the search and replace technique when you add the notion of *backreferences.* The word *backreference* is just a fancy name for a variable inside a search and replace expression that refers to parts of the text that matched the pattern.

Generally when I have a complex problem such as this, I prefer to come up with a simple program that tests out my regular expression. Then if the regular expression is wrong, I can mess with it (er, I mean, *correct the errors*), and then after I have it correct, I can build the real program around it.

Therefore, as a quick example, try this little Perl. (Sorry, I couldn't resist.)

```
$name = "Ingelbert Inguishable";
$name =~ s/([A-Z]\w+)\b ([A-Z]\w+)\b/\2, \1/;
print "$name\n";
```

When you run this, you see the following output, which is what I was hoping for:

```
Inguishable, Ingelbert
```

Here's what the search and replace mess means. First, look at the pattern itself, which starts after the s/ and goes up until the next /:

```
([A-Z]\w+)\b ([A-Z]\w+)\b
```

This pattern searches for an uppercase letter ([A-Z]), followed by any word characters (shown by \w+) up to a word boundary (given by \b). Then I have a space, followed by the same thing again, representing another word starting with an uppercase letter.

But notice that I put parentheses around some parts of the expression. The text that matches the pattern in the first set of parentheses gets saved in a special *backreference* (that is, a temporary variable) called \1 that I can use in the replacement string. The text in the second set of parentheses gets saved in a second backreference called \2.

If you look at the replacement portion, you see the following output:

```
\2, \1
```

In other words, the replacement is the second backreference (that is, the second item found in parentheses), followed by a comma, then a space, and finally the first backreference. And it works!

When you put parentheses around part of an expression, the text that matches that part of the expression gets put in a backreference called \1. In the preceding example, the first set of parentheses matches up with the word Ingelbert, meaning \1 becomes Ingelbert.

The next step is to expand the little program to replace all names. That's easy, with just a few changes. But to make this example more interesting, suppose the file I'm reading is a text file with newlines, and a name can be split in the middle with the first name at the end of one line, and the last name at the beginning of the next. Here's the sample input file I will use:

```
Hello friends, this is Ingelbert Inguishable. Thank you
for coming to our meeting. A special thanks to Salvador
Dalmatian for his outstanding help. Zamamon Ziggly also
helped out considerably.
```

When I started putting together this program, I realized that in the original expression, I have the first and last name always separated by a space. But in this example, I have one instance where they are separated by a newline. If I treat the whole thing as a single-line string (rather than a multiline string), the newlines are considered whitespace, just as spaces are. Thus, I'll modify the expression to use whitespace instead of a single space.

However, when I print out the name in last name, first name format, I want to print out the first and last names with whatever was in between them to preserve the formatting; if a newline was between them, I want to print a newline, not a space. Thus, I'm going to use another backreference, this time for the whitespace between them.

Here's the final program, which I called backref.pl:

```
undef $/;
$_ = <>;
s/([A-Z]\w+)\b(\s+)([A-Z]\w+)\b/\3,\2\1/g;
print $_;
```

To run this program, save the preceding sample text in a file called backref.txt. Then run the program like this:

```
perl backref.pl backref.txt
```

Each name is converted to last name, first name format.

Chapter 4: Grouping and Capturing

In This Chapter

✔ Grouping with alternative words

✔ Capturing text from a match into the $1, $2, $3 variables, and so on

✔ Reading an array of captured text

✔ Preventing side effects of unwanted captures in alternatives

Two important concepts in regular expressions are (betcha can't guess) *grouping* and *capturing*. On a fundamental level, these two topics have little in common, except for one basic point: They both make use of parentheses inside regular expressions.

The idea of *grouping* is that you use parentheses to group together alternative words that you can use in the search. I take up this topic in the first section, "Grouping with Alternative Words." In short, you can specify alternative words in a pattern like `(Mr|Mrs|Ms|Dr)`, which will match `Mr` or `Mrs` or `Ms` or `Dr`.

The idea behind *capturing* is that you may find that a string matches a pattern, and you may want to know which characters in the string matched various parts of the pattern. Using capturing, you can figure out which characters matched and use them later on in your program — or, even later on in the same pattern. I cover this entertaining topic in "Capturing Text from a Match." See you there.

Grouping with Alternative Words

Using regular expressions, you can match *alternative* words. For example, suppose you want to determine if a string matches any of these greetings:

```
Dear Mr. so-and-so:
Dear Ms. so-and-so:
Dear Mrs. so-and-so:
Dear Dr. so-and-so:
```

In other words, you're looking for the word `Dear` followed by a space; `Mr.`, `Ms.`, `Mrs.`, or `Dr.`; a space; any name; and finally a colon.

Everything in this pattern is straightforward except for the prefix, which is an alternative. To show alternatives, separate them with the vertical bar symbol | and put them all inside parentheses. Here's a pattern that works for this example:

```
Dear (Mr|Ms|Mrs|Dr)\. .+:
```

Here's a Perl example that uses this pattern; save this example as `alternative.pl`.

```
$pattern = "Dear (Mr|Ms|Mrs|Dr)\. .+:";

if ("Dear Mr. Blingblankle:" =~ /$pattern/) {
    print "Mr. Blingblankle matches!\n";
}

if ("Dear Mrs. Sternigainagain" =~ /$pattern/) {
    print "Ms. Sternigainagain matches!\n";
}

if ("Dear Ms. Quealblinks:" =~ /$pattern/) {
    print "Ms. Quealblinks matches!\n";
}
```

Notice how I stored the pattern first as a string in a variable, and then used that string as a pattern later by putting the variable's name inside slashes. In Perl, that's the correct way to store a regular expression in a variable: Store it as a string and, when you're ready to use it, put slashes around it.

Here's the same program in PHP:

```
<?php
$pattern = '/Dear (Mr|Ms|Mrs|Dr)\. .+:/';

if (preg_match($pattern,"Dear Mr. Blingblankle:")) {
    print "Mr. Blingblankle matches!\n";
}

if (preg_match($pattern,"Dear Mrs. Sternigainagain")) {
    print "Ms. Sternigainagain matches!\n";
}

if (preg_match($pattern,"Dear Ms. Quealblinks:")) {
    print "Ms. Quealblinks matches!\n";
}
?>
```

When you run either program, you see the following output:

```
Mr. Blingblankle matches!
Ms. Quealblinks matches!
```

Only the first and third comparisons match. Why doesn't the middle one match? Because I purposely left off the colon at the end of the Mrs. Sternigainagain string.

You can see how a pattern such as this would be useful. You can search for salutations, as I did in this example.

Capturing Text from a Match

Matching regular expressions is all fine and dandy, and searching and replacing is pretty exciting, too, but wouldn't it be great if you could somehow take the text that matches a pattern and save it for later? Sure, but you can't.

Just kidding.

You *can* save it for later. All you need to do is surround a part of the pattern with parentheses, and then whatever text matches that part of the pattern is saved in a variable. That sounds pretty easy. Take a look at this simple example from Perl:

```
$str = "This is a great program!";
$str =~ /(.+) is a (.+) program!/;
print "$1\n";
print "$2\n";
```

You can see how the pattern closely resembles the string I'm comparing it to, and that the first .+ part will match up with the word This, and the second .+ part will match up with the word great. The parentheses around each .+ mean that the regular expression engine will capture the text that matches the pattern inside parentheses. The first capture is saved in the $1 variable, the next in $2, and so on, if you have more. (Here, I have only two.) So the preceding program captures the word This to the variable $1 and the word great to the variable $2. Here's the output:

```
This
great
```

Yes, this is great. But what if you don't know how many items will match? Then you can use an array to hold the matches. Here's an example that does this:

```
$str =
    "apples and apricots are best eaten with an ape!";
@list = $str =~ /(ap\w*)/g;
foreach (@list) {
    print "$_\n";
}
```

This pattern looks for all words that start with `ap`. (The `\w` means a word character, and the `g` modifier, which stands for *global,* causes the search to happen as many times as possible.) The assignment line `foreach @list` saves all the matches in the `@list` array. The `foreach` loop then prints out the matches. Here's the output:

```
apples
apricots
ape
```

Now for a more sophisticated example. Suppose you're writing a program that scans every line in a file, searching for lines that match a particular pattern. And suppose that when your program finds a line that matches, the program prints only the part of the line that matches, not the entire line.

When you're searching a file using the program I just described, you're dealing with *patterns,* and as such, with each line you search, the text that matches the pattern may be different. If you were dealing with literal text in your search, it wouldn't make much sense to try to figure out what text matched your pattern: It would be identical to the literal text in your pattern. But a pattern can have wildcards in it. You may specify a pattern such as the following (this is a whole pattern; the word `print` is part of the pattern):

```
print "(.*)";
```

This pattern matches a line such as this:

```
    print "Everybody is a clown";
```

or this, indented differently:

```
        print "This program will eventually end";
```

What does the `.*` portion of the pattern match? It's different in each case. In the first case, it matches `Everybody is a clown`. In the second, it matches `This program will eventually end`.

Here's a Perl program that will open the text file whose name is passed in as a parameter, scan through every line in the file, and print out the text that matches part of the pattern. The pattern is `print "(.*)"`. Therefore, the program will print out the contents of every string constant in a `print` statement. Here's the program, which I called `captureprint.pl`:

```
foreach (<>) {
    if (/print "(.*)";/) {
        print "$1\n";
    }
}
```

This program uses some distinctly Perl techniques. First, I open the file named on the command line using just <>. This crazy construct (that's an understatement) opens the file and reads each line in as an array. The `foreach` loop then cycles through each array member, which is a line of the file. Each line becomes the default variable in the `foreach` loop.

Then I test the regular expression against the default variable (which is the line of text). Because I don't specify a variable in the line `if (/print "(.*)";/) {`, Perl uses the default variable. Then the cool part happens. If the pattern and line match, I print out the data in the `$1` variable. What is `$1`? That's the part I captured inside the parentheses. Tell me that's not one of the coolest things you've seen all year. Okay, so I need to get a life.

To run this program, type `perl captureprint.pl`, followed by the name of a file to read. Because the file is likely to be a code file (you're looking for `print` statements after all), you may type something like this:

```
perl captureprint.pl alternative.pl
```

This prints out the contents of the string constant in every `print` statement found in the file `alternative.pl`. And it works! Here's the output:

```
Mr. Blingblankle matches!\n
Ms. Sternigainagain matches!\n
Ms. Quealblinks matches!\n
```

(The `alternative.pl` file was a program I used in "Grouping with Alternative Words," earlier in this chapter.)

Capturing text with PHP

Here's a quick example of a capture in PHP. Simply use the `preg_match_all` function, like so:

```php
<?php
    preg_match_all(
        "/(a.c).*(g..d)/",
        "My abc soup is good", $words);
    foreach ($words as $str) {
        print "{$str[0]}\n";
    }
?>
```

This prints the following:

```
abc soup is good
abc
good
```

The first capture is the whole pattern, and the following captures are the parts of the pattern in parentheses. But instead of simply printing each element of the array (each element is called $str in the loop), I treat each element itself as an array and print its first element. That's because the $words array is an *array containing three arrays*.

The reason for this is that the preg_match_all function fills the match variable with a fixed number of items in an array: The array contains one element for the entire pattern, and one element for each set of parentheses. Specifically, the preceding call to preg_match_all fills the array $words with three elements: one for the whole pattern, one for (a.c), and one for (g..d). Now look at this slightly more complex example:

```php
<?php
    preg_match_all(
        "/(a.c).(1.3)/",
        "My abc-123 soup is a1c-143 good a2c-153",
        $words);
    foreach ($words as $str) {
        var_dump($str);
    }
?>
```

The whole pattern occurs multiple times in the search string. You can see that abc-123 and a1c-143 and a2c-153 all match. But I still get only three elements in my $words array, regardless of how many times it happens. (And again, each element is itself an array, because $words is an array of arrays.) To show what's happening, I use the var_dump function to dump out the contents of the $str variable in each iteration of the loop. Here's the output:

```
array(3) {
  [0]=>
  string(7) "abc-123"
  [1]=>
  string(7) "a1c-143"
  [2]=>
  string(7) "a2c-153"
}
array(3) {
  [0]=>
  string(3) "abc"
  [1]=>
  string(3) "a1c"
  [2]=>
  string(3) "a2c"
}
array(3) {
  [0]=>
  string(3) "123"
```

```
   [1]=>
   string(3) "143"
   [2]=>
   string(3) "153"
}
```

As expected, the $words array has three elements (one for the whole pattern, one for the (a.c) pattern, and one for the (1.3) pattern). Further, each element is itself an array. The first of these three arrays contains a list of each time the whole pattern matched. Thus you see abc-123, a1c-143, and a2c-153. The second array contains a list of where only the (a.c) pattern matched: abc, a1c, and a2c. The third array contains a list where only the (1.3) pattern matched: 123, 143, and 153.

To better understand the present example, try changing the test string to this:

```
"My abc-123 soup is a1c-143 good a2c-153 a3c-163"
```

This has four instances of each match. You still have only three arrays, but each array now has *four* items.

If you want to see an excellent example of preg_match_all in action, check out Book VII, Chapter 7.

Capturing text with Tcl

Here's a simple example of a capture in Tcl. To capture an individual substring to a variable, add the variable name at the end of the regexp command, like so:

```
% regex {My (a.c) soup} {My abc soup is good} what sub1
1
% puts $what
My abc soup
% puts $sub1
abc
%
```

To capture a set of variables, add the -inline option, like so:

```
% regex -inline {(a.c).*(g..d)} {My abc soup is good}
{abc soup is good} abc good
%
```

This returns a list. The first item in the list is the string that matches the entire pattern. The string is abc soup is good without the My at the beginning. The second item in the list is abc, which matches the first capture. The third item in the list is good, which is definitely a good capture.

Side Effects with Alternatives and Accidental Captures

In programming with regular expressions, you may accidentally capture something. When you use grouping to specify alternatives, you surround your alternatives with a single set of parentheses. And when you have a set of parentheses, like it or not, you're going to capture something. What will you capture? The particular text in the string that matched one of the alternatives.

You may or may not want that. Now suppose you started with a regular expression that included some capturing, and you went on your merry way using the $1 and $2 variables and so on. Then later you modified your regular expression, adding some grouping with alternatives, and suddenly your program messed up. If the group is toward the beginning of your expression and prior to your matching, the $1 will start containing the text from the alternatives.

How can you prevent accidental captures (also known as *side effects*)? Put a question mark and then a colon inside the parentheses surrounding the alternatives. Here's an example that accidentally captures some text:

```
$_ = "Broccoli is good for you!";
@words = /(.+?)\bis (good|bad|ugly) for (.+)!/;
foreach (@words) {
    print "$_\n";
}
```

This example captures the word Broccoli, thanks to the non-greedy capture (.+?)\b. Next, it captures the word good, due to the parentheses around (good|bad|ugly). And finally, it captures the word you, thanks to the (.+) at the end, just before the exclamation mark. Here's the output:

```
Broccoli
good
you
```

But what if you don't want to capture the word good? Then modify the expression just a tad:

```
@words = /(.+?)\bis (?:good|bad|ugly) for (.+)!/;
```

I added the ?: just before the word good. The regular expression engine won't capture what's inside the alternatives list. If you make this change to the preceding broccoli sample, you'll see this revised output:

```
Broccoli
you
```

Regular expressions and this book's examples

You may be interested to know that for some of the examples where I give both a Perl version and a PHP version, I often wrote the Perl version first; then, instead of rewriting it in PHP, I used the regular expression capability of my text editor to modify the program. Then I did some tidying up, but the regular expressions really helped. To accomplish the modifications, I searched on this:

```
((.*) =~ /(.*)/)
```

and I replaced it with this:

```
(preg_match(\2,\1))
```

The goal is to convert a line such as this:

```
if ("Dear Mr. Blingblankle:"
    =~ /$pattern/) {
```

to this:

```
if (preg_match($pattern,"Dear
    Mr. Blingblankle:")) {
```

The only catch to using this regular expression is that the regular expression engine in some text editors treats the parentheses as literals. To use them in grouping, you have to put a backslash in front of them. Yuck. But I did; instead of using the preceding expression as is, I had to modify it slightly so it looked like this:

```
(\(.*\) =~ /\(.*\)/)
```

You'll also notice that I used \1 and \2 for the capture variables. Many editors use a backslash followed by a number to denote the captured variables because the replacement technique is really treated as a backreference.

Book VII
Chapter 4

Grouping and
Capturing

Chapter 5: Joining, Splitting, and Making Up

In This Chapter

✔ **Splitting strings into multiple substrings**

✔ **Splitting in Perl, PHP, and Tcl**

✔ **Obtaining individual characters**

✔ **Joining back together**

A common problem in computer programming is dividing a string into various substrings and then individually processing the different parts. For example, suppose you have an entire paragraph stored in a single string and you want to get an array containing every word in the paragraph.

Sometimes when faced with this problem, the programmer will write a function (or find a function written by somebody else) that will go through a string and break up the string based on spaces. Although this works, it's not very flexible. For example, if you like to put two spaces after each sentence, this may result in a "word" between the two spaces that's really just an empty string. And what about punctuation?

The languages I cover in this book all support various splitting techniques whereby you can split up your strings based not on a fixed character (such as a space) but on a regular expression. Here's a quick example using Perl:

```
$paragraph =
    "This is a paragraph.  It consists of ".
    "several words, and several lines, and ".
    "lots of punctuation!  Sentences are separated ".
    "by two spaces (oh my!).";

@words = split(/\W+/, $paragraph);
foreach (@words) {
    print "$_\n";
}
```

This example uses the split function to divide up the string by words. The regular expression specifies what the separator characters are. You want to separate based on whitespace and punctuation — that is, anything that is not a word character. Therefore, I used the regular expression \W+, which is a regular expression representing one or more non-word characters.

When you run this example, you see a list of all the words in the paragraph. Here are the first three lines:

```
This
is
a
```

. . . and so on. If you look at your output, you'll see that you don't have any blank lines; that is, when the paragraph had two spaces in a row, you didn't end up with a blank "word" that was supposedly between the two spaces. Instead, the split function used the regular expression to match the multiple spaces as a single piece of text, and split on that single piece of text, not within it. (If you want to break this functionality just for fun, remove the + in the regular expression, using \W instead of \W+. Then run the program, and you'll see what I'm talking about.)

In this chapter, I show you how to perform various splits in Perl, PHP, and Tcl. Additionally, I show you how to take the results of a split and combine them together into a single string, a process called a *join*.

You may wonder about some of the practical uses of a split and join. Any time you have a string of data where each data item is separated by some character, you can use a split to divide up the data. For example, if you're reading lines from a comma-separated file created by a spreadsheet program, you can split the lines on the commas by using a line of code like this:

```
@items = split(/,/, $line);
```

Splitting All Over the Place

In the following sections, I show you how to accomplish a split in PHP and Tcl. (The introductory section to this chapter shows you how to split using Perl.) After the language topics, I provide a section that solves a common problem of how to split a string into its individual characters. I show you how to do that in Perl, PHP, and Tcl. And then, finally, I show you how you can modify some of the split functions to obtain not only the array of words, but also information on where the words were in the original string.

Splitting in PHP

The PHP language includes the preg_split function, which is part of the regular expression category of functions. This function behaves just like the

Perl version of the `split` function. However, like the `preg_match` function, you surround your regular expression with slashes and then put the expression inside a quoted string:

```php
<?php
$str = "Hi there, everybody! This is cool.";
$strset = preg_split('/\W+/', $str);
foreach ($strset as $word) {
    print "word: $word\n";
}
?>
```

The `preg_split` function takes the regular expression for the first parameter. (I used single quotes so the backslashes would stay in the string.) The second parameter is the string to split. The function returns an array, which the program then walks through, printing each member.

If you run this program, you may notice a slight problem. Unlike the Perl `split` function, this `preg_split` function in PHP will return an empty word. Here are the lines from the `print` statement:

```
word: Hi
word: there
word: everybody
word: This
word: is
word: cool
word:
```

The final line is empty. But fear not — the `preg_split` function has two additional parameters that give you further options. The first parameter isn't particularly useful; it's a number that lets you limit how many splits the function does. If you don't want to place a limit, pass -1.

The second parameter can be a combination of various constants. The one that is useful here is `PREG_SPLIT_NO_EMPTY`, which prevents the `preg_split` function from returning any empty words. Here's the modified call to `preg_split`:

```php
$strset = preg_split('/\W+/', $str,
    -1, PREG_SPLIT_NO_EMPTY);
```

Two other constants are available for the final parameter: `PREG_SPLIT_OFFSET_CAPTURE` and `PREG_SPLIT_DELIM_CAPTURE`. If you include the first constant, `PREG_SPLIT_OFFSET_CAPTURE`, each item in your array won't be the string; instead, it will be an array itself, containing the string and a number representing the string's position in the original string. For the low-down on the second constant, check out the section "Capturing while splitting," later in this chapter. (You can combine options by putting a vertical bar character, |, between the options.)

Splitting in Tcl

The Tcl language has the command split. However, this command does not use regular expressions. If you want to use regular expressions in a split, you need to use an extra library written to accompany Tcl, called tcllib. The tcllib library is often installed automatically with many Tcl installations.

If your version of Tcl doesn't have the tcllib library installed, you can obtain it by visiting either tcllib.sourceforge.net or www.tcl.tk/software/tcllib/. Both pages offer downloadable files (visit the distributions links) and documentation on using tcllib.

If you have tcllib installed, the following code should work inside of tclsh:

```
% package require textutil
0.6
% set str {Hi there, everybody! This is cool.}
Hi there, everybody! This is cool.
% set result [::textutil::splitx $str {\W+}]
Hi there everybody This is cool {}
```

This code may be a bit cryptic at first, so here's a breakdown:

+ The first % line opens the textutil package, which is part of tcllib.

+ The next % line stores the string Hi there, everybody! This is cool. in the variable str.

+ The third % line calls the splitx command (found in the textutil package), passing as parameters the str variable and the regular expression \W+.

+ The results of the call to splitx are stored in the result variable. The contents of result then appear on the screen. This is a list of six words, plus an empty set.

Why an empty set? This variety of a regex-capable split function adds an empty set if the split pattern is present at the end of the string. With the input string str, the final character (a dot) does match the pattern, resulting in an empty set getting added. The empty set happens, unfortunately, and you probably will just want to ignore it.

Splitting a string into individual characters

If you need to take a string and create an array consisting of the individual characters in the string, you can use the `split` function. To do this, you use an empty pattern for your regular expression. Here's an example in Perl:

```
$string = "abcdefghijklmnopqrstuvwxyz";
@chars = split(//, $string);
foreach (@chars) {
    print "$_\n";
}
```

The regular expression is just `//`, but the slashes are the delimiters, meaning the expression itself is empty: no expression at all.

Here's the same example in PHP:

```
<?php
$string = "abcdefghijklmnopqrstuvwxyz";
$chars = preg_split("//", $string);
foreach ($chars as $char) {
    print "$char\n";
}
?>
```

And finally, here's how you do the same thing in Tcl:

```
package require textutil
set str { abcdefghijklmnopqrstuvwxyz }
set chars [ ::textutil::splitx $str {} ]
foreach char $chars {
    puts $char
}
```

Capturing while splitting

When you split a string, you can also include parentheses inside your regular expression to capture text. However, simply adding the parentheses doesn't automatically cause the various `split` functions to capture text. Rather, you have to add an option.

In PHP, you add the `PREG_SPLIT_DELIM_CAPTURE` option as the fourth parameter in the `preg_split` function. (If you're combining more than one option, separate the options with the vertical bar character as I do in the following example.) Here's a short demonstration:

```
<?php
$str = "Hi there, everybody! This is cool.";
$result = preg_split('/(\W+)/', $str,
    -1, PREG_SPLIT_NO_EMPTY |
    PREG_SPLIT_DELIM_CAPTURE);
foreach ($result as $word) {
    print "word--$word--\n";
}
?>
```

This splits up the $str string and also captures the patterns in the process. Notice I put parentheses around the \W+. Thus, you get the whole string split up: the text separated by the delimiter you specify in the pattern, as well as the delimiters. Remember, the pattern is the word boundaries, which include the usual punctuation characters. Thus, with the PREG_SPLIT_ DELIM_CAPTURE, your final list will also have punctuation characters. (You might want to do this in case you want to join the sentence back together and still have all your punctuation.)

I put two hyphens around $word in the print statement to help you see any spaces in the output. Here's the output:

```
word--Hi--
word-- --
word--there--
word--, --
word--everybody--
word--! --
word--This--
word-- --
word--is--
word-- --
word--cool--
word--. --
```

The first output line is one of the split words. The second output line is the delimiter that followed the first word; this delimiter is just a space. Move down to the fourth line, and you can see that in this case the delimiter is two characters, a comma, and then a space. (You can see the space between the comma and the two hyphens.)

In Perl, you don't need to add any extra options; you just throw in the parentheses, and the party begins. Here's the same program written in Perl; it has the same output as before:

```
$str = "Hi there, everybody! This is cool.";
@result = split(/(\W+)/, $str);
foreach (@result) {
    print "word--$_--\n";
}
```

Joining Together with the Band

The reverse of a split is a *join*. After you have performed a split and you have all your words in an array (or if you merely created an array filled with words), you can easily piece them back together by using a `join` function.

You don't use regular expressions with a `join` function. Instead, you just specify the character or characters to use in between the words when you pull them back together into a string.

Here's an example in Perl:

```
$paragraph =
    "I am bill at at dot com. I ate my kitchen, ".
    "and this is gr e. All th I know school is ".
    "all my brain.";
@words = split(/\W+/, $paragraph);
$final = join('@', @words);
print "$final\n";
```

This example splits apart the `$paragraph` string by words and then pieces all the words back together, putting the @ character between each word. Here's the output filled with secret meaning:

I@am@bill@at@at@dot@com@I@ate@my@kitchen@and
@this@is@gr@e@All@th@I@know@school@is@all@my@brain

The join in PHP is just as easy; you use the somewhat alarmingly titled `implode` function:

```
<?php
$paragraph =
    "I am bill at at dot com. I ate my kitchen, ".
    "and this is gr e. All th I know school is ".
    "all my brain.";
$words = preg_split('/\W+/', $paragraph);
$final = implode('@', $words);
print "$final\n";
?>
```

One problem with `join` (or `implode`, if you prefer more dramatic language) is that you're stuck always inserting the same character string between the words, regardless of what was in the original string you split up. However, if you use the capture method to grab the delimiters as well (refer to the section, "Capturing while splitting," earlier in this chapter), you can use those in the joining of words, as this Perl program demonstrates:

```
$paragraph =
    "I am bill at at dot com. I ate my kitchen, ".
    "and this is gr e. All th I know school is ".
    "all my brain.";
@words = split(/(\W+)/, $paragraph);
$final = join('', @words);
print "$final\n";
```

I added the parentheses around the pattern to capture the delimiters in the array. Also I specified no characters as the delimiter in the `join` function because everything I want to squish back together is in the array itself. When you run this example, you see the same string that `$paragraph` began with.

To accomplish the joining with captured delimiters in PHP, you can still use the `implode` function as before. Simply capture the delimiters using the `PREG_SPLIT_DELIM_CAPTURE` option in the `preg_split` function and then call `implode`, passing an empty string for the delimiter characters.

Chapter 6: Processing Multiple Lines and Files

In This Chapter

✓ **Processing each line in a file**

✓ **Processing a string as a single line or as multiple lines**

✓ **Determining how many lines are in a file**

✓ **Searching all the lines in a file**

✓ **Modifying multiple newlines in a search and replace**

*H*ere's an idea: Suppose that instead of searching for a pattern in a string, you want to search for a pattern in a file. What kinds of issues will you encounter?

Before I answer that, I need to set up some assumptions:

✦ **You're working with a text file.** Regular expressions are for matching text, so a file that contains, for example, compiled C++ code is binary data, and trying to pick compiled code apart by using a big bad regular expression simply doesn't work. In other words, it doesn't make sense to use regular expressions on any type of file but a text file.

✦ **Your text file is organized into lines of text.** That is, if you open the file into a text editor, you see multiple lines, not just one big long line. One big long line is hardly different from a single string.

But what if you have one big long line and you choose the Word Wrap option in your text editor? Most text editors have such an option. In that case, technically you still have only one line of text.

When you have the Word Wrap feature on, you end up with paragraphs of text where each paragraph, although displaying on the screen as multiple lines, is really one long line of text. How do I know this? The answer is my next assumption:

✦ **Each line of text ends with one or two end-of-line characters.**

I say "or two" because different operating systems use different ways to denote the end of a line. Unix uses a single linefeed character, which has ASCII code 10. Windows uses two characters, a carriage return followed by a line feed, which is ASCII code 13 and then 10, respectively. And finally, the Macintosh, not to be outdone, uses just a carriage return, which is ASCII code 13, to end its lines. When you're writing code, you may have seen \r or \n or \r\n inside a string. The \r refers to a carriage return character, or ASCII code 13. The \n refers to the line feed character, which is ASCII code 10. Thus, \r\n generates ASCII code 13 and then 10.

For the purpose of this discussion, I say "a newline" or "the newline character" to refer to whatever end-of-line character (or two) your operating system uses.

Processing Multiline Strings

Why distinguish between multiline and single-line strings? It all comes down to how you want the regular expression engine to interpret the three magical characters ^, $, and . (the dot). By default, these first two characters mean *start of string* and *end of string,* respectively, and the dot character matches any character except newline characters. But if you switch to multiline mode, the ^ and $ suddenly mean *start of line* and *end of line.* In multiline mode, the regular expression engine watches for the newline characters and matches up ^ and $ on a per-line basis. You can also specify a specialized single-line mode, in which case the . matches all characters including newlines. (Normally, as I stated, the dot character doesn't match newlines.)

Here's a good example. To make my point, I'm going to stuff several lines of text into a single string. Here's the Perl code:

```
$a = "Don't eat my computer \nyet. cook it first.\n";
print $a;
print "=========\n";
$a =~ s/^(.*)c(.*)$/$1C$2/mg;
print $a;
```

Look closely at the string. I put a couple \n characters in it; therefore, when you run this, first you'll see the original string print on multiple lines. And to help organize the output, I put a bunch of equal signs on a line by itself to separate the original from the modified string.

Look closely at the regular expression. Remember, as usual, take these things in pieces. The regular expression starts with an s, which means search and replace, and at the end is a g modifier, which means the search and replace will happen as many times as possible. But notice I also put an m after the closing slash in the expression. (They call the m an m *modifier.*) That's the key to magically transforming the search and replace into a multiline format.

The search pattern starts with ^, which in this case means *start of line.* Next comes a (.*), a c, and then another (.*). This will search for the last occurrence of the letter c, and store everything on the line before the c in $1 and everything on the line after the c in $2. (Why does it search for the last occurrence of c? Because the first (. *) is greedy, as all * patterns are unless you follow the * with a ?.)

The next part is the replacement pattern. It is $1M$2. This just spits out the $1 (the stuff before the m), then a capital M, and then the $2 (the stuff after the m). In other words, this expression replaces the last m in each string with a capital M.

When you run the program, you see the following output:

```
Don't eat my cold computer
yet. cook it first.
=========
Don't eat my cold Computer
yet. Cook it first.
```

How many lines are in the file?

I'm going to get *really* picky for a moment. Different programs have different ideas about how many lines exist in a file depending on whether or not the last line in the file has a newline character. (If the last line has a newline character, that means the file ends with the newline character.)

The following is a Perl program that will write out what we humans see as three lines of text:

```
print "abc\n";
print "def\n";
print "ghi";
```

(Notice the final line doesn't have the \n on it.) Save this program as lines.pl and run it like so:

```
perl lines.pl > lines.txt
```

The output is saved to a file called lines.txt. Unix (and the cygwin program on Windows) has a utility called wc, which stands for *word count*. The wc program tells you how many characters, words, and lines are in your file. So how many lines are in lines.txt? Try this:

```
wc -l lines.txt
```

(That's a lowercase L for the parameter, which tells the wc program to count only lines.) I ran this on both a Linux system and a Windows system under cygwin. In both cases, I saw this output:

```
2 lines.txt
```

It says two lines. *Hmm.* However, I then opened the lines.txt output file in Microsoft Word under Windows and chose Tools⇨Word Count. What did I see? Word told me I have *three* lines. Now change the final line in your code to this:

```
print "ghi\n";
```

Running wc this time shows three lines. What does Microsoft Word say I have? *Again* it says I have three lines. But to my eyes, in both cases I see three lines, whether the final line has a \n on it or not!

The ^ and $ now refer to the start and end of the *lines* inside the string, thanks to the m modifier. (Remember, the g modifier causes the replacement to happen as many times as possible.)

What if you have \n characters in your string, but you *want* the ^ and $ characters to signify the start of the string and the end of the string and not the start of the line and end of the line? Remove the m modifier, but don't stop there: Add the s modifier, which means *single line*.

The reason you need to add the s modifier is a slight technicality: The singleline s modifier isn't the opposite of the multiline m modifier, even though the name suggests so. Rather, the s modifier tells the regular expression engine that the . character can match any character including the newline character. Without the s modifier, the . character matches any character *except* the newline character.

Thus, if you test the expression /^.*$/ against the string "Hi/nthere" *with* the s modifier, the .* matches up with all the text inside the string. But *without* the s modifier, the .* matches the H and the i and stops there, not matching the /n or anything that follows it. Thus, here are the rules for the s and m modifiers:

✦ **The s modifier causes the . to match any character including the newline.** Without the s modifier, the . character does not match the newline character.

✦ **The m modifier causes the ^ and $ characters to match the start of the line and end of the line.** Without the m modifier, the ^ and $ characters match the start of the string and end of the string.

As crazy as it sounds, you can use the s and m modifiers together if you want the dot to pick up newlines but still have the ^ and $ mean start and end of line. Thus, you can do some fancy-schmancy stuff like have some expressions cross over onto other lines. For example, you might be searching a text document for somebody's address, which would likely take up multiple lines.

After you understand the ins and outs of processing multiline strings, you can have some fun. You can find every line that contains a certain pattern, and if you want, you can replace those patterns with another string. (And that string can even be made up of the pattern.) Knowing this, you can come up with some seriously complex regular expressions.

If you're reading in text from a file, you have two ways to do it:

✦ You can read in the text line by line and perform a regular expression on each line.

✦ You can read in the whole file as a single string and process it as a multi-line string.

Which way you choose is up to you, but one deciding factor is whether you need to process multiple newlines. The following two sections show two different examples. Each has a different situation, which helps you decide whether you should process the file as a single string.

Searching for All Lines in a File That Contain a Pattern

A common problem in programming is searching for all lines that contain a pattern. You can also replace these lines, which is simply a matter of using a search and replace form of a regular expression. But to keep this example simple, you'll just do a match, meaning you'll locate which lines match the expression and print those lines out.

A program that does this type of searching-each-line operation is usually called a *grep* program. Thus, I will call this program `mygrep.pl`. (Don't call it `grep.pl` because you probably already have a grep program on your system, and you want to keep the names separate.)

In this example, you compare each line to the regular expression. While comparing one line, you really don't care what's in a different line. Thus, I recommend reading the file in line by line (rather than as one big string).

Here's the code that does this; I saved this as `mygrep.pl`:

```
$pattern = $ARGV[0];
$filename = $ARGV[1];
open (INPUT, $filename)
    || die "can't open $filename: $!";
while (<INPUT>) {
    print $_ if /$pattern/;
}
```

This program reads the first command-line argument and stores it in the $pattern variable. It then reads the second command-line argument and stores it in the $filename variable. Next, it tries to open the file named by $filename, storing the file handle in the INPUT variable (or quitting if the program can't open the file).

Then the program grinds through each line in the file. For each line, it performs this somewhat cryptic instruction:

```
print $_ if /$pattern/;
```

This uses the reverse-*if* notation. It performs the print $_ part if the expression is true. The expression in this case is simply a regular expression that operates on the default variable, which contains the line from the file. Thus, this line translates in English to: "If the current line from the file matches the pattern, print out the line."

And that's the grep program. Here's a sample file you can use (save it as grepsample.txt):

```
This is the first line of text.
This is the second Line.
Oh my, how boring.
But the third line doesn't contain anything linear.
That's true. Neither does this line. Oops.
```

To try out the program, type this:

```
perl mygrep.pl [Ll]in grepsample.txt
```

You're searching the grepsample.txt file for the pattern [Ll]in. Here's the output:

```
This is the first line of text.
This is the second Line.
But the third line doesn't contain anything linear.
That's true. Neither does this line. Oops.
```

Modifying Multiple Newlines

You may want to read in a file containing text that has each paragraph on a single line, with no indentations. You can create a new file based on these rules:

✦ Two newlines in a row in the original file result in a new, indented paragraph in the new file.

✦ One newline (not followed by another) results in a new, unindented paragraph.

This is similar to a hard return and soft return in a word processor.

To create a program that accomplishes this, think about the two types of replacements you will have:

✦ Two newlines (or \n\n) turn into a newline and then an indentation. Thus, \n\n is replaced by \n\t.

I use the tab character because that shows up more easily in a book such as this. If I were doing this outside of a book environment, I'd probably prefer a few spaces instead to give me more control over the size of the indentation.

✦ One newline is replaced by . . . let's see . . . one newline. In other words, it doesn't change. That means you have only one replacement to do. Yay! The problem just got easier.

This means the expression must look like this:

```
s/\n\n/\n\t/
```

Because you're looking for multiple newlines, you can't read in the file line by line, processing each line individually. Instead, you need to read in the whole file.

Attempting patterns without regular expressions

Before looking at how to do this hard return and soft return fun using regular expressions, stop and think for a moment how you would do this *without* regular expressions. I've reached the point in my programming career that when I'm confronted with a goal such as this hard return and soft return example, I automatically consider regular expressions because such a job is so much easier with regular expressions. Doing something like this without regular expressions at this point sounds crazy. So how would you do it without? I can't remember, and I'd prefer not to figure it out. Why bother?

Do you need to include the m modifier here? The m modifier determines whether the ^ and $ characters represent the start and end of the string or the start and end of the line. However, in this example it doesn't matter because you won't need the ^ and $ characters. Therefore, go the easy route and leave the m modifier off. (Adding it wouldn't change anything, so I see no reason to include it.)

And what about the s modifier? Again, whether or not the dot character reads newlines doesn't matter because you won't be using the dot character in this example. So leave the s modifier off.

Here's the code:

```
undef $/;
$_ = <>;
s/\n\n/\n\t/;
print $_;
```

Believe it or not, that's the whole thing. Just try that in the C language without regular expressions! The first two lines read in the file named at the command line. This file comes in as one long string and gets put in the default variable. The regular expression on the third line, having no variable names associated with it, operates on the default variable. Then the fourth line prints out the default variable after it's changed.

Save the file as paragraph.pl. Then create a text file containing something like this:

```
This is a paragraph about a paragraph. The paragraph that
    this paragraph is about happens to be the paragraph you
    are reading. What is the paragraph about? I don't know.
But as you read this, you will see that this line is a soft
    return.

This line starts another paragraph because I put two newlines
    at the beginning of it. And that's what this paragraph is
    really all about: Being a paragraph with two newlines at
    the beginning.
```

The first paragraph (starting with This and ending with know.) is on one line of text, with a single newline at the end. The next paragraph (But . . . return) is a single line, but this time it has two newlines at the end. The last paragraph is a single line, and it doesn't matter whether you put a newline at the end.

Save the file as `paragraph.txt`. Then run your program:

```
perl paragraph.pl paragraph.txt
```

You see the modified output:

```
This is a paragraph about a paragraph. The paragraph that
    this paragraph is about happens to be the paragraph you
    are reading. What is the paragraph about? I don't know.
But as you read this, you will see that this line is a soft
    return.
    This line starts another paragraph because I put two
    newlines at the beginning of it. And that's what this
    paragraph is really all about: Being a paragraph with two
    newlines at the beginning.
```

Chapter 7: Processing HTML Files

In this chapter, I offer a handful of examples that deal with processing HTML files using regular expressions in various settings, such as inside a code editor or as a program in different languages. The idea is not to provide a full rundown of everything you can do with HTML; that would span many books. Instead, I show you how I tackled some problems I've encountered and how I used regular expressions to solve these problems. Then you can apply these techniques to your own problems as they arise.

Building a Form Based on a List of Strings

Here's an excellent example of something that may come up. Suppose you have a list of words (such as the columns in a table) and you want to quickly generate a form for easy entry into these columns. This requires transforming lines from something like this:

```
name
email
```

to this:

```
name <input type="text" name="name"><br>
email <input type="text" name="email"><br>
```

You may often have a need for such a conversion in a text editor. Therefore, I show you how to use a text editor with regular expression capabilities to solve this problem. (If you're not using a text editor but are instead writing a program to convert the text, then you really don't need regular expressions;

if you're writing a program, just read through the list, print out `'$colname`
`<input type="text" name="$colname"><br>'` for each line, and forget
regular expressions altogether.)

The search pattern is whatever is on an entire line, which is easy: The pattern is `.*`. Because you want to capture this pattern, put parentheses
around it.

TIP

Check out the documentation for your text editor to determine whether you
need to precede your capture parentheses with backslashes, as in `\(.*\)`.

Thus, depending on your text editor, the pattern becomes this:

`\(.*\)`

or simply this:

`(.*)`

For the replacement text, put the word you captured both at the beginning
and in the middle of your HTML. Your editor will require either `\1` or `$1` to
represent the captured text. Mine uses `\1`, so my replacement text is this:

`\1 <input type="text" name="\1"><br>`

For the Windows SciTE editor, here's what you do:

1. **Select all the text and then press Ctrl+H to open the Search and
    Replace dialog box.**

2. **For the Find What box, type in the pattern `\(.*\)`.**

3. **For the replacement text, type in the preceding replacement text.**

4. **Make sure the Regular Expression box is checked.**

5. **Click Replace All (or just Replace in Selection if you want to replace
    only the selected text).**

    The change happens, and you're done.

For the vi editor, the patterns are the same; instead you use vi's search and
replace command, as follows: Type a colon to access the vi command-
prompt and type the following code:

`:g/\(.*\)/s//\1 <input type="text" name="\1"><br>/g`

Automatically Creating Size Information for IMG Tags

Suppose you have an `.html` file and inside the file are various HTML `img` tags (among other tags). Some of these `img` tags have size information (the length and width of the image), and some don't. And the size information that's present may or may not be correct. But having correct size information in your `img` tags is a good idea; without any size information, the browser will have to wait until the images are downloaded, and then re-render the entire screen. And with incorrect size information, the images will appear distorted.

In this PHP example, I show you how to use regular expressions and image functions to find the `img` tags, snatch out the filenames, obtain the files' width and height information, and then rebuild the `img` tags with the new width and height information. That way you can be assured that:

✦ Every `img` tag has size information (because some `img` tags might not have size information).

✦ The size information is correct for each `img` tag.

When browsers download HTML files containing images, they first download the `.html` files and, at that time, start attempting to draw the HTML, even before the images come down. This is the reason you may want to add size information to your `img` tags. If the browser doesn't know how big the images are, it assumes a small icon size by default. Then after the browser obtains the image information, it re-renders the whole screen. You have probably seen this happen on Web pages while on a slow dialup connection (or during heavy traffic): The page starts to come down, and the text moves all over the place as each new picture appears. Length and width parameters in the `img` tags prevent this from happening.

Like all problems involving text, you can (and should) weigh whether or not regular expressions are the best option. The preceding section includes an example for which you probably wouldn't want to use regular expressions.

In the example in this section, the goal is to extract the filename (along with any options) from the `img` tag. From the extracted options, you can obtain width and height information, if present. Extracting text is a good job for regular expressions, so I'm using regular expressions in this example. (Otherwise, I wouldn't have it in this chapter, but that's beside the point.)

First, Listing 7-1 contains an HTML file named `imgsample.html` that you can use for this example.

Listing 7-1: A File That Contains Several img Tags

```
<html><head><title>Pictures of our trip</title></head>
<body>
This page contains pictures of our trip!<p>
Me on the mountain<br>
<img src="pics\OnMountain.jpg"><p>
Me dropping a rock off the mountain<br>
<img src="pics\dropping.jpg" width="100" height="200"><p>
The rock smashing the ranger's truck<br>
<img src="pics\smashing.jpg" align="middle"><p>
Me running for safety<br>
<img src="pics\running.jpg" alt="Get out!"><p>
My new view<br>
<img src="pics\prison.jpg"><p>
</body></html>
```

This file contains many tags, several of which are img tags. The img tags in this file have different parameters. Now for the regular expression. Although you may be able to do some serious finagling and come up with a single expression to do all the work, keep it simple by dividing up the task. So first you want to find the src parameter from each img tag; Listing 7-2 shows the PHP program that will do this.

Listing 7-2: The imageconvert.php Program

```php
<?php
    if (count($argv) > 0) {
        $filename = $argv[count($argv) - 1];
    }
    else {
        $filename = $_GET['filename'];
    }
    $html = implode("", file($filename));
    $pattern = '/<img.*?>/';
    preg_match_all($pattern, $html, $matches);
    $tags = $matches[0];
    foreach ($tags as $tag) {
        $srcpattern = '/src="(.*?)"/';
        preg_match($srcpattern, $tag, $srcarray);
        $src = $srcarray[1];
        list (,,,$size) = getimagesize($src);
        $hpattern = '/height=".*?"/';
        $newtag = preg_replace($hpattern, '', $tag);
        $wpattern = '/width=".*?"/';
        $newtag = preg_replace($wpattern, '',$newtag);
        $newtag = preg_replace(
            "/\s*>/", " $size>", $newtag);
        $html = str_replace($tag, $newtag, $html);
    }
    print $html;
?>
```

Here are the patterns I'm using in Listing 7-2:

```
/<img.*?>/
```

This pattern finds the `img` tags, because an `img` tag starts with `<img` and ends with `>`. But I'm including the `?` character to ensure the pattern isn't greedy. (Otherwise, if I don't turn off the greediness, the pattern will match everything starting with the `<img` through the final `>` in the file, which is probably the tag `</html>`.)

After extracting each `img` tag, I extract from the tag the source file, using this pattern:

```
/src="(.*?)"/
```

Thanks to the parentheses, this pattern grabs the image filename that is inside double quotes following the `src` parameter. Using that filename along with PHP's image functions, I can determine the dimensions of the image. But the image function I use, `getimagesize`, has a really great feature: This function returns a list, the fourth element of which is a properly formatted string containing the size and width parameters in an HTML tag, like so:

```
width="100" height="100"
```

Yes, `getimagesize` builds this width and height string for us! Next, I use the `/height=".*?"/` pattern inside a call to `preg_replace` remove any existing `height` parameter. (You can see the replacement string I use is just an empty string.) I then do the same with `width`, using the pattern `/width=".*?"/`, to remove the `width` parameter.

Next, I replace the closing angled bracket `>` (as well as any whitespace preceding the angled bracket) with the size string returned by `getimagesize`, along with a new closing angled bracket. Here's the regular expression I use for this replacement:

```
/\s*>/
```

And finally, I use the simple `str_replace` function to replace the entire previous tag with the new tag. Whew!

To run the program from the prompt, try it with the `-q` option to prevent the PHP program from writing out `Content-type` and `X-Powered-By` header information; also, use a redirect to save it to a file like so:

```
php -q imageconvert.php imgsample.html > results.html
```

And here's the output, which shows the fixed version:

```
<html><head><title>Pictures of our trip</title></head>
<body>
This page contains pictures of our trip!<p>
Me on the mountain<br>
<img src="pics/OnMountain.gif" width="100" height="100"><p>
Me dropping a rock off the mountain<br>
<img src="pics/dropping.gif" width="100" height="100"><p>
The rock smashing the ranger's truck<br>
<img src="pics/smashing.gif" align="middle" width="100"
    height="100"><p>
Me running for safety<br>
<img src="pics/running.gif" alt="Get out!" width="100"
    height="100"><p>
My new view<br>
<img src="pics/prison.gif" width="100" height="100"><p>
</body></html>
```

If you're using an earlier version of PHP (before PHP 4.3.0), you'll want to add the following two lines to the very beginning of Listing 7-2:

```
$argv = $_SERVER['argv'] ;
$argc = $_SERVER['argc'] ;
```

The reason for including these two lines is that the `argv` and `argc` global variables exist only in newer versions of PHP.

Extracting All the HTML Text

HTML files look great when viewed in a browser, but what if you want to view them in a text file? Depending on the complexity of the underlying HTML, the file can look pretty messy.

One easy way to view the files is to simply extract the text itself. This method won't work for all HTML files because some files have JavaScript that generates some of the text. But for many HTML files, this will work fine.

In this example, I extract the HTML and build a basic text file. The text file ignores all markup except in the following instances:

✦ It extracts text within the `<body>` tag.

✦ It uses `<br>` and `<p>` tags to generate newline characters.

One of the easiest ways to extract text from HTML is by using regular expressions. The listing is surprisingly short (even shorter than I expected).

I did, however, decide to do multiple regular expressions. The entire code, in Perl, is shown in Listing 7-3; save this as HTMLtoTXT.pl.

Listing 7-3: Code That Extracts the Text from HTML

```
undef $/;
$_ = <>;
($_) = /<body.*?>(.*)<\/body>/s;
s/<p.*?>/\n\n/sg;
s/<br.*?>/\n/sg;
s/<.*?>//sg;
print $_;
```

The first two lines read in the file as a single string and place it in the default variable, $_. The next line yanks out the text between the body tags.

Any HTML tag can have parameters inside it. Even though some don't offer parameters (such as <hr>), technically you're still allowed to put parameters in them (as in <hr a="b">) even though the browser will ignore those parameters. Therefore, you can see in my code that for each pattern for an HTML tag I put a .*? after the tag name. The ? will prevent greediness, stopping at the first >.

After extracting the text outside of the body, you replace each <p> tag with two newlines and each <br> tag with a single newline. Then simply remove the remaining tags. You do each replacement with a separate regular expression.

Finally, you print the resulting string. Here's a sample input file you can use; save this as words.html:

```
<html><head><title>Opportunity</title></head>
<body>
<h1>An Opportunity for You</h1><p>
Like most people, I was born at a <i>very</i>
young age. I then went to school, where I learned
all the skills to make <b>millions</b> of dollars.
Soon after school, I started my own multinational
corporation, and to my delight I didn't just
make <i>millions</i>, but I made <i>billions</i>!
And now, if you send me only $100, I can share with
you this secret of how you can make a lot of money.
(And please don't think that the secret is getting
unsuspecting people to send you $100 as I'm doing
to you. Really! That's not the scam. I mean <i>
plan</i>. <b>Trust me!</b><p>
```

```
Sincerely,<br>
Your Multimillionaire Friend</a>
</body>
</html>
```

To try out the program, type:

```
perl HTMLtoTXT.pl words.html
```

Here's the output:

```
An Opportunity for You


Like most people, I was born at a very
young age. I then went to school, where I learned
all the skills to make millions of dollars.
Soon after school, I started my own multinational
corporation, and to my delight I didn't just
make millions, but I made billions!
And now, if you send me only $100, I can share with
you this secret of how you can make a lot of money.
(And please don't think that the secret is getting
unsuspecting people to send you $100 as I'm doing
to you. Really! That's not the scam. I mean
plan. Trust me!


Sincerely,

Your Multimillionaire Friend
```

You may also want to convert certain HTML entities to their ASCII equivalents. For example, the string < is the HTML equivalent for a less-than character, <. (The reason for this is that the less-than character is normally interpreted as a start-of-tag delimiter. Without this encoding, there is no way to print a less-than character on the browser window.)

To decode HTML entities to their actual characters, add this line to the start of Listing 7-3:

```
use HTML::Entities;
```

And add this line just before the final `print` line to decode the entities before printing:

```
decode_entities($_);
```

Searching Only the Text Portion of an HTML File

What if you want to search a set of HTML files for a certain string, but want to search only the text portion? For example, you may want to look for the word *height,* but you don't want to pick up <img> tags that include a `height` attribute.

You can do this by extracting only the text portion of the HTML (as in the example in the preceding section) and then search only that text for the pattern.

And even better, because you're using regular expressions, you can search for a pattern, not just straight text. (Most Web search engines let you search only for straight text.)

I decided to do this example in Perl because Perl has plenty of handy file and directory functions. Here's the program:

```
use HTML::Entities;

$pattern = $ARGV[0];
print "Finding $pattern\n";

opendir(DIR, ".");
@dirs = grep(/\.htm/, readdir(DIR));
closedir DIR;
foreach (@dirs) {
    undef $/;
    $filename = $_;
    open (MYFILE, $filename);
    $_ = <MYFILE>;
    ($_) = /<body.*?>(.*)<\/body>/s;
    s/<br.*?>/\n\n/sg;
    s/<p.*?>/\n/sg;
    s/<.*?>//sg;
    decode_entities($_);

    @found = /($pattern)/g;
    $count = $#found + 1;
    if (@found) {
        print "$filename: $count\n";
    }
}
```

This code is pretty simple. It uses the HTML::Entities module so that it can search decoded text, not the encoded text. The program takes a pattern as a command-line option; thus, you read the pattern from the @ARGV list into the $pattern variable. Next, you open the current directory. (This program searches only the current directory; you can enhance it to read more if you like.) You read the directory list using the readdir(DIR) function and grep through the list for all items matching the pattern \.htm. (Remember, the backslash before the dot means you're looking for an actual dot. Thus, you're looking for all files that have .htm in them; this includes files that end in .html.) Note that the grep function takes a pattern of its own and searches through every string in the list passed to it, and returns a new list containing only those strings that match the pattern.

At this point, you have a list of files that have .htm in their names. You then use the code from the example in the preceding section to read in the basic text from the .html file. Note that the program reads it into the default variable, $_.

Finally, after you have the text from the file, you scan it for the pattern, using this line:

```
@found = /($pattern)/g;
```

This does a global search through the default variable for the pattern and returns an array of each piece of text in the string that matches the pattern. You don't really care about the exact text that matched the pattern, however; you just want a count. And thus, the final if statement checks if the pattern existed and, if so, prints out how many instances exist.

Here's a sample session:

```
$perl search.pl "C\+\+"
Finding C\+\+
bcpp1-1.html: 9
bcpp1-2.html: 16
news.html: 16
news2.html: 16
temp.html: 2
```

This scans through all the .html files in the current directory, looking for the string C++. (However, the + character is a special pattern character, so precede it with a backslash.) Then you get a list of all the files that contain the string C++.

Chapter 8: Ten Regular Expression Gotchas

In This Chapter

✓ Capturing too much due to greediness

✓ Searching when you meant to replace

✓ Writing code that accidentally ignores backslashes

✓ Omitting delimiters

✓ Confusing singleline, multiline, and the default

*R*egular expressions can be a bit touchy at times. As with any programming language, the regular expression engine has very strict grammar rules. This grammar is even stricter than that of most programming languages, which means you'll probably make a mistake from time to time. In this chapter, I provide you with ten things to watch out for when dealing with regular expressions.

Trying to Cram Multiple Tasks into a Single Expression

Regular expressions are incredibly powerful, but please give them some breathing room. I've seen some enormously complex regular expressions that stretch over 200 characters.

And you know what? These huge regular expressions are almost impossible for us mere humans to read and understand. Okay, once I had a boss chastise me for creating such a monster. But I must admit I was kind of proud of myself.

Please keep your regular expressions simple. If you need to, you can split them up using strings, like so:

```
$datetime = '\d\d\d\d-\d\d-\d\d \d\d:\d\d:\d\d';
$full = "Today is $datetime";

$teststr = "Today is 2005-01-01 08:23:05";
if ($teststr =~ /$full/) {
    print "This is a valid date-time!\n";
}
```

Because of the size of the datetime pattern, I stored it in its own string variable. However, to ensure that the backslashes ended up in the string, I used single quotes for the variable. Then to use the strings in the regular expression, I coded /$full/ so the Perl interpreter would expand $full to create the full regular expression. (Don't simply use $full without the slashes, or it won't work.)

Accidentally Capturing Alternatives

You specify alternatives using (first|second|third|fourth) and so on. The alternatives get parentheses around them, but so do captures. If you're capturing, you will accidentally (or purposely) pick up the alternative in the captures.

If you want to avoid capturing, remember to use (?:first|second|third|fourth). This prevents the text that matches the alternatives from being captured.

Capturing Too Much Due to Greediness

Another problem with capturing is grabbing too much text. This is a common problem when you're trying to parse HTML text. HTML text is filled with tags that start with < and end with >. If you're trying to capture the text in only the first tag in the file, you may accidentally use this expression:

```
/<(.*)>/
```

Unfortunately, this expression picks up text all the way to the end of the final tag, which will either be in the final tag on the current line or in the whole file, depending on your multiline and singleline settings.

Instead, turn off greediness like so:

```
/<(.*?)>/
```

Doing a Search When You Mean to Replace

Remember the differences between matching, searching, and replacing, as well as how you notate each in your language of choice:

+ Matching returns a Boolean in most languages.

+ Searching (usually called capturing) returns an array in most languages.

+ Search and replace returns a modified form of the string.

Perl has some special syntax with these, however. To do a match, test the result of a string compared to a pattern for either true or false. But to capture, Perl saves the captured text resulting from a comparison of a string against a pattern into an array. The array contains the captured text. Other languages (including PHP and Tcl) don't have regular expressions built right into the syntax; instead, you call the regular expression functions.

Writing Code That Accidentally Ignores the Backslashes

This is a problem that affects more areas than just regular expressions, but it's particularly problematic in the regular expression world. In fact, I made this mistake while putting together the samples for this chapter. Look at this string from Perl and see if you can figure out what I did wrong:

```
$datetime = "\d\d\d\d-\d\d-\d\d \d\d:\d\d:\d\d";
```

The problem is that I used double quotes. The double quotes cause backslashes in a string to be interpreted as escape characters for use in the creation of such things as newline characters, \n. To make the backslash actually mean a backslash, use single quotes:

```
$datetime = '\d\d\d\d-\d\d-\d\d \d\d:\d\d:\d\d';
```

When I switched to single quotes, the code worked as expected. Similarly, in Tcl, remember that if you use braces, { and }, no substitutions take place, and you can also avoid the problems I encountered with my $datetime expression in Perl.

Attempting to Use a Feature That's Not Present

Regular expressions are not the same in every language. One mistake I make on occasion is trying to use the \b (word separator) in places where it's not supported.

Tcl doesn't support Perl-style regular expressions completely, even though it has "extended regular expression support." And the regular expression support in various editors may or may not be complete. (The \b pattern is often not supported.) Check your documentation if you aren't sure.

Getting the Uppercase and Lowercase Wrong

This is kind of a simple problem that may seem obvious at first, but I'm talking about uppercase and lowercase in two different situations.

First, it's easy to forget that the string `"George"` will not match the pattern `/george/` or the pattern `/g.*/`. The reason is that `G` doesn't match `g`. By default, the regular expressions are case sensitive. However, you can turn off the case sensitivity by adding the `(?i)` option at the beginning of your pattern, as in `/(?i)george/`.

Another uppercase/lowercase problem sometimes presents its ugly aroma when you're dealing with the various special characters. Remember, for example, that `\w` (lowercase) matches a word character (a letter, digit, or underscore) and `\W` (uppercase) matches anything *but* a word character.

Forgetting to Include the Delimiters (Especially in PHP)

Use the correct delimiters when specifying your regular expressions. For Perl, you use forward slashes. For Tcl, you use braces { and }.

In PHP, your regular expressions are passed to the `preg_` functions as strings, but the strings must contain the slashes at the beginning and the end. Forgetting these slashes is a common source of errors.

Forgetting the Global Option

When doing a replace or when capturing, you need to turn on the global option if you want to pick up all instances of a pattern. Otherwise, by default, you get only the first instance. This can be annoying sometimes, causing its own breed of specially formulated headaches.

In Perl, to specify the global option, add the `g` modifier after the expression.

In PHP, use the `preg_match_all` function instead of the `preg_match` function.

In Tcl, add the `-inline` and `-all` options, like so:

```
% regex -inline -all {(a.c).*(g..d)} {My abc soup is good}
{abc soup is good} abc good
```

This Tcl result is of type `list` and contains three elements, `{abc soup is good}`, `abc`, and `good`. The first element in the list is the subset of the string that completely matched the pattern; the second and third items in the list are the parts that matched the groupings.

Mixing Up Singleline, Multiline, and the Default

Singleline and multiline are not opposites. In Perl regular expressions, the singleline modifier means that the . character will match any character including the newline character. (In other words, if all your lines of text that are separated by \n newlines are held within a single string, adding the singleline modifier will treat the whole string as one line, even though the string has newlines.) The default — when you don't have the singleline modifier present — is that the . character will not match the newline character.

To specify the singleline option in Perl, put an s character after the closing slash of the regular expression, as in this example:

```
/(.*)/s
```

The multiline modifier means that the ^ and $ characters will no longer mean *start of string* and *end of string* respectively, but rather *start of line* and *end of line* within the string. To specify the multiline option, put the m modifier after the regular expression, like so:

```
/(.*)/m
```

To use the multiline and singleline options together, put both m and s (in any order) after the final slash:

```
/(.*)/ms
```

Book VIII

Appendixes

The 5th Wave   By Rich Tennant

"Give him air! Give him air! He'll be okay. He's just been exposed to some raw HTML code. It must have accidently flashed across his screen from the server."

Contents at a Glance

Appendix A: Managing Files with CVS

CVS (Concurrent Versions System) is a standard, free tool for allowing multiple people to work on files (usual source code files) in a project. A central computer maintains the list of files in a *repository,* which is divided into projects. Each project can have a set of directories underneath it.

Normally, the client CVS software is a command-line program. However, you can find various GUI front ends that supposedly make CVS easier to use. My feeling is that CVS is so easy to use for the basic tasks that I almost find the GUI front ends more cumbersome. I prefer to type the CVS commands at the prompt.

CVS is big enough that people can write entire books about it. In this appendix, I just show you what you need to know to use CVS. These are the topics I discuss here:

+ Obtaining a CVS client program

+ Logging on to a CVS server

+ Checking out the files in a project from a repository

+ Adding new files to a project

+ Uploading ("committing") your changed files back into the repository

Additionally, I also include a section on creating a repository for your own local computer.

Taking a Closer Look at CVS

You can *check out* the files of a project in the CVS repository, which means copying the entire directory tree under the project to your own computer. Then you can make changes to various files in the directory and upload your changes back to the CVS system.

Each time you (or any other user) upload a file to the CVS system, CVS keeps a copy of all the previous versions of the file. That way, if necessary, you can go back and look at an earlier version of a file. For example, you may realize that you don't like the change you put in, and you can revert back to an older version, effectively undoing the change. By this regard, CVS is a *version control system*. A typical setup consists of one CVS running on a server, which holds the repository. All users on a development team have a client software program through which they can check out the latest copies, upload their changes, and so on.

If you want to use CVS for your own local projects, you can just run CVS locally. In this mode, your own local copy handles the dirty work of managing the repository; in this mode, you're not using the software in a client/server manner but rather as a stand-alone program.

CVS includes a feature called *branching*. Here's the idea and most common use behind branching: If you release version 1.0 of your product and are well into version 2.0 of your product, and you find a bug in version 1.0, you can go back to version 1.0, fix the bug, and branch off to create a revised version of 1.0, without affecting version 2.0.

Here's another way to look at this example: You finished 1.0 and shipped the product, and all your source code for 1.0 is pretty stable. After the obligatory trip to the Bahamas, you get back and begin work on version 2.0. After two months of work, you and your team members have checked in piles of files to the repository, so the current state of the repository is very different from the way 1.0 was.

But you then discover a bug in version 1.0. You decide you want to fix the bug and ship a patch for version 1.0, without including all the new 2.0 features you've been working on. You check out the entire project for version 1.0, make a change, and start a new branch from version 1.0, where you upload your new files. Now you have two projects that have spawned from version 1.0: The new project 2.0 and the bug-fixed version of 1.0. You can check out either project and build either one independently because CVS keeps track of all the versions.

Getting CVS

CVS is available for many operating systems, including Linux, Solaris, and Windows. You can find a version for your operating system at `www.cvshome.org`. Additionally, you can find another version of CVS for Windows NT/2000/XP at `www.cvsnt.org/`.

If you're interested in *front ends* for CVS (programs with interfaces that are supposed to make CVS easier to use), you can find plenty at `www.wincvs.org/`. (Don't let the name "wincvs" fool you; this isn't just for Windows. Mac and Unix versions are available, too.)

For more CVS tools, check out this page from the main CVS home at
`www.cvshome.org/dev/addons.html`. You can find the official CVS documentation at `www.cvshome.org/docs`.

Using CVS

These are the general steps for using CVS:

1. **Use the CVS command-line tool to log into the CVS server.**

2. **Check out (that is, download) any files you want to obtain.**

3. **Commit (that is, upload) any files you want to put on the server.**

4. **Log out.**

Generally, you use CVS by typing a single CVS command line, which consists of the CVS command, some options for CVS, and a *CVS command*. A CVS command tells CVS what you want to do, such as log in, check out a file, check out a project, commit the files you changed, and log out. Following the command are any options for the command. The command and options all go on a single command line.

To invoke a CVS command, you tell CVS what the command is by typing CVS and the command on the same line.

Preparing CVS

Before you can use CVS, you need to figure out where the CVS repository is located. It might be on your own system in a particular directory, or it might be on a remote server.

After you find the repository, you either save the repository's location in an environment variable called CVSROOT or enter the location on each command line that you use.

In Unix or Linux, if you want to store the location in the CVSROOT environment variable, you can do so like this:

```
CVSROOT=/home/me/MyCVSStuff
export CVSROOT
```

You can either type this in or store it in your `.profile` file on Unix, or the `.bash_profile` file on Linux. On Windows, you can set CVSROOT from the command prompt like this:

```
set CVSROOT=c:\MyCVSStuff
```

**Book VIII
Appendix A**

**Managing Files
with CVS**

Or you can set CVSROOT in the environment variables page of the system properties.

If you're using a remote system, your CVSROOT will more likely look like this: pserver:anonymous@cvs.sourceforge.net:/cvsroot/dev-cpp. (That's one I lifted from the SourceForge open source site, for a project called Dev-C++.)

Alternatively, you can pass the directory name with each CVS command. For example, to log into SourceForge, you can do this:

```
CVSROOT=pserver:anonymous@cvs.sourceforge.net:/cvsroot/dev-cpp
export CVSROOT
cvs login
```

Or you can combine it all on one line, by putting the CVSROOT right on the command line. To do so, you use the -d option:

```
cvs -d pserver:anonymous@cvs.sourceforge.net:/cvsroot/dev-cpp
    login
```

The command format is the same: the word cvs followed by the word login. In between, I include the -d option and the information on the repository. (In the next section, I talk more about the login procedure.)

Logging in to CVS

Before you can use CVS, you need to log in to the remote CVS server. You can use your local client CVS program anytime you want, but before you can check out any files from the CVS server, the server must allow you access.

One thing about CVS that might strike you as strange or awkward is that to log in to CVS, you run the CVS command with the login parameter. Then the CVS command ends, and you end up back at the shell prompt. But you're still logged in. Yes, that's a bit strange: The server remembers who you are, and you can run more CVS commands from the prompt until you have finished you work, after which you can log out.

If you are using CVS for your own local work and aren't connecting to a remote CVS server, you don't need to log in. See "Creating a CVS Repository and Project," later in this chapter, for more information on using CVS locally.

Logging in is easy as long as the format of the command is correct. The login command needs to know the following information:

✦ Who you are

✦ What your password is

✦ The domain name of the system you want to log in to

✦ The project you want to access

If you're using CVS to access an open-source project (such as one on SourceForge), the open-source project Web page will probably show you the CVS command for logging in. I recommend pasting the command from the Web page into the command shell, rather than typing it all in. CVS is picky about its syntax.

To log in to CVS, you use the `login` command, and you set up the `CVSROOT` accordingly. Here's an example:

```
cvs -d me@mydomain.com:/cvsroot/myproject login
```

Here's a closer look at this example:

✦ The username is `me`.

✦ The server you're connecting to is `mydomain.com`.

✦ The project you're accessing is in the repository `/cvsroot/myproject`.

✦ The command is `login`.

You are then prompted for a password.

Checking out an entire project

You might want to check out an entire project for two reasons:

✦ You are new to the project and don't have any of the files.

✦ You want to "get all the latest changes," which means that you want to download any files that have changed since the last time you downloaded the files.

Before checking out a project, make sure you're logged in to the system (if you're required to do so). Then you need to choose a module that you want to check out from the project. (Often projects have only one module named the same as the project.) You can simply type the following line, where `project` is the name of the project you want to check out:

```
cvs checkout project
```

Book VIII
Appendix A

Managing Files
with CVS

Periodically checking out updates

If you're working on a project with multiple people, you don't automatically get everybody else's changes. If other team members make changes to the code and copy the new code into the repository, you periodically need to look for changes.

You can look for changes by moving to the root and checking out the entire project again, like so:

```
cvs -d/MyCVSStuff checkout project
```

The great thing here is that CVS is smart: It knows if you're currently working on some files, and it won't overwrite those files.

Remember that you need to have your CVSROOT stored. If not, include it in the command line like this:

```
cvs -d:pserver:anonymous@cvs.sourceforge.net:/cvsroot/dev-cpp checkout project
```

CVS then runs, downloading all the files into your local directory. Or if your repository is on your own local system, you can use this command:

```
cvs -d/MyCVSStuff checkout project
```

CVS lets you type the word get instead of checkout, if you prefer. Your checkout line looks like this:

```
cvs -d/MyCVSStuff get project
```

Everything is the same; you just say get instead of commit.

Checking out individual files in a project

If you want to check out an individual file in a project, move to the root directory of your project and then check out the file by using the file's entire path name, like so:

```
cvs -d/MyCVSStuff checkout project/src/myfile.cpp
```

project is the name of the project, and /src/myfile.cpp is the path within the project to the file you want to check out, which is myfile.cpp.

Committing your changes (and creating new files)

When you're finished making changes to your file, you can copy the changes back into the repository by using the commit command. This command is easy to use. Make sure you're in the directory where the file sits and type the following line, where myfile.cpp is the file you want to check in:

```
cvs -d/MyCVSStuff commit myfile.cpp
```

This is the interesting part: Before checking in the file, CVS opens a default text editor (usually vi on Unix computers, and Notepad on Windows computers). Inside the text editor, you type a comment describing the changes you made to the file.

Initially, you see information in the text file that's similar to this:

```
CVS: ---------------------------------------------------------
CVS: Enter Log.  Lines beginning with `CVS:' are
CVS: removed automatically
CVS:
CVS: Modified Files:
CVS:     myfile.cpp
CVS: ---------------------------------------------------------
```

This is some default text that tells you what you're doing; CVS doesn't use this text. Type a message at the end, starting on a new, blank line. Your message can extend several lines if you want. Here's an example:

```
CVS: ---------------------------------------------------------
CVS: Enter Log.  Lines beginning with `CVS:' are
CVS: removed automatically
CVS:
CVS: Modified Files:
CVS:     myfile.cpp
CVS: ---------------------------------------------------------
Fixed the bug that was bugging everybody.
Added a new class for removing really bad bugs.
Updated the time to be Y2K compliant.
```

Then save the file and exit. CVS waits for you to finish and then checks in the file for you.

If you're dealing with a new file that you just created, before you can commit the file you must add it to the repository. Yes, this is an extra step, but you're required to do it. Prior to typing the commit command, you need to type an add command:

```
cvs -d/MyCVSStuff add myfile.cpp
```

After this, you can proceed with the commit command.

Checking out files anonymously

If you use an open-source product, and you want to download the entire source tree but aren't a member of the development team, most open-source projects allow anonymous checkout through CVS. This means that you can check out the files as you normally would, but you don't have a username and therefore can't commit any changes that you make. That doesn't mean you can't make any changes; it just means that for now your changes are for your own purposes only and don't become a part of the official source. (However, most open-source projects welcome new developers, which means you can later get a username and check in your changes.)

To check out files anonymously, you follow the instructions on the open-source Web site. For example, SourceForge includes instructions with each project on how to check out the files anonymously. However, the instructions assume you're familiar with CVS. The instruction includes a line for logging in, such as this:

```
cvs -d:pserver:anonymous@cvs.sourceforge.net:/cvsroot/dev-cpp
    login
```

When you're prompted for a password with SourceForge, you simply press Enter. Other open-source sites give you instructions for the password.

But that only logs you in. Next you have to check out the files and then log out. (Please remember to log out.) Some people use the alias `co` instead of `checkout`; `co` means the same as `checkout`. The SourceForge page includes a line for checking out the files, but you need to know the project name:

```
cvs -d:pserver:anonymous@cvs.sourceforge.net:/cvsroot/dev-cpp
    checkout V5
```

In this example, the project name is V5. How did I know that? The developers of each project in SourceForge choose their project names. (The official term is *module,* not *project,* so don't be surprised if you see the word *module* on the SourceForge site.) To figure out what module name the developers used, click the Browse CVS Repository link found on the CVS page of each SourceForge project. (The CVS page is available from the CVS link at the top of each project page.) The Browse CVS Repository link opens a browser version of the repository, where you can see the name of the project. You see several names here, such as the following:

```
Attic/
CVSROOT/
V5/
copying.txt
```

Attic is a special storage place for saving files; that's not the project name. CVSROOT is a special directory used by CVS; again, that's not the project. The only remaining directory here is V5. Thus, that's the project name, and that's how you know what to type at the end of the `checkout` command. Yikes. (The project name has to be a directory, so `copying.txt` isn't the project name because it's a file.) What if there are multiple names besides Attic and CVSROOT? That means the developers are working on multiple projects (or modules).

Logging out

Always remember to log out of your session so that the server knows it can close any open file handles and do all that good stuff that servers do when somebody logs out (like go get a cup of coffee, I suppose). Even if you logged in anonymously, you're still logged in; logging in anonymously simply means that you can't upload files.

To log out, type this line:

```
cvs -d/MyCVSStuff logout
```

That's it; you're free to go.

Creating a CVS Repository and Project

If you're working on a local system and you want to set up your own repository, first you create the root directory with the following line, where `/MyCVSStuff` is the directory you want to use for the repository:

```
mkdir /MyCVSStuff
```

Most likely you won't put the repository in the root; instead, you might do something like this:

```
mkdir /home/MyCVSStuff
```

Next, tell CVS to initialize this directory as a repository:

```
cvs -d/MyCVSStuff init
```

You now have a repository; that was easy. Now you can create a project. I suggest creating an empty directory and any subdirectories you want in the project, such as this:

```
mkdir proj1
cd proj1
mkdir src
mkdir doc
cd ..
```

This creates a project directory called proj1, and two directories under proj1 called src and doc. Then it moves you back to the proj1 directory. From the main proj1 directory, type this:

```
cvs -d/MyCVSStuff import proj1 proj1 start
```

The `import` command creates the new project. Then comes the project name twice. (Advanced users can use different names here for different reasons; if you're interested, check out the online CVS docs for details.) Then you follow with the final option, `start`.

If you've used other version controllers . . .

If you're familiar with other version control systems, you might be disappointed that a major feature is lacking in CVS: file locking. In other version control systems, when you *check out* a file, you get a lock on the file, and nobody else can make changes to their own local copies. (Systems do this by making all the files read-only in the client system's directory and then making the files read-write when you check them out. Thus, you can easily override this feature.) While you have the files checked out, other users can't check them out; the server won't let them. Only after you *check in* your files can somebody else check them out. This prevents multiple people from making changes simultaneously to the same file.

CVS doesn't have this locking feature. When you check out files in CVS, you're getting a local copy of the files. Anyone else can also check out the files and work on the same files you're working on. Thus, the term *check out* means

something different in CVS than in the big powerful version control systems. (However, CVS does have various safety features; for instance, it will notify you if you made changes and somebody else did so that you can merge the changes.)

Some people see this absence of file locking as a problem. But the reality is that CVS is the most-used version control system in the open-source world; it is a fact of life and it requires a slightly different mindset. The creators of CVS realized that their product is used by projects where developers span the entire planet. If one person checks out a file and locks it, leaving others unable to access the file, and then said developer disappears on a month-long vacation (or perhaps an exile?) then the other developers would be stuck. Instead, an alternative idea is that the developers coordinate their work and then merge their work together. Such merging is the way of CVS.

When you type the `import` command, a text editor opens. Enter a description for your project in the text editor. (Put the description on a blank line, not one of the lines that starts with `CVS`.) Then save the file and exit out of the editor.

That creates the project. The project is started, but you don't have anything in it yet. If you want, you can start adding files to the project using the techniques from the section, "Committing your changes (and creating new files)," earlier in the chapter.

Some people have reported having troubles with the `import` command. If you encounter some errors when you try to import a project, try creating the directory in your own local area just off the top of the main CVS directory. From there, create the files and add them as you normally would. If this still doesn't work, a great place on the Web to visit for CVS information is on the CVS main site at `www.cvshome.org`.

Browsing CVS Repositories from the Web

Several free Web server programs are available that let you browse a CVS repository from the Web. While sitting at your client computer, you can open your Web browser, connect to the Web server, and view the projects in the CVS repository. Each project name is a link, and you can click the link to view the files in the project. If you want to see a good example of this, visit any of the projects on SourceForge at `www.sf.net`.

Web browsing is a read-only, anonymous form of CVS. You don't check in files via the Web browser. The idea is for users to be able to easily see the files in the directory and download a few of them.

Although the CVS Web interface is easy to use, don't try to use the Web interface if you're checking out an entire project anonymously. You'll quickly get frustrated because you have to do lots of clicking and saving. Just use the anonymous checkout form of the regular CVS client program; you'll be a much happier person.

To find various Web server programs, please visit `www.cvshome.org/dev/addons.html`.

Appendix B: Understanding Open-Source Licenses

This appendix focuses on open-source licenses. However, before going any further, I want to point out that I am not a lawyer; this is not legal advice. Because I'm not a lawyer, instead of trying to interpret the different licenses for you, I tell you what open source is, what an open-source license is, how you can profit if you offer an open-source license, and what the common open-source licenses are.

What Is Open Source?

People have different opinions on what open source is. In this section, I outline what I think open source means; I'm pretty sure this definition corresponds with the majority of people in the open-source community.

 Open source means that the source code to a product is freely available. Open source does not imply free software. However, most open-source software is free.

People in the open-source community believe that all source code for all software should be freely available. They have good reason for this: They are programmers, and they might really like your software but find that it doesn't exactly meet their needs. Instead of pestering you for a revision, they would like to be able to make the changes themselves.

Such people also feel that community involvement can help a software package evolve. If people with different needs work together on a software package, they can create an even better software package.

What is the distinction between free source and free software? I see this as the fundamental distinction:

+ **Free source** means you can download the source code and compile it for your computer.

+ **Free software** means the product has already been compiled for you.

These two concepts are so similar that many people who provide open-source software provide their software for free. But not everybody does. Linux is one example. I can download all the source code for Linux and build my own Linux box. Or I can go to the Red Hat Web site (www.redhat.com)

and order its version of Linux. At the time of this writing, a premium edition of a Linux server is available for $2,499.00. That's certainly not free, yet Red Hat is one of the front runners in the open-source movement. (Red Hat has several other pricing options on the lower end; I just picked the most expensive one I saw.)

As another example, consider the Perl language. You can easily go to `www.perl.org` and download Perl for your operating system. Or you can download ActiveState's special version of Perl from `www.activestate.com`. Both versions are free. ActiveState makes other versions of Perl that are not free. With these non-free versions, you get other perks and benefits; for example, the Perl Dev Kit includes a nice Visual Debugger. But again, ActiveState is a big member of the open-source movement.

How Do People Make Money?

If you read the previous section, you can see how companies make money: Although their products are open source, companies often supply souped-up versions that are not free. They make money from these products.

But companies can also make money another way if they offer their software for free: They can include optional support packages that are not free. Support is an important issue with many large corporations that are considering purchasing software. Corporations often shy away from free software because support may be unreliable. Some guy named Gunther might be sitting in his garage today writing the software and running from the law tomorrow, nowhere to be found to support his software. Corporations want support. Many open-source developers have recognized this need and have begun offering optional support packages with their free software.

Another way open-source developers make money is by offering corporate licenses. The corporate version of the software is identical to the free version, but the licensing includes a complete installation and documentation on CD, along with various support options.

What Is an Open-Source License?

An open-source license is a special license that you include with your open-source software. This license gives the user certain rights to your software but also limits what the user can do with your software.

Prior to the open-source concept, people who didn't charge for their software would put their software into the *public domain*. This meant that the developers chose not to copyright their software, and anyone could do whatever they wanted with the software. Unfortunately, other users could turn around and sell the public domain software as their own or try to register a copyright for the software under their name. This wasn't a good situation for developers.

People realized that the best way to provide software for free (or, at least, source code for free) was to develop a new kind of license, a license that allowed people to use the software for free, but the original owner still owned the rights to the software. From there, people came up with different methods:

✦ They could distribute free software while keeping their rights but without distributing the code.

✦ They could distribute free software and the code.

✦ They could allow the code to be freely available but charge for the software.

All these methods required different licensing.

Today, most people who want to ship their software for free use the GNU General Public License (GPL). The main idea behind this license is that you create your software and ship it, and anybody can share the software with anybody else for free, provided they include the source code with the product. The whole idea behind *open source* is to keep the source code freely available, so why not ensure that the source code always goes with the product?

Other people use the GNU Lesser Public License (LPL) or use a method known as Copyleft. More recently, people in the GNU community have come up with a license specifically for documentation called GNU Free Documentation License (FDL).

But GNU isn't the only group that has developed an open-source license. Another group is the Mozilla Public License (MPL). (This license is most commonly used with the source code of a browser called Mozilla, which is an offshoot of the original source code used in Netscape.)

As I mentioned in the introduction to this appendix, I'm not going to get into what the different licenses entail because that involves interpreting them. Instead, here are some links where you can find out about these licenses yourself and decide which one is best for you:

✦ All the GNU general licenses are available from the main GNU site at `www.gnu.org/licenses/licenses.html`.

✦ The Mozilla license is available from the main Mozilla site at `www.mozilla.org/MPL/`. This page also has links to some older versions of the license, as well as some modified forms.

Index

B

C

Notes

Notes

FOR DUMMIES®

The easy way to get more done and have more fun

PERSONAL FINANCE

Personal Finance For Dummies
0-7645-5231-7

Investing For Dummies
0-7645-2431-3

Home Buying For Dummies
0-7645-5331-3

Also available:

Estate Planning For Dummies
(0-7645-5501-4)

401(k)s For Dummies
(0-7645-5468-9)

Frugal Living For Dummies
(0-7645-5403-4)

Microsoft Money "X" For
Dummies
(0-7645-1689-2)

Mutual Funds For Dummies
(0-7645-5329-1)

Personal Bankruptcy For
Dummies
(0-7645-5498-0)

Quicken "X" For Dummies
(0-7645-1666-3)

Stock Investing For Dummies
(0-7645-5411-5)

Taxes For Dummies 2003
(0-7645-5475-1)

BUSINESS & CAREERS

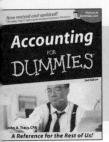
Accounting For Dummies
0-7645-5314-3

Grant Writing For Dummies
0-7645-5307-0

Resumes For Dummies
0-7645-5471-9

Also available:

Business Plans Kit For
Dummies
(0-7645-5365-8)

Consulting For Dummies
(0-7645-5034-9)

Cool Careers For Dummies
(0-7645-5345-3)

Human Resources Kit For
Dummies
(0-7645-5131-0)

Managing For Dummies
(1-5688-4858-7)

QuickBooks All-in-One Desk
Reference For Dummies
(0-7645-1963-8)

Selling For Dummies
(0-7645-5363-1)

Small Business Kit For
Dummies
(0-7645-5093-4)

Starting an eBay Business For
Dummies
(0-7645-1547-0)

HEALTH, SPORTS & FITNESS

Fitness For Dummies
0-7645-5167-1

Golf For Dummies
0-7645-5146-9

Diabetes For Dummies
0-7645-5154-X

Also available:

Controlling Cholesterol For
Dummies
(0-7645-5440-9)

Dieting For Dummies
(0-7645-5126-4)

High Blood Pressure For
Dummies
(0-7645-5424-7)

Martial Arts For Dummies
(0-7645-5358-5)

Menopause For Dummies
(0-7645-5458-1)

Nutrition For Dummies
(0-7645-5180-9)

Power Yoga For Dummies
(0-7645-5342-9)

Thyroid For Dummies
(0-7645-5385-2)

Weight Training For Dummies
(0-7645-5168-X)

Yoga For Dummies
(0-7645-5117-5)

FOR DUMMIES®

A world of resources to help you grow

HOME, GARDEN & HOBBIES

Feng Shui
0-7645-5295-3

Gardening
0-7645-5130-2

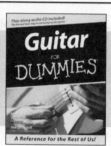

Guitar
0-7645-5106-X

Also available:

Auto Repair For Dummies
(0-7645-5089-6)

Chess For Dummies
(0-7645-5003-9)

Home Maintenance For
Dummies
(0-7645-5215-5)

Organizing For Dummies
(0-7645-5300-3)

Piano For Dummies
(0-7645-5105-1)

Poker For Dummies
(0-7645-5232-5)

Quilting For Dummies
(0-7645-5118-3)

Rock Guitar For Dummies
(0-7645-5356-9)

Roses For Dummies
(0-7645-5202-3)

Sewing For Dummies
(0-7645-5137-X)

FOOD & WINE

Cooking
0-7645-5250-3

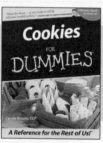

Cookies
0-7645-5390-9

Wine
0-7645-5114-0

Also available:

Bartending For Dummies
(0-7645-5051-9)

Chinese Cooking For
Dummies
(0-7645-5247-3)

Christmas Cooking For
Dummies
(0-7645-5407-7)

Diabetes Cookbook For
Dummies
(0-7645-5230-9)

Grilling For Dummies
(0-7645-5076-4)

Low-Fat Cooking For
Dummies
(0-7645-5035-7)

Slow Cookers For Dummies
(0-7645-5240-6)

TRAVEL

Italy
0-7645-5453-0

Hawaii
0-7645-5438-7

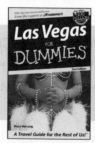

Las Vegas
0-7645-5448-4

Also available:

America's National Parks For
Dummies
(0-7645-6204-5)

Caribbean For Dummies
(0-7645-5445-X)

Cruise Vacations For
Dummies 2003
(0-7645-5459-X)

Europe For Dummies
(0-7645-5456-5)

Ireland For Dummies
(0-7645-6199-5)

France For Dummies
(0-7645-6292-4)

London For Dummies
(0-7645-5416-6)

Mexico's Beach Resorts For
Dummies
(0-7645-6262-2)

Paris For Dummies
(0-7645-5494-8)

RV Vacations For Dummies
(0-7645-5443-3)

Walt Disney World & Orlando
For Dummies
(0-7645-5444-1)

Available wherever books are sold. Go to www.dummies.com or call 1-877-762-2974 to order direct.

FOR DUMMIES®

Plain-English solutions for everyday challenges

FOR DUMMIES®

Helping you expand your horizons and realize your potential

INTERNET

The Internet FOR DUMMIES

0-7645-0894-6

The Internet ALL-IN-ONE DESK REFERENCE FOR DUMMIES

0-7645-1659-0

eBay FOR DUMMIES

0-7645-1642-6

Also available:

America Online 7.0 For Dummies
(0-7645-1624-8)

Genealogy Online For Dummies
(0-7645-0807-5)

The Internet All-in-One Desk Reference For Dummies
(0-7645-1659-0)

Internet Explorer 6 For Dummies
(0-7645-1344-3)

The Internet For Dummies Quick Reference
(0-7645-1645-0)

Internet Privacy For Dummies
(0-7645-0846-6)

Researching Online For Dummies
(0-7645-0546-7)

Starting an Online Business For Dummies
(0-7645-1655-8)

DIGITAL MEDIA

Digital Photography FOR DUMMIES

0-7645-1664-7

Photoshop Elements 2 FOR DUMMIES

0-7645-1675-2

Digital Video FOR DUMMIES

0-7645-0806-7

Also available:

CD and DVD Recording For Dummies
(0-7645-1627-2)

Digital Photography All-in-One Desk Reference For Dummies
(0-7645-1800-3)

Digital Photography For Dummies Quick Reference
(0-7645-0750-8)

Home Recording for Musicians For Dummies
(0-7645-1634-5)

MP3 For Dummies
(0-7645-0858-X)

Paint Shop Pro "X" For Dummies
(0-7645-2440-2)

Photo Retouching & Restoration For Dummies
(0-7645-1662-0)

Scanners For Dummies
(0-7645-0783-4)

GRAPHICS

PowerPoint 2002 FOR DUMMIES

0-7645-0817-2

Photoshop 7 FOR DUMMIES

0-7645-1651-5

Macromedia Flash MX FOR DUMMIES

0-7645-0895-4

Also available:

Adobe Acrobat 5 PDF For Dummies
(0-7645-1652-3)

Fireworks 4 For Dummies
(0-7645-0804-0)

Illustrator 10 For Dummies
(0-7645-3636-2)

QuarkXPress 5 For Dummies
(0-7645-0643-9)

Visio 2000 For Dummies
(0-7645-0635-8)

Available wherever books are sold. Go to www.dummies.com or call 1-877-762-2974 to order direct.